Louisiana Family Law in Comparative Perspective

Louisiana Family Law in Comparative Perspective

Elizabeth R. Carter

A.N. YIANNOPOULOS PROFESSOR OF LAW
JUDGE ANTHONY J. GRAPHIA &
JO ANN GRAPHIA PROFESSOR OF LAW
LOUISIANA STATE UNIVERSITY
PAUL M. HEBERT LAW CENTER

CAROLINA ACADEMIC PRESS
Durham, North Carolina

Print ISBN: 978-1-5310-0686-0
eBook ISBN: 978-1-53100-687-7
LCCN: 2018933193

Carolina Academic Press, LLC
700 Kent Street
Durham, North Carolina 27701
Telephone (919) 489-7486
Fax (919) 493-5668
www.cap-press.com

Printed in the United States of America

Contents

Table of Principal Cases

Preface

At my first conference as a law professor, I was informed by more seasoned (presumably well-meaning) academics that family law was part of the "pink ghetto." The term, of course, refers to those areas of the law considered intellectual backwoods—areas devoid of the scholarly rigor and social prestige of, say, constitutional law or federal courts. In other words, family law is women's work.

Let's set aside, for a moment, the obvious sexist implications of the term. The suggestion that family law is an area that somehow lacks the academic rigor of other areas of law is misinformed, at best. To the contrary, family law involves all of the traditional areas of academic prestige—constitutional law, federal jurisdiction, and civil procedure. On top of those traditionally challenging topics, family law adds additional layers of private law, public policy, and evolving social and political values. This text adds another scholarly consideration—comparative law. American family law is as much of a melting pot and source of innovation as America itself. Some important family law doctrines that are widely accepted in the United States have their roots in the civil law of France, Spain, and even Rome. Similarly, family law in Louisiana has adopted some distinctly common law notions. There are even some aspects of family law that are uniquely American and which have since been exported to other countries.

In the years I have taught family law, I have often warned students that family law is hard. It is quite unlike some of the traditional law school classes where you can study a subject in a vacuum. Family law is more like a blender—all the legal doctrines are combined together at once and it can be messy—just like most families.

This text covers three broad topics: (1) the marriage relationship, (2) the parent-child relationship, and (3) jurisdictional issues. The first three chapters consider the legal regulation of marriage by states and the constitutional implications of that regulation. Chapters 4 through 6 consider some of the many legal consequences of marriage and the effects of defective marriages. Chapters 7 through 9 address divorce and its consequences. Chapter 10 considers the contractual freedom afforded to spouses who wish to modify the default rules governing marriage and divorce. Chapters 11 through 13 involve the creation and establishment of the parent-child relationship and the related constitutional implications. Chapters 14 and 15 discuss two important aspects of parenting—child custody and child support. Finally, Chapters 16 and 17 address important federal and state procedural matters.

Louisiana Family Law in Comparative Perspective

Chapter 1

Introduction to the Legal Regulation of Marriage

A. Historical Perspectives

In recent history, both common law and civil law viewed marriage as a civil—rather than a religious—institution. While both legal systems have long recognized marriage as a civil contract, the legal consequences of that contract have varied considerably across legal systems and have evolved as society has changed. Although the contract of marriage is entered into between the spouses, it has long affected their relationships with the outside world. The following excerpts from Blackstone and Planiol illustrate some of the historical distinctions and similarities between the two legal systems.

Blackstone's writings, which were published in the 1760s, highlight the disabilities a married woman faced as a result of coverture—a legal doctrine that deprived a woman of many basic elements of citizenship and personhood. Many of the legal disabilities of marriage persisted in the United States and in England until the end of the 19th century when they were abolished, at least in part, by the various pieces of legislation dubbed the "Married Women's Property Acts." Yet, many gender inequities continued to exist in marriage long after these acts were abolished. Planiol's writings, which were published in the 1930s, demonstrate a view of marriage and women that is more similar to what is seen today in both common law and civil law jurisdictions in the western world.

Writing in 1931, Professor Daggett made it clear that she believed the civil law was the superior approach.[1] She described the civil law view of marriage as "far kinder than the Common Law notion of a merged personality represented by the husband."[2] The common law, she explained, was "fundamentally wrong and in accord with a more primitive state of society and designed for an age when the position of women entitled them to little education of recognition of any sort...."[3] While the civil law needed only a few "minor adjustments for perfect alignment with changing conditions"; the common law simply could not "be readily adjusted to

---

1. Harriet Spiller Daggett, The Community Property of Louisiana 3 (Louisiana State University Press 1945) (1931).

2. *Id.*

3. *Id.*

meet the social and economic changes of this era."[4] In reading the excerpts from Blackstone and Planiol, consider whether you agree with Professor Daggett.

2 William Blackstone, Commentaries *433–46
OF HUSBAND AND WIFE.

. . . .

Legal Consequences.

By marriage the husband and wife are one person in law; that is the very being or legal existence of the woman is suspended during the marriage, or at least is incorporated and consolidated into that of the husband; under whose wing, protection, and cover, she performs everything; and is therefore called in our law-french a *feme-covert*, *focnina viro co-operta*; is said to be *covert-baron*, or under the protection and influence of her husband, her *baron*, or lord; and her condition during her marriage is called her *coverture*. Upon this principle, of a union of person in husband and wife, depend almost all the legal rights, duties, and disabilities, that either of them acquire by the marriage. . . . The husband is bound to provide his wife with necessaries by law, as much as himself; and, if she contracts debts for them, he is obliged to pay them; but for anything besides necessaries he is not chargeable. . . . If the wife be indebted before marriage, the husband is bound afterwards to pay the debt; for he has adopted her and her circumstances together. If the wife be injured in her person or her property, she can bring no action for redress without her husband's concurrence, and in his name as well as her own: neither can she be sued without making the husband a defendant. . . .

In the civil law the husband and the wife are considered as two distinct persons, and may have separate estates, contracts, debts, and injuries: and therefore in our ecclesiastical courts, a woman may sue and be sued without her husband.

But though our law in general considers man and wife as one person, yet there are some instances in which she is separably considered; as inferior to him, and acting by his compulsion. And therefore all deeds executed, and acts done, by her, during her coverture, are void; except it be a fine or the like matter of record, in which case she must be solely and secretly examined, to learn if her act be voluntary. She cannot by will devise lands to her husband, unless under special circumstances; for at the time of making it she is supposed to be under his coercion. And in some felonies, and other inferior crimes, committed by her, through constraint of her husband, the law excuses her; but this extends not to treason or murder. . . .

These are the chief legal effects of marriage during the coverture; upon which we may observe, that even the disabilities which the wife lies under are for the most part intended for her protection and benefit: so great a favorite is the female sex of the laws of England.

---

4. *Id.*

1 Marcel Planiol, Treatise on the Civil Law

(Louisiana State Law Institute trans. West, 1959)

§ I. RECIPROCAL DUTIES OF THE SPOUSES

892. Enumeration

Marriage engenders special obligations between husband and wife which are the result of their status as spouses. . . .

Among the duties which spring from marriage some are common to both spouses, one is special to the husband (the duty of protection) and one is special to the wife (the duty of obedience). . . .

The duties common to both spouses are, first of all, cohabitation, set forth in Art. 214, and then fidelity, help, and assistance, enumerated in Art. 212.

§ 2. THE MARITAL POWER

919. Laconism of the Texts

The Code does not mention the term marital power in regulating the effects of marriage. It speaks of this power but once, in the title "Of the Marriage Contract." And it does so in order to forbid any attack upon this power, saying that "the spouses cannot derogate from the rights resulting from the marital power upon the person of the wife." (Art. 1388). It is of marital power that Art. 213 speaks when it sets forth that "the husband owes protection to his wife and the wife obedience to her husband." The marital power is thus presented in its double historical aspect, duty of protection imposed upon the husband and a status of protection imposed upon the wife. As an assertion of principle such a text suffices. It is, however, far from satisfactory for the purpose of regulating the consequences flowing from such a definition of principle. This lacuna is filled in but partially by a few texts scattered through the Code. They apply or fix certain of the consequences of marital power. . . .

923. Decadence of the Marital Power

Notwithstanding the force of resistance of traditions, the marital power is growing weaker. In Italy, the Code of 1865 greatly lessened it. It says, it is true, in Art. 131, that the husband is the chief of the family (*capo della famiglia*), that the wife takes his condition and his name, and that she is obliged to follow him wherever he may desire to fix his residence, but it no longer speaks of a duty of general obedience. In Belgium, Laurent boldly proposed to do away with it and to establish the equality of the spouses and the independence of the wife. Even in France such ideas make constant progress. France no longer blindly accepts the statements of Portalis or Pothier when they say that the preponderance of the husband and the subordination of the wife spring from "natural right."

"Marriage is the union of souls," said the First Consul. The modern world looks upon it as an association of two equal beings which cannot last without harmony. Marriage seems to have been for Napoleon nothing but the legal possession, body and soul, of a woman by a man. Perhaps, there should be a golden means found between this species of brutal authority, as Napoleon conceived it, and the absolute suppression of the husband's preponderance. The contemporary "woman's rights" movement is working toward a radical reform which would make marriage itself disappear, or, at all events, cause it to fall into a state of free union, as was the ancient marriage, when Christianity brought about an irresistible movement of reaction. . . .

§ 3. INCAPACITY OF THE MARRIED WOMAN
A. CAUSES OF INCAPACITY
926. Historical Origin

The special incapacity of married women proceeds from a more general incapacity that formerly applied to all women, whether married or not. In primitive communities, where violence and war reigned, woman was too weak to defend herself. She remained under perpetual tutorship. Such was the law of Rome under the Republic. Such were the Germanic customs. This perpetual and general incapacity became attenuated, little by little, with the progress of civilization and of social order. French law, properly so called, never knew it. But if the original incapacity of woman disappeared as regards unmarried women and widows, it continued as regards married women. The same conditions obtained in the Roman Law. The *manus* long survived the tutorship of women who were *sui juris*. It nevertheless finally ceased in time. And during the last centuries of the Empire, no incapacity applied to woman as a result of marriage. They enjoyed the right of free disposition of their property with full capacity to obligate themselves.

927. Modern Theoretical Justification

Woman's incapacity is not a matter connected with her sex. "Her husband's authorization is not based upon the weakness of her judgment, because a married woman's judgment is not weaker than that of unmarried women or widows, who do not require an authorization. . . ." When she becomes wife and mother, a woman may acquire knowledge of business and business experience to the same degree as a man. As Paul Gide put it, her status is thus not one of incapacity but one of dependence. A wife is not incapable because she is a woman, but because she is married. The reason for her incapacity is found in the rights which marriage confers upon her husband. . . .

929. Foreign Law

ENGLISH LAW. It is interesting to compare the movement that has taken place in France with the profound transformation that has gone on in England regarding the condition of the married woman. Until 1870 her personality was merged into that of her husband. A law of August 9, 1870, gave her a partial capacity, analogous to that which results in France from a separation of property. A second act of August 18, 1882 changed from top to bottom the traditional principles of English law and gave the wife complete civil capacity, which she does not as yet enjoy in any other country. . . .

B. Contemporary Legal Definitions of Marriage

See La. Civ. Code art. 86.

Many common law and civil law jurisdictions continue to expressly define marriage as a civil contract. In Louisiana, "[m]arriage is a legal relationship . . . that is created by civil contract."[5] Statutes in many other American states likewise describe marriage as a civil contract.[6] That civil contract continues to carry with it consequences for the spouses in their interactions with each other and with the outside world.

---

5. La. Civ. Code art. 86 (2017).

6. *See, e.g.* Cal. Fam. Code §300 (2017); Iowa Code §595.1A (2017); Kan. Stat. §23-2501 (2017); Mich. Comp. Laws §551.2 (2017); Mo. Rev. Stat. §451.010 (2017); Neb. Rev. Stat. §42-101 (2017); N.M. Stat. §40-1-1 (2017); N.Y. Dom. Rel. Law §10 (2017); Okla. Stat. tit. §43:1 (2017); Wash. Rev. Code §26.04.010 (2017); Wis. Stat. §765.01 (2017).

Chapter 2

Marriage and the U.S. Constitution

Marriage and other intimate relationships are not explicitly addressed by the Constitution. Rather, it is understood that the Tenth Amendment reserves the regulation of marriage and comparable status determinations as a power of the states. As the following materials show, however, other provisions of the Constitution may limit the manner in which states decide to regulate marriage and other intimate relationships. Two of the most common limitations are found in the Equal Protection Clause and the Due Process Clause of the Fourteenth Amendment:

> No state shall make or enforce any law which shall abridge the privileges or immunities of citizens of the United States; nor shall any state deprive any person of life, liberty, or property, without due process of law; nor deny to any person within its jurisdiction the equal protection of the laws.

On occasion, the federal government has enacted laws affecting marriage and other intimate relationships. In these cases, the Due Process Clause of the Fifth Amendment is sometimes implicated: "No person shall be . . . deprived of life, liberty, or property, without due process of law."

A. Marriage as a Fundamental Right

The following cases—*Loving v. Virginia* and *Zablocki v. Redhail*—demonstrate how the Supreme Court has found that marriage is a "fundamental right" protected by the Constitution—and in particular, by equal protection and due process.

Equal Protection. Often, equal protection challenges deal with instances where the state allows (or prohibits) one group of people to engage in a particular activity while not affording similar treatment to another group of people. As demonstrated in the cases that follow, the Supreme Court has developed different tests—or types of scrutiny—in analyzing an equal protection challenge. The most lenient inquiry is the so-called "rational basis review." Under this analysis, the Court will find that a classification is constitutional so long as it is rationally related to a "legitimate state purpose." Some classifications, however, warrant a more stringent type of analysis—so-called "strict scrutiny." If the state classification involves a "suspect classification," then the Court will apply strict scrutiny. Classifications based on race, for example, are usually deemed suspect classifications. For a classification to survive a strict scrutiny review, the state must prove that the law satisfies a compelling state interest and is drawn as narrowly as possible to satisfy that interest. The Court sometimes also applies strict scrutiny to laws that are burdensome to fundamental rights—the same rights that are often protected by substantive due process. Fundamental rights include rights protected by the First Amendment, the right to travel, and, as seen in the marriage cases, the right to privacy and marriage. Other classifications—like those based on gender and legitimacy—have been subjected to intermediate scrutiny. As the name suggests, intermediate scrutiny is more rigorous than a rational basis review and less rigorous than strict scrutiny.

Due Process. Two types of due process are protected by the Due Process Clauses—substantive due process and procedural due process. Procedural due process—as the name implies—requires that the government afford some fair procedure to a citizen before depriving him of life, liberty, or property. The process required, of course, depends on the specific government action contemplated. The more common due process challenge in the family law setting involves substantive due process. The right to substantive due process limits the government's ability to intrude on fundamental rights. For that reason, substantive due process has a considerable amount of overlap with equal protection. Substantive due process, however, does not usually involve the same multi-tiered types of scrutiny seen in the equal protection context. Rather, in determining whether a law is constitutional under a substantive due process challenge, the Court typically tries to balance the fundamental right of the individual with the interest of the government in trying to accomplish some goal. In striking the balance, the Court often considers how well tailored the statute is in accomplishing its goal. If the right that is being burdened is, indeed, a fundamental right, then the Court will typically require the law to be very narrowly tailored. In this respect the analysis can sometimes look similar to a strict scrutiny review.

Loving v. Virginia

388 U.S. 1 (1967)

Mr. Chief Justice WARREN delivered the opinion of the Court.

This case presents a constitutional question never addressed by this Court: whether a statutory scheme adopted by the State of Virginia to prevent marriages between persons solely on the basis of racial classifications violates the Equal Protection and Due Process Clauses of the Fourteenth Amendment. For reasons which seem to us to reflect the central meaning of those constitutional commands, we conclude that these statutes cannot stand consistently with the Fourteenth Amendment.

In June 1958, two residents of Virginia, Mildred Jeter, a Negro woman, and Richard Loving, a white man, were married in the District of Columbia pursuant to its laws. Shortly after their marriage, the Lovings returned to Virginia and established their marital abode in Caroline County. At the October Term, 1958, of the Circuit Court of Caroline County, a grand jury issued an indictment charging the Lovings with violating Virginia's ban on interracial marriages. On January 6, 1959, the Lovings pleaded guilty to the charge and were sentenced to one year in jail; however, the trial judge suspended the sentence for a period of 25 years on the condition that the

Lovings leave the State and not return to Virginia together for 25 years. He stated in an opinion that:

> "Almighty God created the races white, black, yellow, malay and red, and he placed them on separate continents. And but for the interference with his arrangement there would be no cause for such marriages. The fact that he separated the races shows that he did not intend for the races to mix."

After their convictions, the Lovings took up residence in the District of Columbia. On November 6, 1963, they filed a motion in the state trial court to vacate the judgment and set aside the sentence on the ground that the statutes which they had violated were repugnant to the Fourteenth Amendment. The motion not having been decided by October 28, 1964, the Lovings instituted a class action in the United States District Court for the Eastern District of Virginia requesting that a three-judge court be convened to declare the Virginia antimiscegenation statutes unconstitutional and to enjoin state officials from enforcing their convictions. On January 22, 1965, the state trial judge denied the motion to vacate the sentences, and the Lovings perfected an appeal to the Supreme Court of Appeals of Virginia. On February 11, 1965, the three-judge District Court continued the case to allow the Lovings to present their constitutional claims to the highest state court.

The Supreme Court of Appeals upheld the constitutionality of the antimiscegenation statutes and, after modifying the sentence, affirmed the convictions. The Lovings appealed this decision, and we noted probable jurisdiction on December 12, 1966. . . .

Virginia is now one of 16 States which prohibit and punish marriages on the basis of racial classifications. Penalties for miscegenation arose as an incident to slavery and have been common in Virginia since the colonial period. The present statutory scheme dates from the adoption of the Racial Integrity Act of 1924, passed during the period of extreme nativism which followed the end of the First World War. The central features of this Act, and current Virginia law, are the absolute prohibition of a "white person" marrying other than another "white person," a prohibition against issuing marriage licenses until the issuing official is satisfied that the applicants' statements as to their race are correct, certificates of "racial composition" to be kept by both local and state registrars, and the carrying forward of earlier prohibitions against racial intermarriage.

I.

In upholding the constitutionality of these provisions in the decision below, the Supreme Court of Appeals of Virginia referred to its 1955 decision in *Naim v. Naim*, 197 Va. 80, 87 S.E.2d 749, as stating the reasons supporting the validity of these laws. In *Naim*, the state court concluded that the State's legitimate purposes were "to preserve the racial integrity of its citizens," and to prevent "the corruption of blood," "a mongrel breed of citizens," and "the obliteration of racial pride," obviously an endorsement of the doctrine of White Supremacy. The court also reasoned that marriage has traditionally been subject to state regulation without federal intervention, and, consequently, the regulation of marriage should be left to exclusive state control by the Tenth Amendment.

While the state court is no doubt correct in asserting that marriage is a social relation subject to the State's police power . . . the State does not contend in its argument before this Court that its powers to regulate marriage are unlimited notwithstanding the commands of the Fourteenth Amendment. . . . Instead, the State argues that the meaning of the Equal Protection Clause, as illuminated by the statements of the Framers, is only that state penal laws containing an interracial element as part of the definition of the offense must apply equally to whites and Negroes in the sense that members of each race are punished to the same degree. Thus, the State contends that, because its miscegenation statutes punish equally both the white and the Negro participants in an interracial marriage, these statutes, despite their reliance on racial classifications do not constitute an invidious discrimination based upon race. The second argument advanced by the State assumes the validity of its equal application theory. The argument is that, if the Equal Protection Clause does not outlaw miscegenation statutes because of their reliance on racial classifications, the question of constitutionality would thus become whether there was any rational basis for a State to treat interracial marriages differently from other marriages. On this question, the State argues, the scientific evidence is substantially in doubt and, consequently, this Court should defer to the wisdom of the state legislature in adopting its policy of discouraging interracial marriages.

Because we reject the notion that the mere "equal application" of a statute containing racial classifications is enough to remove the classifications from the Fourteenth Amendment's proscription of all invidious racial discriminations, we do not accept the State's contention that these statutes should be upheld if there is any possible basis for concluding that they serve a rational purpose. . . . In these cases, involving distinctions not drawn according to race, the Court has merely asked whether there is any rational foundation for the discriminations, and has deferred to the wisdom of the state legislatures. In the case at bar, however, we deal with statutes containing racial classifications, and the fact of equal application does not immunize the statute from the very heavy burden of justification which the Fourteenth Amendment has traditionally required of state statutes drawn according to race. . . .

There can be no question but that Virginia's miscegenation statutes rest solely upon distinctions drawn according to race. The statutes proscribe generally accepted conduct if engaged in by members of different races. Over the years, this Court has consistently repudiated "[d]istinctions between citizens solely because of their ancestry" as being "odious to a free people whose institutions are founded upon the doctrine of equality. . . ." At the very least, the Equal Protection Clause demands that racial classifications, especially suspect in criminal statutes, be subjected to the "most rigid scrutiny," . . . and, if they are ever to be upheld, they must be shown to be necessary to the accomplishment of some permissible state objective, independent of the racial discrimination which it was the object of the Fourteenth Amendment to eliminate. Indeed, two members of this Court have already stated that they "cannot conceive of a valid legislative purpose which makes the color of a person's skin the test of whether his conduct is a criminal offense. . . ."

There is patently no legitimate overriding purpose independent of invidious racial discrimination which justifies this classification. The fact that Virginia prohibits only interracial marriages involving white persons demonstrates that the racial classifications must stand on their own justification, as measures designed to maintain White Supremacy. We have consistently denied the constitutionality of measures which restrict the rights of citizens on account of race. There can be no doubt that restricting the freedom to marry solely because of racial classifications violates the central meaning of the Equal Protection Clause.

II.

These statutes also deprive the Lovings of liberty without due process of law in violation of the Due Process Clause of the Fourteenth Amendment. The freedom to marry has long been recognized as one of the vital personal rights essential to the orderly pursuit of happiness by free men.

Marriage is one of the "basic civil rights of man," fundamental to our very existence and survival. . . . To deny this fundamental freedom on so unsupportable a basis as the racial classifications embodied in these statutes, classifications so directly subversive of the principle of equality at the heart of the Fourteenth Amendment, is surely to deprive all the State's citizens of liberty without due process of law. The Fourteenth Amendment requires that the freedom of choice to marry not be restricted by invidious racial discriminations. Under our Constitution, the freedom to marry or not marry, a person of another race resides with the individual and cannot be infringed by the State.

These convictions must be reversed. It is so ordered.

Reversed.

Zablocki v. Redhail
434 U.S. 374 (1978)

Mr. Justice MARSHALL delivered the opinion of the Court.

At issue in this case is the constitutionality of a Wisconsin statute, Wis.Stat. §§ 245.10(1), (4), (5) (1973), which provides that members of a certain class of Wisconsin residents may not marry, within the State or elsewhere, without first obtaining a court order granting permission to marry. The class is defined by the statute to include any "Wisconsin resident having minor issue not in his custody and which he is under obligation to support by any court order or judgment." The statute specifies that court permission cannot be granted unless the marriage applicant submits proof of compliance with the support obligation and, in addition, demonstrates that the children covered by the support order "are not then and are not likely thereafter to become public charges." No marriage license may lawfully be issued in Wisconsin to a person covered by the statute, except upon court order; any marriage entered into without compliance with § 245.10 is declared void; and persons acquiring marriage licenses in violation of the section are subject to criminal penalties.

After being denied a marriage license because of his failure to comply with § 245.10, appellee brought this class action under 42 U.S.C. § 1983, challenging the statute as violative of the Equal Protection and Due Process Clauses of the Fourteenth Amendment and seeking declaratory and injunctive relief. The United States District Court for the Eastern District of Wisconsin held the statute unconstitutional under the Equal Protection Clause and enjoined its enforcement. We noted probable jurisdiction . . . and we now affirm. . . .

II

In evaluating §§ 245.10(1), (4), (5) under the Equal Protection Clause, "we must first determine what burden of justification the classification created thereby must meet, by looking to the nature of the classification and the individual interests affected." . . . Since our past decisions make clear that the right to marry is of fundamental importance, and since the classification at issue here significantly interferes with the exercise of that right, we believe that "critical examination" of the state interests advanced in support of the classification is required. . . .

The leading decision of this Court on the right to marry is *Loving v. Virginia*. . . .

Although *Loving* arose in the context of racial discrimination, prior and subsequent decisions of this Court confirm that the right to marry is of fundamental importance for all individuals. . . .

More recent decisions have established that the right to marry is part of the fundamental "right of privacy" implicit in the Fourteenth Amendment's Due Process Clause. In *Griswold v. Connecticut* . . . the Court observed:

> "We deal with a right of privacy older than the Bill of Rights — older than our political parties, older than our school system. Marriage is a coming together for better or for worse, hopefully enduring, and intimate to the degree of being sacred. It is an association that promotes a way of life, not causes; a harmony in living, not political faiths; a bilateral loyalty, not commercial or social projects. Yet it is an association for as noble a purpose as any involved in our prior decisions."

. . . It is not surprising that the decision to marry has been placed on the same level of importance as decisions relating to procreation, childbirth, child rearing, and family relationships. As the facts of this case illustrate, it would make little sense to recognize a right of privacy with respect to other matters of family life and not with respect to the decision to enter the relationship that is the foundation of the family in our society. The woman whom appellee desired to marry had a fundamental right to seek an abortion of their expected child, or to bring the child into life to suffer the myriad social, if not economic, disabilities that the status of illegitimacy brings. . . . Surely, a decision to marry and raise the child in a traditional family setting must receive equivalent protection. And, if appellee's right to procreate means anything at all, it must imply some right to enter the only relationship in which the State of Wisconsin allows sexual relations legally to take place.

By reaffirming the fundamental character of the right to marry, we do not mean to suggest that every state regulation which relates in any way to the incidents of or prerequisites for marriage must be subjected to rigorous scrutiny. To the contrary, reasonable regulations that do not significantly interfere with decisions to enter into the marital relationship may legitimately be imposed. . . . The statutory classification at issue here, however, clearly does interfere directly and substantially with the right to marry.

Under the challenged statute, no Wisconsin resident in the affected class may marry in Wisconsin or elsewhere without a court order, and marriages contracted in violation of the statute are both void and punishable as criminal offenses. Some of those in the affected class, like appellee, will never be able to obtain the necessary court order, because they either lack the financial means to meet their support obligations or cannot prove that their children will not become public charges. These persons are absolutely prevented from getting married. Many others, able in theory to satisfy the statute's requirements, will be sufficiently burdened by having to do so that they will in effect be coerced into forgoing their right to marry. And even those who can be persuaded to meet the statute's requirements suffer a serious intrusion into their freedom of choice in an area in which we have held such freedom to be fundamental.

III

When a statutory classification significantly interferes with the exercise of a fundamental right, it cannot be upheld unless it is supported by sufficiently important state interests and is closely tailored to effectuate only those interests. . . . Appellant asserts that two interests are served by the challenged statute: the permission-to-marry proceeding furnishes an opportunity to counsel the applicant as to the necessity of fulfilling his prior support obligations; and the welfare of the out-of-custody children is protected. We may accept for present purposes that these are legitimate and substantial interests, but, since the means selected by the State for achieving these interests unnecessarily impinge on the right to marry, the statute cannot be sustained.

There is evidence that the challenged statute, as originally introduced in the Wisconsin Legislature, was intended merely to establish a mechanism whereby persons with support obligations to children from prior marriages could be counseled before they entered into new marital relationships and incurred further support obligations. Court permission to marry was to be required, but apparently permission was automatically to be granted after counseling was completed. The statute actually enacted, however, does not expressly require or provide for any counseling whatsoever, nor for any automatic granting of permission to marry by the court, and thus it can hardly be justified as a means for ensuring counseling of the persons within its coverage. Even assuming that counseling does take place — a fact as to which there is no evidence in the record—this interest obviously cannot support the withholding of court permission to marry once counseling is completed.

With regard to safeguarding the welfare of the out-of-custody children, appellant's brief does not make clear the connection between the State's interest and the statute's requirements. At argument, appellant's counsel suggested that, since permission to marry cannot be granted unless the applicant shows that he has satisfied his court-determined support obligations to the prior children and that those children will not become public charges, the statute provides incentive for the applicant to make support payments to his children. This "collection device" rationale cannot justify the statute's broad infringement on the right to marry.

First, with respect to individuals who are unable to meet the statutory requirements, the statute merely prevents the applicant from getting married, without delivering any money at all into the hands of the applicant's prior children. More importantly, regardless of the applicant's ability or willingness to meet the statutory requirements, the State already has numerous other means for exacting compliance with support obligations, means that are at least as effective as the instant statute's and yet do not impinge upon the right to marry. . . . And, if the State believes that parents of children out of their custody should be responsible for ensuring that those children do not become public charges, this interest can be achieved by adjusting the criteria used for determining the amounts to be paid under their support orders.

There is also some suggestion that § 245.10 protects the ability of marriage applicants to meet support obligations to prior children by preventing the applicants from incurring new support obligations. But the challenged provisions of § 245.10 are grossly underinclusive with respect to this purpose, since they do not limit in any way new financial commitments by the applicant other than those arising out of the contemplated marriage. The statutory classification is substantially overinclusive as well: Given the possibility that the new spouse will actually better the applicant's financial situation, by contributing income from a job or otherwise, the statute in many cases may prevent affected individuals from improving their ability to satisfy their prior support obligations. And, although it is true that the applicant will incur support obligations to any children born during the contemplated marriage, preventing the marriage may only result in the children being born out of wedlock, as in fact occurred in appellee's case. Since the support obligation is the same whether the child is born in or out of wedlock, the net result of preventing the marriage is simply more illegitimate children.

The statutory classification created by §§ 245.10(1), (4), (5) thus cannot be justified by the interests advanced in support of it. The judgment of the District Court is, accordingly,

Affirmed.

B. The Right to Privacy and Same-Sex Relationships

In recent decades we have witnessed significant changes in the legal rights afforded to same-sex couples. Legal discrimination against same-sex couples existed at both common law and civil law. Historically, neither system recognized marriages between same sex couples. Many jurisdictions went further—criminalizing same-sex consensual sex (as well as other types of non-procreative sex).

The United States Supreme Court upheld such criminal statutes as recently as 1986. In *Bowers v. Hardwick*, the Supreme Court upheld a Georgia statute criminalizing sodomy.[1] The statute provided that a "person commits the offense of sodomy when he performs or submits to any sexual act involving the sex organs of one person and the mouth or anus of another."[2] After being charged with violating the statute with another man in the privacy of his own home, Hardwick brought suit in Federal District Court challenging the constitutionality of the statute as it related to consensual same-sex sodomy. In an opinion that was highly criticized, and then later reversed, the United States Supreme Court upheld the constitutionality of the statute. In so doing, the Court rejected the notion that homosexual sexual intimacy was a protected fundamental right.

In the years following *Bowers v. Hardwick* (and leading up to *Obergefell v. Hodges*), a myriad of state and federal legislative changes complicated the legal landscape. A 1993 decision by the Hawaii Supreme Court suggested that a prohibition on same-sex marriage might violate the equal protection clause of the state constitution.[3] The decision was rendered moot by a subsequent amendment to the state constitution. Other states, and the federal government, followed suit. As a direct response to issues raised by the Hawaii case, Congress approved the Defense of Marriage Act ("DOMA") in 1996. President Clinton signed DOMA into law after it had been passed by a veto-proof majority of Congress. DOMA had two primary provisions. First, DOMA defined marriage—for all federal law purposes—as being limited to opposite-sex couples—regardless of applicable state law.[4] Second, DOMA provided that states need not recognize same-sex marriages that had been validly entered into in other jurisdictions.[5]

States responded in a variety of ways. At least 40 states—including Louisiana—enacted "mini-DOMAs." The mini-DOMAs consisted of legislation and/or state constitutional amendments that expressly prohibited same-sex marriages and often mirrored the federal law. On the other hand, some states enacted legislation allowing for "domestic partnerships" or "civil unions" for same-sex couples (and in some cases opposite-sex couples too). Sometimes this legal status conferred rights equivalent to

---

1. 478 U.S. 186 (1986).
2. *Id.*
3. Baehr v. Miike, 994 P.2d 566 (1999).
4. 1 U.S.C. § 7 (1997).
5. 28 U.S.C. § 1738C (1997).

marriage; but in other cases, the status was something less than marriage. Some local governments enacted comparable legislation. The City of New Orleans, for example, passed an ordinance in 1993 establishing a "Domestic Partnership Registry" for the city which allowed couples to register (regardless of their sex) and to receive various benefits—including health insurance for the domestic partners of city employees.[6] The New Orleans ordinance withstood subsequent legal challenges despite numerous state laws and a state constitutional provision expressly prohibiting same-sex marriage.[7]

Eventually, some states began to recognize same-sex marriages—but the legal landscape remained complex. California provides an interesting example of this complexity. Consider the following description of California's legal changes:

> In November 2000, the voters of California adopted Proposition 22 through the state's initiative process. Entitled the California Defense of Marriage Act, Proposition 22 amended the state's Family Code by adding the following language: "Only marriage between a man and a woman is valid or recognized in California." Cal. Family Code § 308.5. This amendment further codified the existing definition of marriage as "a relationship between a man and a woman."

> In February 2004, the mayor of San Francisco instructed county officials to issue marriage licenses to same-sex couples. The following month, the California Supreme Court ordered San Francisco to stop issuing such licenses and later nullified the marriage licenses that same-sex couples had received. The court expressly avoided addressing whether Proposition 22 violated the California Constitution.

> Shortly thereafter, San Francisco and various other parties filed state court actions challenging or defending California's exclusion of same-sex couples from marriage under the state constitution. These actions were consolidated in San Francisco superior court; the presiding judge determined that, as a matter of law, California's bar against marriage by same-sex couples violated the equal protection guarantee of Article I Section 7 of the California Constitution. The court of appeal reversed, and the California Supreme Court granted review. In May 2008, the California Supreme Court invalidated Proposition 22 and held that all California counties were required to issue marriage licenses to same-sex couples. From June 17, 2008 until the passage of Proposition 8 in November of that year, San Francisco and other California counties issued approximately 18,000 marriage licenses to same-sex couples.

> After the November 2008 election, opponents of Proposition 8 challenged the initiative through an original writ of mandate in the California Supreme

---

6. *See* Ralph v. City of New Orleans, 4 So. 3d 146 (La. App. 4 Cir. 2009).

7. *See id.*

Court as violating the rules for amending the California Constitution and on other grounds; the California Supreme Court upheld Proposition 8 against those challenges. Strauss leaves undisturbed the 18,000 marriages of same-sex couples performed in the four and a half months between the decision in *In re Marriage Cases* and the passage of Proposition 8. Since Proposition 8 passed, no same-sex couple has been permitted to marry in California.[8]

The three cases below — *Lawrence v. Texas*; *United States v. Winsor*; and *Obergefell v. Hodges* — map the path from the de-criminalization of same-sex relationships to their legal recognition.

Lawrence v. Texas

539 U.S. 558 (2003)

Justice KENNEDY delivered the opinion of the Court.

Liberty protects the person from unwarranted government intrusions into a dwelling or other private places. In our tradition the State is not omnipresent in the home. And there are other spheres of our lives and existence, outside the home, where the State should not be a dominant presence. Freedom extends beyond spatial bounds. Liberty presumes an autonomy of self that includes freedom of thought, belief, expression, and certain intimate conduct. The instant case involves liberty of the person both in its spatial and in its more transcendent dimensions.

I

The question before the Court is the validity of a Texas statute making it a crime for two persons of the same sex to engage in certain intimate sexual conduct.

In Houston, Texas, officers of the Harris County Police Department were dispatched to a private residence in response to a reported weapons disturbance. They entered an apartment where one of the petitioners, John Geddes Lawrence, resided. The right of the police to enter does not seem to have been questioned. The officers observed Lawrence and another man, Tyron Garner, engaging in a sexual act. The two petitioners were arrested, held in custody overnight, and charged and convicted before a Justice of the Peace.

The complaints described their crime as "deviate sexual intercourse, namely anal sex, with a member of the same sex (man)." The applicable state law is Tex. Penal Code Ann. § 21.06(a) (2003). It provides: "A person commits an offense if he engages in deviate sexual intercourse with another individual of the same sex." The statute defines "[d]eviate sexual intercourse" as follows:

"(A) any contact between any part of the genitals of one person and the mouth or anus of another person; or

---

8. Perry v. Schwarzenegger, 704 F. Supp. 2d 921, 927 (2010) (citations omitted).

(B) the penetration of the genitals or the anus of another person with an object."

. . . We granted certiorari . . . to consider three questions:

1. Whether petitioners criminal convictions under the Texas "Homosexual Conduct" law—which criminalizes sexual intimacy by same-sex couples, but not identical behavior by different-sex couples—violate the Fourteenth Amendment guarantee of equal protection of the laws.

2. Whether petitioners' criminal convictions for adult consensual sexual intimacy in the home violate their vital interests in liberty and privacy protected by the Due Process Clause of the Fourteenth Amendment.

3. Whether *Bowers v. Hardwick*, supra, should be overruled.

The petitioners were adults at the time of the alleged offense. Their conduct was in private and consensual.

II

We conclude the case should be resolved by determining whether the petitioners were free as adults to engage in the private conduct in the exercise of their liberty under the Due Process Clause of the Fourteenth Amendment to the Constitution. For this inquiry we deem it necessary to reconsider the Court's holding in *Bowers*.

There are broad statements of the substantive reach of liberty under the Due Process Clause in earlier cases . . . but the most pertinent beginning point is our decision in *Griswold v. Connecticut*, 381 U.S. 479 (1965).

In *Griswold* the Court invalidated a state law prohibiting the use of drugs or devices of contraception and counseling or aiding and abetting the use of contraceptives. The Court described the protected interest as a right to privacy and placed emphasis on the marriage relation and the protected space of the marital bedroom. . . .

After *Griswold* it was established that the right to make certain decisions regarding sexual conduct extends beyond the marital relationship. In *Eisenstadt v. Baird*, 405 U.S. 438 (1972), the Court invalidated a law prohibiting the distribution of contraceptives to unmarried persons. The case was decided under the Equal Protection Clause . . . but with respect to unmarried persons, the Court went on to state the fundamental proposition that the law impaired the exercise of their personal rights. It quoted from the statement of the Court of Appeals finding the law to be in conflict with fundamental human rights, and it followed with this statement of its own:

> "It is true that in *Griswold* the right of privacy in question inhered in the marital relationship . . . . If the right of privacy means anything, it is the right of the individual, married or single, to be free from unwarranted governmental intrusion into matters so fundamentally affecting a person as the decision whether to bear or beget a child."

The opinions in *Griswold* and *Eisenstadt* were part of the background for the decision in *Roe v. Wade*, 410 U.S. 113 (1973). As is well known, the case involved a challenge to the Texas law prohibiting abortions, but the laws of other States were affected as well. Although the Court held the woman's rights were not absolute, her right to elect an abortion did have real and substantial protection as an exercise of her liberty under the Due Process Clause. The Court cited cases that protect spatial freedom and cases that go well beyond it. *Roe* recognized the right of a woman to make certain fundamental decisions affecting her destiny and confirmed once more that the protection of liberty under the Due Process Clause has a substantive dimension of fundamental significance in defining the rights of the person.

In *Carey v. Population Services Int'l*, 431 U.S. 678 (1977), the Court confronted a New York law forbidding sale or distribution of contraceptive devices to persons under 16 years of age. Although there was no single opinion for the Court, the law was invalidated. Both *Eisenstadt* and *Carey*, as well as the holding and rationale in *Roe*, confirmed that the reasoning of *Griswold* could not be confined to the protection of rights of married adults. This was the state of the law with respect to some of the most relevant cases when the Court considered *Bowers v. Hardwick*.

The facts in *Bowers* had some similarities to the instant case. A police officer, whose right to enter seems not to have been in question, observed Hardwick, in his own bedroom, engaging in intimate sexual conduct with another adult male. The conduct was in violation of a Georgia statute making it a criminal offense to engage in sodomy. One difference between the two cases is that the Georgia statute prohibited the conduct whether or not the participants were of the same sex, while the Texas statute, as we have seen, applies only to participants of the same sex. Hardwick was not prosecuted, but he brought an action in federal court to declare the state statute invalid. He alleged he was a practicing homosexual and that the criminal prohibition violated rights guaranteed to him by the Constitution. The Court, in an opinion by Justice White, sustained the Georgia law. . . .

The Court began its substantive discussion in *Bowers* as follows: "The issue presented is whether the Federal Constitution confers a fundamental right upon homosexuals to engage in sodomy and hence invalidates the laws of the many States that still make such conduct illegal and have done so for a very long time." That statement, we now conclude, discloses the Court's own failure to appreciate the extent of the liberty at stake. To say that the issue in *Bowers* was simply the right to engage in certain sexual conduct demeans the claim the individual put forward, just as it would demean a married couple were it to be said marriage is simply about the right to have sexual intercourse. The laws involved in *Bowers* and here are, to be sure, statutes that purport to do no more than prohibit a particular sexual act. Their penalties and purposes, though, have more far-reaching consequences, touching upon the most private human conduct, sexual behavior, and in the most private of places, the home. The statutes do seek to control a personal relationship that, whether or not entitled to formal recognition in the law, is within the liberty of persons to choose without being punished as criminals. . . .

At the outset it should be noted that there is no longstanding history in this country of laws directed at homosexual conduct as a distinct matter. Thus early

American sodomy laws were not directed at homosexuals as such but instead sought to prohibit nonprocreative sexual activity more generally. This does not suggest approval of homosexual conduct. It does tend to show that this particular form of conduct was not thought of as a separate category from like conduct between heterosexual persons. . . .

In summary, the historical grounds relied upon in *Bowers* are more complex than the majority opinion and the concurring opinion by Chief Justice Burger indicate. Their historical premises are not without doubt and, at the very least, are overstated. . . .

As an alternative argument in this case, counsel for the petitioners and some amici contend that *Romer* provides the basis for declaring the Texas statute invalid under the Equal Protection Clause. That is a tenable argument, but we conclude the instant case requires us to address whether *Bowers* itself has continuing validity. Were we to hold the statute invalid under the Equal Protection Clause some might question whether a prohibition would be valid if drawn differently, say, to prohibit the conduct both between same-sex and different-sex participants.

Equality of treatment and the due process right to demand respect for conduct protected by the substantive guarantee of liberty are linked in important respects, and a decision on the latter point advances both interests. If protected conduct is made criminal and the law which does so remains unexamined for its substantive validity, its stigma might remain even if it were not enforceable as drawn for equal protection reasons. When homosexual conduct is made criminal by the law of the State, that declaration in and of itself is an invitation to subject homosexual persons to discrimination both in the public and in the private spheres. The central holding of *Bowers* has been brought in question by this case, and it should be addressed. Its continuance as precedent demeans the lives of homosexual persons. . . .

The doctrine of stare decisis is essential to the respect accorded to the judgments of the Court and to the stability of the law. It is not, however, an inexorable command. . . .

The rationale of *Bowers* does not withstand careful analysis. In his dissenting opinion in *Bowers* Justice STEVENS came to these conclusions:

> "Our prior cases make two propositions abundantly clear. First, the fact that the governing majority in a State has traditionally viewed a particular practice as immoral is not a sufficient reason for upholding a law prohibiting the practice; neither history nor tradition could save a law prohibiting miscegenation from constitutional attack. Second, individual decisions by married persons, concerning the intimacies of their physical relationship, even when not intended to produce offspring, are a form of 'liberty' protected by the Due Process Clause of the Fourteenth Amendment. Moreover, this protection extends to intimate choices by unmarried as well as married persons."

Justice STEVENS' analysis, in our view, should have been controlling in *Bowers* and should control here.

Bowers was not correct when it was decided, and it is not correct today. It ought not to remain binding precedent. *Bowers v. Hardwick* should be and now is overruled. . . .

The judgment of the Court of Appeals for the Texas Fourteenth District is reversed, and the case is remanded for further proceedings not inconsistent with this opinion.

It is so ordered.

United States v. Windsor

133 S. Ct. 2675 (2013)

Justice KENNEDY delivered the opinion of the Court.

Two women then resident in New York were married in a lawful ceremony in Ontario, Canada, in 2007. Edith Windsor and Thea Spyer returned to their home in New York City. When Spyer died in 2009, she left her entire estate to Windsor. Windsor sought to claim the estate tax exemption for surviving spouses. She was barred from doing so, however, by a federal law, the Defense of Marriage Act, which excludes a same-sex partner from the definition of "spouse" as that term is used in federal statutes. Windsor paid the taxes but filed suit to challenge the constitutionality of this provision. The United States District Court and the Court of Appeals ruled that this portion of the statute is unconstitutional and ordered the United States to pay Windsor a refund. This Court granted certiorari and now affirms the judgment in Windsor's favor.

I

In 1996, as some States were beginning to consider the concept of same-sex marriage . . . and before any State had acted to permit it, Congress enacted the Defense of Marriage Act (DOMA). DOMA contains two operative sections: Section 2, which has not been challenged here, allows States to refuse to recognize same-sex marriages performed under the laws of other States.

Section 3 is at issue here. It amends the Dictionary Act in Title 1, § 7, of the United States Code to provide a federal definition of "marriage" and "spouse." Section 3 of DOMA provides as follows:

> "In determining the meaning of any Act of Congress, or of any ruling, regulation, or interpretation of the various administrative bureaus and agencies of the United States, the word 'marriage' means only a legal union between one man and one woman as husband and wife, and the word 'spouse' refers only to a person of the opposite sex who is a husband or a wife." 1 U.S.C. § 7.

The definitional provision does not by its terms forbid States from enacting laws permitting same-sex marriages or civil unions or providing state benefits to residents in that status. The enactment's comprehensive definition of marriage for purposes of all federal statutes and other regulations or directives covered by its terms, however, does control over 1,000 federal laws in which marital or spousal status is addressed as a matter of federal law. . . .

Edith Windsor and Thea Spyer met in New York City in 1963 and began a long-term relationship. Windsor and Spyer registered as domestic partners when New York City gave that right to same-sex couples in 1993. Concerned about Spyer's health, the couple made the 2007 trip to Canada for their marriage, but they continued to reside in New York City. The State of New York deems their Ontario marriage to be a valid one.

Spyer died in February 2009, and left her entire estate to Windsor. Because DOMA denies federal recognition to same-sex spouses, Windsor did not qualify for the marital exemption from the federal estate tax, which excludes from taxation "any interest in property which passes or has passed from the decedent to his surviving spouse." 26 U.S.C. § 2056(a). Windsor paid $363,053 in estate taxes and sought a refund. The Internal Revenue Service denied the refund, concluding that, under DOMA, Windsor was not a "surviving spouse." Windsor commenced this refund suit in the United States District Court for the Southern District of New York. She contended that DOMA violates the guarantee of equal protection, as applied to the Federal Government through the Fifth Amendment. . . .

III

When at first Windsor and Spyer longed to marry, neither New York nor any other State granted them that right. After waiting some years, in 2007 they traveled to Ontario to be married there. It seems fair to conclude that, until recent years, many citizens had not even considered the possibility that two persons of the same sex might aspire to occupy the same status and dignity as that of a man and woman in lawful marriage. For marriage between a man and a woman no doubt had been thought of by most people as essential to the very definition of that term and to its role and function throughout the history of civilization. That belief, for many who long have held it, became even more urgent, more cherished when challenged. For others, however, came the beginnings of a new perspective, a new insight. Accordingly some States concluded that same-sex marriage ought to be given recognition and validity in the law for those same-sex couples who wish to define themselves by their commitment to each other. The limitation of lawful marriage to heterosexual couples, which for centuries had been deemed both necessary and fundamental, came to be seen in New York and certain other States as an unjust exclusion.

Slowly at first and then in rapid course, the laws of New York came to acknowledge the urgency of this issue for same-sex couples who wanted to affirm their commitment to one another before their children, their family, their friends, and their community. And so New York recognized same-sex marriages performed elsewhere; and then it later amended its own marriage laws to permit same-sex marriage. New York, in common with, as of this writing, 11 other States and the District of Columbia, decided that same-sex couples should have the right to marry and so live with pride in themselves and their union and in a status of equality with all other married persons. After a statewide deliberative process that enabled its citizens to discuss and weigh arguments for and against same-sex marriage, New York acted to enlarge the definition of marriage to correct what its citizens and elected representatives perceived to be an injustice that they had not earlier known or understood.

Against this background of lawful same-sex marriage in some States, the design, purpose, and effect of DOMA should be considered as the beginning point in deciding whether it is valid under the Constitution. By history and tradition the definition and regulation of marriage, as will be discussed in more detail, has been treated as being within the authority and realm of the separate States. Yet it is further established that Congress, in enacting discrete statutes, can make determinations that bear on marital rights and privileges. . . .

Though these discrete examples establish the constitutionality of limited federal laws that regulate the meaning of marriage in order to further federal policy, DOMA has a far greater reach; for it enacts a directive applicable to over 1,000 federal statutes and the whole realm of federal regulations. And its operation is directed to a class of persons that the laws of New York, and of 11 other States, have sought to protect. . . .

In order to assess the validity of that intervention it is necessary to discuss the extent of the state power and authority over marriage as a matter of history and tradition. State laws defining and regulating marriage, of course, must respect the constitutional rights of persons, see, e.g., *Loving v. Virginia*, 388 U.S. 1 (1967); but, subject to those guarantees, "regulation of domestic relations" is "an area that has long been regarded as a virtually exclusive province of the States."

The recognition of civil marriages is central to state domestic relations law applicable to its residents and citizens. . . . "[T]he states, at the time of the adoption of the Constitution, possessed full power over the subject of marriage and divorce . . . [and] the Constitution delegated no authority to the Government of the United States on the subject of marriage and divorce."

Consistent with this allocation of authority, the Federal Government, through our history, has deferred to state-law policy decisions with respect to domestic relations. . . .

Against this background DOMA rejects the long-established precept that the incidents, benefits, and obligations of marriage are uniform for all married couples within each State, though they may vary, subject to constitutional guarantees, from one State to the next. Despite these considerations, it is unnecessary to decide whether this federal intrusion on state power is a violation of the Constitution because it disrupts the federal balance. The State's power in defining the marital relation is of central relevance in this case quite apart from principles of federalism. Here the State's decision to give this class of persons the right to marry conferred upon them a dignity and status of immense import. When the State used its historic and essential authority to define the marital relation in this way, its role and its power in making the decision enhanced the recognition, dignity, and protection of the class in their own community. DOMA, because of its reach and extent, departs from this history and tradition of reliance on state law to define marriage. . . .

The Federal Government uses this state-defined class for the opposite purpose — to impose restrictions and disabilities. That result requires this Court now to address whether the resulting injury and indignity is a deprivation of an essential part of the liberty protected by the Fifth Amendment. What the State of New York treats as alike the federal law deems unlike by a law designed to injure the same class the State seeks to protect.

IV

DOMA seeks to injure the very class New York seeks to protect. By doing so it violates basic due process and equal protection principles applicable to the Federal Government. . . . The Constitution's guarantee of equality "must at the very least mean that a bare congressional desire to harm a politically unpopular group cannot" justify disparate treatment of that group. In determining whether a law is motived by an improper animus or purpose, "'[d]iscriminations of an unusual character'" especially require careful consideration. DOMA cannot survive under these principles. The responsibility of the States for the regulation of domestic relations is an important indicator of the substantial societal impact the State's classifications have in the daily lives and customs of its people. DOMA's unusual deviation from the usual tradition of recognizing and accepting state definitions of marriage here operates to deprive same-sex couples of the benefits and responsibilities that come with the federal recognition of their marriages. This is strong evidence of a law having the purpose and effect of disapproval of that class. The avowed purpose and practical effect of the law here in question are to impose a disadvantage, a separate status, and so a stigma upon all who enter into same-sex marriages made lawful by the unquestioned authority of the States.

The history of DOMA's enactment and its own text demonstrate that interference with the equal dignity of same-sex marriages, a dignity conferred by the States in the exercise of their sovereign power, was more than an incidental effect of the federal statute. It was its essence. . . . The stated purpose of the law was to promote an "interest in protecting the traditional moral teachings reflected in heterosexual-only marriage laws." Were there any doubt of this far-reaching purpose, the title of the Act confirms it: The Defense of Marriage. . . .

DOMA writes inequality into the entire United States Code. The particular case at hand concerns the estate tax, but DOMA is more than a simple determination of what should or should not be allowed as an estate tax refund. Among the over 1,000 statutes and numerous federal regulations that DOMA controls are laws pertaining to Social Security, housing, taxes, criminal sanctions, copyright, and veterans' benefits.

DOMA's principal effect is to identify a subset of state-sanctioned marriages and make them unequal. The principal purpose is to impose inequality, not for other reasons like governmental efficiency. . . .

The power the Constitution grants it also restrains. And though Congress has great authority to design laws to fit its own conception of sound national policy, it cannot deny the liberty protected by the Due Process Clause of the Fifth Amendment.

What has been explained to this point should more than suffice to establish that the principal purpose and the necessary effect of this law are to demean those persons who are in a lawful same-sex marriage. This requires the Court to hold, as it now does, that DOMA is unconstitutional as a deprivation of the liberty of the person protected by the Fifth Amendment of the Constitution.

The liberty protected by the Fifth Amendment's Due Process Clause contains within it the prohibition against denying to any person the equal protection of the laws. . . . While the Fifth Amendment itself withdraws from Government the power to degrade or demean in the way this law does, the equal protection guarantee of the Fourteenth Amendment makes that Fifth Amendment right all the more specific and all the better understood and preserved.

The class to which DOMA directs its restrictions and restraints are those persons who are joined in same-sex marriages made lawful by the State. DOMA singles out a class of persons deemed by a State entitled to recognition and protection to enhance their own liberty. It imposes a disability on the class by refusing to acknowledge a status the State finds to be dignified and proper. DOMA instructs all federal officials, and indeed all persons with whom same-sex couples interact, including their own children, that their marriage is less worthy than the marriages of others. The federal statute is invalid, for no legitimate purpose overcomes the purpose and effect to disparage and to injure those whom the State, by its marriage laws, sought to protect in personhood and dignity. By seeking to displace this protection and treating those persons as living in marriages less respected than others, the federal statute is in violation of the Fifth Amendment. This opinion and its holding are confined to those lawful marriages.

The judgment of the Court of Appeals for the Second Circuit is affirmed.

It is so ordered.

Obergefell v. Hodges
135 S. Ct. 2585 (2015)

Justice KENNEDY delivered the opinion of the Court.

The Constitution promises liberty to all within its reach, a liberty that includes certain specific rights that allow persons, within a lawful realm, to define and express their identity. The petitioners in these cases seek to find that liberty by marrying someone of the same sex and having their marriages deemed lawful on the same terms and conditions as marriages between persons of the opposite sex.

I

These cases come from Michigan, Kentucky, Ohio, and Tennessee, States that define marriage as a union between one man and one woman. The petitioners are 14 same-sex couples and two men whose same-sex partners are deceased. The respondents are state officials responsible for enforcing the laws in question. The petitioners claim the respondents violate the Fourteenth Amendment by denying them the right to marry or to have their marriages, lawfully performed in another State, given full recognition. . . .

The petitioners sought certiorari. This Court granted review, limited to two questions. The first, presented by the cases from Michigan and Kentucky, is whether the Fourteenth Amendment requires a State to license a marriage between two people of the same sex. The second, presented by the cases from Ohio, Tennessee, and, again, Kentucky, is whether the Fourteenth Amendment requires a State to recognize a same-sex marriage licensed and performed in a State which does grant that right.

II

Before addressing the principles and precedents that govern these cases, it is appropriate to note the history of the subject now before the Court.

A

From their beginning to their most recent page, the annals of human history reveal the transcendent importance of marriage. The lifelong union of a man and a woman always has promised nobility and dignity to all persons, without regard to their station in life. Marriage is sacred to those who live by their religions and offers unique fulfillment to those who find meaning in the secular realm. Its dynamic allows two people to find a life that could not be found alone, for a marriage becomes greater than just the two persons. Rising from the most basic human needs, marriage is essential to our most profound hopes and aspirations.

The centrality of marriage to the human condition makes it unsurprising that the institution has existed for millennia and across civilizations. Since the dawn of history, marriage has transformed strangers into relatives, binding families and societies together. Confucius taught that marriage lies at the foundation of government This wisdom was echoed centuries later and half a world away by Cicero, who wrote, "The first bond of society is marriage; next, children; and then the family." There are untold references to the beauty of marriage in religious and philosophical texts spanning time, cultures, and faiths, as well as in art and literature in all their forms. It is fair and necessary to say these references were based on the understanding that marriage is a union between two persons of the opposite sex.

That history is the beginning of these cases. The respondents say it should be the end as well. To them, it would demean a timeless institution if the concept and lawful status of marriage were extended to two persons of the same sex. Marriage, in their view, is by its nature a gender-differentiated union of man and woman. This view long has been held—and continues to be held—in good faith by reasonable and sincere people here and throughout the world.

The petitioners acknowledge this history but contend that these cases cannot end there. Were their intent to demean the revered idea and reality of marriage, the petitioners' claims would be of a different order. But that is neither their purpose nor their submission. To the contrary, it is the enduring importance of marriage that underlies the petitioners' contentions. This, they say, is their whole point. Far from seeking to devalue marriage, the petitioners seek it for themselves because of their respect—and need—for its privileges and responsibilities. And their immutable nature dictates that same-sex marriage is their only real path to this profound commitment.

Recounting the circumstances of three of these cases illustrates the urgency of the petitioners' cause from their perspective. Petitioner James Obergefell, a plaintiff in the Ohio case, met John Arthur over two decades ago. They fell in love and started a life together, establishing a lasting, committed relation. In 2011, however, Arthur was diagnosed with amyotrophic lateral sclerosis, or ALS. This debilitating disease is progressive, with no known cure. Two years ago, Obergefell and Arthur decided to commit to one another, resolving to marry before Arthur died. To fulfill their mutual promise, they traveled from Ohio to Maryland, where same-sex marriage was legal. It was difficult for Arthur to move, and so the couple were wed inside a medical transport plane as it remained on the tarmac in Baltimore. Three months later, Arthur died. Ohio law does not permit Obergefell to be listed as the surviving spouse on Arthur's death certificate. By statute, they must remain strangers even in death, a state-imposed separation Obergefell deems "hurtful for the rest of time." He brought suit to be shown as the surviving spouse on Arthur's death certificate.

April DeBoer and Jayne Rowse are co-plaintiffs in the case from Michigan. They celebrated a commitment ceremony to honor their permanent relation in 2007. They both work as nurses, DeBoer in a neonatal unit and Rowse in an emergency unit. In 2009, DeBoer and Rowse fostered and then adopted a baby boy. Later that same year, they welcomed another son into their family. The new baby, born prematurely and abandoned by his biological mother, required around-the-clock care. The next year, a baby girl with special needs joined their family. Michigan, however, permits only opposite-sex married couples or single individuals to adopt, so each child can have only one woman as his or her legal parent. If an emergency were to arise, schools and hospitals may treat the three children as if they had only one parent. And, were tragedy to befall either DeBoer or Rowse, the other would have no legal rights over the children she had not been permitted to adopt. This couple seeks relief from the continuing uncertainty their unmarried status creates in their lives.

Army Reserve Sergeant First Class Ijpe DeKoe and his partner Thomas Kostura, co-plaintiffs in the Tennessee case, fell in love. In 2011, DeKoe received orders to deploy to Afghanistan. Before leaving, he and Kostura married in New York. A week later, DeKoe began his deployment, which lasted for almost a year. When he returned, the two settled in Tennessee, where DeKoe works full-time for the Army Reserve.

Their lawful marriage is stripped from them whenever they reside in Tennessee, returning and disappearing as they travel across state lines. DeKoe, who served this Nation to preserve the freedom the Constitution protects, must endure a substantial burden.

The cases now before the Court involve other petitioners as well, each with their own experiences. Their stories reveal that they seek not to denigrate marriage but rather to live their lives, or honor their spouses' memory, joined by its bond. . . .

III

Under the Due Process Clause of the Fourteenth Amendment, no State shall "deprive any person of life, liberty, or property, without due process of law." The fundamental liberties protected by this Clause include most of the rights enumerated in the Bill of Rights. In addition these liberties extend to certain personal choices central to individual dignity and autonomy, including intimate choices that define personal identity and beliefs.

The identification and protection of fundamental rights is an enduring part of the judicial duty to interpret the Constitution. That responsibility, however, "has not been reduced to any formula." Rather, it requires courts to exercise reasoned judgment in identifying interests of the person so fundamental that the State must accord them its respect. That process is guided by many of the same considerations relevant to analysis of other constitutional provisions that set forth broad principles rather than specific requirements. History and tradition guide and discipline this inquiry but do not set its outer boundaries. That method respects our history and learns from it without allowing the past alone to rule the present.

The nature of injustice is that we may not always see it in our own times. The generations that wrote and ratified the Bill of Rights and the Fourteenth Amendment did not presume to know the extent of freedom in all of its dimensions, and so they entrusted to future generations a charter protecting the right of all persons to enjoy liberty as we learn its meaning. When new insight reveals discord between the Constitution's central protections and a received legal stricture, a claim to liberty must be addressed.

Applying these established tenets, the Court has long held the right to marry is protected by the Constitution. . . .

It cannot be denied that this Court's cases describing the right to marry presumed a relationship involving opposite-sex partners. . . .

Still, there are other, more instructive precedents. This Court's cases have expressed constitutional principles of broader reach. In defining the right to marry these cases have identified essential attributes of that right based in history, tradition, and other constitutional liberties inherent in this intimate bond. And in assessing whether the force and rationale of its cases apply to same-sex couples, the Court must respect the basic reasons why the right to marry has been long protected.

This analysis compels the conclusion that same-sex couples may exercise the right to marry. The four principles and traditions to be discussed demonstrate that the reasons marriage is fundamental under the Constitution apply with equal force to same-sex couples.

A first premise of the Court's relevant precedents is that the right to personal choice regarding marriage is inherent in the concept of individual autonomy. This abiding connection between marriage and liberty is why *Loving* invalidated interracial marriage bans under the Due Process Clause. Like choices concerning contraception, family relationships, procreation, and childrearing, all of which are protected by the Constitution, decisions concerning marriage are among the most intimate that an individual can make. . . .

A second principle in this Court's jurisprudence is that the right to marry is fundamental because it supports a two-person union unlike any other in its importance to the committed individuals. . . . The right to marry thus dignifies couples who "wish to define themselves by their commitment to each other." Marriage responds to the universal fear that a lonely person might call out only to find no one there. It offers the hope of companionship and understanding and assurance that while both still live there will be someone to care for the other.

As this Court held in *Lawrence*, same-sex couples have the same right as opposite-sex couples to enjoy intimate association. *Lawrence* invalidated laws that made same-sex intimacy a criminal act. And it acknowledged that "[w]hen sexuality finds overt expression in intimate conduct with another person, the conduct can be but one element in a personal bond that is more enduring." But while *Lawrence* confirmed a dimension of freedom that allows individuals to engage in intimate association without criminal liability, it does not follow that freedom stops there. Outlaw to outcast may be a step forward, but it does not achieve the full promise of liberty.

A third basis for protecting the right to marry is that it safeguards children and families and thus draws meaning from related rights of childrearing, procreation, and education. The Court has recognized these connections by describing the varied rights as a unified whole: "[T]he right to 'marry, establish a home and bring up children' is a central part of the liberty protected by the Due Process Clause." Under the laws of the several States, some of marriage's protections for children and families are material. But marriage also confers more profound benefits. By giving recognition and legal structure to their parents' relationship, marriage allows children "to understand the integrity and closeness of their own family and its concord with other families in their community and in their daily lives." Marriage also affords the permanency and stability important to children's best interests.

As all parties agree, many same-sex couples provide loving and nurturing homes to their children, whether biological or adopted. And hundreds of thousands of children are presently being raised by such couples. Most States have allowed gays and lesbians to adopt, either as individuals or as couples, and many adopted and foster children have same-sex parents. This provides powerful confirmation from the law itself that gays and lesbians can create loving, supportive families.

Excluding same-sex couples from marriage thus conflicts with a central premise of the right to marry. Without the recognition, stability, and predictability marriage offers, their children suffer the stigma of knowing their families are somehow lesser. They also suffer the significant material costs of being raised by unmarried parents, relegated through no fault of their own to a more difficult and uncertain family life. The marriage laws at issue here thus harm and humiliate the children of same-sex couples.

That is not to say the right to marry is less meaningful for those who do not or cannot have children. An ability, desire, or promise to procreate is not and has not been a prerequisite for a valid marriage in any State. In light of precedent protecting the right of a married couple not to procreate, it cannot be said the Court or the States have conditioned the right to marry on the capacity or commitment to procreate. The constitutional marriage right has many aspects, of which childbearing is only one.

Fourth and finally, this Court's cases and the Nation's traditions make clear that marriage is a keystone of our social order. . . .

There is no difference between same- and opposite-sex couples with respect to this principle. Yet by virtue of their exclusion from that institution, same-sex couples are denied the constellation of benefits that the States have linked to marriage. This harm results in more than just material burdens. Same-sex couples are consigned to an instability many opposite-sex couples would deem intolerable in their own lives. As the State itself makes marriage all the more precious by the significance it attaches to it, exclusion from that status has the effect of teaching that gays and lesbians are unequal in important respects. It demeans gays and lesbians for the State to lock them out of a central institution of the Nation's society. Same-sex couples, too, may aspire to the transcendent purposes of marriage and seek fulfillment in its highest meaning.

The limitation of marriage to opposite-sex couples may long have seemed natural and just, but its inconsistency with the central meaning of the fundamental right to marry is now manifest. With that knowledge must come the recognition that laws excluding same-sex couples from the marriage right impose stigma and injury of the kind prohibited by our basic charter. . . .

[Respondents] assert the petitioners do not seek to exercise the right to marry but rather a new and nonexistent "right to same-sex marriage." *Glucksberg* did insist that liberty under the Due Process Clause must be defined in a most circumscribed manner, with central reference to specific historical practices. Yet while that approach may have been appropriate for the asserted right there involved (physician-assisted suicide), it is inconsistent with the approach this Court has used in discussing other fundamental rights, including marriage and intimacy. *Loving* did not ask about a "right to interracial marriage"; *Turner* did not ask about a "right of inmates to marry";

and *Zablocki* did not ask about a "right of fathers with unpaid child support duties to marry." Rather, each case inquired about the right to marry in its comprehensive sense, asking if there was a sufficient justification for excluding the relevant class from the right.

That principle applies here. If rights were defined by who exercised them in the past, then received practices could serve as their own continued justification and new groups could not invoke rights once denied. This Court has rejected that approach, both with respect to the right to marry and the rights of gays and lesbians. . . .

The right of same-sex couples to marry that is part of the liberty promised by the Fourteenth Amendment is derived, too, from that Amendment's guarantee of the equal protection of the laws. The Due Process Clause and the Equal Protection Clause are connected in a profound way, though they set forth independent principles. Rights implicit in liberty and rights secured by equal protection may rest on different precepts and are not always co-extensive, yet in some instances each may be instructive as to the meaning and reach of the other. In any particular case one Clause may be thought to capture the essence of the right in a more accurate and comprehensive way, even as the two Clauses may converge in the identification and definition of the right. This interrelation of the two principles furthers our understanding of what freedom is and must become.

The Court's cases touching upon the right to marry reflect this dynamic. In *Loving* the Court invalidated a prohibition on interracial marriage under both the Equal Protection Clause and the Due Process Clause. The Court first declared the prohibition invalid because of its unequal treatment of interracial couples. It stated: "There can be no doubt that restricting the freedom to marry solely because of racial classifications violates the central meaning of the Equal Protection Clause." With this link to equal protection the Court proceeded to hold the prohibition offended central precepts of liberty: "To deny this fundamental freedom on so unsupportable a basis as the racial classifications embodied in these statutes, classifications so directly subversive of the principle of equality at the heart of the Fourteenth Amendment, is surely to deprive all the State's citizens of liberty without due process of law." The reasons why marriage is a fundamental right became more clear and compelling from a full awareness and understanding of the hurt that resulted from laws barring interracial unions.

The synergy between the two protections is illustrated further in *Zablocki*. There the Court invoked the Equal Protection Clause as its basis for invalidating the challenged law, which, as already noted, barred fathers who were behind on child-support payments from marrying without judicial approval. The equal protection analysis depended in central part on the Court's holding that the law burdened a right "of fundamental importance." It was the essential nature of the marriage right, discussed at length in *Zablocki* that made apparent the law's incompatibility with requirements of equality. Each concept — liberty and equal protection — leads to a stronger understanding of the other.

Indeed, in interpreting the Equal Protection Clause, the Court has recognized that new insights and societal understandings can reveal unjustified inequality within our most fundamental institutions that once passed unnoticed and unchallenged. . . . .

In *Lawrence* the Court acknowledged the interlocking nature of these constitutional safeguards in the context of the legal treatment of gays and lesbians. Although *Lawrence* elaborated its holding under the Due Process Clause, it acknowledged, and sought to remedy, the continuing inequality that resulted from laws making intimacy in the lives of gays and lesbians a crime against the State. *Lawrence* therefore drew upon principles of liberty and equality to define and protect the rights of gays and lesbians, holding the State "cannot demean their existence or control their destiny by making their private sexual conduct a crime." This dynamic also applies to same-sex marriage. It is now clear that the challenged laws burden the liberty of same-sex couples, and it must be further acknowledged that they abridge central precepts of equality. Here the marriage laws enforced by the respondents are in essence unequal: same-sex couples are denied all the benefits afforded to opposite-sex couples and are barred from exercising a fundamental right. Especially against a long history of disapproval of their relationships, this denial to same-sex couples of the right to marry works a grave and continuing harm. The imposition of this disability on gays and lesbians serves to disrespect and subordinate them. And the Equal Protection Clause, like the Due Process Clause, prohibits this unjustified infringement of the fundamental right to marry.

These considerations lead to the conclusion that the right to marry is a fundamental right inherent in the liberty of the person, and under the Due Process and Equal Protection Clauses of the Fourteenth Amendment couples of the same-sex may not be deprived of that right and that liberty. The Court now holds that same-sex couples may exercise the fundamental right to marry. . . .

V

These cases also present the question whether the Constitution requires States to recognize same-sex marriages validly performed out of State. As made clear by the case of Obergefell and Arthur, and by that of DeKoe and Kostura, the recognition bans inflict substantial and continuing harm on same-sex couples.

Being married in one State but having that valid marriage denied in another is one of "the most perplexing and distressing complication[s]" in the law of domestic relations. Leaving the current state of affairs in place would maintain and promote instability and uncertainty. For some couples, even an ordinary drive into a neighboring State to visit family or friends risks causing severe hardship in the event of a spouse's hospitalization while across state lines. In light of the fact that many States already allow same-sex marriage—and hundreds of thousands of these marriages already have occurred—the disruption caused by the recognition bans is significant and ever-growing.

As counsel for the respondents acknowledged at argument, if States are required by the Constitution to issue marriage licenses to same-sex couples, the justifications for refusing to recognize those marriages performed elsewhere are undermined. The Court, in this decision, holds same-sex couples may exercise the fundamental right to marry in all States. It follows that the Court also must hold—and it now does hold—that there is no lawful basis for a State to refuse to recognize a lawful same-sex marriage performed in another State on the ground of its same-sex character. . . .

The judgment of the Court of Appeals for the Sixth Circuit is reversed.

It is so ordered.

C. Marriage and Religious Beliefs

In *Obergefell*, the Court made it clear that its opinion was not intended to interfere with the fundamental rights afforded by the First Amendment: "Finally, it must be emphasized that religions, and those who adhere to religious doctrines, may continue to advocate with utmost, sincere conviction that, by divine precepts, same-sex marriage should not be condoned." A different, but somewhat related, question arose in the 1800s with respect to polygamy. Must we allow people to marry in a manner consistent with their religious beliefs? In particular, what about polygamy? In *Reynolds v. United States*, the Court answered that question in the negative.

Reynolds is just one piece of the saga between the Mormon Church and the United States Government. The religion—also called the Church of Jesus Christ of Latter Day Saints (or "LDS Church") was founded by Joseph Smith in New York in 1830. Smith and his followers migrated west—establishing settlements in Ohio, Missouri, and Illinois. Smith's religion proved controversial—particularly its belief in plural marriage (a type of polygamy). Smith and his followers repeatedly faced violent conflict—Smith and his brother were killed by a mob during one such conflict in Illinois in 1844. Following Smith's death, Brigham Young became the new leader. As tensions continued to escalate, Young decided to relocate his followers—eventually settling in the Utah territory. The United States government repeatedly attacked the church—often because of the church's belief in plural marriage. In 1857, the United States army invaded the Utah Territory. In 1890 Congress seized most of the church's assets. Eventually, the LDS Church officially repudiated the practice of plural marriage—which helped to facilitate Utah's admission as a state in 1896. Plural marriage has not formed part of the LDS Church doctrine since those early days. A number of splinter groups, however, have continued the practice.

More than a century later, reality television prompted courts and scholars to begin to reconsider the holding in *Reynolds*. The reality show "Sister Wives" premiered in 2010 on the network TLC. The show featured a polygamist family living in Utah—the Brown family. The Browns were members of one of the splinter groups that continued to practice plural marriage. Kody Brown married his first wife, Meri Brown, in 1990. Kody later entered into "spiritual" marriages with wives Janelle, Christine, and Robyn. Once the show aired, Utah police announced an investigation of the family for violations of the state's bigamy statute. Utah's statute provided that "[a] person is guilty of bigamy when, knowing he has a husband or wife, the person purports to marry another person or cohabits with another person."[9]

In some ways, the issues presented by polygamy are similar to those presented by *Lawrence v. Texas* and *Obergefell v. Hodges*. Many states have criminal statutes pertaining to bigamy. Can this type of statute withstand a constitutional challenge following *Lawrence v. Texas*? If not, then does *Obergefell v. Hodges* necessarily lead to the conclusion that states must allow polygamous marriages?

Reynolds v. United States

98 U.S. 145 (1878)

MR. CHIEF JUSTICE WAITE delivered the opinion of the court.

The assignments of error, when grouped, present the following questions. . . .

5. Should the accused have been acquitted if he married the second time, because he believed it to be his religious duty?

. . . On the trial, the plaintiff in error, the accused, proved that at the time of his alleged second marriage he was, and for many years before had been, a member of the Church of Jesus Christ of Latter-Day Saints, commonly called the Mormon Church, and a believer in its doctrines; that it was an accepted doctrine of that church "that it was the duty of male members of said church, circumstances permitting, to practise polygamy; . . . that this duty was enjoined by different books which the members of said church believed to be of divine origin, and among others the Holy Bible, and also that the members of the church believed that the practice of polygamy was directly enjoined upon the male members thereof by the Almighty God, in a revelation to Joseph Smith, the founder and prophet of said church; that the failing or refusing to practise polygamy by such male members of said church, when circumstances would admit, would be punished, and that the penalty for such failure and refusal would be damnation in the life to come." He also proved "that he had received permission from the recognized authorities in said church to enter into polygamous marriage; . . . that Daniel H. Wells, one having authority in said church to perform the marriage ceremony, married the said defendant on or about the time the crime is alleged to have been committed, to some woman by the name of Schofield, and that such marriage ceremony was performed under and pursuant to the doctrines of said church."

Upon this proof he asked the court to instruct the jury that if they found from the evidence that he "was married as charged—if he was married—in pursuance of and in conformity with what he believed at the time to be a religious duty, that the verdict must be 'not guilty.'" This request was refused, and the court did charge "that there must have been a criminal intent, but that if the defendant, under the influence of a religious belief that it was right,—under an inspiration, if you please, that it was

---

9. UTAH CODE § 76-7-101 (1997).

right,—deliberately married a second time, having a first wife living, the want of consciousness of evil intent—the want of understanding on his part that he was committing a crime—did not excuse him; but the law inexorably in such case implies the criminal intent."

Upon this charge and refusal to charge the question is raised, whether religious belief can be accepted as a justification of an overt act made criminal by the law of the land. The inquiry is not as to the power of Congress to prescribe criminal laws for the Territories, but as to the guilt of one who knowingly violates a law which has been properly enacted, if he entertains a religious belief that the law is wrong.

Congress cannot pass a law for the government of the Territories which shall prohibit the free exercise of religion. The first amendment to the Constitution expressly forbids such legislation. Religious freedom is guaranteed everywhere throughout the United States, so far as congressional interference is concerned. The question to be determined is, whether the law now under consideration comes within this prohibition.

The word "religion" is not defined in the Constitution. We must go elsewhere, therefore, to ascertain its meaning, and nowhere more appropriately, we think, than to the history of the times in the midst of which the provision was adopted. The precise point of the inquiry is, what is the religious freedom which has been guaranteed. . . .

Polygamy has always been odious among the northern and western nations of Europe, and, until the establishment of the Mormon Church, was almost exclusively a feature of the life of Asiatic and of African people. At common law, the second marriage was always void (2 Kent, Com. 79), and from the earliest history of England polygamy has been treated as an offence against society. After the establishment of the ecclesiastical courts, and until the time of James I, it was punished through the instrumentality of those tribunals, not merely because ecclesiastical rights had been violated, but because upon the separation of the ecclesiastical courts from the civil the ecclesiastical were supposed to be the most appropriate for the trial of matrimonial causes and offences against the rights of marriage, just as they were for testamentary causes and the settlement of the estates of deceased persons.

By the statute of 1 James I. (c. 11), the offence, if committed in England or Wales, was made punishable in the civil courts, and the penalty was death. As this statute was limited in its operation to England and Wales, it was at a very early period re-enacted, generally with some modifications, in all the colonies. . . . Marriage, while from its very nature a sacred obligation, is nevertheless, in most civilized nations, a civil contract, and usually regulated by law. Upon it society may be said to be built, and out of its fruits spring social relations and social obligations and duties, with which government is necessarily required to deal. In fact, according as monogamous or polygamous marriages are allowed, do we find the principles on which the government of the people, to a greater or less extent, rests. Professor, Lieber says, polygamy leads to the patriarchal principle, and which, when applied to large communities, fetters the people in stationary despotism, while that principle cannot long exist in connection with monogamy. . . . An exceptional colony of polygamists under an exceptional leadership may sometimes exist for a time without appearing to disturb the social condition of the people who surround it; but there cannot be a doubt that, unless restricted by some form of constitution, it is within the legitimate scope of the power of every civil government to determine whether polygamy or monogamy shall be the law of social life under its dominion.

In our opinion, the statute immediately under consideration is within the legislative power of Congress. It is constitutional and valid as prescribing a rule of action for all those residing in the Territories, and in places over which the United States have exclusive control. This being so, the only question which remains is, whether those who make polygamy a part of their religion are excepted from the operation of the statute. If they are, then those who do not make polygamy a part of their religious belief may be found guilty and punished, while those who do, must be acquitted and go free. This would be introducing a new element into criminal law. Laws are made for the government of actions, and while they cannot interfere with mere religious belief and opinions, they may with practices. Suppose one believed that human sacrifices were a necessary part of religious worship, would it be seriously contended that the civil government under which he lived could not interfere to prevent a sacrifice? Or if a wife religiously believed it was her duty to burn herself upon the funeral pile of her dead husband, would it be beyond the power of the civil government to prevent her carrying her belief into practice?

So here, as a law of the organization of society under the exclusive dominion of the United States, it is provided that plural marriages shall not be allowed. Can a man excuse his practices to the contrary because of his religious belief? To permit this would be to make the professed doctrines of religious belief superior to the law of the land, and in effect to permit every citizen to become a law unto himself. Government could exist only in name under such circumstances.

A criminal intent is generally an element of crime, but every man is presumed to intend the necessary and legitimate consequences of what he knowingly does. Here the accused knew he had been once married, and that his first wife was living. He also knew that his second marriage was forbidden by law. When, therefore, he married the second time, he is presumed to have intended to break the law. And the breaking of the law is the crime. Every act necessary to constitute the crime was knowingly done, and the crime was therefore knowingly committed. Ignorance of a fact may sometimes be taken as evidence of a want of criminal intent, but not ignorance of the law. The only defence of the accused in this case is his belief that the law ought not to have been enacted. It matters not that his belief was a part of his professed religion: it was still belief, and belief only. . . .

Upon a careful consideration of the whole case, we are satisfied that no error was committed by the court below.

Judgment affirmed.

Brown v. Buhman

947 F. Supp. 2d 1170 (D. Utah 2013)

(*reversed* on mootness grounds 822 F.3d 1151 (10th Cir. 2016))

CLARK WADDOUPS, District Judge.

INTRODUCTION

Before the court are the parties' cross motions for summary judgment relating to Plaintiffs' facial and as-applied constitutional challenges to Utah's bigamy statute, Utah Code Ann. § 76-7-101 (2013) (the "Statute").... [I]n Part II below the court finds the Statute facially unconstitutional and therefore strikes the phrase "or cohabits with another person" as a violation of the Free Exercise Clause of the First Amendment to the United States Constitution and as without a rational basis under the Due Process Clause of the Fourteenth Amendment, both in light of established Supreme Court precedent. As further analyzed in Part III below, after striking the cohabitation provision the Statute is readily susceptible to a narrowing construction of the terms "marry" and "purports to marry" to remedy the constitutional infirmity of the remainder of the Statute....

FACTUAL BACKGROUND

The court described the relevant facts underlying this lawsuit in its Memorandum Decision and Order dated February 3, 2012 and refers here to that discussion for a general review of the background.

[Author's Note: The facts referred to by the Judge are reproduced here in italics]

Plaintiffs Kody Brown, Meri Brown, Janelle Brown, Christine Brown, and Robyn Sullivan are self-described polygamists that publicly lived in Utah as a plural family. During this time, members of the family have participated in a number of outreach efforts to speak and educate others about their lifestyle. For example, Christine Brown was interviewed on national television by HBO in 2007, participated in the television show 48 Hours in 2008, and spoke to a University of Utah class about polygamy and her polygamist practices in 2009.

Through these and other activities, Plaintiffs became aware that the State of Utah has a policy of not prosecuting individuals for violations of the Anti-Bigamy Statute, except in cases where other crimes accompany the bigamy charge. Relying upon certain assurances of state officials leading up to 2010, the Browns became involved with the television series Sister Wives on TLC, which is a reality show based on their polygamist family.

After the show aired, the Lehi City Police Department began receiving a number of calls inquiring what the department intended to do. The day after the first episode aired, the Lehi City Police Department publicly announced that it was investigating Plaintiffs for bigamy. Similarly, the Utah County Attorney's office stated that the Browns were placed under investigation after its attorneys saw the Sister Wives promotional trailer and commented that the Browns have made it easier for prosecutors because they admitted to felonies on national television. Although prosecutors have left the possibility of other charges open, Plaintiffs' allegations support an inference that these investigations have centered on their bigamist activities. In contrast to the State, Utah County does not have a policy against prosecuting bigamists solely for bigamy. Indeed, since making the initial announcement and remarks, Utah County has remained silent on its intentions to prosecute or not prosecute the Browns under the Statute. Based on these statements, Plaintiffs fled from Utah to Nevada for fear that they would be criminally prosecuted for practicing bigamy. Despite not living and exercising their speech in Utah, they continue to visit relatives and associates in Utah. Once the threat of prosecution is lifted, however, they expect to relocate to the State of Utah.

HISTORICAL BACKGROUND

This decision is fraught with both religious and historical significance for the State of Utah because it deals with the question of polygamy, an issue that played a central role in the State's development and that of its dominant religion, The Church of Jesus Christ of Latter-day Saints (the "LDS Church" or "Mormon Church"). The Brown Plaintiffs are not members of the LDS Church, but do adhere to the beliefs of a fundamentalist church that shares its historical roots with Mormonism. . . .

The court notes that 133 years after *Reynolds*, non-Mormon counsel for Plaintiffs have vigorously advanced arguments in favor of the right of religious polygamists to practice polygamy (through private "spiritual" marriages not licensed or otherwise sanctioned by the state, a relationship to which the court will refer as "religious cohabitation") that would have perhaps delighted Mormon Apostles and polygamy apologists throughout the period from 1852 to approximately 1904. To state the obvious, the intervening years have witnessed a significant strengthening of numerous provisions of the Bill of Rights, and a practical and morally defensible identification of "penumbral" rights "of privacy and repose" emanating from those key provisions of the Bill of Rights, as the Supreme Court has over decades assumed a general posture that is less inclined to allow majoritarian coercion of unpopular or disliked minority groups, especially when blatant racism (as expressed through Orientalism/imperialism), religious prejudice, or some other constitutionally suspect motivation, can be discovered behind such legislation. . . .

Although the object of the decision was the Mormon Church, an institution virtually entirely comprised of white Americans and European immigrants, rather than the "Orient" or a people or institution geographically unique thereto, *Reynolds* invokes this framework because of the comparisons drawn by the Court between Mormons and non-European peoples and their practices, and the Court's views of the nature of the social harm posed by Mormon practices. For the *Reynolds* Court, the comparison with non-European peoples and their practices is precisely what made the Mormons' practice of polygamy problematic.

With this interpretive framework in mind, it is perhaps a bitter irony of the history at issue here that it is possible to view the LDS Church as playing the role of both victim and violator in the saga of religious polygamy in Utah (and America). When the federal government targeted Mormon polygamy for elimination during the half century from the passage of the Morrill Anti-Bigamy Act of 1862 through the Congressional inquiry into the seating of Utah Senator Reed Smoot from 1904 to 1907 the "good order and morals of society" served as an acceptable basis for a legislature, it was believed, to identify "fundamental values" through a religious or other perceived ethical or moral consensus, enact criminal laws to force compliance with these values, and enforce those laws against a targeted group. In fact, with the exception of targeting a specific group, this has remained true in various forms (depending on the particular right and constitutional provision at issue) until the Supreme Court's decision in *Lawrence v. Texas* . . . created ambiguity about the status of such "morals legislation." But the LDS Church was a victim of such majoritarian consensus concerning its practice of polygamy as a foundational and identifying tenet of religious faith. . . . Although the court doubts that *Lawrence* actually must be interpreted to signal the end of the era in which the "good order and morals of society" are a rational basis for majoritarian legislation, there is no question this was the prevailing view in the 1870s. And, in fact, the decades-long "war" by the United States against the LDS Church—beginning with the Republican Party's 1856 platform of abolishing American chattel slavery and Mormon polygamy as the "twin relics of barbarism" and culminating, depending on how one views the historical episode, with either the Enabling Act in 1894 requiring that Utah ensure that "polygamist or plural marriages are forever prohibited" in Utah as a condition for joining the Union as a State, or the seating of Utah Senator Reed Smoot in 1907—was based on a majoritarian consensus that Mormons were indeed "subversive of good order" in their practice of polygamy.

But what exactly was the "social harm" identified by the *Reynolds* Court in the Mormon practice of polygamy that made the practice "subversive of good order"? "Polygamy has always been odious among the northern and western nations of Europe, and, until the establishment of the Mormon Church, was almost exclusively a feature of the life of Asiatic and of African people. . . ." A decade later, the Supreme Court clarified the social harm further, explaining that Mormons were degrading the morals of the country through their religious practices, such as polygamy, which, the Supreme Court declared, constituted "a return to barbarism" and were "contrary to the spirit of Christianity. . . ."

In other words, the social harm was introducing a practice perceived to be characteristic of non-European people—or non-white races—into white American society. . . . Such an assessment arising from derisive societal views about race and ethnic origin prevalent in the United States at that time has no place in discourse about religious freedom, due process, equal protection or any other constitutional guarantee or right in the genuinely and intentionally racially and religiously pluralistic society that has been strengthened by the Supreme Court's twentieth-century rights jurisprudence. . . .

The court need not be entirely bound by the extremely narrow free exercise construct evident in *Reynolds*; that case is, perhaps ironically considering the content of the current case, not controlling for today's ruling that the cohabitation prong of the Statute is unconstitutional. In fact, the court believes that *Reynolds* is not, or should no longer be considered, good law, but also acknowledges its ambiguous status given its continued citation by both the Supreme Court and the Tenth Circuit as general historical support for the broad principle that a statute may incidentally burden a particular religious practice so long as it is a generally applicable, neutral law not arising from religious animus or targeted at a specific religious group or practice.

The court therefore defers to *Reynolds* as binding on the limited question of any potential free exercise right to the actual practice of polygamy. In the religious cohabitation at issue in this case, however, the participants have "consciously chose[n] to enter into personal relationship[s] that [they] knew would not be legally recognized as marriage" even though they "used religious terminology to describe [the] relationship[s]." They make no claim to having entered into legal unions by virtue of their religious cohabitation, having instead "intentionally place[d] themselves outside the framework of rights and obligations that surround the marriage institution." In light of this, despite any applicability of *Reynolds* to actual polygamy (multiple purportedly legal unions), the cohabitation prong of the Statute is not operationally neutral or of general applicability because of its targeted effect on specifically religious cohabitation. It is therefore subject to strict scrutiny under the Free Exercise Clause and fails under that standard. Also, in these circumstances, *Smith*'s hybrid rights exception requires the court to apply a form of heightened scrutiny to Plaintiffs' constitutional claims, including their Due Process claim, since each of those constitutional claims are "reinforced by Free Exercise Clause concerns," in light of the specifically religious nature of Plaintiffs' cohabitation. Alternatively, following *Lawrence* and based on the arguments presented by Defendant in both his filings and at oral argument, the State of Utah has no rational basis under the Due Process Clause on which to prohibit the type of religious cohabitation at issue here; thus, the cohabitation prong of the Statute is facially unconstitutional, though the broader Statute survives in prohibiting bigamy.

[The court goes on to find that: engaging in polygamy is not a fundamental right triggering heightened scrutiny; religious cohabitation does not qualify as a fundamental right triggering heightened scrutiny; cohabitation prong of bigamy statute was neither operationally neutral nor generally applicable, subjecting it to strict scrutiny under the Free Exercise Clause; cohabitation prong of bigamy statute was a facial violation of the Free Exercise Clause; cohabitation prong of bigamy statute violated substantive due process; cohabitation prong of bigamy statute was void for vagueness; and bigamy statute could be saved after striking the cohabitation prong as unconstitutional by adopting narrowing construction of "purports to marry."]

Chapter 3

Marriage Requirements

See La. Civ. Code art. 86-93; 3519-20; La. Rev. Stat. § 9:272-76.

Civil Code article 87 sets forth the basic requirements for a valid marriage in Louisiana: (1) the absence of a legal impediment; (2) a marriage ceremony; and (3) the free consent of the parties expressed at the ceremony. We will consider each requirement in turn.

A. Impediments to Marriage

The first requirement for a valid marriage under Article 87 is the "absence of a legal impediment." Articles 88–90 recognize three legal impediments: (1) an existing marriage; (2) same sex—which is now clearly unconstitutional; and (3) relatedness. These impediments are supposedly based on public policy. But, just how strong is our public policy?

At first blush it may seem that the Full Faith and Credit Clause of the U.S. Constitution would require a state to recognize any marriage validly entered into in another state. Yet, this is not an issue that was fully explored during the era of antimiscegenation laws or during the same-sex marriage cases. There are, however, a number of cases that have considered the validity of out-of-state marriages from a conflict-of-laws perspective. Cases involving conflict-of-laws questions illustrate the strength (or weakness) of the various public policy considerations behind the statutorily recognized impediments to valid marriages.

General conflict-of-laws principles support a pro-marriage (*favor matrimonii*) policy. It is a near universal rule that "[a] marriage which satisfies the requirements of the state where the marriage was contracted will everywhere be recognized as valid unless it violates the strong public policy of another state which had the most significant relationship to the spouses and the marriage at the time of the marriage."[1] Louisiana Civil Code article 3520 takes this approach.

The following case demonstrates the strength (or weakness) of Louisiana's prohibition of marriages between certain relatives.

---

1. Restatement (Second) of Conflict of Laws § 283 (2017).

Ghassemi v. Ghassemi

998 So. 2d 731 (La. App. 4 Cir. 2008)

KUHN, J.

FACTUAL AND PROCEDURAL HISTORY

Plaintiff, Tahereh Ghassemi, filed suit in the East Baton Rouge Parish Family Court (family court) seeking a divorce, spousal support, and a partition of community property. In her petition, she alleged that she and the defendant, Hamid Ghassemi, were married in Bam, Iran in 1976, at which time both parties were citizens of Iran. She further alleged that a son, Hamed, was born of their union in 1977. Ms. Ghassemi contends that in that same year, Mr. Ghassemi entered the United States (U.S.) on a student visa. Ms. Ghassemi avers that when Mr. Ghassemi left Iran in 1977, it was with the understanding that he would return to Iran after he completed his studies or that he would arrange for her and Hamed to join him and establish a residence in the U.S. Unbeknownst to Ms. Ghassemi, after entering the U.S., Mr. Ghassemi contracted a "marriage" with an American woman, allegedly to enhance his legal status in this country. However, this purported "marriage" ultimately ended in "divorce."

The petition further states that, in 1995, Mr. Ghassemi made the necessary applications that allowed Hamed to enter the U.S. as his "son." However, no efforts were made on behalf of Ms. Ghassemi for her to enter the U.S. Subsequently, in 2002, Mr. Ghassemi "married" yet another woman in Baton Rouge, Louisiana, where he had become domiciled. In 2005, through the efforts of her son, Hamed, Ms. Ghassemi finally entered the U.S. as a permanent resident and also settled in Baton Rouge. On May 22, 2006, she filed the present suit.

Mr. Ghassemi responded by filing a peremptory exception pleading the objection of no cause of action. He argued that the purported marriage to Ms. Ghassemi was invalid for various reasons. Specifically, Mr. Ghassemi contended that the marriage was invalid pursuant to section (3) of Article 1045 of the Civil Code of the Islamic Republic of Iran, which provides, in pertinent part, as follows:

> Marriage with the following relations by blood is forbidden, even if the relationship is based on mistake or adultery. . . .

> 3 — Marriage with the brother and sister and their children, or their descendants to whatever generation. . . .

In his pleadings, Mr. Ghassemi posited several arguments in support of his contention that the marriage was invalid, the principal one being that he and Ms. Ghassemi are first cousins. Following a hearing, Mr. Ghassemi's exception was overruled, and the issue of the validity of the marriage was set for a trial on the merits on December 6, 2006, along with Ms. Ghassemi's petition for divorce. . . .

DISCUSSION

I. FINAL JUDGMENT

... The sole issue before us is the same as that presented to the family court: whether an Iranian marriage between first cousins will be recognized in Louisiana.

A. Applicable Law

It is axiomatic that our analysis begins with an examination of the pertinent provisions governing the conflict of laws. Marriage and, specifically, the validity of marriages are topics that, traditionally, have been subsumed under the rubric of status. LSA-C.C. art. 3519, comment (a).

However, Article 3519 only applies to the validity of marriages that do not fall within the ambit of LSA-C.C. art. 3520. LSA-C.C. art. 3519, comment (a). Article 3520, which is more specific, addresses the validity of marriages that are valid in the state where they were contracted or in the state where the parties were first domiciled. Article 3520 purposefully does not encompass marriages that are not valid in either of these states, the validity or invalidity of which must be analyzed under LSA-C.C. art. 3519.12 *See* LSA-C.C. art. 3520, comment (a)....

Comment (b) to Article 3520 explains our state's longstanding policy of "favor matrimonii...."

Thus, it is the public policy of Louisiana that every effort be made to uphold the validity of marriages. Moreover, if a foreign marriage is valid in the state where it was contracted, the marriage is accorded a presumption of validity.

In seeking declaratory relief, Mr. Ghassemi did not argue that a marriage between first cousins is invalid in Iran, where the marriage herein was purportedly contracted. Moreover, we conclude that such a marriage is not prohibited by the Iranian Civil Code article previously cited by Mr. Ghassemi in his peremptory exception pleading the objection of no cause of action. Accordingly, LSA-C.C. art. 3520 is controlling herein, and such a marriage is presumed to be valid. To defeat this presumption, Mr. Ghassemi must prove that the law of another state is applicable and that state's law would invalidate the marriage for reasons of "a strong public policy."

Because both he and Ms. Ghassemi are now domiciled in Louisiana, presumably with no intention of returning to Iran, and because Ms. Ghassemi has sought a divorce in the courts of this state, Mr. Ghassemi essentially argued that Louisiana law would be applicable under LSA-C.C. art. 3519 and asserted, to a considerable extent, that the marriage violates a strong public policy of Louisiana....

Thus, we find that the family court failed to enunciate the appropriate legal standard and further failed to analyze the precise issue before it within the parameters of that standard. The proper legal standard simply requires a two-part inquiry:

(1) Was the marriage valid in the state (Iran) where it was purportedly contracted?

(2) If so, would recognition of the validity of the marriage violate "a strong public policy" of the state whose law would be applicable under LSA-C.C. art. 3519 (Louisiana)?

B. Valid in the state where contracted?

[The court found that first cousin marriages were allowed under Iranian law.]

C. Violation of a strong public policy?

If a marriage is valid where contracted, it is presumed to be valid in this state. To rebut that presumption in the case sub judice, Mr. Ghassemi must prove that the recognition of a foreign marriage between first cousins would violate "a strong public policy" of this state.

Clearly, in determining whether Louisiana has "a strong public policy" against recognizing the validity of a foreign marriage between first cousins, it is appropriate to examine our laws governing marriages that are contracted in this state. . . .

However, the mere fact that a marriage is absolutely null when contracted in Louisiana does not mean that such a marriage validly performed elsewhere is automatically invalid as violative of a strong public policy. For example, comment (b) to LSA-C.C. art. 3520 expressly states, in part: "The word 'contracted' as opposed to the word 'celebrated' is used [in this article] so as not to exclude common-law marriage from the scope of this Article." A common-law marriage is one that is performed without a ceremony. . . . Based on the language in comment (b), LSA-C.C. art. 3520 was clearly intended to encompass foreign common-law marriages, i.e., marriages contracted without a ceremony, even though such a marriage contracted in Louisiana is absolutely null.

Indeed, the jurisprudence is replete with decisions recognizing that if a common-law marriage is contracted in a state whose law sanctions such a marriage, the marriage will be recognized as a valid marriage in Louisiana, even though a common-law marriage cannot be contracted in this state. . . .

Similarly, this state has recognized a foreign marriage contracted by procuration, even though such a marriage would be absolutely null if contracted here. In *U.S. ex rel. Modianos v. Tuttle*, 12 F.2d 927 (E.D.La.1925), the court held that the statute prohibiting marriage by procuration only applied to marriages contracted within Louisiana and that the marriage of a citizen celebrated by proxy in Turkey was valid where it was valid under the laws of that country.

There is no Louisiana jurisprudence addressing the recognition of a foreign marriage between first cousins; however, based on the law of this state, presently and historically, we find that such a marriage, if valid where contracted, is valid in Louisiana and is not a violation of a strong public policy. In finding no violation, we make a clear distinction between the marriage of first cousins and marriages contracted by more closely-related collaterals, i.e., uncle and niece, aunt and nephew, and siblings.

Contrary to assertions made by defense counsel to the family court, marriage between first cousins has not always been prohibited in Louisiana. It was permitted under the Civil Codes of 1804, 1808, and 1825. It was also permitted under the Civil Code of 1870 until its amendment in 1902. . . .

Even so, notwithstanding the prohibitions set forth in former Article 95 (as amended in 1902), the Louisiana Legislature thereafter repeatedly ratified marriages between collaterals in the fourth degree that had been contracted in violation of the prohibition. . . .

Hence, the Louisiana Legislature legalized all marriages between collaterals within the fourth degree that were contracted by citizens of this state before September 11, 1981. . . .

In continually ratifying marriages between collaterals within the fourth degree, notwithstanding our law's express prohibition of such marriages, the legislature voluntarily chose to legalize marriages by Louisiana domiciliaries who had chosen either to ignore Louisiana law or flout it. . . .

There is no reason to apply a different rule to a fugitive marriage performed in another state, rather than a foreign country.

Thus, a marriage contracted in another country or state now must be analyzed without making any distinction as to the parties' domiciliary status at the time the marriage is contracted. Accordingly, a marriage contracted in another state or country where such a marriage is valid is to be analyzed pursuant to LSA-C.C. art. 3520 regardless of whether a person is a domiciliary of Louisiana or of another state or country.

Although no "general" ratifications have occurred since 1981, in 1993, the legislature enacted LSA-R.S. 9:211, which currently provides:

> Notwithstanding the provisions of Civil Code Article 90, marriages between collaterals within the fourth degree, fifty-five years of age or older, which were entered into on or before December 31, 1992, shall be considered legal and the enactment hereof shall in no way impair vested property rights.

In light of all of the foregoing, and for reasons more fully explained below, we are compelled to conclude that Louisiana does not have a strong public policy against recognizing a marriage between first cousins performed in a state or country where such marriages are valid. . . .

However, we emphasize that the instant case involves the marriage of first cousins. Although the previously noted laws, both past and present, applied generally to all collaterals within the fourth degree, we reiterate that in finding no violation of a strong public policy, we make a clear distinction between the marriage of first cousins and marriages contracted between more closely-related collaterals. While the former is commonly accepted, the latter is greatly condemned.

"The marriage of first cousins has historically been regarded as in a different category from that of persons more closely related." A marriage between first cousins neither violates natural law nor is it included in the wider list of prohibited relationships set forth in Chapter 18 of the Bible's Book of Leviticus, the font of Western incest laws.

Thus, while "incestuous" marriages have traditionally constituted an exception to the general rule that a marriage valid where contracted is valid everywhere, that historical exception excludes marriages contracted between first cousins. . . .

Our recognition of this distinction is further buttressed by the fact that relations between first cousins are not encompassed by our criminal incest statute. . . .

Some U.S. states that prohibit first-cousin marriages, including states that consider such marriages void if contracted within the state, have nonetheless recognized such marriages when validly celebrated elsewhere by relying largely on the fact that their respective legislatures had not seen fit to criminalize relations between first cousins, despite prohibiting them from marrying within the state. . . . Based upon the law of Louisiana, first cousins may legally cohabitate, have intimate relations, and even produce children; however, they are merely prohibited from regularizing their union by marriage. This disparity would tend to negate any contention that Louisiana has a strong public policy against marriages between first cousins, since it is in conflict with this state's policy to legally solidify such unions for the good of society at large and for the benefit of any potential posterity.

Furthermore, we note that marriages between first cousins are widely permitted within the western world. "Such marriages were not forbidden at common law." Additionally, no European country prohibits marriages between first cousins. . . . Marriages between first cousins are also legal in Mexico and Canada, in addition to many other countries. . . .

Actually, the U.S. is unique among western countries in restricting first cousin marriages. Even so, such marriages may be legally contracted in Alabama, Alaska, California, Colorado, Connecticut, Florida, Georgia, Hawaii, Maryland, Massachusetts, New Jersey, New Mexico, New York, North Carolina, Rhode Island, South Carolina, Tennessee, Vermont, Virginia, and the District of Columbia. An additional six states, Arizona, Illinois, Indiana, Maine, Utah, and Wisconsin, also allow first cousin marriages subject to certain restrictions.

Accordingly, Louisiana is one of only 25 U.S. states that flatly prohibits such marriages. However, even other states that prohibit marriages between first cousins, have nonetheless found that such marriages do not violate public policy and thus recognize such marriages as valid, if they are valid in the state or country where they were contracted. . . . Like the foregoing courts, we too find that although Louisiana law expressly prohibits the marriages of first cousins, such marriages are not so "odious" as to violate a strong public policy of this state. Accordingly, a marriage between first cousins, if valid in the state or country where it was contracted, will be recognized as valid pursuant to LSA-C.C. art. 3520.

B. Marriage Ceremony

See La. Civ. Code art. 91–92; La. Rev. Stat. §9:201-63.

A marriage ceremony is required for any Louisiana marriage. Lack of a marriage ceremony typically results in an absolute nullity. The Civil Code and the Revised Statutes set forth the various requirements for a legally sufficient ceremony. The few reported decisions that consider the sufficiency of a marriage ceremony demonstrate that some elements—like the ceremony itself—are indispensable. Others—like the competency of the witnesses and the delay for marrying—are apparently less important.

Parker v. Saileau

213 So. 2d 190 (La. App. 3d Cir. 1968)

[Author's Note: At the time this case was decided, Louisiana required 3 witnesses to the marriage ceremony. Current law only requires 2 witnesses.]

Hood, Judge.

This is an action to annul a marriage. It was instituted by Winnie Parker against Kenneth Saileau (sometimes spelled Kenneth Soileau). Judgment was rendered by the trial court dismissing the suit, and plaintiff has appealed.

A wedding ceremony was performed on November 28, 1967, by Rev. Robert C. Carter, a minister of the Gospel, uniting plaintiff and defendant in the bonds of matrimony. Only two persons, other than the parties and the minister, witnessed the ceremony, and the act evidencing the celebration of the marriage was signed only by the parties, the minister and these two witnesses. The ceremony was performed on the day the marriage license was issued, although no waiver of the required 72 hour waiting period had been issued by any proper authority. The parties have not lived together at any time since the wedding ceremony was performed.

Plaintiff alleges as grounds for demanding that the marriage be decreed to be null and void: (1) That the ceremony was not performed in the presence of three witnesses, and the marriage certificate was not signed by three witnesses, as required by LSA-C.C. art. 105; (2) that 72 hours did not elapse between the issuing of the license and the performance of the wedding ceremony, as required by LSA-R.S. 9:203 and LSA-C.C. art. 99, and no waiver of this delay was ever issued; and (3) that there was a lack of consent, as required by LSA-C.C. art. 91.

We direct our attention, first, to the question of whether the marriage should be annulled because it was witnessed by only two, instead of three, witnesses. . . .

Our jurisprudence has been established to the effect that the articles of the Civil Code providing the manner and form in which marriages are to be contracted and celebrated . . . are merely directory to the celebrant, and that the failure to technically observe these formalities does not strike the marriage with nullity.

In *Holmes v. Holmes*, supra, for instance, our Supreme Court said:

"Our code does not declare null a marriage not preceded by a license, and not evidenced by an act signed by a certain number of witnesses and the parties; nor does it make such an act exclusive evidence of a marriage. These laws relating to forms and ceremonies, here regarded as directory to those alone who are authorized to celebrate marriages, are intended to guard against hasty and inconsiderate marriages in defiance of parental authority."

. . . We are convinced that the provisions . . . requiring that the marriage be celebrated in the presence of three witnesses and that the act evidencing the celebration of that marriage be signed by three witnesses, are merely directory to the celebrant, and that the failure to observe these formalities in a wedding ceremony does not strike the marriage with nullity.

In the instant suit we agree with the trial judge that the marriage here at issue is not null and void simply because the wedding ceremony was performed in the presence of only two, instead of three, witnesses and because only two witnesses signed the marriage certificate.

In our opinion the provisions of LSA-R.S. 9:203 and LSA-C.C. art. 99, requiring that there be a delay of 72 hours between the issuance of the license and the performance of the marriage ceremony, also are merely directory, and the failure to observe this requirement does not strike the marriage with nullity.

The minister who performed the ceremony explained that prior to the celebration of the marriage the defendant handed him a document which he described as a "waiver." The minister read the document and interpreted it as being a waiver of the 72 hour delay required by the above cited statutes, whereas it actually was a waiver of the requirement that birth certificates be furnished by the parties. The evidence shows that no waiver of the 72 hour waiting period was ever issued, and that because of a misinterpretation of the above mentioned document the marriage ceremony was performed before that delay had elapsed.

This issue was considered by our Supreme Court in *In re State in Interest of Goodwin,* 214 La. 1062, 39 So.2d 731 (1949). There the court held the marriage to be valid even though the ceremony was performed within the 72 hour waiting period required by LSA-C.C. art . 99. . . .

Penalties are provided for the violation of LSA-R.S. 9:203 and LSA-C.C. art. 99, but there is no statutory provision that the marriage will be void or that it will not be recognized in the event of such a violation. In our opinion a provision to the effect that the marriage will not be recognized if performed within that 72 hour period would have been included in at least one of these two statutes if the legislature had intended that a failure to observe that requirement was to have the effect of invalidating the marriage.

We agree with the trial judge that the marriage may not be annulled on the ground that the 72 hour waiting period required by law was not observed.

Affirmed.

Tennison v. Nevels

965 So. 2d 425 (La. App. 1 Cir. 2007)

McDONALD, J.

Plaintiff, Lisa G. Tennison, petitioned the Twenty-First Judicial District Court for a declaration of nullity of her marriage to Lionel Keith Nevels, which was denied. An appeal was lodged alleging that the trial court erred in not declaring the marriage a nullity because the marriage ceremony failed to be witnessed by two witnesses that meet the requirements of La. R.S. 9:244. For the following reasons, the judgment of the trial court is affirmed.

On June 28, 2005 a marriage license was issued to Lisa Gail Allen and Lionel Keith Nevels. Subsequently, the license certified that Pastor Douglas Prewitt married Lisa and Lionel on July 4, 2005, and that witnesses to the ceremony were Katie Allen and Ashley Allen.

In January 2006, Lisa filed a petition for declaration of nullity of marriage alleging that the ceremony at which she married Lionel was witnessed by her two daughters from a prior marriage, both of whom were minors at the time. Alleging that the marriage ceremony was invalid due to the witnesses being minors, Lisa sought to have the marriage declared an absolute nullity. The trial court heard the matter in March 2006 and denied the motion for nullity, relying on case law wherein marriages were upheld in spite of similarly defective ceremonies.

The Louisiana Civil Code, Title IV, entitled Husband and Wife, provides for the general principles of marriage, nullity of marriage, incidents and effects of marriage, and termination of marriage. The requirements for a valid contract of marriage are: the absence of legal impediment; a marriage ceremony; and the free consent of the parties to take each other as husband and wife, expressed at the ceremony. A marriage is absolutely null when contracted without a marriage ceremony, by procuration, or in violation of an impediment. . . . In the matter before us, all of the legal requirements for a valid marriage are present. None of the deficiencies resulting in an absolutely null marriage are present. The nullity is sought based on a defect in the marriage ceremony.

Our courts are reluctant to invalidate a marriage, and they will not do so unless the law and the facts clearly indicate that it should be annulled. *Parker v. Saileau*, 213 So.2d 190, 194 (La.App. 3rd Cir.1968). Jurisprudence has been established to the effect that the articles of the Civil Code providing the manner and form in which marriages are to be contracted and celebrated are merely directory to the celebrant, and that the failure to technically observe these formalities does not strike the marriage with nullity. The facts of this case do not warrant a deviation from this long-standing jurisprudence.

C. The Marriage Ceremony and Common Law Marriage

See La. Civ. Code art. 91; 3520.

Louisiana's requirement of a marriage ceremony precludes couples from entering into so-called "common law" marriages in Louisiana. This is consistent with the approach taken in the Code Napoléon.

Not all common law jurisdictions recognized common law marriage—and even fewer continue to do so today. Some of Louisiana's neighboring states have allowed common law marriage at some point—leading to inevitable questions in Louisiana. Mississippi recognized common law marriage until 1956. Texas continues to recognize some limited forms of common law marriage. Although spouses have never been allowed to enter into a common law marriage in Louisiana, Louisiana courts have repeatedly been asked to recognize common law marriages entered into in neighboring jurisdictions. *Parish v. Minvielle* demonstrates the approach taken when Louisiana courts are asked to recognize a common law marriage from another state. The case also demonstrates the traditional requirements for the formation of a valid common law marriage.

Common law marriage has become something of an urban myth. There is a common misperception that cohabitation for a period of time (seven years is a popular number) will automatically render a couple "common law spouses." This is simply untrue. A common law marriage is a marriage in which the couple had no marriage ceremony—but in which the couple did meet other substantive requirements. Typically, a couple could confect a valid common law marriage only if they (1) had no existing legal impediments to marriage; (2) agreed to live together as spouses; and (3) held themselves out to their community as a married couple.

There is some variation as to whether the spouses must also be in good faith regarding the validity of the marriage. The question has arisen when two spouses enter into a purported marriage (common law or otherwise) knowing that one of them is still married to someone else. This impediment would, of course, prevent a valid marriage. However, some common-law marriage states have taken the position that the continuance of the purported marriage after removal of the impediment is sufficient to create a valid common law marriage. As will be explored in more detail in the section of this text addressing the putative spouse doctrine, this view runs contrary to Louisiana policy views. Thus, the Louisiana courts impose an additional "good faith" requirement to the typical requirements for a common-law marriage in cases where the issue has arisen. In *Brinson v. Brinson*, the Louisiana Supreme Court explained this approach as follows:

> [I]t would be contrary to the public policy of this state to hold that a bigamous marriage contracted in bad faith in another state may nevertheless produce its civil effects under our law. While this Court has heretofore recognized, as a matter of comity, common-law marriages valid where

contracted, none of the cases has involved a situation like this where the alleged common-law marriage is the outgrowth of a ceremonial marriage, void at its inception and contracted in bad faith by both parties.

It is a well established rule of conflict of laws that the spirit of comity between states does not require a state to recognize a marriage which is contrary to its own public policy. The public policy of this state with respect to the effects produced by a null marriage is to be found in our Civil Code and jurisprudence.

Articles . . . of the Civil Code, which treat of the civil effects of null marriages, affirmatively state that no civil effects can flow from a marriage which is null unless the claimant was in good faith. Hence, since our Code and jurisprudence . . . require absolute good faith on the part of a spouse claiming the civil effects of a bigamous union, it would be inimical to public policy for this Court to conclude that such a relationship, conceived in bad faith, will be given effect in Louisiana merely because it may be sanctioned in the state wherein it existed.[2]

Parish v. Minvielle

217 So. 2d 684 (La. App. 3d Cir. 1969)

FRUGE, Judge.

This is a wrongful death action for the death of Merton R. Parish, brought by Helen Wyble, his surviving widow, by virtue of an alleged common-law marriage contracted in the State of Texas. . . .

The suit arises out of an automobile collision which occurred on November 6, 1957, on U.S. Highway 90 east of the city limits of New Iberia, Iberia Parish, Louisiana.

The collision was between the automobile Mr. Parish was driving and the one that Mrs. Georgie Harry Minvielle, the wife of Leon J. Minvielle, Sr., and the mother of the other defendants, was operating. Both drivers were fatally injured in the accident. [The lower court ruled in that Mrs. Minvielle's negligence was responsible for the accident.]

In regard to the alleged common-law marriage between plaintiff, Helen Wyble, and decedent, Merton R. Parish, the trial court found that under Texas law, the plaintiff and the decedent had entered into a valid common-law marriage, and that therefore, Louisiana courts had to give full faith and credit to the Texas marriage, thereby making Helen Wyble, the legal widow of Merton R. Parish, entitled to recover under L.S.A.-C.C. Art. 2315. . . .

---

2. Brinson v. Brinson, 96 So. 2d 653, 659 (La. 1957). *Accord* Succession of Hendrix, 990 So. 2d 742 (La. App. 5 Cir. 2008).

(4) THE COMMON-LAW MARRIAGE.

It is the principal defense of the defendant-appellees that the plaintiff is not the surviving legal widow of the deceased, Merton R. Parish. They contend that she and Mr. Parish were never legally married.

Plaintiff contends that she is the common-law wife of decedent, recognized as such under the laws of the State of Texas where their union was made in 1938.

The record shows that on April 18, 1938, Helen Wyble left the home of her cousin with whom she was living in Opelousas, Louisiana, and journeyed to Houston, Texas, allegedly to visit with an uncle and aunt, but in reality to visit the decedent Merton R. Parish, a Texan whom she had been dating in Opelousas, since January, 1938. On April 19, 1938, the couple decided to become man and wife and took up residence at the Lee Hotel in Houston, where Mr. Parish had been residing. According to Helen Wyble's testimony, her intention was to live with him and become his common-law wife, there being no impediment to their marriage, neither of them having been married before, and that they lived together from then on until the time of Mr. Parish's death.

Helen Wyble testified that the couple moved to many places, as Mr. Parish's employment required, his being employed as a driller, by Loffland Brothers Inc., and he was hired to go from place to place. The couple obtained passports as husband and wife and went to South America, where they stayed about four years. They opened joint bank accounts in different places, credit accounts, bought property in Louisiana, granting a building and loan association mortgage on it as husband and wife, and filed joint income tax returns. During all the years, the couple held themselves out to friends and relatives as husband and wife.

A Texas attorney, Mr. Sam Williamson, testified by deposition that under the circumstances noted above, under the laws of Texas, there would be no question that the couple would be recognized as husband and wife. He noted that the Texas courts had established three requirements for a valid common-law marriage. . . .

The requirements are:

(1) There must be no legal impediment to the marriage of such persons to each other.

(2) They must agree then and there to become husband and wife, which may be implied, and

(3) They must hold themselves out publicly as husband and wife.

Under the facts of this case, we have no doubt that the union created between the plaintiff and decedent met these requirements. Under the laws of Texas they were, therefore, husband and wife.

Defendants in their briefs state, "It is obvious that both parties were aware that this sort of relationship could not be undertaken in Louisiana, so plaintiff-appellant journeyed to the State of Texas to achieve her purpose."

It is true that Louisiana does not recognize or permit the contracting of common-law marriages in this state, but we are obliged to give effect to such marriages when they are validly contracted in another state. This is commanded by the full faith and credit clause of the United States Constitution, Art. 4, Section 1. . . .

For the foregoing reasons, we are of the opinion that Helen Wyble was, in fact, the legal wife, and now the widow of the decedent, Merton R. Parish.

D. The Marriage Ceremony and Proxy Marriage

See La. Civ. Code art. 91–92.

Marriage by procuration — or "proxy marriage" — is prohibited by Louisiana law. Civil Code article 91 makes it clear that "[t]he parties must be physically present at the ceremony when it is performed." Louisiana's prohibition on proxy marriage is not necessarily consistent with civilian tradition. Nor is proxy marriage really a common law institution. An Illinois court summarized the complicated history of proxy marriage as follows:

> The first time proxy marriages became an issue in the modern United States was during World War I. This was the first war in which large numbers of American men fought across great distances. Some servicemen wanted to be able to marry when they were stationed abroad. Because of this, various American states revived a practice recognized in the old continental law of Europe and in the American colonies through the old English common law.

> Because our analysis goes back to the Middle Ages, we will discuss not only governmental law but also the influence of the Catholic Church on law and culture. The Church traditionally insisted that the parties exchange consent face-to-face in the presence of the Church and get their union blessed by the Church. A failure to observe these requirements did not render the marriage void because Pope Innocent III accepted the Roman view that marriage could be consented to by messenger.

> Over time, the canon laws were superseded by the civil laws. The civil acts aimed to publicize marriages and ensure that marriages were voluntary and deliberate acts of the parties. Marriage by proxy violated the second objective of the civil marriage acts because there was no way to guarantee that a grant of proxy had not been revoked before the ceremony. France leaned against marriage by proxy, through the Napoleonic Code, which did not expressly outlaw proxy marriages but required both parties to be present so the officiate of the ceremony could review the rights and duties of husband and wife. Belgium adopted the Napoleonic Code, but Belgian writers stated that while the code implied a prohibition of marriage by proxy, a ceremony celebrated in such manner could be valid. Italy and Germany expressly outlawed proxy marriage except for their royal families. Austria also prohibited

the practice except by government authorization. In 1916, during World War I, Belgium, France, and Italy all authorized marriage by proxy. All three decrees mentioned the intent of the acts to allow soldiers abroad to marry.

As for the European country most influential on American jurisprudence, England, marriage by proxy was incompatible with English law at the beginning of the twentieth century. The Marriage Act of 1898 prescribed that the parties recite their consent vow in the presence of the registrar or authorized person and multiple witnesses. However, the English law that influenced American jurisprudence was in existence during the colonial period in which marriage by proxy was accepted. With the Reformation, the king's ecclesiastical law equaled or superseded canon law; however, no change on this issue occurred, and canon law's acceptance of marriage by proxy continued in force in England until the eighteenth century.

Proxy marriage was accepted by Roman law, canon law, and ecclesiastical law, but did the policy purposes behind marriage through an agent apply to the American colonies? The conditions the American colonists faced clearly established an ideal situation and need for proxy marriages. Colonists sent to establish a new settlement were often men, and these men left their future brides behind. Thus, the colonists, similar to soldiers serving abroad, had a desire and a need for marriage by proxy. Since marriage by proxy was accepted under English law and accepted on the continent for situations similar to those facing the colonists, marriage by proxy must have existed at common law. This is consistent with the Illinois Supreme Court's assessment that proxy marriage is valid in states still allowing common law marriage.[3]

Proxy marriage is allowed in only a handful of states today—including California, Colorado, Montana, and Texas.[4] Louisiana will apparently recognize a proxy marriage that has been validly entered into in another jurisdiction.[5]

E. Free Consent of the Parties

See La. Civ. Code art. 93.

Like other civil contracts, the contract of marriage requires the free consent of the parties—a concept that applies equally at common law and civil law. Consent is typically expressed by the parties at the marriage ceremony. As it is presently written, Civil Code article 93 expressly recognizes two vices of consent—duress and

---

3. Estate of Crockett, 728 N.E.2d 765 (Ill. App. 5th Dist. 2000).

4. Cal. Fam. Code § 420 (2017); Colo. Rev. Stat. § 14-2-109 (2017); Mont. Code § 40-1-301 (2017); Tex. Fam. Code § 2.006 (2017).

5. *See* United States v. Tuttle, 12 F.2d 927 (E.D. La. 1925); Morris v. Morris, 2010 WL 2342659 (La. App. 1 Cir. 6/11/10) (unpublished opinion).

consent given by a person incapable of discernment. The latter ground is one not seen elsewhere in the Code. The Revision Comments to Article 93 explain that, "[a] 'person incapable of discernment' may include, but is not limited to, a person under the influence of alcohol or drugs, a mentally retarded person, or a person who is too young to understand the consequences of the marriage celebration." Age is considered in more detail in the following section.

The vices of consent set forth in Article 93 are somewhat different from the vices of consent seen elsewhere in the Civil Code. For example, in the context of conventional obligations, the Civil Code provides that "[c]onsent may be vitiated by error, fraud, or duress."[6] In the context of donations inter vivos and mortis causa, the Civil Code recognizes fraud, duress, and undue influence as vices of consent.[7]

The vices of consent are also different than those set forth in the 1870 Code — which provided that consent was not freely given: "(1) When given to a ravisher, unless it has been given by the party ravished, after she has been restored to the enjoyment of liberty; (2) When it is extorted by violence; (3) When there is a mistake respecting the person, whom one of the parties intended to marry."[8] Duress — as it appears in the present law — was intended to carry forward prior jurisprudence relating to consent that was extorted by violence.

There is a dearth of post-revision cases considering Civil Code article 93. The following pre-revision cases may provide some helpful examples. *Parker v. Saileau* presents a factual scenario where a party might seek to claim her consent was vitiated because she was incapable of discernment. *Stakelum v. Terral* illustrates an unsuccessful attempt to invalidate a marriage on duress grounds.

Parker v. Saileau
213 So. 2d 190 (La. App. 3d Cir. 1968)

. . . Plaintiff contends, finally, that the marriage is null because of a failure of consent. She testified that she has been an alcoholic for 20 years, that she had abstained completely for almost 15 years, but that she had gone back to drinking and had been under the influence of alcohol for a period of about two and one-half months immediately prior to the date on which the marriage ceremony was performed.

Plaintiff, a widow 50 years of age, stated that on the morning of November 28, 1967, at defendant's invitation, she accompanied him in his automobile from her home in Tallulah to Eunice, Louisiana, where defendant planned to visit his daughter. She testified that she has no recollection of anything that transpired on that trip, except that when she awoke the next morning she was in a motel room with defendant and she learned at that time that a marriage ceremony had been performed the previous night. The evidence shows that both parties had remained almost fully

---

6. La. Civ. Code art. 1948.

7. La. Civ. Code arts. 1478–79.

8. La. Civ. Code art. 91 (1870).

clothed during the entire night, and that there had been no cohabitation between them. They separated immediately and have not lived together at any time since the ceremony was performed.

Rev. Carter, who performed the marriage ceremony, testified that some time during the afternoon on November 28, 1967, plaintiff and defendant went to his home and informed his wife that they wanted the minister to perform a ceremony uniting them in marriage. They were requested to return about 5:30 or 6:00 that afternoon in order that they could discuss the matter with the minister. The parties returned to the Carter residence at the time suggested, but the minister again delayed them, asking that they return later because he had to eat supper and attend a meeting. They returned about 8:00 that evening and presented the minister with a marriage license and with a request that Rev. Carter perform the marriage ceremony.

The minister then talked to both parties for a period of from 20 to 30 minutes about the prospective marriage before he would consent to perform the ceremony. He testified that during these conversations he could tell that both of the parties had been drinking, but he stated that plaintiff answered the questions that he propounded to her and he concluded that she knew what she was doing. There were only two circumstances which caused him to question the mental attitude of the parties. One was the fact that plaintiff was dressed in slacks. She apologized for the way in which she was dressed, however, and she stated that she realized that it was not the right sort of dress to be worn for such an occasion. The other circumstance was that Mrs. Parker mentioned several times that she needed to get back to Tallulah as soon as possible. Rev. Carter, however, completely satisfied himself after talking to the parties that they fully understood what they were doing and that they were sincere in their desire to get married, and after doing so he proceeded to perform the ceremony.

The trial judge concluded that plaintiff had failed to overthrow the strong presumption of the validity of the marriage. In concluding that the evidence did not show a failure of consent to the marriage, the trial judge said:

> "It is true that plaintiff smelled of alcohol, however, she has not established intoxication to an extent where she would be deprived of the ability to know what she was doing."

Our courts are reluctant to invalidate a marriage, and they will not do so unless the law and the facts clearly indicate that it should be annulled. Also, the established rule is that the trial judge's findings of fact, particularly those involving the credibility of witnesses testifying before him, are entitled to great weight and his conclusions as to the facts will not be disturbed unless found to be clearly erroneous.

In the instant suit the trial judge had the opportunity of observing the demeanor or plaintiff and the other witnesses who testified at the trial. We are unable to say that he erred in his conclusion that plaintiff fully understood what she was doing at the time the marriage ceremony was performed, and that she has not established that there was a failure of consent.

For the reasons herein assigned the judgment appealed from is affirmed. The costs of this appeal are assessed to plaintiff-appellant.

Stakelum v. Terral

126 So. 2d 689 (La. App. 4 Cir. 1961)

YARRUT, Judge.

Plaintiff sues defendant for the annulment of their marriage, claiming he was forced to give his consent by threats of bodily violence and death, both to himself and his parents, by defendant and members of her family. The District Judge dismissed plaintiff's suit, and he has taken this appeal.

The story heard by the District Judge, and read by us from the record, is: Plaintiff and defendant were students attending medical school in New Orleans. Both are in their early "twenties". She hails from a small Texas town, and he is a life-long resident of New Orleans. Having fallen in love, and believing he would marry her, she engaged in premarital sexual intercourse on many occasions. As they sowed, they reaped. She became pregnant and promptly advised him. He promised to marry her, and made several voluntary dates for the ceremony, but, on each occasion, found some excuse for postponement.

When the pregnancy developed to its sixth month, she became panicky and advised her sister in Texas, who was married to a detective on the police force of a large Texas city. Defendant's sister and brother-in-law came to New Orleans to attend the wedding after plaintiff fixed the ceremony for Friday, November 29th. They arrived in New Orleans on Wednesday (27th). Defendant and her brother-in-law spoke to plaintiff over the telephone and asked that he advance the ceremony to the 28th (Thanksgiving Day) because they had to return to Texas on the 29th, but wanted to be present at the wedding. Plaintiff, first reluctant, was persuaded to agree to the 28th. Plaintiff contends he agreed only because defendant and her brother-in-law threatened him and his parents with death.

On the morning of the 28th plaintiff and defendant, with their relatives, embarked by automobile for Mississippi; plaintiff and his parents in one automobile; defendant, her sister and husband (police-detective) in the other. Plaintiff suggested Mississippi as the place for the ceremony. They stopped at Picayune at the office of a Justice of the Peace. He agreed to perform the ceremony, but advised them first to go to Bay St. Louis for a license. Plaintiff and defendant went to Bay St. Louis, obtained the license, returned to Picayune and were there married by the same Justice of the Peace. After the ceremony an unsettled argument ensued between plaintiff and defendant over financial support for herself and the expected baby. All then left the scene of the wedding, plaintiff with his parents for New Orleans; defendant with her sister and husband for Texas. They have been separated ever since.

Having received no word or financial assistance from plaintiff, and being in need of financial assistance for doctor, medical and hospitalization for her pregnancy and delivery, she wrote plaintiff in December, but received no reply. She wrote again in January. This time she threatened to see the District Attorney if he failed to assist her. Plaintiff's only reply was this annulment suit (filed February 10, 1958).

With reference to the threats over the telephone, defendant and her brother-in-law both swear positively no such threats were made. While plaintiff's parents corroborated him regarding the threats, they testified from hearsay, namely, what their son told them had been said to him over the telephone.

Because defendant's brother-in-law usually carried a pistol as a police officer in Texas, plaintiff sought to prove he carried a pistol in New Orleans, concealed on his person at all times, as a constant threat to plaintiff. The officer, his wife and defendant, all swore positively he carried no pistol at any time. Neither plaintiff nor his parents saw a pistol or heard threats on the way to, or during, the wedding ceremony.

The Justice of the Peace testified that, during the ceremony, everything was normal, nobody was frightened, and no threats were made. After the wedding, however, as the parties did not embrace and kiss, he remarked he did not know whether the ceremony was a wedding or a wake. He spoke to plaintiff and his parents in their automobile outside his office. When he repeated the above remark to them, one of them replied they would rather not discuss the matter.

Notwithstanding plaintiff testified defendant had sexual relations with many other fellow-students, not one was produced as a witness. Plaintiff did admit he had intercourse with her on many occasions, both before and after he knew of her pregnancy, yet sought, by innuendo, to show that another of her alleged intimates was responsible.

When plaintiff's parents were asked why they did not notify the police when threatened, they said they did not have time. All they need have done was to refrain from accompanying their son to Mississippi; alerted the New Orleans or Bay St. Louis authorities; or informed the Justice of the Peace before the ceremony, or when he came to their automobile, after the ceremony, to remark that the ceremony appeared to be a wake. Neither defendant nor her brother-in-law was present at that time, so any one of them could have spoken freely, even if previously silent under fear or duress.

It is incredible that a detective of the police force of a large Texas city would, away from home, carry a pistol and threaten death to force the marriage of an "in-law", and thereby suffer possible criminal prosecution and jail sentence, with the resulting loss of his reputation and position as a police officer.

It is also incredible that plaintiff, believing another medical student was responsible for her pregnancy, would continue intercourse with her. His natural reaction, if he were sincere, would have been to shy away and sever all relations. In continuing such relations he, in effect, confessed and affirmed his paternity.

The whole story, as developed by the testimony, convinces us, as it did the District Judge, that no threats of bodily harm or death were ever made; that everything said or done was to appeal to plaintiff's manhood and decency; that plaintiff and his parents had every opportunity to notify the New Orleans or Bay St. Louis police, or the Justice of the Peace.

It is apparent this annulment suit is plaintiff's delayed answer to defendant's demands for financial assistance for herself and baby, with the hope of avoiding that responsibility.

The basic law controlling this case is found in LSA-Civil Code Arts. 91 and 110, to the effect that no marriage is valid when extorted by violence; and that marriages celebrated without the free consent of married persons may be annulled by the one whose free consent was not given, provided the marriage has not been freely consummated after celebration.

We can find no case in our jurisprudence which holds that entreaties to, and persuasion of, the apparent father of their relative's unborn child to do the manly and decent thing by marrying the pregnant mother, is the violence and threats contemplated by the codal articles. . . .

Plaintiff has failed to carry the burden of proving his case by a preponderance of the evidence. We can find no error in the judgment of the District Court and it is affirmed, at the cost of plaintiff.

Affirmed.

F. Free Consent of the Parties: Age Requirement

See La. Child. Code art. 1545.

Like any civil contract, a valid marriage requires the free consent of the parties to be married. The Civil Code directs that this consent must be expressed at the marriage ceremony. Age is an important limitation to free consent, because minors ordinarily are unable to give free consent to a contract—including marriage. However, the situation is somewhat more complex in the marriage setting.

Today, all states have statutory minimum ages for marriage—18 years of age is the most common minimum. In most states, however, there are also exceptions to this minimum that will allow children to marry at a younger age. Typically, parental consent and/or judicial approval is required for such marriages. Some states also require evidence of pregnancy.

Louisiana's approach to child marriage is set forth in Louisiana Children's Code article 1545. Generally, Article 1545 requires a minor to have the written consent of the one of the following: "(1) Both of his parents. (2) The tutor of his person. (3) A person who has been awarded custody of the minor. (4) The juvenile court as provided in Article 1547." If the child is younger than 16, then judicial approval is required—this is a "consent plus" approach. Article 1545 explains that "[a] minor under the age of sixteen must also obtain written authorization to marry from the judge of the court exercising juvenile jurisdiction in the parish in which the minor resides or the marriage ceremony is to be performed."

In Louisiana, a marriage that is performed without the required consents is not necessarily invalid. Rather, it appears that the requirement of prior approval is—like the requirement of a 72-hour delay—merely directory to the officiant. Children's Code article 1545 provides that the "officiant may not perform a marriage ceremony in which a minor is a party" unless the proper prior consents have been obtained. The article makes no mention of the validity of a marriage that occurs without those consents. The Civil Code supports the view that lack of the required consents is merely directory and would result, at most, in a relatively null marriage. Civil Code article 94, which sets forth the grounds for absolute nullity of marriage, does not mention age or the lack of prior parental/judicial consent. Rather, it appears that minority might, at most, result in a relative nullity. Article 95 provides that a marriage is only relatively null "when the consent of one of the parties to marry is not freely given." Article 93 and the accompanying Revision Comments suggest that minority may simply be a vice of consent. Earlier versions of the Civil Code appear to confirm this approach.[9]

Like Louisiana, more than half the states do not have a set age at which children will be prohibited from marrying if appropriate consents are obtained. Critics and scholars have argued that the statutory regimes in most states are insufficient to protect children—especially young girls—from the harms of forced child marriage. The requirement of parental consent, for example, may simply mask what is in fact parental coercion to marry. Evidence of pregnancy may also be evidence of rape—statutory or otherwise.

G. Covenant Marriage

See La. Rev. Stat. § 9:272–76.

In response to the national movement towards no-fault divorce and rising divorce rates, some legislators and scholars began to question whether divorce had become too easy. One outcome of the criticisms of no-fault divorce and changing social mores was the creation of the "covenant marriage." In essence, a covenant marriage is one that is—in some instances—more difficult to terminate by divorce. The history of divorce and the move towards no-fault divorce will be considered in more depth in later chapters. The distinctions between divorce in a "regular" marriage and a covenant marriage will also be considered in more detail in later chapters.

---

9. *See, e.g.,* La. Civ. Code art. 114 (1825).

Covenant marriage does, however, bear mentioning here because there are some additional requirements for entering into covenant marriage.

In addition to Louisiana, two other states (Arizona and Arkansas) have enacted covenant marriage legislation.[10] Entry into a covenant marriage is fairly straightforward and may be accomplished in one of two ways. Couples may elect to enter into a covenant marriage at the outset by (1) obtaining premarital counseling; (2) signing an affidavit in the form set forth by statute; and (3) obtaining the attestation by the counselor confirming that counseling occurred.[11] Couples who are already married may elect to convert their marriage to a covenant marriage by following a similar set of steps. In particular, they should (1) obtain counseling; (2) sign an affidavit; and (3) obtain an attestation by the counselor.[12] The mechanics of having the marriage denoted as a covenant marriage on the marriage license are somewhat different for couples who opt in after already marrying and can be found in the applicable statutes. In either case, the various statutory regimes set forth a list of those people who may serve as counselors and the information that ought to be discussed in that counseling. Generally, counseling may be provided by any religious official or a professional marriage counselor and should "include a discussion of the seriousness of the covenant marriage, communication of the fact that a covenant marriage is a commitment for life, a discussion of the obligation to seek marital counseling in times of marital difficulties, and that they have received and read the [state sanctioned informational pamphlet]."[13]

Apparently, there has been little litigation over the requirements for entry into a covenant marriage because there are only a handful of reported decisions. *Welsh v. Welsh* involves a party who was married before the enactment of the legislation arguing — unsuccessfully — that her marriage became a covenant marriage despite her noncompliance with the statutory requirements. Similar arguments have proven unsuccessful elsewhere.[14] *Short v. Short* involves a couple who apparently intended to have a covenant marriage but failed to comply with the necessary statutory requirements. *Short v. Short* raises an interesting comparative issue. The reasoning in *Short v. Short* relies on a view requiring strict compliance with prescribed statutory formalities — a view that is quite common in civil law and in Louisiana jurisprudence. Such strict compliance views, however, are less prevalent in common law jurisdictions, and similar facts could lead to the opposite conclusion in Arkansas or Arizona.

---

10. Ark. Code § 9-11-801, *et seq.* (2017); Ariz. Rev. Stat. § 25-901, *et seq.* (2017).

11. *See* Ariz. Rev. Stat. § 25-901 (2017); Ark. Code § 9-11-802 (2017); La. Rev. Stat. § 9:273 (2017).

12. *See* Ariz. Rev. Stat. § 25-902 (2017); Ark. Code § 9-11-807 (2017); La. Rev. Stat. § 9:275 (2017).

13. La. Rev. Stat § 9:273 (2017). *Accord* Ariz. Rev. Stat. 25-901 (2017); Ark. Code § 9-11-802-04 (2017).

14. *See,* Stephenson v. Stephenson, 2011 WL 1631953 (Ariz. App. Ct. 4/28/2011) (unpublished decision).

Welsh v. Welsh

783 So. 2d 446 (La. App. 5 Cir. 2001)

PATRICK M. SCHOTT, J. Pro Tem.

Defendant, Doreen B. Welsh, has appealed from a judgment in favor of plaintiff for a divorce pursuant to La. C.C. art. 103. She contends that her 1977 marriage was equivalent to a "covenant marriage," which was not created by the legislature until 1997 and that constitutional principles of due process and equal protection entitle her to the same limitations on divorce as though she were technically a party to a covenant marriage. We reject these arguments and affirm.

At the time of the parties' marriage in 1977, La. C.C. art. 89 provided as follows: "Marriage is a contract intended in its origin to endure until the death of one of the contracting parties; yet this contract may be dissolved before the decease of either of the married persons, for causes determined by law."

In 1997, the legislature adopted the Covenant Marriage Act. . . . This defines a covenant marriage as one entered into by parties "who understand and agree that the marriage between them is a lifelong relationship" This subsection further provides that the couple must have special counseling before entering into a covenant marriage and only when there has been a complete and total breach of the marital commitment may the non-breaking party seek a divorce. The parties to a covenant marriage must make the following declaration of intent: "We do solemnly declare that marriage is a covenant between a man and a woman who agree to live together as husband and wife for as long as they both may live."

Plaintiff argues that the lifelong commitment in the covenant marriage is the same as the one contained in the definition of marriage in the first clause of former La. C.C. art. 89. Consequently, theirs was the equivalent of a covenant marriage even though the Covenant Marriage Act did not come into existence until 20 years after their marriage.

The second clause of La. C.C. art. 89 is ignored by this argument. That clause recognized that the legislature could provide for the grounds of divorce before the death of either party. Plaintiff concedes that the legislature had the authority under this clause to make future changes in the grounds for divorce. Thus, Article 89's lifelong commitment idea was not only significantly tempered by the grounds for divorce that existed when plaintiff was married, but it was subject to subsequent enactments of the legislature which made divorce more easily obtainable. Consequently, marriage under Article 89 was not at all like the covenant marriage created in 1997. The new restrictions on divorce were not even vaguely contemplated by the full provision of Article 89.

The foregoing discussion is dispositive of all of plaintiff's arguments. Hers was not a covenant marriage because that concept did not exist until 20 years after her marriage; and Article 89, while declaring that marriage was a lifelong commitment, gave the parties the right to a divorce for whatever grounds the legislature would provide, including La. C.C. art. 102 under which defendant obtained his divorce. Consequently, plaintiff is not entitled to the same protection or the same procedure in the dissolution of her marriage as she would be if hers were a covenant marriage. Her equal protection and due process arguments are without merit.

Finally, the legislature itself recognized that its newly created covenant marriage was indeed new and distinct from anything that existed before when it created a mechanism for a couple married before 1997 to convert their marriage into a covenant marriage by jointly following the procedure set out in La. R.S. 9:275. Since plaintiff and defendant declined to follow this procedure to designate theirs as a covenant marriage, the Covenant Marriage Act has no application to their marriage. It would be absurd to conclude that these new provisions of the Covenant Marriage Act were somehow thrust upon plaintiff even though he declined to follow the procedure prescribed by the legislature for the Act to apply.

The judgment of the trial court is affirmed.

AFFIRMED.

Short v. Short

77 So. 3d 405 (La. App. 5 Cir. 2011)

FREDERICKA HOMBERG WICKER, Judge.

. . . Ms. Short appeals the judgment wherein the trial judge determined the parties did not enter into a valid Covenant Marriage ("Covenant Marriage judgment"). . . . Finding no manifest error or abuse of discretion in the trial judge's findings, we affirm. . . .

Analysis

Covenant Marriage Judgment

. . . The Covenant Marriage Act, La. R.S. 9:272 et seq., was enacted effective July 15, 1997 by 1997 La. Acts No. 1380. Six weeks later, the office of the registrar of vital records for the Parish of Orleans issued the Shorts' marriage certificate. Nine days later, Reverend John W. Zimmer, Jr. performed the marriage ceremony.

In order to perfect a valid Covenant Marriage, the parties must comply with statutory mandates. In this case, Ms. Short relied on the certified copy of the marriage certificate as proof of a valid Covenant Marriage. In particular, she relied on the parties' signed statement contained therein, stating: "We do hereby declare our intent to contract a Covenant Marriage and, accordingly, have executed a declaration of intent attached hereto." There was, however, no attached documentation and Mr. Short denied signing the statement. The trial judge recognized that as a result of Hurricane Katrina, the New Orleans Parish Bureau of Vital Records could not produce the attached supporting documents, if these existed.

Mr. Short and Reverend Zimmer testified at the hearing. Ms. Short introduced into evidence without objection Reverend Zimmer's affidavit executed on May 17, 2006.

Reverend Zimmer testified that he signed the affidavit attesting that prior to the parties' marriage in 1997, he conducted the marital counseling session with them as required to enter into a Covenant Marriage. The affidavit also stated that the Reverend attested that prior to the marriage between the parties, he signed the attestation clause of the Declaration of Intent to enter into a Covenant Marriage, which had been executed by the parties.

At the hearing, however, Reverend Zimmer testified differently. He testified that he did not specifically recall meeting with these parties or how soon he met with them before performing the ceremony. He was uncertain whether the parties signed a notarized form attesting that they had a discussion with him about the Covenant Marriage. He kept no records of the "very few" Covenant Marriages that he performed. He did not have any informative pamphlets that he either read and/or provided to the parties when he allegedly met with them for the premarital counseling. Reminded that he was under oath, he replied that he could not be certain that he met with Mr. Short for premarital counseling prior to the wedding date in accordance with the Covenant Marriage Act.

Mr. Short testified that he never received premarital counseling from Reverend Zimmer regarding a Covenant Marriage. He stated that the first time he met Reverend Zimmer was the night of the ceremony, although Reverend Zimmer might have been at the rehearsal dinner. He testified that he absolutely never signed a Declaration of Intent to enter into a Covenant Marriage. He did not recall ever seeing a document that was an attestation or affidavit of intent to enter into a Covenant Marriage.

The trial judge concluded that the mandatory requirements for a valid Covenant Marriage were not met: namely, a notarized Declaration of Intent signed by the prospective spouses (La. R.S. 9:273) and premarital counseling (La. R.S. 9:273(A)(2)(a)).

After that ruling, Ms. Short filed a motion for new trial based on alleged newly-discovered evidence. She stated that she discovered a duplicate original of the Declaration of Intent signed by both parties. However, she made no "due diligence" showing nor did she attach the required verified affidavit. At the hearing, Mr. Short's counsel objected to the absence of the required verified affidavit. The trial court properly denied the motion for new trial.

Ms. Short maintains, however, that the supporting documentation was unnecessary because once the certified copy of the certificate of marriage was introduced as a joint exhibit, she met her burden of proving a valid Covenant Marriage. We disagree.

There is no provision in the Covenant Marriage Act stating that the mandatory requirements for a valid Covenant Marriage are met solely by a signed statement of intent on the marriage certificate. Rather, the Covenant Marriage Act mandates special procedures for perfecting such a marriage.

Essential requirements are encompassed within a Declaration of Intent that must be signed by the parties: (1) a detailed recitation of the elements of the Covenant

Marriage contract; the parties' acknowledgement that they have received premarital counseling on the nature, purposes, and responsibilities of marriage; their acknowledgement they have read the Covenant Marriage Act, and they understand that a Covenant Marriage is for life; and, their commitment to each other. (2) An affidavit by the parties that they have received premarital counseling from certain entities, including a minister or clergyman of any religious sect. (3) Premarital counseling, which includes a discussion of the seriousness of Covenant Marriage, communication of the fact that a Covenant Marriage is a commitment for life, a discussion of the obligation to seek marital counseling in times of marital difficulties, and a discussion of the exclusive grounds for legally terminating a Covenant Marriage by divorce or by divorce after a judgment of separation from bed and board. [(4)] An attestation, signed by the counselor and attached to or included in the parties' affidavit, confirming that the parties were counseled as to the nature and purpose of the marriage.

The Act provides that the Declaration shall contain two separate documents, the recitation and the affidavit, the latter of which shall include the attestation either included therein or attached thereto. The Act further provides that the recitation shall be prepared in duplicate originals, one of which shall be retained by the parties and the other, together with the affidavit and attestation, shall be filed as provided in R.S. 9:272(B) ("The application for a marriage license and the Declaration of Intent shall be filed with the official who issues the marriage license.").

Importantly, Mr. Short denied signing the required Declaration of Intent and he also denied receiving the mandated premarital counseling. Reverend Zimmer was uncertain whether the parties signed a notarized form attesting that they had a discussion with him about the Covenant Marriage. Considering Reverend Zimmer's uncertainty and Mr. Short's denial that the parties had the requisite premarital counseling, we find no manifest error in the trial judge's ruling there was no valid Covenant Marriage.

Chapter 4

Incidents of the Marriage Contract

Like many contracts, the contract of marriage creates a host of reciprocal obligations between the parties. Yet, marriage is more than a merely personal contract. It also affects the status of the parties to the contract and their rights and obligations to the outside world. Freedom of contract is somewhat limited in the marriage context. By electing to enter into the marriage contract in the first place, there are certain rules of public order that the parties may not modify by contract. Other incidents of marriage, however, may be modified by the parties. These concepts are true in both the common law and civil law traditions. As will be illustrated in this chapter, there are many instances where the incidents of marriage are the same in both common law and civil law. Often, this is a result of the influence of the church and a shared western legal tradition. Yet, as will also be illustrated in this chapter, some significant historical distinctions between the two legal systems persist today.

The incidents of the marriage contract can be roughly categorized as either "personal" or "patrimonial." The personal effects of marriage include the obligations of support, fidelity, and assistance that married people owe to each other. The personal effects affect not only the spouses, but also their children. Children born to a woman during her marriage are generally presumed to be the biological children of her husband—a notion explored in more detail in later chapters. Personal effects often have real legal consequences. For example, if a spouse breaches the duty of fidelity by committing adultery, he or she may be precluded from seeking spousal support. Adultery is also grounds for divorce in many jurisdictions. The personal effects of marriage are fairly similar in common law and civil law jurisdictions—yet distinctions do exist.

The patrimonial effects of marriage include the various property rights that are affected by the marriage contract or by its termination. In many civil law jurisdictions, married couples are subject to the community property regime which results in the automatic sharing of property acquired during the marriage. The community property regime also affects the division of the spouses' property at death or divorce. Common law, in contrast, did not traditionally recognize any such sharing. Today, both systems generally allow for the patrimonial effects of marriage to be modified by the spouses through contract. The personal effects of marriage, however, often cannot be modified by contract.

A. Personal Effects of Marriage: Mutual Duties of Married Persons

See La. Civ. Code art. 98-100.

Civil Code article 98 sets forth the basic personal effects of marriage in Louisiana. The Code makes the obligations reciprocal on the part of both spouses: "[m]arried persons owe each other fidelity, support, and assistance." These mutual obligations have long been recognized in Louisiana and appeared in the Code Napoléon. Article 212 of the Code Napoléon continues to provide: "*Les époux se doivent mutuellement fidélité secours et assistance.*" Similar language appears in the civil codes of a host of other civil law countries. In some ways, the source articles to current Civil Code article 98 were quite radical for their time. They purported to place the spouses on equal footing with each other during the marriage by describing the marital obligations as identical and reciprocal—regardless of gender. Other articles, however, left no doubt that male preference was still the law of the land.

Traditionally, spouses were also required to live together—and a wife's domicile was deemed to be that of her husband. Article 122 of the Civil Code of 1825, for example, obligated the wife "to live with her husband and to follow him wherever he chooses to reside." In return, the law obligated the husband to "receive [the wife] and to furnish her with whatever is required for the conveniences of life, in proportion to his means and conditions." Planiol explains that this seemingly gendered obligation was better understood as a mutual obligation of cohabitation, which included a reciprocal "conjugal duty" between the spouses.[1]

A host of American states—by statute—impose similar mutual marital obligations on married couples. Article 155 of the California Civil Code of 1872 provided that "Husband and wife contract toward each other obligations of mutual respect, fidelity, and support." Article 155 was, of course, likely based on civil law source provisions.[2] The mutual obligations of "respect, fidelity, and support" are continued verbatim in California law today and have been adopted—often verbatim—by a host of other American states.[3]

Although the mutual obligations the spouses owe to each other are personal—rather than patrimonial—they do have real legal consequences. These obligations can form the basis for a tort suit for loss of consortium. Breach of one of these

---

1. Marcel Planiol, Treatise on the Civil Law *896 (Louisiana State Law Institute trans. West, 1959).

2. The precise origins of this article are somewhat unclear. The most likely sources of inspiration are the Code Napoléon, Louisiana law, and/or the Código Civil para el Distrito Federal (1879). Article 198 of the Código Civil provided: "Los cónyuges están obligados á guardarse fidelidad, á contribuir cada uno por su parte á los objetos del matrimonio y á socorrerse mútuamente."

3. *See, e.g.,* Cal. Fam. Code § 720 (2017); Mont. Code § 40-2-101 (2017); N.M. Stat. § 40-2-1 (2017); N.D. Cent. Code § 14-07-01 (2017); Ohio Rev. Code § 3103.01 (2017); Okla. Stat. tit. 43 § 201 (2017); S.D. Codified Laws § 25-2-1 (2017).

obligations may be grounds for divorce or may preclude a spouse from recovering spousal support. We will explore some of the legal consequences of the personal effects of the mutual spousal obligations in more detail in later sections.

The mutual obligations spouses owe each other are generally considered rules of public order and rules that are essential to the contract of marriage. As such, they typically cannot be waived or modified by contract. *Favrot v. Barnes* is a particularly colorful illustration of this concept. The case also introduces us to the conjugal duty and the view that the conjugal duty—in the modern era—may be part of the duty of fidelity.

Favrot v. Barnes

332 So. 2d 873 (La. App. 4 Cir. 1976)

EDMANN, Judge.

An ex-husband appeals from an alimony award as unwarranted and, alternatively, excessive. Because this court en banc has today decided that an ex-wife must show circumstances which make her unable to support herself by working before she can obtain post-divorce alimony . . . we remand to allow the parties to present evidence on this point.

Entitlement

This prospective husband and wife, in middle age, had each been married before. They executed a pre-marital agreement stipulating separateness of property. We first reject the husband's argument that the agreement's waiver by each of every "claim to the property'" of the other in case of divorce or death is a waiver of alimony. If public policy were to allow such a waiver, this agreement does not constitute one. Alimony to a divorced wife is not a "claim to the property" of the husband; it is a claim against the husband, limited by his "income", C.C. 160.

The spouses had other pre-marital discussions in which, at the husband's instance, they agreed to limit sexual intercourse to about once a week. The husband asserts, as divorce-causing fault, that the wife did not keep this agreement but sought coitus thrice daily. The wife testifies she kept their agreement despite her frustration at not being "permitted" at other times even to touch her husband.

We reject the view that a premarital understanding can repeal or amend the nature of marital obligations as declared by C.C. 119: "The husband and wife owe to each other mutually, fidelity, support and assistance." Marriage obliges the spouses to fulfill "the reasonable and normal sex desires of each other." It is this abiding sexual relationship which characterizes a contract as marriage, rather than, e.g., domestic employer-employee, or landlord-tenant. Persons may indeed agree to live in the same building in some relationship other than marriage. But that is not what our litigants did. They married.

The law does not authorize contractual modification of the "conjugal association" except "[i]n relation to property." C.C. 2327 prohibits alteration of marriage like that agreed to here which the wife allegedly breached: "Neither can husband and wife derogate by their matrimonial agreement from the rights resulting from the power of the husband over the person of his wife. . . ." Nor—because the rights over the person are largely mutual, C.C. 119 and La.Const. art. 1 § 3—can their matrimonial agreement derogate from the power of the wife over the person of her husband.

The fault here alleged by the husband is not, in law, any fault.

B. Personal Effects of Marriage: Surnames

See La. Civ. Code art. 100; La. Rev. Stat. § 9:292; § 13:4751.

The effect of marriage on surnames varies considerably across cultures and across time. In the United States, it is fairly common among opposite-sex spouses for the wife to change her surname to that of her husband's at marriage. A considerable number of women, however, retain their name or elect to hyphenate their names. But, what role does the law play in determining a married person's surname?

Louisiana Civil Code article 100 makes it clear that in Louisiana, "[m]arriage does not change the name of either spouse." Name change requires a legal process in Louisiana—a procedure that is set forth in La. Rev. Stat. § 13:4751. Many married people in Louisiana do not bother with that process, nor do they need to. Article 100 explains that although marriage does not change a person's name, "a married person may use the surname of either or both spouses as a surname." If a married person in Louisiana wants to utilize a new name after marriage, he or she is free to do so. If a person desires to have a different name recognized after marriage on identifying documents (such as a social security card or passport), he or she will typically first request a new social security card reflecting the new name. Generally, the Social Security Administration will issue a new social security card reflecting a chosen married name upon being presented with appropriate evidence—such as a marriage license.[4] A prior legal name change at the state level is not generally required for the issuance of a new social security card. Once the new social security card is obtained, it can be used to effect a name change with other agencies and organizations—such as the passport office and the office of motor vehicles.

Louisiana's approach—which is rooted in the civil law tradition—is radically egalitarian compared to the traditional common law approach. At common law, women were often deemed to bear the surname of their husbands—which was a natural extension of the merger theory of marriage. *Stuart v. Board of Supervisors* and *Welker v. Welker* illustrate some of the distinctions in the common law and civil law views of a woman's name following marriage. The cases are also interesting in that they both consider the effect of customary law in their respective legal traditions.

---

4. 20 C.F.R. § 422.107, 110.

Stuart v. Board of Supervisors involves a married woman seeking to vote in her own name. The court in *Stuart* did not address any constitutional issues raised by the parties. In reading *Stuart*, think about what those constitutional issues might be and how they would likely be resolved today.

Welker v. Welker involves an ex-husband seeking to prevent his ex-wife from continuing to use her married surname. The decision in *Welker* formed the basis of La. Rev. Stat. § 9:292. Unlike Civil Code article 100, that Revised Statute is gendered in nature. In the wake of *Obergefell*, however, it should be understood to be gender neutral in its scope (like Article 100).

Stuart v. Board of Supervisors of Elections for Howard County
295 A.2d 223 (Md. Ct. App. 1972)

MURPHY, Chief Judge.

Mary Emily Stuart and Samuel H. Austell, Jr., were married in Virginia on November 13, 1971 and, shortly thereafter, took up residence in Columbia, Howard County, Maryland. In accordance with the couple's oral antenuptial agreement, Stuart continued, after the marriage, to use and be exclusively known by her birth given ('maiden') name and not by the legal surname of her husband.

On March 2, 1972, Stuart undertook to register to vote in Howard County in her birth given name. After disclosing to the registrar that she was married to Austell but had consistently and nonfraudulently used her maiden name, she was registered to vote in the name of Mary Emily Stuart.

On March 16, 1972 the Board of Supervisors of Elections for Howard County notified Stuart by letter that since under Maryland law "a woman's legal surname becomes that of her husband upon marriage," she was required by Maryland Code, Article 33, § 3–18(c) to complete a "Request for Change of Name" form or her registration would be cancelled. Stuart did not complete the form and her registration was cancelled on April 4, 1972.

Stuart promptly challenged the Board's action by two petitions filed in the Circuit Court for Howard County, the first entitled "Petition to correct [the voter] registry," and the second "Petition to restore name to registry of voters in Howard County." In each petition Stuart maintained that she was properly registered to vote in her birth given name, that being her true and correct name; that under the English common law, in force in Maryland, a wife could assume the husband's name if she desired, or retain her own name, or be known by any other name she wished, so long as the name she used was not retained for a fraudulent purpose; and that since the only name she ever used was Mary Emily Stuart the Board had no right to cancel her voter registration listed in that name.

The petitions were consolidated and an evidentiary hearing was held before Judge T. Hunt Mayfield on May 8, 1972. Evidence was adduced showing that the oral antenuptial agreement between Stuart and Austell that she would retain her maiden name was a matter of great importance to both parties. Stuart testified that her marriage to Austell was "based on the idea that we're both equal individuals and our names symbolize that." There was evidence that prior to the marriage lawyers were consulted on the parties' behalf who indicated that Stuart had the right to retain her own name after the marriage. Stuart testified, and Austell corroborated her testimony, that she would not have gotten married "if . . . (the marriage) would have jeopardized my name." She testified that after the marriage she continued to use her own name on charge accounts, on her driver's license and Social Security registration and in "every legal document I've ever had." "Everybody" she said, "knows me by the name Mary Stuart."

There was evidence showing that the practice of the Board requiring a married woman to use the surname of her husband dated back to 1936; that the practice was a uniform one throughout the State and was adopted to provide some trail of identification to prevent voter fraud; that if a married woman could register under different names the identification trail would be lost; and that the only exception permitted to the requirement that married women register under their husbands' surnames was if the name was changed by court order. . . .

From the court's order denying her petitions to correct the voter registry and to restore her name thereto, Stuart has appealed. She claims on appeal, as she did below, that a woman's surname upon marriage does not become that of her husband by operation of the common law in force in Maryland and that nothing in the provisions of § 3–18(a)(3) and (c) mandates a contrary result.

What constitutes the correct legal name of a married woman under common law principles is a question which has occasioned a sharp split of authorities, crystalized in the conflicting cases of *State ex rel. Krupa v. Green* . . . and *People ex rel. Rago v. Lipsky.* . . . *Green* approved the voter registration of a married woman in her birth given name which she had openly, notoriously and exclusively used subsequent to her marriage, and held that she could use that name as a candidate for public office. The court held:

> "It is only *by custom*, in English speaking countries, that a woman, upon marriage, adopts the surname of her husband in place of the surname of her father."

Lipsky refused to allow a married woman to remain registered to vote under her birth given name on the basis of

> ". . . the long-established custom, policy and rule of the common law among English-speaking peoples whereby a woman's name is changed by marriage and her husband's surname becomes *as a matter of law* her surname."

[The court notes cases supporting both positions in various jurisdictions]

We think the lower court was wrong in concluding that the principles enunciated in *Lipsky* represent the law of Maryland. We have heretofore unequivocally recognized the common law right of any person, absent a statute to the contrary, to "adopt any name by which he may become known, and by which he may transact business and execute contracts and sue or be sued. . . ."

If a married woman may lawfully adopt an assumed name (which, in *Erie*, was neither her birth given name nor the name of her lawful husband) without legal proceedings, then we think Maryland law manifestly permits a married woman to retain her birth given name by the same procedure of consistent, nonfraudulent use following her marriage. In so concluding, we note that there is no statutory requirement in the Code, in either Article 62 (Marriages) or Article 45 (Husband and Wife), that a married woman adopt her husband's surname. Consistent with the common law principle referred to in the Maryland cases, we hold that a married woman's surname does not become that of her husband where, as here, she evidences a clear intent to consistently and nonfraudulently use her birth given name subsequent to her marriage. Thus . . . a married woman may choose to adopt the surname of her husband-this being the long-standing custom and tradition which has resulted in the vast majority of married women adopting their husbands' surnames as their own-the mere fact of the marriage does not, as a matter of law, operate to establish the custom and tradition of the majority as a rule of law binding upon all.

From a study of the English authorities cited to us by the parties and amici curiae, we believe the rule we enunciate today is founded upon the English common law incorporated into the laws of Maryland. . . . The question of English common law was considered by the Ohio Court of Appeals in *State ex rel. Krupa v. Green*, supra, 177 N.E.2d at 619:

> "In England, from which came our customs with respect to names, a woman is permitted to retain her maiden surname upon marriage if she so desires.
>
> "M. Turner-Samuels, in his book on 'The Law of Married Women' at page 345, states:
>
> > 'In England, custom has long since ordained that a married woman takes her husband's name. This practice is not invariable; not compellable by law. . . . A wife may continue to use her maiden, married, or any other name she wishes to be known by. . . .'"

Other English text writers have expressed a similar view of English law:

> "In England (followed by the United States of America) practice has crept in, though apparently comparatively recently, for a woman upon marriage to merge her identity in that of her husband, and to substitute his name for her father's acquiring the new surname by repute. . . ."

Under the common law of Maryland, as derived from the common law of England, Mary Emily Stuart's surname thus has not been changed by operation of law to that of Austell solely by reason of her marriage to him. On the contrary, because of her exclusive, consistent, nonfraudulent use of her maiden name, she is entitled to use the name Mary Emily Stuart unless there is a statute to the contrary. We do not think that the provisions of Article 33, § 3–18(a)(3) and (c), heretofore set forth, require that a married woman register to vote in the surname of her husband unless her name has been changed by legal proceedings. . . .

Nothing in the language of § 3–18(a)(3) or (c) purports to compel *all* married women to register to vote in their husbands' surname. Since Mary Emily Stuart did not undergo a "change of name by marriage," this Section merely requires her to show cause to the Board that she consistently and nonfraudulently used her birth given name rather than her husband's surname following marriage. Although no show cause hearing was held in this case because, as found by the lower court, Stuart had difficulty in contacting the Chairman of the Board, two things are abundantly clear on the record before us: (1) that a show cause hearing, had one been held prior to the critical date specified by the Board, would not have resulted in the registration of Mary Emily Stuart in her maiden name, in light of the uniform practice of the Board, supported by an opinion of the Attorney General of Maryland dated April 7, 1971, and the statements of counsel for the Board at oral argument of the appeal; and (2) that Mary Stuart has amply demonstrated sufficient cause that her registration not be cancelled by proof adduced at the trial, and accepted by the court, that she has consistently and openly, with no intent to defraud, used the name Mary Emily Stuart as her sole and exclusive name after her marriage to Samuel Austell. In view of the impending closing of the voter registration books prior to the November 1972 election, we shall direct that the court below promptly order the Board to restore the name of Mary Emily Stuart to the registry of voters in Howard County. Of course, in so doing, the Board may make whatever cross-reference notation to the fact of Stuart's marriage to Austell that it thinks administratively feasible to meet the avowed needs of voter identification and prevention of dual registrations.

In light of our disposition of the common law issue, we find it unnecessary to reach the constitutional issues raised by the appeal.

Order dismissing petitions vacated; case remanded for the passage of an order in accordance with this opinion; costs to be paid by appellees. Mandate to issue forthwith.

Welcker v. Welcker
342 So. 2d 251 (La. App. 4 Cir. 1977)

Beer, Judge.

Clyde J. Welcker, appellant, seeks injunctive relief to prohibit his divorced wife, nee Beulah Little, from any further use of his surname, "Welcker." Appellee, a retired principal in the New Orleans public school system, contends that she has been generally known, during the seven-year period of her marriage to appellant, and subsequent to the judgment of divorce, as "Beulah Little Welcker." This is the name that she continuously used during her marriage and since the divorce in applying for and maintaining checking accounts, charge accounts, automobile title registration, social security registration, insurance, retirement benefits, etc. Thus, we are confronted by the res nova question of whether or not the dissolution of marriage by divorce forms a basis for injunctive relief in behalf of a former husband seeking to prevent his former wife from using a combination of her Christian name, her family surname and her former husband's surname, such as, in this instance: "Beulah Little Welcker."

In support of their contentions, each of the parties rely upon *Wilty v. Jefferson Parish Democratic Executive Committee.* . . .

However, *Wilty*, supra, though persuasive on several points, is not controlling, for it deals with parties who were separated, not divorced.

Also persuasive but not controlling are . . . these observations of Planiol:

"390. Preservation of the Wife's Patronymic Name

Contrary to the general opinion, marriage does not cause the wife to acquire the name of her husband. Nothing in the law assumes that marriage entails the change of her name, as it does of her nationality. There is, moreover, no reason why it should have this effect, because a name indicates descent. A married woman has, therefore, no name other than that of her family, her maiden name received from her father. It is by it that she should be designated in civil and judicial acts which concern her. And, in practice, most notaries and other draftsmen of acts observe this rule. But her name should be followed by mention of her marriage and by the name of her husband.

392. The Wife's Right to Use Her Husband's Name

A universal right exists to designate a married woman by her husband's name. This usage may be held to have been recognized by the law of February 6, 1893 (Infra No. 395). This does not contradict what has just been said. The wife preserves her patronymic name but she has the right to use her husband's name in all acts of her civil and even of her commercial life. In practice, she often even refers to herself by the 'given name' of her husband.

395. Effect of Divorce

Inasmuch as marriage does not cause a woman to acquire the name of her husband, the question of the divorcee's name is solved in advance. It is asked whether a wife has a right to continue to bear her husband's name after divorce? Evidently, no, because this name did not belong to her even during marriage. If it was given to her, it was solely to attest a fact, her status as a married woman when obtained. The fact having ceased, this designation may no longer be used.

The husband thus has a right to constrain his wife not to use his name any more. He may, for this purpose, apply to the courts and if need be, obtain damages."

On the other hand, we take judicial notice of what is common knowledge, human experience, and ". . . social . . . conditions prevailing in this state. . . ."

Thus, we judicially recognize the generally existent custom under which divorced women are known by a combination of their Christian name, their family surname and their former husband's surname, and, in view of the fact that no express or positive law exists in this jurisdiction, we justifiably look to established custom and equity for assistance in deciding this case. . . .

Significantly, the French civil law acknowledges the legitimacy of custom *praeter legem* (i.e. custom as to a matter not covered by legislation) as a source of law. . . .

On the other hand, we are mindful of our civil law traditions, and, thus, we are also much influenced by Planiol's commentaries and by LSA-C.C. Art. 159, which states that a divorce shall place the parties ". . . in the same situation with respect to each other as if no marriage had ever been contracted between them."

Consequently, we are cognizant that, on one side, are Planiol's commentaries and certain codal implications which validate appellant's contention, and, on the other side, generally established judicially noted custom which validates the contention of appellee.

An additional factor for consideration is our recognition of the right of a divorced woman to revert to the use of her maiden name. . . . Is there, implicit in this recognition, an alternative yet unassailable right to be known by her Christian name, her maiden name and the surname of her former husband?

Although there were no children born of this marriage which was of reasonably short duration (approximately seven years), the effect of our judgment must be considered in light of its effect on all divorced women, childless or otherwise and whose marriages were of short duration or otherwise.

It is doubtful that Planiol could have anticipated present-day mores regarding divorce. Statistically and sociologically, it has, for better or worse, become an important factor in the mainstream of modern life and, thus, has provoked the establishment of its own customs. Important among these is the generally acknowledged acceptability of the use of the husband's surname by his former spouse. We need not burden this opinion with a consideration of the factors which precipitated the establishment of this custom. It is sufficient for our purpose to take judicial notice of its existence and to acknowledge our awareness of the problems that could result from its unwarranted judicial rejection.

We are of the view that appellant has not demonstrated that the trial court erred in its denial of the injunctive relief sought by him, and, thus, we affirm the judgment in all respects. Costs of this appeal are to be borne by appellants, Clyde J. Welcker.

AFFIRMED.

C. Patrimonial Effects of Marriage

See LA. CIV. CODE art. 880-901; 2325-47.

In Louisiana, there are two primary patrimonial effects of marriage: the community property regime and intestate inheritance rights. The second effect—inheritance rights—is common in both civil law and common law jurisdictions. All American states recognize the surviving spouse as an intestate heir of a decedent. Many states—including Louisiana—also limit a testator's ability to disinherit his or her spouse by will. Inheritance rights of surviving spouses are more thoroughly addressed in other courses.

The second patrimonial effect—the community property regime—is uniquely a feature of the civil law tradition. Community property regimes are seen throughout the western world. Nearly every European, Central American, and South American nation employs some system of community property. In the United States, nine states employ community property rules as the default regime: Arizona, California, Idaho, Louisiana, Nevada, New Mexico, Texas, Washington, and Wisconsin. Puerto Rico is also a community property jurisdiction. In a community property system, spouses automatically become concurrent owners of certain types of property. Many community property systems—including those seen in the United States—are ganancial systems of community property. In ganancial systems, assets earned or gained by either spouse during marriage are generally deemed to be community property in which each spouse owns a one-half interest. Premarital property and property acquired by inheritance, in contrast, remains separate. Spouses are often free to opt out of or to otherwise modify the default community property rules by contract.

In the modern era, it can be difficult to appreciate the distinctions between the American community property states and the American separate property (or common law) states. At divorce, the rules governing division of marital property look quite similar. This is no accident. The separate property states devised regimes for dividing assets upon divorce that were heavily influenced by the community property rules. The rules of community property are considered in more detail in other courses.

Chapter 5

Invalid Marriages and the Putative Spouse Doctrine

See La. Civ. Code art. 94–97.

When a marriage is not properly entered into, the result may be a marriage that is either an absolute or relative nullity. In Louisiana, the causes and types of nullity are set forth in the Civil Code. Article 95 provides that "[a] marriage is relatively null when the consent of one of the parties to marry is not freely given." Article 96 provides that "[a] marriage is absolutely null when contracted without a marriage ceremony, by procuration, or in violation of an impediment." Common law is similar in some respects. Defective marriages may be described as either "void" or "voidable," and the effects are roughly equivalent to being an absolute or relative nullity.

As with conventional obligations, absolute and relative nullities yield differing consequences. Due to the unique nature of the marriage contract, however, different rules govern marriages that are nullities than govern conventional obligations. In particular, Louisiana has adopted the civilian putative spouse doctrine, which allows spouses to absolutely null marriages to nonetheless benefit from the civil effects of marriage in certain circumstances. The putative spouse doctrine has also been recognized by a number of other American states—primarily those who also adhere to a system of community property.

A. Relative Nullity/Voidable Marriages

See La. Civ. Code art. 95, 97.

Civil Code article 95 provides that "[a] marriage is relatively null when the consent of one of the parties to marry is not freely given." Article 97 provides that "[a] relatively null marriage produces civil effects until it is declared null." Only certain parties can seek to have a relatively null married declared null. Article 95 provides that a relatively null marriage can only "be declared null upon application of the party whose consent was not free." Despite this language, a 2004 Louisiana appellate decision allowed the heirs of a decedent to challenge the validity of his marriage after his death.[1]

---

1. *See* Succession of Ricks, 893 So. 2d 98 (La. App. 1 Cir. 2004). The court's decision was based—perhaps improperly—on the Code of Civil Procedure rather than the Civil Code. *Ricks* is

Unlike absolutely null marriages, marriages that are merely relative nullities may be confirmed and thereby become valid marriages. Little recent jurisprudence exists contemplating how confirmation may occur. Older cases and the predecessor code articles focused on cohabitation as evidence of confirmation.

Voidable marriages are similar to relatively null marriages. A marriage is typically voidable — rather than void — if there is some lack of consent on the part of one of the parties or some element of fraud.[2] Voidable marriages may only be challenged by the party whose consent was not free. As to the civil effects of marriage, voidable marriages are usually treated as valid marriages until and unless a declaration of nullity is obtained.[3]

B. Absolute Nullity: The Putative Spouse Doctrine

See La. Civ. Code art. 94; 96.

Civil Code article 94 provides that "[a] marriage is absolutely null when contracted without a marriage ceremony, by procuration, or in violation of a legal impediment." Unlike a relatively null marriage, marriages that are absolutely null cannot be confirmed — they are void *ab initio*. As a result, a declaration of nullity is not needed to annul a marriage that is an absolute nullity. Article 94, however, allows "an action to recognize the nullity." The action to declare a marriage an absolute nullity can be brought by any interested person.

The so-called "putative spouse doctrine" is one reason parties may go to the trouble of seeking judicial declarations of nullity in absolutely null marriages. The putative spouse doctrine allows the personal and patrimonial effects of marriage to occur in some instances — even where the marriage is an absolute nullity. In those cases, a declaration of nullity may be needed to terminate the civil effects.

The putative spouse doctrine is commonly traced to cannon law and subsequent development in civil law jurisdictions — particularly France and Spain. The doctrine is an equitable doctrine, which recognizes that in cases where a party is in good faith, declaring the marriage an absolute nullity may work undue hardship. Numerous courts and commentators have reaffirmed this underlying purpose.

A number of states with no community property tradition or other connection to civil law have nonetheless adopted some rule comparable to the putative spouse

---

clearly the outlier in American jurisprudence. *See, e.g.*, Morris v. Goodwin, 148 A.3d 63 (Md. Ct. Spec. App. 2016).

2. *See, e.g.*, Ind. Code § 31-11-0-2 (2017) (young age or mental incompetency); Ind. Code § 31-11-9-3 (2017) (fraud by a party); Minn. Stat. § 518.02 (2017) (mental incapacity, infirmity, incapacitating substances, fraud, age, incapacity to consummate); 23 Penn. Cons. Stat. § 3305 (2017) (young age, incapacitating substances).

3. *See, e.g.*, Watts v. Watts, 547 N.W.2d 466 (Neb. 1996); McConkey v. McConkey, 215 S.E.2d 640 (Va. 1975).

doctrine.[4] Decisions from these states sometimes rely heavily on jurisprudence from Louisiana and other community property jurisdictions.[5] A few states, however, have expressly rejected the doctrine.[6]

As the cases in the following sections illustrate, the putative spouse doctrine arises in a variety of legal settings and continues to be viable today. Both *Rebouche v. Anderson* and *Ceja v. Rudolph & Sletten, Inc.* involve wrongful death actions (in Louisiana and California, respectively). *Mara v. Mara* involves a woman who believed she was divorced as a result of an attorney's fraud—conduct which eventually landed him and others in jail. *Xiong v. Xiong* involves a putative wife who came to the United States from a refugee camp as a child and whose family purported to arrange for her marriage when she was underage.

C. Putative Spouse Doctrine and the Requirement of Good Faith

Good faith of one or both parties is the cornerstone of the putative spouse doctrine. One or both parties must have been in good faith regarding the validity of the marriage at its outset for the doctrine to apply. In Louisiana, Civil Code article 96 makes it clear that the putative spouse doctrine does not operate unless at least one of the parties was in good faith at the outset of the purported marriage. Moreover, the duration of the civil effects afforded by the putative spouse doctrine sometimes hinges on the duration of that good faith. This issue varies by jurisdiction.

In Louisiana, Article 96 explains that "[a]n absolutely null marriage nevertheless produces civil effects in favor of a party who contracted in good faith for as long as that party remains in good faith." This rule is of Spanish origin.[7] The French apparently allowed civil effects to continue—despite a subsequent loss of good faith—until there had been a declaration of nullity.[8] Louisiana has created its own modification to this rule in the case of bigamy. The second sentence of Article 96 explains that "[w]hen the cause of the nullity is one party's prior undissolved marriage, the civil effects continue in favor of the other party, regardless of whether the latter remains in good faith, until the marriage is pronounced null or the latter party contracts a valid marriage." This approach is somewhat more in line with the traditional French approach.

---

4. *See, e.g.*, Alaska Stat. § 25.05.051 (2017); Colo. Rev. Stat. § 14-2-111; Minn. Stat. § 518.055 (2017); Mont. Code § 40-1-404; Neb. Rev. Stat. § 42-378 (2017).

5. *See, e.g.*, Hicklin v. Hicklin, 509 N.W.2d 627 (Neb. 1994) (citing authorities from Louisiana and Texas).

6. *See, e.g.*, Hill v. Bell, 747 S.E.2d 791 (S.C. 2013) ("We decline to adopt the putative spouse doctrine, as it is contrary to South Carolina's statutory law and marital jurisprudence.").

7. *See* La. Civ. Code art. 96, Rev. Comment (b) (1987).

8. *See* 1 Marcel Planiol, Treatise on the Civil Law § 1098 (Louisiana State Law Institute trans. West 1959).

The burden of proof associated with good faith also varies among jurisdictions utilizing the doctrine. In the United States, the good faith of the parties is usually presumed and the burden of proof generally rests on the party seeking to rebut the presumption of good faith. This approach is used elsewhere—but is not universally accepted. For example, Planiol explains that "[c]ertain authors rigorously apply the rule according to which he who desires to profit from an exceptional favor of the law . . . should prove that he fulfills the requisite conditions."[9] In cases of bigamy, some American courts will place the burden on the alleged putative spouse. The courts in *Rebouche v. Anderson* and *Mara v. Mara*, below, clearly adopt that view.

Courts have wrestled with the issue of whether good faith should be a subjective or an objective standard. Most American jurisdictions have concluded that good faith is a subjective standard—rather than an objective one.[10] Yet, objective reasonableness of the belief is still relevant to some extent. The cases below illustrate this struggle. In *Rebouche v. Anderson*, the Louisiana court accurately summarizes the Louisiana approach—which is generally subjective. Louisiana looks for an "honestly reasonable belief" in assessing good faith. In *Ceja v. Rudolph & Sletten, Inc.*, the California Supreme Court concludes that "good faith" is a subjective standard. In doing so, the court rejected a long-standing line of lower court cases that had considered the reasonableness of a person's belief. Both *Rebouch* and *Ceja* make it clear that reasonableness of a belief is not irrelevant to assessing good faith. *Mara* reinforces this view as well.

Rebouche v. Anderson

505 So. 2d 808 (La. App. 2d Cir. 1987)

LINDSAY, Judge.

The plaintiff, Doris D. Rebouche, filed suit against Charles E. Anderson [et als.] for the wrongful death of her alleged husband, Joseph Y. Rebouche. Plaintiff claimed the decedent underwent open heart surgery on November 6, 1984 and that Anderson and Kightlinger, employed by B & B, were operating a heart-lung machine. Plaintiff claimed that the wrong valve was opened, causing the decedent to suffer an air embolism to the brain and brain damage. As a result, the decedent died on January 4, 1985.

B & B Medical filed an exception of no cause or right of action, claiming that Kightlinger and Anderson were not employed by the company and that the plaintiff was not the lawful widow of the decedent. Kightlinger and Anderson also filed an

---

9. 1 MARCEL PLANIOL, TREATISE ON THE CIVIL LAW § 1099 (Louisiana State Law Institute trans. West 1959).

10. *See, e.g.*, Estate of Whyte v. Whyte, 614 N.E.2d 372 (Ill. App. Ct. 1993) ("[W]e consider the subjective attitude as well as the knowledge of the putative spouse. . . ."); Xiong v. Xiong, 800 N.W.2d 187 (Minn. Ct. App. 2011) ("[I]n Minnesota 'good faith' is judged subjectively, while 'reasonable belief' is judged objectively.").

exception of no cause or right of action, asserting that plaintiff was not the lawful widow of the decedent.

A hearing on the exceptions was held and the plaintiff argued she was the putative spouse of the decedent. The trial court sustained the exceptions, finding . . . that plaintiff was not the lawful widow or the putative spouse of the decedent. . . . Plaintiff appealed the trial court judgment. For the following reasons, we affirm.

FACTS

The record indicates that the plaintiff has a sixth grade education and is below normal intelligence. Experts indicated at trial that plaintiff has a mental age of 12 years.

The plaintiff testified that in 1945, when she was 15 years old, she married Johnny Malcolm Wheeler. Two children were born of that marriage. Plaintiff testified the marriage with Wheeler deteriorated, she left Wheeler, and she and the children lived with her parents in Shreveport while plaintiff worked as a waitress in a local eatery. Plaintiff testified that a divorce was obtained from Wheeler, but that her mother took care of everything. Plaintiff's mother was awarded custody of plaintiff's two children.

Plaintiff then married Thomas J. Ramsey around 1955. The couple moved to Baton Rouge, and one child was born of the marriage, Thomas J. Ramsey, Jr. Plaintiff testified that Ramsey treated her cruelly and failed to provide the necessities of life. In 1959, plaintiff left Ramsey and returned to live with her parents in Shreveport. Plaintiff testified that at the time she left, she asked Ramsey if he would get a divorce and claimed he said that he would. However, Ramsey took no action to secure a divorce and in fact the parties did not divorce.

Plaintiff and her son testified that around 1963, Ramsey called Thomas J. Ramsey, Jr. and told him that he had remarried, and he invited the boy to return to Baton Rouge to live with Ramsey and his new wife. The record indicates that Ramsey did not in fact remarry until 1972.

Plaintiff claims she had no communication with Ramsey between the time she left Baton Rouge and her marriage to the decedent, Joseph Y. Rebouche in 1967. The record indicates that the couple and Thomas J. Ramsey, Jr. went to Oklahoma to look at a coon dog and while there decided to get married.

Plaintiff claimed that because Ramsey told her he would obtain a divorce, because Ramsey indicated he had remarried, and because a long period of time had elapsed without communication with Ramsey, she assumed they were divorced and that she was free to marry Rebouche. . . .

GOOD FAITH

The plaintiff argues that the trial court erred in failing to properly apply Louisiana law in determining whether she was entitled to putative spouse status. The plaintiff claims the trial court used an objective analysis rather than the subjective analysis required by Louisiana law. For the following reasons, we conclude that the trial court was not in error in denying the plaintiff putative spouse status. . . .

The good faith required for putative spouse status has been defined as an honest and reasonable belief that the marriage was valid and that no legal impediment to it existed. Good faith consists of being ignorant of the cause which prevents the formation of the marriage, or being ignorant of the defects in the celebration which caused the nullity.

The question of whether a party is in good faith is subjective and depends on all the circumstances presented in any given case. Although the good faith analysis incorporates the objective elements of reasonableness, the inquiry is essentially a subjective one.

If it is shown that a prior marriage has not been dissolved, the burden of proving good faith is on the party whose marriage is under attack. Determination of whether good faith is present is a factual question and the finding of the trial judge is entitled to great weight. That determination will not be overturned unless it is shown to be clearly wrong. Any doubt as to the existence of good faith is to be resolved in favor of a finding of good faith.

There are several factors weighing in favor of plaintiff's claim that she honestly and reasonably believed she was divorced from Ramsey. Plaintiff offered extensive expert testimony to establish that she had an extremely low level of intelligence and has a mental age of approximately 12 years. Plaintiff has worked as a waitress most of her adult life and her tasks were limited to writing down orders and submitting them to the kitchen. She was not required to total the customer's checks. Plaintiff argued that due to her limited education and intelligence she was honest and reasonable in believing that she was divorced from Ramsey. Plaintiff also urged that Ramsey told her he would obtain a divorce and that when Ramsey called the couple's son in 1963 and told him he had remarried, the plaintiff assumed that Ramsey had obtained the divorce. Plaintiff also argued that because such a long period of time passed with no communication from Ramsey, she assumed they were divorced. Plaintiff admitted having undergone a divorce from her first husband, Johnny Wheeler, but argued that her mother took care of the details in those proceedings.

There are also numerous factors weighing against plaintiff's claim that she had an honest and reasonable belief that she was divorced from Ramsey. The plaintiff was 30 years old when she left Ramsey and was the mother of several children. Plaintiff had previously been divorced and in spite of her claim that her mother took care of the divorce proceedings, the record indicates that plaintiff accepted personal service of the divorce petition which was filed against her and signed the affidavit attached to her answer. Plaintiff testified that when she married, she knew that a marriage license was required and that she also knew that a divorce was necessary from Ramsey when she left him.

Plaintiff testified that due to Ramsey's actions, she did not trust him. In light of this fact, there was no reason for her to rely on Ramsey's statement that he would get a divorce. In fact, Ramsey's deposition, which was filed into evidence, brings into question whether Ramsey ever said he would obtain a divorce. Ramsey's deposition indicates that he did not recall any discussion concerning a divorce when he and the plaintiff separated.

Ramsey's deposition also calls into question the content of the telephone conversation between Ramsey and his son in 1963. Ramsey testified that he did not remarry until 1972, and that he did so only after hearing that the plaintiff had obtained a divorce in Arkansas and had remarried.

Plaintiff never checked with Ramsey to be sure a divorce had been obtained before she married Rebouche. Plaintiff argued that the long passage of time with no communication between the parties led her to believe they were divorced. However, even though Ramsey and the plaintiff may not have directly communicated, the reason for the lack of communication was not because Ramsey's whereabouts were not known. Plaintiff knew that Ramsey was in the Baton Rouge area and that Ramsey had a brother-in-law who worked for the U.S. Postal Service in Shreveport. Ramsey testified that this brother-in-law delivered mail to the residence shared by the plaintiff and Rebouche. Ramsey's mother also resided in Shreveport. When the present lawsuit arose and the lack of a divorce from Ramsey became an issue, the plaintiff contacted Ramsey in Baton Rouge and appeared to have little difficulty in doing so.

Plaintiff made much of her lack of education and intelligence at trial; however, plaintiff was not illiterate. She worked much of her adult life as a waitress. Her neighbors and Ramsey testified that they did not notice any limited intellectual ability on the part of the plaintiff.

Given all these factors, it must be determined whether this plaintiff under these circumstances had an honest and reasonable belief that she was divorced from Ramsey. The trial court found that she did not and that finding is entitled to great weight and is not to be overturned unless shown to be clearly wrong. The decision in this case turns largely on the credibility determinations of the trial judge, and those determinations appear to be correct.

Even though this plaintiff had limited education and intelligence, she was acquainted with divorce proceedings and knew that it was necessary to obtain one from Ramsey. She did not personally take action to obtain a divorce. It is disputed whether Ramsey actually said he would obtain a divorce, but in light of plaintiff's distrust of Ramsey, she was unreasonable in relying on any indication he may have offered that he would obtain a divorce. The record also calls into question whether Ramsey relayed to plaintiff in 1963 that he had remarried. In his reasons for judgment, the trial judge indicated that this part of the conversation probably did not occur. In spite of plaintiff's low intelligence, she knew a divorce was necessary, she was distrustful of Ramsey, and she had the ability to contact Ramsey in Baton Rouge to determine whether she and Ramsey were in fact divorced before she married Rebouche. She failed to do this. . . .

From our review of the record and the applicable law, we agree with the trial court that plaintiff did not have an honest and reasonable belief that there was no impediment to her marriage to Rebouche. We must affirm the trial court judgment finding that plaintiff did not have the requisite good faith to entitle her to putative spouse status. . . .

Ceja v. Rudolph & Sletten, Inc.
302 P.3d 211 (Cal. 2013)

BAXTER, J.

. . . .

FACTUAL AND PROCEDURAL BACKGROUND

On September 19, 2007, Robert Ceja (decedent) was killed in an accident at a construction site. Nancy Ceja (plaintiff) filed this wrongful death action against Rudolph & Sletten, Inc. (defendant), claiming she was the putative spouse of decedent. Defendant filed an answer alleging multiple affirmative defenses, including one challenging plaintiff's standing to bring this action as a putative spouse. The parties engaged in discovery, which produced the following evidence.

Decedent and Christina Ceja were wed in 1995. When decedent met plaintiff in 1999, he told plaintiff he was married but separated. In 2001, decedent filed a petition for dissolution of his marriage to Christina, and he started living with plaintiff.

In September 2003, plaintiff and decedent filled out a license and certificate of marriage. The completed document was marked "0" in the space for listing decedent's "number of previous marriages" and was left blank in two other spaces asking how and when any previous marriage had been terminated. Despite knowing of decedent's marriage to Christina, plaintiff signed the "Affidavit" box in the document indicating its contents were "correct and true to the best of our knowledge and belief." A license to marry was issued to plaintiff and decedent on September 24, 2003.

It turns out decedent was still married to Christina when he and plaintiff held their wedding ceremony three days later, on September 27, 2003. On December 31, 2003, the Santa Clara County Superior Court filed a "Notice of Entry of Judgment" and mailed it to the home of plaintiff and decedent. The notice stated that a judgment for dissolution of the marriage between decedent and Christina had been entered on December 26, 2003, and that the judgment was effective as of the date the judgment was filed. The notice also contained a statement—which appeared in a separate box and was printed in boldface type—warning that "[n]either party may remarry until the effective date of the termination of marital status." In January 2004, plaintiff faxed a copy of this court document to decedent's ironworkers union so she could be added to decedent's medical insurance. Decedent's fatal accident occurred over three years later.

As relevant here, defendant moved for summary judgment, contending plaintiff lacked standing to sue for wrongful death as a putative spouse because she did not have the requisite "good faith belief" that her marriage to decedent was valid. . . .

In opposing the motion, plaintiff argued there were triable issues of material fact regarding her status as a putative spouse. She submitted a declaration claiming, among other things, that she understood decedent had filed for "divorce" in 2001 but that she did not know what happened after that because decedent would never discuss the subject. Plaintiff "did not read the marriage certificate in any detail and simply signed the document." She recalled having subsequently faxed a copy of the final divorce papers to the ironworkers union to confirm decedent's final dissolution of marriage, but she "[did] not recall looking specifically at the papers before sending them." Although plaintiff was "unclear on the specific date" of the dissolution, she "absolutely knew" decedent was "divorced from Christina" at the time she faxed the court document and at the time of his accident. Following their well-attended marriage ceremony, plaintiff held herself out as decedent's wife "to all persons at all times." She changed her last name to Ceja, and the two of them wore wedding rings, shared a joint checking account, lived together in the same house as husband and wife, and handled their taxes as married but filing separately. Plaintiff would not have had her wedding on September 27, 2003, had she not believed she would have a legal and valid marriage to decedent. Had she realized at any time that her marriage was invalid, she and decedent "would have simply redone the ceremony. . . ."

DISCUSSION

. . . For the reasons below, we conclude that the good faith inquiry is purely subjective and evaluates the state of mind of the alleged putative spouse, and that the reasonableness of the claimed belief is properly considered as part of the totality of the circumstances in determining whether the belief was genuinely and honestly held.

A. The Subjective Nature of the Good Faith Inquiry

In ordinary usage, the phrase "good faith" is commonly understood as referring to a subjective state of mind. Lay dictionaries, for example, equate good faith with "sincerity" and "honesty." In *People v. Nunn* . . . our court explained that good faith is "ordinarily used to describe that state of mind denoting honesty of purpose, freedom from intention to defraud, and, generally speaking, means being faithful to one's duty or obligation."

. . . Depending on the context, however, good faith may also describe an objective standard requiring a reasonable basis, or alternatively, a standard combining both subjective and objective components. . . . Here, the appropriate context for understanding the phrase as it appears in section 377.60(b) is furnished by the judicially developed putative spouse doctrine. As both parties acknowledge, the wrongful death statute did not include an explicit provision for putative spouses until 1975. But long before any California statute first made reference to putative spouses, our courts began developing the putative spouse concept as a means for enabling a party to an invalid marriage to enjoy certain of the civil benefits of marriage if he or she believed in good faith that the marriage was valid.

When the predecessor to section 377.60 was amended in 1975 to include putative spouses, the Legislature used language nearly identical to the language adopted in 1969 as part of the former Family Law Act. Because codification of the putative spouse doctrine was not meant to restrict the doctrine's application, precodification case law provides the key to ascertaining the Legislature's intent.

Under precodification case law, the good faith inquiry focused exclusively on the state of mind of the alleged putative spouse. The subjective nature of the inquiry was demonstrated by (1) the judicially recognized purpose of the putative spouse doctrine; (2) the types of factors deemed relevant to the inquiry; and (3) judicial review of postmarriage conduct. We address these matters in turn.

Our court made clear from the beginning that the fundamental purpose of the putative spouse doctrine was to protect the expectations of innocent parties and to achieve results that are equitable, fair, and just. To effectuate this purpose, courts applied the doctrine only when the alleged putative spouse's belief in the validity of a marriage was found to have been "genuine," "bona fide," or "honestly" held. By recognizing putative spouse status in cases of genuine, bona fide, or honestly held beliefs, courts adhered to the commonly understood meaning of good faith, i.e., a state of mind denoting honesty of purpose and freedom from intention to defraud.

In evaluating a party's state of mind, courts considered whether efforts were made to create a valid marriage and whether the party was ignorant of the infirmity rendering the marriage void or voidable. Good faith was a question of fact that depended on all the circumstances leading up to and surrounding the invalid marriage, and a party's state of mind when entering the marriage was key. However, a party who married in good faith could lose putative spouse status as of the date the marriage's infirmity was discovered.

Courts assessed a party's efforts to create a valid marriage by looking to the extent of compliance with the legal requisites of a marriage. In determining what inference to draw from a party's efforts or lack thereof, courts deemed it appropriate to consider the party's personal circumstances. For example, lack of personal familiarity and experience with marriage could support a good faith claim where the marriage was not solemnized. Conversely, the circumstance that a plaintiff "lived all her life in California, and had been previously legally married and divorced," was found to undermine a good faith claim where personal vows were exchanged but "[n]o license was procured and no solemnization was had."

Other factors personal to a party, such as age and educational background, also appeared relevant to the good faith inquiry.

Where, as here, a bigamous marriage was involved, the relevant circumstances included the party's personal marital experiences, as well as what the party knew or was told regarding the prior marriage and its supposed termination. In this regard, prior marriage and divorce experience was not a per se bar to a good faith finding. Such experience, however, could either support or undercut a good faith claim, depending on the totality of the circumstances. Good faith could be found if the bigamist, or someone else claiming authoritative factual or legal knowledge, told the prospective spouse that a remarriage could occur because the prior marriage had been legally terminated. On the other hand, good faith claims were rejected where a bigamist told his bride he was not divorced from his wife and where a party was so "thoroughly familiar" with divorce and marriage procedures that she could not have been ignorant of "the farcical solemnization" of her own second divorce or the bogus nature of her attempted third marriage. That courts examined the totality of the circumstances from the personal perspective of the alleged putative spouse supports the inference of a subjective good faith standard.

Finally, precodification decisions typically evaluated whether the parties to an alleged putative marriage acted as if they were married. While the belief a party held when entering the marriage was determinative, postmarriage conduct was viewed as shedding light on the genuineness of that subjective belief. The following types of conduct generally supported a finding of good faith: The parties went through a marriage ceremony and thereafter resided together as a married couple. The parties started a family together or had children from a previous relationship living with them or adopted. The parties held themselves out to the public as married. The parties handled some or all of their finances, earnings, property, and income taxes in a joint manner.

When a party was found credible in asserting a genuine belief in the validity of a marriage, the objective reasonableness of that belief generally was left unaddressed. . . .

B. The Relevance of Reasonableness

Vryonis, decided after the Legislature codified the putative spouse doctrine, was the first California case to hold that a party seeking putative spouse status must demonstrate an objectively reasonable belief in a marriage's validity. . . .

Since *Vryonis* was decided, the [California] Courts of Appeal have been unanimous in holding the good faith inquiry is objective in nature. . . .

We disagree with *Vryonis* and its progeny to the extent they hold good faith is tested by an objective standard that examines whether the facts surrounding the marriage would cause a hypothetical reasonable person to believe in its validity, i.e., a reasonable person test. *Vryonis* reached its conclusion in reliance on case law interpreting good faith in the context of certain criminal law principles, contractual agreements involving banks and car rental agencies, and governmental construction permits. Although an objective test has been found appropriate in those contexts, such a test is at odds with the precodification putative spouse decisions holding good faith is a factual inquiry that assesses a party's credibility and state of mind in light of all the circumstances at issue, including the party's personal background and experience. Indeed, a reasonable person test would make it markedly more difficult to extend the civil benefits of marriage to those parties most in need of the putative spouse doctrine and its protection, namely, those innocents whose youth, inexperience, or lack of education or sophistication contributed to an honest belief in the validity of their marriages. . . .

To summarize, section 377.60(b) defines a putative spouse as "the surviving spouse of a void or voidable marriage who is found by the court to have believed in good faith that the marriage to the decedent was valid." The good faith inquiry is a subjective one that focuses on the actual state of mind of the alleged putative spouse. While there is no requirement that the claimed belief be objectively reasonable, good faith is a relative quality and depends on all the relevant circumstances, including objective circumstances. In determining good faith, the trial court must consider the totality of the circumstances, including the efforts made to create a valid marriage, the alleged putative spouse's personal background and experience, and all the circumstances surrounding the marriage. Although the claimed belief need not pass a reasonable person test, the reasonableness or unreasonableness of one's belief in the face of objective circumstances pointing to a marriage's invalidity is a factor properly considered as part of the totality of the circumstances in determining whether the belief was genuinely and honestly held.

DISPOSITION

The trial court granted summary judgment based on the erroneous assumption that good faith must be tested under the reasonable person standard set forth in *Vryonis*. We affirm the judgment of the Court of Appeal, which concluded to the contrary.

Mara v. Mara

452 So. 2d 329 (La. App. 4 Cir. 1984)[11]

AUGUSTINE, Judge.

. . . .

Concerning the focal question before us—whether Gaudin entered her marriage to Mara in good faith—the trial record reveals the following undisputed facts:

Several years after Gaudin's previous marriage to John P. Buglione in 1960, she became romantically involved with Gustave Mara. The couple decided to get married, and so Gaudin sought a divorce from Buglione in the courts of Alabama. On May 10, 1968, she drove with Mara to Birmingham where, with $350.00 given to her by the defendant, she entered the law office of K.C. Edwards, whose practice was largely devoted to divorces of this kind. There she signed various documents, all purporting to be the vehicles of a legal Alabama divorce. After completing the paperwork, Gaudin paid Edwards the required fee and, in return, received what appeared to be a divorce decree issued by Hon. Bob Moore, Jr. of the Circuit Court of Winston County, Alabama. The decree is impressed with the Seal of the Circuit Court of

---

11. The lawyer and judge involved in Gaudin's divorce were later subjected to various ethical sanctions and convicted of crimes relating to the scheme which took advantage of Gaudin. *See* U.S. v. K.C. Edwards, 458 F.2d 875 (5th Cir. 1972).

Winston County; it is stamped, "Filed 10th day of May 1968," and it contains the signature of the Register of the Court.

Armed with a copy of this ostensibly official divorce judgment, Gaudin returned to Mara's Birmingham hotel room and showed the document to him. Apparently satisfied with these papers, the couple drove back to New Orleans. They were married shortly afterward on June 1, 1968. . . .

In April of 1973, Mara attempted to adopt Gaudin's child by her previous marriage, and finding it necessary to obtain another certified copy of her divorce judgment, he requested this document from the Circuit Court of Winston County, Alabama. Joyce Martin, Register of the Court, responded with a Certificate of Search of Records, stating that the divorce proceeding, *Buglione v. Buglione*, No. 8823, had never been filed. This notice is dated April 23, 1973.

Despite official notice that her first marriage had never been dissolved, Gaudin continued to live with Mara as his wife until approximately one year later, when she left the family home.

On October 10, 1974, Mara filed an action to nullify the marriage, and on April 25, 1975 he obtained a judgment by default.

In September 1975, appellant married her present husband, Warren Gaudin.

The single issue raised by the foregoing facts is whether Gaudin married Mara in the good faith belief that her previous marriage to Buglione had been dissolved by a valid judgment of divorce.

Normally, a spouse who seeks putative status enjoys a presumption that she married in good faith. Good faith, in the context of a putative marriage is an honest and reasonable belief that the marriage was valid and that no legal impediment to it existed. . . . The presumption of good faith is not available, however, to a spouse who has been shown to be previously married and neither widowed nor divorced. To the contrary, such a spouse must bear the burden of proving his or her good faith in contracting the allegedly putative marriage. Whether a spouse enters an invalid marriage in good faith is a question that is largely answerable by the circumstances surrounding the marriage.

Since Gaudin's marriage to Mara was annulled on the ground that her previous marriage to Buglione was never dissolved, appellant now assumes the burden to prove her good faith in marrying Mara; that is, she must prove her reasonable belief that the divorce decree given to her by the Birmingham attorney was valid.

Gaudin insists that she had no cause to doubt the genuineness of her divorce papers until late April 1973, when she and Mara received official notice that the divorce judgment was not on file. Gaudin explained that the Alabama lawyer had defrauded her into believing in the validity of the divorce judgment which he had issued to her, and that she was an easy mark for his trickery and deceit, having only a high school education and no knowledge of divorce law.

Given the undisputed facts of this case, we are satisfied that Gaudin was indeed an unwitting victim of deceit by her Alabama attorney, and that Gaudin entered her marriage to Mara in the belief that her divorce from Buglione was valid. The documents which evidence that divorce were apparently valid, even by the defendant's reckoning, and it is unreasonable to suppose that anyone would willingly pay $350.00 for a divorce knowing that it would be without legal effect. We are impressed, also, with defendant Mara's insistence that he never had cause to question the validity of the divorce, and since we have no reason to think that Gaudin had more knowledge of the Alabama attorney's deceitful practices than Mara did, we would find them both to be good faith victims of fraud.

In connection with this, we note a federal court opinion which sets out in minute detail the unconscionable divorce fraud scheme to which Gaudin briefly referred in her testimony. She called it "the biggest scandal in Alabama for a while". Indeed it was. See *United States v. Edwards*, 458 F.2d 875 (5 Cir.1972).

Having found that Mary Ann Gaudin, at the time of her marriage to Gustave Mara, entertained the good faith and reasonable belief that her divorce from John P. Buglione, Jr. was final and valid, and therefore, that there existed no impediment to her marriage, we conclude that Gaudin is entitled to putative status.

Accordingly, the judgment appealed from is reversed, and the property which is the subject of this dispute is hereby deemed to form part of the putative community which existed between Gustave Mara and his former putative wife, Mary Ann Gaudin. The case is remanded for further proceedings consistent with this opinion.

REVERSED and REMANDED.

D. The Putative Spouse Doctrine and the Ceremony Requirement

See LA. CIV. CODE art. 96, Rev. Comment (d).

Does the putative spouse doctrine apply when the cause of nullity is the lack of a marriage ceremony? This question has created some controversy. Traditionally, the putative spouse doctrine did not apply in cases where there was some defect in the form of the marriage—such as the complete absence of a ceremony. This view made sense in a pure civil law jurisdiction. Planiol explained the traditional approach this way: "no one is presumed not to know the forms of marriage, whereas an impediment may always exist without the spouses knowing of it."[12] Yet, this view had already begun to give way in Planiol's time. As he explained:

---

12. 1 MARCEL PLANIOL, TREATISE ON THE CIVIL LAW § 1104 (Louisiana State Law Institute trans. West 1959).

In present day law, the theory of putative marriages has expanded. The good faith of the spouses can give validity to a marriage, the nullity of which is a vice of form. This change arises from the establishment of new forms instituted for marriage by civil laws and from the different kinds of forms existing in different states. Such differences inevitably bring about irregularities. Within the country itself, the change in its legislation has but a temporary effect. The validity of irregular unions could be recognized as mere temporary expedients. The diversity in the laws of the different states is however a permanent source of mistake.[13]

In Planiol's view, however, the lack of a marriage ceremony was a fatal defect, which precluded the application of the putative spouse doctrine:

It is nevertheless necessary that there have been some kind of celebration. According to the text, it is the marriage "contracted" in good faith that produces its civil effects. It is therefore necessary that there have been at least something that may be considered to be the celebration of marriage. . . . The courts should therefore certainly refuse to accord civil effects to the marriage of anyone who would claim to be married without any act.[14]

The difficulty of the ceremony issue in American jurisdictions was inadvertently predicted at by Planiol when he explained that "[t]he diversity in the laws of the different states is . . . a permanent source of mistake." Not only must American jurisdictions wrestle with confusion arising from the laws of neighboring states, some—like Texas—faced unique issues not present in France or Spain because they recognized both the civilian notion of putative marriage as well as non-ceremonial common law marriages.

Louisiana leaves the question of the ceremony to the discretion of the court and lack of a marriage ceremony is a question of good faith. In other words, the absence of a marriage ceremony is not an absolute bar to the application of the putative spouse doctrine. Traditionally, exceptional facts would need to be present in order to overlook the failure of a ceremony—but recent Louisiana decisions are more forgiving. Revision Comment (e) to Civil Code article 96 alludes to the difficulty Louisiana courts have faced in dealing with this issue. Those cases bear mentioning here as well. *Succession of Marinoni* is a 1935 Louisiana Supreme Court decision in which the court apparently abolished the traditional civil law requirement of a ceremony.[15] The equities certainly favored the putative wife—an Italian immigrant and orphan, who spoke little English, and who was soon courted by a much older man who convinced her they were married despite having no marriage ceremony. The

---

13. 1 Marcel Planiol, Treatise on the Civil Law § 1105 (Louisiana State Law Institute trans. West 1959).

14. 1 Marcel Planiol, Treatise on the Civil Law § 1107 (Louisiana State Law Institute trans. West 1959).

15. Succession of Marinoni, 164 So. 797 (1935).

case was criticized, and later cases—including *Succession of Rossi*—took care to attempt to distinguish *Marinoni* as an outlier.[16]

More recent Louisiana decisions have shown a more liberal view of the ceremony requirement. *Thomason v. Thomason* illustrates this point. *Thomason* also shows how the first sentence of Civil Code article 96 operates with respect to the timing of a putative spouse's loss of good faith.

Like *Marinoni*, a number of putative spouse cases involving no marriage ceremony involve parties who—due to cultural differences—were unfamiliar with American marriage laws. *Xiong v. Xiong*, below, is a contemporary example of such a case out of Minnesota.

Thomason v. Thomason
776 So. 2d 553 (La. App. 3 Cir. 2000)

DOUCET, Chief Judge.

The Defendant, Roger Randolph Thomason, appeals the trial court's determination that, although the marriage was invalid, Barbara Ann Hughes Thomason was in good faith and entitled to the civil effects of marriage as a putative spouse.

Barbara Thomason filed for a divorce in December 1998. In his answer to the petition for divorce, Mr. Thomason stated that no marriage had taken place. A hearing was held on December 6, 1999, at which the following facts were brought to light. The parties met in a sanitarium where both were being treated for tuberculosis. After being released they continued to see each other and on April 5, 1958, Roger asked Barbara to go to Mississippi with him to get married. They went to the courthouse in Port Gibson, Mississippi and obtained a marriage license. At this point the parties' version of events diverge. Barbara testified that they then went to a house and spoke to a man. Although no ceremony was held, she thought this was the justice of the peace and that she was married to Roger. They left the house and checked into a hotel together. She testified that Roger gave her a wedding ring. The next day they returned to Louisiana.

Roger disagreed with this account. At the hearing, he testified that after getting the license they were unable to find a justice of the peace; that they never went to anyone's house but simply checked into a hotel. He testified that he knew no marriage had taken place. It is undisputed that from that time until Barbara left the matrimonial domicile, the two held themselves out as married.

On December 6, 1999, the court held a hearing to determine the issues of marriage and putative spouse status. After hearing the evidence of both parties. The trial court made the following findings:

---

16. *See* Succession of Rossi, 214 So. 2d 223 (La. App. 4 Cir. 1968).

From the testimony of both parties, the Court has determined that even though Barbara Hughes Thomason "believed" that they were married on April 5, 1958, in reality, they were not. It is this Court's opinion that Roger Randolph Thomason took advantage of Barbara's ignorance about marriage and deliberately did not say that they were not married after leaving the home of the justice of the peace and never told Barbara. Although Roger testified that one time during the marriage, he told Barbara that they were not legally married, this Court does not find his testimony to be credible. . . .

This Court has determined that Barbara Ann Hughes Thomason did not know during all the years she was together with Roger that her marriage was defective in the eyes of the law. This does not mean that she is to blame for the marriage not being valid, only that she trusted and loved someone so completely that she never thought they would be deceitful to her.

The court rendered judgment finding that the two were never validly married but that Barbara was in good faith until Roger filed his answer to her petition for divorce and was, therefore, "entitled to the civil effects of the marriage as a putative spouse." Roger appeals.

GOOD FAITH

Roger's first two assignments of error address the existence of good faith on the part of Barbara and the date on which her good faith, if any, ended.

"Good faith" is defined as an honest and reasonable belief that the marriage was valid and that no legal impediment to it existed. "Good faith" consists of being ignorant of the cause which prevents the formation of the marriage, or being ignorant of the defects in the celebration which caused the nullity. The question of whether a party is in good faith is subjective, and depends on all the circumstances present in a given case. Although the good faith analysis test incorporates the objective elements of reasonableness, the inquiry is essentially a subjective one.

Roger testified that because they never found a justice of the peace and never went through a marriage ceremony, Barbara had to know that they were not married. Barbara testified that she thought they were married when they signed the license and saw the man she thought was a justice of the peace. Roger further argues that any good faith belief Barbara had in the validity of the marriage ended when he told her they were not really married shortly before their first child was born. He testified that he told her because he thought they should get married to legitimate the child, but that she did not want to hear it. Barbara testified that the validity of the marriage was never brought into question until Roger filed his answer to the petition.

The determination of whether good faith is present is a factual question and the finding of the trial judge is entitled to great weight on appeal. That factual determination will not be overturned unless it is shown to be clearly wrong. Any doubt as to the existence of good faith is to be resolved in favor of a finding of good faith.

In this case, the trial court apparently based its determination on a credibility evaluation, accepting Barbara's testimony over that of Roger. . . .

In this case, it was not Barbara's testimony which was inconsistent, but Roger's. Throughout his testimony instances of obvious inconsistencies with his deposition testimony were pointed out. Under the circumstances, his credibility is far more questionable than that of Barbara. Therefore, we find no error in the trial court's decision to credit Barbara's testimony. We further find no manifest error in his decision to find that Barbara was in good faith and entitled to the civil benefits of marriage as a putative spouse.

END DATE OF THE COMMUNITY REGIME

Roger further contends that even if Barbara was in good faith until he filed his answer, the trial judge erred in ordering that the community regime be ended retroactive to the date the Defendant filed his answer, that is the date the trial court found that good faith ended. Roger argues that the law requires that the community regime be terminated retroactive to the date of filing the petition for divorce. . . .

However, in this case there will be no judgment of divorce since there was no marriage. The petition for divorce is moot. La.Civ.Code art. 96 provides in pertinent part that: "An absolutely null marriage nevertheless produces civil effects in favor of a party who contracted it in good faith for as long as that party remains in good faith." We agree with the trial court that Barbara remained in good faith until Roger filed his answer to her petition on April 20, 1999. Therefore, the court correctly found that Barbara continued to be entitled to the civil effects of marriage until that date.

PUTATIVE SPOUSE STATUS FOR ROGER THOMASON

Finally, Roger contends that the court found him also to be in good faith and that, as a result, the civil effects of marriage should be extended to him as well. The Defendant misreads the court's judgment. The court, both in its reasons for judgment and in the judgment itself stated that "the actions of both parties constituted good faith." However, a full reading of the reasons makes it clear that the trial court considered that the actions of both parties showed that Barbara was in good faith. The trial judge made no finding that Roger was in good faith. In fact, his findings of fact make it clear that Roger was not in good faith and knew from the beginning that the marriage was not valid. He states, in his written reasons, that: "Roger Randolph Thomason took advantage of Barbara's ignorance about marriage and deliberately did not say that they were not married after leaving the home of the justice of the peace. Roger knew when leaving, that the marriage license was not filed (sic) out by the justice of the peace and never told Barbara." Accordingly, the trial court correctly declined to extend the civil effects of marriage to Roger.

CONCLUSION

For these reasons, the judgment of the trial court is affirmed. Costs of this appeal are to be paid by Roger Thomason.

AFFIRMED.

Xiong v. Xiong

800 N.W.2d 187 (Minn. App. Ct. 2011)

SCHELLHAS, Judge.

Appellant argues that the district court clearly erred by finding that respondent was his putative spouse. Because the record contains evidence of respondent's good-faith belief that she was legally married to appellant, we affirm.

FACTS

On December 8, 2009, respondent Choa Yang Xiong (Yang) commenced this action against appellant Su Xiong (Xiong), seeking determinations of custody, parenting time, child support, spousal maintenance, and division of property on the theory that she was Xiong's putative spouse. Xiong denied that Yang was his putative spouse, and a family-court referee held a trial on the issue.

Based on testimony at the trial, Yang came to the United States of America from a refugee camp in Laos in 1988 when she was about 16 years old. At the refugee camp, Yang learned basic things to prepare her for life in the United States, but she did not learn to speak English. When Yang arrived in the United States, she spoke no English. By 1992, when Yang graduated from high school, she could read only "the easy basic words" in English and could speak "a little"—her high school classes, although taught in English, taught only "basic" things such as numbers, the alphabet, "what tables were, what's a chair[,] [t]he different fruits like apples and oranges, things like that." Yang passed the test required for graduation, but at the time of trial, she could read English only "a little bit, only the easy things." Yang's brothers, who testified at the hearing, confirmed that Yang could not speak any English when she came to the United States. One brother testified that at the time of the hearing, Yang could read and write English at about a sixth- or seventh-grade level and had trouble with difficult words.

Yang met Xiong while she was still in high school. Two weeks after meeting Xiong, in January 1989, the couple had a Hmong cultural marriage ceremony. Each of their families provided a Mej Koob, who "negotiate[ed] regarding the meal, the wedding, and how much the dowry [would] be." The wedding included a ceremony, a meal, and Xiong's payment of a $2,400 dowry. Following the ceremony, the Mej Koob named Xiong and Yang husband and wife and, according to Yang, that was "the end of it." Yang testified that her Hmong wedding was the same as other Hmong cultural weddings that she has attended. Consistent with Yang's testimony, her brothers testified that Xiong and Yang had a Hmong cultural wedding that included Mej Koob and the payment of a dowry.

After their Hmong wedding, the couple began residing together but did not legalize their marriage because Yang was not of legal marrying age. In the Hmong community, the couple described themselves as husband and wife. Xiong's family referred to Yang as "Mrs. Su" because they thought of her as Xiong's wife. But outside the community they described themselves as boyfriend and girlfriend.

Xiong and Yang's families decided that as soon as Yang turned 18, the couple should get a "marriage license." The leader of the Xiong clan testified that he advises clan members that if they get a marriage license, they are legally married in Minnesota. One of Yang's brothers, the leader of the Yang clan, testified that in the 1990s, he told Yang that "she needed to go through a legal marriage ceremony and get a marriage certificate," which he believed included testifying in court. He testified that he understood the difference between a marriage license and a marriage certificate. But Yang testified that in the Hmong language they do not distinguish between the two, that her brother "said something about getting a marriage paper," and that she needed a "marriage paper."

On December 4, 1993, the couple obtained a marriage license from Ramsey County. . . .

Yang recalled that after Xiong completed the paperwork, Yang and Xiong gave their driver's licenses to a woman who told them to raise their right hands and sign something. The woman then handed them the marriage license. Afterwards Xiong told Yang that they "were officially married, all the paperwork was done. And he said we were married culturally and legally, so everything was done. He handed me a paper in an envelope and that was the end of it." Yang did not read the license because she did not have sufficient reading skills to understand it, but she knew it was a marriage license. She "glanced at it with the big writing [that] says marriage license and then [her] name and his name, and [she] just put it in a safe place with [her] important papers." Yang told her father and brothers that she and Xiong were legally married.

When asked whether she went to court and testified as her brother told her to do, Yang answered that she testified at "City Hall"; her understanding was that when the clerk asked her to raise her hand, she was testifying. Yang believed that she and Xiong exchanged vows when they raised their hands and said "yes." Yang testified that she does not know the difference between City Hall and court.

After obtaining the marriage license, Yang referred to Xiong as her husband outside the Hmong community, and she always heard Xiong refer to her as his wife. She never again referred to Xiong as her boyfriend, and she never again heard Xiong refer to her as his girlfriend. Yang's brothers also always heard Yang refer to Xiong as her husband and never heard Xiong refer to Yang as his girlfriend.

Xiong, who had worked as a professional tax preparer, filed joint income-tax returns for the couple. Yang testified that on all legal documents, the couple indicated that they were married and that she was not aware of any document that indicated that they were not married. When Yang applied for naturalization, she reported to the Immigration and Naturalization Service (I.N.S.) that she was married. She also recalled that she brought her marriage license with her to her naturalization interview, as requested, and no one told her that the document was not evidence of marriage. In fact, Yang's certificate of naturalization, dated November 20, 1996, reflects that she is married. Xiong and Yang also bought a house and insurance together as a married couple.

Yang first began to worry that she might not be legally married to Xiong in 2006, when Xiong brought home a second wife. Yang told Xiong that in American culture, he could not have more than one wife. The couple argued, and Xiong told Yang that she was "not even his wife." After the argument, Xiong told Yang that he only made the statement out of anger, did not mean anything by it, and that they were married culturally and legally. Yang believed him. One of Yang's brothers testified that Yang never came to him with any doubts about the legality of her marriage.

In May 2008, Yang contacted a lawyer in anticipation of divorcing Xiong. She had some concerns that they may not be legally married based on the statement Xiong made to her in 2006. The lawyer discovered that although the couple had obtained a marriage license in 1993, it was not returned and no marriage certificate existed. Through an interpreter, the lawyer explained to Yang that she was not legally married in the United States. The lawyer testified that Yang became "very upset" and cried. The lawyer had to repeatedly tell her that she was not legally married. Yang testified that:

> [W]hen I heard the news I fe[lt] very sorry for myself. I wonder[ed] to myself why would my husband mislead me[?] . . . I have a whole bunch of children and it seems like he buried all of us alive. . . . It made me think—because I thought I knew my husband, but when that came about I realized that I didn't know him, I didn't know my husband. It made me, you know, again feel sorry for myself and [I] was overwhelmed with it.

After meeting with the lawyer, Yang tried to talk to Xiong about whether they were legally married, but he said that an "ignorant person like [you] doesn't know anything."

Yang testified that she did not know how to get legally married in Minnesota until sometime after November 3, 2009, when she asked a friend to explain it to her. During cross-examination of Yang, Xiong's lawyer asked her to explain how she could have a good-faith belief that she and Xiong were married if she did not know how to get married. Yang answered, "Because [Xiong] was my husband and he took me to get our marriage license, . . . he spoke English and he was a smart guy. So of course he was my husband and he told me that we were married and of course I would believe him."

Xiong testified at the trial and contradicted almost every point of Yang's testimony. Xiong testified that: Yang spoke English when she came to the United States; Yang could read and write English during high school; Yang was in advanced classes in high school with "American students"; Yang passed "very hard tests" in order to get her diploma; he and Yang were never culturally married because no one documented the gifts and donations; the party was merely to celebrate that they would be living together; the Mej Koobs at the party "just came to help" and did not marry them; he did not pay a dowry to Yang's family; when he and Yang got the marriage license, an official gave Yang a list of judges to contact to perform the ceremony; Yang was dating other men throughout their relationship and did not want to get legally married because she wanted to continue to date; he never referred to Yang as his wife; he referred to her only as his girlfriend; he never heard Yang refer to him as her husband; he filed joint income tax returns only to save money and he and Yang knew that it was wrong; and Yang "forced" him to sign a life-insurance application that he never read and "lots of" other documents indicating they were married.

Following the trial, the district court "unequivocally f[ound] that [Yang's] testimony in her belief that she was legally married to [Xiong] was credible," and "unequivocally [found] that [Xiong's] testimony as to his belief that [Yang] knew, or had reason to know, that the parties were not married [wa]s not credible." The court also found that the parties owned a home together, lived together, had children together, filed joint tax returns, and "came to the Ramsey County Courthouse and obtained a marriage license wherein both parties raised their hand, leading [Yang] to conclude, for that and other reasons testified to, that they were legally married."

Based on the evidence adduced at the evidentiary hearing, the district court found that Yang was "a putative spouse who acquired the rights conferred upon [Xiong's] legal spouse until [Yang] had knowledge of the fact that she was not legally married to [Xiong]" under Minn.Stat. § 518.055 (2010). This appeal follows. . . .

ANALYSIS

Xiong argues that the district court clearly erred by finding that Yang was his putative spouse. Whether a person is a putative spouse is a question of fact. . . . Minnesota's putative-spouse law provides:

> Any person who has cohabited with another to whom the person is not legally married in the good faith belief that the person was married to the other is a putative spouse until knowledge of the fact that the person is not legally married terminates the status and prevents acquisition of further rights. A putative spouse acquires the rights conferred upon a legal spouse, including the right to maintenance following termination of the status. . . .

Minn.Stat. § 518.055. The district court's finding that Yang had a good-faith belief that she was legally married to Xiong is supported by the ample record evidence already described. Although Xiong's testimony contradicted Yang's testimony, the district court discredited Xiong's testimony and credited Yang's. We defer to the district court's assessment of the credibility of witnesses. The evidence is sufficient to support the district court's findings that Yang had a good-faith belief that she was legally married to Xiong and was his putative spouse.

Xiong argues that the putative-spouse doctrine should be applied only when the parties have participated in a wedding ceremony. His argument is flawed for two reasons. First, the argument has no support in the plain language of Minnesota's putative-spouse law, which requires only that (1) the parties cohabit, (2) the parties are not legally married, and (3) the person seeking putative-spouse status have a good-faith belief that the parties were legally married. Second, Yang testified that she believed that the parties were exchanging their wedding vows before the clerk at "City Hall" when they were asked to raise their hands and say "yes," and the district court expressly credited Yang's testimony. Therefore, even if a ceremony were required, Yang had a good-faith belief that a wedding ceremony occurred.

Xiong next argues that Minnesota should apply an objective standard to a putative-spouse claimant's good-faith belief that he or she was legally married. . . . We reject Xiong's argument because in Minnesota, "good faith" is judged subjectively, while "reasonable belief" is judged objectively. The plain language of section 518.055 requires only a "good faith belief," not a "reasonable belief." We therefore determine that the district court correctly used a subjective analysis of Yang's good-faith belief in finding that she was Xiong's putative spouse. . . .

Affirmed.

E. Civil Effects Afforded the Putative Spouse

See La. Civ. Code art. 96.

Civil Code article 96 explains that the good-faith putative spouse is entitled to the civil effects of the marriage. Similarly, the putative marriage will produce "civil effects in favor of a child of the parties." What exactly are those civil effects? The answer varies somewhat by jurisdiction.

In 1973 the Louisiana Supreme Court enumerated the civil effects afforded putative spouses as follows: (1) legitimacy/paternity of children; (2) the right of a putative spouse to claim workmen's compensation from the other spouse's employer; (3) community property rights; (4) spousal inheritance rights; (5) right to the marital portion; and (6) right to claim life insurance proceeds as a surviving spouse.[17] The case went on to hold that alimony/spousal support is a civil effect afforded to a putative spouse. Other cases have considered wrongful death actions and similar tort claims. The states are not in agreement on all of these points.

Children. There is near universal support for treating the children of a putative marriage as marital or legitimate children. Even common law jurisdictions that never adopted a putative spouse doctrine concur on this point. In the modern era, this civil effect is likely less important than it once was—an issue that is explored further in later chapters.

Property Rights. There is also near universal support for a property division in favor of the good faith spouse. Generally, the good faith spouse is entitled to community property rights or to some other equitable division of the marital property. The nuances of this rule vary by jurisdiction and are typically considered in more depth in community property courses. Putative spouse claims sometimes arise after the death of one of the parties to the marriage. Many states afford the putative spouse rights as an intestate heir.

---

17. Cortes v. Fleming, 307 So. 2d. 611 (La. 1973).

Wrongful Death Actions, Workers Compensation, and Similar Claims. There is some disagreement in the area of statutorily created rights such as wrongful death claims and workers compensation claims. Because these rights are typically created by statute, courts have sometimes construed them strictly and only allowed recovery to the persons specifically listed in the statute. Such statutes often include the "spouse" but not the "putative spouse." This harsh treatment has not been accepted in all states. California jurisprudence has long allowed wrongful death claims by putative spouses and now expressly does so by statute.[18] In 1907, the Louisiana Supreme Court refused to allow a putative spouse to bring a wrongful death claim.[19] The court reversed course in 1975 and held that a putative spouse could bring such a claim — expressly reversing its earlier decision.[20]

Alimony/Spousal Support. There is some variation on the issue of spousal support or alimony. Louisiana deems it a civil effect of marriage afforded to putative spouses.[21] It is possible, however, that this rationale no longer applies in the case of final periodic support in light of more recent Louisiana decisions. California affords alimony rights to putative spouses by statute.[22] In 2004, the Nevada Supreme Court specifically adopted the putative spouse doctrine for purposes of dividing community property but refused to extend the doctrine to allow for an award of alimony.[23]

---

18. *See* Kunakoff v. Woods, 332 P.2d 773 (Cal. App. Ct. 1958); Cal. Code Civ. Proc. § 377.60 (2017).

19. Vaughn v. Dalton-Lard Lumber Co. 43 So. 926 (La. 1907).

20. King v. Cancienne, 316 So. 2d. 366 (La. 1975).

21. Cortes v. Fleming, 307 So. 2d 611 (La. 1973).

22. Cal. Fam. Code § 2254 (2017).

23. Williams v. Williams, 97 P.3d 1124 (Nev. 2004).

Chapter 6

Amatory Torts and Related Claims

A. The Amatory Torts: In General

Both contract and tort theories provide modes of recovery when a relationship between spouses (or would be spouses) ends. At common law, a host of actions were once recognized in the family and romance settings—some of which have continued viability today. Some of these actions had comparable civil law analogs. Some actions—like those seeking recovery for seduction or for breach of promise to marry—involved acts leading up to the marriage itself. Others—like alienation of affections—involved the destruction of the marriage relationship. Because of changing social mores, many of these actions have since been abrogated by statute or by jurisprudence. The common law torts of seduction, criminal conversion, and alienation of affections are practically non-existent today.

Seduction was really two torts—both of which involved a man impregnating a woman after convincing her that he would marry her. In some instances, such facts created a cause of action in the woman's parents who could sue to recover damages from the man for the loss of the woman's services and the costs associated with delivering the baby. In some jurisdictions, the woman might also have her own independent tort claim against the man.

Alienation of affections claims are tort actions brought by a spouse against a third party alleged to have caused the dissolution of the marriage—typically the person with whom the other spouse had an affair. The tort was originally based on "the antiquated concept that husbands had a proprietary interest in the person and services of their wives."[1] Today, the tort remains viable in only a handful of states—including Mississippi and North Carolina.

Louisiana does not recognize a cause of action for alienation of affections. In *Moulin v. Monteleone*, the Louisiana Supreme Court set forth several sound reasons for refusing to recognize such an action.[2] Not only was there no comparable right at Spanish or Roman law, the court pointed out that the tort seemed based on the antiquated common law notion that the wife was the husband's chattel. Moreover, damages awarded successful plaintiffs in alienation of affection claims were exemplary or punitive—which is not generally a type of recovery allowed in Louisiana. Finally,

---

1. Helsel v. Noellsch, 107 S.W.3d 231 (Mo. 2003) (*en banc*).
2. 115 So. 447 (La. 1927).

at the time of the decision, Louisiana (like other civil law jurisdictions) did not recognize a cause of action for interference with contract. Marriage, of course, is a civil contract, and the recovery sought was essentially for interference with that contract. These policy justifications remain sound today.

B. Breach of Promise to Marry

See La. Civ. Code art. 1995–98; 2315.

Causes of action for breach of promise to marry lie more in contract than in tort. If marriage is a civil contract, then an engagement must be a type of precatory contract. A cause of action for breach of that promise is one way people might seek compensation for the damage caused by a broken engagement. In many states, breach of promise to marry was abrogated along with the various amatory torts. During that same time period, the popularity of valuable engagement rings increased. At least one scholar has made a compelling case that this was more than just a coincidence. Margaret Brining has argued that women began demanding valuable engagement rings as a type of insurance policy.[3]

Although many jurisdictions have abolished this cause of action along with the heartbalm torts, it remains viable in a number of states — including Louisiana. *Glass v. Wiltz*, below, illustrates the Louisiana approach to breach of promise to marry. The case is also useful for illustrating who is entitled to the engagement ring when an engagement does not result in marriage. *Sanders v. Gore*, which follows *Glass*, places a limit on the right of a party to bring an action for breach. *Sanders* is also notable in that it points out that the Louisiana action for breach of contract to marry is rooted in common law rather than in civil law.

Glass v. Wiltz
551 So. 2d 32 (La. App. 4 Cir. 1989)

Armstrong, Judge.

Defendant, Ann P. Wiltz appeals the trial court's judgment dismissing her reconventional demand for damages against plaintiff for breach of his promise to marry her.

Plaintiff, Lawrence D. Glass, brought suit against defendant, Ann P. Wiltz, seeking the return of a fourteen carat yellow gold diamond ring. The appraised value of the ring is $29,000. The ring was given in contemplation of a future marriage between Mr. Glass and Ms. Wiltz which never took place. After their engagement was terminated, Mr. Glass requested the return of the ring from Ms. Wiltz but to no avail.

---

3. *See generally* Margaret Brining, *Rings and Promises*, 6 J. L. Econ. & Org. 203 (1990).

After trial on the merits, the trial court ordered Ms. Wiltz to return the ring to Mr. Glass and dismissed Ms. Wiltz's reconventional demand for damages for the loss of the ring in the amount of $29,000.00 and for pain and suffering in the amount of $25,000.00. The court wrote in its reasons for judgment that while the record reflected that plaintiff broke the engagement defendant failed to prove any damages as a result of the plaintiff's breach of this promise to marry her. Ms. Wiltz now seeks to have the judgment of the trial court reversed as to its denial of the damages she claimed in her reconventional demand.

A careful study of the law in this area reveals that Louisiana does recognize a cause of action for damages when a party breaches a promise to marry. Ms. Wiltz is not entitled to keep her engagement ring as the law clearly states that a gift in "consideration" of a future marriage is void if the marriage did not take place. One may bring a suit for damages for breach of promise to marry but cannot arbitrarily keep engagement presents as damages. The underlying theory which pervades this subject is that the consummation of the marriage is the end sought, and therefore, the ultimate purpose of all such gifts. Necessarily, the failure of the essential condition on which the gift is made, makes the gift nullable.

Historically such causes of action resulted in damage awards but such cases are rare and recently courts seem reluctant to award damages. . . .

The trend therefore seems to be that courts resist awarding damages in such causes of action unless the injured party can clearly demonstrate that he or she is free from fault and that he or she has suffered damage.

As a result of Mr. Glass' breach of promise, Ms. Wiltz claims that she suffered embarrassment, humiliation, mental anguish and some physical problems. Her testimony at trial was that the emotional trauma of discovering Mr. Glass with another woman caused her to experience a "cerebral assault". It manifested itself in severe head pain, numbness in the face and widening of the eye. Ms. Wiltz offered no medical expert testimony as to her condition. She did produce two half-filled bottles of prescription medicine which she claimed her internist prescribed for her as antidepressant medication. However, she admitted that she did not consistently use the medication because she did not feel that it worked.

Her sole continuing complaint is that she now has a distrust of men that she never had previously. She did not assert that due to this distrust she no longer dated men. To the contrary, she admitted having social relationships with men since her relationship with Mr. Glass terminated. She also maintained that her break-up with Mr. Glass had caused her to be the subject of conversation in their social circle. However, she did not imply that her reputation and social standing had been injured in any way.

Other physical complaints Ms. Wiltz made included weight loss, insomnia, and diarrhea. No evidence was produced to demonstrate the link between Ms. Wiltz's physical problems and her emotional state resulting from Mr. Glass' breach of his promise to marry her. Ms. Wiltz admits that months before she and Mr. Glass stopped seeing each other he informed her that he had changed his mind about marrying her.

She admitted that she continued to wear his engagement ring believing that their engagement was only a charade. At the time she suffered the so-called cerebral assault she no longer believed he intended to marry her. Therefore this ailment and any physical ailments that followed were not linked to his breach of promise to marry but simply to her emotional disappointment following the disintegration of their romance. There is no recovery under the law for such a cause of action.

We find no clear error in the trial court's judgment.

For the foregoing reasons, the trial court's judgment is affirmed.

AFFIRMED.

Sanders v. Gore

676 So. 2d 866 (La. App. 3 Cir. 1996)

KNOLL, Judge.

On September 9, 1994, Brenda Sanders filed suit against Brent Gore, seeking damages for breach of his promise to marry her. On November 4, 1994, Brent Gore filed a peremptory exception of no cause and/or no right of action. The trial court, noting that both parties were married to other persons at the time of the alleged breach, granted defendant's exception. Plaintiff appeals, asserting four assignments of error.

FACTS

The petition of Brenda Sanders alleges the following facts.

In March of 1990, Mrs. Sanders first contacted Mr. Brent Gore, an attorney, concerning a collection matter. Although both Mr. Gore and Mrs. Sanders were married to others at the time, a personal relationship soon developed. In May, 1990, the parties began an adulterous affair that continued until December, 1993.

During the course of the affair, Mr. Gore convinced Mrs. Sanders that he wanted to divorce his wife and marry her. He also convinced her to leave her husband, and in May, 1992, Mrs. Sanders obtained a divorce from her husband of twenty-one years. Mr. Gore represented Mrs. Sanders in the divorce, and she alleges that he was able to obtain a divorce judgment even though she and her husband had not lived separate and apart either prior to or subsequent to the divorce.

In June of 1992, the parties took a trip to Hawaii, where they registered for a promotional tour of time-share condos as "Brent and Brenda Gore." On November 12, 1992, Brent Gore presented an engagement ring to Brenda Sanders and formally asked her to marry him. Ms. Sanders accepted the engagement. The affair continued until December 1993, when Mr. Gore told Ms. Sanders that he was "too weak" to leave his wife. Mr. Gore then told Ms. Sanders that he would not marry her and that their relationship was over.

In September of 1994, Ms. Sanders filed suit for damages arising from their liaison, and from Brent Gore's refusal to leave his wife and marry her. In her petition, plaintiff explicitly details the events leading up to the affair, and recounts their numerous indiscretions. The petition also makes several disparaging remarks about Mr. Gore's marriage, which has survived the affair. Ms. Sanders seeks the recovery of $7,300 in gifts given to the defendant over the course of the relationship. She seeks reimbursement for the costs of remodeling her home, which was refurbished in accord with Mr. Gore's tastes, with a view to becoming their matrimonial domicile. Ms. Sanders also seeks damages for loss of reputation and social standing, mental anguish, humiliation, embarrassment, pain and suffering, loss of financial and emotional support, and the needless break-up of her marriage. . . .

PEREMPTORY EXCEPTION TO BREACH OF A PROMISE TO MARRY

. . . Ms. Sanders' petition is styled as a breach of a promise to marry. Mr. Gore asserts that the fact that the parties were married at the time of the promise operates as a bar to Ms. Sanders' recovery under the contract.

There is little dispute that Louisiana recognizes an action in contract for breach of a promise to marry. The action, as recognized in Louisiana, is of a contractual nature. It is also not disputed that the nature of the contract to marry may in certain situations give rise to nonpecuniary damages for its breach under La.Civ.Code art. 1998. Nevertheless, whether the fact that the parties were married at the time the promise is made operates to nullify the contract is a res nova issue in Louisiana.

We initially note that La.Civ.Code art. 88 specifically provides that a "married person may not contract another marriage." Ms. Sanders argues that this provision is only intended to prevent actual bigamous contracts of marriage, and that a *contrario sensu*, it does not apply to "contracts to contract" a marriage. Although we have no doubt as to the policy considerations behind Article 88, we will assume, arguendo, that it does not prohibit contracts to marry as opposed to contracts of marriage. . . .

As stated by Dr. Harriet S. Daggett, a recognized eminent scholar, the contractual action for breach of a promise of marriage is absent not only in the civil law of France but in all civil law countries. Furthermore, the action, as recognized in Louisiana, has its roots not in the civil law tradition, but in the common law as developed in England in the early 17th century. We therefore find a survey of the common law in this area, although not controlling, relevant to a thorough discussion of the issue.

The contractual nature of the promise of marriage is recognized in the common law. Also recognized, however, is the rule that agreements in derogation of marriage are against public policy. The promise made by Mr. Gore was not merely that he would marry Ms. Sanders, but that he would divorce his wife and marry Ms. Sanders. The dissolution of Mr. Gore's current marriage was a necessary antecedent to him marrying Mrs. Sanders.

It is for the foregoing reasons that the common law has universally recognized that promises of marriage, when made by persons already married, are unenforceable. The only exception to this rule arises when one of the parties successfully conceals his or her current marriage from an innocent party. . . .

Contracts so framed as to have effect only on condition that a divorce between the parties should be granted are generally held illegal, since their object is to interest the party to be benefitted in procuring or permitting a divorce. Thus, a promise to marry made by a man or woman already married, to take effect when he or she has obtained a divorce from his or her present spouse, is illegal and void.

Nevertheless, the recognition that contracts in derogation of marriage are void is not confined to the common law. In the volume on obligations in their Cours de Droit Civil Francais, Aubry and Rau state that:

> In addition to agreements in which the object of the performance promised by one of the parties is an unlawful act and thus the cause itself becomes illegal with regard to the other party, several other agreements may be mentioned whose cause is illegal: . . . promises to dissolve a marriage. . . .

In her brief on this issue, Ms. Sanders argues that "the original common law rationale for Mr. Gore's defense has been undercut by modern views of the state's interest (or lack thereof) in promoting the continued existence of marriage, as reflected by its continued lessening of the burdens of obtaining a divorce." She further states that "[t]here is no longer a public policy, if indeed there ever was one, of preventing couples from divorcing." These statements are sorely misplaced. We find even more bizarre her assertion that "[i]n actuality, statistically, and as a matter of fact, promises of married persons to marry others—even other married persons—is almost as prevalent as, if not more prevalent than, the promise of a single person." While we recognize that divorce is now easier to obtain legally, we also recognize that the institution of marriage is still guarded by public policy provisions.

The State of Louisiana has long recognized the importance to society of the institution of marriage. The family is recognized as the fundamental unit of society. The state, therefore, encourages couples to marry and discourages their divorce. . . .

The case sub judice involves not a simple promise to marry, but a promise to dissolve a marriage and marry another. In fact, this lawsuit was triggered by Mr. Gore's statement that he was "too weak" to leave his wife. Therefore, a primary cause of the contract was the dissolution of Mr. Gore's marriage. This cause was definitely known to Ms. Sanders. The contract sought to be enforced in the case sub judice is in direct opposition to Mr. Gore's obligations under La.Civ.Code art. 98.

Our survey of the law on this issue reveals no jurisprudence or commentary which supports the enforcement of a contract of marriage between persons already married. To the contrary, the jurisprudence of our sister states, the commentary of civilian jurists, Louisiana jurisprudence, and the Louisiana Civil Code support the statement that contracts in derogation of marriage are against public policy. We therefore affirm that the promise to marry by persons already married is unenforceable as against public policy. . . .

Absolutely null contracts are void ab initio, and are treated as if they never existed. . . .

In brief, Ms. Sanders asserts that several theories of recovery, independent of the breach of the promise to marry, apply to the facts alleged in the petition. Although she asserts claims in fraud, detrimental reliance, and abuse of the attorney/client relationship, these causes of action are simply restatements of her action for breach of the marriage promise.

Ms. Sanders asserts that through artifice and fraudulent misrepresentation, Mr. Gore was able to convince her to divorce her husband, renovate her house, and give him expensive gifts. She argues as fraud the fact that he never really intended to leave his wife, and asserts arguments of detrimental reliance. Significantly, however, Mr. Gore never misrepresented to Ms. Sanders that he was married. La.Civ.Code art. 1966 applies to claims of both contract and detrimental reliance and provides that "[a]n obligation cannot exist without a lawful cause." Therefore, an obligation, whether it results from a contract or from detrimental reliance, must have lawful cause. We have already held that the underlying cause for Mr. Gore's promise is against public policy. We also hold that for the same reasons, Ms. Sanders' reliance on that promise is not justified. We therefore find no merit in Ms. Sanders' claim of fraudulently induced detrimental reliance.

Ms. Sanders also alleges an abuse of the attorney/client relationship. Although this court finds Mr. Gore's actions ethically reprehensible, Louisiana law does not prohibit sexual relationships between attorneys and their clients. Also, although Ms. Sanders alleges a conflict of interest in his handling of her divorce, she does not allege that Mr. Gore failed to adequately represent her. Nor is it alleged that Ms. Sanders was unaware of this conflict of interest. In fact, Ms. Sanders specifically alleges in her petition that Mr. Gore told her the reason he wanted her to file for divorce was so that he could marry her. Furthermore, Ms. Sanders does not allege that Mr. Gore's handling of her legal affairs caused her any injury that was independent of her claim for breach of the promise to marry.

For the above reasons, we find that Ms. Sanders failed to state a claim for which the law affords a remedy. . . .

CONCLUSION

We hold that the institution of marriage demands full respect from the law, therefore, as a matter of public policy, agreements to marry by persons already married are absolutely null. The judgment of the trial court is affirmed. All costs of this appeal are assessed to plaintiff-appellant.

AFFIRMED.

C. Amatory Torts and the Putative Spouse Doctrine

At least two Louisiana cases — *Holcomb v. Kincaid* and *Bhati v. Bhati* — have considered whether a putative spouse may seek additional recovery under a tort or contract theory. Interestingly, the cases reached the opposite conclusion, and the briefs in *Bhati* make no reference to *Holcomb*. There are only a handful of recent cases from other jurisdictions that have considered the issue—and the results have been mixed.[4]

Holcomb v. Kincaid

406 So. 2d 650 (La. App. 2 Cir. 1981)

PRICE, Judge.

Plaintiff, Wilma Lee Holcomb, brought this action for fraud against defendant, Eugene Edward Kincaid. The jury awarded her $200,000, and from this judgment defendant has appealed. For the reasons assigned, we reduce the amount awarded to $5,000 and otherwise affirm the judgment.

The allegations of fraud leveled against defendant by plaintiff in this matter arise out of an illegal marriage relationship and its subsequent dissolution after a period of some 12 years.

Plaintiff and defendant, residents of Caddo Parish, were both married to different spouses in 1965 when they decided to get married. Desiring to obtain divorces from their respective spouses as quickly as possible, they moved to Arkansas to establish residence. On the advice of their mutual Arkansas attorney, plaintiff obtained her divorce first, and defendant went into court a month later to obtain his. On June 30, 1965, the judge took the petition for divorce under advisement. On July 2, 1965 plaintiff and defendant were married. Thereafter, on July 16, 1965, the Arkansas judge rendered a decree of divorce in favor of defendant.

In 1977 plaintiff filed for a separation. Defendant reconvened based on abandonment and plaintiff converted her suit to divorce based on adultery. Defendant then reconvened for annulment of the marriage. An annulment was rendered in 1977. At the annulment proceeding the trial judge found plaintiff to be a good faith putative spouse and awarded her alimony. She later received her share of the community property.

Plaintiff filed the present suit, alleging fraud by the defendant for concealing his marital status at the time of their marriage. She prayed for damages for lost wages and retirement pay, humiliation, embarrassment, indignation, and mental anguish and suffering. A jury awarded her a lump sum award of $200,000. Defendant appeals contending (1) plaintiff has no cause of action under La.C.C. Art. 2315; (2) the judgment is clearly contrary to law and evidence; (3) the trial judge erred in not giving an instruction that the jury should consider plaintiff's failure to call witnesses to

---

4. *See, e.g.,* Bradley v. Bradley, 56 A.3d 541 (Ma. Ct. Spec. App. 2012) ("False statements regarding marital status in a bigamy context are actionable as the tort of misrepresentation."); Casey v. Casey, 736 S.W.2d 69 (Mo. Ct. App. 1987) ("Our research has disclosed no Missouri cases recognizing the tort of bigamy.").

corroborate her testimony; and (4) the jury abused its discretion in setting the amount of the award.

On this appeal defendant contends the trial court erred in not sustaining his exception of no cause of action. He contends that Louisiana C.C. Arts. 117 and 118 provide for the exclusive remedies of putative spouses, and since plaintiff has received her share of the community property and is receiving alimony, she has received everything she is legally entitled to as a putative spouse. He further contends that to uphold plaintiff's cause of action and to grant recovery would lead to a variety of tort suits between legal and putative spouses. . . .

The Louisiana jurisprudence has apparently never considered the specific issue here presented-a request for damages because of a fraudulent inducement to marry. However, other jurisdictions that have considered this question have recognized such a cause of action. . . .

All of the cases cited above considered damages only for mental anguish; there was no mention of the offended party having other rights accorded by law for alimony or a division of community property. However, the Supreme Court of Michigan in *Sears v. Wegner*, 150 Mich. 388, 114 N.W. 224 (1907) held there was a cause of action for fraudulent inducement to marry, and awarded support payments for the putative wife and her children in addition to damages for mental anguish and suffering.

Since there is no Louisiana precedent to guide us in resolving this issue, we find the decisions in the other jurisdictions persuasive. Following those decisions, we find that plaintiff's petition does state a cause of action. There is nothing in the wording of C.C. Arts. 117 and 118 that would preclude a cause of action under C.C. Art. 2315. We do not intend by our holding to create additional causes of action in the matrimonial relationship where the rights of the parties are prescribed and restricted by the Civil Code. Our holding is limited to those instances where a person has fraudulently induced another to enter into a marriage contract. There is no public policy reason for limiting a person's right to recover from someone who concealed his marital status from him.

We next consider whether the jury was clearly wrong in finding defendant guilty of fraud. There is documentary proof in the record of defendant obtaining his final divorce decree after his marriage to plaintiff. At the annulment proceeding defendant testified he knew he was not free to marry plaintiff. We conclude there was ample evidence in the record to substantiate the jury's finding of fraud.

Bhati v. Bhati

103 So. 3d 1290 (La. App. 3 Cir. 2012)

PICKETT, Judge.

Midori T. Bhati appeals a judgment of the trial court granting summary judgment in favor of Deo K. Bhati and dismissing her petition for damages arising out of Mr. Bhati's alleged bigamy.

STATEMENT OF THE CASE

Mr. Bhati, a native of India, and Ms. Bhati, a native of Japan, were married in Japan in 1973. They subsequently moved to Louisiana, and both became citizens of the United States. In 2002, they divorced. As a part of the divorce, they litigated the division of community property and Ms. Bhati was awarded final periodic support. In October 2005, Ms. Bhati alleged she learned that Mr. Bhati married a woman in India before their marriage. After investigating the claim, Ms. Bhati filed a lawsuit in June 2006 seeking damages for Mr. Bhati's bigamy. Mr. Bhati filed a motion for summary judgment, arguing that Louisiana does not recognize a cause of action for bigamy. He also argued that the claim was prescribed and barred by res judicata. The trial court heard arguments and, after taking the matter under advisement, granted the motion for summary judgment and dismissed Ms. Bhati's petition.

Ms. Bhati now appeals. . . .

DISCUSSION

. . . The trial court found that La.Civ.Code art. 96 provides the exclusive remedy for damages as a result of a putative marriage. . . . The trial court found that Ms. Bhati, as the good faith party to an absolutely null marriage, received the civil effects of a valid marriage at the time of her divorce. Thus, she has already been compensated for a marriage that was never legally perfected. We agree with the trial court and affirm the judgment entered below.

Ms. Bhati cites cases where damages were sought for the breach of a promise to marry. Those cases cite authority from the nineteenth century where such a claim was recognized by Louisiana courts, but in both instances the claim for damages was denied. In *Glass*, the court found that Ms. Wiltz was unable to show any actual damages arising from the failure of Mr. Glass to marry her. In *Sanders*, this court found that as both Mrs. Sanders and Mr. Gore were married at the time he promised to marry her, a promise to marry was unenforceable as against public policy.

In this case, Ms. Bhati had no reason to believe that her marriage to Mr. Bhati was a nullity until four years after she filed a petition for divorce seeking to end the marriage. She received the civil effects of that marriage. . . . She has failed to allege any facts upon which further relief can be granted under our law.

CONCLUSION

The judgment of the trial court is affirmed. Costs of this appeal are assessed to Midori T. Bhati.

AFFIRMED.

D. Emotional Distress: The New Amatory Tort?

A few states have considered whether emotional distress claims may be brought in factual scenarios that, historically, might have been covered by the amatory torts. Results have been varied.

As a general matter, Louisiana recognizes a cause of action for both intentional and negligent infliction of emotional distress. A handful of Louisiana decisions suggest that such claims may be viable in factual scenarios involving adultery.[5] *Holcomb v. Kincaid*, suggests recovery may be available for the emotional damage caused by bigamy. *Glass v. Wiltz* similarly suggests recovery might be available for breach of a promise to marry.

There are several challenges in actually pursuing one of these claims in any state. Generally, a claim of intentional infliction of emotional distress requires a showing of "extreme and outrageous conduct [that] intentionally or recklessly causes severe emotional distress."[6] A claim of negligent infliction of emotional distress is similar, but requires an additional showing of duty/risk. The duty aspect makes a negligence case rather difficult. Moreover, it can be difficult to demonstrate that the conduct was sufficiently outrageous to justify awarding damages. There are a number of policy considerations in considering the outrageousness of the conduct.

A Utah case — *Jackson v. Brown* — illustrates these policy considerations.[7] Mr. Brown and Ms. Ranay began dating, and Mr. Brown soon proposed. Shortly after the couple had obtained their marriage license, Mr. Brown broke off the engagement. Ms. Jackson later learned he was already married to someone else. The Utah Supreme Court abrogated the cause of action for breach of promise to marry, but allowed Ms. Jackson to move forward with her emotional distress claim. As the court explained:

> As stated above, an earnest decision by one party in a wedding engagement to cancel marriage plans should not be discouraged, let alone legally penalized. Although such a decision may frequently cause some amount of pain for all parties involved, it is not the kind of pain which is susceptible to remedy in the courts. There is not necessarily any legal wrong in it. However, in the case before us today, there are allegations and some evidence that Brown may have acted with the intention of deceiving Jackson and with the knowledge that his actions would cause emotional distress. For instance, Brown has conceded that during the period in question, he was already married; at no time during his relationship with Jackson was he able, legally, to marry her. Yet he proposed, scheduled a ceremony, acquired a license, and apparently offered every appearance of going through with the wedding. He withdrew his promise only hours before the time scheduled for the ceremony. These actions may very well be "considered outrageous and intolerable in that they offend against the generally accepted

---

5. *See* Scarmardo v. Dunaway, 650 So. 2d 417 (La. App. 5 Cir. 1995); Price v. Fuerst, 24 So. 3d 289 (La. App. 3 Cir. 2009).

6. RESTATEMENT (SECOND) OF TORTS § 46 (2017).

7. 904 P.2d 685 (Utah 1995).

standards of decency and morality." Whether such is the case, however, is a question for the trier of fact. Therefore, we hold that the trial court correctly denied Brown's motion to dismiss Jackson's claim of intentional infliction of emotional distress.[8]

---

8. *Id.*

Chapter 7

Divorce Grounds and Procedure

See La. Civ. Code art. 101–05.

A. Divorce: Early History

Debates about the ease of obtaining a divorce are not new. As the following excerpt from Planiol illustrates, depending on the era and the relative political power of the Catholic Church, divorce has at times been unavailable and at other times has been relatively easy to obtain. What is quite clear from Planiol's writing is the influence that the Catholic Church has had with respect to divorce laws.

1 Marcel Planiol, Treatise on the Civil Law
(Louisiana State Law Institute trans. West, 1959)

1132. Old Law

The old law, with which the Catholic Church was in contact, recognized divorce. Roman law, above all, authorized it quite readily, without judicial intervention and without even requiring the reciprocal consent of the parties. Unilateral repudiation was possible by the wife as well as by the husband. Germanic customs, just as the Jewish law, permitted a husband to repudiate his wife, at pleasure and without a specific reason.

1133. Canon Law

The Catholic Church was, from the very beginning, opposed to divorce. This movement originated in the teachings of Jesus Christ, in connection with which there is a remarkable difference among the Evangelists. While Saint Matthew seems to recognize divorce when based upon adultery, Saint Mark and Saint Luke absolutely reject it.

During several centuries, many of the Fathers of the Church, among others Tertullian, authorized divorce conformably with Saint Matthew's text. The thesis of absolute indissolubility was defended by Saint Augustine. It was proclaimed more and more often by the Councils, principally from and after the VIII Century. The triumph of this school of thought ceased to be discussed during the XII Century. Gratian and Pierre Lombard both decided that divorce for adultery is forbidden. . . .

1134. The Reformation

The Reformation brought about during the XVI Century, a strong movement in favor of divorce in Protestant countries. Their law went beyond the text of the Gospel. They authorized divorce in cases other than the adultery of the wife.

1135. The Revolution

The Revolution, which saw in marriage nothing but a civil contract, was necessarily bound to come to divorce. Its reintroduction was contemplated from the time of the Constituent Assembly. It was, however, the Legislative Assembly which arranged the necessary details by the enactment of the law of September 20, 1792. The Legislative Assembly permitted it too easily. First of all it introduced divorce not only by mutual consent but also for mere incompatibility of temperament alleged by one of the two spouses. It then established too many grounds for divorce. Several among them were most debatable, such as emigration, madness and the disappearance of one of the spouses during five years. The Convention . . . made divorce still easier. But confronted by the abuse of this new freedom it quickly returned to the 1792 law. . . .

1136. Regulation of Divorce by Civil Code

The Civil Code retained divorce. It however took precautions for its regulation and in order "to stop the torrent of immorality" due to the revolutionary laws. Divorce for incompatibility of temperament, upon the petition of one of the spouses, was suppressed. Divorce by mutual consent was made more difficult. And the grounds of divorce were reduced from seven to three. These wise measures had a salutary effect. The average number of divorces in Paris fell to 50 a year (75 was the maximum).

1137. Abolition of Divorce in 1816

With the restoration and the Constitution of 1814, the Catholic religion became the state religion. Divorce was thenceforth condemned. . . .

1138. Reestablishment of Divorce

The Constitution of 1830 deprived Catholicism of its attribute of France's sole religion. The logical consequence should have been the reestablishment of divorce. The Chamber of Deputies, during the first year of Louis Philippe's reign, four times passed bills recognizing divorce. They were, however, all of them thrown out by the Chamber of Peers. The Constituent Assembly, in its turn, rejected such a proposal in 1848. It was only 68 years after its abolition, and following a long campaign by M. Niquet, that it was established by a law of July 19, 1884. . . .

1139. Foreign Legislation

Divorce disappeared in Italy with the passing of the French domination. Various publicists and jurists made efforts to reestablish it in 1865. They did not succeed. Art. 148 of the Italian Civil Code sets forth that marriage is dissolved only by the death of one of the spouses. . . .

Divorce is now recognized in most countries of Europe. The only countries which now absolutely forbid it are Italy, Austria, and certain countries of South America. In Hungary non-Catholics may obtain a divorce. It was introduced into Portugal by a law of December 25, 1910, into Czechoslovakia by a law of May 22, 1919, and into Spain by a law of March 2, 1932, with many grounds for divorce.

B. Historic Fault-Based Divorce in the United States

Divorce laws have a complex history in the United States. The relative ease (or difficulty) of obtaining a divorce has long varied from state to state. As is explored in later chapters, the patchwork nature of divorce laws led to the creation of "divorce mills" and a number of United States Supreme Court decisions.

In the early nineteenth century, divorce was exceedingly rare — and essentially unavailable in some states. In a number of southern states — including Louisiana — a divorce quite literally required an act of the legislature. To obtain a divorce, a married person had to receive legislative approval — a process that undoubtedly favored those with considerable means and political connections. For example, the following act was approved by the Louisiana legislature in 1827 during the first session of the 8th Legislature:

> AN ACT To divorce John D. Buckley and his wife Margaret Legg, from the bonds of matrimony.
>
> *Be it enacted by the Senate and House of Representatives of the state of Louisiana, in general assembly convened,* That John D. Buckley and his wife Margaret Legg, be and they are hereby divorced from the bonds of matrimony.
>
> > OCT. LABRANCHE,
> > Speaker of the House of Representatives.
> >
> > AD. BEAUVAIS,
> > President of the Senate.
>
> Approved, February 7, 1827
>
> > H. JOHNSON,
> > Governor of the state of Louisiana.

Louisiana law did allow marriages to be annulled. Louisiana also recognized legal separation — which would put an end to the community property regime and allow the spouses to live separate lives. Legal separation could only be obtained if there was sufficient cause — such as adultery or abandonment. As Civil Code article 136 of the 1870 Code explained: "Separation from bed and board does not dissolve the bond of matrimony, since the separated husband and wife are not at liberty to marry again; but it puts an end to their conjugal cohabitation, and to the common concerns which existed between them."

Eventually, all states moved towards a judicial—rather than legislative—mechanism for divorce. By 1900, judicial divorce was available in every state except South Carolina—which did not allow judicial divorce until 1948. In order to obtain a divorce, one spouse was required to sue the other and successfully establish some type of fault on the part of the other spouse. Fault grounds varied by state—but most states recognized adultery as grounds for divorce. Abandonment and cruelty were also common grounds for divorce.

Before a major revision in 1990, Louisiana provided for a two-part system for divorce. Article 139 allowed for an immediate divorce in the case of adultery or felony conviction. Alternatively, the spouses could first seek a separation for one of the grounds enumerated in Article 138 and live apart for at least a year without reconciliation. At that time, the couple could return to court and seek a divorce. The grounds remained largely unchanged from the 1900s and are still relevant today for purposes of determining a spouse's entitlement to final periodic spousal support. Articles 138 and 139—as they appeared before their 1990 repeal—are reproduced at the end of this section.

In the era of fault-based divorce, couples devised a number of schemes to circumvent onerous state laws. Some married people traveled to other jurisdictions to obtain divorces—Nevada was a popular divorce mill for a number of years. This approach could be cost prohibitive and subject to legal challenges. Some couples would agree ahead of time that one of them would sue the other for divorce on some fault ground even if no such fault existed. A few enterprising spouses tried catch their significant others in compromising positions in order to claim adultery.

As spouses tried to circumvent the rules, a variety of doctrines evolved to prevent them from accomplishing their goals. Under the doctrine of collusion, a court could refuse to grant a divorce if the court found the parties had some agreement to fail to make a valid defense, to manufacture a ground for divorce, or to otherwise provide false testimony in order to obtain a divorce. Spouses who were unable to sufficiently cooperate in order to obtain a collusive divorce might still face hurdles. Under the doctrine of recrimination, a court could refuse to grant a divorce if both parties had committed some fault—a sort of contributory negligence approach to divorce. Evidence of condonation of the bad behavior or of reconciliation could also preclude a divorce.

As social mores and our understanding of marriage and divorce changed, there was a national push towards no-fault divorce. Of course, the movement was not without controversy—impassioned arguments were made on both sides. Today, no-fault divorce is available in every state as well as in a number of other countries. In 1970, California became the first state to enact no-fault divorce legislation. New York, the last state to join the movement, did not enact no-fault divorce laws until 2010. Louisiana's change occurred in 1990.

La. Civ. Code art. 138. Grounds for separation from bed and board
[REPEALED 1990]

Separation from bed and board may be claimed reciprocally for the following causes:

1. In case of adultery on the part of the other spouse;

2. When the other spouse has been convicted of a felony and sentenced to death or to imprisonment at hard labor in the state or federal penitentiary;

3. On account of habitual intemperance of one of the married persons, or excesses, cruel treatment, or outrages of one of them toward the other, if such habitual intemperance, or such ill-treatment is of such a nature as to render their living together insupportable;

4. Of a public defamation on the part of one of the married persons towards the other;

5. Of the abandonment of the husband by his wife or the wife by her husband;

6. Of an attempt of one of the married persons against the life of the other;

7. When the husband or wife has been charged with a felony, and shall actually have fled from justice, the wife or husband of such fugitive may claim a separation from bed and board, on producing proofs to the judge before whom the action for separation is brought, that such husband or wife has actually been guilty of such felony, and has fled from justice;

8. On account of the intentional non-support by the husband of his wife who is in destitute or necessitous circumstances, or by the wife of her husband who is in destitute or necessitous circumstances;

9. When the husband and wife have voluntarily lived separate and apart for one year and no reconciliation has taken place during that time. . . .

La. Civ. Code art. 139. Grounds for divorce
[REPEALED 1990]

Immediate divorce may be claimed reciprocally for one of the following causes:

1. Adultery on the part of the other spouse.

2. Conviction of the other spouse of a felony and his sentence to death or imprisonment at hard labor.

Divorce may be granted to either spouse after a separation from bed and board in accordance with the provisions of Section 302 of Title 9 of the Louisiana Revised Statutes of 1950.

C. Divorce in the Era of No-Fault

See La. Civ. Code art. 101–05; 159.

States vary considerably in their implementation of no-fault divorce. A majority of states have both fault and no-fault divorce provisions. Common fault grounds today include adultery, abandonment, imprisonment, and abuse — yet individual state variations persist.[1] A handful of states repudiated fault-based divorce in its entirety. In these states, adultery and similar fault-based grounds are no longer statutorily available grounds for divorce. Rather, these states generally only allow divorce for "irreconcilable differences" or similar grounds.[2] Of course, adultery or some other "fault" might very well be the basis for the couple's irreconcilable differences. Whether that "fault" will come before the court depends on the state.

In California, for example, the courts do not adjudicate whether a party was at fault. But, the courts do determine whether the marriage is broken, and evidence of adultery or other misconduct may be relevant for making that determination. A California appellate court summarized the law as follows:

> It is well settled the decision that a marriage is irretrievably broken does not need to be based on objective facts. . . . The California Legislature, in adopting no-fault divorce in 1969, recognized the divorce proceedings were already highly adversarial in nature and it was not helpful to issues of child custody and division of property to force one party to prove why they made the personal and necessarily subjective decision to end the marriage.
>
> For this reason, the code "offers no precise definition or guidelines to measure the existence of 'irreconcilable differences.' Instead, it simply requires the court to determine there are 'substantial reasons for not continuing the marriage and which make it appear the marriage should be dissolved.'" The irreconcilable differences ground is purposely broad. It is intended to represent the actual reasons underlying marital breakdowns and at the same time make irrelevant questions of "fault" or misconduct by either party. . . . It is sufficient evidence for a party to subjectively decide the marriage is over and there is no hope of reconciliation.

---

1. *See, e.g.*, Ala. Code § 30-2-1 (2017) (physical incapacity, adultery, 7 years imprisonment, crime against nature, drug/alcohol addiction, incompatibility, domestic violence); Ark. Code § 9-12-301(2017) (impotence, felony conviction, habitual drunkenness, cruel and barbarous treatment, adultery); Ind. Code § 31-15-2-3 (2017) (irretrievable breakdown, felony conviction, impotence, and incurable insanity); Tex. Fam. Code § 6.001–007 (2017) (insupportable cruelty, adultery, felony conviction, abandonment, confinement in mental hospital).

2. *See, e.g.*, Ariz. Rev. Stat. § 25-314 (2017) ("irretrievably broken" or "one or both of the parties desire to live separate and apart"); Cal. Fam. Code § 2310 (2017) ("irreconcilable differences"); Wash. Rev. Code § 26.09.030 (2017) ("irretrievably broken"); Wis. Stat. § 767.315 (2017) ("irretrievable breakdown").

The determination of irreconcilable differences is "not a ministerial one," and trial courts should not make such findings perfunctorily. Determination of this issue necessarily poses a question of fact. . . .[3]

In a number of states, the fact that the parties have lived separate and apart for some prescribed period of time will serve as sufficient evidence of the breakdown of the marriage, and the court need not make any further inquiry.[4] These "waiting periods" can be quite lengthy—making an immediate fault-based divorce an attractive option for some spouses.

As part of the reform movement, a handful of states also discarded the notion of legal separation. As the earlier excerpts from Planiol explained, legal separation does not terminate the marriage relationship. Rather, separation merely allows the parties to begin separating their finances and to move forward with independent lives. In many states—including Louisiana—legal separation existed long before divorce was readily available. Once judicial divorce was available, many states retained the notion of legal separation. In some cases, a spouse could seek either a legal separation or a divorce. In other cases, legal separation might be a necessary prerequisite to a divorce. Louisiana is one of the handful of states that eliminated the notion of legal separation as part of its reform movement. Yet, as will examined in more detail later, the concept persists in the case of covenant marriages.

Today, Louisiana allows both fault and no-fault grounds for divorce. The fault grounds are set forth in Civil Code article 103 and include adultery, felony conviction, and abuse. The fault-based grounds essentially allow the spouses to obtain an "immediate" divorce. They may also have some significance in spousal support determinations. Louisiana's no-fault approach to divorce simply requires that the spouses live separate and apart for the requisite period of time. Civil Code article 103.1 sets forth the time periods. There are two procedural methods for obtaining a no-fault divorce in Louisiana—often called 102 or 103 divorces after the applicable code articles. In a 102 no-fault divorce, one of the spouses files a petition for divorce and then the couple lives separate and apart for the requisite time period. Once that period has elapsed, the spouse returns to court and is typically given an immediate divorce. In a 103 no-fault divorce, the spouses first live separate and apart for the requisite period of time. Once that time period elapses, one of the spouses may go to court and seek a divorce from the other.

Although the time required for both 102 and 103 no-fault divorces is the same, there are some significant distinctions. Civil Code article 159 explains that the "judgment of divorce terminates a community property regime retroactively to the date of the filing of the petition in the action in which the judgment of divorce is rendered." Therefore, the termination of the community property regime can occur

---

3. Marriage of Greenway, 158 Cal. Rptr. 3d 364 (4th Dis. 2013).
4. *See, e.g.*, Ark. Code § 9-12-301 (2017) (18 months); Conn. Gen. Stat. § 46b-40 (2017) (18 months); Wis. Stat. § 767.315 (2017) (12 months).

much earlier in a 102 no-fault divorce than in a 103 no-fault divorce. The distinction is also relevant for spousal support, because pre-filing fault will preclude a claim for final periodic support, whereas post-filing fault usually will not.

The following sections will first consider Louisiana's fault-based divorce options and then Louisiana's no-fault regime. The following sections do not consider the abuse-based grounds for divorce in Louisiana because those are relatively recent additions to the Civil Code and there are not yet any reported decisions considering issues they might raise.

D. Adultery as Grounds for Divorce

Adultery is probably the oldest and most widespread grounds for divorce. It was also considered a crime in many jurisdictions. In Louisiana, as in many states, adultery remains a basis for an immediate divorce. As a policy matter, why do we allow a divorce in the case of adultery? The policy justifications have changed over time and have evolved alongside the evolution of marriage more generally.

For many years, adultery required some type of sexual act that could result in pregnancy. The law viewed the primary harm caused by adultery as the possible adulteration of the family bloodline—particularly the husband's bloodline. The emotional harm inflicted on the jilted spouse was a secondary concern. This view was true in both the common law and civil law tradition. As one court explained:

> As known to the common law . . . adultery consisted of sexual intercourse by a man, married or single, with a married woman not his wife. The circumstance on which adultery depended at common law was the possibility of introducing spurious issue; in other words, its tendency to adulterate the issue of an innocent husband and turn the inheritance away from his own blood to that of a stranger.[5]

Planiol expressed a similar view:

> When the wife has a lover, if she has children, they will be the legitimate children of her husband. He may bring a suit in disavowal, but the proof necessary to drive out of the family the children who are not his, may often fail him. Herein lurks a great danger which does not affect the deceived husband alone. The adultery of the wife compromises the base upon which the legitimate family rests.[6]

For this reason, the wife's adultery was sometimes treated more severely than the husband's. In a number of states, a single act of adultery on the part of the husband was insufficient grounds for divorce. The same was not true for the wife.

---

5. State v. Bigelow, 92 A. 978 (Vt. 1915).

6. 1 MARCEL PLANIOL, TREATISE ON THE CIVIL LAW § 900 (Louisiana State Law Institute trans. West 1959).

As society began to place greater value on the emotional connection between the spouses, courts were asked to reconsider the harms caused by adultery. If the harm caused by adultery was the harm to the couple's relationship, then perhaps limiting the definition of adultery to procreative sexual acts was too restrictive. As a result, courts have struggled to define which sexual acts constitute adultery—and the outcomes can be inconsistent.

For example, in the era before same-sex marriage was universally legal, courts struggled to decide whether same-sex affairs constituted adultery for legal purposes. Some courts limited adultery to procreative acts—excluding homosexual affairs from the definition of adultery.[7] Other state courts reached the opposite conclusion, holding that "both extramarital homosexual, as well as heterosexual relations constitute adultery."[8] Courts also dealt with the (sometimes) related issue of whether specific sexual acts—like oral sex—could constitute adultery. This issue is explored in *Menge v. Menge*, below.

A significant issue in recent cases of adultery is the question of proof. Intimate sexual activity tends to occur behind closed doors, and an accused spouse often has a disincentive to admit his or her adultery. In reading the cases below, consider the types of proof offered to support the claims of adultery. Similarly, consider the evidentiary weight afforded to a spouse's own admission of adultery. Why is additional evidence usually required?

Menge v. Menge
491 So. 2d 700 (La. App. 5 Cir. 1986)

Bowes, Judge.

. . . Danny Menge filed a petition for divorce on March 13, 1985, alleging that Mrs. Menge was guilty of adultery and requesting custody of the couple's minor daughter. . . .

At trial, Mrs. Menge denied having ever engaged in sexual intercourse with a certain named individual. She testified that she and the other man got undressed and into bed together, and engaged in certain enumerated "sexual activities", which did not include sexual intercourse.

Charles Many, a private detective engaged by Mr. Menge, testified that he observed the defendant and other man together on four occasions: once they drove to LaPlace and back, at which time they were kissing and embracing. On the other occasions, the detective stated that the man and Mrs. Menge were inside her apartment for various unspecified periods of time, with the lights out. Insofar as we can determine, Mrs. Menge's 15-month old daughter was also in the apartment on those occasions.

---

7. In re Blanchflower, 834 A.2d 1010 (N.H. 2003).
8. Owens v. Owens, 274 S.E.2d 484 (Ga. 1981). *Accord* Patin v. Patin 371 So. 2d 682 (Fla. 1979); Adams v. Adams, 357 So. 2d 881 (La. App. 1 Cir. 1978); RGM v. DEM, 410 S.E.2d 564 (S.C. 1991).

Patrick Walsh, another detective, testified that, in one instance, he observed the man drive to Mrs. Menge's apartment and briefly enter; then he drove to a nearby parking lot where he left his car and walked back to the apartment. The lights inside went off for somewhat less than an hour, whereupon Mrs. Menge drove the man back to his car. Other observations by the detective were of the two outside in the automobile on two other occasions. The only other witness was Mrs. Menge's sister, whose testimony was equivocal at best.

On appeal, Mrs. Menge seeks to distinguish between the acts to which she admitted and "sexual intercourse", averring that her actions did not constitute adultery. We disagree.

. . . [T]he [Louisiana] Supreme Court approached a "definition" of adultery when it stated:

> It must be alleged that the offending party was guilty of adultery, or was guilty of having sexual connection or intercourse, which mean the same thing.

> Black's Law Dictionary, 5th Edition (1979) defines adultery as "voluntary sexual intercourse of a married person with a person other than the offender's husband or wife."

> Webster's New Collegiate Dictionary, A. & C. Merriam Co., Copyright 1981, defines sexual intercourse as: "(1) heterosexual intercourse involving penetration of the vagina by the penis: coitus; (2) intercourse involving genital contact between individuals other than penetration of the vagina by the penis."

Mrs. Menge, then, seeks to limit the definition of adultery to coitus. We do not interpret the applicable law so narrowly. Louisiana law and jurisprudence does not define adultery per se. . . . However, our law recognizes another species of adultery, which is homosexual adultery. . . . Homosexual adultery, by its very definition, does not include coitus. We find that the acts to which Mrs. Menge admitted, specifically the commission of "oral sex", constitutes adultery within the meaning of Civil Code Article 139.

Further, we find that a conclusion on the part of the trial court that Mrs. Menge and her partner did not limit themselves merely to oral sex is justified. . . . The testimony of Mrs. Menge and the private detectives (who, defendant admitted, "told the truth") prove that opportunity knocked more than once. The burden of proof required in adultery cases is the requirement of evidence so convincing that it excludes all other reasonable hypotheses than that of guilt of adultery. It would be fatuous of this court to believe that human passion, kindled in so frank a manner as Mrs. Menge confessed, would not be ultimately consummated.

We recognize that the testimony of private detectives must be carefully considered and accepted with extreme caution and that an admission of adultery, without other evidence, is generally insufficient proof upon which to dissolve a marriage.

However, we find that the direct admissions of Mrs. Menge give probative and corroborative value to the statements of the detectives, and vice versa.

We therefore conclude that the trial judge was correct, and certainly committed no manifest error, in his finding that Mrs. Menge was guilty of adultery.

Tidwell v. Tidwell

152 So. 3d 1045 (La. App. 2 Cir. 2014)

WILLIAMS, J.

The plaintiff, Ashlee Tidwell ("Ashlee"), appeals a judgment granting the defendant a divorce. The trial court found that the defendant had proved by a preponderance of evidence that the plaintiff committed adultery. For the following reasons, we affirm.

FACTS

Ashlee and Todd Tidwell ("Todd") were married in October 1995, in Ouachita Parish, Louisiana. The parties have two children, who were 17 and 12 years old at the time of trial. In December 2012, Ashlee and Todd met Glenn Northcott ("Glenn") at a party and they began visiting often with Glenn at his houseboat on the Ouachita River. Ashlee began sending an increasing number of text messages to Glenn. In February 2013, Ashlee remained at Glenn's houseboat after the other guests left and did not return home until early in the morning. On March 8, 2013, while Todd was at home, Ashlee went out for the evening with Glenn and another couple, Kathy and Karl Porter. Ashlee and Glenn spent the night at the Porters' home.

On April 16, 2013, Ashlee filed for divorce under LSA-C.C. art. 102. . . . Todd filed an answer and reconventional demand under LSA-C.C. art. 103(2), alleging that Ashlee had committed adultery and was at fault in the breakdown of the marriage. . . .

At the divorce hearing, Ashlee did not appear and her deposition was introduced into evidence. Todd and two private investigators testified about the number of meetings between Ashlee and Glenn at her residence and his houseboat. After hearing the testimony, the trial court issued oral reasons finding that based upon the totality of the circumstances, Todd had proved by a preponderance of evidence that Ashlee had committed adultery. The court rendered judgment in favor of Todd Tidwell, granting a divorce based upon adultery. Ashlee Tidwell appeals the judgment.

DISCUSSION

Ashlee contends the trial court erred in applying the preponderance of evidence burden of proving adultery. Ashlee argues that this court should conduct a de novo review of the record because the trial court committed legal error in applying the incorrect burden of proof.

A divorce shall be granted on the petition of a spouse upon proof that the other spouse has committed adultery. Generally, a petitioner has the burden of proving his claims by a preponderance of the evidence. A spouse may establish the other spouse's adultery by indirect or circumstantial evidence as well as by direct evidence. If circumstantial evidence alone is relied upon, then the proof must be so convincing as to exclude any other reasonable hypothesis but that of guilt of adultery. The facts and circumstances must lead fairly and necessarily to the conclusion that adultery has been committed as alleged in the petition.

In the present case, Ashlee's deposition was admitted into evidence. During her testimony, she admitted to having sex with Northcott a number of times after the date that her petition for divorce was filed. . . . Consequently, we cannot say the trial court erred in requiring that Todd prove Ashlee's adultery by a preponderance of the evidence. This assignment of error lacks merit.

Ashlee contends the trial court was clearly wrong in finding sufficient evidence to prove that she committed adultery. She argues that Todd did not prove adultery because the private investigators' testimony failed to corroborate her admission of a sexual relationship with Northcott. . . .

An admission of adultery, without other evidence, is generally insufficient proof upon which to dissolve a marriage. Absent other evidence, the fact that a man and a woman are alone together does not necessarily justify presuming that the encounter is for romantic or sexual reasons. A trial court's credibility evaluation in an adultery case is entitled to substantial weight on review.

In the present case, Jan Marino testified that she was an investigator hired to conduct surveillance of Ashlee for one week in May 2013. Marino stated that on May 10, 2013, at 9:30 a.m. she saw Northcott's vehicle parked at Ashlee's residence. Marino testified that they left the home together at 12:45 p.m. in Ashlee's vehicle and drove to the Highland Yacht Club, where Northcott's boat was located. Marino stated that she saw Ashlee's vehicle parked near the boat at 1:45 p.m. Marino testified that she checked the lot each subsequent hour during the day and Ashlee's vehicle remained in the same parking space until she ended her surveillance at midnight.

Another investigator, Donna Caldwell, testified that she took over for Marino at 12:15 a.m. and saw Ashlee's vehicle in the parking lot. Caldwell stated that at 1:30 a.m., she observed Northcott standing beside the vehicle talking with Ashlee, who was in the driver's seat.

During her deposition, Ashlee was asked about an occasion on April 20, 2013, when she was seen at the boat late at night. She denied having sex with Northcott that night and stated she did not know the date when their sexual relationship began. . . .

The record shows that Ashlee admitted to having sex with Northcott during the marriage and that their sexual relationship could have begun in May 2013. The testimony of the investigators indicated that Ashlee was alone with Northcott in the boat for many hours on May 10, 2013. She acknowledged being on the boat with him that day. Although by itself, evidence that a man and a woman are alone does not necessarily mean that the meeting is for sexual reasons, here Ashlee admitted to having sex with Northcott on his boat, but she did not specify the date. The authority cited by Ashlee in her brief does not support her assertion that the circumstantial evidence can corroborate her admission of adultery only if she specifically admitted to having sex on the same date she was observed going to the boat with Northcott.

After hearing the evidence and weighing the credibility of the witnesses, the trial court found that Todd satisfied his burden of proving that Ashlee committed adultery by a preponderance of the evidence based upon Ashlee's admission of adultery coupled with the testimony concerning the times and places of her meetings with Northcott. After reviewing the record as a whole, we cannot say the trial court's factual determination in this close case was clearly wrong. Thus, the assignment of error lacks merit. . . .

AFFIRMED.

E. Commission of a Felony as Grounds for Divorce

A number of states continue to recognize criminal activity as a type of fault sufficient to award a divorce to the other spouse. The nuances vary by state.

Why should we allow divorce in the case of a criminal conviction? Some Louisiana cases have suggested this is a public policy matter but have not done much to elaborate on that policy. Planiol offers some additional guidance:

> The stigma flowing from condemnation to a serious penalty falls indirectly upon the spouse of the convict. It is proper that this spouse, thus affected by the unworthiness of the convict, should be able to obtain the rupture of the marriage and have nothing more in common with such a spouse. This ground for divorce is peremptory, just as adultery. The court has no discretionary power and cannot refuse the divorce.[9]

Cases from other states suggest that common law arrived at a similar justification. In *Ness v. Ness*, for example, the South Dakota Supreme Court explained that conviction of a felony evidenced a "lack of character," caused a "blemish on the family relationship," and was therefore grounds to "sever the marital ties."[10]

Louisiana Civil Code article 103 requires conviction of a felony and sentencing to death or imprisonment at hard labor. Only a handful of reported decisions have examined the Louisiana approach. But, those cases that have examined the Louisiana approach have answered many of the possible questions left open by the statute.

In *McKee v. McKee*, the court suggested that a pre-marital felony conviction and prison term was not a basis for divorce, because the relevant facts occurred before the marriage.[11] In *Nickels v. Nickels*, the court explained that a spouse is entitled to an immediate divorce even if the other spouse is challenging the conviction on appeal:

---

9. 1 MARCEL PLANIOL, TREATISE ON THE CIVIL LAW § 1171 (Louisiana State Law Institute trans. West 1959).

10. 110 N.W.2d 128 (N.D. 1961).

11. 262 So. 2d 211 (La. App. 2 Cir. 1972).

> To entitle a spouse to an immediate divorce, the statute requires only the "... conviction ... of a felony and his sentence to ... imprisonment at hard labor." It does not require all delays for appeal to have expired, or that the convicted spouse actually serve any of the sentence. The conviction and sentencing alone are sufficient to provide the grounds for divorce, and the public policy underlying this ground for divorce is satisfied by this initial determination of guilt and sentencing.[12]

Relying, in part, on *Nickels*, the court in *Kitchen v. Kitchen* similarly allowed a wife to obtain an immediate divorce where her husband was convicted of a felony but eventually received a suspended sentence:

> We are in agreement that conviction and sentencing alone are sufficient to satisfy the requirements of [the Civil Code] regardless of whether the sentence is ever enforced. We do not believe the legislative intent was to allow convicted felons to circumvent the edicts imposed by [the Civil Code] simply because whatever sentence they initially received was later suspended. The fact that a sentence is suspended does not lessen the impact of a conviction, nor does the granting of a suspension negate the fact that the convicted felon was sentenced and carries that sentence with him. We do not believe that the public policies ... would best be served by allowing a convicted felon, sentenced to hard labor, to abrogate [the Civil Code] simply because his sentence was suspended.[13]

Scheppf v. Scheppf held that "entry of a guilty plea to the commission of a crime is tantamount to conviction for the commission of that crime for purposes of [divorce]."[14]

At least two questions remain unanswered by the existing Louisiana jurisprudence. First, what is the effect of a felony conviction in another jurisdiction? Does it matter whether the offense would constitute a felony in Louisiana? Secondly, is divorce available where both spouses have been convicted of a felony—perhaps even one they committed together?

F. Living Separate and Apart Continuously: No-Fault in Louisiana

No-fault divorces in Louisiana require a showing that the spouses have lived separate and apart continuously for the requisite period of time. The time periods have been amended by the legislature on occasion. The requirements of the applicable Code articles are fairly straightforward—yet, some questions have arisen.

---

12. 347 So. 2d 510 (La. App. 2 Cir. 1977). *Accord* Tauzier v. Tauzier, 466 So. 2d 565 (La. App. 5 Cir. 1985).

13. 480 So. 2d 494 (La. App. 5 Cir. 1985).

14. 430 So. 2d 370 (La. App. 3 Cir. 1983).

Gibbs v. Gibbs, below, considers whether the separation must be voluntary on the part of both parties. In a later section dealing with reconciliation, we will consider just how continuous the separation needs to be. *Lemoine v. Lemoine* illustrates what has become a widely accepted understanding of the phrase "living separate and apart continuously" in Louisiana. As a result of *Lemoine* and similar cases, most petitions for no-fault divorce in Louisiana will allege that the spouses have "lived separate and apart continuously, without reconciliation" for the requisite time period. Reconciliation is explored in more detail in the next chapter.

Gibbs v. Gibbs

711 So. 2d 331 (La. App. 2 Cir. 1998)

Patricia Gibbs appeals the judgment of the trial court granting her husband Michael a divorce under La. C.C. art. 103. Patricia contends that the trial court improperly granted the divorce because she and Michael had not lived separate and apart for six months prior to the filing of the petition for divorce as required by art. 103. For the following reasons, we affirm the judgment of the trial court.

FACTS

On July 9, 1996, Michael filed his petition seeking a judgment of divorce based on his having lived separate and apart from Patricia in excess 6 months at the time of the filing of the petition. . . .

At trial on March 3, 1997, Michael testified that he physically separated from his wife and moved to Dallas on July 24, 1995. Michael stated that, although initially the move was temporary to find work, after three or four months he resolved not to return to live with his wife. He returned to Shreveport for brief visits, the longest being 3 hours when he waxed the family car prior to his return with it to Dallas. According to Michael, he and Patricia did not live together or have sex with each other after he moved to Dallas. He continued to live in Dallas until the time of the trial, but he had not worked since November 7, 1995, due to an injury.

Patricia testified that she had no knowledge of her husband's intention to live separate and apart for the purpose of divorce until she was served with the petition for divorce. She stated that Michael returned a few times for visits, and although she confirmed the absence of any conjugal relations, she said that Michael hugged her during some of those visits. By all accounts, the last contact that the couple had was in February 1996, when Michael obtained the family car for his use.

Diane Allen, the Gibbs' adult daughter, testified that she had no knowledge that her father intended to separate from her mother until the service of the divorce petition. She described her father's visits with her and her mother as infrequent, brief and never overnight. She indicated she had no knowledge of her parents having any conjugal relations during this time, but she stated that she saw her parents hug during a few of the visits.

Joyce Bridwell testified that Michael had lived with her in Dallas since July 1995. To her knowledge he had not reconciled or lived with his wife since that time.

A neighbor, Mr. Wodke, also described Michael's visits as infrequent, brief and never overnight. He also stated that Michael hugged Patricia on their parting during the "early 1996" visit in which he obtained the car.

The trial judge indicated in his ruling that he was "clearly convinced that they have been separated for the requisite length of time." He granted the divorce and found the claim for alimony pendente lite to be moot.

DISCUSSION

. . . The "living separate and apart" contemplated as a ground for divorce must be voluntary on the part of at least one of the parties and continuous for the period required. In discussing LSA-R.S. 9:301, the predecessor of art. 103, the Louisiana Supreme Court stated:

> . . . from the point in time that a party evidences an intention to terminate the marital association, when coupled with actual physical separation, the statutorily required separation period begins to run. And that is so regardless of the cause of the initial physical separation.

Patricia contends that she and Michael had not lived separate and apart for the required six months prior to the filing of the petition for divorce on July 9, 1996. Michael testified that when he originally traveled to Dallas in July 1995 he did not intend to live separate and apart from Patricia, but his intentions changed in about the third or fourth month after his move to Dallas. As a result, Michael had the intention of living separate and apart from Patricia from at least December 1995.

Michael never resided in the matrimonial domicile after his move to Dallas. Both Patricia and Michael testified that his visits to the former matrimonial domicile were infrequent after the move to Dallas (no more than 4–5 visits) and that the duration of these visits was short (the longest being 3 hours). While Michael may have hugged Patricia during some of these visits, both parties testified that they did not engage in sexual intercourse with each other after Michael's move to Dallas. In addition, although Michael did not work from November 7, 1995, the date of his injury, until March 3, 1997, the date of trial, he continued to live in Dallas with Ms. Bridwell.

We believe from the foregoing that the trial judge could reasonably have concluded that Michael had evidenced his intent to terminate the marital relationship. We are precluded from setting aside a trial court's findings of fact unless those findings are clearly wrong. We find no reason to overturn the trial court's factual finding in the present case.

CONCLUSION

For the foregoing reasons, the judgment of the trial court is affirmed.

Lemoine v. Lemoine

715 So. 2d 1244 (La. App. 3 Cir. 1998)

THIBODEAUX, Judge.

. . . .

II. FACTS

Brenda and Henry Lemoine physically separated on February 18, 1997, when Mr. Lemoine moved out of the marital domicile. On that same date, Mr. Lemoine filed a Petition for Divorce and Other Relief requesting that he be granted a divorce pursuant to La. Civ. Code art. 102 once all legal delays and requirements of law had been met. Mrs. Lemoine was personally served on February 24, 1997. On March 11, 1997, she filed an Answer and Reconventional Demand for a divorce pursuant to La. Civ. Code art. 102, as well. . . .

On August 25, 1997, 187 days after filing the Petition for Divorce and Other Relief, Mr. Lemoine filed a Motion for Final Divorce, requesting Mrs. Lemoine be required to show cause why a Judgment of Divorce should not be rendered. Mr. Lemoine alleged that 180 days had elapsed since service of process had been made on Mrs. Lemoine, and that 180 days had elapsed before the filing of his rule to show cause. He also asserted that the parties had lived separate and apart continuously with no reconciliation since the filing of his Petition for Divorce and Other Relief. Mrs. Lemoine answered and denied Mr. Lemoine's allegations that they had lived separate and apart continuously since the initial separation.

The Lemoines traveled out of town together on four occasions on overnight trips after their separation. It was also established at the trial that Mr. Lemoine stayed overnight with Mrs. Lemoine at the former marital domicile on at least four occasions after the separation, during which time they resumed sexual relations. The parties and their son testified that Mr. Lemoine's visits were intermittent, although he sometimes stayed for a few days at a time. Mr. Lemoine rented a separate residence during their separation, and stated he never intended to return to the marital domicile. Further, he always brought his clothes with him whenever he stayed overnight, and never moved any of his possessions back into the home. At the conclusion of the hearing, the court stated orally:

> The court does not find reconciliation in this case. There was no intent, really, to-or a meeting of the minds where reconciliation was achieved. Occasional sexual encounters or going out, interacting in a sociable manner, that, itself, does not constitute a reconciliation. In fact, this Court sees that as quite mature.
>
> The actions no [sic] not constitute reconciliation. The reason being that the Court believes that the purpose of the encounters was, perhaps, to bring this to an amicable end, with a property settlement dispute between the parties, and not necessarily to restore and renew marriage on a permanent basis, as required for the defense of reconciliation to a divorce action. . . .

The trial court rendered judgment in favor of Mr. Lemoine granting him a divorce pursuant to La. Civ. Code art. 102. Mrs. Lemoine appealed.

III. LAW AND DISCUSSION

. . . .

Living Separate and Apart Continuously

As stated above, the divorce action at issue in this case is that delineated by La. Civ. Code art. 102 . . .

It is clear from the record that Mr. Lemoine's Motion for Final Divorce was filed after the requisite 180 days had elapsed after the service of his Petition for Divorce and Other Relief upon Mrs. Lemoine. The only other proof necessary for a final divorce in this case is evidence that the parties lived separate and apart continuously for at least 180 days prior to the filing of the rule to show cause. Mrs. Lemoine contends that this requirement was not met and the divorce should not have been granted because the court failed to recognize that she and Mr. Lemoine did not live separate and apart continuously for 180 days as required by the Civil Code, but instead, erroneously granted the divorce based solely upon a finding of no reconciliation having taken place during the 180 day waiting period.

"Living separate and apart" for purposes of obtaining a final divorce means that the parties live apart in such a manner that those in the community are aware of the separation. The Lemoines occupied separate dwellings during the requisite time period, although they did interact intermittently in the marital home and elsewhere. The record reflects that Mr. Lemoine rented a separate home, kept all of his major personal belongings at his separate home, was absent for weeks at a time from the marital home, and never remained at the marital home for more than a few nights at a time on the sporadic occasions in which he visited. This court is satisfied that they lived apart in such a manner that their separation was visible in the community and that others were aware of the separation. The trial court also orally stated that it believed the parties lived separate and apart for six months. The court's finding was espoused in the midst of its discussion of the intermittent sexual encounters between the couple and Mr. Lemoine's occasional overnight visits at the marital home. Although the court spoke of these actions in terms of whether they were evidence of a reconciliation between the parties, we cannot say that the court was erroneous in doing so.

The trial court appropriately considered the issue of reconciliation in its determination of whether the divorce should be granted. Reconciliation is a defense that may be asserted to extinguish a cause of action for divorce pursuant to La. Civ. Code art. 102. La. Civ. Code art. 104. As we stated in *Veron v. Veron* . . . :

> [W]e find that the mandate set forth in *Nethken v. Nethken*, 307 So.2d 563 (La.1975), a case involving a LSA-R.S. 9:302 (now repealed) divorce based upon no reconciliation for a period of six months or more following a judgment of separation, still holds true as to the right to a divorce after the passing of a prescribed statutory time without reconciliation.

The Louisiana Supreme Court stated in *Nethken, supra*, at page 566:

> Such a divorce decree is founded entirely upon the absolute right of either spouse to obtain the divorce on the proof merely that there has been no reconciliation during the probation period allowed by statute.

Further, the 1990 Revision Comments to La.Civ.Code art. 102, subsections (c) and (e), address the appropriateness of a consideration of reconciliation when seeking this divorce action. They state in pertinent part:

> (c) The defense of reconciliation and the various procedural defenses implicit in this Article . . . should be raised at the hearing on the rule to show cause provided for in Code of Civil Procedure Article 3952 (added 1990).

> (e) An action under this Article may be defeated by proof that the parties have reconciled during the one hundred eighty day period. *See* C.C. Art. 104, infra (rev. 1990).

The trial court did not commit error in considering whether the parties reconciled. In fact, we find that it applied the appropriate test for determining whether the Lemoines were entitled to a final divorce pursuant to La.Civ.Code art. 102. The determination consists of finding whether the parties lived separate and apart continuously for 180 days, without reconciliation, after the service of such a petition on the other party or, the signing of a waiver of service by the other party. Reconciliation occurs when there is a mutual intent to reestablish the marital relationship on a permanent basis. "The motives and intentions of the parties to restore and renew the marital relationship is a question of fact determined by the trial judge from the totality of the circumstances." The trial court's finding that no reconciliation took place, is reasonably supported by the record and is not manifestly erroneous. Therefore, we do not find that the trial court committed error during its determination of whether a final divorce should be rendered in this case, as we find no substantive difference between living separate and apart and failing to reconcile under La. Civ. Code art. 102. . . .

AFFIRMED.

G. Divorce and Separation in Covenant Marriage

See La. Rev. Stat. § 9:307–09.

One of the purposes of the covenant marriage legislation was to make divorce more difficult for those parties electing to have a covenant marriage. In many respects, the covenant marriage statutes revive Louisiana's prior divorce laws. For example, legal separation remains an option for couples in a covenant marriage, and the grounds for separation and for divorce are quite similar to those that existed under the earlier legislation. On the other hand, some of the grounds for separation and divorce in covenant marriage—namely adultery, living separate and apart, felony conviction, and abuse—are nearly identical to the grounds that exist for regular marriages. The period of time required for living separate and apart, however, is longer in the case of a covenant marriage. The covenant marriage statutes also retain the concepts of abandonment and cruel treatment—both of which existed under previous law.

Covenant marriage adds an additional requirement to the divorce and separation process—the requirement of counseling. Louisiana Revised Statute § 9:307 makes it clear that separation or divorce is only available "subsequent to the parties obtaining counseling." This requirement is waived by statute in cases of abuse. *Johnson v. Johnson*, below, considers the counseling requirement.

Johnson v. Johnson
168 So. 3d 641 (La. App. 1 Cir. 2014)

Pettigrew, J.

. . . .

BACKGROUND FACTS AND PROCEDURAL HISTORY

Mr. and Ms. Johnson were married on April 18, 2003, and entered into a covenant marriage. They had two minor children born of that marriage: one on May 12, 2004, and the other on August 17, 2005. The parties physically separated on July 19, 2013, and have lived separate and apart without reconciliation since that time.

On July 23, 2013 (four days after the alleged physical separation of the parties), Ms. Johnson filed a petition for separation or in the alternative, divorce. . . .

Mr. Johnson filed a peremptory exception raising the objection of no cause of action, alleging that Ms. Johnson was seeking a separation or divorce prior to the couple engaging in marital counseling, as required by La. R.S. 9:307 relative to covenant marriages. Mr. Johnson sought a judgment to be rendered in his favor and denying all of Ms. Johnson's claims. As mentioned above, the trial court rendered a final judgment on July 9, 2014, sustaining Mr. Johnson's exception and dismissing Ms. Johnson's claims.

PEREMPTORY EXCEPTION OF NO CAUSE OF ACTION

The function of the peremptory exception raising the objection of no cause of action is to test the legal sufficiency of a pleading by determining whether the law affords a remedy on the facts alleged in the pleading. The exception is triable on the face of the pleadings, and, for the purpose of determining the issues raised by the exception, the well-pleaded facts in the petition must be accepted as true. The burden of demonstrating that a petition fails to state a cause of action is upon the mover. In reviewing a trial court's ruling sustaining an exception of no cause of action, appellate courts conduct a de novo review, because the exception raises a question of law, and the trial court's decision is based only on the sufficiency of the petition.

In his exception, Mr. Johnson asserted that Ms. Johnson's petition was premature and stated no viable cause of action against him for divorce or separation, because the statutory provision for covenant marriages, requiring the parties to engage in counseling prior to filing for a legal separation or divorce, had not been met. In the memorandum he filed in support of the exception, Mr. Johnson also challenged Ms. Johnson's petition as failing to state a viable cause of action on the basis of the insufficient amount of time that the parties had been physically separated (one month) at the time of the filing of the petition.

Ms. Johnson does not deny entering into a covenant marriage with Mr. Johnson. In fact, she alleges such in her petition. In that petition, Ms. Johnson alleged she was seeking a separation from bed and board pursuant to La. R.S. 9:307B(6), relative to covenant marriages, because of the cruel treatment of Mr. Johnson, or in the alternative, pursuant to La. R.S. 9:307B(5), upon the passage of the requisite period of time (two years) of living separate and apart without reconciliation. She additionally alleged that she would "receive counseling as required by La. R.S. 9:307(C)."

In sustaining the exception and dismissing Ms. Johnson's claims, the trial court issued the following written reasons:

> The Court, considering the briefs filed by both parties in this matter, grants the defendant, Joey J.E. Johnson's exception of No Cause of Action.

> In brief to this court, counsel for Ms. Johnson states that the trial court, in a status conference, questioned whether the covenant marriage act, specifically, La. R.S. 9:308, prohibited the parties from suing for child custody and support; and the parties submitted briefs on that issue. The transcript of the hearing in this matter is not included in the record before this court. However, counsel for Ms. Johnson further indicates in brief to this court that the trial court's expressed reason for sustaining the exception was its belief that marital counseling was a statutory prerequisite to the filing of a petition for separation/divorce for parties in a covenant marriage. . . .

APPLICABLE LAW/DISCUSSION/ANALYSIS

The Covenant Marriage Act, La. R.S. 9:272 et seq., was enacted by 1997 La. Acts No. 1380, effective July 15, 1997. That act, with regard to divorce, in La. R.S. 9:272C provides a covenant marriage may be terminated by divorce only upon one of the exclusive grounds enumerated in La. R.S. 9:307. . . .

However, La. R.S. 9:308A allows spouses in a covenant marriage to sue each other for "causes of action pertaining to spousal support or the support or custody of a child while the spouses are living separate and apart, although not judicially separated." Moreover, La. R.S. 9:293 makes spouses in a covenant marriage "subject to all the laws governing married couples generally and to the special rules governing covenant marriages." Additionally, La. R.S. 9:291 expressly preserves to parties of a covenant marriage the right to sue on causes of action pertaining to contracts or arising out of the civil code provisions governing matrimonial regimes, "and for causes of action pertaining to spousal support or the support or custody of a child while the spouses are living separate and apart."

We have reviewed all of the applicable law and agree with Ms. Johnson, none of the statutes relating to marital regimes, covenant marriage, divorce or separation require the filing of a divorce petition as a prerequisite to the filing of an action to enforce the obligation of spouses to support one another or their children. . . .

While we recognize that, in furtherance of the intent and purpose of the Covenant Marriage Act, the act includes a statutory requirement that couples who enter into such marriage receive counseling prior to obtaining a judgment of divorce or a judgment of separation; nothing in that act or in any other statute or case in Louisiana jurisprudence requires the parties to obtain counseling prior to filing a suit stating a valid cause of action for incidentals to divorce, particularly child support and custody, and including spousal support. Indeed, provisions within the Covenant Marriage Act itself, i.e., La. R.S. 9:308A, La. R.S. 9:291 and La. R.S. 9:293, indicate that causes of action incidental to divorce (such a spousal and child support, and custody), and even the cause of action for divorce or separation, are viable, notwithstanding that counseling is required before a judgment of separation or divorce can be rendered. Thus, Ms. Johnson has stated a cause of action. . . .

H. Conflicts of Law

See La. Civ. Code art. 3521.

As we will study in more detail in later chapters, a court's jurisdiction to render a divorce decree is typically predicated on the domicile of one (or both) of the spouses within the state. Although courts are often called upon to apply the laws of other states in rendering decisions, questions of domicile and of the marital status of a domiciliary are generally considered important public policy issues of the state in which the spouse (or spouses) is domiciled. As a result, Louisiana Civil Code article 3521 adopts what is probably the majority rule: "A court of this state may grant a divorce or separation only for grounds provided by the law of this state."

Blackburn v. Blackburn presents and interesting example of how a court might view a covenant marriage in a state without any comparable legislation.

Blackburn v. Blackburn
180 So. 3d 16 (Ala. Ct. Civ. App. 2015)

Thomas, Judge.

Karen Lincecum Blackburn ("the wife") and David Blackburn ("the husband") were married on November 6, 2004, in Louisiana. The parties later moved to Mobile; it is undisputed that the parties were residents of Alabama when this action commenced. On January 11, 2013, the husband filed a complaint seeking a divorce in the Mobile Circuit Court ("the trial court"), alleging as grounds incompatibility of temperament and an irretrievable breakdown of the marriage. On January 16, 2013, the wife filed an answer to the complaint and a counterclaim seeking a divorce in which she alleged incompatibility of temperament and that the husband had committed acts of domestic violence.

. . . On July 11, 2013, the wife filed a "motion to enforce the covenant marriage contract," in which she asserted that the parties had been married subject to the Louisiana Covenant Marriage Act ("the Act") . . . and that the provisions of the Act governed the divorce action between the parties. After a hearing, the trial court entered an order on September 6, 2013, denying the wife's motion to enforce the parties' covenant-marriage contract. . . .

It is undisputed that the parties in the present case entered into a covenant marriage when they married in Louisiana.

Our research reveals that neither the appellate courts of this state, nor of any other state, have addressed the issue whether a state that does not have laws specifically providing for covenant marriages, such as Alabama, must apply the covenant-marriage law of another state during divorce proceedings initiated by parties who are now domiciled in the non-covenant-marriage state. Faced with this issue of first impression, we must consider the feasible options for its resolution. One option is to determine that our courts do not have subject-matter jurisdiction to grant a divorce to parties who entered into a covenant marriage. However . . . the matter presently before us undoubtedly concerns a marriage, as recognized by this state, albeit with statutory limitations regarding the dissolution of that marriage. We, therefore, conclude that a court of this state is not precluded from exercising jurisdiction of a divorce action between parties who initially entered into a covenant marriage in a different state.

Having determined that the trial court had jurisdiction to grant the parties a divorce, the next question is whether a court of this state is required to apply the Act to parties who participated in a covenant marriage in Louisiana but who subsequently relocated their domicile to Alabama. Although there is no caselaw on point, as a matter of law,

> "[u]nder our system of law, judicial power to grant a divorce—jurisdiction, strictly speaking—is founded on domicil. . . . The framers of the Constitution were familiar with this jurisdictional prerequisite, and since 1789 neither this Court nor any other court in the English-speaking world has questioned it. Domicil implies a nexus between person and place of such permanence as to control the creation of legal relations and responsibilities of the utmost significance. The domicil of one spouse within a State gives power to that State, we have held, to dissolve a marriage wheresoever contracted."

. . . We also find in the Restatement (Second) of Conflict of Laws § 285 (1971), that "[t]he local law of the domiciliary state in which the action is brought will be applied to determine the right to divorce." We further note that our supreme court has stated that "[t]he State is a silent party to divorce actions, public policy is involved and the integrity of the court's decrees are involved." Moreover, the drafter of the Act concedes in an article that she coauthored that Louisiana ceases to be an "interested state" if neither party has retained domicile in Louisiana.

The only authority cited by the wife in her appellate brief for this issue is caselaw standing for the proposition that parties may agree that laws of a state other than Alabama govern their prenuptial agreement. Even if we were to construe the document the parties executed as a prenuptial agreement, we also note that the "authority of a court . . . to grant [a] divorce[] is purely statutory." We further note that, pursuant to La. Civ. Code, art. 3521, a Louisiana court "may grant a divorce or separation only for grounds provided by the law of [Louisiana]." We find no basis, statutory or otherwise, for a court of this state to grant a divorce based upon the laws of a state other than Alabama.

Section 30-2-1(7) and (9), Ala. Code 1975, empowers the circuit courts of this state to divorce married persons for "a complete incompatibility of temperament" or "an irretrievable breakdown of the marriage." It is undisputed that the parties were domiciled in Alabama when the husband initiated this action and that the husband, and the wife in her counterclaim, asserted incompatibility as a ground for a divorce. Moreover, our legislature has previously considered, and thus far rejected, the implementation of covenant marriage in Alabama. Given that the parties availed themselves of the laws of this state in their initial filings for a divorce, and that the laws of this state do not provide for a covenant marriage, we conclude that the trial court did not err when it denied the wife's motion to enforce the parties' covenant-marriage contract. . . .

Based upon the foregoing, the judgment of the trial court divorcing the parties is affirmed.

AFFIRMED.

Chapter 8

Affirmative Defenses and Exceptions to Divorce

The Civil Code expressly contemplates one defense or exception to the divorce action — reconciliation. Article 104 provides that the "cause of action for divorce is extinguished by the reconciliation of the parties." The cases in the first section of this chapter consider what constitutes reconciliation and the applicable burdens of proof. Reconciliation is recognized as an affirmative defense in both common law and civil law.

A related question is whether there may be any additional defenses or exceptions to the divorce action. Historically, most jurisdictions recognized additional defenses including recrimination, condonation, collusion, and connivance. It is conceivable that these defenses may still be available in appropriate cases. Condonation, for example, has a significant overlap with reconciliation and seems, at least implicitly, recognized in some reconciliation cases.

A. Civil Code Article 104: Reconciliation

See LA. CODE CIV. PROC. art. 921–23, 927; LA. CIV. CODE art. 104.

Reconciliation is not defined with specificity in the Louisiana Civil Code. However, there is jurisprudence and scholarly writing exploring the subject. Planiol explains that "[t]here is reconciliation when the offended spouse has consented to forgive the offender . . . [and] the wrongdoing of the other is condoned."[1] French law intentionally vested the courts with the authority to determine what facts might establish a reconciliation — and Louisiana takes the same approach. Most often, evidence "of reconciliation is the resumption of the life in common, when it has been temporarily broken."[2] As the cases below demonstrate, the effect of reconciliation is to wipe the slate clean. Planiol explained that reconciliation "produces the effect of an amnesty which wipes out the past."[3] In other words, if a spouse has grounds for divorce — whether fault based or no-fault based — a subsequent

---

1. 1 MARCEL PLANIOL, TREATISE ON THE CIVIL LAW § 1208 (Louisiana State Law Institute trans. West 1959).
2. *Id.*
3. *Id.*

reconciliation will preclude a court from granting a divorce. Common law takes a similar view.

Generally, resumed cohabitation and other facts suggesting resumption of a married life will serve as evidence of reconciliation. Sexual relations between the parties are also indicative of reconciliation—but not always determinative. In *Million v. Million*, a case where the husband apparently repeatedly raped his wife during their separation, the court explained as follows:

> The evidence in this case vividly illustrates the error of an absolute rule which would deem one or several isolated acts of sexual intercourse as conclusively establishing reconciliation.
>
> Reconciliation is the voluntary resumption or reestablishment of the relationship which formerly existed between the parties. While sexual intercourse constitutes strong evidence that the relationship has been resumed, proof of one act or of several isolated acts of sexual intercourse is not necessarily conclusive of the issue of reconciliation.
>
> The issue of reconciliation under C.C. art. [104] is an issue of fact to be determined in each particular case by consideration of all the activities of the parties and by all of the circumstances of the case. In order to establish a reconciliation which will break the continuity of a period of separation or constitute a condonation or forgiveness of past behavior, the overall circumstances must show a mutual intention by the parties to voluntarily resume their marital relationship.[4]

Because reconciliation is a somewhat subjective question, thorny issues can arise. It can be difficult to determine whether the parties truly intended to reconcile. As a policy matter, the law favors reconciliation and wants to encourage spouses to reconcile. On the other hand, the courts do not want to unduly punish a spouse who attempts a failed reconciliation.

At first blush, it may seem odd that a spouse would bother with the time and expense of litigating the issue of reconciliation—particularly where both spouses clearly want the divorce. The issue usually comes down to money. A successful reconciliation defense will delay the date of the ultimate divorce—which may result in a more favorable division of community property or a longer interim spousal support award. It often affects final periodic spousal support as well. As we will explore in more detail later, final periodic support is only available to a spouse who is free from fault at the time of the filing of divorce. A reconciliation will have wiped out any earlier fault and allow recovery.

On occasion, a particularly conniving spouse will try to trick the other spouse into a reconciliation in order to obtain a financial advantage. In *Tablada v. Tablada*, for example, Mr. Tablada "first initiated reconciliation talks with [Mrs. Tablada] on the

---

4. 352 So. 2d 325 (La. App. 4 Cir. 1977).

same evening that he learned he was going to have to pay alimony pendite lite and that a private investigator's report existed which indicated he was involved in an adulterous relationship."[5] The trial court found this "highly suspicious" and noted that although Mrs. Tablada's efforts at reconciliation were sincere, Mr. Tablada's were not. On appeal, the court affirmed the trial court's finding that there was no reconciliation because Mr. Tablada had no genuine intent to reconcile with Mrs. Tablada.

Oriheula v. Oriheula involves an interesting fact scenario where the spouses apparently reconciled without ever actually resuming living together — an outcome that would likely be untenable in the era when women were required to live with their husbands as one of their marital duties.

Oriheula v. Oriheula

184 So. 3d 182 (La. App. 5 Cir. 2015)

Robert A. Chaisson, Judge.

In this domestic proceeding, the sole issue presented is whether the trial court erred in finding that the parties had not reconciled, and granting a divorce pursuant to the provisions of La. C.C. art. 102. For the reasons that follow, we reverse the judgment of divorce granted by the trial court.

FACTS AND PROCEDURAL HISTORY

Ivan Orihuela and Gina Orihuela (hereinafter referred to by her maiden name of Signorelli) were married on December 26, 2007, and they thereafter established their matrimonial domicile in Jefferson Parish. On April 29, 2014, Mr. Orihuela filed a petition for divorce pursuant to La. C.C. art. 102. On May 5, 2014, Mr. Orihuela and Ms. Signorelli began living separate and apart. On the same date, Ms. Signorelli filed an answer and reconventional demand for divorce pursuant to La. C.C. art. 102.

On January 7, 2015, Ms. Signorelli filed a motion for rule to show cause why divorce should not be granted under the provisions of La. C.C. art. 102 on the basis that the parties had been living separate and apart for the requisite period of time. On February 9, 2015, the court conducted a hearing on the rule to show cause. Both Ms. Signorelli and Mr. Orihuela testified at the hearing, and much of the testimony was undisputed regarding the circumstances surrounding their relationship subsequent to the filing of the divorce petition.

According to Ms. Signorelli, the last day that she and Mr. Orihuela lived together was May 5, 2014. However, despite living separate and apart, the two maintained regular contact and had many conversations about reconciling. They routinely went to lunch or dinner together, engaged in sexual relations on numerous occasions, and spent nights at each other's houses. She admitted that she had a key to his house, had knowledge of the alarm codes, and had gone there on one or two occasions even when Mr. Orihuela was not home. She acknowledged that at one point, they went to the

---

5. 590 So. 2d 1357 (La. App. 5 Cir. 1991).

store and bought various toiletries for her to keep at his house when she spent the night. Ms. Signorelli also testified that they went on brief trips together, including one in December of 2014, to celebrate their wedding anniversary. Although she claimed that the trip "became very disastrous," she acknowledged that they went out to dinner to celebrate their anniversary and that Mr. Orihuela bought her jewelry on that trip.

In addition, Ms. Signorelli testified that Mr. Orihuela took out a life insurance policy naming her as the beneficiary in September of 2014, that they still have a joint checking account, and that on occasion, he has paid her rent as well as some of her credit card bills and expenses. During her testimony, Ms. Signorelli acknowledged that subsequent to the filing of the divorce petition, she "probably" texted Mr. Orihuela numerous times that she loved him and also sent him a birthday card in January of 2015 professing her love for him and representing herself as his wife. She further admitted that in January of 2015, the two were having discussions about continuing the rule to show cause hearing. While acknowledging in her testimony all the time she spent with Mr. Orihuela, she claimed that there was no reconciliation between them. Ms. Signorelli denied telling Mr. Orihuela that she wanted to reconcile or move back in together and further denied representing herself as Mrs. Orihuela to any third parties. She asserted that she made her decision not to reconcile since the filing of the divorce petition and also asserted that at no time since their physical separation did she present herself as someone who had reconciled with Mr. Orihuela.

Mr. Orihuela also testified at the hearing regarding the circumstances surrounding their relationship subsequent to the filing of the divorce petition. He maintained that ever since he filed for divorce, the two have been trying to reconcile and have spent a lot of time together. They ate out often, went to plays, and took trips together. According to Mr. Orihuela, he treated Ms. Signorelli as his wife and bought her lavish gifts for her birthday, Christmas, and anniversary. They engaged in sexual relations and spent nights at each other's houses. In addition, they portrayed themselves to others as husband and wife. Mr. Orihuela asserted in his testimony that the intent at all times was to reconcile, but they planned on living separate and apart until the lease on her rental house expired. Mr. Orihuela testified that they talked about continuing the January hearing on the rule to show cause, but then they got into an argument on January 27, 2015, which effectively ended their reconciliation.

After considering the evidence presented, the trial judge granted the motion for divorce and stated, in part, as follows:

> All right. Submitted by both parties, and the issue before the Court is reconciliation. Number one, have the parties lived separate and apart for six months prior to divorce? Yes, you have. So the question is have the parties reconciled. At this time, the Court finds that there was no reconciliation. There was no intent really or a meeting of the minds of the parties where reconciliation is concerned.

Occasionally, the parties appeared to have had sexual intercourse. They went out. They interacted in a social manner. And that in itself does not constitute reconciliation. With reconciliation, you have to have a meeting of the minds, and I didn't find that in this situation. Did the parties attempt to reconcile? Yes, it appears that the parties attempted to reconcile. Did the parties reconcile? Again, I don't think the parties reconciled.

On March 20, 2015, Mr. Orihuela filed a motion for appeal from the divorce judgment. In his appellate brief, he argues that the trial court erred in finding that the parties had not reconciled and in thereafter granting a judgment of divorce pursuant to La. C.C. art. 102. We agree with this argument.

DISCUSSION

It is well settled that a court of appeal may not set aside a trial court's or a jury's finding of fact in the absence of manifest error or unless it is clearly wrong. . . .

In the present case, the trial court found that a reconciliation had not occurred and thereafter granted the parties a divorce based on living separate and apart for the requisite period of time pursuant to La. C.C. art. 102. Mr. Orihuela contends that the evidence presented at the hearing showed that there was mutual intent to restore the marital relationship, and therefore, the trial court erred in finding that a reconciliation had not occurred.

La. C.C. art. 104 makes clear that the cause of action for divorce is extinguished by the reconciliation of the parties. In order to constitute reconciliation, the parties must intend to reestablish their marriage. The law is clear that reconciliation is an issue of fact to be decided by the trial court after careful consideration of the particular facts and circumstances of each particular case. The overall circumstances of the case must show a mutual intention to resume their marital relationship in order for an alleged reconciliation to interrupt the continuity of a period of separation. The trial court has much discretion and its factual findings are accorded very substantial weight on review.

At the hearing on the rule to show cause, the testimony surrounding the circumstances of their relationship subsequent to the filing of the divorce petition was basically undisputed. Although the parties began living separate and apart on May 5, 2014, it is clear that they maintained regular contact and spent an extensive amount of time together. In particular, they went to lunch and dinner regularly, went on a couple of brief trips together, engaged in sexual relations, and spent nights at each other's houses. It is further undisputed that the two celebrated their wedding anniversary, that he bought her jewelry and other items, that he paid her rent as well as some of her expenses on occasion, and that he took out a life insurance policy naming her as the beneficiary.

The only disputed testimony at the hearing revolved around the parties' intent to restore their marital relationship. Ms. Signorelli testified that since the filing of the divorce petition, she never intended to reconcile with Mr. Orihuela, and she made her intention clear to him. In contrast, Mr. Orihuela testified that the intent was clearly to resume the marital relationship. He maintained that he and Ms. Signorelli have been trying to reconcile since he filed the petition for divorce and that they planned to resume living together after the lease on her rental house had expired. After considering this conflicting testimony on their intentions, the trial court determined that there "was no intent really or a meeting of the minds of the parties where reconciliation is concerned."

We acknowledge that the appellate court generally does not disturb the factual findings of the trial court. However, the record in this case, including both the testimony and evidence presented, is replete with proof that both parties intended to reconcile. Ms. Signorelli, in her testimony, admitted that the parties had many conversations about reconciling and that there were numerous attempts at reconciling. In addition, Mr. Orihuela presented several text messages, which Ms. Signorelli acknowledged sending to him, showing that she clearly had the intent to reconcile. In particular, we note Ms. Signorelli sent Mr. Orihuela a text message telling him, "Thanks for a great day . . . Was sad to see U go . . . You almost have me to the point of a complete reconciliation." In other text messages, she spoke of what she wanted from their relationship, implored him not to leave her, and asked him if he was going to continue the rule to show cause hearing. Ms. Signorelli also admitted that she "probably" texted Mr. Orihuela numerous times that she loved him. In addition, Ms. Signorelli admitted giving Mr. Orihuela a birthday card in January of 2015, in which she professed her love for him and represented herself as his wife.

Although we are reluctant to reverse a trial court's factual findings, we are compelled to do so in the instant case as the record undoubtedly supports a determination that the parties reconciled. Accordingly, for the reasons set forth herein, we reverse the judgment of divorce granted by the trial court.

REVERSED.

B. Other Defenses: Recrimination, Collusion, Condonation, Connivance

Before the era of no-fault divorce, the doctrines of recrimination, collusion, condonation, and connivance often operated like reconciliation. In Louisiana, it is not entirely clear whether these doctrines have continued viability. Because fault-based divorces do still exist in Louisiana and because the issue of fault is often relevant to spousal support, there is an argument that these doctrines are not entirely irrelevant. Of all of them, condonation seems to come up most often—likely because it falls along the spectrum of reconciliation.

Recrimination has not been viable in Louisiana for some time. In *Thomason v. Thomason*, below, the Louisiana Supreme Court abrogated the doctrine more than a decade before the no-fault divorce legislation.

Thomason v. Thomason

355 So. 2d 908 (La. 1978)

Dixon, Justice.

This suit for divorce because of the conviction and sentence of the spouse to imprisonment at hard labor was brought by relatrix, Rachael Hotard Thomason. Respondent husband answered, reconvening for divorce because of the adultery of his wife. The trial judge rejected the demands of both parties because of "mutual fault."

Only the wife appealed. The Court of Appeal affirmed the judgment against her, finding that "our doctrine of comparative rectitude dictates that neither shall prevail. . . ."

At trial on December 1, 1976 it was established that the parties were married September 23, 1973 and had one child. Records were introduced to show that Mr. Thomason was charged by bill of information with armed robbery on January 30, 1975, pled guilty to simple robbery on July 1, 1976, and was sentenced to serve five years at hard labor. He had been in the custody of the State since his arrest in January, 1975. Mrs. Thomason had been living with John Eady since September of 1975 and had a child by him. . . .

The trial court, in properly considering both Mrs. and Mr. Thomason's claims for divorce, found "equal mutual fault" and thus dismissed both causes of action. The trial judge was applying the doctrine of recrimination, which requires the denial of relief to a complainant who has been guilty of conduct which would entitle the other spouse to a divorce.

This court-created doctrine has been long established in our jurisprudence and is based on the equitable idea that he who comes into court with unclean hands cannot obtain relief. The application of the recrimination doctrine which denies the divorce to both parties results in punishing the two equally guilty parties by sentencing them to live in a married state after they have both proved their incompatibility.

Certain policy arguments have been advanced for retention of the recrimination doctrine: (1) promotion of marital stability, (2) deterrence of immorality, (3) promotion of financial security for women, and (4) prevention of subsequent bad marriages. These considerations, which might have been reasonable in ages past, can no longer justify its application. Two parties seeking divorce have already demonstrated an inclination to breach their marriage contract; it is doubtful that forcing them to remain married would be conducive to the family concept. Instead of promoting stability and discouraging bad marriages, it tends to lead to increased hatred between the parties, infidelity, the destruction of home life to the detriment of the children, and perhaps fosters cruelty and physical violence. Instead of curbing immoral conduct, the parties are allowed to continue illicit relationships with the court's consent. We do not understand that the doctrine of recrimination strengthens the institution of marriage or serves any useful social purpose. The law should not prevent the termination of a defunct marriage even, or especially, where both parties are at fault.

If a divorce is possible where one party is guilty, there is all the more reason to grant a divorce where both are guilty. The judicially created doctrine of recrimination in divorce is therefore abrogated by the court, acknowledging the legislative abrogation of the doctrine in separation cases.

For the foregoing reasons . . . [t]here is now judgment in favor of Mrs. Thomason granting her a divorce from Hugh Montgomery Thomason, III, at his cost.

C. Other Defenses: Mental Illness

A handful of Louisiana cases have suggested that mental illness might be a viable defense in a divorce based on adultery or relevant to some other issue of fault. *Eppling v. Eppling* explained the rule as follows:

> Actions that would normally be construed as fault contributing to the separation are excused when involuntarily induced by a preexisting mental illness. However, the mental illness must be shown to have caused the behavior which would otherwise constitute marital fault.[6]

In *Seltzer v. Seltzer*, Mrs. Seltzer argued (unsuccessfully) that her adultery should be excused due to her mental illness.[7] Although both parties and the experts were in agreement that Mrs. Seltzer was mentally ill, the court did not believe that the mental illness actually caused Mrs. Seltzer to engage in the affair. Nonetheless, the court seemed to concede that with the right facts, the defense might be viable.

Doane v. Benenate, below, is a more recent case involving mental illness and the relevance of fault to a spousal support award. In reading the case, consider whether the court might also be swayed by the doctrine of condonation. That is, did the husband condone his wife's bad behavior?

Doane v. Benenate

671 So. 2d 523 (La. App. 4 Cir. 1996)

BARRY, Judge.

Natalie Benenate Doane appeals the denial of permanent alimony. We hold that Mrs. Doane's alleged fault was due to mental illness, reverse the judgment, and remand.

Facts

Mr. and Mrs. Doane married in 1978. Mr. Doane filed for a divorce based on living separate and apart for six months (La.C.C. art. 102). A divorce was rendered on August 30, 1994. Mrs. Doane filed for permanent alimony and alleged she was not at fault.

---

6. 537 So. 2d 814 (La. App. 5 Cir. 1989).
7. 584 So. 2d 710 (La. App. 4 Cir. 1991).

The court found Mrs. Doane was mentally troubled for years before the divorce, was under psychiatric care, and

> [e]ven prior to her breakdown in 1988 Natalie Doane told August Doane that she did not love him and that she felt sorry for him.

The court held Mrs. Doane was not free from fault and not entitled to permanent alimony.

Mrs. Doane's appeal asserts that her continuing mental illness during the marriage precludes a finding of "fault."

Permanent Alimony

Freedom from fault is necessary for permanent alimony.

A spouse claiming permanent alimony must show he or she was not at fault in the breakup of the marriage. That spouse need not be totally blameless and the trial court's finding of fact will not be disturbed unless manifestly erroneous. . . .

Because the statutory law does not specify "fault" as a basis to deny permanent alimony, "fault" is now determined according to our jurisprudence. Legal fault consists of serious misconduct which caused the marriage's dissolution.

Mr. Doane testified he left the marital domicile in April 1993 because the marriage had declined, Mrs. Doane often said she did not love him, the couple did not communicate, and their sexual relations declined. He said Mrs. Doane asked him to leave on more than one occasion. He claims that Mrs. Doane's expressions of lack of love and her requests that he leave the domicile support the finding that Mrs. Doane was at fault.

Mrs. Doane submits that her conduct was caused by mental illness. Actions of one spouse toward another that normally constitutes cruel treatment are excused when involuntarily induced by a preexisting physical or mental illness. . . .

Jurisprudence requires that the mental illness pre-date the misconduct. *Miller v. Miller* . . . considered whether the wife's psychological illness excused her fault in the separation (alimony was not at issue). *Miller* held that the wife's illness did not excuse her conduct of cursing her husband, pouting, sleeping in a separate bedroom and denying her husband sexual relations because the misconduct commenced long before the wife became ill.

However, reconciliation that follows misconduct which constitutes "fault" renders moot the issue of previous fault. *Doran v. Doran* . . . did not involve mental illness but considered the effect of reconciliation to a party's fault. *Doran* affirmed dismissal of the wife's claim for permanent alimony because she failed to show necessitous circumstances, but in dicta considered the wife's fault where the couple lived together following her extramarital affair.

> The effect of a reconciliation between the parties is to effectively "wipe the slate clean" and make the issue of previous fault of the parties moot as to any cause of action subsequent to the reconciliation. . . .

The record establishes that Mrs. Doane had a schizoaffective disorder at the time of the separation. Mr. and Mrs. Doane testified that Mrs. Doane has been mentally ill and was hospitalized for a "breakdown" in 1988. Dr. Kenneth Purcell, psychiatrist, first examined Mrs. Doane in February 1990. He diagnosed a schizoaffective disorder and said Mrs. Doane had auditory hallucinations which affect her interpersonal relationships and decrease her ability to handle stress.

The record shows that Mrs. Doane's misconduct pre-dated the diagnosis of her mental illness. Prior to her 1988 hospitalization Mrs. Doane asked Mr. Doane to leave and said she did not love him and she married him out of pity and fear. Mrs. Doane testified it was her "other personality" that told Mr. Doane that she did not love him.

However, the Doanes lived together as husband and wife for six years after her 1988 breakdown and three years after she saw Dr. Purcell. Mr. Doane testified that after 1988 Mrs. Doane's statements became more frequent and she hit him. The parties reconciled after Mrs. Doane's initial misconduct. Mrs. Doane's post-1988 conduct caused Mr. Doane to leave.

Mrs. Doane's conduct was directly related to her illness. She had a "mental" breakdown in 1988; however, Mr. Doane lived with her until 1993. Her mental illness precluded a finding of fault. The trial court clearly erred by finding Mrs. Doane's at fault.

We reverse and remand for further proceedings.

REVERSED AND REMANDED.

Chapter 9

Spousal Support

See LA. CIV. CODE art. 111–18.

A. Evolution of Spousal Support Laws

Spousal support—also called alimony or maintenance—is recognized in both common law and civil law. The justifications for such awards, however, have varied over time and from court-to-court. Traditionally, spousal support awards were based on the husband's obligation to support his wife—and to some extent this justification remains in a gender-neutral form. Spousal support has also been justified on partnership and public fisc theories. For example, the Florida Supreme Court explained that spousal support "is awarded on the theory that marriage is a partnership to which the wife has contributed and when she withdraws from it she is entitled to reimbursement that she may not become a public charge."[1] In more recent years, a rehabilitative theory of alimony has taken hold. To enable a spouse to become self-reliant, some courts have crafted alimony awards by looking at the time and cost needed for a spouse to obtain an education or job skills.

Most states recognize two types of spousal support—interim support (or alimony pendite lite) and final periodic support (or permanent alimony). The interim support is financial support awarded during the pendency of the divorce litigation, and it often has a different theoretical basis than final support. Final periodic support is financial support awarded after the divorce. In many states, including Louisiana, final support awards are only available to the innocent spouse. Some scholars have observed that, by tying spousal support awards to guilt or innocence, states are impliedly embracing a punishment or reward theory of alimony.

Until 1979, spousal support statutes in many states were gender specific—alimony was only available to the wife. Louisiana took this approach as well. Interestingly, the source articles of the Code Napoléon were gender neutral, and Planiol clearly endorsed the view that spousal support could be awarded to either spouse. In *Orr v. Orr*, below, the Supreme Court held that gender-specific support statutes could not withstand a constitutional challenge. In reading *Orr v. Orr*, compare the type of

---

1. Chestnut v. Chestnut, 33 So. 2d 730 (Fla. 1948).

151

scrutiny the court applies in an equal protection case involving a gender classification to cases involving racial classifications, like *Loving v. Virginia*.

Orr v. Orr

440 U.S. 268 (1979)

Mr. Justice BRENNAN delivered the opinion of the Court.

The question presented is the constitutionality of Alabama alimony statutes which provide that husbands, but not wives, may be required to pay alimony upon divorce. . . .

We now hold the challenged Alabama statutes unconstitutional and reverse. . . .

II

In authorizing the imposition of alimony obligations on husbands, but not on wives, the Alabama statutory scheme "provides that different treatment be accorded . . . on the basis of . . . sex; it thus establishes a classification subject to scrutiny under the Equal Protection Clause. . . ." The fact that the classification expressly discriminates against men rather than women does not protect it from scrutiny. "To withstand scrutiny" under the Equal Protection Clause, " 'classifications by gender must serve important governmental objectives and must be substantially related to achievement of those objectives.' " We shall, therefore, examine the three governmental objectives that might arguably be served by Alabama's statutory scheme.

Appellant views the Alabama alimony statutes as effectively announcing the State's preference for an allocation of family responsibilities under which the wife plays a dependent role, and as seeking for their objective the reinforcement of that model among the State's citizens. We agree, as he urges, that prior cases settle that this purpose cannot sustain the statutes. *Stanton v. Stanton*, 421 U.S. 7, 10 (1975), held that the "old notio[n]" that "generally it is the man's primary responsibility to provide a home and its essentials," can no longer justify a statute that discriminates on the basis of gender. "No longer is the female destined solely for the home and the rearing of the family, and only the male for the marketplace and the world of ideas." If the statute is to survive constitutional attack, therefore, it must be validated on some other basis.

The opinion of the Alabama Court of Civil Appeals suggests other purposes that the statute may serve. Its opinion states that the Alabama statutes were "designed" for "the wife of a broken marriage who needs financial assistance." This may be read as asserting either of two legislative objectives. One is a legislative purpose to provide help for needy spouses, using sex as a proxy for need. The other is a goal of compensating women for past discrimination during marriage, which assertedly has left them unprepared to fend for themselves in the working world following divorce. We concede, of course, that assisting needy spouses is a legitimate and important governmental objective. We have also recognized "[r]eduction of the disparity in economic condition between men and women caused by the long history of discrimination against women . . . as . . . an important governmental objective." It only remains, therefore, to determine whether the classification at issue here is "substantially related to achievement of those objectives."

Ordinarily, we would begin the analysis of the "needy spouse" objective by considering whether sex is a sufficiently "accurate proxy" for dependency to establish that the gender classification rests "'upon some ground of difference having a fair and substantial relation to the object of the legislation.'" Similarly, we would initially approach the "compensation" rationale by asking whether women had in fact been significantly discriminated against in the sphere to which the statute applied a sex-based classification, leaving the sexes "not similarly situated with respect to opportunities" in that sphere. But in this case, even if sex were a reliable proxy for need, and even if the institution of marriage did discriminate against women, these factors still would "not adequately justify the salient features of" Alabama's statutory scheme. Under the statute, individualized hearings at which the parties' relative financial circumstances are considered already occur. There is no reason, therefore, to use sex as a proxy for need. Needy males could be helped along with needy females with little if any additional burden on the State. In such circumstances, not even an administrative-convenience rationale exists to justify operating by generalization or proxy. Similarly, since individualized hearings can determine which women were in fact discriminated against vis-à-vis their husbands, as well as which family units defied the stereotype and left the husband dependent on the wife, Alabama's alleged compensatory purpose may be effectuated without placing burdens solely on husbands. Progress toward fulfilling such a purpose would not be hampered, and it would cost the State nothing more, if it were to treat men and women equally by making alimony burdens independent of sex. "Thus, the gender-based distinction is gratuitous; without it, the statutory scheme would only provide benefits to those men who are in fact similarly situated to the women the statute aids," and the effort to help those women would not in any way be compromised.

Moreover, use of a gender classification actually produces perverse results in this case. As compared to a gender-neutral law placing alimony obligations on the spouse able to pay, the present Alabama statutes give an advantage only to the financially secure wife whose husband is in need. Although such a wife might have to pay alimony under a gender-neutral statute, the present statutes exempt her from that obligation. Thus, "[t]he [wives] who benefit from the disparate treatment are those who were . . . nondependent on their husbands." They are precisely those who are not "needy spouses" and who are "least likely to have been victims of . . . discrimination," by the institution of marriage. A gender-based classification which, as compared to a gender-neutral one, generates additional benefits only for those it has no reason to prefer cannot survive equal protection scrutiny.

Legislative classifications which distribute benefits and burdens on the basis of gender carry the inherent risk of reinforcing the stereotypes about the "proper place" of women and their need for special protection. Thus, even statutes purportedly designed to compensate for and ameliorate the effects of past discrimination must be carefully tailored. Where, as here, the State's compensatory and ameliorative purposes are as well served by a gender-neutral classification as one that gender classifies and therefore carries with it the baggage of sexual stereotypes, the State cannot be permitted to classify on the basis of sex. And this is doubly so where the choice made by the State appears to redound—if only indirectly—to the benefit of those without need for special solicitude.

III

Having found Alabama's alimony statutes unconstitutional, we reverse the judgment below and remand the cause for further proceedings not inconsistent with this opinion. That disposition, of course, leaves the state courts free to decide any questions of substantive state law not yet passed upon in this litigation. Therefore, it is open to the Alabama courts on remand to consider whether Mr. Orr's stipulated agreement to pay alimony, or other grounds of gender-neutral state law, bind him to continue his alimony payments.

Reversed and remanded.

B. Interim Spousal Support: In General

Civil Code articles 111–13 contemplate two types of support awards—interim spousal support and final periodic support. Those articles also make it clear that marital fault is irrelevant for purposes of interim spousal support. Article 113 explains that an award of interim spousal support should be "based on the needs of [the] party, the ability of the other party to pay, any interim allowance or final child support obligation, and the standard of living of the parties during the marriage." Article 113 also imposes time limitations on the possible duration of interim support. The basic considerations for awarding interim spousal support in Louisiana—needs, ability to pay, and standard of living during the marriage—are quite similar to the statutory considerations set forth in other states. Generally, the burden of proof is with the party seeking the support. *Molony v. Harris* and *McFall v. Armstrong*, below, are fairly representative examples of the facts a court should consider in making an award of interim support.

Molony v. Harris
51 So. 3d 752 (La. App. 4 Cir. 2010)

TERRI F. LOVE, Judge.

This appeal arises from a petition for divorce. The trial court denied Meredith Harris' request for interim spousal support. We find that the trial court did not abuse its discretion in denying interim spousal support and affirm.

FACTUAL BACKGROUND AND PROCEDURAL HISTORY

Duncan Molony filed for a divorce from Meredith Harris. Mr. Molony also sought judicial resolution of ancillary matters, including interim spousal support. . . .

The trial court denied Ms. Harris' request for interim spousal support and found that Ms. Harris did not have the requisite need for an award of interim spousal support. In addition, the trial court stated that Mr. Molony had "minimal ability" to pay interim spousal support to Ms. Harris, but that Mr. Molony's ability to pay was offset by the fact that Ms. Harris' work hours were reduced because of her AA attendance. Ms. Harris timely sought a devolutive appeal, which was granted.

STANDARD OF REVIEW

"The trial court is vested with much discretion in determining awards of spousal support." "Such determinations will not be disturbed absent a clear abuse of discretion." As to interim spousal support specifically, "[a]n abuse of discretion will not be found if the record supports the trial court's conclusions about the means of the payor spouse and his or her ability to pay."

Factual findings shall not be set aside absent manifest error. To substantiate reversal, the appellate court must find from the record that there is no reasonable factual basis for the finding of the trial court and that the record establishes that the finding is clearly wrong or manifestly erroneous.

INTERIM SPOUSAL SUPPORT/La. C.C. art. 113

As her sole assignment of error, Ms. Harris alleges that the trial court erred in failing to award interim spousal support.

An award of interim spousal support is governed by La. C.C. art. 113. . . . Thus, the trial court examines the parties' circumstances utilizing three criteria when determining whether interim spousal support is warranted: 1) the claimant's need, 2) the other spouse's ability to pay, and 3) the standard of living of the parties during the marriage.

CLAIMANT'S NEED

Ms. Harris asserts that the trial court erred in failing to award interim spousal support.

"A spouse demonstrates a need for alimony pendente lite if she demonstrates that she lacks sufficient income to maintain the style or standard of living that she enjoyed while residing with [sic] other spouse during the marriage." "Interim spousal support is specifically designed to maintain the status quo during litigation and, as such, the burden is on the claimant to prove her entitlement to such support."

Calculation of Ms. Harris' Adjusted Gross Income

Ms. Harris also contends that the trial cot erroneously imputed her income by not deducting from her gross receipts all of the business expenses reflected on her tax return. However, Mr. Molony's expert CPA, Kern Schaffer (who was properly disclosed as an expert witness prior to trial), opined that several of the business expenses claimed by Ms. Harris on her 2007 tax return were inflated to artificially reduce her actual adjusted gross income. Mr. Schaffer also noted that Ms. Harris' S-Corporation taxes did not seem to be set up correctly because the corporation should be paying

Social Security. The trial court has wide discretion in imputing income to a claimant spouse where that spouse's income is uncertain. "[W]here there is conflict in the testimony, reasonable evaluations of credibility and reasonable inferences of fact should not be disturbed upon review, even though the appellate court may feel that its own evaluations and inferences are as reasonable." Accordingly, the trial court did not err in its factual finding as to Ms. Harris' adjusted gross income.

Calculation of Ms. Harris' Net Income

Ms. Harris asserts that the trial court erred in calculating her net monthly income. Ms. Harris' calculations of her net monthly income differ from the calculations of the trial court, primarily because the trial court did not recognize all of the business expenses claimed by Ms. Harris. As previously noted, the trial court's discretion includes the ability to impute an adjusted gross income to Ms. Harris based on the evidence and testimony presented at trial. Because the trial court and Ms. Harris began with differing figures for Ms. Harris' adjusted gross income, Ms. Harris and the trial court also reach different figures for Ms. Harris' net monthly income after deducting her recurring monthly expenses.

Ms. Harris, in her calculations, deducted her telephone, internet, and fax expenses twice, once as a business expense in determining her adjusted gross income, and again as a recurring monthly expense in determining her net monthly income. Accordingly, the trial court had the discretion to allow Ms. Harris to deduct her telephone, internet, and fax expenses once and the trial court made that deduction when computing Ms. Harris' adjusted gross income.

Further, Ms. Harris points to the fact that she offered testimony that her monthly credit card payments total $2,000.00, as opposed to the $1,000.00 reflected on her Income and Expense Affidavit. Ms. Harris claims that the trial court failed to acknowledge the additional monthly expense in the amount of $1,000.00, and thereby erred in calculating her net monthly income. However, given the wide latitude the trial court has in making factual findings when presented with conflicting evidence and testimony, the trial court's decision to allow Ms. Harris a $1,000.00 monthly credit card expense does not constitute reversible error.

The trial court also noted that Ms. Harris receives between $3,000 and $4,000 from her mother every month. Ms. Harris offered testimony tentatively describing the money received from her mother as an advance on her inheritance. Ms. Harris testified that she used the money from her mother to pay the shortfall between her monthly income and her monthly expenses. However, on cross-examination, Ms. Harris testified that she used the money from her mother to pay her legal bills.

The trial court's determination was based on the evidence submitted and testimony offered by both parties as to Ms. Harris' actual net monthly income. As such, we do not find that the trial court abused its discretion or committed manifest error.

Ms. Harris' Gross Income for Child Support and Spousal Support

Ms. Harris asserts that the trial court erred in its calculation of her adjusted gross income because it attributed different figures to her in the judgment awarding child support and in the reasons for judgment denying interim spousal support. In the judgment awarding child support, the trial court imputes an adjusted gross income of $5,684.85 to Ms. Harris; meanwhile, in the reasons for judgment denying interim spousal support, the trial court did not specify what adjusted gross income was imputed to Ms. Harris. Rather, the reasons for judgment denying interim spousal support only reflects the gross income imputed to Ms. Harris (in the amount of $6,666.00) and the net income imputed to Ms. Harris (in the amount of $6,460.03).

The record, when viewed in its entirety, indicates that the trial court did make mathematical errors in both the judgment awarding child support and the reasons for judgment denying interim spousal support. These errors, however, do not result in a significant reduction or inflation of Ms. Harris' adjusted gross income for spousal support purposes. Had the trial court properly ascribed those business expenses of Ms. Harris, which it recognized as legitimate, to her gross income in the judgment awarding child support (as it did in the reasons for judgment denying interim spousal support), then the difference between the figures in the two judgments would be inconsequential. Accordingly, the mathematical errors made by the trial court amount to harmless error.

Inclusion of Child Support from Previous Marriage

Ms. Harris contends that the trial court committed legal error by including the child support she receives from a child born prior to her marriage to Mr. Molony when calculating her monthly income. Ms. Harris presents two grounds upon which she bases her argument that the trial court erred in this regard. First, Ms. Harris points to La. R.S. 9:315(C)(3)(d)(i), which specifies that the determination of a parent's gross income should not include child support received for purposes of determining that parent's child support obligation. Ms. Harris ignores the fact that La. R.S. 9:315 references child support and that spousal support is the subject of a different section of La. R.S. Title 9.7 Consequently, La. R.S. 9:315(C)(3)(d)(i) does not apply to the trial court's determination of Ms. Harris' income for spousal support purposes.

. . . . Ms. Harris claims that the trial court did not include Ms. Harris' expenses for her child from a previous marriage in calculating her total monthly expenses, and for this reason the trial court erred by including her child support as income. The record reveals, however, that the trial court took into account Ms. Harris' expenses for her other child when it calculated her total monthly expenses. In doing so, the trial court followed *Pellerin*, where this Court recalculated interim spousal support to include child support as a part of the claimant spouse's means of meeting monthly expenses where the claimant spouse's expenses include expenses of the child for which support payments are received.

Attributing Full-Time Earning Capacity to Ms. Harris

Ms. Harris alleges that the trial court abused its discretion in finding that Ms. Harris was not voluntarily underemployed, but acknowledges her inability to work full-time due to her court ordered attendance at AA meetings but nevertheless imputing a full-time earning capacity. Ms. Harris argues that although the trial court found Ms. Harris was not voluntarily underemployed, it effectively treated her that way when it offset her reduced working hours by Mr. Molony's marginal ability to pay interim spousal support. Mr. Molony counters that it was within the trial court's discretion to consider Ms. Harris' reduced work hours, and that the trial court was correct to not prejudice Mr. Molony because of Ms. Harris' need to attend AA meetings.

The trial court specifically found that "but for Ms. Harris' addiction, she would more likely than not increase her number of patients." [sic] As such, "Mr. Molony should not be penalized at this time for Ms. Harris' inability to work full time due to her alcoholism." This Court has previously held that a trial court's determination of an interim spousal support award "requires consideration of . . . the claimant spouse's immediate employment history and capacity for self support." The record supports the reasonableness of the trial court's finding that Ms. Harris would be capable of earning additional monetary support were it not for her alcoholism. The trial court found that Mr. Molony had little ability to pay and decided not to penalize him because of Ms. Harris' need to attend AA meetings, which the trial court found lowered her income. Therefore, we do not find an abuse of discretion.

. . . . Because Ms. Harris failed to prove her need for interim spousal support, it was within the trial court's discretion to conclude that Ms. Harris had no need for interim spousal support based on the evidence and testimony.

SPOUSE'S ABILITY TO PAY

The ability of the spouse to pay interim spousal support exists if money remains after all monthly expenses have been paid, which includes deducting from that spouse's net monthly income the combined monthly expenses for that spouse and his or her children, including any child support obligation. Further, the payor spouse's inability to pay precludes an award of interim spousal support to the claimant spouse even where the claimant has demonstrated need.

Calculation of Mr. Molony's Income

Ms. Harris asserts that the trial court erred in relying on Mr. Molony's testimony regarding his income, as opposed to the paycheck stub that was offered into evidence. Ms. Harris claims that Mr. Molony's gross monthly income is $9,324.45 based upon the $4,303.59 reflected on Mr. Molony's April 15, 2009 paystub for that pay period. Ms. Harris insists that Mr. Harris is paid every two weeks, or 26 pay periods per year, which is the basis for her calculation of his monthly income ($4,303.59 times 26, divided by 12). Mr. Molony testified, however, that he is paid twice per month, not every two weeks. Further, Mr. Molony's April 15, 2009 paystub reflects a pay period of April 1, 2009, through April 15, 2009, which means he is paid twice per month, for a total of only 24 pay periods per year. Accordingly, Ms. Harris' assertion regarding Mr. Molony's gross monthly income is without merit.

Moreover, it is within the trial court's discretion, based on the evidence and testimony before it, to make a determination regarding Mr. Molony's income. The record reveals that the gross monthly income imputed by the trial court to Mr. Molony, $8,240.45, does differ from the base earnings reflected on Mr. Molony's April 15, 2009 paycheck for that pay period. Testimony was offered, however, that Mr. Molony had received two one-time bonuses in 2009 totaling $5,619.69, and the $8,240.45 figure accepted by the trial court was based on Mr. Molony's annual salary with those bonuses added into the calculation ($5,619.69 added to $94,500.00, divided by 12). Thus, the trial court's finding is reasonably supported by the record and should not be overruled.

Lastly, Ms. Harris argues that Mr. Molony's paycheck deductions for his 401k, medical insurance coverage, dental insurance coverage, and vision insurance coverage should be added back into his net monthly income since those deductions are elective. Ms. Harris fails to acknowledge that Mr. Molony's paycheck deduction for medical insurance coverage for herself and the parties' minor child provides a benefit to her and the child of the sort that this Court has previously found to be a form of indirect support. As to Mr. Molony's 401k deduction, this Court found that a trial court should not require the payor spouse to cease contributing to his or her retirement savings plan in order to pay interim spousal support.

Calculation of Mr. Molony's Monthly Expenses

Ms. Harris contends that the trial court should have considered Mr. Molony's alleged expense sharing with his sister. Mr. Molony testified that he was not currently paying rent to his sister, although the monthly rent was an accruing obligation, and that the rent payment was inclusive of electricity, water, gas, and cable. Because of his testimony that he was not current on his rent obligation, the trial court added the amount of Mr. Molony's monthly rent obligation, $400.00, back into his net monthly income.

Ms. Harris claims that the trial court should have also disallowed certain other monthly expenses claimed by Mr. Molony because he is living with his sister rent-free. Those expenses, totaling $370.92, are not included in Mr. Molony's rent obligation. . . .

Ms. Harris also states that the trial court was ambiguous regarding its calculation of Mr. Molony's net income, specifically whether and how the trial court included the tax credit Mr. Molony claimed for the parties' minor child. The tax credit Ms. Harris refers to was from the 2008 tax year, and Ms. Harris fails to demonstrate how a tax credit from 2008, would affect Mr. Molony's net income in 2009.

Overall, Ms. Harris asserts that the trial court erred in calculating Mr. Molony's monthly income. While Mr. Molony is a salaried, W-2 employee, his receipt of two one-time bonuses was factored into the trial court's determination of his gross monthly income. The trial court found that Mr. Molony's monthly expenses were greater than his monthly income. The trial court then added Mr. Molony's rent back into his income because Mr. Molony testified that he was not paying rent even though it was an accruing obligation. Thus, the trial court found that Mr. Molony had a small monthly budgetary surplus. In its reasons for judgment, the trial court's final determination as to Mr. Molony's ability to pay was that "Mr. Molony has the ability to pay, but not by much."

However, the trial court further noted that Ms. Harris was not working full-time due to her attendance at AA meetings and individual therapy sessions, and that "Mr. Molony should not be penalized at this time for Ms. Harris' inability to work full time due to her alcoholism." The earning capacity of the claimant spouse may properly be considered by the trial court in determining whether interim spousal support should be awarded to the claimant. "Once a spouse establishes that she has insufficient income for maintenance, the trial court may award a sum for that spouse's support proportioned to the needs of the claimant spouse and the means of the other spouse." "An abuse of discretion will not be found if the record supports the trial court's conclusions about the means of the payor spouse and his or her ability to pay." Thus, it was within the trial court's discretion to deny Ms. Harris an award of interim spousal support based on the evidence presented of Mr. Molony's ability to pay.

STANDARD OF LIVING OF THE PARTIES

"Interim spousal support is specifically designed to maintain the status quo during litigation. . . ." The trial court, in the reasons for judgment, stated that Ms. Harris and Mr. Molony went on vacations about once per year during the marriage, and that they would go out to eat once a month or once every other month before their separation. The trial court noted that Ms. Harris vacationed twice since the separation. Because the trial court gave due consideration to Ms. Harris' standard of living both before and after the separation, it was not an abuse of discretion for the trial court to deny Ms. Harris interim spousal support.

The record reasonably supports the findings of the trial court. Considering the minor mathematical errors made by the trial court, its denial of interim spousal support to Ms. Harris was proper based on the evidence and testimony presented because those mathematical errors did not amount to prejudicial error. Given the applicable standard of review and the deference that must be given to factual determinations made by the trial court where those findings are reasonably supported by the record, we do not find that the trial court abused its discretion.

DECREE

For the above mentioned reasons, we find that the trial court did not err and affirm the denial of interim spousal support.

AFFIRMED.

McFall v. Armstrong

50 So. 3d 904 (La. App. 5 Cir. 2010)

CLARENCE E. McMANUS, Judge.

This is an appeal by Mr. McFall from the trial court's judgment awarding Ms. McFall interim spousal support. For the reasons which follow, we affirm the trial court's judgment in part and amend in part.

STATEMENT OF THE CASE

Joseph and Shannon McFall were married on April 16, 1994. Joseph McFall filed a petition for divorce on October 15, 2009. On November 2, 2009, Shannon McFall filed an answer and reconventional demand in which she sought interim periodic spousal support. Ms. McFall had also filed a petition for protection from abuse in the trial court on September 22, 2009. That petition was dismissed by the trial court, but then later reinstated by the trial court. Mr. McFall filed an appeal from the trial court's judgment reinstating Ms. McFall's petition for protection from abuse. In an opinion dated June 29, 2010, this Court reversed the trial court's decision finding the matter was not properly reinstated after dismissal.

A hearing was held on November 30, 2009 and the issue of interim spousal support was addressed. The trial court issued a written judgment and reasons for judgment on December 15, 2009 awarding Ms. McFall interim spousal support of $1,075.00 per month, retroactive to September 22, 2009. The trial court also awarded her exclusive use of the family home, payment of her car loan and insurance, and payment of the mortgage during the pendency of the proceedings, subject to a one-half rental rate credit in the community property partition. . . .

DISCUSSION

Mr. McFall appeals the trial court's award of interim spousal support of $1,075.00 per month. . . .

Interim Spousal Support

The trial court awarded Ms. McFall $1,075.00 per month for interim spousal support. A court may award interim periodic support to a spouse in a divorce proceeding based on the needs of that spouse, the ability of the other spouse to pay, and the standard of living of the spouses during the marriage. Interim spousal support is designed to assist the claimant spouse in sustaining the same style or standard of living that he or she enjoyed while residing with the other spouse, pending the litigation of the divorce. The needs of the claimant spouse have been defined as "the total amount sufficient to maintain her in a standard of living comparable to that enjoyed by her prior to the separation, limited only by the husband's ability to pay," and the claimant spouse has the burden of proving his or her need. The trial court is vested with much discretion in determining awards of spousal support and these determinations will not be disturbed absent a clear abuse of discretion.

Following the hearing, the trial court found Ms. McFall has needs beyond her imputed income and Mr. McFall has the ability to pay. Ms. McFall was not employed at the time of the hearing. She had previously worked as a certified medical assistant; however, she had not worked in this position since 1995 and had not maintained her certifications. The trial court found her skills were obsolete or of no use. Thus, the trial court imputed minimum wage to Ms. McFall as income potential.

We find the trial court did not abuse its discretion in reaching this conclusion. Even if Ms. McFall returned to work, she would most likely not be able to return to the same position at the same salary she was previously at as a certified medical assistant. Additionally, she no longer has the certifications necessary to work in the same position. Therefore, the trial court correctly imputed an income potential of minimum wage to Ms. McFall.

Next, the trial court determined Mr. McFall's income and benefits to be in excess of $90,000.00 per year. Mr. McFall claimed he only earned $56,680.00 per year. However, based on his testimony and demeanor in the courtroom, the trial court found him to be "anything but credible." The trial court found that Mr. McFall owns two SpeeDee Oil Change franchises and owns concession vending machines that operate at each franchise location. The trial court also found that Mr. McFall has unreported cash business. Additionally, Mr. McFall uses business funds to pay the note and insurance on the family vehicle, family cell phones, and family health insurance. The tax returns presented by Mr. McFall indicate an income over $90,000.00. Mr. McFall disputes this amount, claiming he earns significantly less. However, the trial court questioned his credibility and clearly did not give great weight to his testimony. Therefore, we find no abuse of the trial court's discretion in determining Mr. McFall's income to be more than $90,000.00.

We also agree with the trial court that Ms. McFall does have a need for spousal support. Ms. McFall presented an income and expense statement showing monthly expenses of $4,311.00. These expenses are necessary to maintain the same standard of living as the couple enjoyed prior to the separation. Further, Mr. McFall has the ability to pay spousal support, based on his income established by the trial court and discussed above. Thus, we find the trial court did not abuse its discretion by awarding $1,075.00 per month to Ms. McFall for interim periodic spousal support. . . .

In accordance with the above, we affirm the trial court's award of interim spousal support to Ms. McFall in the amount of $1,075.00 per month. . . .

C. Duration of Interim Spousal Support

As the name suggests, interim spousal support is designed to be time-limited in its duration. Yet, parties have a real incentive to extend the length of an interim award for as long as possible. Interim awards are sometimes more generous than final periodic support awards. Also, while fault is a complete bar to receiving a final periodic support award in Louisiana, fault is irrelevant to interim spousal support awards.

Therefore, a party who is ineligible for final periodic support due to some fault has an incentive to extend an interim award for as long as possible.

In general, an interim support award will terminate upon the rendition of the divorce judgment. There are, however, several caveats to that rule. If a claim for final spousal support is pending when the judgment of divorce is issued, then Article 113 provides that the interim support award terminates upon the earlier of "rendition of a judgment awarding or denying final spousal support or one hundred eighty days from the rendition of judgment of divorce." The article also allows extension beyond one hundred eighty days for "good cause shown."

A 2014 amendment to Article 113 also allows interim awards to have a longer duration when a divorce is granted on abuse grounds set forth in Article 103(4) or 103(5).

Only a handful of reported decisions have considered what is meant by "good cause." A couple of cases have suggested that disability or the inability of a spouse to find employment for reasons beyond his or her control might constitute good cause. On the other hand, courts have also said that extensions should not be used merely as a means to punish a party for some wrongdoing during litigation. In *Roan v. Roan*, the court explained that: "We do not think that the legislature intended interim support provisions of Article 113 to be used as a remedy or punishment for dilatory discovery responses."[2] *Hogan v. Hogan*, below, seems to modify the rule in *Roan* when the conduct has been particularly egregious.

Hogan v. Hogan

178 So. 3d 1013 (La. App. 2 Cir. 2015)

GARRETT, J.

Richard Russell Hogan ("Russ") appeals from a trial court judgment which awarded interim spousal support in favor of his former wife, Jill Adams Hogan, in the amount of $3,800 per month and ordered that it be paid beyond the statutory 180-day period. . . . We affirm the trial court judgment.

INTRODUCTION

Contested domestic cases are never amicable. However, what occurred in this case is beyond the pale. To understand why we are affirming the decisions made below, especially the extension of the period of time for payment of interim spousal support, it is—unfortunately—necessary to review in detail the factual and procedural background leading up to the protracted hearing and the evidence adduced at that hearing. Unlike many domestic cases that take years to resolve and are handled by multiple judges, this case is somewhat unique. The same judge presided over this matter from the beginning through all the events resulting in the instant appeal. Thus, the trial court had the full benefit of being well versed and completely familiar with

---

2. 870 So. 2d 626 (La. App. 2 Cir. 2004).

the entire sordid picture and all of the machinations that occurred before, during, and after the dissolution of the parties' marriage.

FACTUAL AND PROCEDURAL BACKGROUND

Russ and Jill married in Ruston in September 2007. Two children were born of this marriage: a son (DOB 12/09), and a daughter (DOB 12/10). It was Jill's first marriage and Russ's second. He had another daughter from his first marriage, who was about 10 years older than his son with Jill. Unfortunately, the parties' marriage was marred by Russ's repeated infidelities, substantial substance abuse, and reckless financial shenanigans.

When the parties met in 2005, Russ was an agent for American Family Life Assurance Company (AFLAC). In February 2007, Jill—who had been working for a medical supply company—got her license to sell insurance and began working for AFLAC also. By this time, Russ had been promoted to district sales coordinator (DSC). However, due to their relationship and the resulting conflict of interest, Jill had to cultivate her own clients without his assistance. Later that year, Russ was promoted to regional sales coordinator (RSC); his region covered a large portion of North Louisiana. Due to an extramarital affair with one of his insurance agents and lying to his boss, Russ lost his position as RSC in early 2010. The couple briefly separated due to Russ's cheating, but reconciled. In March 2010, Russ accepted a DSC position in Jacksonville, Florida, and the family moved there in April 2010. However, during her pregnancy with their daughter, Jill had to move back to Louisiana to maintain her medical insurance coverage with Blue Cross/Blue Shield of Louisiana. She and their son moved in with her mother in Monroe in August 2010. While Jill was away, Russ engaged in an affair with a woman named Julia. He was also frequenting strip clubs and using drugs. By his own admission at trial, he was "definitely spending lots of money" during this time period. In February 2011, Russ decided to take a DSC position in Orlando, a fact that Jill learned only when she read about it on Russ's Facebook page. Jill made plans to pack up the Jacksonville house for the move to Orlando. However, on March 16, 2011, Jill learned of Russ's affair with Julia after calling a frequently dialed number she found on Russ's cell phone records.

Jill filed for divorce on March 18, 2011, in Ouachita Parish. She sought joint custody of the children and designation as the domiciliary parent. She also requested interim spousal support and, upon its termination, final periodic spousal support. When Jill traveled to Jacksonville with her father to retrieve household and personal belongings, she discovered that Russ had taken most of these items; she later learned that he had placed them in storage under the name of yet another woman. . . .

On July 27, 2011, Jill filed an amended petition for divorce, in which she alleged in detail Russ's adultery with various women and the "double life" he led during their marriage. Jill recounted how insurance coverage issues forced her to stay in Monroe while pregnant with their daughter and how she later learned about his activities in Florida during her absence. She asserted that, during this time period, Russ had minimal contact with his family, missing holidays on the ground that he could not afford to travel to Louisiana to see them. However, during the same time period, he spent significant funds on alcohol, drugs, and strip clubs. She alleged that in March 2011, Julia confirmed her relationship with Russ and provided Jill with hundreds of texts and photos, documenting a lengthy affair and Russ's reckless lifestyle, which allegedly included the daily intake of excessive alcohol and the use of multiple drugs, such as cocaine, Lortab, marijuana, crystal meth, Xanax and Adderall.

Jill further asserted that she and her family had provided for all of the children's care and financial support since March 2011, and that Russ had terminated the children's health insurance coverage. She further alleged that Russ had issues with alcohol. She expressed concern as to the children's safety in their father's custody, particularly in light of the people with whom he associated. She requested drug testing under La. R.S. 9:331.1. On the issue of physical abuse, Jill alleged several episodes of violence, including some which occurred when she was pregnant. She sought relief under La. R.S. 9:364 of the Post-Separation Family Violence Relief Act, which disqualifies a parent with a history of family violence from being awarded sole or joint custody of children and restricts visitation. She specifically requested that Russ be denied visitation with the children until after his completion of a treatment program.

While the divorce proceedings were in the early stages, Russ met Brandie Jager, a waitress in Mississippi who was 14 years his junior. A week after they met in May 2011, Brandie drove to Florida to stay with him. In June 2011, she moved into the $2,000-a-month furnished house he was renting in a gated community on an Orlando golf course. Brandie was unemployed, and Russ paid all her expenses and provided her with a cell phone. She later accompanied him on several luxurious trips—including one to Hawaii and another to Deer Valley, Utah, where they stayed at the St. Regis Hotel. They dined lavishly, both at restaurants and while entertaining at home. Russ bought Brandie expensive gifts, including $200 sunglasses. He also treated himself to such amenities as $200 sunglasses and a couple of $600 tattoos.

In June 2011, Russ sent Jill a check for $500; it was the first money he had paid for his children's support since the divorce filing. In the meantime, Jill had been forced to apply for food stamps in order to feed their two young children and herself. . . .

Russ continued living with Brandie. In November 2011, Brandie opened a bank account in her name, into which Russ began depositing money. That same month, Jill's car, a Dodge Charger given to her by Russ for Christmas 2009, was repossessed because Russ stopped making the payments on it. (He later testified that he was "upset" with Jill and assumed she could borrow her mother's car.) Also in November 2011, Russ quit his lucrative job in Orlando and moved back to Ruston to "fight [Jill's] ass," as he declared in an email. Brandie accompanied him. . . .

Despite his substantial arrearages, Russ continued to make large, frivolous purchases instead of paying his support obligations. In May 2012, Russ borrowed $10,000 to buy a Nissan Altima for Brandie. He admitted at trial that the monthly notes on Brandie's Altima were higher than those on Jill's repossessed Charger. Next he spent

$15,000 on a speedboat which, according to Brandie's testimony, cost $100 every time they filled up the gas tank. The record also indicates that Russ bought a used Jeep in May 2012 for $1,800 and then sold it at a loss for about $1,400 in August 2012. All of these purchases were financed by loans obtained through AFLAC. . . .

In May 2013, Russ paid $1,600 cash for an engagement ring Brandie picked out at Zales. In June 2013, he signed up for a one-year membership at Anytime Fitness, agreeing to pay dues of $443.40, plus another $960.00 for a six-month personal trainer/nutrition program. . . .

INTERIM SPOUSAL SUPPORT

Russ contests several aspects of the trial court's award of interim spousal support. . . .

Duration

Russ further contends that the trial court erred in extending the interim spousal support award beyond the 180-day period of La. C.C. art. 113 because Jill did not file a motion or rule for an extension. He also argues that the extension was punitive and not based on "good cause." Although he never raised this issue below in any pleadings or arguments presented to the trial court, he now seeks to have the interim spousal support terminated as of the date of the divorce in March 2013, or 180 days thereafter. . . .

Whether "good cause" exists for the extension of interim support must be determined on a case-by-case basis. It must constitute, if not a compelling reason, certainly a reason of such significance and gravity that "it would be inequitable to deny an extension of such support." "Good cause" pursuant to La. C.C. art. 113 "requires an affirmative showing by the party seeking an extension of interim support that the extension is really and genuinely needed, and the purpose for which it is sought is legitimate, not calculated to cause hardship or to obtain as much spousal support as possible for as long as possible."

Russ also argues that the extension of interim spousal support by the trial court should be reversed because Jill did not request the extension by filing a rule to extend. In support of this, he cites *Roan, supra*, where this court found the trial court abused its discretion in finding the delay from incomplete discovery was good cause to retroactively extend interim spousal support when no motion to extend had been filed. However, we factually distinguish *Roan*, which was in a totally different procedural posture. There, a hearing was actually held on the issue of permanent periodic spousal support. The issue was when to end payment for the interim spousal support and when to begin the permanent periodic spousal support. The payor spouse was paying the interim spousal support ordered by the trial court, and he received a credit for his overpayment. Also, the delays in *Roan* were attributable to both litigants and no motions to compel or for contempt were filed to remedy the discovery issues.

Jill requested both interim spousal support and final periodic spousal support in her original divorce pleading. Review of the record shows that the trial on the support issues was delayed due to Russ's failure to supply his financial information, as well as his mistress's refusal to answer questions during her deposition and supply her financial records. These matters had to be sorted out through rules to compel and contempt proceedings before the financial issues could go forward and be litigated. Trial on the objections to the HOC recommendations, including the issue of interim spousal support, and the contempt motions finally began in July 2013, within 180 days of the March 2013 divorce. After several days of taking evidence, the matter was continued by agreement to September 16, 2013, which was still within the 180-day post-divorce period. However, to accommodate the knee surgery of Russ's counsel, the matter was then continued to November 22, 2013. The trial then continued on that date, which was more than 180 days after the divorce became final, without Russ ever asserting any objection to the lack of a rule to extend. We note that La. C.C. art. 113 itself does not specifically require the filing of an additional pleading to request an extension of the 180-day period.

We further observe that Russ never objected to the continuation of the March 2012 temporary order in the divorce judgment rendered in March 2013, which expressly maintained the temporary order. He never filed any motions to terminate or revoke interim spousal support or to have a hearing set on the issue of entitlement to permanent periodic spousal support, although procedural vehicles were certainly available to him under Louisiana law.

We find that the facts of this case demonstrate "good cause" for an extension of the interim spousal support. While a certain amount of financial gamesmanship and withholding of support is sadly typical in some domestic cases, the lengths to which Russ has gone to avoid his financial responsibilities, and to deliberately cause financial hardship for Jill, are outrageous. As a result of his machinations, she is destitute — which was unquestionably his intent — and the continuation of interim spousal support is "really and genuinely needed," as provided in *Roan*, supra. The trial court recognized the great severity of the situation and, after careful consideration of all factors, took the only measure it felt would be effective. Based upon the extreme conduct in this particular case, we find no error on the part of the trial court in its imposition of interim spousal support for a period beyond the 180-day statutory period.

D. Final Periodic Spousal Support: Fault and Burden of Proof

Unlike interim support, freedom from fault is relevant to determining an award of final periodic support. Civil Code 112 makes it clear that only a spouse who "has not been at fault prior to the filing of a petition for divorce" can seek final periodic support. As the cases and the comments make clear, the concept of fault includes both the fault grounds that are sufficient for divorce — such as adultery — as well as other types of fault that lead to the deterioration of the marital relationship.

Comment (c) to Civil Code article 111 specifically incorporates the fault grounds that were sufficient for divorce or separation under prior law. Those grounds include habitual intemperance, cruel treatment, public defamation, abandonment, and intentional nonsupport. Some of these, of course, remain grounds for divorce in a covenant marriage. Reconciliation often plays a role in these cases. A reconciliation following some fault sufficient to preclude an award of spousal support will wipe the slate clean and allow the spouse to bring a support claim.

Louisiana is not alone in considering the issue of fault for purposes of spousal support. Most states continue to consider marital fault—an approach that has been criticized by a number of scholars.

In Louisiana, and as is illustrated in *Hutson v. Hutson*, the spouse seeking spousal support generally bears the burden of proving that he or she is free from fault in the dissolution of the marriage. Proving freedom from any fault is a somewhat strange burden—as the cases demonstrate. *Lagars v. Lagars* illustrates an exception to the general rule where the divorce was already rendered on some fault ground—like adultery—in which case the burden shifts.

Hutson v. Hutson

908 So. 2d 1231 (La. App. 2 Cir. 2005)

STEWART, J.

Thomas Ray Hutson, seeks reversal of the of the trial court's judgment finding his former spouse, Gladys Hutson, free from fault in the dissolution of the marriage for the purposes of awarding final periodic spousal support. For the reasons set forth below, we affirm the judgment of the trial court.

FACTS

Thomas Ray Hutson ("Mr. Hutson"), and Gladys May Dampier Claunch Hutson ("Ms. Hutson"), were married on September 27, 1985, in Hamburg, Arkansas, and subsequently established a matrimonial domicile in Ouachita Parish. No children were born of the marriage. On August 28, 2003, Mr. Hutson filed for divorce, pursuant to La. C.C. art. 102, in the Fourth Judicial District Court for the Parish of Ouachita. On September 22, 2003, Ms. Hutson filed an answer and reconventional demand in which she alleged that she was free from fault in the break up of the marriage and was in need of final periodic support. Mr. Hutson filed an answer to the reconventional demand generally denying Ms. Hutson's assertion that she was free from fault in the break up of the marriage, but made no factual allegations as to any conduct on her part which would constitute fault.

On March 11, 2004, Mr. Hutson filed a rule for a final judgment of divorce and a determination on the issue of fault in the break up of the marriage. At the hearing, the court heard from the parties and various friends and relatives as to the circumstances surrounding the break up of the marriage.

Mr. Hutson testified that during the marriage, Ms. Hutson subjected him to criticism and nagging "almost daily." She criticized his children and his fishing, and she nagged him about doing yard work. Mr. Hutson indicated that his children quit coming to the house, but he did not explain how this was attributable to Ms. Hutson since he admitted she never criticized the children in their presence. He also indicated he quit fishing because she would tease him when he did not catch anything.

Mr. Hutson also alleged that Ms. Hutson constantly accused him of having extramarital affairs. However, his testimony reflected that Ms. Hutson was more inquisitive than accusatory about his relationships with other women. He also testified that Ms. Hutson controlled the family finances, but gave no testimony that he was in disagreement with the arrangement.

He testified that the parties did not have sexual relations or share a bedroom during the last two years of their marriage, but he admitted that it was because he did not want to have anything to do with "somebody that just, uh, is a bitch." He admitted that about a year before Ms. Hutson moved out of the matrimonial domicile, he told her he did not love her anymore. He testified that he was relieved when she moved out and admitted that he never asked her to return. Even though she moved out, Mr. Hutson stated he believed that Ms. Hutson did not want a divorce.

The court also heard from Lisa Woods, a self-described estranged niece of Ms. Hutson's. After admitting that she had not been on speaking terms with her aunt for four years, she testified that her aunt was very controlling and insulting. Most of her testimony was based on hearsay as she was not a witness to the day-to-day events in the marriage. And while she undeniably had no kind words for her estranged aunt from a personal perspective, her testimony is less than instructive on the fault issue.

Mr. Hutson also submitted the testimony of his son, Clint Hutson who testified that he had not been out to his father's home in six years. Therefore testimony could not corroborate any of his father's allegations as to Ms. Hutson being the source of any problems in the marriage or between Clint and his father.

Lastly, Mr. Hutson submitted the testimony of Carolyn Morris, the woman who has been his barber for the past 15 years and with whom Ms. Hutson allegedly accused him of having an affair. Morris confirmed that Ms. Hutson, who was also a client, always made Mr. Hutson's haircut appointments. Morris testified that the Hutsons hardly spoke about each other while getting their hair cut. However, Mr. Hutson would occasionally tell her of Ms. Hutson's jealous streak, and Ms. Hutson was sometimes critical of Mr. Hutson's inability to repair things around the house.

After the parties separated and divorce proceedings were initiated, Mr. Hutson asked Morris to dinner. After the parties' outing, Ms. Hutson accused Morris of having an affair with Mr. Hutson, which Morris denied.

On Ms. Hutson's behalf, the trial court heard from Candy Edwards, her granddaughter, who testified that she was a frequent guest in the Hutsons' home and even vacationed with the parties on occasion. Ms. Edwards stated that she never witnessed

the parties argue or raise their voices at each other. She also noted that her grandmother performed the majority of the household chores including the cooking, cleaning and laundry. She also prepared breakfast for Mr. Hutson and packed him a
lunch every day even after he told her that he did not love her anymore. She worked
in her garden and even mowed occasionally. Ms. Edwards denied ever hearing her
grandmother voice suspicions about her husband's fidelity prior to the parties'
separation.

Ms. Edwards' testimony was substantively corroborated by Judy Fondren, Ms.
Hutson's sister who lived on the parties' property between 1987 and 1989. Ms. Fondren believed the parties had a good marriage and never witnessed any bickering,
nagging or arguing between the parties.

The trial court also heard from two of the parties' neighbors, Gay Montgomery
and Beverly Powell. Both women testified that they spent a considerable amount of
time in the presence of the parties. Both witnesses testified about their perception
that the parties had a good marriage and that Ms. Hutson was an attentive spouse
who regularly cooked and kept a clean house. Neither witness could recall hearing
the parties argue, or hearing Ms. Hutson nagging or berating Mr. Hutson. They also
denied ever hearing Ms. Hutson voice suspicions about whether her husband was
having an extramarital affair prior to their separation.

Lastly, the trial court heard from Ms. Hutson herself. Ms. Hutson testified that
she and Mr. Hutson had a good relationship during their marriage until he told her
he did not love her anymore and moved out of their bedroom. She cooked, cleaned
and did the laundry. She worked in her garden and helped with the mowing. She also
handled the family finances without objection from Mr. Hutson until the very end
of their 18-year marriage. She also testified that while she had some persistent health
problems, she never refused him sex unless she was acutely ill.

Ms. Hutson testified that while she and Mr. Hutson's daughter had a somewhat
strained relationship at the outset, she generally had a good relationship with his
children. She denied that they fought or argued on a regular basis, or that she accused
him of having affairs. She also affirmatively stated that she did nothing to break up
the marriage and that it broke down when he told her that he did not love her and
wanted a divorce.

At the conclusion of the hearing, the trial court rendered a judgment of divorce.
A final judgment of divorce was signed on May 14, 2004. The trial court ordered the
parties to submit briefs on the issue of fault and took the matter under advisement.
On June 3, 2004, the trial court issued reasons for judgment finding that there was
insufficient evidence to support a finding that Ms. Hutson was at fault in the break
up of the marriage. In its ruling, the trial court stated that Mr. Hutson failed to meet
his burden that Ms. Hutson was at fault. A written judgment to this effect was signed
on June 21, 2004, and certified as final by the trial court. Mr. Hutson took an appeal
from that judgment. This court subsequently dismissed that appeal and remanded

the matter to the trial court after concluding that the certification of the judgment as final was inappropriate. . . .

DISCUSSION

Burden of Proof

First, we address Mr. Hutson's assignment of error regarding the misapplication of the burden of proof by the trial court. The jurisprudence is unequivocal on the issue of who bears the initial burden on the fault question in final periodic support proceedings. The burden is squarely on the claimant spouse who must show that she is free from fault in the dissolution of the marriage. In brief, Ms. Hutson concedes that the trial court erred in placing the initial burden on Mr. Hutson to prove that she was at fault in the break up of the marriage.

[handwritten margin note: burden of proof]

Where one or more trial court legal errors interdict the fact-finding process, and the record is otherwise complete, the reviewing court should make its own independent de novo review and assessment of the record. Because the trial court's misplacement of the initial burden in the present case prevented it from making a finding of fact on whether Ms. Hutson met the burden of proving her freedom from fault, we will conduct a de novo review of the record.

[handwritten margin note: de novo review for legal error]

The jurisprudence provides little guidance on how a claimant spouse is to perform the task of proving freedom from fault. While the case law indicates that the burden can be shifted to the non-claimant spouse when the divorce is obtained on the basis of adultery of the non-claimant spouse . . . there is no indication of how one shifts the burden when a divorce is obtained on the basis of living separate and apart for the requisite period of time.

Ms. Hutson presented evidence in the form of her own testimony and that of her niece, sister and neighbors. She affirmatively stated that she did nothing to break up the marriage. Her niece, sister and neighbors, who had been exposed to the couple at various times throughout the marriage, testified that Ms. Hutson had been a good wife who performed her fair share of the household duties. They testified that the parties rarely argued, and they denied witnessing any of the nagging which Mr. Hutson alleges plagued their marriage.

We find that this evidence is sufficient to establish freedom from fault in instances where the divorce is not obtained on the fault grounds delineated in La. C.C. art. 103. Ms. Hutson made a prima facie showing that she was not at fault in the break up of the marriage by presenting testimony to support her version of the events leading to the break up of the marriage. Such a prima facie showing was sufficient to meet her initial burden of proof. Once that burden was met, the burden shifted to Mr. Hutson to prove conduct on the part of the claimant spouse which rises to the level of fault.

Fault

Fault is a threshold issue in a claim for spousal support. In a proceeding for divorce or thereafter, the court may award final periodic support to a party free from fault prior to the filing of a proceeding to terminate the marriage, based on the needs of that party and the ability of the other party to pay. La. C.C. art. 111. Statutory law does not specify what constitutes fault so as to bar an award of final periodic support. However, the jurisprudence has characterized the necessary conduct as synonymous with the fault grounds which previously entitled a spouse to a separation under former La. C.C. art. 138 or the fault grounds which currently entitle a spouse to a divorce under La. C.C. art. 103.

Prior to its repeal, Article 138 provided the grounds for separation which included adultery, habitual intemperance, excesses, cruel treatment or outrages, making living together insupportable, and abandonment. La. C.C. art. 103 currently entitles a spouse to seek a fault-based divorce on the basis of the other spouse's adultery or conviction of a felony sentence punishable by death or hard labor. A spouse who petitions for permanent support need not be totally blameless in the marital discord. Only misconduct of a serious nature, providing an independent contributory or proximate cause of the break up, equates to legal fault. A party is not deprived of alimony due to a reasonably justifiable response to the other spouse's initial acts. A spouse who perceives infidelity may become quarrelsome or hostile. Such a reasonable reaction does not constitute legal fault. The commission of adultery causes the break up, not the reaction. A spouse who reacts should not be precluded from receiving alimony solely because of his or her own response.

The only two grounds raised by Mr. Hutson in relation to potential fault on the part of Ms. Hutson were cruel treatment and abandonment. In order to prove abandonment, a party must show that the other party has withdrawn from the common dwelling without lawful cause or justification, and the party has constantly refused to return to live with the other. Mr. Hutson did not satisfy these requirements because he admitted that he had told his wife he did not love her, was relieved when she moved out of the house and had never asked her to return.

To prove cruel treatment, Mr. Hutson needed to show a continued pattern of mental harassment, nagging and griping by one spouse directed at the other so as to make the marriage insupportable as mere bickering and fussing do not constitute cruel treatment for purposes of denying alimony. We find that Mr. Hutson's allegations as to the amount of nagging he endured during the marriage, which were not corroborated by his own witnesses and were contradicted by ample testimony from Ms. Hutson's witnesses, do not rise to the level of cruel treatment.

While many spouses may be tempted to characterize repeated requests to perform household chores such as mowing and yard work as cruel treatment, the level testified to by Mr. Hutson falls far short of that which would be required to make a marriage insupportable. Also, the record does not support Mr. Hutson's contentions that Ms. Hutson repeatedly accused him of infidelity. She denied having any such suspicions before the parties separated, and no one recalled Ms. Hutson ever confiding any such suspicions. Nor does the record support his contention that Ms. Hutson alienated him from his children. Even Mr. Hutson's own son would not corroborate the allegation. All in all, the evidence failed to establish a continued pattern of mental harassment.

CONCLUSION

For the foregoing reasons, the judgment of the trial court awarding final periodic support to Ms. Hutson in the amount of $900.00 per month is hereby affirmed. Costs of this appeal are to be borne by Mr. Hutson.

AFFIRMED.

Lagars v. Lagars

491 So. 2d 5 (La. 1986)

MARCUS, Justice.

Jimmy Lee Lagars filed suit for absolute divorce based on living separate and apart continuously for a period of one year. Katherine Kennedy Lagars answered denying that Mr. Lagars was entitled to a divorce and reconvened seeking a divorce in her favor on the ground of adultery and seeking post-divorce alimony in the amount of $750.00 per month. In her reconventional demand, Mrs. Lagars did not allege her freedom from fault in the dissolution of the marriage, and in his answer to the reconventional demand, Mr. Lagars did not assert that Mrs. Lagars was at fault.

At trial, Mr. Lagars admitted his adultery. The exact nature, extent and duration of the adulterous relationship, however, was not shown. No evidence was presented as to the precise date that the Lagars physically separated, and it is unclear whether Mr. Lagars committed adultery prior to the separation. Mrs. Lagars presented no evidence to show her freedom from fault in causing either the physical separation or the divorce of the parties, and Mr. Lagars presented no evidence to show Mrs. Lagars' fault, other than his brief statement that the separation occurred due to her "griping all the time."

The trial judge rendered a judgment in favor of Mrs. Lagars granting her a divorce on the ground of adultery, but denied her request for alimony. He reasoned that Mrs. Lagars had the burden of proving her freedom from fault, and that she failed to introduce any evidence on this issue. Mrs. Lagars' motion for a new trial was denied by the trial judge. Mrs. Lagars appealed. The court of appeal affirmed, finding that a spouse who claims post-divorce alimony must prove, by a preponderance of the evidence, freedom from fault, even though the divorce is granted because of the adultery of the other spouse. The court determined that since Mrs. Lagars failed to produce any evidence on this issue, she did not meet her burden of proof. On application of Mrs. Lagars, we granted certiorari to review the correctness of that decision.

The sole issue presented for our consideration is whether a spouse seeking post-divorce alimony in a suit for divorce on the ground of adultery, where there has been no judicial separation, must prove his or her freedom from fault in order to obtain post-divorce alimony. . . .

The instant case presents a res nova issue to this court, that is, whether a spouse seeking post-divorce alimony in a suit for divorce on the ground of adultery, where there has been no judicial separation, must prove his or her freedom from fault in order to obtain post-divorce alimony. . . .

We conclude that when there has been no judicial separation, a spouse claiming post-divorce alimony in an action for divorce based on adultery is entitled to alimony, if in need, if the claimant spouse obtains a judgment of divorce in his or her favor, unless the other spouse affirmatively defends and proves that the claimant spouse was at fault. We reach this conclusion because when there has been no judicial separation, the divorce is the first fault determination between the parties, and the judgment of divorce based on the adultery of the non-claimant spouse carries with it the implication that the claimant spouse was not at fault. This implication satisfies the burden of proof on the claimant spouse to show his or her freedom from fault. . . . There is a possibility, however, that the misconduct of the claimant spouse was also a cause of the separation or divorce, and the other spouse should be able to defeat the claim for alimony by affirmatively proving the fault of the claimant spouse. Hence, in the instant case, in order to defeat Mrs. Lagars' claim for post-divorce alimony, if she can show that she is in need, Mr. Lagars must affirmatively prove by a preponderance of the evidence that Mrs. Lagars was at fault under one of the grounds for separation or divorce under La.Civ.Code arts. 138(1)–(8) or 139. . . .

DECREE

For the reasons assigned, the judgments of the courts below are reversed, and the case is remanded to the district court for further proceedings consistent with the views herein expressed and in accordance with law.

E. Fault: Cruel Treatment

Cruel treatment is one of the more common fault issues litigated today. As the following cases demonstrate, cruel treatment is behavior that is sufficiently severe on the part of one spouse that it renders living together insupportable. Further, the cruel treatment must be shown to be the proximate cause for the deterioration of the marriage. But, where is the line between ordinary marital spats and conduct constituting cruel treatment? Some older cruel treatment cases involved actions that amounted to spousal abuse. Recent revisions to the Civil Code articles dealing with divorce make abuse an independent ground for divorce in some cases. As some of the cases below demonstrate, actions that would otherwise constitute cruel treatment do not preclude spousal support when they are provoked by the other spouse or are a response to the other spouse's bad behavior.

Wolff v. Wolff

966 So. 2d 1202 (La. App. 3 Cir. 2007)

GENOVESE, Judge.

In this domestic case, Defendant, Elizabeth B. Wolff, seeks reversal of the trial court's judgment finding that she was not free from fault in the dissolution of her marriage to Plaintiff, Christopher K. Wolff, and thus precluded from final periodic spousal support. For the reasons set forth below, we affirm the judgment of the trial court. . . .

ASSIGNMENT OF ERROR

In her sole assignment of error, Ms. Wolff argues that the trial court incorrectly denied her request for final periodic spousal support.

LAW AND DISCUSSION

Ms. Wolff contends that the trial court erred in its acceptance of Mr. Wolff's testimony that she was unjustifiably jealous, accusatory, and cruel towards Mr. Wolff as a basis for finding that she was not free from fault in the break-up of the marriage. We disagree. . . .

Mr. Wolff argues that Ms. Wolff was unjustifiably jealous, and years of her accusations of infidelity showed a pattern of mental harassment and cruel treatment towards him which rendered their marriage unsupportable. According to Mr. Wolff's testimony, Ms. Wolff harassed him about recurring dreams she had about him and a former schoolmate, and she accused him of having affairs with at least two women. Mr. Wolff denied ever committing adultery. Mr. Wolff contends that the evidence, or lack thereof, supports the trial court's finding that Ms. Wolff failed to prove her freedom for fault. We agree.

Ms. Wolff asserts that the trial court erred by relying on Mr. Wolff's testimony that she nagged him incessantly in concluding that she was not free from fault in the dissolution of the marriage. Ms. Wolff testified that she was a dutiful wife and mother, and that she never initiated an argument with Mr. Wolff. She claimed that not until the night before he left did Mr. Wolff ever tell her that he was unhappy with her as a wife, or that she was too jealous. He never complained about her either being a nag, being insecure, or being accusatory. In fact, Ms. Wolff denied being either unreasonably jealous or unjustly accusatory. Ms. Wolff admitted to having an on-going argument with Mr. Wolff over his hiring of their mutual friend, Mrs. Charity Naquin (Mrs. Naquin); however, Ms. Wolff denied being unreasonable.

According to Ms. Wolff, Mr. Wolff was overly flirtatious and would openly flaunt his attraction to other women in front of her. Ms. Wolff admitted that on these occasions she would voice her displeasure; however, she denied overreacting, nagging, or bickering incessantly.

Mrs. Tina Ormsby (Mrs. Ormsby) testified on behalf of Ms. Wolff; however, her testimony did not corroborate Ms. Wolff's testimony. Mrs. Ormsby admitted to witnessing Ms. Wolff's jealousy and nagging. Further, she also witnessed Ms. Wolff's efforts to make Mr. Wolff angry and jealous.

Mrs. Naquin was called to testify on behalf of Mr. Wolff. Her testimony corroborated Mr. Wolff's assertion that Ms. Wolff was jealous. In fact, Mrs. Naquin testified that Ms. Wolff told her that she was not happy with Mr. Wolff because he had employed her against her (Ms. Wolff's) wishes. According to Mrs. Naquin, Ms. Wolff stated that until Mr. Wolff terminated Mrs. Naquin's employment, she, Ms. Wolff, was going to make his life "a living hell." It is noteworthy that Ms. Wolff did admit telling this to Mrs. Naquin; however, she denied actually making Mr. Wolff's life such.

Considering the evidence, law, and jurisprudence, we do not find that the trial court clearly erred or was manifestly erroneous in finding that Ms. Wolff failed to affirmatively prove her freedom from fault and that her continued pattern of mental harassment rendered their marriage insupportable.

DECREE

For the foregoing reasons, the judgment denying Ms. Wolff final periodic spousal support is affirmed. Costs of this appeal are assessed against Defendant/Appellant, Elizabeth B. Wolff.

Cauthron v. Cauthron

113 So. 3d 232 (La. App. 1 Cir. 2013)

THERIOT, J.

In this divorce case, the wife appeals a trial court judgment denying her request for final periodic support. We affirm. . . .

DISCUSSION

Louisiana Civil Code article 112 provides that the court may award final periodic support to a spouse who has not been at fault and is in need of support. The burden of proving freedom from fault is upon the claimant. To constitute fault sufficient to deprive a spouse of final periodic support, the spouse's misconduct must not only be of a serious nature, but it must also be an independent, contributory, or proximate cause of the separation. Such acts are synonymous with the fault grounds that previously entitled a spouse to a separation or divorce, i.e., adultery, conviction of a felony, habitual intemperance or excesses, cruel treatment or outrages, public defamation, abandonment, an attempt on the other's life, status as a fugitive, and intentional non-support. As with any factual finding, a trial court's findings of fact relative to the issue of fault in domestic cases are entitled to great weight and will not be overturned on appeal absent manifest error.

At the close of Mrs. Cauthron's case, Mr. Cauthron moved for an involuntary dismissal of her claim for final periodic support in accordance with La. C.C.P. art. 1672(B). . . . The court granted the involuntary dismissal, finding that

Mrs. Cauthron was guilty of cruel treatment which caused the breakup of the marriage. On appeal, Mrs. Cauthron alleges that the court erred in granting the involuntary dismissal because there was no evidence offered to support the court's factual conclusions that she was guilty of cruel treatment and that her cruel treatment of her husband caused the marriage to fail. . . .

Although the only testimony offered on the issue of fault was Mrs. Cauthron's, she had the burden of proving that she was free from fault, and there was sufficient support for the court's conclusion in her testimony on cross-examination. Mrs. Cauthron admitted on cross-examination that her husband was concerned with her misuse of prescription drugs; that she criticized her husband in front of his friends; that she slept in a separate bedroom from her husband; that her heavy smoking had resulted in cigarette burns on their furniture and floors; and that she had been arrested for damaging their neighbors' plants and surveillance equipment as part of an ongoing feud with the neighbors. Mrs. Cauthron also admitted that she did not accompany her husband to the hospital for a heart catheterization because she was babysitting her young grandson.

Furthermore, when Mr. Cauthron was hospitalized in 2010 for an ulcerated toe and doctors were considering amputation, she admitted that she just dropped him off at the hospital rather than staying with him. Although she did visit him in the hospital during this three or four day stay, she brought her young grandson with her so she could babysit him. Finally, immediately prior to filing for divorce, Mr. Cauthron travelled to Mexico to have gastric bypass surgery in an effort to get his weight and diabetes under control. Although he asked his wife to accompany him for the surgery, she chose not to go with him because she needed to babysit her grandson. Within days of returning from Mexico, Mr. Cauthron filed for divorce.

The court concluded that Mrs. Cauthron was guilty of cruel treatment of her husband because her "cavalier attitude towards his health" was an "absolute sign that she didn't care," and her refusal to accompany him to Mexico for surgery was the "final straw" that led to the dissolution of the marriage. Given the evidence before the court, we cannot say that the court's findings were manifestly erroneous. Because Mrs. Cauthron failed to carry her burden of proving that she was free from fault in the breakup of the marriage, the court did not err in granting the involuntary dismissal of her claim for final periodic support.

CONCLUSION

The judgment denying Mrs. Cauthron's claim for final periodic support is affirmed. Costs of this appeal are to be borne by the appellant, Marlene Yancovich Cauthron.

AFFIRMED.

Diggs v. Diggs

6 So. 3d 1030 (La. App. 3 Cir. 2009)

SULLIVAN, Judge.

Ex-husband appeals the trial court's determination that his ex-wife proved she is entitled to final periodic support. For the following reasons, we affirm the judgment of the trial court.

Facts

Jeffrey and Cheryl Diggs were married June 3, 1995. One daughter was born of their marriage. On August 8, 2006, Cheryl filed for divorce as provided in La.Civ.Code art. 102. A judgment of divorce was granted on April 12, 2007.

Ancillary to the divorce, Cheryl sought final periodic support, claiming she was disabled and free from fault prior to filing for divorce. In his answer, Jeffrey admitted Cheryl was disabled but denied she was free from fault in causing the divorce. At trial, Cheryl testified that she suspected for a long time during the marriage that Jeffrey was having an affair. In 2005, she hired a private investigator whose investigation confirmed her suspicions. Cheryl's attorney cross-examined Jeffrey about emails written to him in 2002 to establish that the affair was ongoing at that time. The emails were suggestive of an intimate relationship between Jeffrey and the author.

Cheryl further testified that she was concerned about possibly contracting sexually-transmitted diseases from the beginning of the marriage and that she continuously asked Jeffrey if he was having an affair. According to Cheryl, Jeffrey always denied having an affair until he was faced with the evidence obtained by the private investigator. Cheryl also testified that she and Jeffrey went to counseling because of her suspicions and that while Jeffrey's behavior improved during counseling, it reverted to what it had been prior to the counseling when the counseling ended.

Jeffrey admitted that the author of the suggestive emails was a woman he and Cheryl knew and that he had an affair with her, but he claimed the affair did not begin until December 2005. He testified that in 2002 he and the author were just friends and that the emails were the author's way of "joking." Jeffrey also testified that throughout their marriage, Cheryl was mean and controlling of him, their daughter, and his daughter who lived with them. He complained that she was verbally abusive, was not affectionate, and would push him away when he tried to show her affection. He testified that she told him in 2001 she did not love him and that she did not support him in his work or personal endeavors. Jeffrey described Cheryl as being cold and distant to his family, friends, and guests, including his boss. He further testified that after she was home full time due to her disability, she essentially did nothing in their home for him or the children, although her disability did not prevent her from doing so.

According to Jeffrey, he initiated counseling in 2001 to address his concerns, but it did not help. He claimed that he did not divorce Cheryl because he did not want his children to grow up in a home without both parents like he did. Jeffrey also claimed that Cheryl put him out of their home by having the door locks changed and changing the alarm system code.

Cheryl denied that she locked Jeffrey out of their home, but she did not deny his descriptions of her behavior toward him, the children, and others during the course of the marriage.

The trial court determined that Cheryl proved she is entitled to final periodic support. It found her suspicions of an affair were warranted in light of the suggestive emails and that her mean behavior was excusable under the circumstances. Jeffrey appeals, claiming that he and Cheryl were at fault in causing the breakup of their marriage.

Discussion

Jeffrey urges that the trial court improperly found his adultery to be the sole, independent, and proximate cause of the failure of the marriage without considering Cheryl's habitually cruel behavior as an independent and proximate cause of the dissolution of marriage.

A spouse seeking final periodic support must "affirmatively prove" she is free from causing the failure of the marriage. To meet this burden, she must prove she did not commit misconduct that is an "independent, contributory or proximate cause of the failure of the marriage." Habitual intemperance or excesses and cruel treatment or outrages are examples of fault that can defeat a claim for final periodic support. However:

> A party is not deprived of alimony due to a reasonable justifiable response to the other spouse's initial acts. A spouse who perceives infidelity may become quarrelsome or hostile. Such a reasonable reaction does not constitute legal fault. The suspicion of adultery causes the breakup and not the reaction. A spouse who reacts should not be precluded from receiving alimony solely because of his or her own response. . . .

The trial court observed that Jeffrey's description of Cheryl's behavior equated to habitual intemperance and cruel treatment and that if he had left the marriage before entering into an affair, its opinion would have been different. However, the trial court also determined that while Cheryl did not have proof of Jeffrey's affair until 2005, the emails were of a "serious and intimate nature" that warranted her suspicions of adultery and justified the habitual intemperance and meanness described by Jeffrey.

We agree with the trial court's determination that Cheryl's behavior constituted cruel treatment and fault as contained in La.Civ.Code arts. 111 and 112, but we cannot reverse the trial court's determination that Cheryl established this behavior was a response to Jeffrey's affair unless the record establishes that the determination was an abuse of discretion. The trial court was faced with a credibility determination. It accepted Cheryl's testimony that she was suspicious of Jeffrey having an affair from the beginning of the marriage and found her testimony credible. Without documents or objective evidence that contradicts Cheryl's testimony, we cannot reverse the trial court's credibility determination unless it is "so internally inconsistent or implausible on its face, that a reasonable fact-finder would not credit the witness's story." The record does not contain such evidence; therefore, we cannot reverse the trial court's determination.

Conclusion

The judgment of the trial court is affirmed, and all costs are assessed to Jeffrey Diggs.

AFFIRMED.

F. Fault: Abandonment

Abandonment constitutes legal fault for purposes of final periodic support. As the following cases demonstrate, it is not enough to simply show that a spouse left the marital home. The party asserting abandonment must also show that the other spouse consistently refused to return and that the other spouse had no lawful cause for leaving. Legal cause for abandonment includes the various fault grounds that would otherwise preclude spousal support. Abandonment can be a challenging issue in the age of no-fault divorce. Did one spouse abandon the other, or were the spouses simply living separate and apart for purposes of obtaining a divorce?

Ashworth v. Ashworth

86 So. 3d 134 (La. App. 3 Cir. 2012)

Thibodeaux, Chief Judge.

The defendant, Larry Ashworth, appeals from a judgment finding the plaintiff, Katherine Ashworth, free from fault in their divorce. He further appeals from a judgment awarding her $200.00 per month in final spousal support. Finding no abuse of discretion by the trial court, we affirm the judgments appealed. . . .

IV.

LAW AND DISCUSSION

The court is given authority to award spousal support "to a party who is in need of support and who is free from fault prior to the filing of a proceeding to terminate the marriage." La.Civ.Code art. 111. Fault that precludes spousal support includes misconduct of a serious nature that is "an independent contributory or proximate cause of the separation." "Fault continues to mean misconduct [that] rises to the level of one of the previously existing fault grounds for legal separation or divorce." La.Civ.Code art. 111, Comment (C). Prior to its repeal, La.Civ.Code art. 138 provided grounds for separation as adultery, habitual intemperance, excesses, cruel treatment or outrages, making living together insupportable, and abandonment.

Here, Larry asserts that Katherine abandoned the matrimonial domicile and that it was error for the trial court to find her free from fault on the basis of Larry's failure to ask her to return. This argument has no merit.

Abandonment

Abandonment can serve as grounds for fault only if one of the parties withdrew from the matrimonial domicile without lawful cause and constantly refused to return. Under the second element, if a spouse has cause or justification for leaving, that spouse is not guilty of abandonment. Likewise, the third element, a constant refusal to return, is essential. For abandonment, "a party cannot merely show that the spouse left the common dwelling and then rely upon the spouse's failure to prove a case grounded upon fault."

Katherine testified at trial that, approximately ten days before the separation, she happened to drive down a street and saw a woman sitting with Larry in his truck. When she stopped to ask what was going on, Larry told her not to ask questions and to go home. Katherine testified that she went to her mother's house instead and was told by her brother and her niece that Larry was giving the girl in the truck, and her roommate, money in exchange for sex. Katherine testified that other people confirmed Larry's infidelity. The couple argued, and Katherine subsequently told Larry to leave. Larry refused to go without a court order.

On October 31, 2007, Katherine packed and left the couple's domicile. Larry admitted at trial that he never asked Katherine to return. By the end of January 2008, Larry had a girlfriend living with him in the domicile with whom he admitted sexual relations. He allowed her to remove his wife's name from the mailbox and insert her own. In April 2008, Larry drove his girlfriend to his wife's location and allowed her to drive Katherine's car away in front of Katherine's friends. Katherine testified that this event extinguished her hopes of reconciliation. Subsequently, Katherine filed for divorce on September 30, 2008.

It is undisputed that Katherine was the one to leave the couple's domicile in October 2007. Therefore, the first criterion for abandonment is present. However, under the second criterion, if she had justification or lawful cause to leave, she is without fault for abandonment. Lawful cause which justifies the withdrawal from the common dwelling is that which is substantially equivalent to a cause giving the withdrawing spouse grounds for a separation. However, under *Von Bechman v. Von Bechman*, 386 So.2d 910, there is no requirement that Katherine prove Larry's adultery.

Katherine suspected adultery based upon what she had seen and heard. Katherine saw the woman with Larry in the truck and confronted them. She testified that her brother had a cell phone picture of the woman with Larry in his truck and a recording of Larry's complaint when a simultaneous call came in from Katherine, which Katherine saw and heard. Katherine further testified that she had a picture indicating infidelity, but the camera was stolen. She also testified that the roommate of the woman in the truck had admitted giving Larry sexual favors for money. Larry admitted to seeing the "ladies" and paying utility bills for the roommate but denied sexual relations. His trial testimony was spurious and unconvincing.

The trial court found that, based upon what Katherine had seen, what she had been told, and what had been admitted, Katherine had a reasonable belief that Larry was being unfaithful and that she was justified in leaving. The trial court had also heard testimony by the roommate of the woman in the truck. Both women appeared to have drug problems, as the woman in the truck was in drug rehabilitation, and Larry admitted that he suspected the roommate of having drug problems. In court, the roommate denied sexual relations with Larry and denied talking to "Kat" in years. The judge made it clear that she did not believe that the roommate had spoken a word of truth.

Domestic issues turn largely on evaluations of witness credibility, and the trial judge has much discretion in such matters. Here, the trial court obviously made credibility determinations and found that Katherine's withdrawal from the common dwelling was justified. This decision was within the trial court's discretion.

The third criterion for abandonment is that the abandoned spouse desired the other spouse's return and the exiting spouse constantly refused to return to the matrimonial domicile.

In *Von Bechman*, the Louisiana Supreme Court found that, where the husband changed the locks on the domicile a month after the wife's departure, told her he was happier once she had left, and never requested that she return, the claim for abandonment was properly dismissed. Similarly here, both Katherine and Larry testified that Larry never asked Katherine to return and that he had a live-in girlfriend within three months of Katherine's departure. Further, Larry's actions regarding the girlfriend's name on the mailbox and the girlfriend's use of the family vehicle indicate that Larry did not desire Katherine's return. These events occurred well before Katherine filed for divorce. Moreover, Katherine testified that Larry finally indicated that he did not know why he was unfaithful but that he was happy in his current situation.

Larry argues that Katherine told friends and family that he was having sex with crack whores and that this conduct made continuing to live with her insupportable; therefore, he never asked her to return. Larry puts the cart before the horse. A party is not precluded from receiving spousal support due to a reasonable, justifiable response to the other spouse's initial acts. The Louisiana Supreme Court has held:

> An association which implies adultery naturally brings on marital discord. A spouse who perceives infidelity may become quarrelsome or hostile. Such a reasonable reaction does not constitute legal fault. The suspicion of adultery causes the break-up and not the reaction. A spouse who reacts should not be precluded from receiving alimony solely because of his or her response. . . .

Larry testified that, until a week before the separation, he and Katherine had a good relationship; he never suspected her of adultery, and there was no misconduct of any kind on her part. Accordingly, the evidence yields no basis for convincing us that Katherine was at fault for the dissolution of the couple's marriage, and we find, like the trial court, that Katherine has proved her freedom from fault in the separation and divorce. . . .

Schmitt v. Schmitt

28 So. 3d 537 (La. App. 4 Cir. 2009)

PATRICIA RIVET MURRAY, Judge.

FACTUAL AND PROCEDURAL BACKGROUND

On June 18, 1993, the parties were married, having dated for nine years. . . . Both parties had been married before and both had children from their prior marriages. No children were born of this marriage.

DISCUSSION

The sole issue on appeal is whether the trial court erred in denying Mrs. Schmitt's request for final periodic support. . . .

In this case, Mr. Schmitt contends that Mrs. Schmitt's fault consisted of abandonment. The essential elements required to establish abandonment are withdrawal from the common dwelling, absence of lawful cause for the withdrawal, and refusal of the spouse who withdrew to return to live with the other. It is undisputed that Mrs. Schmitt withdrew from the common dwelling and that she refused, despite Mr. Schmitt's requests, to return. The only element in dispute is her absence of lawful cause for withdrawing.

Although in determining entitlement to final periodic support the fault of the spouse from whom support is sought generally is not pertinent. However, an exception is recognized when the ground for establishing fault on the part of the claimant spouse is abandonment. Cruel treatment by the other spouse may be sufficient to constitute lawful cause to leave. To prove cruel treatment a party needs to show a continued pattern of mental harassment, nagging, and griping by one spouse directed at the other so as to make the marriage insupportable. . . . "When the degree of spousal fussing and bickering . . . allows the finding of a pattern of harassment, unbraiding, nagging and griping, a determination by the trial court of cruel treatment has been found supported by the record." However, "[m]ere friction or dissatisfaction in the relationship or incompatibility between the spouses, however intense, is not enough to constitute cruel treatment or lawful cause for abandonment." Each must be decided on its own facts.

In this case, Mrs. Schmitt contends that Mr. Schmitt's conduct and treatment far exceeded reasonable bickering between average married couples and rose to the level of cruel treatment. She further contends that a series of incidents can lay the foundation for one spouse leaving the other and that such was the case here. Mr. Schmitt, on the other hand, contends that the parties had the same day to day garden variety problems experienced in all long term marriages and that their mere bickering and fussing was not sufficient to constitute cruel treatment. Although the trial court did not provide reasons for judgment, it apparently found that Mrs. Schmitt lacked justification to leave.

Mrs. Schmitt acknowledges that her burden of establishing that the trial court was manifestly erroneous in finding her at fault is a difficult one. Nonetheless, she contends that there is no support in the record for the trial court's finding. Rather, she contends that the testimony of the parties coupled with the two letters Mr. Schmitt wrote to her in July 2007 establish that she was a good wife, why the marriage failed, and her freedom from fault. She contends that Mr. Schmitt's letters constituted judicial confessions under La. C.C. art. 1853 of his fault that in turn justified her abandoning him.

. . . In this case, Mr. Schmitt testified that in the two letters he wrote what he thought Mrs. Schmitt wanted to hear; he "was apologizing for being unkind at times and selfish at times just as people are in all marriages." He thus contends that the nice things that he said about Mrs. Schmitt in the letters do not prove that she was justified in leaving. We agree. The letters, although relevant, were not dispositive of the issue of whether Mrs. Schmitt was free from fault. Rather, the letters have to be read in the context in which they were written: a husband begging his wife to return. The evidence before the trial court thus consisted primarily of the parties' conflicting testimony.

The record reflects that Mr. Schmitt was a pharmacist and made about five times more than she made in her job as a dental hygienist. Mr. Schmitt testified that he was overly generous in that he paid almost all of the household expenses, including electricity, gas, water, phone, car insurance, life insurance, medical insurance, homeowner's insurance, cars that he bought for Mrs. Schmitt, car repairs, and house repairs. He also paid Mrs. Schmitt's income taxes. Mr. Schmitt acknowledged that he did not pay any of her uncovered medical expenses. Mr. Schmitt also acknowledged that he was not overly generous in terms of taking Mrs. Schmitt out to eat and things of that nature. Although Mrs. Schmitt admitted that he regularly bought her Christmas presents, she testified that she had to beg Mr. Schmitt to buy food for the holidays and that he rarely bought her clothes. She testified that when they came home from their honeymoon he told her he was not going to take her on any more vacations.

At some time before 2003, Mrs. Schmitt left Mr. Schmitt for about three months. Her reason for leaving the first time was because he was becoming a monster, out of control, locked her out of the bedroom many times, kicked her in bed, called her the worse wife, told her she was a horrible person, and threatened to take her car (which was in his name). Her reason for returning was that he promised that he was going to work on his issues: being respectful to her; and being more generous, kind, and loving, especially patient. According to Mrs. Schmitt, he worked on these things for about two weeks after she returned and then he got worse than ever.

During the period of 2003 to 2005, Mrs. Schmitt had three back surgeries and one neck surgery. Mrs. Schmitt testified that after her surgeries Mr. Schmitt did not help her and that he expected her to do the cooking and cleaning. In his deposition Mr. Schmitt agreed that he did not help his wife after the surgeries, but at trial he disagreed. Mr. Schmitt acknowledged that he flushed Mrs. Schmitt's prescription pain medication (Percocet) down the toilet. He explained that she promised him that she would not take Percocet because it is highly addictive. She told him that the drug

reconciliation

was prescribed to her by mistake. He further explained that he flushed the Percocet down the toilet because he felt it was in her best interest not to take it.

In response to the trial court's question of whether she believed she was at fault for the break up of the marriage, Mrs. Schmitt testified "[a]bsolutely not" and that she did everything she could to make the marriage work. Mrs. Schmitt testified that the reason she left in 2007 was because Mr. Schmitt was treating her worse, condemning her, being more controlling, and continually screaming. She cited two things that prompted her departure in 2007. First, she stated that when Mr. Schmitt's stockbroker would come over, she would have to go in the other room because Mr. Schmitt did not want her to know anything about his money. Second, Mr. Schmitt told her not to talk to anybody in his family and that they thought she was weird.

Mr. Schmitt described their marital problems as normal type problems that any couple married for a long time experiences. He testified that their marriage had its ups and downs. He further testified that his wife on occasion was displeasing to him. He noted that she had bizarre behaviors, including leaving the front door unlocked, claiming that an eighteen-wheeler truck backed up into her on the interstate, and setting a pillow on fire. He characterized Mrs. Schmitt as a little absent minded and "[a] lot careless."

Mrs. Schmitt testified that Mr. Schmitt was jealous of her family and her relationship with them. She testified that Mr. Schmitt is very obsessive compulsive and that he knew she was "scatter-brained" when he married her. She also described herself as clumsy.

The parties agree that Mr. Schmitt never physically abused or harmed Mrs. Schmitt. They also agree that throughout the marriage they continued to sleep together and to have sex; Mrs. Schmitt never denied Mr. Schmitt sex. Mrs. Schmitt testified that she believed in sexual healing and that she took her marriage vows seriously.

Based on our review of the record, we do not find that Mrs. Schmitt satisfied her burden of establishing her freedom from fault. In light of the conflicting testimony and facts presented at the hearing and considering the vast discretion provided the trial court, we cannot conclude that the trial court's factual finding of fault on her part was manifestly erroneous. . . .

DECREE

For the foregoing reasons, the judgment of the trial court is affirmed.

AFFIRMED.

G. Fault: Habitual Intemperance

Habitual intemperance is similar to cruel treatment—and the two are often alleged simultaneously. In order to constitute legal fault, the habitual intemperance must be so severe that it renders living together unsupportable and it must be shown to be the proximate cause of the deterioration of the relationship.

Jenkins v. Jenkins

882 So. 2d 705 (La. App. 2 Cir. 2004)

Moore, J.

. . . .

FACTS

Frank Jenkins and Brenda Eldridge were married on September 16, 1983 — his fourth and her first, although two of Frank's marriages were to the same woman. At the time Frank married Brenda, he had two sons, ages 19 and 17, and a daughter, Lindsey, age 2, from his previous marriage to Judy Bennett Jenkins. Frank had custody of Lindsey every other weekend. . . .

The first signs of marital discord occurred near the end of the summer of 2000 when Brenda moved out of the house on August 29. She filed for a divorce on September 20, 2000, but the couple reconciled in January, 2001 after being separated for approximately five months. As part of their agreement to reconcile, Brenda signed a partition agreement waiving any future right to alimony and the home in exchange for $50,000, which was never paid. One year later, on March 21, 2002, Brenda moved out again and filed for divorce on April 15, 2002. She sought interim and permanent spousal support. . . .

Frank now appeals alleging that the court erred in finding that Brenda was without fault. . . .

DISCUSSION

The court issued a "ruling and judgment," stating that it rendered judgment based upon consideration of the law, testimony and documentary evidence. The trial judge assigned no separate oral or written reasons for judgment detailing the factual basis for ruling that Brenda Jenkins was without fault in the dissolution of the marriage and the factual basis for awarding her $700 per month permanent alimony, while denying all other requests for relief. . . .

Fault

. . . Frank contends that Brenda was totally at fault in the dissolution of the 19-year marriage, and that he was without fault. Brenda abandoned him when she moved out of the matrimonial domicile and refused to return. This abandonment, he argues, caused the dissolution of the marriage. . . .

It is undisputed that Brenda moved out of the matrimonial domicile, and she had no plans to return. She testified as much. Frank testified that on one occasion he suggested that she return home and be a "decent wife." On the other hand, he also admitted at trial that he once told his former brother-in-law, whose wife (Brenda's sister) had also left him, that they may find that it's better that "the bitches are gone." Notwithstanding this remark, if we assume that Brenda refused to return, the sole question regarding the issue of abandonment is whether Brenda had lawful cause for leaving.

Lawful Cause

Brenda alleged in her petition and testified at trial that the cause of the physical separation and divorce was Frank's excessive drinking, which she said led to physical and verbal abuse directed at her. She testified his drinking began every afternoon around 2:00 o'clock at the trailer park with his brother L.C., and by the time Frank came home around 5:30 or 6:00, there was a personality change. He would have an additional three or four more drinks after he came home. She said when he was drinking, Frank verbally degraded her, accused her of infidelity, called her a "fucking bitch," and told her she could "carry her ass" if she did not like it. She testified that he pulled her hair and pinched her. On one occasion, she said he grabbed her hair and twisted her arm behind her back when she tried to walk away from him after they had been arguing about alcohol.

Brenda admitted that she sometimes drank two or three cocktails when they were at a party or holiday occasion, but denied that she drank excessively or ever became obnoxious from drinking. She said that she sometimes would go weeks without drinking, and has never drunk alcohol on a daily basis. She admitted that she received a DWI when she was a teenager.

Frank denied that he drank excessively or ever abused Brenda. He admitted that he drank two or three cocktails each evening during the marriage, but claimed that Brenda matched him drink for drink. Frank said that toward the end of the marriage, Brenda became very cold towards him and then left him without any reason. He says he was never physically or verbally abusive to Brenda.

Both parties tried to corroborate their testimony with testimony of friends and relatives:

Russell Fleeman, Brenda and Frank's one-time brother-in-law married to Brenda's sister, testified that he never saw Brenda drink in excess or act obnoxiously or rudely. Regarding Frank's statement to him after their wives had left them, he quoted Frank as saying, "I don't give a fuck what's happened to the bitches." He said that although he observed Frank in social settings, he was not measuring what Frank drank. He never observed Frank abusing Brenda.

Terry Jenkins, Frank's daughter-in-law by marriage to Frank's son, Vance, testified that she had never seen Brenda drink to excess or to the point that she was impaired. On the other hand, she stated that she and her husband no longer have a relationship with Frank because of his drinking. Nor do they allow Frank to have a relationship with his grandchildren. She has observed Frank drunk and using vulgar language. She does not allow her children to visit or stay with Frank because of his excessive drinking. When the couple was married, she only allowed the kids to go to the camp when Brenda was there because Brenda would not be drinking. Prior to the separation and divorce, she and her husband visited on holiday occasions. She admitted that her relationship with Frank, as well as Vance's, relationship with him, was strained due to Frank's drinking. She said Vance told her that Frank once offered to build him a house and take the kids from her if he would "divorce the bitch."

Lisa Ginn, Brenda's sister, testified that she has seen Brenda drink on occasions but never to excess. However, she has observed Frank drink excessively at the camp and saw him stumble and fall at the camp on Labor Day three years earlier from drunkenness. She has heard Frank verbally abuse Brenda. She said she called in January of 2002 and asked if Brenda was there. She testified that Frank responded by saying, "She's here. I'm looking at the bitch." She said Frank made crude comments, and recalled one such particularly gross comment he made to her pregnant daughter.

Other evidence of Frank's behavior was introduced in the record, including the pleadings in the divorce filed by his former wife, Judy Bennett Jenkins and also an incident at the trailer park involving the police. The former divorce pleadings contained allegations against Frank of behavior similar to the allegations by Brenda, namely, that Frank accused Judy of infidelity, of pulling her hair, and using degrading and abusive language to her. Ouachita Parish Sheriff's deputy James Hindmon testified that in August of 2002, he was called out to investigate an alleged battery committed by Frank Jenkins on a juvenile, and in which his report indicated that he, Hindmon, detected the smell of alcohol on Frank. The deputy recalled that he detected a strong smell of alcohol coming from Frank and from his brother L.C., when he interviewed each of them. He did not perform an intoxication test, but he observed that Frank had "glassy, watery eyes." No arrests, however, resulted from the investigation.

Judy Bennett Jenkins was married to Frank twice and is the mother of Lindsey. Judy testified that Frank used abusive language toward her during her marriages to Frank in the late seventies. She stated that the allegations in her divorce pleadings that Frank had accused her of infidelity were true. Although she remembered that Frank drank, she could not remember if he drank every night. Judy also testified that Brenda once called her and accused her of lying about the allegations that Frank had abused her and told her that Frank was a wonderful husband and had never done anything like that.

Lindsey Jenkins testified that her father only drank socially in the evening, and said Brenda drank with him. She said that she had seen Brenda mock her father and recalled a few incidents in which Brenda hurt her feelings when she was a child. She also said she heard Brenda speak badly about her father. Lindsey admitted that she was financially dependent on her father.

L.C. Jenkins testified that he lives in the trailer park owned by his brother. He said that normally they would not drink until after working hours at 5:00. He said that he saw Brenda consuming alcohol on the same occasions that he saw Frank drinking and never saw them together in which she was not drinking along with Frank. He testified that he never saw Frank speak or act abusively toward Brenda.

Glinda Jenkins, L.C.'s wife, corroborated much of L.C.'s testimony. She said that Frank and Brenda had engaged in social drinking together for as long as she had known them and had never observed Frank being abusive toward Brenda.

Ray Jenkins, another brother of Frank Jenkins said he had observed Frank and Brenda drink socially. He had never seen Frank verbally or physically abuse Brenda on the occasions that he visited their home.

Lane Jenkins, one of Frank's sons who also lived in the trailer park, testified that he had never seen or heard his father physically or verbally abuse Brenda. He said that alcohol consumption was only socially in the evening, and Frank and Brenda both participated. Lane also contradicted Terry Jenkins' testimony that they did not have alcohol in their home.

Several of the above witnesses testified that Brenda spent a minimal amount of time with Frank during his hospital recuperation lasting several days.

To justify or establish lawful cause for leaving the common dwelling, the withdrawing spouse must make a showing which is substantially equivalent to a cause giving rise to grounds for separation under the former LSA-C.C. art. 138. Habitual intemperance or excesses, cruel treatment or outrages were included among the causes serving as "fault" grounds for separation under former Article 138.

It is well-settled that it is not the quantity of alcohol but rather the extent and habitualness of intoxication that constitutes "habitual intemperance" for purposes of "fault." Proof of intoxication on two or three occasions does not establish habitual intemperance.

In *Broderick*, Chief Justice O'Niell stated that

> habitual intemperance—like ill-treatment of one of the spouses toward the other—is not a just cause for a separation from bed and board unless such habitual intemperance, or such ill treatment, is of such a nature as to render their living together insupportable. And the question whether the habitual intemperance, or ill-treatment, in any given case, is of such a nature as to render the living together of the parties to the marriage unbearable, — or "insupportable" . . . —is a question for the Court, and not for either of the parties to decide. In deciding that question, in any given case, the court must consider the habits of the complaining party, and his or her conduct towards the other party to the marriage.

Regarding acts of cruelty, it has been held that where the conduct of a spouse is calculated permanently to destroy the peace of mind and happiness of the other so as to utterly destroy the objects of matrimony, a judgment of separation may be granted on grounds of cruelty.

The trial court in this case did not state for the record the factual determinations and credibility determinations upon which it based its conclusion that Brenda was not at fault and therefore implicitly finding that she was justified in leaving the house. Nevertheless, we conclude that the trial court must have found that Brenda had just cause for moving out of the matrimonial domicile based upon Frank's habitually excessive drinking and abusive language toward Brenda. The testimony supports a finding that Brenda drank on occasion with Frank, but not to excess and not with the same resultant personality change Frank underwent when he continued to drink. Brenda apparently complained to Frank about the excessive drinking to no avail, and it is obvious he does not believe he has a drinking problem. Frank's habitual, excessive consumption of alcohol followed by abusive language toward his wife seemed calculated to utterly destroy Brenda's peace of mind and happiness rendering the marriage unsupportable. For this reason, we conclude that the trial court did not err in finding that Brenda was without fault in the dissolution of the marriage. . . .

Matthews v. Matthews

184 So. 3d 173 (La. App. 5 Cir. 2015)

Fredericka Homberg Wicker, Judge.

In this divorce action, appellant, Todd Matthews, complains of the trial court's judgment finding appellee, Dawn Rogers Matthews, free from fault in the dissolution of their marriage and awarding her final periodic spousal support. For the reasons fully discussed herein, we affirm the trial court's judgment. . . .

Discussion and Analysis

. . . .

Freedom from Fault

In his first assignment of error, Mr. Matthews argues that the trial court erred in awarding final periodic spousal support to Ms. Rogers, because Ms. Rogers failed to prove that she was free from fault prior to the filing of the petition for divorce. Mr. Matthews argues that Ms. Rogers' testimony that she smoked marijuana on a daily basis constitutes evidence of habitual intemperance or excess, which is fault precluding an award of final periodic spousal support in her favor. Mr. Matthews asserts that, in awarding final periodic spousal support in favor of Ms. Rogers, the trial court erroneously relied on a finding that Mr. Matthews was at fault in the dissolution of the marriage, rather than a finding that Ms. Rogers was free from fault, as required by La. C.C. arts. 111 and 112. As evidence of the trial court's error, Mr. Matthews cites the trial court's written reasons for judgment, wherein the trial court opined that it "[was] more persuaded that Mr. Matthews' budding relationship and vision of a future with Wendy Barrios was the impetus for his departure from the matrimonial domicile."

Permanent spousal support may only be awarded to a spouse who has not been at fault in the termination of the marriage. . . . Under La. C.C. art. 112, a spouse seeking permanent spousal support has the burden of proving freedom from fault. Fault which will preclude support contemplates conduct or substantial acts of commission or omission by a spouse violative of his or her marital duties or responsibilities. Spouses seeking support need not be perfect to be free from legal fault; rather, to constitute fault which will prohibit a spouse from permanent support, the spouse's conduct must be not only of a serious nature but must also be an independent contributory or a proximate cause of the separation.

The habitual intemperance or excessiveness of a spouse may constitute fault precluding a final spousal support award to that spouse. Though we have traditionally defined "habitual intemperance or excessiveness" in relation to a spouse's alcohol consumption, there is Louisiana jurisprudence affirming a trial court's finding of fault based, in part, on a spouse's marijuana use. . . . In the context of alcohol abuse, we have defined habitual intemperance as "that degree of intemperance from the use of intoxicating liquor which disqualifies the person a great portion of the time from properly attending to business, or which would reasonably inflict a course of great mental anguish upon an innocent party." Applying this same definition in the analogous context of marijuana consumption, the jurisprudence is clear that the consumption must be to such an extent that it substantially interferes with the spouse's marital duties or inflicts great mental anguish upon the other spouse.

Prior to, and during, the hearing on Mr. Matthews' Motion to Set Fault for Trial, Ms. Rogers admitted to smoking marijuana on a daily basis to increase her appetite and counteract her anorexia. Mr. Matthews testified that he was aware of Ms. Rogers' marijuana consumption prior to their marriage and that he was aware that Ms. Rogers continued to smoke marijuana throughout the entirety of their marriage. Though Mr. Matthews testified that he voiced concerns to Ms. Rogers about her marijuana use, he also testified that he never voiced his concerns to anyone other than Ms. Rogers. Ms. Rogers disputed that claim, and testified that she never heard any complaints from Mr. Matthews regarding her marijuana use. Roy Rogers, Ms. Rogers' father and the husband of Mr. Matthews' mother, testified that he had never heard any complaints from Mr. Matthews about Ms. Rogers' marijuana use, nor was he aware that Ms. Rogers smoked marijuana before the commencement of these proceedings.

Moreover, Mr. Matthews admitted that Ms. Rogers performed all of the tasks typically expected of a homemaker, including cleaning the family home, washing clothes, cooking for the family, helping the couple's two children with their homework, and bringing the children to appointments. Mr. Matthews testified that he never disposed of Ms. Rogers' marijuana, never monitored Ms. Rogers' activity with the children, and never filed for divorce prior to the filing of the instant proceeding. Other than Mr. Matthews, the only witness who noted Mr. Matthews' displeasure with Ms. Rogers' marijuana habit was her sister, Nora Dalgo, who testified that she could tell Mr. Matthews did not approve of Ms. Rogers' marijuana use because "he would walk away from it" and she could tell he was not happy with Ms. Rogers because of "the way he walked away."

Regarding the couple's sexual intimacy, Mr. Matthews testified that during the six month period prior to their separation, the instances of sexual intercourse between the couple diminished. Mr. Matthews also admitted that during this time Ms. Rogers was recovering from two surgeries and that during this period he began communicating online with another woman, Wendy Barrios, with whom he eventually began a sexual relationship and with whom he cohabitated at the time of the hearing. During examination related to Wendy Barrios, Mr. Matthews claimed that, though he communicated online with Ms. Barrios prior to the couple's separation, he never met her in person until April 22, the same day on which he moved into her home. Ms. Rogers testified that the only times she denied Mr. Matthews' sexual advances were when he was too intoxicated, which she testified were frequent during the last three years of their marriage. Again, Nora Dalgo provided some corroboration for Mr. Matthews' claim, testifying that Ms. Rogers told her that in the year before their separation the couple was not having sex. However, Ms. Dalgo also testified that Ms. Rogers complained to her about Mr. Matthews' frequent alcohol intoxication.

In its written reasons for judgment, the trial court first noted that Ms. Rogers was credible and sincere, becoming visibly emotional during her testimony, while Mr. Matthews seemed defensive and evasive during portions of his testimony and that, despite his claim that he moved into the home of Wendy Barrios without first meeting her and did not begin a sexual relationship with her until after filing his petition, he failed to call Ms. Barrios to testify to those facts. The trial court found that there was no dispute that Ms. Rogers smoked marijuana daily to increase her appetite, but that all of the testimony established that she was a dutiful wife and mother and that few people were even aware of Ms. Rogers' marijuana use until after the couple's separation. Accordingly, the trial court found that "Ms. [Rogers] has met her burden and is free from fault," and opined that the more likely reason for the dissolution of the marriage was Mr. Matthews' relationship with Wendy Barrios.

In the area of domestic relations, much discretion must be vested in the trial judge and particularly in evaluating the weight of evidence which is to be resolved primarily on the basis of the credibility of witnesses. . . .

Though Ms. Rogers admitted to using marijuana frequently throughout the entirety of the marriage and refusing sexual intercourse with Mr. Matthews at times when he was intoxicated, Mr. Matthews produced little evidence to lend credibility to his claim that these issues caused the dissolution of the marriage. Aside from Mr. Matthews' own testimony, the only corroboration for his claims came from the testimony of Nora Dalgo, who seemed confused several times throughout the proceedings and offered little factual support for her conclusions. The trial court found Ms. Rogers to be a credible witness who was sincere in her testimony and Mr. Matthews to be defensive and evasive during his testimony. We find no manifest error in those determinations.

We do not opine, by way of this decision, on the propriety of marijuana use, nor does our decision reject a spouse's marijuana consumption as a basis for a finding of marital fault that might preclude an award of final periodic spousal support. However, we find no error in the trial court's determination that Ms. Rogers' marijuana consumption was not the proximate cause for the dissolution of the marriage. The testimony elicited at trial established that Ms. Rogers fulfilled her marital duties as a wife and mother, regardless of her marijuana consumption, and Mr. Matthews offered no evidence to the contrary. Moreover, Ms. Rogers frequently used marijuana before and throughout the entirety of the couple's marriage, and Mr. Matthews offered little evidence that he voiced any objection to it until Ms. Rogers sought spousal support. Therefore, we find no error in the trial court's award of final periodic spousal support in favor of Ms. Rogers.

Accordingly, we find this assignment of error lacks merit.

H. Fault: Public Defamation

Only a handful of reported decisions in Louisiana involve public defamation as a fault relative to divorce. As the following cases demonstrate, a claim of fault due to public defamation requires that a spouse show that the alleged defamatory statement was (1) false; (2) made publicly to person to whom the accuser has no legitimate excuse to talk about the subject of the accusations; (3) not made in good faith; and (4) made with malice.

Thibodeaux v. Thibodeaux
525 So. 2d 69 (La. App. 3 Cir. 1988)

Doucet, Judge.

Defendant, Eugene Thibodeaux, appeals from a judgment awarding plaintiff, Ethel Rae Cormier Thibodeaux, permanent periodic alimony at the rate of $150.00 per month. . . .

On appeal defendant contends that the trial court erred in not finding that plaintiff was at fault in causing the dissolution of the marriage, thus precluding her from receiving permanent alimony. . . .

Defendant next contends that the plaintiff publicly defamed him, and under La.C.C. art. 138(4), and the applicable jurisprudence, this constitutes fault sufficient to preclude her from receiving alimony. We will examine the issue of defamation even though, as we have discussed above with reference to alleged cruel treatment (accusations of infidelity), any public defamation could not, we feel, have been considered a serious and independent contributory or proximate cause of the marital breakup.

To establish a public defamation as contemplated in C.C. art. 138(4) it is necessary to prove the alleged defamatory statement was: (1) false; (2) made publicly to a person to whom the accuser has no legitimate excuse to talk about the subject of the accusations; (3) not made in good faith; and (4) made with malice.

As we have previously discussed, plaintiff's accusations were not totally unfounded and her suspicions were justifiably aroused. However, without regard to truth or falsity, there is no evidence that any statements made to others by the plaintiff were made with malice. Plaintiff, a beautician, apparently confided to her fellow beautician her belief that defendant was dating other women. There is nothing in the record to suggest that this was done with malice or was anything other than one person seeking sympathy or advice from another. A fellow employee of defendant testified that while he was working one day plaintiff came and asked him if "that woman" left. On another occasion as this same individual was walking past the parties' residence, plaintiff asked him "what woman Eugene was talking to." Again, we can discern no evidence of malice on the part of the plaintiff in making these vague inquiries and there is nothing to indicate that plaintiff acted other than in good faith. In view of these facts and circumstances and the applicable law and jurisprudence we find no error in the trial court's failure to find fault on the part of the plaintiff on the grounds of public defamation.

Cardinale v. Cardinale
397 So. 2d 54 (La. App. 2 Cir. 1981)

JASPER E. JONES, Judge.

Defendant and plaintiff in reconvention, Janice Lee Cardinale, appeals a judgment denying her a separation from her husband, plaintiff, John W. Cardinale, Jr. We affirm.

Plaintiff sued defendant for a divorce on the grounds of adultery. Plaintiff alleged that on April 12, 1980 defendant was seen with an unnamed white male at the Lost and Found Bar. He also alleged that defendant danced with this man and then met him later at her apartment where at 12:07 a. m. the lights were extinguished until 1:30 a. m.

Defendant denied these allegations and reconvened for a separation on the grounds of public defamation and "of excesses and cruelty."

The trial judge rejected plaintiff's demands for a divorce because he failed to prove defendant committed adultery. He also found defendant failed to show excesses and cruelties as would entitle her to a separation, and that she did not prove public defamation. The trial judge concluded she could not use the allegation of adultery in the divorce petition as a basis for a separation on the grounds of public defamation. . . .

Shortly after the separation between the parties, which occurred April 5, 1980, plaintiff hired private detectives to follow his wife and after plaintiff obtained the report from these investigators he instituted his suit for divorce on the grounds of adultery on April 23, 1980. . . .

The fact that appellant admitted going to a bar with another man and staying there with him for some time before he carried her back to her apartment on the night of the alleged adultery, together with the fact that plaintiff had been forced to trial without having available the investigators whom he employed, are circumstances which we conclude adequately support the trial judge's conclusions that appellant did not establish her cause of action for a separation on the ground of defamation. The fact that plaintiff's attorney failed to subpoena the investigators before trial cannot establish that plaintiff's allegations of adultery were made with malice, nor do these allegations standing alone establish that plaintiff made them with malice.

Judgment is AFFIRMED at defendant's cost.

I. Fault: Post-Separation Fault

Civil Code article 111 provides that, to be entitled to final periodic support, a spouse must be "free from fault prior to the filing of a proceeding to terminate the marriage." In the case of a divorce based on living separate and apart under Civil Code article 103, this can create a tricky issue of timing. Any legal fault—including cruel treatment or adultery—that occurs during a period of living separate and apart but before filing for divorce can preclude a spousal support award. For that reason, it may be advisable for a spouse who anticipates seeking spousal support to seek a divorce under Civil Code article 102, rather than 103.

Brehm v. Brehm

685 So. 2d 377 (La. App. 5 Cir. 1996)

DALEY, Judge.

In this proceeding for permanent alimony, appellant Milton Brehm appeals the trial court's finding that his wife was free from fault in the breakup of their marriage. On appeal, he cites as error the trial court's failure to find that she either abandoned the marital domicile, or that she was guilty of post separation fault. After thorough review of the record and applicable law, we find that the trial court erred in finding Mrs. Brehm free from fault, and reverse the trial court's judgment. . . .

The parties, Mr. Brehm and Carmela Brehm, were married for approximately 30 years, and had four daughters, all of whom were of majority at the time of this divorce suit. The record shows that Mrs. Brehm left the matrimonial domicile in August, 1993. She filed a Rule to Show Cause why Divorce Should Not be Granted and Motion for Permanent Alimony on January 13, 1994. A judgment of divorce was granted on October 24, 1994, reserving the issue of alimony. The trial on alimony took place on August 28–31, 1995. The trial court found that both parties were free from fault in the marriage's breakup. The trial court issued written reasons for judgment, which read as follows:

> Under the provision of Louisiana Civil Code Article 112, the spouse who seeks alimony after divorce must be free of fault in the breakup or dissolution of the marriage. Therefore the issues regarding freedom from fault must be an initial determination in these proceedings and prior to an award of permanent alimony. . . .

> From testimony and evidence presented at trial, the marriage appeared to be a normal and healthy one during the first ten years. However, the testimony varies regarding the stability of the marriage during its later years.

> On one hand there is testimony that Mr. Brehm was a very controlling individual who placed severe limitations on his wife, insofar as things she could and could not do within their own home. There is further testimony that Mrs. Brehm suffered from constant verbal abuse by her husband as well. And that her husband had drawn an imaginary line in their marital bed

which she was forbidden to cross. Overall the testimony suggests that in August of 1993, Mrs. Brehm had reached the breaking point where she could no longer live under such conditions. She had in effect reached the point where she had developed a "Somatiform [sic] Disorder" which affected her mental and physical well being. This condition ultimately forced her to leave the marital domicile according to her testimony.

On the other hand there is testimony that early in the marriage, Mr. Brehm was told by his wife that she no longer loved him. Other testimony suggests that the parties had no visible or unusual problems during the marriage. The parties exercised by walking together and engaged in other various activities together. Their marriage appeared to be a happy and ideal one up until the day Mrs. Brehm left the matrimonial domicile in August of 1993. Although she had previously left the home in July of 1993, she returned within twenty-four hours of leaving.

There is further testimony that during her August departure, Mr. Brehm nor their children knew her whereabouts nor understood her reason for leaving the matrimonial domicile so suddenly. This unannounced departure caused Mr. Brehm to undergo severe stress as a result of not knowing where his wife had gone.

Upon her brief return to the family home, Mrs. Brehm proceeded to break all of the family china and set her wedding dress on fire. The expert testimony suggests that this type of behavior was a symbolic act of seeking release and relief from "marital maladjustment".

This Court finds it inconceivable that the symptoms which were manifested by Mrs. Brehm, according to expert testimony, resulted from a healthy or normal marriage. Obviously, there was a deterioration that took place during the course of this marriage. The Court is unable to determine from the evidence and testimony presented, if the breakup of the marriage is the fault of either of the parties of if perhaps it is merely the result of the everchanging roles, responsibilities, and expectations of spouses who grow apart rather than together as a basic unit of our society.

Therefore, it is the finding of this Court that the defendant, Milton L. Brehm, Jr. as well as the plaintiff, Carmela C. Brehm, are free of fault in causing the dissolution of the marriage.

The appellant argues that the court should have found that Mrs. Brehm abandoned the matrimonial domicile in August of 1993, and was therefore at fault in the marriage's breakup. The appellant further contends that her acts of breaking the china and setting her wedding dress on fire were acts of post-separation cruelty, constituting fault sufficient to preclude her entitlement to permanent alimony. In her appellate brief, Mrs. Brehm argues that any actions by her that would constitute fault should be excused by her mental condition. . . .

POST-SEPARATION FAULT

Next, Mr. Brehm argues that the trial court should have found Mrs. Brehm guilty of post-separation fault: specifically, her acts of breaking the family china and setting her wedding dress on fire in the front yard.

Post-separation fault on the part of one spouse will preclude that spouse from receiving permanent alimony, but in order to preclude an award of permanent alimony, the post-separation fault must be of a magnitude that it would, if standing alone, constitute grounds for divorce.

Approximately one month after the initial separation, Mrs. Brehm notified Mr. Brehm that she was returning to the home to retrieve her clothing and some personal belongings. Prior to her arrival, Mr. Brehm divided up the china and crystal so that she could take her half, and he photographed all the clothing in her dressers and closet. When Mrs. Brehm arrived, she carried out the china and crystal, which she then dropped on the sidewalk in front of the home. At some point she mutilated several family pictures by cutting Mr. Brehm out of the pictures. She found her wedding dress and attempted to set it on fire in the front yard, while Mr. Brehm and at least one of their daughters watched. She then dragged the dress to her sister's house two blocks away, where the fire was put out.

Mrs. Brehm testified that she set the wedding dress on fire because of all her negative feelings regarding her marriage. Dr. Jordan testified that the above acts were symbolic acts regarding her anger and sense of futility about her marriage, and were essentially symbolic acts of wanting to end the relationship. Both the doctor and Mrs. Brehm testified that her acts were not committed with the intent to cause hurt to Mr. Brehm, but were rather a breakdown on her part caused by her anger and extremely negative feelings. The doctor pointed out that Mrs. Brehm destroyed items that belonged to her, not to Mr. Brehm. In the case of the wedding dress, that item is one that many women form a strong sentimental attachment to that men do not. Had she wanted to hurt Mr. Brehm, the doctor said it would have been more likely that she would have destroyed items that belonged solely to him.

We find that Mrs. Brehm's acts do not constitute post-separation fault. They were not committed with the purpose of humiliating or hurting Mr. Brehm. Nor do we find that these acts, on their own, are of such a magnitude that they would constitute grounds for divorce.

Accordingly, we reverse the trial court's judgment, and find that Mrs. Brehm's abandonment of the matrimonial domicile constituted legal fault, precluding her from receiving permanent alimony. The parties are to bear their own costs of this appeal.

REVERSED.

J. Final Periodic Support: Factors to Determine Award

Civil Code article 112 sets forth the factors a court should consider in determining an award of final periodic support. The factors set forth in article 112 are, for the most part, not particularly unique. Many other states have statutes with similar illustrative factors a court should consider in making an award of spousal support.[3] The use of an illustrative list of factors gives courts a considerable amount of latitude in crafting support awards—making litigation unpredictable. This is especially true when spousal support is compared to child support—for which clearer mathematical guidelines exist.

The following cases illustrate some of the factors courts consider in determining the amount and duration of a final spousal support award.

Rhymes v. Rhymes
125 So. 3d. 377 (La. 2013)

KNOLL, Justice.

This final periodic spousal support case presents the *res nova* issue of whether homeschooling of children born of the marriage is a factor the trial court can consider when awarding final support pursuant to La. Civ.Code art. 112. . . .

FACTS

Timothy John Rhymes and Dina Constantin Rhymes, who are both mechanical engineers, were married on September 1, 1990. Dina gave birth to their first child, Lucy Annette Rhymes, on April 13, 1999. At that time, by the parents' mutual consent, Dina stopped working to stay home with the child. On February 3, 2003, the couple's second child, Jack William Rhymes, was born. Perceiving the public school system in Baton Rouge to be inadequate and the private school system too expensive, the parties decided Dina would homeschool the children. Dina has instructed the children since they were five years of age and continued to do so at the time of trial in this matter. . . .

DISCUSSION

The sole issue before this Court is whether homeschooling is a legal factor in determining final support. As this issue is strictly a legal one involving the interpretation of our Civil Code provisions, we review the lower courts' rulings under the de novo standard. Moreover, our analysis is guided by well-established rules of statutory construction. . . .

Significantly, both of these Civil Code provisions [Arts. 111 and 112] focus explicitly on the needs of the moving spouse and the ability of the other to pay, rather than on the needs of the children. In this regard, the statutory provisions on child

---

3. *See, e.g.*, GA. CODE § 19-6-5 (2017); MD. CODE § 11-106 (2017); TENN. CODE § 36-5-121 (2017).

support and custody do not come into play, and the award of final support is controlled by the provisions quoted above, most particularly La. Civ.Code art. 112.

Under its provisions, the trial court must consider all relevant factors as the Louisiana Law Institute's employment of the term "shall" in the first sentence of paragraph B denotes: "The court shall consider all relevant factors in determining the amount and duration of final support." It then goes on to list several factors the court may consider, including such concerns as the health and age of the parties, their earning capacity, and their financial obligations. However, as evident in the clear and unambiguous use of the permissive "may" in the second sentence of paragraph B, this list is merely illustrative, not exhaustive or exclusive, requiring the trial court to consider each individual spouse and his or her corresponding needs and circumstances. Therefore, while homeschooling is not included as a specific factor for consideration, there is no specific legal exclusion of homeschooling as a consideration, and so, it can be considered under the clear and unambiguous provisions of La. Civ. Code art. 112, if it is relevant. The trial court erred as a matter of law in failing to consider homeschooling as a factor given the facts of this case.

Whether it is a relevant factor is to be determined on a case-by-case basis. Much as a court considers the effect of custody upon a party's earning capacity, we find the court may likewise consider the effect the duties and obligations associated with homeschooling have on the earning capacity of the parent undertaking the children's instruction.

In the present case, there is no dispute Dina is free from fault or that Timothy can afford to pay. The contentious issue is whether Dina, a mechanical engineer, is in need of support.

The record evidence undisputedly shows the parties agreed Dina would forego her career as a mechanical engineer to stay home to care for and educate the children. The parties further stipulated the children would continue to be homeschooled by Dina, and the evidence at trial elicited from the court-appointed educational evaluator showed the children were well-educated and thriving in their homeschool environment. The proffered testimony further shows Dina's obligation to homeschool the children has an effect on her earning capacity as she spends approximately 27.5 hours per week on school work—instructing the children in world history, geography, literature, math, physics, language arts, creative expression, handwriting, typing, and German. While Timothy urges his withdrawal of his objection to the continued homeschooling of his children does not equate to his approval of same, it is not disputed Dina continues to homeschool the children by stipulation of the parties as reflected in the record. Therefore, we agree with Judge Conery that Dina's homeschooling should be a factor considered in the determination of her final support award according to La. Civ.Code art. 112.

Accordingly, we vacate the judgments of the lower courts as to this issue only and remand this matter to the District Court to consider homeschooling as a factor in determining final support in this case.

CONCLUSION

In summary, we find a trial court must consider all relevant factors in determining final support. Homeschooling the children of the marriage may be a relevant consideration in this determination. In the present case, we find the District Court erred as a matter of law in failing to consider homeschooling as a factor in the determination of final support for Dina. Accordingly, we vacate the judgments of the lower courts as to this issue only and remand this matter to the District Court for further proceedings consistent with this opinion. . . .

VACATED and REMANDED TO THE DISTRICT COURT.

Pierce v. Pierce

945 So. 2d 908 (La. App. 2 Cir. 2006)

LOLLEY, J.

. . . .

FACTS

Fern and Jimmy Pierce separated after 44 years of marriage. Fern and Jimmy were 65 years old when the divorce was granted, both free of fault, on March 23, 2005. Beginning in 1975, Jimmy, a master plumber, and Fern earned their living from their business, Jimmy L. Pierce Plumbing and Heating Co., Inc., until it ceased to be a formally working corporation in 2001. In 2002, Fern and Jimmy started working for D & J Pierce, Inc., a company which was incorporated by their son and had received assets from the former Jimmy L. Pierce Plumbing and Heating Co., Inc. Due to financial hardship, the son was unable to pay any salary to his parents after March 31, 2005. Although Jimmy retired, he continued to work for his son unpaid and was provided with a truck, gasoline, and a cell phone.

At the time of the trial for spousal support, Jimmy was drawing $1,275.00 per month and Fern was drawing $774.00 per month both from Social Security benefits. The trial court noted that a partition of the couple's assets had not yet occurred. In awarding retroactive interim spousal support the trial court took into consideration Jimmy's earning capacity and awarded Fern the sum of $962.96. However, based on only the current income from Social Security the trial court awarded Fern $425.00 per month in permanent periodic spousal support. Fern now appeals the permanent periodic spousal support award.

LAW AND DISCUSSION

Fern contends that the trial court erred in failing to consider Jimmie's earning capacity and therefore awarded an inadequate sum for permanent periodic spousal support.

Once freedom of fault is established, the basic tests for the amount of spousal support are the needs of that spouse and the ability of the other spouse to pay. The award for final periodic spousal support is governed by La. C.C. art. 112. . . .

The eight specific factors listed in La. C.C. art. 112 are not exclusive. The relative financial positions of the parties and the standard of living during the marriage are not listed in La. C.C. art. 112 but can be relevant factors. Article 112 also limits the amount to not exceed one-third of the obligor's net income. The trial court is vested with great discretion in making post-divorce alimony determinations, and its judgment will not be disturbed absent a manifest abuse of discretion.

Fern argues that the trial court should have considered Jimmy's earning capacity, as it did for interim spousal support, resulting in an increased sum of permanent spousal support. Fern contends that since Jimmy is in good health and continues to work and perform physical labor associated with the work he was doing as a plumber, earning capacity should have been considered.

The trial court questioned Jimmy's ability to maintain an earning capacity given his age, high blood pressure, and retirement status. Since there was no proof of other income, the trial court determined the amount of $425.00 per month based only on his Social Security benefits.

Our review of the record, as noted by the trial court, reveals that Jimmy and Fern Pierce fell onto some hard times due to bad investments while doing business as Jimmy L. Pierce, Plumbing and Heating Co., Inc. resulting in much of their assets being encumbered by a sizable judgment. Furthermore, while the son has been operating the business, other issues arose and he was unable to pay his parents a salary due to the poor financial state of the business. Because a partition of the community assets has not yet occurred, we cannot look to the potential earnings from the various pension and retirement funds alluded to by Jimmy.

It is clear that Fern is in financial need and unable to work in light of her poor health. However, it is also apparent that while Jimmy can work, he is able to do limited physical labor and helps his son oftentimes in a supervisory capacity. The trial court explained that there is no way to determine how long Jimmy could work and did not think it appropriate to impute a salary for the purposes of permanent periodic spousal support. The trial court thoroughly reviewed all factors involved and relevant case law, in addition to extensive factual findings at the conclusion of the hearing. Although we recognize Fern's necessitous circumstances, we do not find that the trial court was manifestly erroneous in awarding $425.00 for permanent periodic spousal support.

CONCLUSION

For the foregoing reasons, we affirm the amount for permanent periodic spousal support set forth by the trial court. Costs of this appeal shall be split equally among the parties.

AFFIRMED.

Drury v. Drury

883 So. 2d 465 (La. App. 2 Cir. 2004)

Drew, J.

Kurt Drury appeals a judgment awarding Betty Jo Drury $600.00 per month in permanent periodic spousal support. We affirm.

FACTS

Betty Jo Drury ("Betty") and Kurt Drury ("Kurt") were married on March 5, 1973. The couple eventually established a matrimonial domicile in Shreveport, Louisiana, where they resided when these proceedings commenced. The couple's only child, Marci Brooks, is of the age of majority. On December 24, 2000, Donald moved out of the matrimonial domicile to pursue a relationship with a woman he had met on the internet. . . .

DISCUSSION

Kurt argues that the trial court erred in imputing Betty with earning potential of $350.00 per month when the evidence showed that she was earning more than that at the time of trial, and that the trial court compounded that error by failing to consider the imputed income in calculating the amount of support it ultimately awarded Betty. Both of these arguments are without merit.

At the time of trial, Betty was 65 years old and had suffered from and had surgery for carpal tunnel syndrome in both hands. She had also suffered from breast cancer in 1998, for which she underwent a mastectomy. In November of 2002, Betty was diagnosed with rheumatoid arthritis in her hands and feet. While she spent most of the marriage caring for the needs of her disabled husband, she did work part-time at Hallmark stocking cards. At the time of trial, Betty was still employed by Hallmark, but had provided her notice of resignation effective May 2, 2003. Betty's decision to retire was due to her continuing health problems, especially the recent arthritis diagnosis. She testified that she had tried to retire several months earlier, but stayed on while a co-worker recovered from hip surgery.

Betty's W-2s for the years 2000, 2001, and 2002 showed that she had an average gross monthly income of $537.16 in 2000, $825.48 in 2001, and $1,055.21 in 2002. Betty explained that the increase in income was a result of her working more hours than she did during the marriage. She testified that she was required to take on the additional work to make ends meet. Nevertheless, the trial court found that Betty would be unable to continue her employment with Hallmark due to her age and ongoing health problems and, thus, declined to attribute her with the income she had been earning from that employment. The trial court did find, however, that she should be able to maintain some form of part-time employment and imputed income to her in the amount of $350.00 per month. . . .

It is axiomatic that in determining a spouse's earning capacity, one of the enumerated factors in La. C.C. art. 112, the court must look to that spouse's age, health, education, and employment experience. After reviewing the entire record and considering the totality of the circumstances, we do not find that the trial court erred in finding that Betty would be unable to continue to earn an income at the same level she had in the three preceding years. Betty was 65 (an age when most people are retiring) and suffered from numerous health problems, described in the testimony of both Betty and her daughter. Her health problems were further confirmed by documentation of the numerous prescription medications Betty was required to take. Continuing the repetitive work associated with her job re-stocking greeting cards for Hallmark would be detrimental to Betty's physical welfare. Accordingly, it was not an abuse of the trial court's discretion to impute Betty with an average monthly income of $350.00 per month on the basis that she could find some form of part-time work which would not aggravate her health problems.

Kurt's contention that the trial court failed to include this $350.00 in Betty's monthly income when calculating the award of final support is without merit. The trial court found that Betty's allowable expenses amounted to $1,816.00 per month. In adding $350.00 per month to Betty's monthly social security income of $905, the trial court would have arrived at a total monthly income of $1,255.00, which is $561.00 less than Betty's monthly expenses. There is no rigid formula by which a final support award is to be made, and we do not find that the award of $600.00 per month was an abuse of the trial court's discretion.

Kurt further argues that the trial court erred in awarding Betty final periodic support when her inability to financially provide for herself is due in part to her imprudent depletion of assets. Specifically, Kurt relies on evidence regarding two events: first, Betty's withdrawal of $20,000.00 from a community account just after the parties' separation and, second, Betty's receipt of $26,000.00 from the sale of a home. Betty testified that some of these funds were donated to her children and her church, and to purchase a vehicle and a home. Kurt argues that the sums donated to her children and church to the detriment of her ability to support herself should preclude her from receiving alimony.

The evidence shows that Betty withdrew $20,000.00 from a community account prior to the parties' physical separation in December of 2000. She then donated $5,000.00 apiece to each of her two children, put $5,000.00 down on the purchase of a Saturn automobile, used some funds to retain an attorney, and gave money to her church.

The evidence also shows that the parties had a community interest in a home located on Booth Drive, with a monthly mortgage note of $538.00. Kurt deeded the property to Betty, who sold it and received approximately $18,000.00 in proceeds. Betty then purchased a cabin on Camp Joy for $22,000.00, for which she made a down payment of $16,000.00 and borrowed an additional $6,000.00. Betty eventually sold the Camp Joy cabin for $26,000.00. The record is unclear as to what her payoff on the Camp Joy cabin was. She then made a down payment of $4,000.00 toward the purchase of a new home on Wells Island and financed approximately $30,000.00 of the purchase price. Her current monthly note on the Wells Island home is $301.00, approximately $235.00 less than the mortgage note on the matrimonial domicile.

A spouse claiming support is required to deplete her liquid assets to some extent before she may be entitled to post-divorce support. In determining the extent of any depletion of assets, the court must apply a rule of reasonableness in light of factors such as the value and liquidity of the assets, ages and health of the parties and their relative ability, education, and work experience. The court must be cautious of the probable long-term effects when contemplating depletion of assets.

The evidence supports the trial court's conclusions that the disposition of assets complained of by Kurt was not unreasonable and that Betty should not be required to deplete her remaining liquid assets before being awarded final support. Betty's use of community funds to replace her vehicle, retain an attorney, and donate money to her children and church was not unreasonable. Betty testified that she put $5,000.00 down on the purchase of an automobile to replace the inoperable vehicle with which she had been left. She then donated a total of $10,000.00 to her children ($5,000 each). She used part of the remainder to retain an attorney, an expense which became necessary as a result of Kurt's actions. As noted by the trial court, one might question whether Betty was the best manager of her money, but the evidence does not support the conclusion that she "squandered" her funds or that her dispositions were made in bad faith.

The record is unclear as to the exact amount of money Betty was left with after the series of transactions that began with the sale of the matrimonial home and ended with her purchase of the Wells Island home. Viewed in a light most favorable to Kurt, Betty could have retained as much as $20,000.00. However, even assuming this to be the case, we find that the trial court did not err in finding that Betty should not be required to deplete these assets. Considering Betty's various medical complications and advancing age, she is likely to encounter various expenses which she will not be able to afford on her monthly social security income and final periodic support. Accordingly, we find this argument to be without merit.

DECREE

At appellant's costs, the judgment is AFFIRMED.

K. Final Periodic Support: Limitation on Award

Unlike interim spousal support, which has no statutory cap, Civil Code article 112 imposes an upper limit on the amount of an award for final periodic support. Generally, "the sum awarded may not exceed one-third of the obligor's net income." A similar limitation appeared in the Code Napoléon and in earlier Louisiana law. Issues can arise, of course, in determining the exact numerical value of the obligor's net income.

Neff v. Neff

162 So. 3d 732 (La. App. 3 Cir. 2015)

GENOVESE, Judge.

. . . .

FACTS AND PROCEDURAL HISTORY

Mr. and Mrs. Neff were married on August 4, 1990, and were granted a judgment of divorce on March 24, 2014. Incidental to the divorce proceedings, Mrs. Neff filed a Rule for Final Spousal Support on March 18, 2014, which came before the trial court on July 7, 2014. Following a hearing, the trial court issued written reasons for judgment, finding Mrs. Neff to be free from fault in the dissolution of the marriage and awarding her final periodic spousal support of $750.00 per month retroactive to March 18, 2014. Mr. Neff appeals. . . .

LAW AND DISCUSSION

Louisiana Civil Code Article 111 provides authority for a trial court's award of final periodic spousal support. Louisiana Civil Code Article 112(A) governs how such a determination is to be made by a trial court and provides that "[w]hen a spouse has not been at fault prior to the filing of a petition for divorce and is in need of support, based on the needs of that party and the ability of the other party to pay, that spouse may be awarded final periodic support" in accordance with La. Civ.Code art. 112(C). . . .

Also to be considered is Mr. Neff's ability to pay. According to the record, Mr. Neff has remarried and has another child. His current living situation includes maintaining credit card debt and the payment of two car notes, which he is able to do while his current wife does not work. Mr. Neff earns $6,344.00 per month and receives $960.00 in disability for a total annual income of over $87,000.00. . . .

Mr. Neff also complains of the $750.00 per month award in his third assignment of error. Specifically, he contends that the amount is greater than one-third of his net income, in violation of La. Civ.Code art. 112(D). Mr. Neff asserts that his monthly gross income is $7,304.00, from which $2,486.35 is deducted. He also itemizes his monthly expenses as $8,696.17, thereby creating a deficiency of $1,392.17. Therefore, he concludes that one-third of his net income is actually a negative number.

As Mrs. Neff notes, Mr. Neff's own Income and Expense Affidavit reflects a $4,817.58 net income. Additionally, if "typical[,]" his paychecks substantiate nearly $10,000.00 in overtime pay. Mrs. Neff concludes that Mr. Neff is making $76,128.00 per year, plus he receives $11,520.00 in disability payments per year, for a total of $87,648.00 per year. Mrs. Neff compares and contrasts this amount to her income of $20,800 per year "if she only worked her daytime job[.]"

Based upon the record, we do not find the amount of $750.00 per month in final periodic spousal support to be excessive, especially considering the trial court's express and legitimate reliance on Mr. Neff's lack of credibility. The record is void of corroborating proof of his purported expenses and contains significant contradictory information as to his income. We find no abuse of the trial court's discretion in its award of $750.00 per month of final periodic spousal support for Mrs. Neff. We likewise find that said amount is not in excess of one-third of Mr. Neff's income in violation of La. Civ.Code art. 112. . . .

AFFIRMED AS AMENDED.

Jones v. Jones
804 So. 2d 161 (La. App. 2 Cir. 2001)

GASKINS, J.

The plaintiff, John H. Jones, appeals a trial court judgment ordering him to pay final periodic spousal support to the defendant, Evelyn J. Jones, in the amount of $2,000.00 per month. In the alternative, he claims that the amount of alimony is factually and legally insupportable. We affirm in part and amend in part the trial court judgment. . . .

AMOUNT OF FINAL PERIODIC SUPPORT

Mr. Jones argues that the trial court award of $2,000.00 per month in final periodic support is excessive. He contends that this amount exceeds one-third of his net monthly income, a result prohibited by La. C.C. art. 112(B). He also claims that the award exceeds the needs of Mrs. Jones and takes into account expenses which may not be claimed in awarding final periodic support. These arguments have merit.

La. C.C. art. 112B provides that the sum awarded for final periodic support shall not exceed one-third of the obligor's net income. Mr. Jones correctly argues that the trial court award of $2,000.00 per month exceeds one-third of his net income. The trial court stated that the award of final periodic spousal support was based upon Mr. Jones' earnings in 2000. His W-2 form shows income of $94,578.03. Mr. Jones' pay records show that in 2000, he had tax deductions in the amount of $31,541.32, leaving a net income of $63,036.71. His monthly net income was $5,253.06. One-third of this amount is $1,751.02. This is the maximum amount of final periodic support that may be awarded in this case. Therefore, the trial court award of $2,000.00 per month in final periodic spousal support exceeds the maximum and must be amended. . . .

AFFIRMED IN PART; AMENDED IN PART; AFFIRMED AS AMENDED.

L. Modification and Termination of Spousal Support Award

See LA. CIV. CODE art. 114–17.

States vary considerably on the rules governing the duration and modification of spousal support awards.

Modification. As a general matter, spousal support awards may be later modified by a court if there has been a change in circumstances. Generally, a significant increase or decrease in either (1) the ability of the obligor to pay; or (2) the needs of the obligee will be relevant to a modification. Of course, the applicable burden of proof and other details vary by state. Louisiana allows modification (or termination) when there has been a material change in circumstances. However, Civil Code article 114 provides that the "subsequent remarriage of the obligor spouse shall not constitute a change of circumstances." This reflects a policy decision that the obligor should not be able to reduce his or obligations to a first spouse by contracting a subsequent marriage. Not all states have such an inflexible view. Article 116 also allows contractual modification and waiver of final spousal support—a topic that is taken up in the next section.

Termination. Support awards are often limited in duration. Nonetheless, many states have additional default rules pertaining to termination. The three most common causes for termination are (1) death of a party, (2) remarriage of a party, and (3) cohabitation of the obligee.

Most states agree that remarriage of the obligee terminates the support obligation.[4] A number of states, however, expressly permit the parties to deviate from this rule by private agreement, by court order, or by both.[5] Louisiana Civil Code article 115 makes it clear that remarriage of the obligee causes an automatic termination of the spousal support award—no judicial decree is needed. The theoretical justification for terminating spousal support upon the remarriage of the obligee is that the new spouse has assumed the support obligation. Interestingly, Planiol did not support the automatic termination rule: "It should not be assumed that alimony ceases by operation of law in the case of a second marriage, upon the theory that the obligation to succor devolves upon the new spouse."[6] As is discussed in more detail in the next section, Article 116 allows contractual modification of final spousal support (but not interim support).

Not all obligees remarry right away (or ever). Some of them, nonetheless, proceed to cohabitate with another person with whom they have a romantic relationship. Most states will view a subsequent cohabitation by the obligee as grounds for modification or termination of the support obligation, but the details vary. In California, for example, cohabitation creates a rebuttable presumption that there is a decreased need for spousal support.[7] In Virginia, courts are supposed to terminate spousal support if there is evidence of cohabitation for one year or more, unless there is evidence that

---

4. *See, e.g.,* MD. CODE FAMILY LAW § 11-108 (2017); VA. CODE § 20-110 (2017).

5. *See, e.g.,* CAL. FAM. CODE § 4337 (2017); HAW. REV. STAT. § 580-51 (2017); N.D. CENT. CODE § 14-05-24.1 (2017).

6. 1 MARCEL PLANIOL, TREATISE ON THE CIVIL LAW § 1261-4 (Louisiana State Law Institute trans. West 1959).

7. CAL. FAM. CODE § 4323 (2017).

termination would be unconscionable.[8] A handful of states take the approach adopted by Louisiana, which permits termination provided there are facts sufficient to prove cohabitation. Article 115 provides that the obligation of support "is extinguished upon . . . a judicial determination that the obligee has cohabited with another person of either sex in the manner of married persons."

Death of a party receives varying treatment. In a number of states—including Louisiana—death of either party typically terminates the award.[9] Some states will nonetheless allow the automatic termination rule to be modified by court order, by agreement of the parties or by both.[10] A few states take the opposite approach and allow support obligations to survive death in some instances. In Tennessee, for example, lump sum alimony awards survive the death of the obligor.[11]

Almon v. Almon, below, illustrates some of the factors a Louisiana court will look to in order to decide whether an obligee is cohabitating with another person in the manner of married persons. *Williams v. Poore* is a modification case that illustrates, again, the application of the factors set forth in Article 112.

Almon v. Almon

943 So. 2d 1113 (La. App. 1 Cir. 2006)

WHIPPLE, J.

This matter is before us on appeal by John Almon from a judgment of the trial court dismissing his rule to terminate permanent spousal support with prejudice. For the following reasons, we affirm. . . .

DISCUSSION

The appellate court's review of factual findings is governed by the manifest error-clearly wrong standard. The two-part test for the appellate review of a factual finding is: 1) whether there is a reasonable factual basis in the record for the finding of the trial court; and 2) whether the record further establishes that the finding is not manifestly erroneous. . . .

Louisiana Civil Code article 115, which governs the extinguishment of spousal support obligations provides, as follows: "The obligation of spousal support is extinguished upon the remarriage of the obligee, the death of either party, or a judicial determination that the obligee has cohabited with another person of either sex in the manner of married persons."

---

8. Va. Code § 20-109 (2017).

9. *See, e.g.*, Md. Code Family Law § 11-108 (2017).

10. *See, e.g.*, Me. Rev. Stat. § 951-A (2017); Ohio Rev. Code § 3105.18 (2017); Or. Rev. Stat. § 3105.18 (2017); Wash. Rev. Code § 26.09.170 (2017).

11. Tenn. Code § 36-5-121.

Article 115 was last amended by Acts 1997, No. 1078, § 1, effective January 1, 1998. As discussed in *Arnold v. Arnold*, 2002-0819 (La.App. 1st Cir.4/2/03), 843 So.2d 1167, 1171, prior to the application of 1997 La. Acts No. 1078, article 112(A)(4) provided that "[p]ermanent periodic alimony . . . terminates if the spouse to whom it has been awarded remarries or enters into open concubinage." However, the phrase "open concubinage" is no longer used in the Louisiana Civil Code to identify a manner of extinguishment of the spousal support obligation. Instead, with regard to the modification or extinguishment of a spousal support obligation, LSA-C.C. art. 115 requires "a judicial determination that the obligee has cohabited with another person of either sex in the manner of married persons."

According to Revision Comment (e), the new language used in article 115, i.e., "cohabited with another person . . . in the manner of married persons[,] means to live together in a sexual relationship of some permanence . . . It does not mean just acts of sexual intercourse." The phrase further "obviates the difficulties of proving absence of concealment" inherent in the term "open concubinage." See LSA-C.C. art. 115, Revision Comment (e); see also *Arnold*, 843 So.2d at 1171.

In rendering its findings, the trial court stated as follows:

> Article 115 states cohabitated (sic) in the manner of married persons. I went to Webster's Dictionary and looked up cohabit and cohabiting. The archaic version is to dwell or abide in company. The second definition says to dwell or live together as husband and wife. In the United States, at the common law, marriage is presumed when a man and woman have cohabitated permanently together being reputed by those who know them to be husband and wife and admitting the relationship. The presumption is removed if the relationship is proved to have been an-of illicit origin.

> The evidence shows clearly that Mr. Perine came to the house of Mrs. Almon, her testimony is originally as a friend to help her out with a child who was anorexic and this man would go feed the child. Then she said she felt some obligation to him, apparently when he needed a place to live, because of what he had done to help her. She freely admitted that he slept in her house, but she says he slept downstairs and kept his clothing in the garage. And she freely admitted that they engaged in sex occasionally.

> I've already said that my view of marital sex is archaic, and it is. [Counsel for Mr. Almon]'s example of if somebody went on a cruise and had sex, that was not living like married people. What if they went on a cruise every weekend, would that still not be married people or what if you went on a cruise with a different partner every weekend? I mean, I just think that sex in this country has become casual, not to my liking, but apparently it has become casual.

> According to Webster and the common law, and I know we're a civil law jurisdiction, but you have to hold yourself out to be a married person. And

I don't think that happened here. And having basically no case law from Louisiana to go on, I'm going to find that while Mrs. Almon had this man to share her house, not necessarily her bedroom, and occasionally had sex with him, that it did not rise to a manner of married persons, and I'm going to deny the rule to terminate permanent alimony.

On appeal, Mr. Almon argues the trial court misinterpreted and misapplied the provisions of LSA-C.C. art. 115. In support, he cites to an isolated statement by the trial court in its oral reasons, "you have to hold yourself out to be a married person," and argues that the article does not require proof that Mrs. Almon held herself out as being married to the person with whom she is living in order to be deemed to be "living in the manner of a married person."

After a complete reading of the trial court's reasons, we find that Mr. Almon has taken this statement out of context. A reading of the reasons in their entirety shows that the trial court correctly applied the standard set forth in the article. Moreover, we find the record supports the court's factual finding "that while Mrs. Almon had this man to share her house, not necessarily her bedroom, and occasionally had sex with him, that it did not rise to a manner of married persons." Thus, the trial court properly denied the rule to terminate permanent spousal support.

Mr. Almon further argues that . . . "living together in the manner of married persons simply means to 'live together in a sexual relationship of some permanence.'" While living together in a sexual relationship of some permanence is certainly a factor, the statute does not provide for extinguishment of a spousal obligation, where, as here, the evidence establishes only random acts of sexual intercourse. After thorough review of Arnold and Booth, we find Mr. Almon's reliance on these cases misplaced, as the instant case is factually distinguishable.

At the hearing, Mrs. Almon testified that Mr. Terry Perine lived in her home for approximately one year, from the latter part of 2003 to December of 2004, and also for a few months prior to 1999 when Mr. Perine was released from a rehab program, because he had nowhere else to stay. Mrs. Almon testified that she allowed him to reside there because she felt obligated to Mr. Perine and felt that she owed him a "big favor" because he had helped Mrs. Almon by coming to feed her daughter, who suffered from anorexia, when Mrs. Almon was working at night. She stated that when circumstances arose that Mr. Perine had nowhere else to stay, she allowed him to live in her home. In return, although Mrs. Almon did not insist that Mr. Perine pay a specific amount as rent, Mr. Perine agreed to help Mrs. Almon pay for her monthly medication, pay for groceries, and perform repairs and small jobs around her home. Mrs. Almon testified that on many occasions, Mr. Perine would tell her "This is my last job, then I'm going to leave." Mrs. Almon stated that initially she would reply that that was fine with her. However, Mrs. Almon further testified that she became dissatisfied with the financial arrangements in return for housing after he expressed his desire that she "give him part of the house" in return for the repairs he made. In explaining why he had resided on the premises for the time period at issue, she stated that Mr. Perine would always begin working on a new repair project in the house despite knowing that Mrs. Almon did not want him to continue to live there.

Mrs. Almon testified that during the time in question, Mr. Perine did not share Mrs. Almon's bedroom. He did not keep his belongings, i.e., clothes and toiletries, in her bedroom. Instead, during the time he lived at Mrs. Almon's home, he slept downstairs and kept his clothing in the garage in a laundry basket. Mrs. Almon testified that she did not want or allow Mr. Perine to share her bedroom, and, in fact, kept an outside lock on her bedroom door to keep Mr. Perine out of her bedroom. Mrs. Almon described one occasion wherein she was forced to file a complaint with the police after Mr. Perine attempted to cut through the lock on her bedroom door. This incident occurred shortly before Mrs. Almon terminated their financial arrangements and asked Mr. Perine to move out of the residence.

Although Mrs. Almon testified that they had engaged in sexual relations on occasion at the commencement of his residency, she never committed to having any type of romantic relationship with him because they were not involved in such a relationship. Mrs. Almon stated that they stopped having sexual relations early on because there was no affection involved in it. Mrs. Almon further testified that she and Mr. Perine did not "date," they were not an "item," and they did not attend parties or social functions together as a "couple." Mrs. Almon did not consider or introduce Mr. Perine as her "boyfriend," nor did she consider them a "couple." Mrs. Almon testified that they never discussed marriage and stated that she had not engaged in nor expected to have any long-term or other relationship with Mr. Perine, other than noted above.

A thorough review of the record and testimony contained therein reveals that Mrs. Almon and Mr. Perine did not "live together in a sexual relationship of some permanence" as contemplated by the statute. See LSA-C.C. art. 115, Revision Comment (e). Moreover, although Mrs. Almon testified that she and Mr. Perine had engaged in sexual relations on occasion in the early part of his residing in her home, "cohabited . . . in the manner of married persons," does not mean just acts of sexual intercourse. Considering the record in its entirety, the record does not support a finding that Mrs. Almon and Mr. Perine were cohabiting with one another "in the manner of married persons" as required by LSA-C.C. art. 115 to warrant the termination of Mr. Almon's permanent spousal support obligation.

Accordingly, we find no error in the trial court's factual findings and determinations herein, which are amply supported by the record.

CONCLUSION

Based on the above and foregoing reasons, the judgment of the trial court dismissing Mr. Almon's rule to terminate permanent spousal support with prejudice is affirmed. Costs of this appeal are assessed against Mr. Almon.

AFFIRMED.

Williams v. Poore

55 So. 3d 953 (La. App. 4 Cir. 2011)

Patricia Rivet Murray, Judge.

. . . .

FACTUAL AND PROCEDURAL BACKGROUND

On September 14, 1998, Mr. Poore and Ms. Williams were divorced after thirty-three years of marriage. At the time of the divorce, the parties had two major children. On the same date as the divorce, the parties entered into a consent judgment that provided for Mr. Poore to pay Ms. Williams permanent spousal support in the amount of $1,500.00 per month. . . . [Mr. Poore paid until 2009. Mr. Poore now argues a change in circumstances entitles him to a reduction.]

DISCUSSION

The principal issue on appeal is whether the trial court erred in modifying the final spousal support award. . . .

Material change in circumstances

The party seeking to modify a spousal support award has the burden of proving "a material change in circumstances of one of the parties between the time of the previous award and the time of the rule for modification of the award." La. R.S. 9:311(A); La. C.C. art. 114. The party must show either "a change in the obligee's needs or the obligor's ability to pay." A trial court's determination of whether a material change in circumstances has been established will not be disturbed on appeal absent an abuse of discretion.

According to the official revision comments to Article 114, "[t]he court should make the determination whether periodic support will be modified or terminated based on the changed circumstances of either party." In so doing, "[t]he court should consider the relevant factors listed in Article 112. . . ."

In this case, the trial court was presented with evidence regarding Mr. Poore's income and Ms. Williams' needs and found that Mr. Poore met his burden of establishing a material change in circumstances. The trial court gave the following reasons for its finding:

> During Mr. Poore's Rule to Modify, he testified that he lost his job with Carson Wagonlit Travel. Mr. Poore stated that he worked for Carlson Wagonlit for nineteen years and received a severance package in the area of $41,000.00. Mr. Poore recently obtained employment, earning $60,000.00 per year. Mr. Poore introduced an income and expense statement, demonstrating a monthly net income of $6,945.17. He reported that his monthly expenses total $7,788.95. A majority of Mr. Poore's monthly expenses are related to outstanding credit card bills. He stated that he incurred these bills as a result of helping the parties' adult son, Christopher Poore, who had and continues to have financial trouble.

Ms. Williams testified that she has not worked in ten (10) years. She reported that she is on medication which prevents her from working. Ms. Williams stated that her sole source of support is the $1,500.00 spousal support payment. She attached a monthly income and expense statement dated November 30, 2009. At that time, she reported monthly expenses of $2,607.00. Ms. Williams reported her total assets to be $244,900.00. Ms. Williams indicated that she is also helping their son. She stated that Christopher plans on moving in with her in the near future. Ms. Williams acknowledged that Mr. Poore has helped their son in the past.

On appeal, Ms. Williams contends that Mr. Poore failed to prove a material change in circumstances for two reasons. First, she contends that he failed to prove a decrease in his income by a legal certainty. Rather, she contends that when he filed the rule to modify the spousal support (November 2009) he was actually making more money than when he entered the consent judgment (August 1998). Although Mr. Poore was unemployed when he filed his rule to modify, he received a severance package equal to six months of his prior salary, which was $98,000.00 a year. Moreover, he recommenced employment in January 2010 earning $60,000.00 a year. As a result, she contends that when he filed his rule to modify his annual income actually was equal to at least $98,000.00, which is more than he was making when the consent judgment was entered.

Second, Ms. Williams contends that the trial court erred in considering Mr. Poore's financial support of Christopher Poore, the parties' major son, as a living expense. In support, she cites the well-settled jurisprudence holding that the financial support of a major child is not considered a living expense of a party for purposes of determining spousal support. Regardless, she emphasizes that Mr. Poore testified that he was no longer financially supporting Christopher Poore when he filed his rule to modify.

Mr. Poore counters that the trial court correctly found a material change in circumstances based on the evidence regarding his loss of his job, his monthly income and expenses, and his financial troubles as a result of helping his major son. He further contends that the trial court also correctly considered that Ms. Williams had not worked in ten years and correctly concluded that she had an earning capacity because she was not disabled in such a way as to prevent her from working.

In finding Mr. Poore met his burden of establishing a material change in circumstances, the trial court weighed the credibility of the witnesses — Mr. Poore and Ms. Williams — and properly considered all of the pertinent Article 112 factors. Insofar as Mr. Poore's income, the record reflects his present income at Travelcorp is only $60,000.00 a year. Although he received a one-time severance from Carlson when he was terminated from his previous employment, the severance is not part of his current income. Moreover, he used a large portion of the severance to catch up on the arrearages that he owed Ms. Williams, which in September 2009 totaled $8,750.00. We further note that Mr. Poore testified that since 1998 his expenses have dramatically increased and that his current monthly expenses exceed his current monthly income.

The relevance of Mr. Poore's support of his major son was that it was identified as the primary cause of Mr. Poore's large credit card balances. However, as Ms. Williams acknowledges, when Mr. Poore filed his motion to modify the spousal support, he was no longer financially supporting their major son. At the time of the hearing, Ms. Williams testified that she was providing financial support to their son. Given both parties acknowledge that they have each financially supported their major son, this factor, even if considered, is neutral.

One of the Article 112 factors the trial court could have considered was the age of the parties. Given her age—sixty-three at the time of the hearing—Ms. Williams acknowledged that she was eligible to apply for Social Security benefits. However, she testified that she elected to wait until age sixty-eight or seventy in order to collect higher Social Security benefits. On the other hand, one of sources of Mr. Poore's current income is his Social Security benefits.

Another Article 112 factor the trial court could have considered is the lengthy duration of the marriage—thirty-three years. Although this factor initially may have supported a spousal support award to Ms. Williams to help her adjust, we find, as Mr. Poore asserted in his motion, that "[t]he period of time for the recipient [Ms. Williams] to adjust to the divorce is long past due." In this regard, we note that both parties acknowledged that Mr. Poore has paid Ms. Williams approximately $200,000.00 in spousal support over the last decade.

In sum, the record reflects that the trial court, in accord with La. C.C. art. 112, considered all the relevant factors testified to in court by the parties and correctly concluded that Mr. Poore met his burden of establishing a material change in circumstances. However, "[a] finding of change in circumstances does not automatically result in a modification or termination of support." Rather, the effect of a finding of a change in circumstances is to "shift the burden to the party opposing the modification or termination of alimony to prove need and the relevant [Article] 112 factors." The next issue we must address is whether, as Ms. Williams contends, the trial court erred in determining her need was only $700.00 per month and that she had the ability to work.

Need and ability to work

Ms. Williams contends that she established her need through her testimony that she was unemployed, that her principal source of income was the spousal support of $1,500.00 a month, and that her expenses totaled $2,607.00 a month. She contends that the trial court's findings that her need was only $700.00 a month and that she was able to work were erroneous in two respects.

First, she contends that the trial court erred in relying on the fact she had total assets of $244,900.00. In support, she cites the principle that it is unjust to punish a former spouse for her prudent handling of her financial affairs. Contrary to Ms. Williams' contention, the trial court's consideration of the fact that she had significant assets was not improper. A parties' means, including the liquidity of those means, is an Article 112 factor. . . .

Second, Ms. Williams contends that the trial court erred in excluding from evidence her exhibit — an uncertified letter from her treating physician, Dr. Billings — regarding her mental condition and inability to work. The trial court correctly ruled that the uncertified correspondence from Ms. Williams' treating physician could not be introduced into evidence. In so ruling, the trial court expressly indicated that if the correspondence was certified it would have been admissible. Given the lack of proper evidence of her inability to work, the trial court found that "Ms. Williams is not disabled in such a manner that would prevent her from working."

The trial court's ruling excluding the uncertified letter and imputing income to Ms. Williams for purposes of modifying the spousal support award is supported by the jurisprudence. In *Williams*, supra, this court outlined the following pertinent principles:

- "A spouse claiming the inability to work for the purpose of computing alimony bears the burden of proving that disability by a preponderance of the evidence;"
- The spouse's "own self-serving testimony regarding his or her inability to work is insufficient proof of the inability;"
- The spouse claiming such an inability must present corroborating evidence, such as a certified doctor's report or a doctor's expert testimony;
- "Except perhaps in a case where the spouse's obvious mental or physical disability renders that spouse impaired, a trial court abuses its discretion in finding that a spouse is unable to work on the basis of that spouse's own self-serving testimony alone;"
- When a non-working spouse fails to establish an inability to work, the trial court is required to impute some income to that spouse; and
- "In determining the amount of income to impute to such a non-working spouse claiming alimony, the trial court should consider that spouse's employment history, physical and mental health, age, and education. La. C.C. art. 112."

In this case, Ms. Williams' testimony that she was diagnosed as bipolar and manic depressive was insufficient to establish a disability that rendered her unable to work. Nor was this an obvious mental or physical disability. Given Ms. Williams' failure to introduce proper evidence of her inability to work, the trial court was required to impute income to her by considering the relevant Article 112 factors. Considering all the relevant factors, including the assets of the parties and Ms. Williams' earning capacity, the record supports the trial court's reduction of Ms. Williams' spousal support to $700.00 per month.

DECREE

For the forgoing reasons, the judgment of the trial court is affirmed.

AFFIRMED.

Chapter 10

Matrimonial Agreements

Louisiana enjoys a unique historical acceptance of marriage contracts. As a result of Louisiana's French and Spanish legal heritage, marriage contracts have been recognized and widely accepted since the 1700s. Both the 1808 and 1870 codifications expressly allowed marriage contracts and regulated their form and content. Louisiana law continues to expressly approve of a variety of marriage contracts. In contrast, common law jurisdictions traditionally viewed marriage contracts less favorably. Many common law jurisdictions accepted and enforced marriage contracts regulating the distribution of property upon the death of a spouse—and particularly contracts that waived one spouse's rights in the estate of the other spouse. In the case of second marriages, for example, these contracts presumably facilitated family harmony by protecting the inheritance rights of the children of the first marriage. However, common law jurisdictions treated marriage contracts regulating the relationship between the spouses or division of property at divorce with overt hostility. Unlike Louisiana, most states lacked statutes specifically addressing marriage contracts that were effective at some time earlier than the death of a spouse. Moreover, many courts believed these types of marriage contracts violated public policy by encouraging divorce. As views of marriage, divorce, and family changed, marriage contracts gained greater acceptance in common law jurisdictions.

Responding to these changes and concerns of lack of uniformity of state treatment of marriage contracts, the Uniform Law Commission drafted the Uniform Premarital Agreement Act (UPAA) in 1983. At least twenty-six jurisdictions have enacted some version of the UPAA. The UPAA grants spouses broad freedom to contract regarding the economic consequences of marriage. However, many substantive requirements and evidentiary burdens of the UPAA are more onerous than the laws in Louisiana. On the whole, the UPAA continues to treat marriage contracts with a greater degree of suspicion than Louisiana law.

A. Form and Timing Requirements

See La. Civ. Code art. 2325–33; UPAA § 2.

Louisiana Civil Code article 2331 requires that matrimonial agreements be executed in the form of an authentic act or an act under private signature duly acknowledged. If a matrimonial agreement gratuitously re-characterizes separate property as community property, then it most likely must be in the form of an authentic act.

Consistent with Louisiana's public records doctrine, Louisiana Civil Code article 2332 provides that a matrimonial agreement is not effective with respect to third parties until it is filed for recordation in the appropriate conveyance records. Unfortunately, no state-wide registration is available and spouses owning property in multiple parishes may have to record their matrimonial agreement in multiple locations. Article 2332 explains that the agreement is "effective toward third persons as to immovable property, when filed for registry in the conveyance records of the parish in which the property is situated and as to movables when filed for registry in the parish or parishes in which the spouses are domiciled." Spouses entering into post-nuptial agreements face additional burdens. Article 2329 requires court approval for post-nuptial agreements that modify or terminate the legal regime of community property. Article 2329 requires a "joint petition and a finding by the court that this serves their best interests and that they understand the governing principles and rules." Spouses are free to enter into a post-nuptial agreement that opts in to the default matrimonial regime without the necessity of court approval. Article 2329 also contains an exception for married couples who move into Louisiana from another state: "During the first year after moving into and acquiring a domicile in this state, spouses may enter into a matrimonial agreement without court approval."

The UPAA simply requires that the agreement "be in writing and signed by both parties." As the comment to § 2 of the UPAA explains, however, many states impose additional requirements that are similar to Louisiana's notary requirement. The UPAA does not address the topic of post-nuptial agreements. A more recent model act — the Uniform Premarital and Marital Agreements Act (the UPMAA) does address post-nuptial agreements and imposes essentially the same requirements as the UPAA imposes on premarital agreements. To date, only a couple of states have enacted the UPMAA.

Rush v. Rush and *Muller v. Muller* illustrate the importance of meeting the form requirements prior to the actual marriage. As is shown by *Dornemann v. Dornemann*, however, common law jurisdictions are sometimes more lenient with the timing of the form requirements.

Rush v. Rush

115 So. 3d 508 (La. App. 1 Cir. 2013)

KUHN, J.

This appeal was taken by appellant, Lynn E. Peuschold, from a judgment declaring a purported matrimonial agreement to be valid as to form. For the following reasons, we convert this appeal into a supervisory writ, reverse the trial court judgment, and render declaratory judgment in favor of appellant.

PROCEDURAL BACKGROUND

On January 30, 1993, Ms. Peuschold, and appellee, Randall C. Rush, signed a matrimonial agreement purporting to establish a separation of property regime between them during their contemplated marriage. The document was executed before a notary, but was not signed by witnesses. Thereafter, the parties were married on February 18, 1993, and two children were born of the marriage.

On August 31, 2011, Mr. Rush filed a petition for divorce in which he alleged that the parties were separate in property due to the prenuptial matrimonial agreement they executed. On September 30, 2011, over eighteen years after the parties married, Mr. Rush executed an acknowledgement by authentic act of his signature on the 1993 matrimonial agreement. In response to Mr. Rush's request for admission of facts, Ms. Peuschold admitted that she signed the matrimonial agreement, but stated that her response was not "deemed an acknowledgement of any nature or kind under oath."

In her answer to the divorce petition, Ms. Peuschold denied that a separate property regime existed, and she filed a reconventional demand asserting that the matrimonial agreement was invalid as to form. Additionally, on January 13, 2012, she filed a petition for declaratory judgment seeking a declaration that the matrimonial agreement was invalid and that a community of acquets and gains existed between the parties. Ms. Peuschold asserted that the agreement was invalid as to form because it was neither an authentic act due to the lack of witnesses, nor was it an act under private signature duly acknowledged by both spouses. She further alleged that the agreement was invalid due to vices of consent.

At a hearing limited to the issue of the alleged vices of form, the trial court considered the dispositive issue to be whether Ms. Peuschold's admission that she signed the matrimonial agreement operated as an acknowledgement of the agreement under La. C.C. art. 1836, which sets forth the manner in which private acts may be acknowledged. Concluding that it did, the trial court rendered judgment that the matrimonial agreement was valid as to form. Without reasons, the trial court designated the judgment as a final judgment pursuant to La. C.C.P. art. 1915(B)(1). Ms. Peuschold now appeals, alleging in three assignments of error that the trial court erred in finding the matrimonial agreement valid as to form. . . .

VALIDITY OF THE MATRIMONIAL AGREEMENT

Ms. Peuschold argues that, in finding the matrimonial agreement valid as to form, the trial court ignored the requirements of La. C.C. art. 2329. Specifically, she argues that La. C.C. art. 2331, which sets forth the form requirements for matrimonial agreements, must be read in conjunction with the temporal requirement of Article 2329 that spouses who wish to enter into a matrimonial agreement during marriage modifying or terminating a matrimonial regime must obtain court approval. Since the matrimonial agreement at issue was not acknowledged until over eighteen years after the parties' marriage and no court approval was obtained, she asserts it was invalid as to form. We agree.

Under Articles 2329 and 2331, parties may enter into a matrimonial agreement either before or during marriage concerning all matters not prohibited by public policy. Article 2331 requires that such matrimonial agreements be "made by authentic act or by an act under private signature duly acknowledged by the spouses." Additionally, although Article 2331 does not impose a temporal requirement for the spousal acknowledgements, Article 2329 requires that, in order for spouses to enter into a matrimonial agreement that modifies or terminates a matrimonial regime during marriage, the spouses must file a joint petition and obtain court approval for the agreement.

Since both Articles 2329 and 2331 deal with the execution of matrimonial agreements, they must be read in pari materia. *See* La. C.C. art. 13. When two statutes can be reconciled by a fair and reasonable interpretation, the court must read the statutes so as to give effect to each. Further, due to the strong legislative policy against spouses giving up their community rights during marriage without judicial supervision, the formalities of Article 2329 must be construed stricti juris.

In the instant case, it is undisputed that the matrimonial agreement is not in authentic form due to the absence of witnesses. *See* La. C.C. art. 1833. Nevertheless, the trial court accepted Mr. Rush's argument that the 1993 matrimonial agreement was valid as to form under Article 2331 because it was an act under private signature duly acknowledged by both spouses, Mr. Rush's acknowledgement being an authentic act executed on September 30, 2011, and Ms. Peuschold's acknowledgement consisting of her admission during discovery that she signed the agreement. The trial court erred in doing so.

Regardless of whether Ms. Peuschold's admission that she signed the matrimonial agreement operated as an acknowledgement, that admission occurred during the existence of the marriage, as did Mr. Rush's own acknowledgement. Thus, even though the parties executed the matrimonial agreement by private act prior to their marriage, they did not perfect all of the elements of form required by Article 2331 prior to their marriage. Therefore, no valid matrimonial agreement existed at the time that the parties entered into marriage, and a community of acquets and gains was created by operation of law. Nor could the mere acknowledgement of the private act during the marriage validate the matrimonial agreement, since Article 2329, which must be strictly construed, mandates that spouses can only modify or terminate a matrimonial regime during marriage by filing a joint petition and obtaining court approval. No such joint petition was filed or court approval obtained in the instant case. Accordingly, we find that the 1993 matrimonial agreement was invalid as to form due to the failure of the parties to comply with the requirements of Articles 2329 and 2331.

CONCLUSION

For the reasons assigned, we grant this writ and reverse the judgment of the trial court. Additionally, we hereby render judgment in favor of Lynn E. Peuschold, and against Randall C. Rush, declaring that a community of acquets and gains existed between the parties during their marriage because the January 30, 1993 matrimonial agreement they executed is invalid due to lack of proper form. All costs of this appeal are assessed to Mr. Rush.

WRIT GRANTED; REVERSED AND RENDERED.

Muller v. Muller

72 So. 3d 364 (La. App. 5 Cir. 2011)

SUSAN M. CHEHARDY, Judge.

Plaintiff/appellant, Amy Strong Muller ("Mrs. Muller"), appeals a judgment of the district court denying her petition to have a premarital matrimonial agreement declared null and void ab initio. Mrs. Muller alleged in her petition that she and her then fiance', Carl Muller Jr. ("Mr. Muller"), entered into the agreement on April 7, 1995 in St. John the Baptist Parish, and the agreement was duly recorded on that same day. The couple was married on the following day, April 8, 1995. The record indicates that the marriage broke down at some point, although their marital status at the time of the hearing indicates the couple was not yet divorced.

Mrs. Muller's original petition indicated that the agreement was "executed before a notary", but was not in authentic form or duly acknowledged by the parties, in accordance with La. C.C. art. 2331. Specifically, she urged that although the agreement bore the signature of a notary, there were no witnesses to the party's signatures, and as a result the agreement should be set aside for lack of proper form. Mrs. Muller filed a Motion for Summary Judgment, which was converted to an ordinary proceeding, and the matter went to trial on the merits on November 19, 2009. Following the trial that took place in November 2009, the trial court orally granted judgment in favor of Mrs. Muller, but the judgment was not reduced to writing.

Although the date is unclear from the record, at some point before the judgment was reduced to writing the trial court decided to reconsider its earlier ruling, granted a new trial on its own motion, and reheard the matter on January 13, 2010. Following that hearing, the trial court, in a judgment dated April 6, 2010, denied Mrs. Muller's petition finding the agreement to be valid. Mrs. Muller appeals.

At the hearing in January 2010 that forms the basis of this appeal, Mr. Muller testified that he could not recall who presented whom with the actual premarital matrimonial agreement, that he did not recall if he or Mrs. Muller prepared it, whether he obtained the form from an attorney, or if he downloaded it from a computer. He remembered taking the document to a notary, but admitted that there were no witnesses present when he executed the document. He denied Mrs. Muller's allegation that the agreement was signed by her at home prior to the time he brought it to the notary. He did not remember who had the agreement recorded. Mr. Muller could not recall whether or not he worked for several years following the marriage, although he did "cash jobs" sometimes "as long as I stayed under the federal limit." He did not recall if he had gone back to work in 1997, or exactly where he worked from 1997 till the parties moved their matrimonial domicile to Mississippi in 1999.

Mrs. Muller testified that the primary reason for the premarital matrimonial agreement was Mr. Muller's concern that her income would be used to calculate an increase in child support for Mr. Muller's child from a previous marriage. Mrs. Muller testified that Mr. Muller downloaded the form from the computer in their home, and presented it to her for her signature the day before their planned nuptials. She testified that she believed he would not marry her if she did not sign it. She testified that there was no one present at their home when she signed the document and, after she executed the agreement, Mr. Muller took the document to a notary with whom he was familiar, who notarized it. However, no witnesses signed the agreement. She did not testify as to how the document came to be recorded. Mrs. Muller testified that, once they were married, Mr. Muller never mentioned the premarital matrimonial agreement again.

According to the testimony of both parties, while they did observe certain formalities of a separate property regime, such as separate bank accounts and separate tax returns, they both testified that they acquired several pieces of real estate during the marriage, and that none of the acts of sale referenced or mentioned the premarital matrimonial agreement. Mrs. Muller also testified that she utilized a substantial portion of her income, and a separate property inheritance from her uncle, to pay expenses on renovation and upkeep of their joint properties, and to pay loans and other obligations that directly benefited Mr. Muller.

Following the second trial in this matter, the trial court entered judgment with written reasons dated April 6, 2010. While the trial court determined that the agreement had not been signed before a notary or two witnesses, and, as such, the premarital agreement was invalid as an authentic act, the trial court found that the agreement was valid as an act under private signature, duly acknowledged. The court reasoned that, the act was duly acknowledged because, in open court, Mrs. Muller twice admitted the signature as her own before numerous witnesses. The trial court went on to state that *Ritz v. Ritz*, a case from this Court,

> arbitrarily assumes that because all elements of an authentic act must be met *before* the marriage, then the same must be applied to all elements of an act under private signature duly acknowledged. . . . Pertinent statutory law is devoid of any reference to such requirement. . . . The 5th Circuit in *Ritz* combined two ideas that should not be combined and created a requirement that simply does not exist.

The trial court further held, "The agreement benefitted both parties and was executed prior to the marriage. Therefore, the policy concern that necessitates court approval for agreements made during the marriage does not apply in this case."

La. C.C. art. 2331 states, "A matrimonial agreement may be executed by the spouses before or during marriage. It shall be made by authentic act or by an act under private signature duly acknowledged by the spouses." La. C.C. art. 2329 states, in pertinent part,

> Spouses may enter into a matrimonial agreement that modifies or terminates a matrimonial regime during marriage *only* upon joint petition and a finding by the court that this serves their best interests, and that they understand the governing principles and rules. They may, however, subject themselves

to the legal regime by a matrimonial agreement at any time without court approval. (Emphasis added.)

In the case before us, the trial court incorrectly concludes, as a matter of law, that La. C.C. art. 2329 is inapplicable to this matter. The dictates of La. C.C. art. 2329 are not mere policy concerns, but a mandate made part of a statutory enactment that casts a suspicious eye on the establishment of a separation of property regime effected during the marriage. The codal requirement that any party entering into an agreement that modifies or terminates the matrimonial regime after marriage must do so by joint petition and a finding by a court that the modification is in the best interest of both parties, is without exception. The factual circumstances of this or any other case cannot act to vitiate its requirements.

In *Ritz v. Ritz, supra,* this Court was faced with a factual situation similar to the matter now before us. Mr. and Mrs. Ritz entered into a premarital matrimonial contract that evidence showed failed as an authentic act. In considering whether or not the document sufficed as an act under private signature, we stated in *Ritz*:

> Mr. Ritz avers that because Mrs. Ritz admitted in court, as well as in her deposition, that she signed the document, the contract has been duly *acknowledged* and thus qualifies as an act under private signature. However, there is *nothing* in the record to indicate that *any* acknowledgment took place prior to or even during the marriage. We note that La. C.C. art. 2331, *supra,* has made *acknowledgment* a *requisite* to the validity of a matrimonial contract under private signature. Except for the exception stated in [La. C.C.] art. 2329, *supra,* just as all requirements of a pre-marital authentic act *must* be met *prior* to the marriage, so too, must all elements of an act under private signature *duly acknowledged* be done *prior,* or antecedent, to the marriage.

We find that the trial court's abrogation of the *Ritz* case was in error. The case before us presents no single fact that deviates from *Ritz,* and its premise remains sound. Both Mr. and Mrs. Muller testified that the document in question was executed prior to their marriage. Yet, even the trial court found that Mrs. Muller's signature was not properly witnessed by the notary and, as such, the document is not in authentic form.

Further, the record does not indicate that Mr. or Mrs. Muller duly acknowledged the matrimonial agreement before the marriage.

The issue is whether a party can duly acknowledge a signature on a premarital matrimonial agreement after the marriage. Here, Mrs. Muller did admit that her signature was on the premarital matrimonial document. However, as in *Ritz,* we note that "all elements of an act under private signature duly acknowledged be done prior, or antecedent, to the marriage." We hold that a post-nuptial acknowledgement cannot vitiate the mandate of La. C.C. art. 2329 that any matrimonial agreement entered into during the marriage to modify or terminate a matrimonial regime must be by joint petition, and after a finding by the court that the agreement serves the best interests of the parties. For these reasons, the ruling of the trial court is reversed, and the premarital matrimonial agreement between these parties is declared to be null and void ab initio. Costs of these proceedings are assessed against the appellee, Mr. Muller.

REVERSED

Dornemann v. Dornemann

850 A. 2d 273 (Conn. 2004)

WINSLOW, J.

FACTUAL BACKGROUND

Maryann H. Dornemann, the plaintiff, has moved to preclude evidence of the parties' premarital agreement at the divorce trial. The special defense of the defendant, Michael Dornemann, claims that the premarital agreement governs the central issues in the divorce. The plaintiff asserts that the premarital agreement is unenforceable for four reasons. First, written financial disclosures were not attached to it. Second, it was executed by the plaintiff as the result of undue influence and lack of free will. Third, it was not signed by the defendant and, therefore, was not in proper form. Fourth, and finally, it was not delivered to the plaintiff after signature by the defendant. The court heard testimony and received exhibits on January 7, January 8, January 9, February 18, February 27 and March 4, 2004.

The more credible evidence leads to the following factual findings. The plaintiff, whose maiden name was Maryann Hegel, grew up in Tennessee. After three years of college in Tennessee, she attended a fine arts school in Florida and received an associate's degree in interior design. The plaintiff worked as a model, then a restaurateur. The plaintiff freelanced as an interior designer and lived in her own apartment on 71st Street in New York City when she met the defendant on a blind date on September 25, 1995.

The defendant is a German national. He has a master's degree in business administration and a Ph.D. in economics. When the parties met, the defendant was involved in mergers and acquisitions with Bertelsmann AG and was an active member of its executive board. He is now chief executive officer of BMG Entertainment, which is a ten billion dollar global music and television business.

The parties' dating in the latter part of 1995, included two trips to Europe. The defendant owned residences and vacation homes in various parts of Europe and the United States. In January 1996, the defendant ended his relationship with a former girlfriend. Shortly thereafter, the plaintiff gave up her work and her apartment and moved into the defendant's New York apartment. She also traveled with the defendant to some of his other homes, in Europe and in the United States. The parties discussed the possibility of marriage three or four times in 1996. The defendant made it clear that a prenuptial agreement would be a necessity if he were to remarry. He had been married twice before and had required a prenuptial agreement each time.

When the parties were staying at one of the defendant's two homes in Aspen, Colorado in January 1997, the plaintiff told the defendant that she was pregnant. The parties decided to marry. They telephoned their families to announce the engagement. Shortly thereafter, the defendant reminded the plaintiff that a prenuptial agreement was a necessity. Without such an agreement, he would support the child, but he would not marry the plaintiff. The plaintiff loved the defendant, she was pregnant and she wanted to marry as soon as possible. She did not wish her pregnancy to be physically apparent to others on her wedding day. The parties set April 13, 1997 as the wedding date. The defendant urged the plaintiff to hire a lawyer to provide advice regarding the prenuptial contract.

The defendant retained his corporate lawyer, Aydin Caginalp, in January 1997. Caginalp used attorney Ben Fraser as Connecticut counsel for further advice in this matter. On February 19, 1997, the defendant conveyed to Caginalp the name and telephone number of the plaintiff's lawyer. The plaintiff had selected attorney Alicia Gany at the recommendation of the plaintiff's sister. Gany solicited the advice and assistance of another New York attorney, Harold Meyerson, and a Connecticut family law specialist, attorney Samuel Schoonmaker. The plaintiff instructed her accountant in Tennessee to remit financial information to Gany. Conceptual discussions between the parties took place in February. Between February 19 and March 10, Caginalp made seven different drafts of the prenuptial contract. He provided his fourth draft to Gany on February 28.

By the time the defendant left for a business trip to Germany on February 27, 1997, he had seen two or three early drafts of the prenuptial agreement. The parties and their attorneys had had further negotiations about the agreement. Changes were made through drafts five and six, culminating in draft seven on March 10. The changes varied from grammatical corrections to substantive matters, such as an increase in the amount of the up-front lump sum payment to the plaintiff in the event of divorce. The plaintiff traveled to Zermatt, Switzerland on March 3, 1997. The defendant joined the plaintiff in Zermatt on March 4. The parties left Zermatt for Munich, Germany on March 14. Both parties communicated with their respective lawyers regarding the terms of the prenuptial agreement and the financial disclosures while they were in Zermatt and Munich. Gany advised the plaintiff not to sign the premarital agreement in its draft seven version. Gany acknowledged in a letter to the plaintiff that the plaintiff was determined to sign the premarital agreement despite Gany's advice to the contrary.

On March 10, 1997, Caginalp forwarded, by Federal Express, two originals of the premarital agreement to the defendant in Munich, together with instructions for the execution of the documents before a notary or before two witnesses. Financial statements were not attached to the original documents. Financial information had been remitted separately between the attorneys. The defendant's disclosure was detailed in over one hundred pages, supplemented by a four-page precis. The attorneys, in turn, remitted financial information to their respective clients prior to March 17, 1997. On March 10, 1997, Gany sent to the plaintiff in Europe a letter from Schoonmaker, the consulting Connecticut attorney, summarizing the defendant's financial condition.

Caginalp had no further contact with Gany after March 10, and no further communications with the defendant regarding the prenuptial contract until the current court proceedings. Caginalp never received any signed copy of the prenuptial contract. Gany had no further contact with Caginalp after March 10, and no further communications with the plaintiff regarding the prenuptial contract until the plaintiff was about to commence divorce proceedings. Gany never received any signed copy of the prenuptial contract.

The defendant's office arranged an appointment with a notary in Munich for Monday, March 17, 1997, when the parties were to execute the prenuptial agreement. Because the defendant was called away on business in Luxembourg and Gütersloh at the last minute, only the plaintiff kept the appointment with the notary. She knew that the defendant would not marry her without a prenuptial agreement in place. She chose to proceed with the signing of the agreement because she wanted to marry the defendant. She took the blank documents to the notary, and she executed two originals of the prenuptial contract on March 17, 1997 (the Munich versions). She spent a few days in Nice, France, and then returned to Munich on Friday, March 21. The defendant also returned to Munich on March 21, and took possession of the partially executed contracts that day. At the end of the weekend, the defendant went to Paris and the plaintiff went to New York City. The defendant returned to New York City on Thursday, March 27.

Through the end of March 1997, the parties' descriptions of events are essentially the same. There is no reconciling the parties' separate accounts concerning the execution of, and control over, the prenuptial documents after March 1997. It is certain that one of the parties is lying. The plaintiff asserts that she never saw the Munich versions after March 21, 1997, until February 2003. She denies that the defendant ever gave back to her a Munich version of the prenuptial agreement. She denies that the defendant ever provided to her a copy of the prenuptial agreement signed by him.

In February 2003, the plaintiff was contemplating divorce. While the defendant was away on business, the plaintiff went to the parties' safe in their Greenwich home, found the two Munich versions, left one in the safe, and took one out. The two Munich versions were the only prenuptial documents in the safe when she looked there. The defendant had signed neither Munich version. On March 6, 2003, the plaintiff took a Munich version with her for her divorce consultation with a Manhattan lawyer. She left with her lawyer the Munich version she had removed from the safe in February.

The defendant has quite a different story. He explains that his New York office acquired two additional blank originals of the prenuptial agreement from Calginalp. The defendant asserts that he took the two blank originals to a restaurant on April 1, 1997, where he met his friend and business associate, Douglas Diamond. He signed the two originals that day, and Diamond signed them as a witness (the Diamond counterparts). The defendant gave one of the Diamond counterparts to the plaintiff that same day and instructed her to combine it with the Munich version to make a completely executed agreement. The defendant does not explain satisfactorily why it was necessary for him to sign separate blank originals, instead of the Munich versions. He cites his busy schedule as the reason for his disregard of the instructions of his attorney as to the execution of the prenuptial agreement before a notary or two witnesses.

In December 2002, the defendant was planning a climbing expedition to Cerra Aconcagua in the Andes. He wanted to review the provisions of his will. He claims that he went to the safe in the Greenwich home, took out his will and his Diamond counterpart of the prenuptial agreement, and made copies of those two documents. He says that he then replaced the will and the original Diamond counterpart in the safe. He did not look in the safe again until April 2003. He kept the copies of the two documents in a file folder for later reference and departed for Argentina on January 24, 2003, for the seventeen-day expedition. After the defendant returned from Argentina, he joined his wife in Antigua for one week and Vermont for a few more days. The parties returned to Greenwich on Monday, February 24. The defendant then reviewed the copied documents as he flew to Europe for business purposes on February 25, 2003. He left the copies in his office safe in Munich.

The defendant learned on April 12, 2003, that his wife wanted a divorce. The divorce writ was served upon him on April 15, 2003. He then looked in the Greenwich safe for the prenuptial agreement. He says he did not find his Diamond counterpart, but only a Munich version. When he returned to Germany on April 23, 2003, he retrieved his copy of the Diamond counterpart. The defendant testified that he showed his copy of the Diamond counterpart to his lawyer in May 2003, but did not give the copy to him at that time. The defendant's lawyer testified that the defendant told him in May 2003, about a prenuptial document signed by the defendant in the presence of a witness, but did not show it to him at that time.

Shortly after the divorce action commenced, the defendant's attorney, Arnold Rutkin, thought that the plaintiff might try to disavow the validity of the prenuptial contract. Rutkin advised the defendant to sign his Munich version without dating his signature. The defendant signed the document at his home in Greenwich in June 2003 (the Greenwich version). It was the Greenwich version that the defendant attached to his answer and special defense for his pleadings in the present case.

The defendant showed the copy of the Diamond counterpart to his lawyers for the first time in November 2003. The defendant's lawyers provided a copy of the Diamond counterpart to the plaintiff's attorneys at the beginning of December 2003, in a packet of discovery materials. Prior to that time, the defendant and his attorneys had not disclosed to the plaintiff's attorneys the claim that the Diamond counterpart existed. At a deposition on December 19, 2003, the defendant also provided, as an exhibit, a copy from Caginalp's file of the letter and blank prenuptial agreement that Caginalp had sent to Munich in March 1997.

The plaintiff's description of the finding of the Munich versions in the Greenwich safe and her actions thereafter is credible. The defendant's testimony and that of Douglas Diamond is not convincing. The defendant's account is incongruous. He intended the prenuptial contract to be in place and valid prior to the April 13, 1997 wedding. For reasons known only to him, he delayed his own execution of the documents until 2003. He did not sign any version of the premarital agreement prior to the marriage of the parties.

The validity of prenuptial contracts in Connecticut is governed, since October 1, 1995, by the Connecticut Premarital Agreement Act (the act). General Statutes § 46b–36a et seq. Prior to the act, our Supreme Court had set forth the standards for determining the validity of a prenuptial agreement in *McHugh v. McHugh*, 181 Conn. 482, 436 A.2d 8 (1980), as follows: "The validity of an antenuptial contract depends upon the circumstances of the particular case. . . . Antenuptial agreements relating to the property of the parties, and more specifically, to the rights of the parties to that property upon the dissolution of the marriage, are generally enforceable where three conditions are satisfied: (1) the contract was validly entered into; (2) its terms do not violate statute or public policy; and (3) the circumstances of the parties at the time the marriage is dissolved are not so beyond the contemplation of the parties at the time the contract was entered into as to cause its enforcement to work injustice." The act endorses, clarifies and codifies the *McHugh* standards. . . .

III

The plaintiff asserts that the defendant's failure to sign the premarital agreement prior to the marriage renders the contract invalid. The act defines "premarital agreement" as "an agreement between prospective spouses made in contemplation of marriage." General Statutes § 46b–36b. Although the definition does not specify that the agreement must be written, General Statutes § 46b–36c states that the agreement "shall be in writing and signed by both parties."

The act expressly shifts to the party, who questions the validity of the agreement, the burden of proving why the agreement should not be enforced. General Statutes § 46b–36g. That section does not specify as a reason for lack of enforcement a failure to sign the document by the party seeking to enforce it. The omission of such a ground for nonenforcement raises a question as to whether the requirement of § 46b–36c, that the agreement be in writing and signed by both parties, is mandatory or directory.

"[D]efinitive words, such as must or shall, ordinarily express legislative mandates of a nondirectory nature." Yet in the context of time and notice requirements, the Connecticut appellate courts have often found the word "shall" to be directory rather than mandatory. In particular, where a requirement is expressed in affirmative terms, unaccompanied by negative words, and there is no language that expressly invalidates any action taken after noncompliance with the statutory provisions, the Supreme Court has ruled that statutory language should be construed as directory. Although the issue implicated by the construction of § 46b–36c is not one of deadlines for filing documents or proper procedures for giving notice, the issue is, nevertheless, procedural. The question is whether a signature on the document by the party seeking enforcement is essential to the purpose of the statute. "In order to determine whether a statute's provisions are mandatory [the courts] have traditionally looked beyond the use of the word 'shall' and examined the statute's essential purpose."

It is a fundamental objective of the court to give effect to the intent of the legislature. "In seeking to discern that intent, [the court will] look to the words of the statute itself, to the legislative history and circumstances surrounding its enactment, to the legislative policy it was designed to implement, and to its relationship to existing legislation and common law principles governing the same general subject matter." "[A] statute is not to be construed so as to thwart its [intended] purpose."

The wording of § 46b–36c is affirmative. Affirmative terms, unaccompanied by negative words, are an indication of directory intent rather than mandatory intent on the part of the legislature. "The test to be applied in determining whether a statute is mandatory or directory is whether the prescribed mode of action is the essence of the thing to be accomplished, or in other words, whether it relates to a matter of substance or a matter of convenience. . . . If it is a matter of substance, the statutory provision is mandatory. If, however, the legislative provision is designed to secure order, system and dispatch in the proceedings, it is generally held to be directory, especially where the requirement is stated in affirmative terms unaccompanied by negative words."

The act contains no language expressly invalidating agreements that fail to comply with the dual signing provision. Although § 46b–36g sets forth four circumstances under which the agreement "shall not be enforceable," the lack of a signature by the enforcing party is not among those circumstances. When the statute itself recites no adverse consequence for failure to comply with a procedural matter, the legislative purpose may be deemed to be directory.

There is useful legislative history for the act. When the joint judiciary committee of the General Assembly held public hearings on March 17, 1995, the committee took testimony from Edith F. McClure of the Family Law Committee of the Connecticut Bar Association. The Family Law Committee of the Bar Association drafted the act. The statement of purpose from the Family Law Committee of the Connecticut Bar Association began as follows: "The purpose of the proposed Act is to achieve by legislation a statement of public policy recognizing the efficacy of agreements for the management and control of property and personal rights and obligations of spouses. . . . The purpose of the Act is to provide certainty as to the enforceability of the provisions in premarital agreements. . . ." "[T]estimony before legislative committees may be considered in determining the particular problem or issue that the legislature sought to address by the legislation. . . . This is because legislation is a purposive act . . . and, therefore, identifying the particular problem that the legislature sought to resolve helps to identify the purpose or purposes for which the legislature used the language in question."

"In determining whether the use of the word 'shall' is mandatory or directory, the test is whether the prescribed mode of action is of the essence of the thing to be accomplished. . . . That test must be applied with reference to the purpose of the statute." The signature of the party seeking enforcement of the terms of the contract is not a necessity. So long as he performs his obligations under the contract, his signature is superfluous from a practical point of view. In the present case, the defendant married the plaintiff. In so doing, he acted in reliance upon the plaintiff's signing of the premarital agreement. The certainty-of-enforceability purpose of the statute is achieved when the person who is disavowing the validity of the document has signed it intelligently and willingly. Having reaped the benefit of the signing, the plaintiff may not now disavow the burdens she assumed as her part of the contract. "One enjoying rights is estopped from repudiating dependent obligations which he has assumed; parties cannot accept benefits under a contract fairly made and at the same time question its validity."

A colloquy that took place on the floor of the House of Representatives on May 23, 1995, addressed issues relating to technical noncompliance with the act as opposed to substantive noncompliance. As the proponent of the act, Representative Ellen Scalettar of the 114th assembly district responded, through Deputy Speaker Wade A. Hyslop, Jr., to questions put by Representative Richard O. Belden of the 113th assembly district:

"[Representative Belden]: Mr. Speaker, just a question, through you to the proponent please. Mr. Speaker, with the enactment of this legislation, if somebody had signed some other agreement or it didn't comply with this statute, would it have the legal effect of a contract anyway? Through you, Mr. Speaker. . . .

"[Representative Scalettar]: Through you, Mr. Speaker. Yes, it would still be a valid contract. In fact, the bill specifically provides in Section 10 that it will not be deemed to affect the validity of any premarital agreement made prior to the effective date of the Act. . . .

"[Representative Belden]: Then, through you, Mr. Speaker, how about a separate agreement made after the effective date that did not entirely comply with the legislation before us? . . .

"[Representative Scalettar]: Through you, Mr. Speaker. I think the noncompliance would be subject to interpretation by the courts in that circumstance. The language is very broadly written. And I can't really foresee a circumstance where this bill, if enacted, would prevent enforcement of an agreement. . . .

"[Representative Belden]: Thank you, Mr. Speaker. What I'm attempting to get into the record here is whether this is a mandate that the only way you can have a premarital agreement in the state of Connecticut is by following this statute or whether or not two consenting adults following a standard contract type format could, in fact, enter into any type of agreement they care to and still be valid. And that's what I'm trying to get in the record, Mr. Speaker, through you to Representative Scalettar. If I perchance decided to, if for some reason, was single and decided to marry next year and entered into a contract that was different than the requirements of this file, would it be enforceable? Through you, Mr Speaker. . . .

"[Representative Scalettar]: Through you, Mr. Speaker. It's very difficult to answer in the abstract. I believe that most agreements would be enforceable because I can't, as I said, I can't really foresee circumstances where the conditions would be in such noncompliance as to render the agreement invalid. But, for example, if the agreement adversely affected the rights of a child, which is in violation of the statute, I do not believe that would be enforceable. It would depend on the actual terms of the agreement."

Representative Belden used the word "mandate" to question whether the intent of the act was to supplant common law premarital contracts or merely to steer the process into a standardized form. The discussion that took place on the floor of the House suggests that the legislature intended to do the latter. Shortly after the dialogue between Representatives Belden and Scalettar, the act passed the House with no dissenting vote.

The legislative history confirms that the purpose of the act is to recognize the legitimacy of premarital contracts in Connecticut, not to constrain such contracts to a rigid format so as to limit their applicability. The legislature's use of the word "shall" in §46b–36c is directory rather than mandatory as to the signature of the party seeking to enforce the premarital agreement. A signature by the party seeking to enforce the contract is a matter of convenience rather than a matter of substance. It is the signature of the party seeking to invalidate the force of the contract that is of the essence in order to assure enforceability.

The act was not enacted in derogation of the common law. Prior to the passage of the act, Connecticut had recognized the efficacy and usefulness of contracts between persons proposing to marry. To interpret §46b–36c as mandatory, as to the signature of the enforcing party, would impose a procedural burden upon premarital agreements that neither goes to the essence of the contracts nor serves any useful public policy. The defendant's signature on the premarital agreement was not required for the formation of the contract. Its absence from the contract is not a material omission. The parties intended to be bound by the terms of the premarital agreement regardless of the fact that the defendant had not signed the document.

CONCLUSION

The plaintiff has shown that the defendant failed to deliver to her before the marriage a version or counterpart signed by the defendant. The plaintiff signed the premarital agreement before a notary on March 17, 1997. The defendant did not sign the premarital agreement prior to the marriage of the parties. The defendant demonstrated his acceptance of the premarital agreement by marrying the plaintiff on April 13, 1997. Since the court finds that the defendant acted in reliance upon the premarital agreement by marrying the plaintiff, the question of delivery of the contract to the plaintiff after signature by the defendant is moot. Delivery of an original or counterpart of a prenuptial agreement to each signing party is not a requirement for validity under common law or under § 46b–36a et seq.

The plaintiff's claim that enforcement of the premarital agreement would be unconscionable has been reserved and will be addressed at the trial of the present case. The plaintiff executed a prenuptial agreement, after adequate financial disclosures, willingly and voluntarily. There was no coercion or undue influence. The defendant's failure to sign the contract prior to the marriage did not invalidate the contract. He assented to the bargain by marrying the plaintiff on April 13, 1997.

The plaintiff's motion in limine to preclude evidence of the parties' premarital agreement is denied.

B. Substance of Agreements

See La. Civ. Code art. 116, 2329–30; UPAA § 3.

Louisiana Civil Code article 2329 allows spouses to enter into matrimonial agreements "as to all matters that are not prohibited by public policy." Civil Code article 2330 provides some express examples of the limits of contractual freedom. That article prohibits spouses from using a matrimonial agreement to "renounce or alter the marital portion." It also provides that the spouses may not limit with respect to third persons the right that one spouse alone has under the legal regime to obligate the community or to alienate, encumber, or lease community property." Generally, spouses are free to modify or opt out of the community property regime — and this is a common motivation for a marriage contract in Louisiana. Article 2330 simply mandates that the rules governing the management of community property cannot be altered by contract to the extent that third parties are entitled to rely on those management rules.

The ability of spouses to use a matrimonial agreement to modify or waive the obligation of spousal support has caused a fair amount of litigation in Louisiana and elsewhere. Today, Civil Code article 116 permits couples to modify or waive the obligation of final spousal support in an authentic act or act under private signature duly acknowledged by the spouses — such as a matrimonial agreement. Jurisprudence is clear, however, that interim support may not be modified or waived in the same manner. *McAlpine v. McAlpine*, below, illustrates the Louisiana approach.

Section 3 of the UPAA also sets forth rules governing the content of premarital agreements. The rules are similar to those in Louisiana. Section 3 clearly permits the spouses to modify the ownership of their property in a number of manners and "allows the modification or elimination of spousal support." In practice, most states agree that final spousal support or its equivalent can be modified or waived by a marriage contract. States vary, however, with respect to the waiver or modification of interim spousal support. A number of states take the same position Louisiana takes and prohibit waiver of interim support while allowing waivers of final support. Others allow waiver, or modification, or both.

McAlpine v. McAlpine

679 So. 2d 85 (La. 1996)

VICTORY, Justice.

. . . .

FACTS AND PROCEDURAL HISTORY

About a week prior to their marriage in 1989, Michael McAlpine and Jonnie Fox signed an antenuptial agreement which provided for a separate property regime and for a waiver of alimony pendente lite and permanent alimony. The agreement provided, inter alia, that Jonnie Fox would receive $25,000 at divorce if the parties were married less than six years and $50,000 if they were married six years or more, regardless of fault or need on the part of Jonnie Fox. The parties were divorced on May 18, 1992. On October 5, 1992, Jonnie Fox McAlpine filed a rule to show cause why she (1) should not be awarded permanent alimony pursuant to article 112 of the Louisiana Civil Code, and (2) should not have a Mercedes Benz automobile returned to her, claiming it to be a gift to her from Mr. McAlpine. . . .

We now conclude that permanent alimony was not enacted to protect the public interest, but for the benefit of individuals. Further, we conclude that if protection of the public interest was ever a proper consideration for permanent alimony, that day has long since passed.

DISCUSSION

Article 6 of the Code Napoleon, the original source of LSA-C.C. art. 7, provides "one may not by private conventions derogate from the force of laws which concern public order and good morals." Planiol explains that this test gives a necessary sanction to a great number of legal provisions which do not specifically define their degree of authority. The law very often sets forth a rule without saying whether or not it permits derogations from its provisions. . . .

Nowhere in Planiol do we find a reference to permanent alimony as enacted for the public interest or order. Rather, Planiol states:

> Divorce having destroyed the marriage, no effects of it should continue. Upon what idea is founded persistence of the obligation of support between two persons who have nothing in common? Its basis is found in a principle already mentioned more than once. Whatever act of man causes damage to another obliges him by whose fault it happened to repair it, says Art. 1382. As long as the marriage lasted it gave each of the spouses an acquired position upon which each could count. The community of life permitted the spouse without means to share the welfare of the other. Suddenly through no fault of the spouse in question, he or she find himself or herself devoid of resources and plunged into poverty. It is manifestly in such a case as this that

the guilty party should be made to bear the consequences of his wrongful acts.

It is thus seen that the responsibility for alimony is based upon a concept entirely foreign to Art. 212. It is no longer a duty due by a spouse to a spouse because there are no longer any spouses. The duty is to make pecuniary amends for the consequences of an illicit act. This obligation subsisting after divorce partakes, in the highest degree, of the nature of an indemnity. It is intended to restore to the spouse without means something of the resources of which he or she is thenceforth deprived through the other's fault.

This indemnity nevertheless merely counterbalances the privation of the right of support which was vested in the spouse. It becomes transformed into alimony. This is why alimony follows the general rules applicable to alimentary pensions.

Prior to 1855, a wife, after obtaining divorce, was not entitled to alimony in Louisiana. In 1855, article 160 was adopted, granting alimony only to "the wife who had obtained the divorce out of the property of her husband, not to exceed one-third of her husband's income." Thus, the husband would have been proven to be "at fault" under then article 138 of the Civil Code because our law then allowed divorce only based on fault and did not allow a divorce for merely living separate and apart prior to 1916. When no-fault divorce was first recognized by Act 269 of 1916, allowing either party to obtain a divorce, there was no provision in LSA-C.C. art. 160 allowing alimony to a not-at-fault wife where the husband obtained the divorce based on seven years of living separate and apart. Thus, in 1928, article 160 was amended to allow alimony to the wife who proves she has not been at fault, where the husband obtained the "no-fault" divorce based on seven years of living separate and apart. This eliminated the required "fault" of the husband in granting alimony to the wife. In 1934, article 160 was amended to substitute the phrase "seven years or more" to "for a certain period of time" in light of the fact that the Legislature had reduced the seven year requirement to four years, and would later reduce it to two years, in 1938. The period is now 180 days from the service of a filed petition for divorce or six months. LSA-C.C. arts. 102 and 103. In 1979, article 160 was amended to allow alimony to the "spouse" who has not been at fault. Present article 112 is article 160 of the Louisiana Civil Code of 1870, as amended by Acts 1986, No. 229, Sec. 1. LSA-C.C. art. 112, Editor's note. Thus, we see from the beginning of alimony in Louisiana that "fault" played an extremely important role, as Planiol said it did in French law.

In *Player*, we characterized alimony after divorce as a "pension," stating as follows:

As the marriage is forever dissolved, there is no obligation arising from it. The law accords, not alimony in such a case, but a pension, to the unfortunate spouse who has obtained the divorce. This pension becomes revocable in case it should become unnecessary, and in case the wife should contract a second marriage.

Player was cited by this Court in 1940 for the proposition that alimony after divorce "is in the nature of a pension accorded by law to the wife without fault against whom a judgment of divorce has been rendered." The Court in *Fortier* went even further and called this alimony a "pure gratuity" to be granted "in the discretion of the court."

In *Hays v. Hays* . . . the husband argued that, since divorce dissolved the bonds of matrimony and thus his obligation to support his wife, and since permanent alimony was "a mere gratuity," an award of permanent alimony constituted a taking of his property for private purposes in violation of the federal and state constitutions. We disagreed and explained our definition of "gratuity" in the context of permanent alimony:

> By this statement this court meant that after divorce there no longer exists an obligation under the marriage contract for the husband to support and maintain his wife, as this contract has been dissolved. In other words, the court had in mind that the wife after divorce no longer has the absolute right to demand of her divorced husband support and assistance since the dissolution of the marriage contract relieved him of that obligation; that consequently the right of the wife to be awarded alimony under Article 160 does not flow from the marriage contract, and that insofar as this contract is concerned, the alimony is a gratuity in the nature of a pension. However, the court's statement cannot be construed to mean that there is no obligation on the divorced husband to pay alimony under certain circumstances.

> Divorce is not one of the inalienable rights granted by the federal or the state Constitution, and the lawmakers of the state may make laws regulating divorce and impose conditions under which a citizen of this state may obtain a divorce. Alimony is incidental and related to divorce, and its imposition is within the power which the lawmakers have to regulate and impose conditions for a divorce. Consequently, when the Legislature enacted Article 160 of the Civil Code, it was simply saying to a citizen of this state, as it had a constitutional right to do, that if cause exists for a divorce, it may be had subject to the condition that the court may in certain specified circumstances require the husband to pay alimony. By paying this alimony the husband is discharging an obligation imposed upon him by the court under authority of law, and his property is in no sense being unconstitutionally taken.

. . . In light of the history of article 160, and courts' and commentators' interpretation of article 160, we must consider whether alimony after divorce is a "law enacted for the public interest" such that any waiver would be an absolute nullity. While other laws governing marriage and children are often enacted for the public interest and non-waivable, an examination and comparison of the laws in this area that have, and have not, been declared non-waivable provides valuable insight.

In *Holliday v. Holliday*, 358 So.2d 618, 620 (La.1978), we held prenuptial waivers of alimony pendente lite void as contrary to the public policy of this State, expressed in LSA-C.C. arts. 119, 120 and 148, that a husband should support and assist his wife during the existence of the marriage. We held that this legal obligation of support, as well as the fact that the conditions affecting entitlement to alimony pendente lite could not be foreseen at the time antenuptial agreements are entered, overrides the premarital anticipatory waiver of alimony. We noted that we expressed no opinion on the antenuptial waiver of permanent alimony, reserving it for another day.

Thus, alimony pendente lite is based on the statutorily imposed duty of the spouses to support each other during marriage. See LSA–C.C. art. 98 ("Married persons owe each other fidelity, support, and assistance.") We have historically noted the difference between alimony pendente lite and permanent alimony. Comment (e) to LSA-C.C. art. 98 states that "[t]he spouses' duties under this Article, as a general rule are matters of public order from which they may not derogate by contract." On the other hand, there is no corresponding statutory duty of support mandating permanent alimony between former spouses.

While we have held that alimony pendente lite is a law enacted for the public interest, the reasoning behind Justice Calogero's argument in the *Holliday* dissent, that alimony pendente lite is not a law of public order, is really applicable to permanent alimony. Justice Calogero dissented, stating as follows:

> Neither am I persuaded by relator's contention and the majority's inference that alimony pendente lite is, in the public interest, essential to avoid a wife's becoming a social burden and/or ward of the state. This attitude is a demeaning one which is inconsistent with the realities of the day. It is simply not correct to assume that all, or most, women are incapable of financial independence but must, instead, be wholly dependent upon either their husbands or the state.
>
> Furthermore, in this case, as in almost all marriages where the spouses have entered into an antenuptial agreement, there is no community of acquets and gains. The wife thus has the same control over her property between separation and divorce as she had prior to separation and prior to marriage. An antenuptial waiver by the wife of alimony pendente lite would make the wife no more of a burden on the state than she was prior to marriage. I therefore view alimony pendente lite as a right which is provided for the benefit of the individual and not for the protection of public order and good morals.

In today's world, more women than ever are in the workforce and are capable of financial independence. Further, a waiver of permanent alimony would make the spouse incapable of financial independence no more of a burden than he or she was before marriage.

The Civil Code limits spouses' rights, before and during marriage, to renounce or alter the marital portion or the established order of succession. The legislature determined that these rules were rules of public order that may not be derogated by agreement. We believe that had the legislature intended to limit spouses' rights to waive post-divorce alimony in the same way, it would have made this clear. Instead, the Civil Code contains no prohibition against the waiver of post-divorce alimony.

Further, the Civil Code limits individuals' rights in other areas where a derogation of such rights would result in the individual becoming a public burden. An individual is forbidden from divesting himself of all his property by a donation inter vivos. Also, the right to contract not to compete is limited. "Both of these situations demonstrate the underlying state concern that a person cannot by convention deprive himself of the ability to support himself." But, as stated in the above case note, alimony is distinguishable:

> To assume that a wife's waiver of alimony automatically occasions the danger that she will become a ward of the state is to assume that the only revenue which married women have is the salary earned by their husbands. Such an assumption is unrealistic in light of modern social trends. . . .

> Because waiver of alimony presents a severely limited likelihood that a spouse will become a ward of the state, this public interest should not be considered a public policy unlawfully contravened by the antenuptial waiver of alimony after divorce.

Clearly, a waiver of permanent alimony does not deprive a spouse of his or her ability to support herself.

In other situations involving spouses, waivers in certain areas are clearly allowed. The Civil Code gives spouses, before or during marriage, the right to enter into a matrimonial agreement as to all matters that are not prohibited by public policy. LSA-C.C. art. 2329. A "matrimonial agreement" is defined as "a contract establishing a regime of separation of property or modifying or terminating the legal regime." LSA-C.C. art. 2328. Thus, parties, before or during marriage, can waive their right to the legal regime. As with permanent alimony, this deprives a spouse of the other's earnings and property acquired during marriage that would otherwise become community property, and potentially involves greater consequences on the part of the non-earning spouse than would a waiver of permanent alimony, which is limited to one-third of the other spouse's income and is only to provide sufficient means for support. . . .

Another situation where waiver is allowed is post-separation waivers of alimony. . . .

To allow post-separation waivers of permanent alimony and not prenuptial waivers, as violative of the public order, would be incongruous. Either permanent alimony is a law established for the protection of the public interest, and, as such, a waiver of such is an absolute nullity under article 7, or it is not. On original hearing, "[w]e distinguish[ed] without overruling" most of the above cases allowing waivers of permanent alimony in post-separation agreements because there, "unlike in an antenuptial agreement, the conditions which affect entitlement to alimony after divorce can be foreseen at the time of the contract." "Thus, the spouse who may be placed in necessitous circumstances by the agreement is in a much better position to protect him or herself and the risk that the spouse may become a ward of the state is significantly reduced." However, on reconsideration, we find that such a distinction is not justified under article 7 of the Civil Code, which decrees any act in derogation of a law enacted for the protection of the public interest is an absolute nullity. The concept of foreseeability is generally not a requirement for valid contracts.

Finally, to hold that antenuptial waivers of permanent alimony are invalid as a matter of public policy would be illogical because permanent alimony is granted only to spouses not-at-fault. Surely the grant of permanent alimony to "innocent" spouses and not "guilty" spouses cannot be a law enacted for the public interest under LSA-C.C. art. 7. Is it really arguable that the state has an interest in keeping not-at-fault divorced spouses off state support but has no such interest in keeping at-fault divorced spouses off the public dole? It is much more probable that the legislature in originally providing for permanent alimony did it not to keep needy ex-wives off public support, but to attempt to rectify the loss suffered by an innocent wife at the hands of an at-fault husband. If preventing divorced spouses from becoming a public burden was really a law enacted for the public interest it probably would have applied to all wives (now spouses), innocent or not.

Our holding today is in accordance with the majority of states that now hold that antenuptial waivers of permanent alimony are not per se invalid as against public policy. As stated by two family law commentators, since 1970, with the advent of no-fault divorce and the changes in society that such laws represent, public policy has changed and the traditional rule that prenuptial waivers of permanent alimony were void ab initio has given way to the more realistic view that such agreements are valid and enforceable under certain conditions. Rather than encouraging divorce, these agreements provide couples with the opportunity to plan for the future and safeguard their financial interests. Without this option, potential spouses may choose to live together informally without the benefit of marriage. Thus, these agreements may actually encourage marriage in some instances.

CONCLUSION

We conclude that permanent alimony is not a law enacted for the public interest. Rather, it was enacted to protect individuals, i.e., not-at-fault divorced spouses in need. Thus, the prohibition found in article 7 of the Civil Code does not apply. . . .

C. Grounds for Challenging Agreements: Consent and Voluntariness

See La. Civ. Code art. 2328; UPAA § 6.

No special capacity rules exist for matrimonial agreements in Louisiana. Revision Comment (b) to Civil Code article 2328 explains that the general obligations rules applicable to other contracts apply to matrimonial agreements. Spouses are presumed to have capacity to execute matrimonial agreements, and the validity of an agreement depends on the free consent of both spouses. Error, fraud, and duress are the only grounds available for challenging consent. Unlike some other jurisdictions, validity of the prenuptial agreement is unaffected by failure of the parties to obtain separate legal representation. However, lack of separate representation is sometimes an important factor in determining whether a party's consent was vitiated by fraud, error, or duress.

In some respects, Louisiana's approach to capacity and consent is more lenient than the approach taken under the UPAA and the adopting jurisdictions. The UPAA addresses capacity by explaining when an agreement is not enforceable. Specifically, Section 6 of the UPAA provides that "a premarital agreement is not enforceable if a party against whom enforcement is sought" is able to prove that "the party did not execute the agreement voluntarily." Voluntariness is similar to the requirement of free consent and can generally be challenged on the grounds of fraud, duress, or mistake. In adopting the UPAA, some states added additional requirements. California Family Code § 1615, for example, provides that premarital agreements are deemed involuntary unless the court makes certain findings of fact. The court must find that the parties were represented by independent counsel (or gave an informed waiver and met other requirements) and the parties must have had at least seven days between being presented with the agreement and signing the agreement. Louisiana has no corresponding waiting period or requirement for independent representation, as illustrated in *Weinstein v. Weinstein*, below. Although many states have adopted the UPAA, the state-by-state implementation of the Act and its interpretation sometimes varies considerably. *Mamot v. Mamot* and *In re Shanks*, below, illustrate this point.

Weinstein v. Weinstein

62 So. 3d 878 (La. App. 3d Cir. 2011)

PAINTER, Judge.

Defendant, Linda Allen Weinstein, appeals the trial court's judgment regarding the existence of a community regime between her and her former husband, John Haas Weinstein, and the amount of child support to be paid for their minor child. For the following reasons, we affirm in part and reverse in part.

FACTS AND PROCEDURAL HISTORY

John and Linda were married on August 8, 1986. On August 7, 1986, the day before the wedding, they signed a separation of property agreement. Two children were born of the marriage, only one of whom was a minor at the time of the ruling from the child support hearing appealed herein. On August 7, 1997, they filed a joint petition to affirm an agreement establishing a community property regime. On that same day, an order was signed recognizing the agreement establishing a community property regime. They separated in March 2004, and a judgment of divorce was signed on April 1, 2005.

On January 21, 2010, after a lengthy hearing, the trial court rendered a partial final judgment finding that the prenuptial agreement was effective in creating a separation of property regime between the parties. The judgment also granted a motion for involuntary dismissal as to the claims that the trial court order established a community regime in August 1997. Linda appeals.

DISCUSSION

. . . .

Prenuptial Agreement

Linda next asserts that the trial court erred in finding the prenuptial agreement to be valid and in granting the motion for involuntary dismissal in that regard. She argues that she signed the contract as a result of fraud on the part of John and that John was in violation of the rules of professional conduct in that he was her lawyer at the time they entered into the contract and was prohibited from contracting with her where they had differing interests in the contract.

Consent, which is necessary for the formation of a valid contract, may be vitiated by error, fraud, or duress. La. C.C. art. 1948. In order to establish that a party's consent to a contract has been vitiated due to error, the error must concern a cause without which the obligation would not have been incurred and that cause was known or should have been known to the other party. La. C.C. art. 1949. Cause is defined as the reason why a party obligates himself. La. C.C. art. 1967.

Error may concern a cause when it bears on the nature of the contract, or the thing that is the contractual object or a substantial quality of that thing, or the person or the qualities of the other party, or the law, or any other circumstance that the parties regarded, or should in good faith have regarded, as a cause of the obligation.

La. C.C. art. 1950. However, in order to establish that a party's consent has been vitiated due to fraud, the error need not concern the cause of the obligation, but it must concern a circumstance that has substantially influenced the party's consent. La. C.C. art. 1955.

Louisiana Civil Code Article 1953 defines fraud as "a misrepresentation or a suppression of the truth made with the intention either to obtain an unjust advantage for one party or to cause a loss or inconvenience to the other." Further, "[f]raud need only be proved by a preponderance of the evidence and may be established by circumstantial evidence." La.Civ.Code art. 1957. In support of her allegations of fraud, Linda introduced into evidence a diary entry by John written approximately ten years after his marriage in which he examined his feelings about his marriage and ways in which he felt he could or could have improved his relationship with his wife and his failures in so doing. The trial court did not feel that this document was evidence of fraud, and we cannot say that it rises to the level of indicating "a misrepresentation or a suppression of the truth made with the intention either to obtain an unjust advantage for one party or to cause a loss or inconvenience to the other" at the time the marriage agreement was entered.

Linda further asserts that John violated the rules of professional conduct by entering into a marriage contract with her while he was acting as her attorney. As John notes, there is no positive law prohibiting an attorney from entering a prenuptial agreement with a client. However, John argues that his representation of her in connection with her prior divorce did not encompass representation as to the prenuptial contract. We agree that to assert a conflict in this regard, Linda had the burden of showing that John's representation extended to the prenuptial contract.

The relationship between an attorney and his client is purely contractual in nature and results only from a clear and express agreement between the parties. Establishment of an attorney-client relationship is adequately proven when it is shown that the advice and assistance are sought and received in matters pertinent to his profession or when the agreement of representation has been made under conditions acceptable to both parties.

While it is well established that the existence of an attorney-client relationship depends to a great degree on the client's subjective belief that it exists, the belief must be reasonable. Additionally, "[a]greement of an attorney to represent a client as to a particular matter does not create an agency relationship as regards other business affairs of the client."

It is uncontested that John, as well as several other attorneys, represented Linda in connection with a prior divorce. However, our examination of the record does not reveal enough proof to show that the scope of that representation extended to the prenuptial agreement. The record does not contain any testimony from Linda as to her subjective belief in this regard, nor did she introduce a contract evidencing an attorney-client relationship in connection with the prenuptial agreement.

Additionally, the record shows that Linda received advice to seek separate legal representation with regard to the prenuptial agreement and chose not to follow that advice. Counsel for Linda called Anthony Fazzio, an attorney practicing in Lafayette, Louisiana, to testify at the hearing on the marital regime. In response to questioning by counsel for Linda, Fazzio testified as follows: John was a friend since law school, and he had occasionally been co-counsel on cases with John. He enrolled as counsel on Linda's prior divorce at John's request. John and Linda showed up at his office without an appointment, and Linda asked to speak to him in private and told him that John wanted her to sign a prenuptial agreement. He asked her if she understood that he was a friend of John's. He further instructed her that she should get someone to read the document and prepare it from her point of view. He told her that while it would protect her if anyone sued John, it would also keep her from sharing in his successes, and she responded by saying that she was not interested in John's money. A short time later, John and Linda came back, and the agreement was signed and notarized in front of witnesses.

In light of the evidence of record, we find no error in the trial court's ruling with regard to the validity of the prenuptial agreement and in granting the motion for involuntary dismissal in that regard.

Attorney-Client Privilege

Linda next asserts that the trial court erred in finding that there was no attorney-client privilege between Linda and attorneys Shepton Hunter, John Haas Weinstein, Anthony Fazzio, and David L. Carriere as to the prenuptial agreement. However, we find no error in this finding. We have already found that Linda failed to carry her burden of showing that John was acting as her legal representative in connection with the prenuptial agreement. Further, there is no evidence that David Carriere ever acted as Linda's legal representative. With regard to the attorney-client privilege, if any, arising out of an attorney-client relationship between Linda and either Fazzio or Hunter, we find that Linda waived any such privilege by calling them as witnesses and questioning them concerning potentially privileged matters. La.Code. Evid. art. 502 provides that the holder of a privilege may waive it by disclosing the privileged information or by consenting to its disclosure. Linda consented to the disclosure of any information testified to by Fazzio and Hunter at her behest. . . .

Mamot v. Mamot

813 N.W. 2d 440 (Neb. 2012)

HEAVICAN, C.J.

The Howard County District Court entered a decree of dissolution of the marriage of Kevin B. Mamot and Valara Mamot. The court determined that the premarital agreement entered into by the parties, although unconscionable, was valid and enforceable. The court divided the assets and entered an order regarding child support. Valara appeals, and Kevin has filed a cross-appeal. We reverse, and remand for further proceedings.

I. BACKGROUND

Kevin and Valara began living together in Kevin's house near St. Libory, Nebraska, in 2003. Valara had two children from a previous relationship, and Kevin had one child from a previous relationship who lived with him. Kevin and Valara had two children together, twin daughters who were born on June 30, 2008.

The couple planned to get married on June 17, 2006, and discussed signing a premarital agreement prior to the marriage. Kevin testified that he and Valara had talked about his financial worth from the beginning of their relationship and that Valara knew from the time they started dating that his net worth was more than $1 million. Valara testified that she was unaware of the actual value of Kevin's assets, but she believed one of his businesses was worth more than $2 million. The parties eventually signed a premarital agreement, the contents of which will be discussed below, but Valara claimed that she did not see Kevin's financial statement prior to signing the agreement.

On April 28, 2010, Valara filed a petition for legal separation, in which she alleged that the premarital agreement was invalid because (1) it was not executed as contemplated by the parties, (2) it is unconscionable as a matter of law, (3) it is against public policy, and (4) the parties subsequently waived its terms and provisions. . . .

The trial court entered a decree of dissolution on May 27, 2011. The court determined that Valara executed the premarital agreement voluntarily; that she had time for an independent review of the premarital agreement, although she chose not to consult with independent counsel; that there was no convincing evidence that Valara was surprised that Kevin would require the premarital agreement; and that there was no evidence of an inequality of bargaining power between the parties. The trial court also found that Valara did not meet her burden to establish Kevin's failure to fully disclose his assets.

The court then considered whether the premarital agreement was unconscionable. It found that the language of the premarital agreement "clearly defies the basic underpinnings of the marital relationship." The court also found that the premarital agreement as written "truly makes Valara an 'indentured servant', toiling with day-to-day activities with no possibility of accumulating any assets under the circumstances existing and the agreement as written." The court determined that the premarital agreement "is one-sided, evidences overreaching, and demonstrates sharp dealing not consistent with the obligations of marital partners to deal fairly with each other." The court found that the premarital agreement is unconscionable, but that "unconscionability alone does not make the [agreement] unenforceable."

The court found that Valara did not carry her burden to prove that before execution of the premarital agreement, (1) she was not provided a fair and reasonable disclosure of Kevin's property or financial obligations; (2) she did not voluntarily and expressly waive, in writing, any right to disclosure; and (3) she did not have, or reasonably could not have had, an adequate knowledge of Kevin's property or financial obligations. . . .

IV. ANALYSIS

The primary issue before us is the enforceability of the premarital agreement. We are governed by Nebraska's version of the Uniform Premarital Agreement Act, which was adopted by Nebraska in 1994. The act authorizes parties who are contemplating marriage to contract with respect to matters including the rights and obligations of each party in any property of the other, the disposition of property upon divorce, and the modification or elimination of spousal support. The contract cannot be in violation of public policy or in violation of statutes imposing criminal penalties. . . .

As the party opposing enforcement of the premarital agreement, Valara has the burden to prove that the premarital agreement is not enforceable. Pursuant to § 42-1006, Valara must prove either that she did not voluntarily execute the premarital agreement or that the premarital agreement was unconscionable when it was executed. If she seeks to prove that the premarital agreement was unconscionable, Valara must prove three conditions: that before execution of the agreement, (1) she was not provided a fair and reasonable disclosure of Kevin's property or financial obligations; (2) she did not voluntarily and expressly waive, in writing, her right to disclosure of Kevin's property and financial obligations beyond the disclosure provided; and (3) she did not have, or reasonably could not have had, an adequate knowledge of Kevin's property or financial obligations.

1. DID VALARA VOLUNTARILY SIGN AGREEMENT?

We turn first to the question of whether Valara voluntarily executed the premarital agreement. Neither the Uniform Premarital Agreement Act nor corresponding Nebraska statutes define "voluntarily," and this court has not previously considered the term as related to a premarital agreement. The Nebraska Court of Appeals was asked to review such an agreement in *Edwards v. Edwards.* That court relied on the California Supreme Court's interpretation of "voluntarily" as used in the Uniform Premarital Agreement Act. The California court identified the following factors that a court might consider:

(1) "coercion that may arise from the proximity of execution of the agreement to the wedding, or from surprise in the presentation of the agreement";

(2) "the presence or absence of independent counsel or of an opportunity to consult independent counsel";

(3) "inequality of bargaining power — in some cases indicated by the relative age and sophistication of the parties";

(4) "whether there was full disclosure of assets"; and

(5) the parties' understanding of the "rights being waived under the agreement or at least their awareness of the intent of the agreement."

The Nebraska Court of Appeals noted that other jurisdictions have also relied on the California court's interpretation of "voluntarily." We shall use these factors in our review of the Mamot agreement.

(a) Coercion or Surprise

Kevin and Valara lived together for 3 years prior to their marriage. Their wedding was scheduled to be held June 17, 2006. Both had signed premarital agreements for earlier marriages. They each testified as to the sequence of events that led to the premarital agreement at issue.

Valara testified that Kevin hinted about a premarital agreement several times before the marriage, but that the subject was usually dropped. Valara said she eventually agreed to a premarital agreement and told Kevin that if he had an agreement drawn up, she would have it reviewed by the attorney who drafted the premarital agreement for her previous marriage.

Valara stated that around June 9, 2006, Kevin came home for lunch and presented Valara with two copies of the premarital agreement, which Kevin told her she needed to read and sign. Valara noted that there was no signature page and was no financial statement listing the parties' assets, which she believed were normally included in a premarital agreement. Kevin also testified that no financial statements were attached to the copy he presented to Valara. Kevin told Valara he would obtain a financial statement form for her. Valara said that she and Kevin signed the premarital agreement and that Kevin took both copies with him, preventing her from further reviewing the document. That evening, Kevin gave Valara a financial statement form to complete, and she filled it out that night. Valara said she had no part in the preparation of the premarital agreement and did not have any contact with the attorney who drafted it.

Valara stated that Kevin returned a few days later with one copy of the premarital agreement, which had a signature page attached. Valara told Kevin that they needed to list their assets and that she needed to have her attorney review the agreement, but Kevin said there was no time. Kevin reportedly said, "You've got to get this signed otherwise we're not getting married Saturday." Kevin did not contradict this statement, and he testified that Valara had had "plenty of time" to have the document reviewed by an attorney because she was not working outside the home at the time.

Valara signed the document on June 12, 2006, but it was not notarized. Valara said that she asked for a copy of the signed document but that she did not receive it until a month or two later. She stated that the copy she received did not have any financial attachments or a signature page.

Kevin said he and Valara began talking about the premarital agreement 3 or 4 months before the marriage because Valara had been married previously and he had been married twice, and both had used premarital agreements in their previous marriages. A letter dated June 3, 2006, which accompanied the premarital agreement, directed the parties to attach financial statements, sign the premarital agreement, and return the original to Kevin's attorney. Each party retained a copy.

Kevin testified that Valara had sufficient time to have an attorney review the premarital agreement before she signed it because she was not working outside the home. Kevin acknowledged that the premarital agreement was not notarized because there was not enough time to go to town to have it signed. Kevin said that he was in a hurry to sign it, but that Valara "had all day if she wanted somebody to look at it or go through it" and that Valara "could have had anybody look at it that she wanted."

The record suggests that Valara may not have been surprised at the idea of a premarital agreement, but it appears that she was surprised when Kevin actually presented it to her. The parties had discussed an agreement, but there is no indication that there had been recent discussions regarding the matter.

In order to get married in the Catholic church, which was Kevin's faith, it was necessary for Kevin to obtain an annulment of his second marriage. Valara testified that they started the annulment process in 2003 and that it was completed in 2006. Once the annulment was approved, Kevin and Valara set their wedding date for June 17, 2006, and she began making wedding plans.

Valara testified that she and Kevin each had two attendants at the wedding. About 20 members of their immediate families were at the church, and about 150 guests were present at the reception, which included a dance with music provided by a disk-jockey. The parties' children were involved in the wedding.

The signed copy of the premarital agreement is dated June 12, 2006, which was the Monday prior to the wedding. Based on these facts, it is reasonable to find that Valara felt coerced into signing the agreement when Kevin presented it to her during the noon hour and told her she needed to sign it immediately or there would be no wedding. Kevin did not dispute these facts, which indicate a level of coercion. By that date, Valara had already paid for or made commitments to pay for invitations, the reception hall, flowers, a diskjockey, and wedding attire for the children. If the wedding were canceled, Valara would have been subjected to public embarrassment and possible financial loss.

At the time of the wedding, Valara had quit her job and was a homemaker taking care of three children. Kevin and Valara lived on an acreage outside of St. Libory, an unincorporated community in Howard County. Although Kevin testified that she had time to have the agreement reviewed by a professional, the reality is that she had only a few hours between when Kevin presented her with the agreement and when he returned and expected her to sign it. During that short time, she would have been required to attempt to find an attorney who would immediately review the agreement and advise her as to whether she should sign it. It is reasonable to believe that Valara felt she had no choice but to sign the agreement or the wedding would not take place as planned. Valara has met her burden to show that she was coerced into signing the premarital agreement after Kevin delivered the ultimatum that she needed to sign the agreement or there would be no wedding.

(b) Independent Counsel

The record shows that the premarital agreement was prepared by Kevin's attorney at Kevin's request. Valara was not represented by independent counsel. Although Valara testified that she told Kevin she would have her attorney review the agreement, she stated that once Kevin presented the document to her, she did not have an opportunity to have it reviewed. Valara stated that Kevin told her that his attorney would "take care" of her. Kevin testified that he told Valara to consult with her own lawyer. Because both parties were busy, Valara told Kevin to have an agreement prepared because they both wanted such an agreement.

The dated copy of the agreement was signed on June 12, 2006, which was 5 days prior to the wedding. That time might have been sufficient for Valara to consult with an attorney. However, according to Valara's testimony, Kevin did not allow sufficient time for review when he first presented the premarital agreement to her. Kevin gave the document to her when he was home for lunch and expected her to sign it immediately. Kevin did not dispute Valara's testimony and asserted that Valara "had all day" if she wanted someone to review the agreement.

As noted above, Kevin and Valara lived on an acreage outside a small community. In order to obtain professional advice about the premarital agreement, Valara would have been required to first locate an attorney who would be willing to review it. The attorney would be required to agree to review the document in a short period of time. Valara would possibly have had to travel to meet with the attorney. A premarital agreement can be a complicated legal document that requires careful consideration of its provisions. At best, Kevin expected Valara to sign the agreement with only a few hours to consider it. Valara had fewer than 5 days before the wedding in which to seek legal advice—5 days in which she was also planning the wedding. The record supports a finding that Valara did not have a sufficient opportunity to have the premarital agreement reviewed by independent counsel. Thus, Valara has met her burden to show this factor, which weighs in favor of finding that Valara did not voluntarily sign the agreement.

(c) Inequality in Bargaining Power

The California Supreme Court identified inequality of bargaining power as another factor for a court to consider. It noted that in some cases, this inequality may be shown by the relative age and sophistication of the parties. A California appeals court has also considered a disparity in the parties' income and their respective assets at the time they entered into a premarital agreement as an indication of an inequality of bargaining power. We therefore review the record to consider whether there was an inequality of bargaining power.

Prior to the marriage, Valara worked for 6 years in medical administration and medical underwriting. She worked full time until January 1, 2006, when she began working 30 hours per week. In May, Valara's employer asked her to return to full-time work. But she quit on June 1 because Kevin said, "There's plenty to do around the house, you can fix it up, you can keep the yard up." Valara stated that she was not pleased about quitting and that she "love[d her] job."

Valara said that during the marriage, she had no way to earn income except by helping her grandmother on a farm and keeping financial records for her father. Valara said she earned about $1,500 to $2,000 per year from her grandmother and $2,000 to $3,000 per year from her father. She used that money to pay for gas, school lunches, clothing for the children, and groceries. Kevin provided her with $1,000 per month, which she used to pay the mortgage on a house she was renting out.

Valara spent a great deal of time working with Kevin's 14-year-old son from a previous marriage who had difficulties at school and was eventually given psychiatric medication. Valara claimed to have worked with him for 4 to 6 hours each night until he was in the sixth grade. Valara stated that she helped Kevin in his professional life by doing whatever he asked of her, whether it was driving a truck or preparing meals for employees.

Kevin owns interests in three business organizations: one-half of a trucking company, one-half of a land and cattle company, and one-third of a feedlot company. There was also evidence that Kevin actively trades in the commodities market. Thus, it appears that Kevin is more sophisticated in business matters than is Valara. She was an employee in the insurance industry while Kevin was self-employed and actively involved in three business interests.

The record also suggests a disparity in the parties' income and assets at the time they entered into the agreement. Kevin had a much greater net worth at the time the agreement was signed. Testimony was offered that he was worth more than $1 million and possibly more than $2 million when the parties married. Prior to the marriage, Valara earned between $23,000 and $32,000 annually and had a retirement account worth $18,000. Valara quit her job just prior to the wedding.

There was also an inequality in the bargaining power of the two parties. While Valara had some business experience, she worked as an hourly employee for an insurance company. Kevin had partial ownership in three companies, serving as president of at least one of them, and traded in the commodities market. After Valara quit working outside the home, she was a homemaker who took care of five children as well as the house. Valara met her burden to show an inequality in the bargaining power of the two parties.

(d) Full Disclosure

The parties disputed whether there was adequate disclosure of assets prior to the signing of the premarital agreement and whether financial statements were attached to the premarital agreement when it was signed.

Valara stated that she did not see Kevin's financial statement before she signed the agreement and that she had no idea that Kevin had a net worth in excess of $2 million. However, Kevin said that he and Valara had talked about his financial worth from the beginning of their relationship and that she understood she would be "financially set." Kevin believed Valara knew from the time they started dating that he had a net worth in excess of $1 million. Kevin asserted that Valara had an opportunity to see his financial statement before signing the premarital agreement. Although Valara admitted that she completed a financial statement, she maintained it was not a part of the premarital agreement.

The trial court noted that Valara testified she reminded Kevin on more than one occasion that the financial statements needed to be attached to the premarital agreement. Kevin provided the financial statement form for Valara to complete. There is no definitive evidence to show whether Kevin fully disclosed his assets to Valara prior to the signing of the premarital agreement. We have only the conflicting testimony of the two parties. As the trial court noted, the attorney who drafted the premarital agreement was not called as a witness to help explain whether the financial statements were attached to the premarital agreement.

In a review de novo on the record, an appellate court reappraises the evidence as presented by the record and reaches its own independent conclusions with respect to the matters at issue. We determine that Valara did not meet her burden to show that she was not aware of the extent of Kevin's financial holdings before the agreement was signed.

(e) Parties' Understanding of Rights Being Waived or Awareness of Intent
of Agreement

It is clear that both parties were aware of the purpose and intent of premarital agreements because each had entered into such agreements in earlier marriages. Valara demonstrated an understanding that assets are "[u]sually" listed "within the [agreement]." However, having an understanding of the intent of a premarital agreement and understanding the rights being waived by the actual language of the agreement are not the same.

The premarital agreement provided that each party would retain sole ownership of all his or her property, "now owned or hereafter acquired by him or her, free and clear of any claim of the other." In the event of divorce, the parties agreed that neither would make any claim

> to any property now owned or hereafter acquired by the other party or to any separate property of the other party or to any appreciation or increase in value of such property during the marriage or to any property generated, earned or purchased by the other party as his or her sole and separate property.

The separate property of the parties was defined as all property belonging to each party at the commencement of the marriage, property "acquired by a party out of the proceeds or income from property owned at the commencement of the marriage or attributable to appreciation in value of said property, whether the enhancement in value is due to market conditions or to the services, skills or efforts of either party." The agreement also provided that any property "now owned or hereafter acquired in a party's name alone" shall be that party's separate property.

As the trial court determined, the agreement purported to "isolate as separate property" that which was owned by Kevin at the time of the marriage, but it also sought "to reach into the future to prevent any marital interest arising from income produced as a result of his ownership of these assets." The agreement left Valara as a homemaker who took care of the children with "no possibility of accumulating any assets under the circumstances existing and the agreement as written."

The trial court stated that the language of the agreement "defies" the basic underpinnings of the marital relationship, which should be "a partnership where both parties through their mutual efforts obtain assets subject to equitable division in the event of a dissolution." Under this agreement, Valara was an "'indentured servant.'"

The premarital agreement is a complex legal document which uses specialized terminology that might not be easily comprehended by a person unfamiliar with the law. We find no evidence to suggest that Valara fully understood the terms of the agreement. Valara met her burden to demonstrate that she did not have a complete understanding of the rights she was waiving in signing the premarital agreement.

2. AGREEMENT WAS NOT VOLUNTARILY SIGNED

This court reviews the trial court's determinations de novo, but we are also reminded that the trial court's determinations are initially entrusted to its discretion and will normally be affirmed absent an abuse of that discretion. As noted above, in a review de novo on the record, an appellate court reappraises the evidence as presented by the record and reaches its own independent conclusions with respect to the matters at issue.

We have reviewed the record as it relates to the question of whether Valara voluntarily entered into the premarital agreement, and we find that the trial court abused its discretion in finding that she did. Taking into consideration the factors identified in Edwards, we find that Valara was coerced into initially signing the document, during a lunch hour just a few days before the wedding and after the wedding invitations had been sent and she had already spent money on wedding preparations. Kevin told her she needed to sign the agreement or the wedding would not take place. Valara did not have an adequate opportunity to have independent counsel review the document. Although Kevin testified that Valara "had all day," that she had "plenty of time" to have the agreement reviewed because she was not working outside the home at the time, and that "she could have went [sic] to town" and "could have had anybody look at it that she wanted," it is unrealistic to believe Valara had the time and wherewithal to adequately review the agreement.

The record supports a finding that there was a disparity in the parties' income and their respective assets at the time they entered into the agreement, which indicates an inequality of bargaining power. Valara met her burden to show that she did not understand that by signing the agreement, she was waiving her right to full disclosure of Kevin's premarital property and giving up any claim to Kevin's property obtained during the marriage. The sole factor for which Valara did not meet her burden is whether there was a full disclosure of assets prior to the signing of the agreement. The evidence on that issue is in conflict.

After completing our de novo review, we find that Valara met her burden to show that she did not sign the premarital agreement voluntarily, and therefore, it is unenforceable.

Pursuant to § 42-1006, the party challenging a premarital agreement must show either that the agreement was not signed voluntarily or that it was unconscionable. If the challenging party seeks to show that the agreement was unconscionable, that party must also prove that he or she was not provided a fair and reasonable disclosure of the other party's property or financial obligations; that the challenging party did not voluntarily and expressly waive, in writing, any right to disclosure of the other party's property or financial obligations beyond the disclosure provided; and that the challenging party did not have, or reasonably could not have had, an adequate knowledge of the other party's property or financial obligations. Because we find that Valara did not sign the agreement voluntarily, we need not further address whether it was unconscionable. . . .

In re Shanks

758 N.W.2d 506 (Iowa 2008)

HECHT, Justice.

This case provides the first occasion for this court to determine the validity of a premarital agreement under Iowa Code section 596.8. Upon further review of the court of appeals' affirmance of the district court's order denying a request for specific performance of a premarital agreement, we conclude the agreement was voluntarily executed, conscionable, and enforceable. Accordingly, we vacate the decision of the court of appeals, affirm in part and reverse in part the district court's judgment, and remand this case for further proceedings.

I. Background Facts and Proceedings.

Randall Shanks is an attorney with a successful personal injury and workers' compensation practice in Council Bluffs. Teresa Shanks holds an associate degree in court reporting and a Bachelor of Science degree in marketing management. She has been employed in various roles, including a position in the marketing department of a casino, and employment as a bookkeeper, secretary, and office manager in Randall's law office.

Randall and Teresa were married in Jamaica on April 23, 1998. This was a second marriage for both parties. Randall had two children and Teresa had three children from prior marriages. While contemplating marriage, Randall and Teresa discussed Randall's goal of preserving his current and future assets for his children in the event their marriage were to end by his death or a divorce. Randall suggested they enter a premarital agreement, and Teresa agreed, stating she was not marrying Randall for his money.

In late March or early April 1998, Randall drafted a premarital agreement and presented it to Teresa by April 13, ten days before their wedding. The first draft proposed the parties would maintain separate ownership of their assets acquired before and during the marriage, and provided the parties did not intend to hold jointly-owned property except a marital home and a joint checking account. The draft included a mutual waiver of alimony and provided for the equitable division of only jointly-owned property in the event of a divorce. The draft further contemplated Randall would maintain $500,000 in life insurance coverage on his life, and name Teresa as the beneficiary.

Upon receiving the draft, Teresa asked Randall several questions. He responded to them, but insisted Teresa should seek independent legal advice as to the meaning and legal effect of the proposed agreement. Teresa consulted a friend, who referred her to Edith Peebles, an attorney licensed only in Nebraska. Randall did not know Peebles, but when her office requested a copy of the draft, he revised the document to identify Peebles as the lawyer advising Teresa in the matter.

Peebles requested Lisa Line, an associate in her law firm, review the draft on April 16. Line made several handwritten notations on the document, including an exclamation that the proposed agreement would force Teresa to "waive all rights as spouse!" in Randy's pension assets. When Line realized the prenuptial agreement was between two Iowa residents who planned to reside in Iowa, she suggested Peebles should advise Teresa to have an Iowa-licensed attorney review the document. When they met on April 16, Peebles advised Teresa to seek Iowa-licensed counsel. Peebles's firm charged ninety dollars for the legal services rendered to Teresa.

After her meeting with Peebles on the 16th, Teresa returned the document to Randall and requested he make the changes and clarifications suggested in Line's handwritten notes. She did not heed Peebles's advice to seek Iowa counsel. Randall made some revisions, gave the new draft to Teresa, and again told her to review it with her lawyer.

Despite Randall's urging that she have her lawyer review the revised draft, Teresa did not seek further counsel from Peebles or any other attorney. Randall attached to the revised agreement separate schedules listing the assets of each party, the parties signed the agreement on April 17, and they departed for Jamaica the next day. As we have already noted, Randall and Teresa were married in Jamaica on April 23, 1998.

The marriage later failed, and Randall filed a petition requesting its dissolution on November 23, 2004. Randall sought, and Teresa opposed, enforcement of the premarital agreement. The district court bifurcated the trial, first taking up the question of the enforceability of the premarital agreement. After a trial of that matter, the court found Teresa's execution of the agreement was involuntary, and therefore concluded the accord was unenforceable under Iowa Code section 596.8(1) (providing a premarital agreement is not enforceable if the person against whom enforcement is sought proves the agreement was not executed voluntarily).

Following a subsequent trial on property division, spousal support, and attorney fees, district court dissolved the parties' marriage, divided the marital assets, and awarded Teresa spousal support for a term of only two months. The decree allocated to Teresa assets valued at $86,755 and ordered Randall to pay Teresa a total of $150,000 in three equal installments payable on April 1, 2006, September 1, 2006, and January 1, 2007. The decree made no award for attorney fees beyond the judgment entered earlier against Randall for temporary attorney fees.

Randall appealed, challenging both the ruling denying his request for enforcement of the premarital agreement and the property division ordered in the dissolution decree. Teresa cross-appealed, claiming equity requires for her a more favorable property division, more substantial spousal support, and an additional award for attorney fees. The court of appeals affirmed the district court's decisions in all respects. We granted further review to address the validity of the premarital agreement. . . .

III. Discussion.

In Iowa, premarital agreements executed on or after January 1, 1992, are subject to the requirements of the Iowa Uniform Premarital Agreement Act (IUPAA), codified in Iowa Code chapter 596. Iowa Code § 596.12. The IUPAA provides three independent bases for finding a premarital agreement unenforceable:

A premarital agreement is not enforceable if the person against whom enforcement is sought proves any of the following:

(1) The person did not execute the agreement voluntarily.

(2) The agreement was unconscionable when it was executed.

(3) Before the execution of the agreement the person was not provided a fair and reasonable disclosure of the property or financial obligations of the other spouse; and the person did not have, or reasonably could not have had, an adequate knowledge of the property or financial obligations of the other spouse. . . .

Id. § 596.8. The IUPAA is modeled after the Uniform Premarital Agreement Act (UPAA), which was drafted by the National Conference of Commissioners on Uniform State Laws in 1983. A primary goal of the UPAA was to increase the certainty of enforceability of premarital agreements. In the absence of instructive Iowa legislative history, we look to the comments and statements of purpose contained in the Uniform Act to guide our interpretation of the comparable provisions of the IUPAA.

A. Voluntariness.

The district court found the premarital agreement in this case was not executed voluntarily because Randall, as an attorney, had substantially greater power under the circumstances and Teresa did not receive the advice of independent Iowa counsel. In making that finding, the district court relied on our decision in *Spiegel*, which established that waivers of rights in premarital agreements executed prior to the adoption of the IUPAA are not enforceable if they were not "knowing and voluntary." In *Spiegel*, we undertook a "procedural fairness" analysis to determine whether the agreement was "fairly, freely and understandingly entered into" by the parties.

While broad notions of procedural fairness were relevant to our determination of voluntariness challenges to premarital agreements executed prior to January 1, 1992, the IUPAA has significantly altered and clarified the voluntariness inquiry for agreements executed after that date. In contrast to the "knowing and voluntary" test of "procedural fairness" applied in Spiegel, section 596.8(1) requires only that the agreement be executed voluntarily. Neither the IUPAA nor the UPAA defines the term "voluntarily." Black's Law Dictionary defines "voluntarily" as "[i]ntentionally; without coercion." In *Spiegel*, we intimated that a voluntarily executed premarital agreement was one free from duress and undue influence. We believe this is the appropriate formulation of the voluntariness inquiry under IUPAA as well. We therefore hold proof of duress or undue influence is required under section 596.8(1) to establish a premarital agreement was involuntarily executed.

Teresa testified she executed the agreement voluntarily. Upon our de novo review, we conclude Teresa failed to establish duress or undue influence.

1. Duress.

There are two essential elements to a claim of duress in the execution of a contract: (1) one party issues a wrongful or unlawful threat and (2) the other party had no reasonable alternative to entering the contract. Here, Randall informed Teresa he would not get married again without a premarital agreement. We rejected the argument that such an ultimatum was wrongful or unlawful in *Spiegel*. Additionally, similar to the bride-to-be in *Spiegel*, Teresa had the reasonable alternative of cancelling the wedding in the face of such a threat. These facts fall far short of a showing of duress sufficient to support a finding that Teresa involuntarily executed the agreement.

2. Undue influence.

We stated the standard for undue influence in *Spiegel*:

> Undue influence is influence that deprives one person of his or her freedom of choice and substitutes the will of another in its place. "[M]ere importunity that does not go to the extent of controlling the will of the grantor does not establish undue influence." Freedom from undue influence is presumed.

The district court found Randall's position as a lawyer, and his status as Teresa's fiancée and employer, put Randall in such a position of power over Teresa that she was willing to put her full faith in his judgment in drafting the agreement. Despite the potential for abuse inherent in the parties' complex relationship, we find the evidence presented was insufficient to establish undue influence.

Although Teresa testified that Randall subtly encouraged her not to take the second draft to an attorney, the district court found this testimony incredible. We credit the district court's credibility determination and find Randall encouraged Teresa to seek the advice of counsel as to both drafts of the agreement. The facts presented here simply do not demonstrate the "improper or wrongful constraint, machination, or urgency of persuasion" required for a finding of undue influence. We are not persuaded that Randall's will was substituted for Teresa's own judgment in deciding to sign the agreement.

Having found the premarital agreement was not a product of duress or undue influence, we conclude Teresa has failed to prove she executed the agreement involuntarily. . . .

D. Grounds for Challenging Agreements: Unconscionability

Most states allow matrimonial agreements to be set aside if they are unconscionable. Section 6 of the UPAA expressly provides that an agreement may be unenforceable if it was "unconscionable when it was executed." Louisiana, in accordance with its civil law tradition, does not generally recognize unconscionability as grounds for annulling contracts. In common law, unconscionability is a question of law to be decided by the court. The Comment to Section 6 of the UPAA explains that this standard "includes protection against onesidedness, oppression, or unfair surprise." Furthermore, "in the context of negotiations between spouses as to the financial incidents of their marriage, the standard includes protection against overreaching, concealment of assets, and sharp dealing not consistent with the obligations of marital partners to deal fairly with each other." Unconscionability alone will not invalidate the prenuptial agreement under the UPAA. Rather, the party challenging the agreement must prove:

> the agreement was unconscionable when it was executed and, before execution of the agreement the party:
>
> (i) was not provided a fair and reasonable disclosure of the property or financial obligations of the other party;
>
> (ii) did not voluntarily and expressly waive, in writing, any right to disclosure of the property or financial obligations of the other party beyond the disclosure provided; and
>
> (iii) did not have, or reasonably could not have had, an adequate knowledge of the property or financial obligations of the other party.

The practical effect of Section 6 is to require a full disclosure of the assets and liabilities of both spouses at the time the agreement is executed or a waiver of that disclosure. Louisiana has no comparable requirement. However, many Louisiana prenuptial agreements include waiver language nonetheless. Presumably, inclusion of this language is designed to avoid conflicts of law issues in the subsequent enforcement of the agreement.

Not all jurisdictions have implemented the UPAA's provisions on unconscionability verbatim. Some states, for example, make lack of financial disclosure or waiver an independent ground for invalidating an agreement. In other words, an agreement may be invalid if it was unconscionable *or* if there was no financial disclosure.

Unconscionability, as defined by the UPAA, can lead to some curious outcomes. In *Marsocci v. Marsocci* below, the court enforces an agreement it deems unconscionable because there was an adequate financial disclosure.

Marsocci v. Marscocci
911 A.2d 690 (R.I. 2006)

Justice GOLDBERG, for the Court.

This case came before the Supreme Court on November 1, 2006, on cross-appeals by the plaintiff, Debra L. Marsocci (Debra or plaintiff), and the defendant, David A. Marsocci (David or defendant), from a Family Court decision pending entry of final judgment of divorce. The defendant appeals the trial justice's decision that invalidated a premarital agreement (agreement) based on unconscionability, involuntariness, and lack of fairness. The defendant also assigns error to the amount of child support awarded to the plaintiff. In her appeal, the plaintiff argues that the Family Court erred in its equitable distribution of assets and alleges that she should have been awarded one-half of the marital estate, rather than the one-third that the trial justice ordered.

For the reasons stated in this opinion, we vacate the judgment and remand this case to the Family Court for further proceedings consistent with this opinion.

Facts and Travel

The facts in this case are largely undisputed. Debra L. Tetreault and David A. Marsocci were married on August 26, 1995. On August 22, 1995, four days before the wedding, the parties signed a premarital agreement. At that time, David was represented by counsel; Debra was not. However, both parties declared that the other had "fully disclosed [his or her] present approximate net worth" and that each party "had full opportunity for review of [the] agreement and both parties acknowledge their understanding of the effect and content" of it. As his separate property, David listed six parcels of real estate, both developed and undeveloped, three vehicles, and a business checking account; however, no specific values were assigned to these assets. Debra had no assets. The agreement was signed by the parties and properly witnessed. Their son, Matthew, was born six months later.

In July 2002, Debra filed a complaint for absolute divorce. . . .

Before addressing the distribution of the couple's assets, the Family Court sought to determine whether the premarital agreement was valid and enforceable. The trial justice declared that as the party challenging the validity of the agreement, Debra had a "heavy burden." She also noted that it was Debra's contention that the agreement was not enforceable because property that was described as separate property at the time of the marriage had transmuted into marital property. David insisted that the agreement was valid and disputed Debra's claim of an interest in the real estate that he owned.

In Rhode Island, the enforceability of premarital agreements is controlled by the Uniform Premarital Agreement Act (UPAA), G.L.1956 § 15-17-6. The trial justice declared that it was incumbent upon Debra to prove, by clear and convincing evidence, that:

> "[T]he agreement was not executed voluntarily; that the agreement was unconscionable when it was executed, as well as before; that the party [challenging the agreement] was not provided a fair and reasonable disclosure of the property or financial obligations of the other party, and did not expressly waive, in writing, any right to disclosure of the property or financial obligations of the other party beyond the disclosure already provided."

With respect to the issue of voluntariness, the trial justice looked for guidance to and relied upon the California statutory definition of voluntariness, which contains a presumption that a premarital agreement was not voluntary "unless the Court finds, among other things, that the party against whom enforceability is sought . . . if unrepresented . . . was fully informed of the terms and basic effects of the agreement, as well as the rights and obligations he or she is giving up."

The trial justice found that each asset David had listed was unaccompanied by a dollar value; nor was there a written waiver of Debra's right to disclosure of the value of her husband's property and his financial obligations. She stated that although there was scant testimony about the circumstances under which it was executed, the agreement could "speak for itself." She then went on to note that although representation by separate counsel is not required, when, as here, a party is unrepresented, "it is vital to the validity of the prenuptial agreement that there be full and specific information regarding the assets and the obligations of each signator[y]" and that in this case "[t]here is no information contained in this agreement as to the values of any of Mr. Marsocci's assets."

The Family Court then addressed the question of unconscionability and declared that unconscionability relates to "the negotiations between the parties [designed] to protect against over-reaching, concealment of assets and sharp dealing." The trial justice declared that premarital agreements must be scrutinized closely because of the nature of the fiduciary relationship between the parties, a relationship that does not exist between parties to traditional arms-length contracts. She noted that this agreement provides that Debra "has nothing and agrees to end up with nothing after her marriage; the so-called after-acquired property clause." She further found that a "prenuptial agreement in which one party acquires all to the exclusion of the other party is not a substantively fair agreement" and that it "defies the basic underpinnings of the marital relationship; namely, that marriage is a partnership where both parties through their mutual efforts obtain assets subject to equitable distribution in the event they cease getting along."

The court then went on to find by clear and convincing evidence that:

> "the agreement was not only involuntarily executed due to the failure of the agreement to fully disclose the value of Mr. Marsocci's assets and the lack of any waiver of said information signed by Mrs. Marsocci, but further due to the fact that the agreement is unconscionable . . . [and demonstrates] over-reaching and sharp dealing."

. . . Both parties appealed, and it is these appeals that are now before this Court. . . .

The Premarital Agreement

In Rhode Island, the enforceability of a premarital agreement is governed by the Uniform Premarital Agreement Act as codified in § 15-17-6. Section 15-17-6 states:

> "(a) A premarital agreement is not enforceable if the party against whom enforcement is sought proves that:
>
> "(1) That party did not execute the agreement voluntarily; and
>
> "(2) The agreement was unconscionable when it was executed and, before execution of the agreement, that party:
>
>> "(i) Was not provided a fair and reasonable disclosure of the property or financial obligations of the other party;
>>
>> "(ii) Did not voluntarily and expressly waive, in writing, any right to disclosure of the property or financial obligations of the other party beyond the disclosure provided; and

"(iii) Did not have, or reasonably could not have had, an adequate knowledge of the property or financial obligations of the other party.

"(b) The burden of proof as to each of the elements required in order to have a premarital agreement held to be unenforceable shall be on the party seeking to have the agreement declared unenforceable and must be proven by clear and convincing evidence.

"(c) If a provision of a premarital agreement modifies or eliminates spousal support and that modification or elimination causes one party to the agreement to be eligible for support under a program of public assistance at the time of separation or marital dissolution, a court, notwithstanding the terms of the agreement, may require the other party to provide support to the extent necessary to avoid that eligibility.

"(d) An issue of unconscionability of a premarital agreement shall be decided by the court as a matter of law. . . ."

Unconscionability

The "issue of unconscionability of a premarital agreement shall be decided by the court as a matter of law." Section 15-17-6(d). In addressing this element, the trial justice found that the agreement was unconscionable because Debra was unrepresented by counsel and "effectively [gave] up any interest in any assets obtained during the marriage, but for the marital domicile[.]" Although the parties to a premarital agreement may proceed without counsel, this is a factor that is relevant to a finding of unconscionability. The trial justice also found that "[a] prenuptial agreement in which one party acquires all to the exclusion of the other party is not a substantively fair agreement and defies the basic underpinnings of the marital relationship[.]" We agree.

The agreement respecting the parties' separate property interests provides:

"Such ownership and use of Prior Property shall include income, interest, rents, dividends, and stock splits, which said income shall be considered prior acquired property.

"Such separate ownership of assets shall also apply to any substitutions and replacements of such Prior Property obtained from the proceeds of disposition of such Prior Property during the marriage."

The trial justice noted that David's business, both at the time the agreement was executed and at the time of the divorce, involved "selling one property and purchasing another, and mortgaging one to obtain another, and so on and so forth, using the rent for same to pay his personal and his marital debt." The language of the agreement purports to isolate as separate property not only the actual holdings explicitly listed as David's "Prior Property," but also seeks to reach into the future to prevent a marital interest arising from income produced as a result of David's ownership of these assets, notwithstanding the fact that this income comprised the majority of David's earnings throughout the marriage. Given the nature of David's business at the time the agreement was executed and throughout the course of the marriage, we agree with the trial justice that this language clearly "defies the basic underpinnings of the marital relationship; namely, that marriage is a partnership where both parties through their mutual efforts obtain assets subject to equitable distribution in the event they cease getting along[,]" and as such was unconscionable at the time it was executed. Unconscionability alone, however, will not defeat a premarital agreement.

Disclosure

Finally, the Family Court justice rested her decision on a finding that "[t]here is no information contained [within the] agreement as to the values of any of Mr. Marsocci's assets." The UPAA does not require that the assets and financial obligations of the parties be set forth in the agreement. Rather, a party's failure to provide a fair and reasonable disclosure of the property or financial obligations to the other party is a factor that must be proven by clear and convincing evidence to defeat the agreement. Although brief and lacking in detail, David's assets were listed in an addendum to the agreement, and each party acknowledged that the other had "fully disclosed [his or her] present approximate net worth[.]" We deem this acknowledgement to constitute adequate compliance with the mandate that each party be provided with "a fair and reasonable disclosure of the property or financial obligations of the other party[.]" Section 15-17-6(a)(2)(i).

After careful review of the agreement and the record in this case, we are of the opinion that Debra failed to establish, by clear and convincing evidence, all of the elements set forth in § 15-17-6. Thus, we hold that the agreement is valid and shall control the apportionment of assets between the parties. We are of the opinion, however, that the agreement does not preclude the Family Court from assigning the appreciation in value or an interest in David's property that increased in value as a result of the efforts of either spouse during the marriage under § 15-5-16.1(b).

Although counsel for defendant strenuously argued before this Court that the assets listed in the agreement and their proceeds or substitutions were forever frozen as David's separate property and, as such, should be immune to transmutation and active appreciation, he is incorrect. Premarital assets that were transmuted into marital assets and any appreciation of David's assets resulting from marital efforts are marital property subject to equitable distribution. Accordingly, we vacate the judgment and remand this case for further proceedings, including a valuation and equitable distribution of those assets comprising the marital estate. . . .

Conclusion

For the reasons stated, the defendant's appeal is sustained in part. The judgment of the Family Court is vacated. The papers in the case are remanded to the Family Court for further proceedings in accordance with this decision.

Chapter 11

Parents, Children, and the Constitution

A. Parental Authority

The Supreme Court has repeatedly recognized that parents have a fundamental right to the care, custody, and nurture of their children. Parental autonomy is a fundamental—but not unlimited—right. The government also has an interest in ensuring that children are protected from abuse and ensuring the general health and welfare of its citizens—a notion sometimes called *parens patriae*. Most developed nations, for example, have enacted laws aimed at preventing the abuse and endangerment of children. As the following cases demonstrate, parental autonomy cases often involve the difficult balance between the fundamental rights of parents and the interest of the state.

Stanley v. Illinois, the first case below, involves the constitutionality of an Illinois statute that presumed unwed fathers were unfit parents and allowed the state to remove children from the parent without a prior hearing. *Stanley* involves both procedural due process and equal protection under the Fourteenth Amendment. *Stanley* also illustrates one of many instances in which the law has discriminated against non-marital parents and children—an issue we will examine again.

Wisconsin v. Yoder, the second case below, is an important decision involving religious objections to compulsory education laws for children. Like some of the marriage cases, *Yoder* involves a fundamental liberty interest recognized by the Fourteenth Amendment. In this case, that liberty interest involves both parental autonomy generally as well as religious freedom protected by the First Amendment. *Yoder* reaffirms the importance of those liberty interests. In reading *Yoder*, consider how it might apply to other types of parental autonomy questions that do not always involve a religious component—such as decisions regarding homeschooling, vaccinations, and discipline.

Santosky v. Kramer considers the procedural due process rights of parents in state proceedings to terminate parental rights because of abuse or neglect. Again, the court is asked to balance the constitutionally protected liberty interest parents have in their children against the *parens patriae* role of the state in protecting children from abuse and neglect.

Stanley v. Illinois

405 U.S. 645 (1972)

Mr. Justice WHITE delivered the opinion of the Court.

Joan Stanley lived with Peter Stanley intermittently for 18 years, during which time they had three children. When Joan Stanley died, Peter Stanley lost not only her but also his children. Under Illinois law, the children of unwed fathers become wards of the State upon the death of the mother. Accordingly, upon Joan Stanley's death, in a dependency proceeding instituted by the State of Illinois, Stanley's children were declared wards of the State and placed with court-appointed guardians. Stanley appealed, claiming that he had never been shown to be an unfit parent and that since married fathers and unwed mothers could not be deprived of their children without such a showing, he had been deprived of the equal protection of the laws guaranteed him by the Fourteenth Amendment. . . .

Stanley presses his equal protection claim here. The State continues to respond that unwed fathers are presumed unfit to raise their children and that it is unnecessary to hold individualized hearings to determine whether particular fathers are in fact unfit parents before they are separated from their children. We granted certiorari. . . .

I

Issue

⟵ . . . Is a presumption that distinguishes and burdens all unwed fathers constitutionally repugnant? We conclude that, as a matter of due process of law, Stanley was entitled to a hearing on his fitness as a parent before his children were taken from him and that, by denying him a hearing and extending it to all other parents whose custody of their children is challenged, the State denied Stanley the equal protection of the laws guaranteed by the Fourteenth Amendment.

II

Illinois has two principal methods of removing nondelinquent children from the homes of their parents. In a dependency proceeding it may demonstrate that the children are wards of the State because they have no surviving parent or guardian. In a neglect proceeding it may show that children should be wards of the State because the present parent(s) or guardian does not provide suitable care.

The State's right—indeed, duty—to protect minor children through a judicial determination of their interests in a neglect proceeding is not challenged here. Rather, we are faced with a dependency statute that empowers state officials to circumvent neglect proceedings on the theory that an unwed father is not a "parent" whose existing relationship with his children must be considered. "Parents," says the State, "means the father and mother of a legitimate child, or the survivor of them, or the natural mother of an illegitimate child, and includes any adoptive parent," but the term does not include unwed fathers.

Under Illinois law, therefore, while the children of all parents can be taken from them in neglect proceedings, that is only after notice, hearing, and proof of such unfitness as a parent as amounts to neglect, an unwed father is uniquely subject to the more simplistic dependency proceeding. By use of this proceeding, the State, on showing that the father was not married to the mother, need not prove unfitness in fact, because it is presumed at law. Thus, the unwed father's claim of parental qualification is avoided as "irrelevant."

In considering this procedure under the Due Process Clause, we recognize, as we have in other cases, that due process of law does not require a hearing "in every conceivable case of government impairment of private interest." [*Cafeteria and Restaurant Workers Union etc. v. McElroy*] explained that "[t]he very nature of due process negates any concept of inflexible procedures universally applicable to every imaginable situation" and firmly established that "what procedures due process may require under any given set of circumstances must begin with a determination of the precise nature of the government function involved as well as of the private interest that has been affected by governmental action."

The private interest here, that of a man in the children he has sired and raised, undeniably warrants deference and, absent a powerful countervailing interest, protection. It is plain that the interest of a parent in the companionship, care, custody, and management of his or her children "come[s] to this Court with a momentum for respect lacking when appeal is made to liberties which derive merely from shifting economic arrangements."

The Court has frequently emphasized the importance of the family. The rights to conceive and to raise one's children have been deemed "essential," "basic civil rights of man," and "[r]ights far more precious . . . than property rights." "It is cardinal with us that the custody, care and nurture of the child reside first in the parents, whose primary function and freedom include preparation for obligations the state can neither supply nor hinder." The integrity of the family unit has found protection in the Due Process Clause of the Fourteenth Amendment, the Equal Protection Clause of the Fourteenth Amendment, and the Ninth Amendment.

Nor has the law refused to recognize those family relationships unlegitimized by a marriage ceremony. The Court has declared unconstitutional a state statute denying natural, but illegitimate, children a wrongful-death action for the death of their mother, emphasizing that such children cannot be denied the right of other children because familial bonds in such cases were often as warm, enduring, and important as those arising within a more formally organized family unit. . . .

These authorities make it clear that, at the least, Stanley's interest in retaining custody of his children is cognizable and substantial.

For its part, the State has made its interest quite plain: Illinois has declared that the aim of the Juvenile Court Act is to protect "the moral, emotional, mental, and physical welfare of the minor and the best interests of the community" and to "strengthen the minor's family ties whenever possible, removing him from the custody of his parents only when his welfare or safety or the protection of the public cannot be adequately safeguarded without removal. . . ." These are legitimate interests, well within the power of the State to implement. We do not question the assertion that neglectful parents may be separated from their children.

But we are here not asked to evaluate the legitimacy of the state ends, rather, to determine whether the means used to achieve these ends are constitutionally defensible. What is the state interest in separating children from fathers without a hearing designed to determine whether the father is unfit in a particular disputed case? We observe that the State registers no gain towards its declared goals when it separates children from the custody of fit parents. Indeed, if Stanley is a fit father, the State spites its own articulated goals when it needlessly separates him from his family.

. . . It may be, as the State insists, that most unmarried fathers are unsuitable and neglectful parents. It may also be that Stanley is such a parent and that his children should be placed in other hands. But all unmarried fathers are not in this category; some are wholly suited to have custody of their children. This much the State readily concedes, and nothing in this record indicates that Stanley is or has been a neglectful father who has not cared for his children. Given the opportunity to make his case, Stanley may have been seen to be deserving of custody of his offspring. Had this been so, the State's statutory policy would have been furthered by leaving custody in him.

. . . [I]t may be argued that unmarried fathers are so seldom fit that Illinois need not undergo the administrative inconvenience of inquiry in any case, including Stanley's. The establishment of prompt efficacious procedures to achieve legitimate state ends is a proper state interest worthy of cognizance in constitutional adjudication. But the Constitution recognizes higher values than speed and efficiency. Indeed, one might fairly say of the Bill of Rights in general, and the Due Process Clause in particular, that they were designed to protect the fragile values of a vulnerable citizenry from the overbearing concern for efficiency and efficacy that may characterize praiseworthy government officials no less, and perhaps more, than mediocre ones.

Procedure by presumption is always cheaper and easier than individualized determination. But when, as here, the procedure forecloses the determinative issues of competence and care, when it explicitly disdains present realities in deference to past formalities, it needlessly risks running roughshod over the important interests of both parent and child. It therefore cannot stand.

. . . The State's interest in caring for Stanley's children is de minimis if Stanley is shown to be a fit father. It insists on presuming rather than proving Stanley's unfitness solely because it is more convenient to presume than to prove. Under the Due Process Clause that advantage is insufficient to justify refusing a father a hearing when the issue at stake is the dismemberment of his family.

III

The State of Illinois assumes custody of the children of married parents, divorced parents, and unmarried mothers only after a hearing and proof of neglect. The children of unmarried fathers, however, are declared dependent children without a hearing on parental fitness and without proof of neglect. Stanley's claim in the state courts and here is that failure to afford him a hearing on his parental qualifications while extending it to other parents denied him equal protection of the laws. We have concluded that all Illinois parents are constitutionally entitled to a hearing on their fitness before their children are removed from their custody. It follows that denying such a hearing to Stanley and those like him while granting it to other Illinois parents is inescapably contrary to the Equal Protection Clause.

The judgment of the Supreme Court of Illinois is reversed and the case is remanded to that court for proceedings not inconsistent with this opinion. It is so ordered.

Reversed and remanded.

Wisconsin v. Yoder

406 U.S. 205 (1972)

Mr. Chief Justice BURGER delivered the opinion of the Court.

On petition of the State of Wisconsin, we granted the writ of certiorari in this case to review a decision of the Wisconsin Supreme Court holding that respondents' convictions for violating the State's compulsory school-attendance law were invalid under the Free Exercise Clause of the First Amendment to the United States Constitution made applicable to the States by the Fourteenth Amendment. For the reasons hereafter stated we affirm the judgment of the Supreme Court of Wisconsin.

Respondents Jonas Yoder and Wallace Miller are members of the Old Order Amish religion, and respondent Adin Yutzy is a member of the Conservative Amish Mennonite Church. They and their families are residents of Green County, Wisconsin. Wisconsin's compulsory school-attendance law required them to cause their children to attend public or private school until reaching age 16 but the respondents declined to send their children, ages 14 and 15, to public school after they complete the eighth grade. The children were not enrolled in any private school, or within any recognized exception to the compulsory-attendance law, and they are conceded to be subject to the Wisconsin statute.

. . . The trial testimony showed that respondents believed, in accordance with the tenets of Old Order Amish communities generally, that their children's attendance at high school, public or private, was contrary to the Amish religion and way of life. They believed that by sending their children to high school, they would not only expose themselves to the danger of the censure of the church community, but, as found by the county court, also endanger their own salvation and that of their children. The State stipulated that respondents' religious beliefs were sincere.

In support of their position, respondents presented as expert witnesses scholars on religion and education whose testimony is uncontradicted. They expressed their opinions on the relationship of the Amish belief concerning school attendance to the more general tenets of their religion, and described the impact that compulsory high school attendance could have on the continued survival of Amish communities as they exist in the United States today. The history of the Amish sect was given in some detail, beginning with the Swiss Anabaptists of the 16th century who rejected institutionalized churches and sought to return to the early, simple, Christian life deemphasizing material success, rejecting the competitive spirit, and seeking to insulate themselves from the modern world. As a result of their common heritage, Old Order Amish communities today are characterized by a fundamental belief that salvation requires life in a church community separate and apart from the world and worldly influence. This concept of life aloof from the world and its values is central to their faith.

A related feature of Old Order Amish communities is their devotion to a life in harmony with nature and the soil, as exemplified by the simple life of the early Christian era that continued in America during much of our early national life. Amish beliefs require members of the community to make their living by farming or closely related activities. Broadly speaking, the Old Order Amish religion pervades and determines the entire mode of life of its adherents. Their conduct is regulated in great detail by the Ordnung, or rules, of the church community. Adult baptism, which occurs in late adolescence, is the time at which Amish young people voluntarily undertake heavy obligations, not unlike the Bar Mitzvah of the Jews, to abide by the rules of the church community.

Amish objection to formal education beyond the eighth grade is firmly grounded in these central religious concepts. They object to the high school, and higher education generally, because the values they teach are in marked variance with Amish values and the Amish way of life; they view secondary school education as an impermissible exposure of their children to a "wordly" influence in conflict with their beliefs. The high school tends to emphasize intellectual and scientific accomplishments, self-distinction, competitiveness, worldly success, and social life with other students. Amish society emphasizes informal learning-through-doing; a life of "goodness," rather than a life of intellect; wisdom, rather than technical knowledge, community welfare, rather than competition; and separation from, rather than integration with, contemporary worldly society.

Formal high school education beyond the eighth grade is contrary to Amish beliefs, not only because it places Amish children in an environment hostile to Amish beliefs with increasing emphasis on competition in class work and sports and with pressure to conform to the styles, manners, and ways of the peer group, but also because it takes them away from their community, physically and emotionally, during the crucial and formative adolescent period of life. During this period, the children must acquire Amish attitudes favoring manual work and self-reliance and the specific skills needed to perform the adult role of an Amish farmer or housewife. They must learn to enjoy physical labor. Once a child has learned basic reading, writing, and elementary mathematics, these traits, skills, and attitudes admittedly fall within the category of those best learned through example and "doing" rather than in a classroom. And, at this time in life, the Amish child must also grow in his faith and his relationship to the Amish community if he is to be prepared to accept the heavy obligations imposed by adult baptism. . . .

The Amish do not object to elementary education through the first eight grades as a general proposition because they agree that their children must have basic skills in the "three R's" in order to read the Bible, to be good farmers and citizens, and to be able to deal with non-Amish people when necessary in the course of daily affairs. They view such a basic education as acceptable because it does not significantly expose their children to wordly values or interfere with their development in the Amish community during the crucial adolescent period. While Amish accept compulsory elementary education generally, wherever possible they have established their own elementary schools in many respects like the small local schools of the past. In the Amish belief higher learning tends to develop values they reject as influences that alienate man from God.

On the basis of such considerations, Dr. Hostetler testified that compulsory high school attendance could not only result in great psychological harm to Amish children, because of the conflicts it would produce, but would also, in his opinion, ultimately result in the destruction of the Old Order Amish church community as it exists in the United States today. The testimony of Dr. Donald A. Erickson, an expert witness on education, also showed that the Amish succeed in preparing their high school age children to be productive members of the Amish community. He described their system of learning through doing the skills directly relevant to their adult roles in the Amish community as "ideal" and perhaps superior to ordinary high school education. The evidence also showed that the Amish have an excellent record as law-abiding and generally self-sufficient members of society. . . .

I

There is no doubt as to the power of a State, having a high responsibility for education of its citizens, to impose reasonable regulations for the control and duration of basic education. Providing public schools ranks at the very apex of the function of a State. Yet even this paramount responsibility was, in *Pierce*, made to yield to the right of parents to provide an equivalent education in a privately operated system. There the Court held that Oregon's statute compelling attendance in a public school from age eight to age 16 unreasonably interfered with the interest of parents in directing the rearing of their off-spring, including their education in church-operated schools. As that case suggests, the values of parental direction of the religious upbringing and education of their children in their early and formative years have a high place in our society. Thus, a State's interest in universal education, however highly we rank it, is not totally free from a balancing process when it impinges on fundamental rights and interests, such as those specifically protected by the Free Exercise Clause of the First Amendment, and the traditional interest of parents with respect to the religious upbringing of their children so long as they, in the words of *Pierce*, "prepare [them] for additional obligations."

It follows that in order for Wisconsin to compel school attendance beyond the eighth grade against a claim that such attendance interferes with the practice of a legitimate religious belief, it must appear either that the State does not deny the free exercise of religious belief by its requirement, or that there is a state interest of sufficient magnitude to override the interest claiming protection under the Free Exercise Clause. Long before there was general acknowledgment of the need for universal formal education, the Religion Clauses had specifically and firmly fixed the right to free exercise of religious beliefs, and buttressing this fundamental right was an equally firm, even if less explicit, prohibition against the establishment of any religion by government. The values underlying these two provisions relating to religion have been zealously protected, sometimes even at the expense of other interests of admittedly high social importance. . . .

The essence of all that has been said and written on the subject is that only those interests of the highest order and those not otherwise served can overbalance legitimate claims to the free exercise of religion. We can accept it as settled, therefore, that, however strong the State's interest in universal compulsory education, it is by no means absolute to the exclusion or subordination of all other interests.

II

We come then to the quality of the claims of the respondents concerning the alleged encroachment of Wisconsin's compulsory school-attendance statute on their rights and the rights of their children to the free exercise of the religious beliefs they and their forbears have adhered to for almost three centuries. In evaluating those claims we must be careful to determine whether the Amish religious faith and their mode of life are, as they claim, inseparable and interdependent. A way of life, however virtuous and admirable, may not be interposed as a barrier to reasonable state regulation of education if it is based on purely secular considerations; to have the protection of the Religion Clauses, the claims must be rooted in religious belief. Although a determination of what is a "religious" belief or practice entitled to constitutional protection may present a most delicate question, the very concept of ordered liberty precludes allowing every person to make his own standards on matters of conduct in which society as a whole has important interests. Thus, if the Amish asserted their claims because of their subjective evaluation and rejection of the contemporary secular values accepted by the majority, much as Thoreau rejected the social values of his time and isolated himself at Walden Pond, their claims would not rest on a religious basis. Thoreau's choice was philosophical and personal rather than religious, and such belief does not rise to the demands of the Religion Clauses.

Giving no weight to such secular considerations, however, we see that the record in this case abundantly supports the claim that the traditional way of life of the Amish is not merely a matter of personal preference, but one of deep religious conviction, shared by an organized group, and intimately related to daily living. That the Old Order Amish daily life and religious practice stem from their faith is shown by the fact that it is in response to their literal interpretation of the Biblical injunction from the Epistle of Paul to the Romans, "be not conformed to this world. . . ." This command is fundamental to the Amish faith. Moreover, for the Old Order Amish, religion is not simply a matter of theocratic belief. As the expert witnesses explained, the Old Order Amish religion pervades and determines virtually their entire way of life, regulating it with the detail of the Talmudic diet through the strictly enforced rules of the church community. . . .

As the record so strongly shows, the values and programs of the modern secondary school are in sharp conflict with the fundamental mode of life mandated by the Amish religion; modern laws requiring compulsory secondary education have accordingly engendered great concern and conflict. The conclusion is inescapable that secondary schooling, by exposing Amish children to worldly influences in terms of attitudes, goals, and values contrary to beliefs, and by substantially interfering with the religious development of the Amish child and his integration into the way of life of the Amish faith community at the crucial adolescent stage of development, contravenes the basic religious tenets and practice of the Amish faith, both as to the parent and the child. . . .

In sum, the unchallenged testimony of acknowledged experts in education and religious history, almost 300 years of consistent practice, and strong evidence of a sustained faith pervading and regulating respondents' entire mode of life support the claim that enforcement of the State's requirement of compulsory formal education after the eighth grade would gravely endanger if not destroy the free exercise of respondents' religious beliefs.

III

Neither the findings of the trial court nor the Amish claims as to the nature of their faith are challenged in this Court by the State of Wisconsin. Its position is that the State's interest in universal compulsory formal secondary education to age 16 is so great that it is paramount to the undisputed claims of respondents that their mode of preparing their youth for Amish life, after the traditional elementary education, is an essential part of their religious belief and practice. . . .

Wisconsin concedes that under the Religion Clauses religious beliefs are absolutely free from the State's control, but it argues that "actions," even though religiously grounded, are outside the protection of the First Amendment. But our decisions have rejected the idea that religiously grounded conduct is always outside the protection of the Free Exercise Clause. It is true that activities of individuals, even when religiously based, are often subject to regulation by the States in the exercise of their undoubted power to promote the health, safety, and general welfare, or the Federal Government in the exercise of its delegated powers. But to agree that religiously grounded conduct must often be subject to the broad police power of the State is not to deny that there are areas of conduct protected by the Free Exercise Clause of the First Amendment and thus beyond the power of the State to control, even under regulations of general applicability. . . .

Nor can this case be disposed of on the grounds that Wisconsin's requirement for school attendance to age 16 applies uniformly to all citizens of the State and does not, on its face, discriminate against religions or a particular religion, or that it is motivated by legitimate secular concerns. A regulation neutral on its face may, in its application, nonetheless offend the constitutional requirement for governmental neutrality if it unduly burdens the free exercise of religion. . . .

We turn, then, to the State's broader contention that its interest in its system of compulsory education is so compelling that even the established religious practices of the Amish must give way. . . .

The State advances two primary arguments in support of its system of compulsory education. It notes, as Thomas Jefferson pointed out early in our history, that some degree of education is necessary to prepare citizens to participate effectively and intelligently in our open political system if we are to preserve freedom and independence. Further, education prepares individuals to be self-reliant and self-sufficient participants in society. We accept these propositions.

However, the evidence adduced by the Amish in this case is persuasively to the effect that an additional one or two years of formal high school for Amish children in place of their long-established program of informal vocational education would do little to serve those interests. . . .

It is neither fair nor correct to suggests that the Amish are opposed to education beyond the eighth grade level. What this record shows is that they are opposed to conventional formal education of the type provided by a certified high school because it comes at the child's crucial adolescent period of religious development. . . .

The State, however, supports its interest in providing an additional one or two years of compulsory high school education to Amish children because of the possibility that some such children will choose to leave the Amish community, and that if this occurs they will be ill-equipped for life. . . .

There is nothing in this record to suggest that the Amish qualities of reliability, self-reliance, and dedication to work would fail to find ready markets in today's society. Absent some contrary evidence supporting the State's position, we are unwilling to assume that persons possessing such valuable vocational skills and habits are doomed to become burdens on society should they determine to leave the Amish faith, nor is there any basis in the record to warrant a finding that an additional one or two years of formal school education beyond the eighth grade would serve to eliminate any such problem that might exist.

The requirement for compulsory education beyond the eighth grade is a relatively recent development in our history. Less than 60 years ago, the educational requirements of almost all of the States were satisfied by completion of the elementary grades, at least where the child was regularly and lawfully employed. The independence and successful social functioning of the Amish community for a period approaching almost three centuries and more than 200 years in this country are strong evidence that there is at best a speculative gain, in terms of meeting the duties of citizenship, from an additional one or two years of compulsory formal education. Against this background it would require a more particularized showing from the State on this point to justify the severe interference with religious freedom such additional compulsory attendance would entail.

We should also note that compulsory education and child labor laws find their historical origin in common humanitarian instincts, and that the age limits of both laws have been coordinated to achieve their related objectives. In the context of this case, such considerations, if anything, support rather than detract from respondents' position. The origins of the requirement for school attendance to age 16, an age falling after the completion of elementary school but before completion of high school, are not entirely clear. But to some extent such laws reflected the movement to prohibit most child labor under age 16 that culminated in the provisions of the Federal Fair Labor Standards Act of 1938. It is true, then, that the 16-year child labor age limit may to some degree derive from a contemporary impression that children should be in school until that age. But at the same time, it cannot be denied that, conversely, the 16-year education limit reflects, in substantial measure, the concern that children under that age not be employed under conditions hazardous to their health, or in work that should be performed by adults. . . .

In these terms, Wisconsin's interest in compelling the school attendance of Amish children to age 16 emerges as somewhat less substantial than requiring such attendance for children generally. For, while agricultural employment is not totally outside the legitimate concerns of the child labor laws, employment of children under parental guidance and on the family farm from age 14 to age 16 is an ancient tradition that lies at the periphery of the objectives of such laws. There is no intimation that the Amish employment of their children on family farms is in any way deleterious to their health or that Amish parents exploit children at tender years. Any such inference would be contrary to the record before us. Moreover, employment of Amish children on the family farm does not present the undesirable economic aspects of eliminating jobs that might otherwise be held by adults.

IV

Finally, the State . . . argues that a decision exempting Amish children from the State's requirement fails to recognize the substantive right of the Amish child to a secondary education, and fails to give due regard to the power of the State as parens patriae to extend the benefit of secondary education to children regardless of the wishes of their parents. . . .

This case, of course, is not one in which any harm to the physical or mental health of the child or to the public safety, peace, order, or welfare has been demonstrated or may be properly inferred. The record is to the contrary, and any reliance on that theory would find no support in the evidence.

Contrary to the suggestion of the dissenting opinion of Mr. Justice DOUGLAS, our holding today in no degree depends on the assertion of the religious interest of the child as contrasted with that of the parents. It is the parents who are subject to prosecution here for failing to cause their children to attend school, and it is their right of free exercise, not that of their children, that must determine Wisconsin's power to impose criminal penalties on the parent. The dissent argues that a child who expresses a desire to attend public high school in conflict with the wishes of his parents should not be prevented from doing so. There is no reason for the Court to consider that point since it is not an issue in the case. The children are not parties to this litigation. The State has at no point tried this case on the theory that respondents were preventing their children from attending school against their expressed desires, and indeed the record is to the contrary. The State's position from the outset has been that it is empowered to apply its compulsory-attendance law to Amish parents in the same manner as to other parents — that is, without regard to the wishes of the child. That is the claim we reject today.

Our holding in no way determines the proper resolution of possible competing interests of parents, children, and the State in an appropriate state court proceeding in which the power of the State is asserted on the theory that Amish parents are preventing their minor children from attending high school despite their expressed desires to the contrary. . . . On this record we neither reach nor decide those issues.

. . . [T]his case involves the fundamental interest of parents, as contrasted with that of the State, to guide the religious future and education of their children. The history and culture of Western civilization reflect a strong tradition of parental concern for the nurture and upbringing of their children. This primary role of the parents in the upbringing of their children is now established beyond debate as an enduring American tradition. If not the first, perhaps the most significant statements of the Court in this area are found in *Pierce v. Society of Sisters*, in which the Court observed:

> "Under the doctrine of *Meyer v. Nebraska* . . . we think it entirely plain that the Act of 1922 unreasonably interferes with the liberty of parents and guardians to direct the upbringing and education of children under their control. As often heretofore pointed out, rights guaranteed by the Constitution may not be abridged by legislation which has no reasonable relation to some purpose within the competency of the State. The fundamental theory of liberty upon which all governments in this Union repose excludes any general power of the State to standardize its children by forcing them to accept instruction from public teachers only. The child is not the mere creature of the State; those who nurture him and direct his destiny have the right, coupled with the high duty, to recognize and prepare him for additional obligations."

. . . To be sure, the power of the parent, even when linked to a free exercise claim, may be subject to limitation under *Prince* if it appears that parental decisions will jeopardize the health or safety of the child, or have a potential for significant social burdens. But in this case, the Amish have introduced persuasive evidence undermining the arguments the State has advanced to support its claims in terms of the welfare of the child and society as a whole. The record strongly indicates that accommodating the religious objections of the Amish by forgoing one, or at most two, additional years of compulsory education will not impair the physical or mental health of the child, or result in an inability to be self-supporting or to discharge the duties and responsibilities of citizenship, or in any other way materially detract from the welfare of society.

In the fact of our consistent emphasis on the central values underlying the Religion Clauses in our constitutional scheme of government, we cannot accept a parens patriae claim of such all-encompassing scope and with such sweeping potential for broad and unforeseeable application as that urged by the State.

V

For the reasons stated we hold, with the Supreme Court of Wisconsin, that the First and Fourteenth Amendments prevent the State from compelling respondents to cause their children to attend formal high school to age 16. . . .

In light of this convincing showing, one that probably few other religious groups or sects could make, and weighing the minimal difference between what the State would require and what the Amish already accept, it was incumbent on the State to show with more particularity how its admittedly strong interest in compulsory education would be adversely affected by granting an exemption to the Amish.

Nothing we hold is intended to undermine the general applicability of the State's compulsory school-attendance statutes or to limit the power of the State to promulgate reasonable standards that, while not impairing the free exercise of religion, provide for continuing agricultural vocational education under parental and church guidance by the Old Order Amish or others similarly situated. The States have had a long history of amicable and effective relationships with church-sponsored schools, and there is no basis for assuming that, in this related context, reasonable standards cannot be established concerning the content of the continuing vocational education of Amish children under parental guidance, provided always that state regulations are not inconsistent with what we have said in this opinion.

Affirmed.

Santosky v. Kramer
455 U.S. 745 (1982)

Justice BLACKMUN delivered the opinion of the Court.

Under New York law, the State may terminate, over parental objection, the rights of parents in their natural child upon a finding that the child is "permanently neglected." The New York Family Court Act § 622 requires that only a "fair preponderance of the evidence" support that finding. Thus, in New York, the factual certainty required to extinguish the parent-child relationship is no greater than that necessary to award money damages in an ordinary civil action.

Today we hold that the Due Process Clause of the Fourteenth Amendment demands more than this. Before a State may sever completely and irrevocably the rights of parents in their natural child, due process requires that the State support its allegations by at least clear and convincing evidence.

I

A

New York authorizes its officials to remove a child temporarily from his or her home if the child appears "neglected," within the meaning of Art. 10 of the Family Court Act. Once removed, a child under the age of 18 customarily is placed "in the care of an authorized agency," usually a state institution or a foster home. At that point, "the state's first obligation is to help the family with services to . . . reunite it. . . ." But if convinced that "positive, nurturing parent-child relationships no longer exist," the State may initiate "permanent neglect" proceedings to free the child for adoption.

. . . Termination denies the natural parents physical custody, as well as the rights ever to visit, communicate with, or regain custody of the child.

New York's permanent neglect statute provides natural parents with certain procedural protections. But New York permits its officials to establish "permanent neglect" with less proof than most States require. Thirty-five States, the District of Columbia, and the Virgin Islands currently specify a higher standard of proof, in parental rights termination proceedings, than a "fair preponderance of the evidence. . . ." The question here is whether New York's "fair preponderance of the evidence" standard is constitutionally sufficient.

B

Petitioners John Santosky II and Annie Santosky are the natural parents of Tina and John III. In November 1973, after incidents reflecting parental neglect, respondent Kramer, Commissioner of the Ulster County Department of Social Services, initiated a neglect proceeding under Fam.Ct.Act § 1022 and removed Tina from her natural home. About 10 months later, he removed John III and placed him with foster parents. On the day John was taken, Annie Santosky gave birth to a third child, Jed. When Jed was only three days old, respondent transferred him to a foster home on the ground that immediate removal was necessary to avoid imminent danger to his life or health.

In October 1978, respondent petitioned the Ulster County Family Court to terminate petitioners' parental rights in the three children. Petitioners challenged the constitutionality of the "fair preponderance of the evidence" standard specified in Fam.Ct.Act § 622. The Family Court Judge rejected this constitutional challenge . . . and weighed the evidence under the statutory standard. . . . The judge later held a dispositional hearing and ruled that the best interests of the three children required permanent termination of the Santoskys' custody.

Petitioners appealed, again contesting the constitutionality of § 622's standard of proof. . . .

II

Last Term in *Lassiter v. Department of Social Services* . . . this Court, by a 5–4 vote, held that the Fourteenth Amendment's Due Process Clause does not require the appointment of counsel for indigent parents in every parental status termination proceeding. The case casts light, however, on the two central questions here—whether process is constitutionally due a natural parent at a State's parental rights termination proceeding, and, if so, what process is due.

In *Lassiter*, it was "not disputed that state intervention to terminate the relationship between [a parent] and [the] child must be accomplished by procedures meeting the requisites of the Due Process Clause." The absence of dispute reflected this Court's historical recognition that freedom of personal choice in matters of family life is a fundamental liberty interest protected by the Fourteenth Amendment.

The fundamental liberty interest of natural parents in the care, custody, and management of their child does not evaporate simply because they have not been model parents or have lost temporary custody of their child to the State. Even when blood relationships are strained, parents retain a vital interest in preventing the irretrievable destruction of their family life. If anything, persons faced with forced dissolution of their parental rights have a more critical need for procedural protections than do those resisting state intervention into ongoing family affairs. When the State moves to destroy weakened familial bonds, it must provide the parents with fundamentally fair procedures.

In *Lassiter*, the Court and three dissenters agreed that the nature of the process due in parental rights termination proceedings turns on a balancing of the "three distinct factors" . . . the private interests affected by the proceeding; the risk of error created by the State's chosen procedure; and the countervailing governmental interest supporting use of the challenged procedure. While the respective *Lassiter* opinions disputed whether those factors should be weighed against a presumption disfavoring appointed counsel for one not threatened with loss of physical liberty . . . that concern is irrelevant here. Unlike the Court's right-to-counsel rulings, its decisions concerning constitutional burdens of proof have not turned on any presumption favoring any particular standard. To the contrary, the Court has engaged in a straight-forward consideration of the factors identified . . . to determine whether a particular standard of proof in a particular proceeding satisfies due process.

. . . *Addington* [*v. Texas*] teaches that, in any given proceeding, the minimum standard of proof tolerated by the due process requirement reflects not only the weight of the private and public interests affected, but also a societal judgment about how the risk of error should be distributed between the litigants.

Thus, while private parties may be interested intensely in a civil dispute over money damages, application of a "fair preponderance of the evidence" standard indicates both society's "minimal concern with the outcome," and a conclusion that the litigants should "share the risk of error in roughly equal fashion." When the State brings a criminal action to deny a defendant liberty or life, however, "the interests of the defendant are of such magnitude that historically and without any explicit constitutional requirement they have been protected by standards of proof designed to exclude as nearly as possible the likelihood of an erroneous judgment." The stringency of the "beyond a reasonable doubt" standard bespeaks the "weight and gravity" of the private interest affected, society's interest in avoiding erroneous convictions, and a judgment that those interests together require that "society impos[e] almost the entire risk of error upon itself. . . ."

This Court has mandated an intermediate standard of proof—"clear and convincing evidence"—when the individual interests at stake in a state proceeding are both "particularly important" and "more substantial than mere loss of money." Notwithstanding "the state's 'civil labels and good intentions,'" the Court has deemed this level of certainty necessary to preserve fundamental fairness in a variety of government-initiated proceedings that threaten the individual involved with "a significant deprivation of liberty" or "stigma. . . ."

III

In parental rights termination proceedings, the private interest affected is commanding; the risk of error from using a preponderance standard is substantial; and the countervailing governmental interest favoring that standard is comparatively slight. Evaluation of the three *Eldridge* factors compels the conclusion that use of a "fair preponderance of the evidence" standard in such proceedings is inconsistent with due process.

A

. . . *Lassiter* declared it "plain beyond the need for multiple citation" that a natural parent's "desire for and right to 'the companionship, care, custody, and management of his or her children'" is an interest far more precious than any property. When the State initiates a parental rights termination proceeding, it seeks not merely to infringe that fundamental liberty interest, but to end it. "If the State prevails, it will have worked a unique kind of deprivation. . . . A parent's interest in the accuracy and justice of the decision to terminate his or her parental status is, therefore, a commanding one."

In government-initiated proceedings to determine juvenile delinquency, civil commitment, deportation, and denaturalization, this Court has identified losses of individual liberty sufficiently serious to warrant imposition of an elevated burden of proof. Yet juvenile delinquency adjudications, civil commitment, deportation, and denaturalization, at least to a degree, are all reversible official actions. Once affirmed on appeal, a New York decision terminating parental rights is final and irrevocable. Few forms of state action are both so severe and so irreversible.

Thus, the first *Eldridge* factor—the private interest affected—weighs heavily against use of the preponderance standard at a state-initiated permanent neglect proceeding. We do not deny that the child and his foster parents are also deeply interested in the outcome of that contest. But at the factfinding stage of the New York proceeding, the focus emphatically is not on them. . . .

However substantial the foster parents' interests may be, they are not implicated directly in the factfinding stage of a state-initiated permanent neglect proceeding against the natural parents. . . . For the foster parents, the State's failure to prove permanent neglect may prolong the delay and uncertainty until their foster child is freed for adoption. But for the natural parents, a finding of permanent neglect can cut off forever their rights in their child. Given this disparity of consequence, we have no difficulty finding that the balance of private interests strongly favors heightened procedural protections.

B

Under *Mathews v. Eldridge*, we next must consider both the risk of erroneous deprivation of private interests resulting from use of a "fair preponderance" standard and the likelihood that a higher evidentiary standard would reduce that risk. Since the factfinding phase of a permanent neglect proceeding is an adversary contest between the State and the natural parents, the relevant question is whether a preponderance standard fairly allocates the risk of an erroneous factfinding between these two parties.

In New York, the factfinding stage of a state-initiated permanent neglect proceeding bears many of the indicia of a criminal trial. The Commissioner of Social Services charges the parents with permanent neglect. They are served by summons. The factfinding hearing is conducted pursuant to formal rules of evidence. The State, the parents, and the child are all represented by counsel. The State seeks to establish a series of historical facts about the intensity of its agency's efforts to reunite the family, the infrequency and insubstantiality of the parents' contacts with their child, and the parents' inability or unwillingness to formulate a plan for the child's future. The attorneys submit documentary evidence, and call witnesses who are subject to cross-examination. Based on all the evidence, the judge then determines whether the State has proved the statutory elements of permanent neglect by a fair preponderance of the evidence.

At such a proceeding, numerous factors combine to magnify the risk of erroneous factfinding. Permanent neglect proceedings employ imprecise substantive standards that leave determinations unusually open to the subjective values of the judge. In appraising the nature and quality of a complex series of encounters among the agency, the parents, and the child, the court possesses unusual discretion to underweigh probative facts that might favor the parent. Because parents subject to termination proceedings are often poor, uneducated, or members of minority groups, such proceedings are often vulnerable to judgments based on cultural or class bias.

The State's ability to assemble its case almost inevitably dwarfs the parents' ability to mount a defense. No predetermined limits restrict the sums an agency may spend in prosecuting a given termination proceeding. The State's attorney usually will be expert on the issues contested and the procedures employed at the factfinding hearing, and enjoys full access to all public records concerning the family. The State may call on experts in family relations, psychology, and medicine to bolster its case. Furthermore, the primary witnesses at the hearing will be the agency's own professional caseworkers whom the State has empowered both to investigate the family situation and to testify against the parents. Indeed, because the child is already in agency custody, the State even has the power to shape the historical events that form the basis for termination.

The disparity between the adversaries' litigation resources is matched by a striking asymmetry in their litigation options. Unlike criminal defendants, natural parents have no "double jeopardy" defense against repeated state termination efforts. If the State initially fails to win termination, as New York did here, it always can try once again to cut off the parents' rights after gathering more or better evidence. Yet even when the parents have attained the level of fitness required by the State, they have no similar means by which they can forestall future termination efforts.

Coupled with a "fair preponderance of the evidence" standard, these factors create a significant prospect of erroneous termination. A standard of proof that by its very terms demands consideration of the quantity, rather than the quality, of the evidence may misdirect the factfinder in the marginal case. Given the weight of the private interests at stake, the social cost of even occasional error is sizable. . . .

C

Two state interests are at stake in parental rights termination proceedings — a parens patriae interest in preserving and promoting the welfare of the child and a fiscal and administrative interest in reducing the cost and burden of such proceedings. A standard of proof more strict than preponderance of the evidence is consistent with both interests.

"Since the State has an urgent interest in the welfare of the child, it shares the parent's interest in an accurate and just decision" at the factfinding proceeding. As parens patriae, the State's goal is to provide the child with a permanent home. Yet while there is still reason to believe that positive, nurturing parent-child relationships exist, the parens patriae interest favors preservation, not severance, of natural familial bonds. "[T]he State registers no gain towards its declared goals when it separates children from the custody of fit parents."

The State's interest in finding the child an alternative permanent home arises only "when it is clear that the natural parent cannot or will not provide a normal family home for the child." At the factfinding, that goal is served by procedures that promote an accurate determination of whether the natural parents can and will provide a normal home.

Unlike a constitutional requirement of hearings, or court-appointed counsel, a stricter standard of proof would reduce factual error without imposing substantial fiscal burdens upon the State. As we have observed, 35 States already have adopted a higher standard by statute or court decision without apparent effect on the speed, form, or cost of their factfinding proceedings.

Nor would an elevated standard of proof create any real administrative burdens for the State's factfinders. New York Family Court judges already are familiar with a higher evidentiary standard in other parental rights termination proceedings not involving permanent neglect. New York also demands at least clear and convincing evidence in proceedings of far less moment than parental rights termination proceedings. We cannot believe that it would burden the State unduly to require that its factfinders have the same factual certainty when terminating the parent-child relationship as they must have to suspend a driver's license.

IV

The logical conclusion of this balancing process is that the "fair preponderance of the evidence" standard prescribed by Fam.Ct.Act § 622 violates the Due Process Clause of the Fourteenth Amendment. The Court noted in *Addington*: "The individual should not be asked to share equally with society the risk of error when the possible injury to the individual is significantly greater than any possible harm to the state." Thus, at a parental rights termination proceeding, a near-equal allocation of risk between the parents and the State is constitutionally intolerable. The next question, then, is whether a "beyond a reasonable doubt" or a "clear and convincing" standard is constitutionally mandated. . . .

A majority of the States have concluded that a "clear and convincing evidence" standard of proof strikes a fair balance between the rights of the natural parents and the State's legitimate concerns. We hold that such a standard adequately conveys to the factfinder the level of subjective certainty about his factual conclusions necessary to satisfy due process. We further hold that determination of the precise burden equal to or greater than that standard is a matter of state law properly left to state legislatures and state courts.

We, of course, express no view on the merits of petitioners' claims. At a hearing conducted under a constitutionally proper standard, they may or may not prevail. Without deciding the outcome under any of the standards we have approved, we vacate the judgment of the Appellate Division and remand the case for further proceedings not inconsistent with this opinion.

B. Non-Marital Children

Both common law and civil law have a long history of discrimination against non-marital children. Non-marital children traditionally had inferior inheritance rights than marital children in both legal systems. Yet, distinctions existed and, for a time, some civil law systems were more forgiving than the common law. But, distinctions were sometimes complex. *Pettus v. Dawson,* an 1891 decision of the Texas Supreme Court, highlights some of these issues.[1] Elijah Garrett died intestate in 1836. His closest surviving relative was his mother—Catherine Lesher. Ms. Lesher was not married when she gave birth to Garret. By the time of the case, Ms. Lesher had died, and her other, "legitimate," children sought to be declared owners of the property. Under

---

1. 17 S.W. 714 (Tex. 1891).

common law, the outcome would be simple. As a non-marital child, Mr. Garrett could not inherit property from his parents nor could they inherit property from him. But, because of the timing of the events, the Texas court had to consider civil law.

The main questions in this case must be disposed of as arising under the civil law of Spain and Mexico, which prevailed in Texas at the time of the death of the said Elijah L. Garrett. There was but one rule at common law. All illegitimate children were bastards, and a bastard was regarded as the first of his family, *nullius filius*, and was incapable of either receiving or transmitting an inheritance, except to his own legitimate children. But the civil law, though originally holding to the same rule, became relaxed, and out of this relaxation grew up a distinction between illegitimate children, which gave rise to much uncertainty about what at different periods was the law. "The Roman law distinguished between the offspring of that concubinage which it tolerated as an inferior species of matrimony, and the spurious brood of adultery, prostitution, and incest." A distinction was made between offspring the issue of frailty and prostitution. The offspring of concubines, who resided in the same house with the father, were called *naturales*, and could be legitimated in one of the various modes provided by law. Care should be taken not to confound the meaning of the different words used. At common law the word "bastard" applied to all illegitimate children. Under the civil law, while it was sometimes loosely so applied, there is quite a distinction. We will not follow the adoption of the civil law in the Gothic countries of France and Germany further than to notice that in France a bastard could not inherit at all, unless legitimated by the marriage of his father and mother. The mode of legitimation by letters patent from the prince was abrogated by the Code Napoleon. As adopted in Spain, the civil law was modified and provided methods by which natural children could be legitimated so as to inherit from their fathers. In the Spanish civil law the word *bastardo* meant and was applied to the sons of fathers who could not contract matrimony when the son was begotten. Bastards, as thus defined, could not inherit from the father; nor could they become legitimated. But such as were not *danado*, or the offspring of an adulterous, sacrilegious, or incestuous intercourse, were permitted to inherit from the mother. Here we find another distinction taken from the Roman civil law, which called such offspring *spurii*, or spurious children. We use the word "bastard" indiscriminately, but under the civil law Elijah L. Garrett would be the "spurious" offspring of his mother, Catherine Lesher. Although, as before stated, the word *bastardo* was used in the Spanish civil law ordinarily as applying to any illegitimate son, still the character of bastard offspring capable of inheriting from the mother was called *espurio*, or spurious, the class *danado y punible ayuntamiento* being excluded. The right of the spurious bastard (*bastardo espurio*) to inherit from his mother is fully recognized in the Spanish civil law, and the right is reciprocal. The law conferring this right is omitted from Moreau and Carleton's translation of Partidas as not applicable to Louisiana, where bastards were excluded from inheritance by the Civil Code. But it remained a part of the Spanish civil law as introduced into Mexico. We think that the difficulty in determining the question in this state arises chiefly from want of familiarity with a system of foreign laws, and the fact that we do not readily distinguish between the French civil law as adopted in Louisiana and the Spanish civil law as adopted in Mexico, all of which, having its origin in the Roman Civil Law, became modified by the countries through which it passed. Although it is now more than half a century since the common law was substituted for the civil law in this state, this is the first time the precise question has been before the supreme court. We are of the opinion that Mrs. Lesher could and did inherit from her bastard son."

As the forgoing excerpt makes clear, even the terminology used to describe non-marital children was stigmatizing. In more recent years, courts and legislatures began moving away from the use of such language. The law itself has also changed. Today, non-marital children generally enjoy the same inheritance rights and rights to child support as marital children.

Several important Supreme Court decisions relating to the rights of non-marital children arose out of Louisiana. In *Levy v. Louisiana*, below, the U.S. Supreme Court held that Louisiana's wrongful death statute ran afoul of equal protection in allowing only marital children to bring wrongful death actions with respect to a deceased parent. In *Labine v. Vincent*, 401 U.S. 532 (1971), the Court seemed to retreat from its position in *Levy*. *Labine* involved a challenge to Louisiana's intestate inheritance laws which treated marital and non-marital children differently. *Labine* upheld the constitutionality of Louisiana's law. Just a few years later, however, the Court reconsidered. In *Trimble v. Gordon*, below, the Court considered the constitutionality of an Illinois statute that contemplated disparate schemes of intestate inheritance for marital and non-marital children. Although the holding in *Trimble* was favorable to non-marital children, the Court clearly refused to apply strict scrutiny to the issue. The *Trimble* decision is also helpful in illustrating the various types of legal rights that may be affected by a legal parent-child relationship.

Levy v. Louisiana
391 U.S. 68 (1968)

Mr. Justice DOUGLAS delivered the opinion of the Court.

Appellant sued on behalf of five illegitimate children to recover, under a Louisiana statute for two kinds of damages as a result of the wrongful death of their mother: (1) the damages to them for the loss of their mother; and (2) those based on the survival of a cause of action which the mother had at the time of her death for pain and suffering. Appellees are the doctor who treated her and the insurance company.

We assume in the present state of the pleadings that the mother, Louise Levy, gave birth to these five illegitimate children and that they lived with her; that she treated them as a parent would treat any other child; that she worked as a domestic servant to support them, taking them to church every Sunday and enrolling them, at her own expense, in a parochial school. . . .

We start from the premise that illegitimate children are not "nonpersons." They are humans, live, and have their being. They are clearly "persons" within the meaning of the Equal Protection Clause of the Fourteenth Amendment.

While a State has broad power when it comes to making classifications, it may not draw a line which constitutes an invidious discrimination against a particular class. Though the test has been variously stated, the end result is whether the line drawn is a rational one.

In applying the Equal Protection Clause to social and economic legislation, we give great latitude to the legislature in making classifications. Even so, would a corporation, which is a "person," for certain purposes, within the meaning of the Equal Protection Clause be required to forgo recovery for wrongs done its interests because its incorporators were all bastards? However that might be, we have been extremely sensitive when it comes to basic civil rights and have not hesitated to strike down an invidious classification even though it had history and tradition on its side. The rights asserted here involve the intimate, familial relationship between a child and his own mother. When the child's claim of damage for loss of his mother is in issue, why, in terms of "equal protection," should the tortfeasors go free merely because the child is illegitimate? Why should the illegitimate child be denied rights merely because of his birth out of wedlock? He certainly is subject to all the responsibilities of a citizen, including the payment of taxes and conscription under the Selective Service Act. How under our constitutional regime can he be denied correlative rights which other citizens enjoy?

Legitimacy or illegitimacy of birth has no relation to the nature of the wrong allegedly inflicted on the mother. These children, though illegitimate, were dependent on her; she cared for them and nurtured them; they were indeed hers in the biological and in the spiritual sense; in her death they suffered wrong in the sense that any dependent would.

We conclude that it is invidious to discriminate against them when no action, conduct, or demeanor of theirs is possibly relevant to the harm that was done the mother.

Reversed.

Trimble v. Gordon

430 U.S. 762 (1977)

Mr. Justice POWELL delivered the opinion of the Court.

At issue in this case is the constitutionality of § 12 of the Illinois Probate Act which allows illegitimate children to inherit by intestate succession only from their mothers. Under Illinois law, legitimate children are allowed to inherit by intestate succession from both their mothers and their fathers.

I

Appellant Deta Mona Trimble is the illegitimate daughter of appellant Jessie Trimble and Sherman Gordon. Trimble and Gordon lived in Chicago with Deta Mona from 1970 until Gordon died in 1974, the victim of a homicide. On January 2, 1973, the Circuit Court of Cook County, Ill., had entered a paternity order finding Gordon to be the father of Deta Mona and ordering him to pay $15 per week for her support. Gordon thereafter supported Deta Mona in accordance with the paternity order and openly acknowledged her as his child. He died intestate at the age of 28, leaving an estate consisting only of a 1974 Plymouth automobile worth approximately $2,500.

Shortly after Gordon's death, Trimble, as the mother and next friend of Deta Mona, filed a petition for letters of administration, determination of heirship, and declaratory relief in the Probate Division of the Circuit Court of Cook County, Ill. That court entered an order determining heirship, identifying as the only heirs of Gordon his father, Joseph Gordon, his mother, Ethel King, and his brother, two sisters, and a half brother. All of these individuals are appellees in this appeal, but only appellee King has filed a brief.

The Circuit Court excluded Deta Mona on the authority of the negative implications of § 12 of the Illinois Probate Act, which provides in relevant part:

> "An illegitimate child is heir of his mother and of any maternal ancestor, and of any person from whom his mother might have inherited, if living; and the lawful issue of an illegitimate person shall represent such person and take, by descent, any estate which the parent would have taken, if living. A child who was illegitimate whose parents inter-marry and who is acknowledged by the father as the father's child is legitimate."

If Deta Mona had been a legitimate child, she would have inherited her father's entire estate under Illinois law. In rejecting Deta Mona's claim of heirship, the court sustained the constitutionality of § 12. . . .

We noted probable jurisdiction to consider the arguments that § 12 violates the Equal Protection Clause of the Fourteenth Amendment by invidiously discriminating on the basis of illegitimacy and sex. We now reverse. As we conclude that the statutory discrimination against illegitimate children is unconstitutional, we do not reach the sex discrimination argument.

II

In *Karas*, the Illinois Supreme Court rejected the equal protection challenge to the discrimination against illegitimate children on the explicit authority of *Labine v. Vincent*. . . . The court found that § 12 is supported by the state interests in encouraging family relationships and in establishing an accurate and efficient method of disposing of property at death. The court also found the Illinois law unobjectionable because no "insurmountable barrier" prevented illegitimate children from sharing in the estates of their fathers. By leaving a will, Sherman Gordon could have assured Deta Mona a share of his estate.

Appellees endorse the reasoning of the Illinois Supreme Court and suggest additional justifications for the statute. In weighing the constitutional sufficiency of these justifications, we are guided by our previous decisions involving equal protection challenges to laws discriminating on the basis of illegitimacy. "[T]his Court requires, at a minimum, that a statutory classification bear some rational relationship to a legitimate state purpose." In this context, the standard just stated is a minimum; the Court sometimes requires more. "Though the latitude given state economic and social regulation is necessarily broad, when state statutory classifications approach sensitive and fundamental personal rights, this Court exercises a stricter scrutiny. . . ."

Appellants urge us to hold that classifications based on illegitimacy are "suspect," so that any justifications must survive "strict scrutiny." We considered and rejected a similar argument last Term in *Mathews v. Lucas*. . . . As we recognized in *Lucas*, illegitimacy is analogous in many respects to the personal characteristics that have been held to be suspect when used as the basis of statutory differentiations. We nevertheless concluded that the analogy was not sufficient to require "our most exacting scrutiny." Despite the conclusion that classifications based on illegitimacy fall in a "realm of less than strictest scrutiny," *Lucas* also establishes that the scrutiny "is not a toothless one," a proposition clearly demonstrated by our previous decisions in this area.

III

The Illinois Supreme Court prefaced its discussion of the state interests served by § 12 with a general discussion of the purpose of the statute. Quoting from its earlier opinions, the court concluded that the statute was enacted to ameliorate the harsh common-law rule under which an illegitimate child was *filius nullius* and incapable of inheriting from anyone. Although § 12 did not bring illegitimate children into parity with legitimate children, it did improve their position, thus partially achieving the asserted objective. The sufficiency of the justifications advanced for the remaining discrimination against illegitimate children must be considered in light of this motivating purpose.

A

The Illinois Supreme Court relied in part on the State's purported interest in "the promotion of [legitimate] family relationships." Although the court noted that this justification had been accepted in *Labine*, the opinion contains only the most perfunctory analysis. This inattention may not have been an oversight, for § 12 bears only the most attenuated relationship to the asserted goal.

In a case like this, the Equal Protection Clause requires more than the mere incantation of a proper state purpose. No one disputes the appropriateness of Illinois' concern with the family unit, perhaps the most fundamental social institution of our society. The flaw in the analysis lies elsewhere. As we said in *Lucas*, the constitutionality of this law "depends upon the character of the discrimination and its relation to legitimate legislative aims." The court below did not address the relation between

§ 12 and the promotion of legitimate family relationships, thus leaving the constitutional analysis incomplete. The same observation can be made about this Court's decision in *Labine*, but that case does not stand alone. In subsequent decisions, we have expressly considered and rejected the argument that a State may attempt to influence the actions of men and women by imposing sanctions on the children born of their illegitimate relationships.

In *Weber* we examined a Louisiana workmen's compensation law which discriminated against one class of illegitimate children. Without questioning Louisiana's interest in protecting legitimate family relationships, we rejected the argument that "persons will shun illicit relations because the offspring may not one day reap the benefits of workmen's compensation." Although *Weber* distinguished *Labine* on other grounds, the reasons for rejecting this justification are equally applicable here:

> "The status of illegitimacy has expressed through the ages society's condemnation of irresponsible liaisons beyond the bonds of marriage. But visiting this condemnation on the head of an infant is illogical and unjust. Moreover, imposing disabilities on the illegitimate child is contrary to the basic concept of our system that legal burdens should bear some relationship to individual responsibility or wrongdoing. Obviously, no child is responsible for his birth and penalizing the illegitimate child is an ineffectual as well as an unjust way of deterring the parent."

The parents have the ability to conform their conduct to societal norms, but their illegitimate children can affect neither their parents' conduct nor their own status.

B

The Illinois Supreme Court relied on *Labine* for another and more substantial justification: the State's interest in "establish[ing] a method of property disposition." Here the court's analysis is more complete. Focusing specifically on the difficulty of proving paternity and the related danger of spurious claims, the court concluded that this interest explained and justified the asymmetrical statutory discrimination against the illegitimate children of intestate men. The more favorable treatment of illegitimate children claiming from their mothers' estates was justified because "proof of a lineal relationship is more readily ascertainable when dealing with maternal ancestors." Alluding to the possibilities of abuse, the court rejected a case-by-case approach to claims based on alleged paternity.

The more serious problems of proving paternity might justify a more demanding standard for illegitimate children claiming under their fathers' estates than that required either for illegitimate children claiming under their mothers' estates or for legitimate children generally. We think, however, that the Illinois Supreme Court gave inadequate consideration to the relation between § 12 and the State's proper objective of assuring accuracy and efficiency in the disposition of property at death. The court failed to consider the possibility of a middle ground between the extremes of complete exclusion and case-by-case determination of paternity. For at least some significant categories of illegitimate children of intestate men, inheritance rights can be recognized without jeopardizing the orderly settlement of estates or the dependability of titles to property passing under intestacy laws. Because it excludes those categories of illegitimate children unnecessarily, § 12 is constitutionally flawed.

The orderly disposition of property at death requires an appropriate legal framework, the structuring of which is a matter particularly within the competence of the individual States. In exercising this responsibility, a State necessarily must enact laws governing both the procedure and substance of intestate succession. Absent infringement of a constitutional right, the federal courts have no role here, and, even when constitutional violations are alleged, those courts should accord substantial deference to a State's statutory scheme of inheritance.

The judicial task here is the difficult one of vindicating constitutional rights without interfering unduly with the State's primary responsibility in this area. Our previous decisions demonstrate a sensitivity to "the lurking problems with respect to proof of paternity," and the need for the States to draw "arbitrary lines . . . to facilitate potentially difficult problems of proof." "Those problems are not to be lightly brushed aside, but neither can they be made into an impenetrable barrier that works to shield otherwise invidious discrimination." Our decision last Term in *Mathews v. Lucas* . . . provides especially helpful guidance.

In *Lucas* we sustained provisions of the Social Security Act governing the eligibility for surviving children's insurance benefits. One of the statutory conditions of eligibility was dependency on the deceased wage earner. Although the Act presumed dependency for a number of categories of children, including some categories of illegitimate children, it required that the remaining illegitimate children prove actual dependency. The Court upheld the statutory classifications, finding them "reasonably related to the likelihood of dependency at death." Central to this decision was the finding that the "statute does not broadly discriminate between legitimates and illegitimates without more, but is carefully tuned to alternative considerations."

Although the present case arises in a context different from that in *Lucas*, the question whether the statute "is carefully tuned to alternative considerations" is equally applicable here. We conclude that § 12 does not meet this standard. Difficulties of proving paternity in some situations do not justify the total statutory disinheritance of illegitimate children whose fathers die intestate. The facts of this case graphically illustrate the constitutional defect of § 12. Sherman Gordon was found to be the father of Deta Mona in a state-court paternity action prior to his death. On the strength of that finding, he was ordered to contribute to the support of his child. That adjudication should be equally sufficient to establish Deta Mona's right to claim a child's share of Gordon's estate, for the State's interest in the accurate and efficient disposition of property at death would not be compromised in any way by allowing her claim in these circumstances. The reach of the statute extends well beyond the asserted purposes.

C

The Illinois Supreme Court also noted that the decedents whose estates were involved in the consolidated appeals could have left substantial parts of their estates to their illegitimate children by writing a will. The court cited *Labine* as authority for the proposition that such a possibility is constitutionally significant. The penultimate paragraph of the opinion in *Labine* distinguishes that case from *Levy v. Louisiana* because no insurmountable barrier prevented the illegitimate child from sharing in her father's estate. "There is not the slightest suggestion in this case that Louisiana has barred this illegitimate from inheriting from her father." The Court then listed three different steps that would have resulted in some recovery by *Labine's* illegitimate daughter. *Labine* could have left a will; he could have legitimated the daughter by marrying her mother; and he could have given the daughter the status of a legitimate child by stating in his acknowledgment of paternity his desire to legitimate her. In *Weber* our distinction of *Labine* was based in part on the fact that no such alternatives existed, as state law prevented the acknowledgment of the children involved.

Despite its appearance in two of our opinions, the focus on the presence or absence of an insurmountable barrier is somewhat of an analytical anomaly. Here, as in *Labine*, the question is the constitutionality of a state intestate succession law that treats illegitimate children differently from legitimate children. Traditional equal protection analysis asks whether this statutory differentiation on the basis of illegitimacy is justified by the promotion of recognized state objectives. If the law cannot be sustained on this analysis, it is not clear how it can be saved by the absence of an insurmountable barrier to inheritance under other and hypothetical circumstances.

By focusing on the steps that an intestate might have taken to assure some inheritance for his illegitimate children, the analysis loses sight of the essential question: the constitutionality of discrimination against illegitimates in a state intestate succession law. If the decedent had written a will devising property to his illegitimate child, the case no longer would involve intestate succession law at all. Similarly, if the decedent had legitimated the child by marrying the child's mother or by complying with the requirements of some other method of legitimation, the case no longer would involve discrimination against illegitimates. Hard questions cannot be avoided by a hypothetical reshuffling of the facts. If Sherman Gordon had devised his estate to Deta Mona this case would not be here. . . .

D

Finally, appellees urge us to affirm the decision below on the theory that the Illinois Probate Act, including § 12, mirrors the presumed intentions of the citizens of the State regarding the disposition of their property at death. Individualizing this theory, appellees argue that we must assume that Sherman Gordon knew the disposition of his estate under the Illinois Probate Act and that his failure to make a will shows his approval of that disposition. We need not resolve the question whether presumed intent alone can ever justify discrimination against illegitimates, for we do not think that § 12 was enacted for this purpose. The theory of presumed intent is not relied upon in the careful opinion of the Illinois Supreme Court examining both the history and the text of § 12. This omission is not without significance, as one would expect a state supreme court to identify the state interests served by a statute of its state legislature. Our own examination of § 12 convinces us that the statutory provisions at issue were shaped by forces other than the desire of the legislature to mirror the intentions of the citizens of the State with respect to their illegitimate children.

To the extent that other policies are not considered more important, legislators enacting state intestate succession laws probably are influenced by the desire to reflect the natural affinities of decedents in the allocation of estates among the categories of heirs. A pattern of distribution favoring brothers and sisters over cousins is, for example, best explained on this basis. The difference in § 12 between the rights of illegitimate children in the estates of their fathers and mothers, however, is more convincingly explained by the other factors mentioned by the court below. Accepting in this respect the views of the Illinois Supreme Court, we find in § 12 a primary purpose to provide a system of intestate succession more just to illegitimate children than the prior law, a purpose tempered by a secondary interest in protecting against spurious claims of paternity. In the absence of a more convincing demonstration, we will not hypothesize an additional state purpose that has been ignored by the Illinois Supreme Court.

IV

For the reasons stated above, we conclude that § 12 of the Illinois Probate Act cannot be squared with the command of the Equal Protection Clause of the Fourteenth Amendment. Accordingly, we reverse the judgment of the Illinois Supreme Court and remand the case for further proceedings not inconsistent with this opinion.

So ordered.

C. Recognition as a Parent

One issue raised by *Stanley v. Illinois* is what steps are required to be recognized as a parent for legal purposes. In *Stanley*, the father's biological relationship was not in question. As we will explore in more detail later, state law sets forth a comprehensive scheme for determining the biological parentage of children. For example, there is near universal agreement that a woman's husband is presumed to be the father of any child born to her during the marriage. This is an old legal presumption — one that predates modern medical practices. Advances in reproductive technology and DNA testing have raised new legal questions regarding parental rights. The Supreme Court has only begun to scratch the surface of this complicated legal area.

Michael H. v. Gerald D., below, considers the constitutionality of the presumptive paternity of a husband in the face of conclusive evidence that another man is the child's biological father. *Pavan v. Smith*, below, considers a somewhat related issue—the right of a same-sex spouse to benefit from the presumption of parentage.

Michael H. v. Gerald D.
491 U.S. 110 (1989)

Justice SCALIA announced the judgment of the Court and delivered an opinion, in which THE CHIEF JUSTICE joins, and in all but footnote 6 of which Justice O'CONNOR and Justice KENNEDY join.

Under California law, a child born to a married woman living with her husband is presumed to be a child of the marriage. Cal.Evid.Code Ann. § 621 (West Supp.1989). The presumption of legitimacy may be rebutted only by the husband or wife, and then only in limited circumstances. The instant appeal presents the claim that this presumption infringes upon the due process rights of a man who wishes to establish his paternity of a child born to the wife of another man, and the claim that it infringes upon the constitutional right of the child to maintain a relationship with her natural father.

I

The facts of this case are, we must hope, extraordinary. On May 9, 1976, in Las Vegas, Nevada, Carole D., an international model, and Gerald D., a top executive in a French oil company, were married. The couple established a home in Playa del Rey, California, in which they resided as husband and wife when one or the other was not out of the country on business. In the summer of 1978, Carole became involved in an adulterous affair with a neighbor, Michael H. In September 1980, she conceived a child, Victoria D., who was born on May 11, 1981. Gerald was listed as father on the birth certificate and has always held Victoria out to the world as his daughter. Soon after delivery of the child, however, Carole informed Michael that she believed he might be the father.

In the first three years of her life, Victoria remained always with Carole, but found herself within a variety of quasi-family units. In October 1981, Gerald moved to New York City to pursue his business interests, but Carole chose to remain in California. At the end of that month, Carole and Michael had blood tests of themselves and Victoria, which showed a 98.07% probability that Michael was Victoria's father. In January 1982, Carole visited Michael in St. Thomas, where his primary business interests were based. There Michael held Victoria out as his child. In March, however, Carole left Michael and returned to California, where she took up residence with yet another man, Scott K. Later that spring, and again in the summer, Carole and Victoria spent time with Gerald in New York City, as well as on vacation in Europe. In the fall, they returned to Scott in California.

In November 1982, rebuffed in his attempts to visit Victoria, Michael filed a filiation action in California Superior Court to establish his paternity and right to visitation. In March 1983, the court appointed an attorney and guardian ad litem to represent Victoria's interests. Victoria then filed a cross-complaint asserting that if she had more than one psychological or de facto father, she was entitled to maintain her filial relationship, with all of the attendant rights, duties, and obligations, with both. In May 1983, Carole filed a motion for summary judgment. During this period, from March through July 1983, Carole was again living with Gerald in New York. In August, however, she returned to California, became involved once again with Michael, and instructed her attorneys to remove the summary judgment motion from the calendar.

For the ensuing eight months, when Michael was not in St. Thomas he lived with Carole and Victoria in Carole's apartment in Los Angeles and held Victoria out as his daughter. In April 1984, Carole and Michael signed a stipulation that Michael was Victoria's natural father. Carole left Michael the next month, however, and instructed her attorneys not to file the stipulation. In June 1984, Carole reconciled with Gerald and joined him in New York, where they now live with Victoria and two other children since born into the marriage.

In May 1984, Michael and Victoria, through her guardian ad litem, sought visitation rights for Michael pendente lite. To assist in determining whether visitation would be in Victoria's best interests, the Superior Court appointed a psychologist to evaluate Victoria, Gerald, Michael, and Carole. The psychologist recommended that Carole retain sole custody, but that Michael be allowed continued contact with Victoria pursuant to a restricted visitation schedule. The court concurred and ordered that Michael be provided with limited visitation privileges pendente lite.

On October 19, 1984, Gerald, who had intervened in the action, moved for summary judgment on the ground that under Cal.Evid.Code § 621 there were no triable issues of fact as to Victoria's paternity. This law provides that "the issue of a wife cohabiting with her husband, who is not impotent or sterile, is conclusively presumed to be a child of the marriage." The presumption may be rebutted by blood tests, but only if a motion for such tests is made, within two years from the date of the child's birth, either by the husband or, if the natural father has filed an affidavit acknowledging paternity, by the wife.

[The state courts held in favor of Gerald.]

Before us, Michael and Victoria both raise equal protection and due process challenges. We do not reach Michael's equal protection claim, however, as it was neither raised nor passed upon below. . . .

III

We address first the claims of Michael. At the outset, it is necessary to clarify what he sought and what he was denied. California law, like nature itself, makes no provision for dual fatherhood. Michael was seeking to be declared the father of Victoria. The immediate benefit he evidently sought to obtain from that status was visitation rights. But if Michael were successful in being declared the father, other rights would follow—most importantly, the right to be considered as the parent who should have custody, a status which "embrace[s] the sum of parental rights with respect to the rearing of a child, including the child's care; the right to the child's services and earnings; the right to direct the child's activities; the right to make decisions regarding the control, education, and health of the child; and the right, as well as the duty, to prepare the child for additional obligations, which includes the teaching of moral standards, religious beliefs, and elements of good citizenship." All parental rights, including visitation, were automatically denied by denying Michael status as the father. While Cal.Civ.Code Ann. §4601 places it within the discretionary power of a court to award visitation rights to a nonparent, the Superior Court here, affirmed by the Court of Appeal, held that California law denies visitation, against the wishes of the mother, to a putative father who has been prevented by §621 from establishing his paternity.

Michael raises two related challenges to the constitutionality of §621. First, he asserts that requirements of procedural due process prevent the State from terminating his liberty interest in his relationship with his child without affording him an opportunity to demonstrate his paternity in an evidentiary hearing. We believe this claim derives from a fundamental misconception of the nature of the California statute. While §621 is phrased in terms of a presumption, that rule of evidence is the implementation of a substantive rule of law. California declares it to be, except in limited circumstances, irrelevant for paternity purposes whether a child conceived during, and born into, an existing marriage was begotten by someone other than the husband and had a prior relationship with him.

As the Court of Appeal phrased it:

> "The conclusive presumption is actually a substantive rule of law based upon a determination by the Legislature as a matter of overriding social policy, that given a certain relationship between the husband and wife, the husband is to be held responsible for the child, and that the integrity of the family unit should not be impugned."

Of course the conclusive presumption not only expresses the State's substantive policy but also furthers it, excluding inquiries into the child's paternity that would be destructive of family integrity and privacy.

This Court has struck down as illegitimate certain "irrebuttable presumptions." Those holdings did not, however, rest upon procedural due process. A conclusive presumption does, of course, foreclose the person against whom it is invoked from demonstrating, in a particularized proceeding, that applying the presumption to him will in fact not further the lawful governmental policy the presumption is designed to effectuate. But the same can be said of any legal rule that establishes general classifications, whether framed in terms of a presumption or not. In this respect there is no difference between a rule which says that the marital husband shall be irrebuttably presumed to be the father, and a rule which says that the adulterous natural father shall not be recognized as the legal father. Both rules deny someone in Michael's situation a hearing on whether, in the particular circumstances of his case, California's policies would best be served by giving him parental rights. Thus, as many commentators have observed, our "irrebuttable presumption" cases must ultimately be analyzed as calling into question not the adequacy of procedures but—like our cases involving classifications framed in other terms—the adequacy of the "fit" between the classification and the policy that the classification serves. We therefore reject Michael's procedural due process challenge and proceed to his substantive claim.

Michael contends as a matter of substantive due process that, because he has established a parental relationship with Victoria, protection of Gerald's and Carole's marital union is an insufficient state interest to support termination of that relationship. This argument is, of course, predicated on the assertion that Michael has a constitutionally protected liberty interest in his relationship with Victoria.

It is an established part of our constitutional jurisprudence that the term "liberty" in the Due Process Clause extends beyond freedom from physical restraint. . . .

In an attempt to limit and guide interpretation of the Clause, we have insisted not merely that the interest denominated as a "liberty" be "fundamental" (a concept that, in isolation, is hard to objectify), but also that it be an interest traditionally protected by our society. As we have put it, the Due Process Clause affords only those protections "so rooted in the traditions and conscience of our people as to be ranked as fundamental." Our cases reflect "continual insistence upon respect for the teachings of history [and] solid recognition of the basic values that underlie our society. . . ."

This insistence that the asserted liberty interest be rooted in history and tradition is evident, as elsewhere, in our cases according constitutional protection to certain parental rights. Michael reads the landmark case of *Stanley v. Illinois* . . . as establishing that a liberty interest is created by biological fatherhood plus an established parental relationship—factors that exist in the present case as well. We think that distorts the rationale of those cases. As we view them, they rest not upon such isolated factors but upon the historic respect—indeed, sanctity would not be too strong a term—traditionally accorded to the relationships that develop within the unitary family. In *Stanley*, for example, we forbade the destruction of such a family when, upon the death of the mother, the State had sought to remove children from the custody of a father who had lived with and supported them and their mother for 18 years. . . .

Thus, the legal issue in the present case reduces to whether the relationship between persons in the situation of Michael and Victoria has been treated as a protected family unit under the historic practices of our society, or whether on any other basis it has been accorded special protection. We think it impossible to find that it has. In fact, quite to the contrary, our traditions have protected the marital family (Gerald, Carole, and the child they acknowledge to be theirs) against the sort of claim Michael asserts.

The presumption of legitimacy was a fundamental principle of the common law. Traditionally, that presumption could be rebutted only by proof that a husband was incapable of procreation or had had no access to his wife during the relevant period. . . . The primary policy rationale underlying the common law's severe restrictions on rebuttal of the presumption appears to have been an aversion to declaring children illegitimate, thereby depriving them of rights of inheritance and succession, and likely making them wards of the state. A secondary policy concern was the interest in promoting the "peace and tranquillity of States and families," a goal that is obviously impaired by facilitating suits against husband and wife asserting that their children are illegitimate. . . .

We have found nothing in the older sources, nor in the older cases, addressing specifically the power of the natural father to assert parental rights over a child born into a woman's existing marriage with another man. Since it is Michael's burden to establish that such a power (at least where the natural father has established a relationship with the child) is so deeply embedded within our traditions as to be a fundamental right, the lack of evidence alone might defeat his case. But the evidence shows that even in modern times—when, as we have noted, the rigid protection of the marital family has in other respects been relaxed—the ability of a person in Michael's position to claim paternity has not been generally acknowledged. . . .

Moreover, even if it were clear that one in Michael's position generally possesses, and has generally always possessed, standing to challenge the marital child's legitimacy, that would still not establish Michael's case. As noted earlier, what is at issue here is not entitlement to a state pronouncement that Victoria was begotten by Michael. It is no conceivable denial of constitutional right for a State to decline to declare facts unless some legal consequence hinges upon the requested declaration. What Michael asserts here is a right to have himself declared the natural father and thereby to obtain parental prerogatives. What he must establish, therefore, is not that our society has traditionally allowed a natural father in his circumstances to establish paternity, but that it has traditionally accorded such a father parental rights, or at least has not traditionally denied them. Even if the law in all States had always been that the entire world could challenge the marital presumption and obtain a declaration as to who was the natural father, that would not advance Michael's claim. Thus, it is ultimately irrelevant, even for purposes of determining current social attitudes towards the alleged substantive right Michael asserts, that the present law in a number of States appears to allow the natural father—including the natural father who has not established a relationship with the child—the theoretical power to rebut the marital presumption. What counts is whether the States in fact award substantive parental rights to the natural father of a child conceived within, and born into, an extant marital union that wishes to embrace the child. We are not aware of a single case, old or new, that has done so. This is not the stuff of which fundamental rights qualifying as liberty interests are made.

In *Lehr v. Robertson*, a case involving a natural father's attempt to block his child's adoption by the unwed mother's new husband, we observed that "[t]he significance of the biological connection is that it offers the natural father an opportunity that no other male possesses to develop a relationship with his offspring," and we assumed that the Constitution might require some protection of that opportunity. Where, however, the child is born into an extant marital family, the natural father's unique opportunity conflicts with the similarly unique opportunity of the husband of the marriage; and it is not unconstitutional for the State to give categorical preference to the latter. . . .

IV

We have never had occasion to decide whether a child has a liberty interest, symmetrical with that of her parent, in maintaining her filial relationship. We need not do so here because, even assuming that such a right exists, Victoria's claim must fail. Victoria's due process challenge is, if anything, weaker than Michael's. Her basic claim is not that California has erred in preventing her from establishing that Michael, not Gerald, should stand as her legal father. Rather, she claims a due process right to maintain filial relationships with both Michael and Gerald. This assertion merits little discussion, for, whatever the merits of the guardian ad litem's belief that such an arrangement can be of great psychological benefit to a child, the claim that a State must recognize multiple fatherhood has no support in the history or traditions of this country. Moreover, even if we were to construe Victoria's argument as forwarding the lesser proposition that, whatever her status vis-à-vis Gerald, she has a liberty interest in maintaining a filial relationship with her natural father, Michael, we find that, at best, her claim is the obverse of Michael's and fails for the same reasons.

Victoria claims in addition that her equal protection rights have been violated because, unlike her mother and presumed father, she had no opportunity to rebut the presumption of her legitimacy. We find this argument wholly without merit. We reject, at the outset, Victoria's suggestion that her equal protection challenge must be assessed under a standard of strict scrutiny because, in denying her the right to maintain a filial relationship with Michael, the State is discriminating against her on the basis of her illegitimacy. Illegitimacy is a legal construct, not a natural trait. Under California law, Victoria is not illegitimate, and she is treated in the same manner as all other legitimate children: she is entitled to maintain a filial relationship with her legal parents.

We apply, therefore, the ordinary "rational relationship" test to Victoria's equal protection challenge. The primary rationale underlying § 621's limitation on those who may rebut the presumption of legitimacy is a concern that allowing persons other than the husband or wife to do so may undermine the integrity of the marital union. When the husband or wife contests the legitimacy of their child, the stability of the marriage has already been shaken. In contrast, allowing a claim of illegitimacy to be pressed by the child — or, more accurately, by a court-appointed guardian ad litem — may well disrupt an otherwise peaceful union. Since it pursues a legitimate end by rational means, California's decision to treat Victoria differently from her parents is not a denial of equal protection.

The judgment of the California Court of Appeal is

Affirmed.

Pavan v. Smith

137 S. Ct. 2075 (2017)

PER CURIAM.

As this Court explained in *Obergefell v. Hodges*, the Constitution entitles same-sex couples to civil marriage "on the same terms and conditions as opposite-sex couples." In the decision below, the Arkansas Supreme Court considered the effect of that holding on the State's rules governing the issuance of birth certificates. When a married woman gives birth in Arkansas, state law generally requires the name of the mother's male spouse to appear on the child's birth certificate—regardless of his biological relationship to the child. According to the court below, however, Arkansas need not extend that rule to similarly situated same-sex couples: The State need not, in other words, issue birth certificates including the female spouses of women who give birth in the State. Because that differential treatment infringes *Obergefell*'s commitment to provide same-sex couples "the constellation of benefits that the States have linked to marriage," we reverse the state court's judgment.

The petitioners here are two married same-sex couples who conceived children through anonymous sperm donation. Leigh and Jana Jacobs were married in Iowa in 2010, and Terrah and Marisa Pavan were married in New Hampshire in 2011. Leigh and Terrah each gave birth to a child in Arkansas in 2015. When it came time to secure birth certificates for the newborns, each couple filled out paperwork listing both spouses as parents—Leigh and Jana in one case, Terrah and Marisa in the other. Both times, however, the Arkansas Department of Health issued certificates bearing only the birth mother's name.

The department's decision rested on a provision of Arkansas law, Ark.Code § 20-18-401 (2014), that specifies which individuals will appear as parents on a child's state-issued birth certificate. "For the purposes of birth registration," that statute says, "the mother is deemed to be the woman who gives birth to the child." § 20-18-401(e). And "[i]f the mother was married at the time of either conception or birth," the statute instructs that "the name of [her] husband shall be entered on the certificate as the father of the child." § 20-18-401(f)(1). There are some limited exceptions to the latter rule—for example, another man may appear on the birth certificate if the "mother" and "husband" and "putative father" all file affidavits vouching for the putative father's paternity. But as all parties agree, the requirement that a married woman's husband appear on her child's birth certificate applies in cases where the couple conceived by means of artificial insemination with the help of an anonymous sperm donor.

The Jacobses and Pavans brought this suit in Arkansas state court against the director of the Arkansas Department of Health—seeking, among other things, a declaration that the State's birth-certificate law violates the Constitution. The trial court agreed, holding that the relevant portions of § 20-18-401 are inconsistent with *Obergefell* because they "categorically prohibi[t] every same-sex married couple . . .

from enjoying the same spousal benefits which are available to every opposite-sex married couple." But a divided Arkansas Supreme Court reversed that judgment, concluding that the statute "pass[es] constitutional muster." In that court's view, "the statute centers on the relationship of the biological mother and the biological father to the child, not on the marital relationship of husband and wife," and so it "does not run afoul of *Obergefell*." Two justices dissented from that view, maintaining that under *Obergefell* "a same-sex married couple is entitled to a birth certificate on the same basis as an opposite-sex married couple."

The Arkansas Supreme Court's decision, we conclude, denied married same-sex couples access to the "constellation of benefits that the Stat[e] ha[s] linked to marriage." As already explained, when a married woman in Arkansas conceives a child by means of artificial insemination, the State will—indeed, must—list the name of her male spouse on the child's birth certificate. And yet state law, as interpreted by the court below, allows Arkansas officials in those very same circumstances to omit a married woman's female spouse from her child's birth certificate. As a result, same-sex parents in Arkansas lack the same right as opposite-sex parents to be listed on a child's birth certificate, a document often used for important transactions like making medical decisions for a child or enrolling a child in school.

Obergefell proscribes such disparate treatment. As we explained there, a State may not "exclude same-sex couples from civil marriage on the same terms and conditions as opposite-sex couples." Indeed, in listing those terms and conditions—the "rights, benefits, and responsibilities" to which same-sex couples, no less than opposite-sex couples, must have access—we expressly identified "birth and death certificates." That was no accident: Several of the plaintiffs in *Obergefell* challenged a State's refusal to recognize their same-sex spouses on their children's birth certificates. In considering those challenges, we held the relevant state laws unconstitutional to the extent they treated same-sex couples differently from opposite-sex couples. That holding applies with equal force to § 20-18-401.

Echoing the court below, the State defends its birth-certificate law on the ground that being named on a child's birth certificate is not a benefit that attends marriage. Instead, the State insists, a birth certificate is simply a device for recording biological parentage—regardless of whether the child's parents are married. But Arkansas law makes birth certificates about more than just genetics. As already discussed, when an opposite-sex couple conceives a child by way of anonymous sperm donation—just as the petitioners did here—state law requires the placement of the birth mother's husband on the child's birth certificate. And that is so even though (as the State concedes) the husband "is definitively not the biological father" in those circumstances. Arkansas has thus chosen to make its birth certificates more than a mere marker of biological relationships: The State uses those certificates to give married parents a form of legal recognition that is not available to unmarried parents. Having made that choice, Arkansas may not, consistent with *Obergefell*, deny married same-sex couples that recognition.

The petition for a writ of certiorari and the pending motions for leave to file briefs as amici curiae are granted. The judgment of the Arkansas Supreme Court is reversed, and the case is remanded for further proceedings not inconsistent with this opinion.

It is so ordered.

Chapter 12

Biological Filiation

Filiation—like marriage—is a status determination that has a variety of important legal consequences. Civil Code article 178 explains that "[f]iliation is the legal relationship between a child and his parent." Filiation affects inheritance rights and the right to bring certain legal actions—as demonstrated by *Levy v. Louisiana*. Filiation is also important in child support and child custody proceedings.

States take a variety of approaches to determining parentage of children. All states recognize that a parent-child relationship may be established by adoption—a topic considered in the next chapter. States also recognize that a parent-child relationship may be established through a biological relationship. To that end, Civil Code article 179 provides that "[f]ilitaion is established by proof of maternity or paternity or by adoption."

Historically, proof of maternity was fairly straightforward. Proof of paternity, however, could be more complicated. New reproductive technologies and the increased ease of genetic testing have further complicated the legal landscape and, in many cases, state law has yet to adapt to scientific reality. State law has also been slow to adapt, in some cases, to constitutional mandates—as demonstrated in *Pavan v. Smith*. Moreover, biological relationship is not always required to establish proof of maternity or paternity. Keep these limitations in mind as you read the cases and materials that follow as well as the corresponding state laws.

A number of states have implemented some version of the Uniform Parentage Act or have laws that are heavily influenced by the Act. The following materials will, on occasion, use the Uniform Parentage Act as a basis for comparison. States laws have also been heavily influenced by federal law. In order to remain eligible for federal funding for various services relating to child and spousal support enforcement, federal law requires states to enact various laws pertaining to paternity of children.[1]

A. Maternity

See La. Civ. Code art. 184; La. Rev. Stat. § 9:391.1; Uniform Parentage Act § 201.

Historically, the question of biological maternity rarely posed any significant legal question. Evidence that a woman gave birth to a particular child was sufficient to

---

1. 45 C.F.R. § 302.70 (2017).

prove that she was the biological mother of the child. The Louisiana Civil Code continues to take this approach. Article 184 provides that "[m]aternity may be established by a preponderance of the evidence that the child was born to a particular woman, except as otherwise provided by law." The "except as otherwise provided by law" language leaves open the possibility that Louisiana could enact a legislative scheme recognizing maternity in cases of assisted reproduction using donated eggs or embryos and/or where the child was carried by a surrogate. However, Louisiana has struggled to enact comprehensive legislation in this arena. As a result, parents utilizing assisted reproductive technologies are sometimes left in a legal gray area. For example, Louisiana Revised Statute § 9:391.1 will allow a child conceived after the death of the biological mother through the use of assisted reproductive technologies to be filiated with that biological mother under certain circumstances. Presumably, such a scenario would require a gestational surrogate and it is unclear what rights, if any, the gestational surrogate might have to the child under Louisiana law.

Section 201 of the Uniform Parentage Act is more modern. Like Louisiana, the Act provides that maternity may be established by several means including the "woman's having given birth to the child." The Act also contemplates that maternity may be established when the child was born to another woman under a gestational surrogacy agreement.

B. Presumptive Paternity of Marital Children

See La. Civ. Code art. 185–86, 88; La. Rev. Stat. § 9:391.1; Uniform Parentage Act § 201.

Both common law and civil law have long recognized a strong presumption that the husband of a woman who gives birth to a child is the biological father. Traditionally, this presumption was quite strong. Courts in Louisiana and in other states often referred to it as one of the "strongest presumptions in law." In the age where a child's legal rights hinged on whether he was "legitimate" or "illegitimate," this presumption could be incredibly powerful. Although non-marital children are no longer treated so severely, the presumption of paternity stemming from marriage to the mother is still significant.

Historically, the presumption of the husband's paternity was quite difficult to overcome. As the Supreme Court explained in *Michael H. v. Gerald D:*

> The presumption of legitimacy was a fundamental principle of the common law. Traditionally, that presumption could be rebutted only by proof that a husband was incapable of procreation or had had no access to his wife during the relevant period. As explained by Blackstone, nonaccess could only be proved "if the husband be out of the kingdom of England (or, as the law somewhat loosely phrases it, extra quatuor maria [beyond the four seas]) for above nine months. . . ." And, under the common law both in England and here, "neither husband nor wife [could] be a witness to prove access or

nonaccess." The primary policy rationale underlying the common law's severe restrictions on rebuttal of the presumption appears to have been an aversion to declaring children illegitimate, thereby depriving them of rights of inheritance and succession, and likely making them wards of the state. A secondary policy concern was the interest in promoting the "peace and tranquillity of States and families," a goal that is obviously impaired by facilitating suits against husband and wife asserting that their children are illegitimate.[2]

Like common law, the Code Napoléon and early Louisiana law permitted the husband to rebut the presumption of paternity where he was physically separated from his wife during the time of conception or where he was impotent due to an accident. Impotence due to natural causes was not generally grounds for disavowal for policy reasons. As Planiol explained: "The law refuses to consider natural impotence as a ground for disavowal [because] [i]t is subject to errors and its attestation would bring about too many scandals."[3]

As *Michael H. v. Gerald D.* suggests, the presumption of paternity in the father and the difficulty in rebutting the presumption was supported by two public policy concerns. First, public policy favored "legitimacy" of children. Second, public policy favored family harmony and the marital unit. Louisiana has long recognized these policies as well. Yet, changing social mores and the relative ease and increased reliability of paternity tests have forced courts and legislatures to temper the rules relating to the presumption of paternity in the husband.

Like most states, Louisiana continues to recognize marriage to the mother at the time of birth as a basis for presuming paternity. Louisiana law—following a tradition implemented by the Code Napoléon—also applies this presumption when children are born within 300 days of the date of the dissolution of the marriage. This period of time was deliberately longer than the typical pregnancy. Planiol explains the rationale as follows:

> According to our old law the courts had complete discretionary power in passing upon the matter as one of fact to be decided according to circumstances and their personal judgment. Some decisions held that a pregnancy could have lasted twelve months, fifteen months and even longer. And thus were children declared legitimate born more than a year after the death of their mother's husband. The compilers of the Civil Code did not desire to leave such an important matter to the caprice of courts, in as much as judicial decisions had shown that special considerations had produced astounding results. The matter was referred to Fourcroy. He was asked to fix,

---

2. Michael H. v. Gerald D., 491 U.S. 110 (1989).

3. MARCEL PLANIOL, TREATISE ON THE CIVIL LAW *1431 (Louisiana State Law Institute trans. West, 1959).

according to scientific data, the extreme duration of pregnancies, both as regard their length and their brevity.

When the compilers of the Code thus had serious information in hand, they extended somewhat the limits of pregnancy in order to favor legitimacy. They wanted to be certain that they would not deprive any legitimate child of its just due. And they also desired to have round figures which could be easily applied. Here are those they adopted (Art. 312 and Art. 314). The shortest pregnancies last at least 180 days. The longest last at most 300 days. The Code was drawn up under the Republican calendar, under which all months were of 30 days. It is thus seen that the legal duration of pregnancies is at least 6 months and not more than 10 months.[4]

Common law, in contrast, relied on judicial discretion regarding the duration of pregnancy—leading, predictably, to some inconsistent results. A Kentucky court held that a child born 324 days following a marriage was presumed to be the child of the former husband—a remarkably long period of gestation.[5] An Ohio court similarly recognized the paternity of a child born 324 days after the wife last had sex with her husband.[6] A Washington court recognized a child born 336 days following a couple's separation as presumptively the child of the husband.[7] Yet, a Massachusetts court opined that "it is matter of common knowledge that a period of gestation of three hundred and five days is highly unusual and improbable."[8] Many courts took judicial notice that pregnancy ought to last 280 days—and a number of states later reinforced that rule by statute. The 1973 Uniform Parentage Act—perhaps inspired by Louisiana—rejected the 280-day rule and replaced it with a 300-day period.

Louisiana presumes the paternity of the husband in several instances. Civil Code article 185 explains that the "husband of the mother is presumed to be the father of the child born during the marriage or within three hundred days from the date of the termination of the marriage." When there are conflicting presumptions due to the mother's remarriage, Louisiana resolves the issue of paternity in favor of the first husband. Article 186 explains that "[i]f a child is born within three hundred days from the day of the termination of a marriage and his mother has married again before his birth, the first husband is presumed to be the father." That article goes on to explain that the presumption shifts to the second husband if the first husband obtains a judgment of disavowal. Paternity is also presumed in certain cases of assisted conception. Article 188, which applies to a married woman who becomes pregnant by artificial insemination, precludes the husband from disavowing "a child born to his wife as a result of an assisted conception to which he consented." Similarly, Revised

---

4. Marcel Planiol, Treatise on the Civil Law *1376 (Louisiana State Law Institute trans. West, 1959).

5. Ousley v. Ousley, 261 S.W.2d 817 (Ky. App. Ct. 1953).

6. Powell v. State, 95 N.E. 660 (Ohio 1911).

7. Pierson v. Pierson, 214 P. 159 (Wash. 1923).

8. Commonwealth v. Kitchen, 11 N.E.2d 482 (Mass. 1937).

Statute § 9:391.1 deems children who are conceived after the death of the husband using his gametes to be filiated with him under certain circumstances.

C. Presumptive Paternity of Non-Marital Children

See LA. CIV. CODE art. 195–96; LA. REV. STAT. § 9:392–93; UNIFORM PARENTAGE ACT § 201, 301–02.

Federal law requires states to implement procedures for the voluntary acknowledgement of non-marital children. Federal law also requires the states to implement laws that provide that such a "voluntary acknowledgement of paternity creates a rebuttable or, at the option of the State, conclusive presumption of paternity. . . ."[9] Additionally, states must implement "[p]rocedures under which a voluntary acknowledgement must be recognized as a basis for seeking a support order without requiring any further proceedings to establish paternity."[10] To that end, both Louisiana law and the Uniform Parentage Act contemplate certain factual situations that will give rise to a presumption of paternity for non-marital children. As a general matter, for a man to be considered the presumptive father of a non-marital child, he must undertake some affirmative step of acknowledging the child in order to invoke the presumption.

These affirmative steps may seem quite technical and appear to impose a high burden on fathers of non-marital children who want to establish their paternity. To help obviate this problem, federal law requires states to implement various voluntary paternity acknowledgment programs aimed at assisting and encouraging people to execute voluntary acknowledgements—including hospital-based programs.[11] Louisiana, like other states, has established such a program, and many acknowledgements are likely signed at the hospital near the time of birth with the assistance of hospital personnel.

Louisiana recognizes two factual situations where non-marital children will be presumed to be the filiated with a particular man. First, Louisiana Civil Code article 195 establishes a presumption of paternity where the couple marries after the woman has given birth to a child. If the man also acknowledges the child in an authentic act, he will be presumed to be the father of the child. The strength of this presumption and its effects are comparable to the presumption of paternity afforded to fathers of marital children. Earlier versions of Article 195 permitted acknowledgement in either the form of an authentic act or by signing the birth certificate. Section 204(a)(4) of the Uniform Parentage Act has a similar provision. The Uniform Act is also more lenient. Section 204(a)(5) establishes a presumption of paternity where the man

---

9. 45 C.F.R. § 302.70 (2017).

10. *Id.*

11. *See* 45 C.F.R. § 302.70.

"resided in the same household with the child and openly held out the child as his own" for the first two years of the non-marital child's life.

Second, Louisiana Civil Code article 196 allows a man to establish his presumptive filiation with respect to a non-marital child—without marrying the mother—by acknowledging the child by authentic act. Earlier versions of Article 196 permitted acknowledgement in either the form of an authentic act or by signing the birth certificate. Unlike the other presumptions of paternity, this acknowledgement creates a presumption that "can be invoked only on behalf of the child." This phrase can be a bit confusing. Louisiana Revised Statute § 9:392.1 provides some explanation. Under the statute, an acknowledgement of paternity is "deemed to be a legal finding of paternity and is sufficient to establish an obligation to support the child and to establish visitation without the necessity of obtaining a judgment of paternity." This rule is consistent with the federal requirement regarding the strength and effect of the presumption. But, this rule is only applicable to custody, visitation, and support proceedings. As a result, the man is deemed the father for those purposes, but not for other purposes such as wrongful death and inheritance actions. Louisiana could have made this presumption comparable to the presumption afforded fathers of marital children had it chosen to do so. As it stands, in proceedings like wrongful death actions and inheritance issues, the presumption may be invoked on behalf of the child—the child is entitled to the presumption that he is the biological child of the man and entitled to inherit from him or bring a wrongful death proceeding. On the other hand, the man is not entitled to that same presumption. As *Udomeh v. Joseph*, below, illustrates, the man who desires to establish his paternity of a nonmarital child for purposes other than child support, custody, and visitation must bring an avowal action. The Uniform Parentage Act similarly contemplates a method of acknowledgement of paternity by non-marital fathers. The Louisiana Revised Statutes set forth the required contents of an authentic act of acknowledgement. However, *Succession of Dangerfield*, below, explains that compliance these requirements is not strictly necessary for a valid act of acknowledgement.

Udomeh v. Joseph
103 So. 3d 343 (La. 2011)

KNOLL, Justice.

This civil case presents the issue of whether an alleged biological father may bring a wrongful death and survival action for his illegitimate child, where the father has not filed a timely avowal action, but filed his wrongful death and survival petition asserting his paternity within the peremptive period of La. Civ. Code art. 198. In resolving this issue, we are called upon to decide whether the filiation requirements of La. Civ. Code art. 198 apply to actions under La. Civ. Code arts. 2315.1 and 2315.2.

After the death of the minor child, S.U., plaintiff, Fidel Udomeh, filed a wrongful death and survival action against defendants, Sandra Joseph and the State of Louisiana through the Department of Social Services and the Louisiana State University

Health System, University Medical Center-Lafayette (collectively "state defendants"), alleging he was the child's biological father. The state defendants filed a peremptory exception of no right of action; although the wrongful death and survival petition was filed within one year of S.U.'s death, Udomeh had not brought an avowal action under La. Civ. Code art. 198 to prove his paternity. The District Court granted the state defendants' exception, dismissing the case with prejudice. The Court of Appeal affirmed, holding Udomeh was not a proper beneficiary for a wrongful death and survival action, as he had failed to file an avowal action within one year of S.U.'s death. We granted this writ to address the correctness vel non of the appellate court's decision.

For the following reasons, we find, while Udomeh was required to file an avowal action in order to bring a wrongful death and survival action, under Louisiana's fact-pleading system, Udomeh's petition pled sufficient facts to state an avowal action.

Accordingly, the judgments of the lower courts are reversed.

FACTS AND PROCEDURAL HISTORY

Plaintiff, Fidel Udomeh, alleges he and defendant, Sandra Joseph, were the biological parents of a minor child, S.U., who was born on June 16, 1997. Udomeh and Joseph were never married and separated early in S.U.'s life. Udomeh, however, contends he maintained an active presence in S.U.'s life and held himself out to the community as his father. Additionally, Udomeh states he voluntarily paid child support until Joseph sought state-mandated child support in 2001.

In February 2006, Udomeh learned Joseph had taken S.U. to a tall building in Baton Rouge and attempted to commit suicide with her son by jumping off of the building. S.U. was able to persuade his mother from taking their lives. Subsequently, Joseph voluntarily committed herself for psychiatric treatment at Vermillion Hospital in Lafayette, and was released a few days later. Udomeh made a formal complaint to the State of Louisiana, through the Department of Social Services ("LDSS"), seeking an investigation and protection for S.U. In response, LDSS issued a form letter stating it was "unable to investigate the situation because it does not meet the legal and policy definition of child abuse or neglect."

In January 2009, while at a restaurant in Lafayette, Joseph experienced another psychotic episode with S.U. in her custody. Local police were called to the restaurant and escorted Joseph to University Medical Center ("UMC") for treatment. UMC released Joseph shortly thereafter, with S.U. in her custody. Joseph, an employee of LDSS, also began exhibiting strange and erratic behavior at work, prompting several coworkers to file witness accounts, complaints, and incident reports with LDSS. One coworker stated Joseph's behavior should be addressed "as soon as possible, especially since she is the sole caregiver for a minor child."

On February 21, 2009, Joseph drove S.U. to Grand Coteau and ordered him out of the vehicle. Joseph then intentionally and repeatedly ran S.U. over with her vehicle, killing him.

On September 8, 2009, Udomeh filed the instant wrongful death and survival action against Joseph, LDSS, and UMC, alleging the state defendants acted negligently by failing to take any action to protect S.U. Both LDSS and UMC argued Udomeh was precluded from bringing suit, as he had not first filed an avowal action under La. Civ. Code art. 198. Initially, LDSS filed a declinatory exception of insufficient service of process. Subsequently, LDSS filed an answer on September 10, 2010, asserting peremptory exceptions of no cause of action and no right of action or, in the alternative, a dilatory exception of lack of procedural capacity. UMC filed an answer raising no exceptions, but later filed a peremptory exception of no right of action.

The trial court granted the state defendants' exceptions of no right of action and/or lack of procedural capacity and dismissed Udomeh's claims against LDSS and UMC with prejudice.

The Court of Appeal affirmed, holding Udomeh was not a proper beneficiary to bring a wrongful death and survival action, as he did not file an avowal action within one year of S.U.'s death. . . .

DISCUSSION

La. Civ. Code art. 198

To recover under a claim for wrongful death and survival, a plaintiff must fall within the class of persons designated as a beneficiary under La. Civ. Code arts. 2315.1 and 2315.2. When the decedent leaves no surviving spouse or child, the decedent's surviving father and mother are the proper beneficiaries to bring a wrongful death and survival action.

Filiation is the legal relationship between a child and his parent. La. Civ. Code art. 178. Filiation is established by proof of maternity, paternity, or adoption. La. Civ. Code art. 179. Prior to 2004, the Civil Code did not provide a process for a biological father to establish parentage of his illegitimate child. Our jurisprudence, however, recognized a biological father's right to establish paternity by means of an avowal action. In 2004, the Louisiana Legislature enacted former La. Civ. Code art. 191, which permitted a man to establish his paternity of a child, even if the child was presumed to be the child of another man. Shortly thereafter, through the enactment of Act 192 of 2005, the Legislature comprehensively revised Title VII of Book I of the Civil Code, regarding the law of filiation. As part of this revision, the Legislature enacted La. Civ. Code art. 198, which provided, in relevant part:

> A man may institute an action to establish his paternity of a child at any time except as provided in this Article. The action is strictly personal.
>
> *   *   *
>
> In all cases, the action shall be instituted no later than one year from the day of the death of the child.
>
> The time periods in this Article are peremptive.

In the present case, S.U. died on February 21, 2009. While Udomeh filed a wrongful death and survival action on September 8, 2009, he did not file an avowal action prior to February 2010, when his right to bring a paternity action was extinguished.

Udomeh argues a putative father is not required to establish filiation under La. Civ. Code art. 198 in order to bring wrongful death and survival actions on behalf of his illegitimate child. La. Civ. Code arts. 2315.1 and 2315.2 merely provide "[t]he surviving father and mother of the deceased" may bring a wrongful death or survival action if the decedent "left no spouse or child surviving." Thus, neither of these statutes required Udomeh to establish paternity pursuant to La. Civ. Code art. 198.

[The court included the following language in a footnote to the forgoing paragraph: "Although Udomeh is listed as the father on S.U.'s birth certificate, this is insufficient to establish paternity. Under La. Civ. Code art. 196, a man may create a presumption of paternity by *signing* the birth certificate of a child not filiated to another man. The presumption, however, can be invoked only on behalf of the child, and the acknowledgment does not create a presumption in favor of the man who acknowledges the child."]

We disagree. The Louisiana Civil Code is a general system of law promulgated by legislative authority, and effect must be given to all of its provisions as such. Its various articles form parts of a complete system and must be construed with reference to each other and harmonized with its general purpose. The Code is "a self sufficient and logically interdependent enactment, to be construed as a whole, and to regulate entirely the relationships and incidents within its scope." Thus, it is incorrect to conclude the Code's filiation articles have no bearing on wrongful death and survival actions, simply because La. Civ. Code arts. 2315.1 and 2315.2 do not explicitly reference La. Civ. Code art. 198.

While this Court has not specifically addressed the application of La. Civ. Code art. 198 to La. Civ. Code arts. 2315.1 and 2315.2, we have repeatedly applied the filiation provisions of the Code to determine the proper beneficiaries for wrongful death and survival actions.

In *Chatelain v. State, Dept. of Transp. & Dev.,* 586 So.2d 1373 (La. 1991), this Court applied former La. Civ. Code art. 209, governing a paternity action by a child, to determine if a child of the decedent was a proper party to bring a wrongful death and survival action. We noted "[t]he critical requirement for classification of a person as a child under Article 2315 is the biological relationship between the tort victim and the child. The child with a biological connection to the tort victim, whether a legitimate, legitimated or illegitimate child, has the right to bring an action for wrongful death and survival damages." However, we noted "when the child is neither legitimate at birth nor subsequently legitimated by the parent, Article 209 imposes a time limitation for establishing the filiation necessary to qualify as a child under Article 2315." Thus, under this Court's jurisprudence, a party bringing a wrongful death and survival claim must establish filiation in accordance with the requirements and temporal limitations of the Civil Code.

Further, the revision comments to La Civ. Code art. 198 indicate a putative father must timely file an avowal action pursuant to Article 198 in order to bring a wrongful death and survival action. One purpose of the temporal restrictions of Article 198 is "that a father who failed during a child's life to assume his parental responsibilities should not be permitted unlimited time to institute an action to benefit from the child's death." La. Civ. Code art. 198, Official Revision Comments (d).

Accordingly, we conclude the filiation provisions of La. Civ. Code art. 198 apply to actions under La. Civ. Code arts. 2315.1 and 2315.2. A putative father must file a timely avowal action in order to maintain a wrongful death and survival action for the death of his illegitimate child.

Additionally, we note it is too late for Udomeh to amend his petition to also bring an avowal action along with his wrongful death claim. The temporal limitations of La. Civ. Code art. 198 are peremptive, and this Court has held "relation back of an amended or supplemental pleading . . . is not allowed to avoid the running of a peremptive period." Therefore, Udomeh cannot amend his petition, as his right to bring an avowal action was extinguished in February 2010.

Fact-Pleading

Although Udomeh's petition does not specifically request a judgment of paternity, under Louisiana's fact-pleading system, we find Udomeh has pled the material facts necessary to state an avowal action, while giving fair notice to defendants that his paternity is at issue in this action.

Louisiana's Code of Civil Procedure uses a system of pleading based upon the narration of factual allegations. "No technical forms of pleading are required. All allegations of fact of the petition, exceptions, or answer shall be simple, concise, and direct, and shall be set forth in numbered paragraphs." La. Code Civ. Proc. art. 854.

Under La. Code Civ. Proc. art. 862, except in cases of a default judgment,

> a final judgment shall grant the relief to which the party in whose favor it is rendered is entitled, even if the party has not demanded such relief in his pleadings and the latter contain no prayer for general and equitable relief.

Article 862 permits courts to render substantive justice on the basis of facts pleaded and to refuse to permit a denial of substantive rights due to technical defects of language or characterization of the case. "So long as the facts constituting the claim or defense are alleged or proved, the party may be granted any relief to which he is entitled under the fact-pleadings and evidence." However, due process requires adequate notice to the parties of the matters to be adjudicated.

Although Article 862 abolished the "theory of the case" pleading requirement, La. Code Civ. Proc. art. 891 provides a petition "shall contain a short, clear, and concise statement of all causes of action arising out of, and of the material facts of, the transaction or occurrence that is the subject matter of the litigation." In order to plead "material facts" within Louisiana's fact-pleading system, the pleader must "'state what act or omission he or she will establish at trial, such as the fact the defendant failed to deliver goods by a designated date, exceeded the speed limit, or failed to pay workers' compensation benefits although the evidence in his or her possession clearly established a compensable injury and disability.'"

In the present case, Udomeh's petition refers to S.U. as Udomeh's "minor child" and "minor son" and alleges:

> Petitioner, FIDEL UDOMEH, and Defendant, SANDRA JOSEPH, were the biological parents of their minor child, the late S.U., who was born on June 16, 1997. Petitioner and Defendant were never married, but the paternity of the child has been established since birth.

> Petitioner and SANDRA JOSEPH separated from one another early in the child's life, but Petitioner maintained an active role as father in his son's life at all pertinent times.

After reviewing the petition, we find Udomeh has set forth the material facts necessary for an avowal action. As noted above, a pleader must set forth the act or omission he or she will establish at trial. Here, the petition alleges a biological relationship between the pleader and the child, as well as his support and acknowledgement of the child. These allegations provided the state defendants with adequate notice of the issue of Udomeh's paternity. . . .

Additionally, allowing Udomeh to proceed with a paternity suit does not offend the policies underlying La. Civ. Code art. 198. As noted earlier, one purpose of the statute's one-year peremptive period is to prevent a father who failed to assume parental responsibilities during the child's lifetime from having unlimited time to bring a wrongful death and survival action. Further, where the child is presumed to be the child of another man, the biological father must quickly institute an avowal action "to protect the child from the upheaval of such litigation," where the child lives in an existing, intact family or has become attached to his presumed father. The present case, however, does not involve either of these factual scenarios. Udomeh alleges he acknowledged and supported his child during his lifetime and no other man is presumed to be S.U.'s father.

We conclude Udomeh's petition sets forth sufficient facts to state an avowal action and provide notice to defendants of the issue of Udomeh's paternity. This is in accord with La. Code Civ. Proc. art. 862 and the general rules that pleadings should be construed in such a manner as to achieve substantial justice, and harsh, technical rules of pleading are not favored. As Udomeh filed his petition within one year of S.U.'s death, his avowal action is timely under La. Civ. Code art. 198, and his right to bring an avowal action is not perempted as long as the present action is pending. As the determination of whether a party has pled sufficient facts under Article 862 to be entitled to certain relief must necessarily be decided on a case-by-case basis, our ruling in this particular matter is limited to the facts adduced in this record. . . .

DECREE

For the foregoing reasons, the judgments of the lower courts are reversed and this case is remanded to the District Court for further proceedings.

REVERSED; REMANDED.

Succession of Dangerfield

207 So. 3d 427 (La. App. 1 Cir. 2016)

WELCH, J.

Ezzard Bowman, in his capacity as the executor of the Succession of Joseph Dangerfield, appeals a judgment declaring that Bridgette Shropshire had been formally acknowledged by Joseph Dangerfield, the decedent, and recognizing her as an heir of Mr. Dangerfield. For reasons that follow, we affirm the judgment of the trial court.

BACKGROUND

Mr. Dangerfield died on September 8, 2003. Mr. Dangerfield's succession was opened in August 2004, and Mr. Bowman, the natural son of Mr. Dangerfield, was subsequently appointed as the executor of the succession. Mr. Dangerfield's widow, Edith Dangerfield, produced for probate a document dated October 30, 2002, which purported to be the last will and testament of Mr. Dangerfield; however, by judgment signed on April 8, 2014, the trial court determined that the document was not valid as the last will and testament of Mr. Dangerfield. Thus, the effect of the trial court's judgment was that Mr. Dangerfield died intestate. See La. C.C. art. 880.

Thereafter, almost ten years after Mr. Dangerfield's succession was opened, Ms. Shropshire filed a petition seeking to be recognized as an heir of Mr. Dangerfield. After a hearing, the trial court rendered judgment in favor of Ms. Shropshire declaring that she had been formally acknowledged by Mr. Dangerfield and that she be recognized as an heir of Mr. Dangerfield. An amended judgment in conformity with the trial court's ruling was signed on April 28, 2016, and it is from this judgment that Mr. Bowman has appealed, challenging the trial court's determination that Ms. Shropshire had been formally acknowledged by Mr. Dangerfield.

LAW AND DISCUSSION

. . . Under the Louisiana Civil Code, there are three ways of establishing paternal filiation, or a legal relationship between a father and child: (1) the presumption of paternity due to a marriage to the mother (La. C.C. arts. 185, 186 and 195); (2) in the absence of a marriage, the presumption of paternity based on a formal acknowledgement by the father (La. C.C. art. 196); or (3) in the absence of a marriage between the parents or a formal acknowledgment, by the institution of a legal proceeding to prove filiation (La. C.C. art. 197).

Pertinent to this appeal is the formal acknowledgement set forth in La. C.C. art. 196. Louisiana Civil Code article 196 provides, in pertinent part, that "[a] man may, by authentic act or by signing the birth certificate, acknowledge a child not filiated to another man;" such an "acknowledgement creates a presumption that the man who acknowledges the child is the father." "An authentic act is a writing executed before a notary public or other officer authorized to perform that function, in the presence of two witnesses, and signed by each party who executed it, by each witness, and by each notary public before whom it was executed." La. C.C. art. 1833(A).

In this case, the trial court determined that Ms. Shropshire had been formally acknowledged by Mr. Dangerfield based on an Act of Donation Inter Vivos ("the act of donation"), which was executed in East Baton Rouge Parish before a notary and two witnesses on May 12, 2003. In the act of donation, Mr. Dangerfield "declared'. . . [t]hat Donee, [Ms.] Shropshire, is the daughter of [Mr. Dangerfield]" and that he was donating a particularly described piece of immovable property in East Baton Rouge Parish to Ms. Shropshire "in consideration of the love and affection that he bears for [Ms.] Shropshire."

In addition, the trial court relied on the factually similar case of *Mayfield v. Mayfield*, 511 So.2d 1285, 1286 (La. App. 2nd Cir. 1987), wherein the second circuit court of appeal addressed the issue of whether an authentic act of donation of immovable property could satisfy the requirements set forth in the civil code for a formal acknowledgement. In *Mayfield*, before the death of the decedent, Croford Mayfield, in 1977, the decedent and his legitimated daughter, Norma Mayfield, formally donated, by authentic act, a piece of real estate to James Mayfield in 1975, declaring therein that the donation was made "in consideration of the natural love and affection they have for their son and brother, respectively, James Mayfield." The court determined that the 1975 donation from the decedent and his legitimized daughter satisfied, in form and in substance, the requirements for a formal acknowledgment set forth in former La. C.C. art. 203, which provided that "[t]he acknowledgement of an illegitimate child shall be made by a declaration executed before a notary public, in the presence of two witnesses, by the father and mother or either of them, or it may be made in the registering of the birth or baptism of such child." The court further stated that the absence of the word "acknowledgment" in the authentic act did not preclude a finding that the authentic act was a formal acknowledgement. Thus, the court held that the 1975 donation was legally sufficient as a formal acknowledgment under former La. C.C. art 203.

Based on the holding in *Mayfield* and the authentic form of the act of donation wherein Mr. Dangerfield attested that Ms. Shropshire was his daughter, the trial court rendered judgment declaring that Ms. Shropshire had been formally acknowledged by Mr. Dangerfield and that she was entitled to be recognized as his heir. On appeal, Mr. Bowman does not dispute that the act of donation meets the legal requirements of an authentic act under La. C.C. art. 1833(A); rather he contends that the substance of the authentic act of donation was insufficient to satisfy the legal requirements for a formal acknowledgement.

First, Mr. Bowman contends that the trial court ignored the requirements set forth in La. R.S. 9:392, which was enacted after the *Mayfield* decision in 1987. Mr. Bowman argues that La. R.S. 9:392 sets forth substantive requirements for a formal acknowledgement, which are in addition to the requirements set forth in the civil code, and that the act of donation does not contain these additional substantive requirements. . . .

The determination as to whether, as Mr. Bowman suggests, La. R.S. 9:392 sets forth substantive requirements for a formal acknowledgement that are in addition to the requirements set forth in the civil code is a matter of statutory interpretation. The fundamental question in all cases involving statutory interpretation is legislative intent. Further, according to the general rules of statutory interpretation, our interpretation of any statutory provision begins with the language of the statute itself. When a law is clear and unambiguous and its application does not lead to absurd consequences, its language must be given effect, and its provisions must be construed so as to give effect to the purpose indicated by a fair interpretation of the language used. Unequivocal provisions are not subject to judicial construction and should be applied by giving words their generally understood meaning. Words and phrases must be read with their context and construed according to the common and approved usage of the language. . . .

Paragraph A of La. R.S. 9:392 provides that "[p]rior to the execution of an acknowledgment of paternity" pursuant to the civil code, "the notary shall provide" the party making the acknowledgment "orally" and "in writing" of specific legal rights and obligations with respect to acknowledgment, as well as the circumstances under and time limits within which the acknowledgement can be rescinded. Giving these words and phrases their generally prevailing meaning, we cannot say that this paragraph imposes substantive requirements (in addition to those set forth in the civil code) that must be contained within the act of acknowledgement; rather, we find that it clearly and unambiguously imposes a duty on the notary—prior to the execution of a declaration of acknowledgement—to provide specific notice to the party making the acknowledgment of the legal consequences of the act.

On the other hand, paragraph B specifically provides that "[i]n addition to the general requirements of" the civil code, "a declaration of acknowledgment . . . shall include the social security numbers of the father and mother;" however, the "[f]ailure to recite a party's social security number . . . shall not affect the validity of the declaration." Based on the clear and unambiguous terms of paragraph B, we find that it does set forth a substantive requirement for an act of acknowledgment, i.e., the social security numbers of the father and mother, which is in addition to the general requirements of an act of acknowledgement set forth in the civil code. However, paragraph B further sets forth, clearly and unambiguously, that the failure to include a party's social security number does not affect the validity of the acknowledgment—in other words, the failure to include this additional substantive requirement in the act of acknowledgment does not affect the validity of it.

Therefore, reading La. R.S. 9:392 in conjunction with the rules of statutory construction, we find that paragraph A (La. R.S. 9:392(A)) does not set forth substantive requirements for a formal acknowledgement which must be set forth in the acknowledgement; it imposes a duty on the notary to inform the person signing the acknowledgment of the legal consequences of the act prior to its execution. However, we find that paragraph B (La. R.S. 9:392(B)) does set forth a substantive requirement for a formal acknowledgement, which is in addition to the general requirements set forth in the civil code. Notably, in this case, the act of donation sets forth the social security numbers of both Ms. Shropshire and Mr. Dangerfield, but it does not contain the social security number of Ms. Shropshire's mother. However, pursuant to the express terms of La. R.S. 9:392(B), the failure of the act of donation to include the mother's social security number does not affect the validity of Mr. Dangerfield's formal acknowledgement of Ms. Shopshire. Thus, Mr. Bowman's argument that the act of donation was insufficient to constitute a formal acknowledgment because it failed to include the substantive requirements of La. R.S. 9:392 lacks merit.

Next, citing *Turner v. Busby*, 883 So.2d 412, 418, Mr. Bowman argues that in order for an authentic act acknowledging paternity to serve as a formal acknowledgment, the act must reveal an intent to legitimize by notarial act. He claims that the act of donation did not express or reveal an intent to legitimize Ms. Shropshire, therefore it cannot constitute a formal acknowledgment. However, we find no merit to Mr. Bowman's argument that a formal acknowledgment must express an intent to legitimize, and we find that his reliance on *Turner* for such argument is misplaced. *Turner*, which was decided in 2004 (prior to the 2005 La. Acts, No. 192 repeal of former La. C.C. arts. 178–211 and the amendment and reenactment of those articles to now comprise La. C.C. arts. 184–198), makes no such holding or statement. In addition, his argument confuses two separate and distinct legal concepts under the former provisions of the civil code relative to a legal relationship between parent and child, i.e., former La. C.C. arts. 178–211. . . .

Accordingly, Turner provides no support for Mr. Bowman's argument that an authentic act acknowledging paternity must reveal an intent to legitimize in order to serve as a formal acknowledgment lacks merit. An act to legitimate pursuant to former La. C.C. art. 200 and an act of acknowledgement pursuant to former La. C.C. art. 203 were two separate and distinct legal concepts with different legal consequences. The intent to legitimize or legitimate was an element of an act to legitimate; it was not a required element of an act of or a formal acknowledgment under former La. C.C. art. 203. Likewise, the intent to legitimate cannot be a required element of an act of acknowledgement under La. C.C. art. 196. . . .

Accordingly, based on our review of the record and applicable law, including the Mayfield decision discussed hereinabove, we find no error in the trial court's conclusion that the act of donation was an authentic act and that the statement therein by Mr. Dangerfield that Ms. Shropshire was his daughter satisfied in form and in substance the legal requirements set forth in La. C.C. art. 196 for a formal acknowledgment. Although the act of donation does not set forth the social security number of Ms. Shropshire's mother, as required by La. R.S. 9:392(B), the failure to include that information does not affect the validity of Mr. Dangerfield's formal acknowledgment. Therefore, the judgment of the trial court declaring that Ms. Shropshire had been formally acknowledged by Mr. Dangerfield and that she was entitled to be recognized as his heir is affirmed.

CONCLUSION

For all of the above and foregoing reasons, this appeal is maintained and the April 28, 2016 amended judgment of the trial court is affirmed.

All costs of this appeal are assessed to the appellant, Ezzard Bowman.

D. Establishing Paternity: Avowal Actions

See La. Civ. Code art. 197–98; Uniform Parentage Act § 201; § 601–12.

Both Louisiana and the Uniform Parentage Act contemplate various situations where a party may go to court and obtain a judicial declaration establishing paternity. These types of proceedings arise for a variety of reasons. As illustrated in *Udomeh v. Joseph*, above, the father of a non-marital child might need to bring an avowal action in order to inherit from his child or in order to bring a wrongful death action on behalf of his child. Similarly, the child of a decedent might bring an action seeking to establish his filiation with the decedent for inheritance purposes if the child has not already been acknowledged by the decedent. Alternatively, the child (acting through his mother, guardian, or through a state agency such as the Louisiana Department of Children and Family Services) may bring an action to establish paternity for purposes of obtaining child support and other financial benefits.

Federal law requires that states "permit the establishment of paternity of a child at any time before the child attains 18 years of age."[12] In other words, children (or their legal representatives) must be allowed to establish paternity at any time until they reach the age of majority. Louisiana is one of a handful of states that is quite lenient in its implementation of the federal law. Civil Code article 197 allows a child to bring an action to establish paternity at any time. The only time limitation imposed in Louisiana is when the action is brought after the alleged father's death and the action is being brought for succession purposes — an issue not addressed by the federal law. In those cases, the action is subject to a one-year peremptive period commencing on the date of death of the alleged father. Section 606 of the Uniform Parentage Act takes a similar approach. Under both schemes, it is immaterial whether the child is already filiated with another man. This can lead to a somewhat curious outcome in Louisiana where a child is legally filiated with two men — so-called "dual paternity."

Both Louisiana and the Uniform Parentage Act also allow a man to bring his own avowal action to establish his biological paternity with respect to a child. Louisiana and the Uniform Parentage Act differ somewhat with respect to the timing and circumstances under which such an action may be brought — and an examination of actual state laws reveals considerable variation among the states. Civil Code article 198 generally allows a man to bring an avowal action at any time. If the child is already filiated with another man, both Louisiana and the Uniform Parentage Act limit the alleged father's ability to bring an avowal action. These limitations — as well as those implemented in other states — represent legislative attempts to balance difficult policy considerations. As *Michael H. v. Gerald D.* illustrated, a number of states previously imposed a complete ban on the ability of a man believing he was the biological father to bring an avowal action where there was already a presumptive father. That approach

---

12. 42 U.S.C. § 666(a)(5)(A)(i) (2017).

has largely come to an end. Like Louisiana, states more often give alleged fathers a short window of time to seek to establish paternity when the child is presumptively the child of another man. Revision Comment (e) to Article 198 explains the policy as follows:

> Requiring that the biological father institute the avowal action quickly is intended to protect the child from the upheaval of such litigation and its consequences in circumstances where the child may actually live in an existing intact family with his mother and presumed father or may have become attached over many years to the man presumed to be his father.

In an effort to balance the various policy concerns, Article 198 establishes a one-year peremptive period for avowal actions. Generally, peremption commences on the date of the child's birth. However, if the mother deceived the father regarding his paternity in bad faith, then peremption commences from the earlier of: (a) the date he knew or should have known of his paternity; or (b) 10 years from the birth of the child. In any event, the action must be brought within one year of the child's death. The action is also strictly personal to the father.

The following cases explore the bad faith deception exception to Article 198's one-year peremptive period. They also vividly demonstrate the conflicting policy considerations legislatures grapple with in attempting to craft laws to address complicated issues that often involve competing public policy concerns.

Suarez v. Acosta

194 So. 3d 626 (La. App. 5 Cir. 2016)

JUDE G. GRAVOIS, Judge.

INTRODUCTION

Plaintiff/appellant, Carlos Suarez, appeals the trial court's June 2, 2015 judgment that maintained defendant/appellee, Alvin Acosta's, peremptory exception of prescription/peremption in this paternity/avowal action brought by Mr. Suarez. For the following reasons, we affirm.

FACTS AND PROCEDURAL HISTORY

Alvin Acosta and Suyapa Casco Acosta ("Suyapa") were married on January 21, 2007. On February 14, 2007, Adriana Acosta was born to Suyapa. Mr. Acosta is listed as Adriana's father on her birth certificate. On April 24, 2012, Suyapa died of leukemia.

On February 13, 2015, Mr. Suarez filed a "Petition for Paternity Suit, Child Custody and Child Support" against Mr. Acosta. Pertinent to his paternity/avowal suit, Mr. Suarez alleged that prior to the Acostas' marriage, he maintained a relationship with Suyapa that resulted in the conception and birth of Adriana. He further alleged that he was "intentionally deceived" by Suyapa as to his status as Adriana's biological father. In March of 2014, he was told by a co-worker, Trenella Daigs, that he was Adriana's biological father. As a result of learning this information, "he underwent DNA testing." According to the petition, "the results of the DNA test proved with 99.999999% certainty" that Mr. Suarez is Adriana's biological father. Thus, Mr. Suarez alleges that he could not have known that Adriana was his child until he received the DNA test results proving his paternity.

In response, on March 25, 2015, Mr. Acosta filed exceptions of no cause and/or no right of action, and prescription and/or peremption as to Mr. Suarez's paternity/avowal action concerning Adriana. A hearing on the exceptions was held before the domestic commissioner on April 15, 2015.

Both Mr. Acosta and Mr. Suarez testified at the hearing before the domestic commissioner. Mr. Acosta testified that he met Suyapa in 2004 when they both worked at Pep Boys. They became engaged in 2006 and married in 2007. They had two children, Adriana and Gabriella. Mr. Acosta testified that his name is on both children's birth certificates, and they both call him "Daddy." Mr. Suarez also worked at Pep Boys. Mr. Acosta testified that during the time he and Suyapa were dating and later married, Mr. Suarez and Suyapa were "best friends," and Mr. Suarez would call her "every day to tell her good morning." However, as far as Mr. Acosta knew, there was no ongoing sexual relationship between Mr. Suarez and Suyapa.

Mr. Acosta further testified that on January 23, 2007, two days after he and Suyapa were married and before Adriana was born, he received a call from a lady claiming to be Mr. Suarez's girlfriend who informed him that Suyapa was calling Mr. Suarez and claiming that Adriana was Mr. Suarez's child. Mr. Acosta called Suyapa to ask her about these claims. She told him to "hold on," and a few minutes later, Mr. Acosta received a call from Mr. Suarez. According to Mr. Acosta, during their phone conversation, after learning that Mr. Acosta and Suyapa had gotten married, Mr. Suarez told Mr. Acosta that the child was his, and he was going to force Mr. Acosta to take a DNA test. Thereafter, sometime between that phone call and when Adriana was born, while Mr. Acosta was picking Suyapa up from work, Mr. Suarez personally confronted Mr. Acosta. During their confrontation, Mr. Suarez first claimed that Suyapa had been with him that morning. He then told Mr. Acosta that if the baby was born on a specific due date, then it was his child, and he was going to force Mr. Acosta to take a DNA test. Mr. Acosta testified that he did not talk to Mr. Suarez again until after Suyapa passed away, more than five years later. To his knowledge, prior to this suit, Mr. Suarez did not bring any legal action or make a formal request for a DNA test, though Mr. Suarez could have found Mr. Acosta if he needed to.

Mr. Suarez testified before the domestic commissioner that he met Suyapa at Pep Boys sometime in 1997 or 1998, and he began having a sexual relationship with her sometime in late 2001 or 2002. It was an "on and off thing." He admitted to having sex with Suyapa in 2006, even after she became pregnant. Once Adriana was born, they no longer had a physical relationship. He testified that he spoke to Mr. Acosta in 2005 or 2006, but "[he didn't] think [he] made any threats or any allegations of [him] being the father," because he had not yet learned Suyapa was pregnant. When he learned that she was pregnant, he asked her twice if the child was his, and she told him that the child was not his. He testified that both conversations that Mr. Acosta testified about "never happened." He also testified that he did not learn that he was the child's father until a co-worker told him of such in March of 2014. According to

Mr. Suarez, his coworker was told this information by Suyapa sometime before her death and by her mother, Mrs. Casco, and when asked about proof, Mr. Suarez stated that they were "real close friends." He further testified that he saw Suyapa after Adriana was born and has seen Adriana since she was born "maybe once or twice a month." When the domestic commissioner asked him if he had any suspicions that the child might be his when he saw her, he said no because "she didn't look like [him.]"

At the end of the hearing, the domestic commissioner orally granted the exception of prescription/peremption; he issued a written judgment to that effect on April 20, 2015. On April 17, 2015, Mr. Suarez filed an objection to the domestic commissioner's order and requested an evidentiary hearing before the district court. The hearing before the district court was held on May 19, 2015. . . .

At the conclusion of the hearing, the trial court orally sustained the domestic commissioner's granting of the exception of prescription/peremption and held that Mr. Suarez's paternity/avowal action was deemed perempted and was accordingly dismissed. A judgment to that effect was signed on June 2, 2015. On September 17, 2015, Mr. Suarez filed the Motion for Devolutive Appeal and Notice of Appeal. This appeal followed. . . .

ASSIGNMENT OF ERROR NUMBER THREE

In his third and final assignment of error, Mr. Suarez argues that the trial court committed manifest error in finding that Mr. Suarez was perempted from claiming paternity of the minor child. . . .

La. C.C. art. 185 states that the husband of the mother is presumed to be the father of a child born during the marriage. Since Mr. Acosta and Suyapa were married at the time of Adriana's birth, Mr. Acosta is presumed to be Adriana's father. Considering this, Mr. Suarez was required to file his paternity/avowal action within one year of Adriana's birth, unless he was "in bad faith deceived" by Suyapa regarding his paternity. Mr. Suarez argues that he was deceived, and he did not learn that he was the child's father until after he was told such by a coworker in March of 2014 and subsequently had a DNA test performed. Thus, he argues that his suit filed in February 2015 was timely.

At the hearings, Mr. Suarez testified that he had an on and off again physical relationship with Suyapa from late 2001 or 2002 until the minor child was born and admitted to having had sex with Suyapa in 2006 and continued to have sex with her even after she became pregnant. When he learned Suyapa was pregnant, Mr. Suarez testified that he asked her a couple of times if the child was his, and she told him no. He admitted to seeing Suyapa after the child was born and admitted to continually seeing the child as often as once or twice a month since the child's birth. He alleges, however, that he did not have any reason to doubt Suyapa, and it was only later, after Suyapa's death, when a co-worker told him the child was his, did he get a DNA test and learn that he was the father.

Mr. Acosta presented different facts. According to Mr. Acosta, he was approached twice, before the baby was even born, by Mr. Suarez who claimed the child was his and he was going to force Mr. Acosta to take a DNA test. Though Mr. Suarez knew where to find Mr. Acosta if he so needed, Mr. Suarez did not make any formal request for a DNA test or take any legal action until eight years after these incidents allegedly occurred. . . .

The trial court found that Mr. Suarez knew or should have known that he was Adriana's biological father at least eight years before he filed this suit, and thus his paternity/avowal action was perempted. Based on the evidence presented, we cannot say that the trial court's findings of fact in this regard are manifestly erroneous or clearly wrong. Further, in light of the conflict between the testimony of Mr. Suarez and that of Mr. Acosta, we cannot say that the trial court's evaluations of credibility and inferences of fact in this case were unreasonable. Accordingly, we find no error in the trial court's ruling that Mr. Suarez's paternity/avowal action was perempted. This assignment of error is without merit.

CONCLUSION

For the foregoing reasons, we affirm the trial court's judgment sustaining Mr. Acosta's exception of prescription/preemption.

MOTION TO DISMISS APPEAL DENIED: AFFIRMED

Leger v. Leger

215 So. 3d 773 (La. App. 3 Cir. 2015)

SAVOIE, Judge.

Appellant John Jerome Fontenot appeals the ruling of the trial court, wherein the court ruled that he did not have a right to avow his paternity of Gracelynn Leger pursuant to Louisiana Civil Code article 198. For the following reasons, we affirm.

Michael Leger and Danielle Gotreaux Leger were married in 2007. Three children were born during the marriage—Michael Joseph Leger, III, born January 4, 2007, Gracelynn Ann Leger, born August 21, 2012, and Emilee Camille Leger, born March 1, 2014. In the fall of 2011, John Jerome Fontenot, a local veterinarian, and Danielle Leger had an affair. During that time, Danielle became pregnant with Gracelynn Leger. Dr. Fontenot submitted to a DNA test in October 2012, just two months after the birth, to determine whether he was the father of Gracelynn. The results indicated that there was a 99.99% percent probability that Dr. Fontenot was Gracelynn's father.

Michael and Danielle separated in August 2013. Danielle was pregnant with Emilee at the time of the separation. When Emilee was born in March 2014, the Department of Children and Family Services ("DCFS") removed her from Danielle's care because she tested positive for cocaine. Michael was working offshore at the time of the birth. When the infant was removed, a DCFS worker contacted Dr. Fontenot to take custody of Gracelynn because he was identified by Danielle's mother as the father of Gracelynn.

On March 3, 2014, Michael was served with a petition for custody of Gracelynn, which alleged that Dr. Fontenot was Gracelynn's father. This was when Michael first became aware of the affair between Dr. Fontenot and Danielle and, that he might not be Gracelynn's father.

Danielle also told Michael that he was not the father of the newborn Emilee. Danielle told DCFS that Emilee was Dr. Fontenot's child. However, DNA testing confirmed that Emilee was, in fact, the biological child of Michael.

Eventually, all three children were placed in Michael's custody. During a hearing officer's conference on the petition for custody in April 2014, the parties agreed on a visitation schedule for Dr. Fontenot and Gracelynn. No further action was taken in that matter.

In May 2014, Michael filed a petition for divorce against Danielle alleging adultery. Dr. Fontenot filed a Petition for Intervention, for Paternity, Custody, and Alternatively, Visitation. In the petition, Dr. Fontenot alleged that he was unable to file a timely avowal action because he feared for the safety of Danielle and Gracelynn. . . .

The trial court ruled that La. Civ. Code art. 198 precluded Dr. Fontenot from establishing paternity of Gracelynn. The exception of preemption was granted. Dr. Fontenot now appeals.

ASSIGNMENT OF ERROR NUMBER ONE

. . . Generally, an avowal action may be brought at any time. However, La. Civ. Code art. 198 establishes a time period for filing such an action in two instances— if the child is presumed to be the child of another man and if the child dies. The first scenario applies to the instant case. "The husband of the mother is presumed to be the father of a child born during the marriage[.]" Louisiana Civil Code Article 198 specifies that an action must be instituted "within one year from the day of the birth of the child" in this instance.

Michael and Danielle were married at the time of Gracelynn's birth. In accordance with the above statute, Dr. Fontenot had one year from the birth of Gracelynn to file his avowal action. He did not do so. There is one exception to the one year time period. If the mother, in bad faith, deceives the father concerning his paternity, the father must institute an action within one year from the day he knew or should have known of the birth of the child or within ten years of the child's birth, whichever first occurs.

It is Dr. Fontenot's contention that his avowal action was timely due to this exception. He believed that Danielle and Gracelynn would be in physical danger if he were to expose the fact that he was Gracelynn's father. This was the reason he delayed the institution of the avowal action. He argues that the exception found in La. Civ. Code art. 198 should extend to these circumstances. We disagree.

While Dr. Fontenot's situation is unfortunate, the law is clear. Only "if the mother in bad faith deceived the father of the child regarding his paternity" does the exception apply. There is no evidence that Danielle deceived Dr. Fontenot regarding his paternity. She may have deceived Dr. Fontenot regarding the consequences of disclosing his paternity; however, Dr. Fontenot knew he was Gracelynn's father. Within two months of Gracelynn's birth, Dr. Fontenot submitted to a DNA test that clearly showed he was the child's father. Furthermore, in his petition for intervention, Dr. Fontenot acknowledges that he knew that he is Gracelynn's father for more than a year since her birth.

Even if we were to conclude that Danielle deceived Dr. Fontenot regarding his paternity, which we do not, the law requires that "the action shall be instituted within one year from the day the father knew or should have known of his paternity, or within ten years from the day of the birth of the child, whichever first occurs." It is fair to say that Dr. Fontenot knew or should have known that he was Gracelynn's father when the DNA testing was conducted in October 2012. This avowal action was filed in May 2014. Therefore, even if the exception applied, Dr. Fontenot's avowal action would still be untimely. . . .

DECREE

For the foregoing reasons, the judgment of the trial court is affirmed. Costs of these proceedings are assessed to Appellant John Jerome Fontenot.

AFFIRMED.

E. Rebutting the Presumption of Paternity: Disavowal Actions and Contestation Actions

See La. Civ. Code art. 187–94; Uniform Parentage Act § 606–09.

In some instances, a presumptive father may wish to rebut the presumption of paternity and essentially disestablish his paternity of a particular child. The child or the child's mother might likewise desire to rebut the presumptive paternity of a particular man. Both the Uniform Parentage Act and Louisiana law permit legal adjudications rebutting presumptive paternity. Again, the two regimes differ in some significant respects, and an examination of laws enacted in other states reveals even greater variety.

Louisiana allows a presumptive father's paternity to be rebutted by two different types of actions: (1) the disavowal action, and (2) the contestation action. Civil Code articles 187–90 set forth the rules governing the disavowal action. That action is brought by either the presumptive father or by his successors following his death. Like avowal actions, the Civil Code sets forth various time limits for bringing disavowal actions. Again, this reflects a legislative attempt to strike a balance between competing public policy concerns.

Article 189 addresses the disavowal action of a man who is a presumptive father due to his marriage to the mother. In general, the husband's action is subject to a one-year liberative prescription. This prescriptive period begins to run from the later of (a) the birth of the child, or (b) "the day the husband knew or should have known that he may not be the biological father of the child." There is an exception to this general rule where the spouses lived separate and apart for 300 days preceding the child's birth. In that case, "prescription does not commence to run until the husband is notified in writing that a party in interest has asserted that the husband is the father of the child." *Pociask v. Mosely*, below, considers the meaning of that exception.

Article 190 considers the prescriptive periods applicable when the disavowal action is brought by an heir or legatee — usually for inheritance purposes. Again, the action is subject to a one-year liberative prescription. The starting point for the prescriptive period depends on whether the prescription had already begun to run under Article 190 before the presumptive father's death. If so, then the successor's action is "subject to a liberative prescription of one year [that] . . . commences to run from the day of the death of the husband." If, however, prescription had not yet begun to run (perhaps because the presumptive father lived separate and apart from the mother, because he predeceased the child, or because he did not know he was not the father before his death), then the successor's "prescription commences to run from the day the successor is notified in writing that a party in interest has asserted that the husband is the father of the child."

Civil Code articles 191–94 set forth the contestation action. Article 191 explains that the contestation action is "an action to establish both that her former husband is not the father of the child and that her present husband is the father." Thus, the action addresses the scenario presented in Article 186 where a woman has remarried and gives birth within 300 days of the termination of her prior marriage. Article 186 provides that the first husband is presumed to be the father in that case. The contestation action allows the mother to bring an action to essentially establish paternity in the second husband and disestablish paternity in the first husband. The relevant Civil Code articles set forth rules regarding the applicable time limits and the specific nature of the judgment that the court should issue.

Pociask v. Moseley
122 So. 3d 533 (La. 2013)

Guidry, Justice.

In this disavowal action, the district court granted summary judgment in favor of the plaintiff, Derek Alan Pociask, and allowed him to disavow paternity of the minor child, J.M. The appellate court reversed and rendered judgment in favor of the defendant, Kere Moseley, finding the plaintiff's action was prescribed under Article 189 of the Civil Code of Louisiana, and dismissing the action with prejudice. We granted the plaintiff's application for supervisory writs, and for the reasons set forth below, we reverse the court of appeal's decision and reinstate the judgment of the district court.

FACTS AND PROCEDURAL HISTORY

Kera Moseley and Derek Pociask were married on October 11, 1997, in New Orleans. One child, E.P., was born of the marriage on April 4, 1999. The parties physically separated on April 30, 2006. On March 15, 2007, Ms. Moseley gave birth to another child, J.M. Following a hearing on Ms. Moseley's rule to show cause on

May 14, 2007, the district court rendered a judgment of divorce. On July 15, 2008, Mr. Pociask was notified by the State of Louisiana that Ms. Moseley had asserted he is the father of J.M. . . .

On January 20, 2011, the parties entered into a consent judgment, whereby the district court ordered that J.M. submit to a DNA test within ten days. The results of the DNA test revealed that the plaintiff was not the biological father of J.M. . . .

DISCUSSION

. . . The motions for summary judgment at issue here arise in the context of a petition for disavowal of paternity. The defendant has asserted a defense of prescription, asserting the plaintiff's disavowal action was not filed within one year of the birth of the child, nor did the parties live separate and apart continuously for three hundred days immediately preceding the birth of the child, such that the suspensive exception to the one-year limitation in La. Civ. Code art. 189 is similarly unavailing to the plaintiff. The issue thus presented in the instant case is whether the former husband timely filed his petition for disavowal of paternity. . . .

It is a longstanding principle of our civil law tradition that the husband of the mother is presumed to be the father of a child born either during the marriage or within three hundred days from the date of the termination of the marriage. La. Civ. Code art. 185. However, the husband may disavow paternity of the child by clear and convincing evidence that he is not the father, though the testimony of the father must be corroborated by other evidence. La. Civ. Code art. 187. The petition for disavowal of paternity must be brought within the time limitations set forth in La. Civ. Code art. 189, which provides as follows:

> The action for disavowal of paternity is subject to a liberative prescription of one year. This prescription commences to run from the day the husband learns or should have learned of the birth of the child.

There is an exception suspending this time limitation contained in the second paragraph of La. Civ. Code art. 189:

> Nevertheless, if the husband lived separate and apart from the mother continuously during the three hundred days immediately preceding the birth of the child, this prescription does not commence to run until the husband is notified in writing that a party in interest has asserted that the husband is the father of the child.

In *Gallo*, we explained that the policy embodied in the restrictive provisions of the Louisiana Civil Code dealing with the action to disavow is "to protect innocent children, born during marriage, against scandalous attacks upon their paternity by the husband of the mother, who may be seeking to avoid paternal obligations to the child." Thus, "the traditional and historical position of Louisiana jurisprudence was to zealously guard and enforce the presumption of paternity" created by the Civil Code. "The fundamental ends achieved by such court action were preservation of the family unit, avoidance of the stigma of illegitimacy, and aversion to the disinheritance that resulted from a successful disavowal action. . . ."

In 1999 . . . this court noted that once the bonds of matrimony are dissolved by divorce, the state's interest in preserving the marital family wanes. We observed in *Gallo* that, "[a]lthough some rights spring from the dissolution of a lawful marriage, today's realities are that illegitimacy and 'broken homes' are neither rarities nor stigmas as in the past." In *Gallo*, we pointed to then-recent changes in this area of the law, which included legislation making the presumption regarding paternity rebuttable instead of conclusive; Louisiana's recognition of dual paternity; and the acceptance of DNA testing as conclusive scientific evidence of biological paternity. . . .

A similarly liberalizing legislative change was effected in the second paragraph of La. Civ. Code art. 189, to suspend the time period for filing the disavowal action if the husband continuously lived separate and apart from the mother during the three hundred days immediately preceding the birth of the child. No such suspension of prescription was provided for until the 1999 amendment, which incorporated the living separate and apart language long used in the codal articles governing divorce. See La. Civ. Code arts. 102 and 103. This suspension for filing the disavowal action was incorporated into the Law Institute's revision of Article 189 and has been continued in the 2005 legislation. The professed intent behind these changes in the law of filiation is to bring legal and biological paternity into closer association.

With this history in mind, we turn to the issue at hand: whether the overnight visit between the parties in this case interrupted the three-hundred day requirement for the parties to live separate and apart continuously. The plaintiff argues the phrase "living separate and apart continuously" is a term of art within the family law context which has a long and settled interpretation for obtaining a "no fault" divorce under La. Civ. Code arts. 102 or 103, that is, no longer living openly as husband and wife. The plaintiff argues that in applying this requirement, Louisiana courts have recognized impermanent or intermittent visits, or even sexual intercourse, between separated spouses will not serve to interrupt the continuity of a legal separation. The plaintiff argues the jurisprudence establishes that, to prove reconciliation interrupting the continuity of separation, the overall circumstances must show a mutual intention by the parties to voluntarily resume their marital relationship. Here, the plaintiff argues, there was no evidence in the record that the parties had reconciled or even had attempted to reconcile. Moreover, to obtain the divorce, the defendant attested that the parties had lived separately and apart continuously from the plaintiff from April 30, 2006, through May 14, 2007, the day of the hearing on the rule to show cause. Thus, the plaintiff argues, the exception in Art. 189 applies, and his petition was timely filed within one year of being given notice in writing by the State that a party in interest had asserted that he is the father of the child.

The defendant on the other hand argues there remains a strong public policy in Louisiana to favor the legitimacy of children. . . . Thus, she contends the court of appeal properly applied a strict construction of the prescription article on disavowing paternity. She further contends the appellate court properly declined to read the prescription article, La. Civ. Code art. 189, in pari materia with the articles on divorce, La. Civ. Code arts. 102 and 103, because the purposes and public policy considerations behind disavowal actions and divorce actions are vastly different. The defendant contends the provisions on paternity and divorce do not pertain to the same subject matter and the language therein should be interpreted as having the meaning that best conforms to the purpose of the law, citing La. Civ. Code art. 10.

The fundamental question in all cases of statutory interpretation is legislative intent and the ascertainment of the reason or reasons that prompted the legislature to enact the law. The rules of statutory construction are designed to ascertain and enforce the intent of the legislature. Legislation is the solemn expression of legislative will, and therefore, interpretation of a law involves primarily a search for the legislature's intent. When a law is clear and unambiguous and its application does not lead to absurd consequences, the law shall be applied as written and no further interpretation may be made in search of the intent of the legislature.

The meaning and intent of a law is determined by considering the law in its entirety and all other laws on the same subject matter and placing a construction on the provision in question that is consistent with the express terms of the law and with the obvious intent of the legislature in enacting it. The statute must, therefore, be applied and interpreted in a manner that is consistent with logic and the presumed fair purpose and intention of the legislature in passing it. This is because the rules of statutory construction require that the general intent and purpose of the legislature in enacting the law must, if possible, be given effect. It is presumed the intent of the legislature is to achieve a consistent body of law.

La. Civ. Code art. 13 provides that, where two statutes deal with the same subject matter, they should be harmonized if possible. It is a well-settled rule of statutory construction that all laws dealing with the same subject matter must be construed in pari materia. Statutes are in pari materia — pertain to the same subject matter — when they relate to the same person or thing, to the same class of persons or things, or have the same purpose or object.

We hold that the phrase "living separate and apart continuously" in the divorce articles and the disavowal action article found in our Civil Code should be read in pari materia. The codal articles on divorce and those on filiation and disavowal of paternity are found in Book 1 of our Civil Code, entitled "Of Persons," and clearly relate or pertain to the same class of persons, that is, families in some state of flux, and to the same or strikingly similar objects, that is, the dissolution of marital and filial relationships. Although Articles 102 and 103 apply the subject language in setting forth grounds for divorce without fault, and Article 189 applies the subject language in delineating a time limitation for liberative prescription of the disavowal action, they both involve the husband and wife living separate and apart continuously in the context of a dissolving marital or filial relationship. Further, as in this case, a disavowal action is most often precipitated by a divorce between the mother and the presumed legal father. Simply stated, but for the marriage, there would be no disavowal action under Art. 189. Therefore, it is logical to interpret a provision or language in the disavowal article similarly to the same provision or language in the divorce articles.

Finally, the legislature, when it amended Art. 189 in 1999 and reenacted it in 2005, was certainly aware of the phrase "living separate and apart continuously" as used in the divorce articles, which language had been long and consistently interpreted and applied by the courts of this state such that the phrase has acquired a "peculiar and appropriate meaning" in the area of family law. "Technical words and phrases, and such others as may have acquired a peculiar and appropriate meaning in the law, shall be construed and understood according to such peculiar and appropriate meaning." La. Rev. Stat. 1:3. There is no indication, and the parties have not directed us to any legislative history, that, when the legislature adopted the subject phrase found in the divorce articles for use in the disavowal action article—first in 1999 and then again in 2005, it intended a different meaning to apply. While we continue to adhere to our policy of strictly construing the codal provisions dealing with filiation, we cannot ignore either the context of the known terms and phrases employed by the legislature in creating an exception to the running of the time limitation for a disavowal action or the trend of the legislative changes in this area of the law.

Accordingly, reading La. Civ. Code art. 189 in pari materia with La. Civ. Code arts. 102 and 103, we find the district court correctly concluded that one overnight visit in the former matrimonial domicile when both parties were present did not interrupt the three-hundred-day time period required for the former husband to live separate and apart continuously from the mother to avail himself of the exception to the running of prescription set forth in Art. 189. There is no dispute the parties maintained separate residences in different states commencing from their separation on April 30, 2006, when the plaintiff moved to Pittsburgh, Pennsylvania, through the date of the birth of the child on March 15, 2007, 319 days later. The mother, in obtaining the divorce, attested she had lived separate and apart from the plaintiff from April 30, 2006, through the date of the divorce on May 14, 2007. Aside from the one night visit on or about May 25, 2006, in which the parties were present in the former matrimonial domicile, there is no evidence the parties did not hold themselves out to the community as living separate and apart. There are no allegations of cohabitation, sexual relations or reconciliation that might serve to defeat or interrupt the requirement of living separate and apart for three hundred days. Thus, we find no error in the district court's determination that the parties had lived separate and apart continuously for the three hundred days immediately preceding the birth of the child.

Accordingly, the district court properly denied the defendant's motion for summary judgment and granted the plaintiff's motion for summary judgment, allowing him to disavow paternity of the minor child J.M. The plaintiff established that he had lived separate and apart continuously from the mother for the three hundred days immediately preceding the birth of the child on March 15, 2007. He was first given notice on July 15, 2008, that the mother had asserted he was the father of J.M.

and that the mother was seeking child support. The plaintiff timely filed his disavowal petition on August 19, 2008, well within the one-year time limitation provided for in Art. 189. Because there is no dispute that the plaintiff is not the biological father of the child, summary judgment in favor of the plaintiff was warranted.

CONCLUSION

After reviewing the law and jurisprudence, we hold the court of appeal erred in not reading La. Civ. Code art. 189 in pari materia with La. Civ.Code arts. 102 and 103 before determining whether the husband and mother had lived separate and apart continuously for the three hundred days immediately preceding the birth of the child. The district court correctly found that one overnight visit, absent any allegation of cohabitation, sexual relations, or reconciliation, did not serve to interrupt the three-hundred day period. Thus, the district court properly denied the defendant's motion for summary judgment and granted summary judgment in favor of the plaintiff, Derek Alan Pociask, and allowed him to disavow paternity of the minor child, J.M. For the reasons set forth above, we reverse the court of appeal's decision and reinstate the judgment of the district court.

REVERSED; DISTRICT COURT'S JUDGMENT REINSTATED

Chapter 13

Filiation by Adoption

A. Origins and Legal Effects of Adoption

See LA. CIV. CODE art. 199; LA. REV. STAT. § 9:461; LA. CHILD. CODE § 1256.

Adoption has ancient legal roots in the civil law tradition. Historically, adoption was a means of ensuring that a person had an heir to inherit his property. The adoption of boys or young men by wealthy Romans without male heirs was fairly common. Although the adoption resulted in the adopted child being considered the child of the adoptive parents, his social and economic ties to his biological family were not always severed. Nor was adoption typically something that took place in secret. For example, a number of Roman emperors succeeded to power as a result of adoption — including Augustus, Caligula, and Nero. These emperors, like many other Roman adoptees, were related to their adoptive fathers in some other manner as well. Augustus was adopted by his maternal great-uncle Julius Caesar. Caligula was the great-nephew and then adopted son of Tiberius. Nero was adopted by his grand-uncle Claudius after Claudius married Nero's mother and, thus, had also become Nero's stepfather.

The notion of adoption as a means of providing an entirely new family for a child is a relatively new concept. Although the notion of adoption originated in the civil law (and was unknown to common law), our modern understanding of adoption is rooted in a uniquely American tradition. Massachusetts is credited with implementing the first modern adoption law. The Adoption of Children Act of 1851 exhibited some civil law notions — like the right of adopted children to inherit from their adoptive parents. The law also added some new considerations by requiring the court to determine whether the proposed adoptive parents were able to provide adequately for the child. As the American notion of adoption took hold, courts and legislatures also began to require that adoption records be sealed and that the fact of an adoption remain secret — something that has begun to change in recent years.

American courts have routinely recognized the civil law origins of the law of adoption. As the following excerpt demonstrates, American courts have looked to Louisiana sources to gain a better understanding of the civilian tradition.

> The common law made no provision for the adoption of children, and we can get no light from that source. The Roman law made provision for adopting children, and the provisions of that law, as revised and changed by Justinian, formed a complete system. The adopted child was, as that law

declared, "assimilated, in many points, to a son born in lawful matrimony." That law preserved to the child all the family rights resulting from his birth, and secured to him all the family rights produced by the adoption. The Supreme Court of Louisiana, in discussing this subject, says: "And the effect was such, that the person adopted stood not only himself in relation of child to him adopting, but his children became the grandchildren of such person." At another place the court said: "Now, when in an enabling or permissive statute, the Legislature has used a word so familiar in its ordinary acceptation, and so well known in the sources of our law, does it become the judiciary to say that it has not such meaning, because the law-giver has not himself expressly defined the sense in which he intended the word should be taken?" It is also said: "The law-giver ought not to be supposed ignorant of this state of things, or to use a term in a more restricted sense than it was formerly known to our laws." It is true that the remarks of the court apply with rather more force to a State which has adopted the civil law than to one where the common law prevails, but they, nevertheless, declare a general principle which has a place in all enlightened systems of jurisprudence, for it is established law that where a rule is borrowed from another body of laws, courts will look to the source from which it emanated to ascertain its effect and force. If, as the civil law so fully provided, a child of the adoptive son stood in the relation of grandchild to the adoptive father, then the son himself must stand as the child of that father. The statute of Massachusetts makes some exceptions as to the child's status, and it was held that the adoptive child as to property of the adoptive father stood as a natural child, save in so far as the exceptions declared otherwise, the court saying: "The adopted child, in this case, therefore, in construing her father's settlement, must be regarded in the light of a child born in lawful wedlock, unless the property disposed of by the settlement falls within one of the exceptions."[1]

Today, adoption is a widely recognized method of establishing filiation. Louisiana Civil Code article 199 explains that "the adopting parent becomes the parent of the child for all purposes and the filiation between the child and his legal parent is terminated, except as otherwise provided by law." Today, this view is nearly universal in western legal systems. Louisiana Children's Code article 1256 reinforces this point:

> . . . the parents of the child whose rights have not been previously terminated by a surrender or a judgment of termination and all other blood relatives of the adopted child are relieved of all their legal duties and divested of all their legal rights with regard to the adopted child including the right of inheritance from the adopted child and his lawful descendents, and the adopted child and his lawful descendents are relieved of all legal duties and divested of all legal rights with regard to the parents and other blood relatives.

---

1. Humphries v. Davis, 100 Ind. 274 (Ind. 1885).

The second sentence of Civil Code article 199, however, is less well accepted. In Louisiana, "[t]he adopted child and his descendants retain the right to inherit from his former legal parent and the relatives of that parent." In other words, Louisiana continues to adhere to the traditional Roman view that adoption does not entirely sever the biological parent-child relationship. Rather, adopted children are entitled to inherit from both their biological family and their adoptive family — placing adopted children in a favorable position. Few American states take this approach.

Louisiana gives special consideration to the inheritance rights of children adopted by stepparents. The rule is essentially the same regardless of whether the adoption occurs when the child is a minor or an adult. In the case of adult adoptions, Revised Statute § 9:461 provides that "if the adoptive parent is married to a parent of the adopted child at the time of the adoption or was married to a parent at the time of the death of the parent, the relationship of that parent and his relatives to the adopted child shall remain unaltered and unaffected by the adoption." Similarly, in the case of the adoption of a minor by a stepparent, Children's Code article 1256 provides that "[i]f the adoptive parent is married to a blood parent of the adopted child, the relationship of that blood parent and his blood relatives to the adopted child shall remain unaltered and unaffected by the adoption." Some other states have enacted similar rules for step-parent adoptions.

B. Equitable Adoption

More than half the states recognize the legal doctrine of "equitable adoption" or "adoption by estoppel." This doctrine applies where a putative parent never begins or completes the legal process needed to adopt a child, but nevertheless treats the child as though he or she had been adopted. Most cases involving the doctrine of equitable adoption involve inheritance or similar rights following the death of the putative parent. The California Supreme Court summarized the doctrine as follows:

> In its essence, the doctrine of equitable adoption allows a person who was accepted and treated as a natural or adopted child, and as to whom adoption typically was promised or contemplated but never performed, to share in inheritance of the foster parents' property. "The parents of a child turn him over to foster parents who agree to care for him as if he were their own child. Perhaps they also agree to adopt him. They do care for him, support him, educate him, and treat him in all respects as if he were their child, but they never adopt him. Upon their death he seeks to inherit their property on the theory that he should be treated as if he had been adopted. Many courts would honor his claim, at least under some circumstances, characterizing the case as one of equitable adoption, or adoption by estoppel, or virtual adoption, or specific enforcement of a contract to adopt." The doctrine is widely applied to allow inheritance from the adoptive parent: at least

27 jurisdictions have so applied the doctrine, while only 10 have declined to recognize it in that context.[2]

In *Roche v. Big Moose Oil Field Truck Service*, below, the Louisiana Supreme Court rejected the doctrine of equitable adoption. In *Lankford v. Wright*, below, the North Carolina Supreme Court considers the purpose and history of equitable adoption and decides whether the doctrine should be recognized in North Carolina.

Roche v. Big Moose Oil Field Truck Service

381 So. 2d 393 (La. 1980)

CALOGERO, Justice.

This is a wrongful death action by a surviving wife, individually and as tutrix of her adopted children, for the death of her husband and the children's prospective adoptive father who was killed while unloading a truck owned by Big Moose Oil Field Truck Services. Named as one group of defendants are the driver of the truck, Big Moose, and their insurer (the Big Moose defendants). A second group of defendants includes certain executive officers and employees of Fred Wilson Drilling Company and their insurer (the Fred Wilson defendants). We granted writs (375 So.2d 658 (La.1979)) to resolve the following issues:

1) Whether the minor children have a right of action for the wrongful death of decedent when the final decree of adoption was not rendered before his death.

2) Whether plaintiff under R.S. 23:1102 is required to intervene in the prior suit filed by the workman's compensation insurer against the tortfeasor rather than proceed in her own separate suit?

Plaintiff Alice C. Roche and the decedent Joseph Daniel Roche were married in 1968. They had no children. In 1974 the Juvenile Court for the Parish of Calcasieu decreed William David Robinson and Dawn Rochelle Robinson to be abandoned and awarded their custody to the Louisiana Health and Human Resources Administration for placement, in the best interest of the children. The children had been living with the Roches since April 21, 1972 as their foster children. . . .

On appeal the Third Circuit affirmed the trial court's ruling that the minor children have no right of action because they were not adopted at the time of decedent's death, and affirmed the dismissal of Mrs. Roche's action on the ground that R.S. 23:1102 requires that she intervene in the compensation insurer's previously filed suit. . . .

To determine whether these minor children have a right of action for the wrongful death of Joseph Roche, we must examine Article 2315 of the Louisiana Civil Code which creates the survival and wrongful death actions and the classes of beneficiaries

---

2. Estate of Ford, 82 P.3d 747 (Ca. 2004).

who in the order of preference may recover damages thereunder. The first class of beneficiaries includes "the surviving spouse and child or children of the deceased."

Adopted children were first included as beneficiaries by Acts 1948, No. 333, § 1 which amended Article 2315 to extend the right of action to children who were adopted. The article was again amended in 1960 to its present form to provide that the word child as used in that article includes a child "by adoption." Whether we can find that the word child also includes a child for whom a petition of adoption has been filed but whose adoption is not final is the issue here.

In *Bertrand v. State Farm Fire and Casualty Co.*, 333 So.2d 322 (La.App. 3rd Cir. 1976), an analogous situation was presented. There a mother had surrendered her minor child to the child's maternal grandparents for adoption. After an interlocutory decree but before a final decree of adoption, the child drowned. Both the child's mother and his maternal grandparents sued for damages for wrongful death. The Court of Appeal held that because the grandparents were not the mother and father of the child "by adoption" within the meaning of Civil Code Article 2315 (because the final decree of adoption had not been rendered), the child's mother rather than the prospective adoptive parents had the right of action under Article 2315.

It is well-settled in the jurisprudence that the right of action created by Article 2315 may be extended only to the beneficiaries named in the statute and that the classes of beneficiaries must be strictly construed. . . .

In the instant case the minor children are not the "children" of the decedent "by adoption" within the meaning of Article 2315. Although they may have been dependent upon decedent for support and affection, they are neither his biological nor his adoptive "children." We therefore can not find that they have a right of action under Article 2315 for his death.

In brief plaintiffs present the following additional arguments:

1. That the minor children even if not the adopted children of decedent suffered no less than if their prospective adoptive father had died after the final decree of adoption than before because they were totally dependent upon him for income, support, guidance and affection;

2. That Mr. and Mrs. Roche had committed themselves twice through contract with the Department of Public Welfare to provide for the care and financial support of the children;

3. That the doctrine of equitable adoption which is recognized in some common law jurisdictions should be applied in this case;

4. That the prospective adoptive children should be treated under the law at least as well as illegitimate children who in *Levy v. Louisiana*, were afforded the right to recover for the wrongful death of their mother upon whom they were dependent;

5. That the children should be treated as "posthumous children" who being born after the death of their father are accorded all the legal rights of legitimate children.

We have considered each of plaintiffs' arguments and try as we might to find a legal basis for holding that the minor children have a right of action, we can reach no other conclusion than that the arguments have no merit. None of these equitable considerations, separately or together, serve to make these children the adoptive children of decedent within the meaning of Article 2315. Furthermore the common law cases relying on the doctrine of equitable adoption (which cases represent only two of the common law jurisdictions) are of no assistance in the interpretation of Article 2315. The argument based on *Levy v. Louisiana,* is also unpersuasive because the holding in that case was based on a finding that the restrictive interpretation of Article 2315 which excluded illegitimate biological children from the class of beneficiaries was invidiously discriminatory on the basis of birth. The children in the instant case are not decedent's biological children; therefore *Levy* is inapposite.

Plaintiffs' argument that the children should be treated just as would a decedent's posthumous children is possibly their best argument. While we recognize that there is some analogy between a fetus in its mother's womb which is born after the death of its father and a prospective adoptive child whose adoption had been petitioned for but which is scheduled to become final only a month after the prospective father's death, the rule that Article 2315 be strictly interpreted requires that we not expand the classes of beneficiaries by analogy. Moreover, the analogy between the two is a weak one. In the case of a fetus which subsequent to the father's death is born alive, the father can do nothing to prevent the child's birth or status, unlike the present case in which the decedent Joseph Roche could have withdrawn his consent prior to the final adoption decree. Additionally the posthumous child's being born alive is unaffected by and unrelated to the event which gives rise to its Article 2315 rights the death of its father. The prospective adoptive child's claim, on the other hand, is directly related to and dependent upon the father's continued concurrence in the adoption, a matter affected by and in fact prevented by his pre-adoption death . . .

Decree

For the foregoing reasons the judgments of the district court and the Court of Appeal are affirmed insofar as they dismissed the action brought on behalf of the minor children. . . . The case is remanded to the district court for further proceedings consistent with this opinion.

JUDGMENTS AFFIRMED IN PART; REVERSED IN PART; REMANDED.

Lankford v. Wright

489 S.E.2d 604 (N.C. 1997)

Frye, Justice.

The sole issue in this case is whether North Carolina recognizes the doctrine of equitable adoption. We hold that the doctrine should be recognized in this state, and therefore, we reverse the decision of the Court of Appeals.

Plaintiff, Barbara Ann Newton Lankford, was born to Mary M. Winebarger on 15 January 1944. When plaintiff was a child, her natural mother entered into an agreement with her neighbors, Clarence and Lula Newton, whereby the Newtons agreed to adopt and raise plaintiff as their child. Shortly thereafter, plaintiff moved into the Newton residence and became known as Barbara Ann Newton, the only child of Clarence and Lula Newton.

The Newtons held plaintiff out to the public as their own child, and plaintiff was at all times known as Barbara Ann Newton. Plaintiff's school records referred to plaintiff as Barbara Ann Newton and indicated that Clarence and Lula Newton were her parents. Plaintiff's high-school diploma also referred to plaintiff as Barbara Ann Newton. After Clarence Newton died in 1960, the newspaper obituary listed Barbara Ann Newton as his surviving daughter. Later, with Lula Newton's assistance, plaintiff obtained a Social Security card issued to her under the name of Barbara Ann Newton.

After plaintiff joined the Navy, plaintiff and Lula Newton frequently wrote letters to each other. In most of the letters, plaintiff referred to Lula Newton as her mother and Lula Newton referred to plaintiff as her daughter. Lula Newton also established several bank accounts with plaintiff, where Lula Newton deposited money plaintiff sent to her while plaintiff was in the Navy. On several occasions, plaintiff took leaves of absence from work to care for Lula Newton during her illness.

In 1975, Lula Newton prepared a will. When she died in 1994, the will was not accepted for probate because some unknown person had defaced a portion of the will. The will named plaintiff as co-executrix of the estate and made specific bequests to plaintiff. Since the will could not be probated, Lula Newton died intestate.

After Lula Newton's death, plaintiff filed for declaratory judgment seeking a declaration of her rights and status as an heir of the estate of Lula Newton. Defendants, the administrators and named heirs of Lula Newton, filed a motion for summary judgment. The trial court granted defendants' motion. The North Carolina Court of Appeals affirmed the order granting summary judgment, reasoning that plaintiff was not adopted according to N.C.G.S. §§ 48–1 to –38 and that North Carolina does not recognize the doctrine of equitable adoption. This Court granted plaintiff's petition for discretionary review, and we now conclude that the doctrine of equitable adoption should be recognized in North Carolina. . . .

Equitable adoption is a remedy to "protect the interest of a person who was supposed to have been adopted as a child but whose adoptive parents failed to undertake the legal steps necessary to formally accomplish the adoption." The doctrine is applied in an intestate estate to "give effect to the intent of the decedent to adopt and provide for the child." It is predicated upon principles of contract law and equitable enforcement of the agreement to adopt for the purpose of securing the benefits of adoption that would otherwise flow from the adoptive parent under the laws of intestacy had the agreement to adopt been carried out; as such it is essentially a matter of equitable relief. Being only an equitable remedy to enforce a contract right, it is not intended or applied to create the legal relationship of parent and child, with all the legal consequences of such a relationship, nor is it meant to create a legal adoption.

Adoption did not exist at common law and is of purely statutory origin. Equitable adoption, however, does not confer the incidents of formal statutory adoption; rather, it merely confers rights of inheritance upon the foster child in the event of intestacy of the foster parents. In essence, the doctrine invokes the principle that equity regards that as done which ought to be done. The doctrine is not intended to replace statutory requirements or to create the parent-child relationship; it simply recognizes the foster child's right to inherit from the person or persons who contracted to adopt the child and who honored that contract in all respects except through formal statutory procedures. As an equitable matter, where the child in question has faithfully performed the duties of a natural child to the foster parents, that child is entitled to be placed in the position in which he would have been had he been adopted. Likewise, based on principles of estoppel, those claiming under and through the deceased are estopped to assert that the child was not legally adopted or did not occupy the status of an adopted child.

Further, the scope of the doctrine is limited to facts comparable to those presented here. Thirty-eight jurisdictions have considered equitable adoption; at least twenty-seven have recognized and applied the doctrine. A majority of the jurisdictions recognizing the doctrine have successfully limited its application to claims made by an equitably adopted child against the estate of the foster parent. By its own terms, equitable adoption applies only in limited circumstances. The elements necessary to establish the existence of an equitable adoption are:

(1) an express or implied agreement to adopt the child,

(2) reliance on that agreement,

(3) performance by the natural parents of the child in giving up custody,

(4) performance by the child in living in the home of the foster parents and acting as their child,

(5) partial performance by the foster parents in taking the child into their home and treating the child as their own, and

(6) the intestacy of the foster parents.

These elements, particularly the requirement of intestacy, limit the circumstances under which the doctrine may be applied. Specifically, the doctrine acts only to recognize the inheritance rights of a child whose foster parents died intestate and failed to perform the formalities of a legal adoption, yet treated the child as their own for all intents and purposes. The doctrine is invoked for the sole benefit of the foster child in determining heirship upon the intestate death of the person or persons contracting to adopt. Whether the doctrine applies is a factual question, and each element must be proven by clear, cogent, and convincing evidence.

In this case, the evidence in the record tends to show that the above elements can be satisfied by clear, cogent, and convincing evidence. The record demonstrates that the Newtons agreed to adopt plaintiff; that the Newtons and plaintiff relied on that agreement; that plaintiff's natural mother gave up custody of plaintiff to the Newtons; that plaintiff lived in the Newtons' home, cared for them in their old age, and otherwise acted as their child; that the Newtons treated plaintiff as their child by taking her into their home, giving her their last name, and raising her as their child; and that Mrs. Newton died intestate several years after Mr. Newton died. These facts fit squarely within the parameters of the doctrine of equitable adoption and are indicative of the dilemma the doctrine is intended to remedy. . . .

The dissent points out that a minority of jurisdictions have declined to recognize the doctrine of equitable adoption. However, we again note that an overwhelming majority of states that have addressed the question have recognized and applied the doctrine. More importantly, it is the unique role of the courts to fashion equitable remedies to protect and promote the principles of equity such as those at issue in this case. We are convinced that acting in an equitable manner in this case does not interfere with the legislative scheme for adoption, contrary to the assertions of the dissent. Recognition of the doctrine of equitable adoption does not create a legal adoption, and therefore does not impair the statutory procedures for adoption.

In conclusion, a decree of equitable adoption should be granted where justice, equity, and good faith require it. The fairness of applying the doctrine once the prerequisite facts have been established is apparent. Accordingly, we reverse the Court of Appeals' decision which affirmed the trial court's entry of summary judgment for defendants and remand to the trial court for further proceedings not inconsistent with this opinion.

REVERSED AND REMANDED.

C. Availability of Children for Adoption

See La. Child. Code art. 1015, 1101 *et seq.*

Children may become eligible for adoption following an involuntary termination proceeding. In an involuntary termination proceeding, the court terminates the parental rights of the biological parents—generally against the objections of the biological parents. Louisiana Children's Code articles 1001 *et seq.* set forth a comprehensive legislative scheme for the involuntary termination of parental rights. As in other states, parental rights can only be terminated in fairly serious cases involving abuse, neglect, or criminal conduct. A number of procedural safeguards are built in to the legislative scheme in an effort to balance the various competing interests.

Children may also become available for adoption when the biological parents agree to voluntarily surrender their rights to the child and to allow the child to be adopted. Louisiana Children's Code article 1101 *et seq.* sets forth a comprehensive legislative scheme for the voluntary surrender of parental rights. As in other states, the statutes aim to ensure that the biological parents' consent to a voluntary surrender is both informed and truly voluntary. Often, the consent requirements differ with respect to mothers and fathers. Further, the consent requirements sometimes differ when the father is a presumptive father due to marriage to the mother. Louisiana draws these distinctions in Children's Code article 1193. As demonstrated by *In re R.E.*, below, this approach has withstood constitutional challenge.

In re R.E.

645 So. 2d 205 (La. 1994)

DENNIS, Justice.

We are called upon to decide the proper allocation of the burden of proof when an alleged natural father opposes the surrender of his child for adoption in accordance with Louisiana Children's Code Articles 1130 et seq. After R.E., an unwed mother, duly surrendered Q.P.E., her newborn child, for adoption, T.P.L., the alleged natural father, was notified and he timely filed his notice of opposition to the adoption.

After a hearing, the trial court found that T.P.L. had forfeited his parental rights and decreed that his rights are terminated. On appeal, the court of appeal reversed and remanded the case for a new hearing, holding that the trial court erred in failing to require that the parties supporting the surrender prove the natural father's unfitness by clear and convincing evidence. On remand, the trial court maintained T.P.L.'s opposition, declared that no adoption can take place without his consent, and granted him custody of the child, finding that the natural father's unfitness had been proved by clear and convincing evidence, but concluding that under the court of appeal's decision such a finding was insufficient to support a termination of parental rights.

Beacon House Adoption Services, Inc., the adoption agency, Linda C. Fowler, the attorney and curator ad hoc for Q.P.E., and the Louisiana Department of Social Services have intervened and applied to this court for supervisory writs.

We grant writs of supervisory control, reverse and remand the case to the trial court for a new determination consistent with law and this opinion.

Although an unwed father's biological link to his child does not, in and of itself, guarantee him a constitutional stake in his relationship with that child, such a link combined with a substantial parent-child relationship will do so. When an unwed father demonstrates a full commitment to the responsibilities of parenthood and an ability to participate beneficially in the rearing of his child, his interest in personal contact with his child acquires substantial protection under the state and federal due process clauses.

Under the statutory scheme implementing these principles, the unwed father is afforded notice and a hearing at which he has an opportunity to demonstrate his biological link and substantial relationship with the child. In accordance with this court's decision in *In re B.G.S.*, the statutes contemplate that the unwed father's constitutionally protected interest in a parent-child relationship does not come into existence until the father demonstrates his fitness for parental responsibilities, commitment to those responsibilities, concrete actions taken to grasp his opportunity to be a father, and the potential for him to make a valuable contribution to the child's development. The burden of proof is upon the putative father to show the preservation of his opportunity to establish parental rights by proving these interrelated elements by a preponderance of the evidence. If the father carries this burden, his parental rights become established, no adoption may be granted without his consent, and custody of the child will be granted to him. If the father fails to carry this burden, his parental rights are not brought into existence, and the court shall decree that the father's rights to oppose the adoption are terminated.

In our opinion, this statutory framework affords the unwed father all of the process due him under the state and federal constitutions. . . . It is true that, when fully established, the protected liberty interest of natural parents in their right to the care, custody, and management of their children cannot be terminated by the state unless it supports its allegations by at least clear and convincing evidence . . . and that due process may require that no person shall lose such a fully established right unless the state has borne the burden of producing the evidence and convincing the fact finder that the essential elements have been proved. But this is not a proceeding initiated or supported by the state to terminate a natural parent's established parental rights. This is an adoption case between private litigants, and under the circumstances herein the unwed father does not have a fully established protected right to a parental relationship with his child until he demonstrates his fitness and commitment according to the standards provided by law and our decisions. Due process guarantees him notice, hearing and an adequate opportunity to make such a showing; it does not require, however, that he be presumed fit and committed to parental responsibilities or that the burden of proving otherwise be allocated to the parties supporting the surrender and adoption of the child. Indeed, under the Supreme Court's decision in *Lehr v. Robertson*, supra, and this court's decision in *In re B.G.S.*, supra, the burden of proof is clearly allocated to the father to show that he has acquired an established parental right.

The court of appeal exceeded its authority in ordering that the child be placed temporarily in custody of the Louisiana Department of Social Services pending the determination of whether the natural father may successfully oppose the surrender and adoption. Beacon House is an "agency," viz., a private agency or institution licensed for the placement of children for adoption. When the child's mother executed an authentic act of voluntary surrender of the child to Beacon House, that agency became the legal custodian of the child. Beacon House continues to be the legal custodian pending either an adoption or a proper determination that the unwed father has established his parental rights and is entitled to legal custody.

The pleadings, trial court reasons for judgment, and the briefs of the parties indicate that proper application of the foregoing precepts to the evidence in this case may warrant a finding that the unwed father failed to carry his burden of proving his fitness for parental responsibilities, commitment to those responsibilities, and potential for making a valuable contribution to the child's development. In the interest of expediting this proceeding involving the custody and adoption of an infant however, we will not send for a full record or attempt to make a determination of the facts at this level. Instead, we vacate the judgments below and remand the case to the trial court for an expeditious hearing and decision consistent with law and this opinion after taking any additional evidence as the trial court deems advisable. Custody of the child is restored to the Beacon House pending the trial court's decision.

It is so ordered.

REVERSED AND REMANDED TO TRIAL COURT.

D. Adult Adoption

See LA. CIV. CODE art. 212–14; LA. REV. STAT. §9:461.

Most states, including Louisiana, allow the adoption of adults as well as children. Adult adoptions are usually subject to fewer procedural and logistical hurdles than the adoption of minors because of the different policy considerations involved. Requirements vary by state—but many states require some sort of court approval for an adult adoption to take place. Some states additionally require evidence of a pre-existing parent-child relationship. Some states also require that the consent of certain parties be obtained and/or that they receive notice. These parties may include biological parents, the spouse of the adoptee, or the spouse of the adoptor. Other states have no such requirement.

Adult adoptions—like their Roman predecessors—are often used as a means of ensuring inheritance rights. Yet, the inheritance rights of persons adopted as adults vary considerably from state-to-state. Most jurisdictions agree that persons adopted as adults may inherit from their adoptive parents. Some states, however, limit the inheritance rights to property transferred directly from the adoptive parent. In other words, the adopted adult may inherit from his adoptive parent—but not from the adoptive parent's relatives. States also vary with respect to whether the adopted adult may continue to inherit from his or her biological family.

In many respects, Louisiana's adult adoption scheme is quite liberal. For years, all that was needed to effect an adult adoption was an authentic act. Concerns over undue influence and fraud prompted a change in Louisiana. Presently, Civil Code article 212 allows an adult to be adopted by a stepparent without judicial authorization. Other adult adoptions, however, require court approval. The inheritance rights of adults adopted in Louisiana are generally the same as adopted minors.

Chapter 14

Child Custody

A. Historical Evolution of Child Custody Laws

Virtually all developed nations have adopted a legal regime that seeks to award child custody in accordance with the child's best interests—and a host of international treaties and similar conventions mandate such rules. This was not always the case. At both common law and civil law, children were essentially considered property belonging to their fathers. For a time, the father's rights were near absolute, and the mother had few, if any, rights to her children. By the time of Planiol, this harsh approach had begun to change. Although the father presumptively was entitled to the custody of children, in appropriate circumstances, custody might be granted to the mother. As Planiol explained, custody sometimes depended on which spouse was deemed at fault in the divorce or separation as well as the interests of the children:

> The grounds which justify divorce imply the moral depravity of at least one of the spouses. It is but proper that such a spouse should be deemed to be an unworthy father or mother. Nevertheless, if the interests of the children are not adversely affected, the court should respect the agreements made by the parents regarding the custody of the children. . . .

> The first thing to be done is to remove the children from the guilty spouse whose influence might be disastrous. Art. 302 therefore provides that the children should be confided to the spouse who obtained the divorce. The court has discretionary power when the divorce has been pronounced on account of reciprocal wrongs.

> This is not however an absolute rule. The same article reserves the right to the court to order that the children be confided to the other spouse, although guilty, or that they be turned over to a third person. The court is therefore free to do what it thinks is in the interest of the children. It may, for example give the boys to the father and the girls to the mother, or confide to the latter those young children needing maternal care or which may perhaps be not yet weaned.[1]

Common law, perhaps influenced by the civil law, likewise tempered its harsh approach. As the Tennessee Supreme Court explained:

---

1. MARCEL PLANIOL, TREATISE ON THE CIVIL LAW *1275–76 (Louisiana State Law Institute trans. West, 1959).

That the father is entitled upon the principles of the common law to the exclusive custody of his children is not, and can not be, controverted; and that, if he have it, a court of common law will not deprive him of it but for an abuse of his trust affecting their persons, either by improper violence or improper restraint, and which would justify the issuance of a writ of habeas corpus for their protection. . . . The probability is that the rigid principles of the common law would have restored the possession of a minor child to the father under all the circumstances; for, as has been observed, this would have been in conformity with the social principle. But, if it ever were so, it is so no longer, and perhaps the mitigation, so far as it has extended, is adopted from the civilians. The mitigation of the principle is "that the court is not bound, in a proceeding upon habeas corpus, to deliver the child to the father, but may act upon its discretion according to the circumstances of the particular case." The first, and, so far as we at present know, the earliest, case referred to in support of this position is the case of *The King v. Delaval* and others, decided by Lord Mansfield, in 3 Burr. 1434. The predilections of that jurist for the civil code, and his strong disposition to engraft its principles upon the rude stem of the common law, are well known. However, the principle thus laid down has been so repeatedly recognized, both in England and the United States, that it is now at all events a part of the common law. . . . The principle being thus established that the court is not bound by a fixed principle of right to restore a child to its father, but may, at its discretion, withhold it, the question occurs, Under what circumstances may that discretion be exercised? This must of necessity, in many instances, be a thing difficult for judicial determination, as no fixed and determinate principles can be established upon the subject—every case resting upon its own peculiar circumstances. It is to be observed that in all cases the interest and welfare of the child is the great leading object to be attained, and, therefore, if it be of an age sufficiently matured to judge for itself, the court will free itself from the responsibility of determining the controversy by leaving it at liberty to go where it pleases. But, if it be not of such an age, the court will judge for it. There are certain principles upon the subject recognized by all the authorities, and controverted by none; such as, if the father be unworthy or incapable, morally or physically, to take care of the child, if there be apprehensions of improper restraint, the court will not restore the possession to him.[2]

Today, all American jurisdictions award custody in accordance with the "best interests of the child." Generally, this standard requires the court to consider a number of statutorily prescribed or jurisprudentially determined factors to determine what custodial arrangement will best meet the interests of the child. Historically, it was common to grant sole custody to one parent and award visitation to the other

---

2. State v. Paine, 23 Tenn. 523 (1843).

parent. This approach is less common today, because courts and legislatures have come to understand that, in most cases, shared parental responsibility will best benefit the child. In many states, a shared custodial arrangement is presumed to be in the child's best interest.

B. Child Custody in Louisiana

See La. Civ. Code art. 105, 131–137, 152 and 256; La. Rev. Stat. § 9:335–36.

The Louisiana Civil Code contemplates differing approaches to child custody depending on whether the child is a marital child. Custody of non-marital children, Article 256 explains, depends on whether the father has acknowledged the child. Article 131, in contrast, sets forth a custody regime for children of divorcing parents. In practice, courts apply Article 131 and the articles that follow it in custody decisions involving both marital and non-marital children.

In determining custody, the court is directed to consider the best interests of the child. Article 134 sets forth a variety of factors to assist the court in making that determination. Article 132 expresses a preference that the parents agree to the custody arrangement. Where the parents agree, "the court shall award custody in accordance with their agreement unless the best interest of the child requires a different award." Article 132 also expresses a clear preference for joint custody. If no agreement is reached or if the agreement is not in the best interest of the child, Article 132 directs the court to "award custody to the parents jointly." Sole custody in one parent is only permitted where it is "shown by clear and convincing evidence to serve the best interest of the child."

Civil Code article 133 contemplates awarding custody to a non-parent in certain extreme circumstances. Custody in a non-parent is only permitted where "an award of joint custody or sole custody to either parent would result in substantial harm to the child." In such a case, the court is directed to "award custody to another person with whom the child has been living in a wholesome and stable environment, or otherwise to any other person able to provide an adequate and stable environment."

The Civil Code also contemplates an award of visitation rights to a non-custodial parent. Article 136 provides that a non-custodial parent "is entitled to reasonable visitation rights unless the court finds, after a hearing, that visitation would not be in the best interest of the child." Article 136 also contemplates awarding visitation rights to non-parents under extraordinary circumstances.

If the court awards joint custody, Revised Statute § 9:335 directs the court to issue a "joint custody implementation order" which sets forth, among other things, the allocation of physical and legal custody of the child. Additionally, the joint custody implementation order should generally specify which parent is designated as the "domiciliary parent"—a position that affords greater decision making rights to that parent.

The interaction between the provisions of the Civil Code contemplating joint custody and Revised Statute § 9:355 can be confusing. The Louisiana Supreme Court has explained the interaction as follows:

> The term "custody" is usually broken down into two components: physical or "actual" custody and legal custody. The typical joint custody plan will allocate time periods for physical custody between parents so as to promote a sharing of the care and custody of the child in such a way as to ensure the child of frequent and continuing contact with both parents. Legal custody, by contrast, has previously been defined as "the right or authority of a parent or parents, to make decisions concerning the child's upbringing." Pursuant to this definition, both parents remained legal custodians of the child regardless of which parent had physical custody of the child at a given time under the typical joint custody plan. Joint legal custody thus involved a sharing of the responsibilities concerning the child including decisions about education, medical care, discipline and other matters relating to the upbringing of the child.
>
> With the enactment of [La. Rev. Stat. § 9:355] however, the decision-making rules have changed. Presently, when parties are awarded joint custody, the court must designate a domiciliary parent unless the implementation order provides otherwise, or for other good cause shown. . . .
>
> The domiciliary parent has the authority to make all decisions affecting the child unless an implementation order otherwise provides. All major decisions made by the domiciliary parent concerning the child are subject to judicial review upon motion by the non-domiciliary parent. In this judicial review, it is presumed all major decisions made by the domiciliary parent are in the best interest of the child. Therefore, the burden of proving they are in fact not in the best interest of the child is placed on the non-domiciliary parent who opposes the decision. Non-major decisions are not subject to judicial review. The domiciliary parent is also the parent with whom the child primarily resides. . . .
>
> Notwithstanding the domiciliary parent's right to make all decisions affecting the child however, [La. Rev. Stat. § 9:356] nevertheless obligates the parents to exchange information concerning the health, education, and welfare of the child and to confer with one another in exercising decision-making authority. Moreover, in instances where the requirements for not designating a domiciliary parent are met, Title VII of Book I of the Civil Code governs the rights and responsibilities of parents with joint legal custody.[3]

---

3. Evans v. Lungrin, 708 So. 2d 731 (La. 1998).

C. Best Interest of the Child; Generally

The following cases illustrate some of the factors a court may consider in determining the best interest of the child and the application of the relevant civil code articles. The cases also illustrate some ancillary issues. In *Wilson v. Finley*, a teenage couple had a non-marital child while they were both sophomores in high school. For years, they had informally agreed to a custody arrangement without any apparent court or governmental involvement. The parents found themselves in court years later to establish an initial custody arrangement once challenges arose with the informal plan. *Martinez v. Lagos* is similar in that the parents—who were never married to each other—did not find themselves in court fighting over an initial custody arrangement until the child was six years old. Both cases illustrate how, in many cases, parents might simply formulate their own custody arrangements outside of the legal system. These cases also illustrate that courts apply Civil Code article 131 to both marital and non-marital custody arrangements. Finally, *Kirsch v. Kirsch* involves an award of sole custody to one parent with visitation granted to the other.

Wilson v. Finley
146 So. 3d 282 (La. App. 2 Cir. 2014)

WILLIAMS, J.

In this child custody dispute, the mother, Shareese L. Finley, appeals a trial court judgment awarding primary domiciliary custody of the minor child to the father, Richard Demarcus Wilson, Sr. For the following reasons, we affirm.

FACTS

Richard Demarcus Wilson, Sr. ("Richard") and Shareese L. Finley ("Shareese") are the parents of the minor child, "R.J.," who was born on February 24, 2007. At the time of R.J.'s birth, Richard and Shareese were sophomores in high school. Richard's mother, Judy Wilson ("Mrs. Wilson") took care of R.J. while Richard and Shareese continued with school and school-related extracurricular activities. Richard and his parents testified that by the end of 2007, Shareese allowed R.J. to live with them "due to the unstable situation with [Shareese]'s family and her living arrangements." However, Shareese denied allowing R.J. to live with the Wilson family. She testified that R.J. lived with both her and Richard, alternating weeks between the Wilson home and her grandmother's home.

Richard and Shareese graduated from high school in 2009. Both were offered scholarships to attend college—Richard was offered athletic scholarships from various universities; Shareese received a TOPS scholarship which would pay her tuition to a college or university in the state of Louisiana. Richard decided to attend Southern University in Baton Rouge, while Shareese chose to attend Grambling State University in Grambling. The parties decided that R.J. would live with Richard's parents while Richard and Shareese attended college. Pursuant to the oral agreement, Richard's parents would take care of R.J. from Sunday evenings until Friday evening;

Shareese would care for him from Friday evening until Sunday evening, during holiday breaks and during the summer months.

During the trial, the evidence was virtually undisputed that Richard played college football and rarely came home on weekends when he was in college in Baton Rouge. However, the testimony varied with regard to how often Shareese came to get R.J. from the Wilsons' home on weekends.

Nevertheless, the agreement remained in place until 2011. According to the testimony presented at trial, Mrs. Wilson called Richard and Shareese and told them they needed to formulate a plan to assume responsibility for caring for R.J. because she and her husband were "getting tired." At that point, Shareese and her aunt, LaChandon Finley, met with Mrs. Wilson to address the issue. Initially, Shareese suggested having R.J. come to Ruston to live with her in her off-campus apartment. However, due to her nursing school schedule, the plan was not feasible because on at least one day of the week, she did not have anyone to care for R.J. According to Shareese, her "Plan B" was to have R.J. remain in Monroe and live with her aunt.

Meanwhile, Richard considered dropping out of college to return home to care for R.J. After contemplating the alternatives, Mrs. Wilson decided that it was best for R.J. to remain in her home; Richard and Shareese agreed. At some point, Richard decided to return to Monroe to "take care of [his] responsibility as a man" and assume the care of R.J. For the 2011–2012 school year, Richard transferred to Grambling State University, resided at home with his parents and R.J., and commuted to Grambling for classes. Subsequently, he was offered a scholarship to play football at Grambling and moved into an apartment in Ruston. Richard then sustained a football injury and moved back to Monroe to live with his parents. At that time, according to Richard and his parents, he assumed the day-to-day care of R.J., doing tasks such as helping R.J. get dressed for school, helping him with homework in the evenings, volunteering for certain activities at the school and coaching some of R.J.'s sporting activities. Richard continued with his studies at Grambling, commuting from Monroe to Grambling for classes.

On March 27, 2013, Richard filed a petition seeking primary domiciliary custody of R.J. Thereafter, the trial court entered an interim custody order, awarding domiciliary custody to Richard; Shareese was granted "liberal visitation." Following a conference, the hearing officer recommended that the parties be awarded joint custody, with Richard designated as the domiciliary parent. Shareese objected to the hearing officer's report, and a trial to determine the custody of R.J. was held.

During the hearing, the evidence established the following: R.J. was a student at Robinson Elementary School; he was well-behaved; he made good grades; Shareese was employed full-time at Glenwood Regional Medical Center; Shareese had her own apartment in Ruston and received government housing assistance; Richard was a full-time college student; he resided with R.J. at his parents' home; he was not employed.

R.J.'s teachers from pre-kindergarten and kindergarten testified at trial. R.J.'s pre-kindergarten teacher testified that he had not met Shareese. He stated that Richard came to the school to check on R.J.'s progress, and Richard and his parents attended parent/teacher conferences. R.J.'s kindergarten teacher testified that Richard participated in R.J.'s education and he came to the school for parent lunches and field day activities. She further testified that Shareese picked up R.J. from school "maybe two times" and attended his kindergarten graduation. However, the teacher testified that she did not recall discussing R.J.'s progress in school with Shareese.

The testimony at trial varied with regard to who provided for R.J. financially. Shareese testified that she purchased "everything" R.J. needed, including "all" of his school clothes and supplies, Christmas gifts and birthday presents. She also stated that she paid for all of his birthday parties, while Richard never purchased anything for R.J. She and her witnesses testified that she spent as much as $500 per year on school clothes and at least $700 per year on Christmas gifts.

Conversely, Richard and his parents testified that Shareese never provided any financial support for R.J.'s care. Richard and his mother testified that Shareese received benefits through the Supplemental Nutrition Assistance Program ("SNAP"), in part, by claiming R.J. as a dependent on her application. They also testified that the only contribution Shareese made for R.J.'s care was that she allowed Mrs. Wilson to use her SNAP card to purchase food for R.J. in the amount of $65 per month. According to the Wilsons, Richard purchased R.J.'s school clothes and supplies and paid his school fees. They admitted that Richard and Shareese both purchased Christmas gifts for R.J.

It appears that the relationship between the parties became volatile and deteriorated when, in January 2013, Mrs. Wilson informed Shareese that she would be claiming R.J. as a dependent on her federal and state income tax returns because he resided with her. Prior to that year, Shareese had been claiming R.J. as a dependent and receiving both the child tax credit and earned income credit, although he primarily resided with the Wilsons.

Following a three-day hearing, the trial court awarded the joint custody of R.J. to the parties, with Richard being designated the primary domiciliary parent. The court also ordered that the recommendations of the hearing officer be maintained.

Shareese appeals.

DISCUSSION

Shareese contends the trial court erred in awarding primary domiciliary custody to Richard. She argues that the court erred in finding that Richard is in a better position to provide food, clothing and medical care to R.J. She points out that, at the time of the hearing, Richard was unemployed, had a very limited employment history and lived with his parents, who had filed Chapter 13 bankruptcy proceedings. Shareese further argues that at the time of the trial, she had a full-time job and her own apartment.

It is well settled in our statutory and jurisprudential law that the paramount consideration in any determination of child custody is the best interest of the child. The court is to consider all relevant factors in determining the best interest of the child.

The trial court is not bound to make a mechanical evaluation of all of the statutory factors listed in LSA-C.C. art. 134, but should decide each case on its own facts in light of those factors. These factors are not exclusive, but are provided as a guide to the court, and the relative weight given to each factor is left to the discretion of the trial court.

LSA-R.S. 9:335(A)(2)(b) provides that, to the extent feasible and in the best interest of the child, physical custody of the child should be shared equally. However, the law is clear: substantial time, rather than strict equality of time, is mandated by the legislative scheme providing for joint custody of children.

The trial court has vast discretion in deciding matters of child custody and visitation. Therefore, the trial court's determination will not be disturbed on appeal, absent a clear showing of an abuse of discretion. As long as the trial court's factual findings are reasonable in light of the record when reviewed in its entirety, the appellate court may not reverse, even though convinced it would have weighed the evidence differently if acting as the trier of fact.

In the instant case, all of the witnesses testified that R.J. is a bright, well-adjusted child and is flourishing academically and socially. Richard testified that he is a good parent to R.J.; Shareese testified that she is a good parent to R.J. They both agreed that the previous custody and visitation schedule had worked in the past.

In weighing the factors set forth in LSA–C.C. art. 134, the trial court noted the following findings:

- Both parents were college students.

- Both parents had "significant" love, affection and emotional ties with R.J.

- Both parents had the capacity and disposition to provide R.J. with love, affection and spiritual guidance and to continue his education and rearing.

- Neither parent had the ability to independently provide food, clothing, medical care for R.J.

- Richard's family had been financially providing for R.J. most of the child's life.

- Richard returned to live with his parents to help rear R.J. while continuing his education.

- R.J. had lived with Richard's family "most of his life."

- Richard's family provided a nurturing and stable environment for R.J.

- It was in the best interest of R.J. to continue in the family unit with Richard's family.

- R.J. attended elementary school in the district in which Richard's family lived and he is an "A" student.

- Richard attends to R.J.'s day-to-day needs and activities.

The trial court acknowledged that Shareese is receiving housing assistance while she is attending college. However, the court noted that if her assistance ended, she may not be able to provide a home for R.J. The court also expressed its concern that Shareese was contemplating applying to medical school. It concluded that Shareese's plans for a more stable future had been "derailed by the fact that [she] failed out of nursing school." The court further concluded:

> [T]he best interest of R.J. is for him to maintain where he is[.]

> * * *

> [I] think to take a child who is well-adjusted, happy, loving, good student, healthy, by all regards, and to remove him into a place that would only potentially be that way, only speculatively be that way, but also could potentially be disruptive to that—what has been clearly against his best interest.

We have reviewed this record in its entirety and we are convinced, as was the trial court, that both Richard and Shareese are loving parents. However, the paramount goal in child custody cases is to reach a decision which serves the best interest of the child. The trial court observed the demeanor of the parties and the witnesses and expressly noted that both parties loved R.J. However, the trial court's conclusion that Richard, with the continued assistance of his parents, was able to provide a stable and safe living environment for R.J. is supported by the facts of this case.

The trial court also considered the prior physical custody arrangement established by the parties and the willingness of Richard and his parents to foster a relationship between R.J. and his mother. It is apparent that the court endeavored to fashion a custody plan for R.J. which would continue his close relationship with both parents, and yet ensure his safety and stability. Moreover, the custody and visitation schedule ordered by the trial court is markedly similar to the previous custody arrangement agreed upon by the parties.

Based on the record before us, we find that the trial court did not abuse its discretion in concluding that it was in R.J.'s best interest to award primary domiciliary custody to Richard, with liberal visitation in favor of Shareese.

CONCLUSION

For the above reasons, the judgment of the trial court is affirmed. Costs of the appeal are assessed to the appellant, Shareese L. Finley.

AFFIRMED.

Martinez v. Lagos

142 So. 3d 231 (La. App. 5 Cir. 2014)

STEPHEN J. WINDHORST, Judge.

Plaintiff, Leyman Jose Martinez, appeals from that portion of the trial court's decision awarding custody of the minor child. We affirm the judgment of the trial court. . . .

The parties in this case spoke Spanish and English. They testified at the hearing through an interpreter.

Ms. Lagos and Mr. Martinez were never married. At the hearing on the issue of custody, Ms. Lagos testified that she and Mr. Martinez resided together for around 18 months after their daughter was born. For the next three years, she and the child lived together without incident. The child was six at the time of the custody hearing.

Ms. Lagos further testified that she owns a two bedroom condominium. Originally, Mr. Martinez had been providing $300.00 per month for child support, but then he reduced the amount to $150.00. She was having difficulty making the mortgage payment, so she rented the second bedroom to her uncle's stepson. She testified that her tenant spends most of his time away, and that he does not drink. He smokes cigarettes, but never around the child, and always goes outside. Ms. Lagos stated that the child has her own bed in Ms. Lago's bedroom, and that the child has sufficient privacy. Ms. Lagos further testified that her work schedule was flexible and that she could adjust it around the schedule of the child.

At the time of the hearing, the child had graduated from kindergarten and was in first grade. Her report card was introduced to show that she made good grades in kindergarten. According to Ms. Lagos, she makes sure the child's homework is completed, and when she (Ms. Lagos) needs help in explaining, she contacts her niece, who can read and speak English. The child speaks and comprehends English very well. Ms. Lagos further stated that when the child was with Mr. Martinez, her homework would not be completed, or it would be incorrect.

Mr. Martinez testified that he and Ms. Lagos were still able to work together after he moved, and that difficulties did not start to arise until December of 2010, when he started dating his wife. He saw his daughter less often after his marriage in December of 2011, until a hearing officer put a custody and visitation schedule in place in September of 2012. Mr. Martinez further alleged that Ms. Lagos did not meet him when he brought the child to her, but only left her door open at the condominium, as if "she didn't want to receive" the child. Ms. Lagos testified that she left her door open, but did not approach Mr. Martinez because he would berate her in front of the child.

Also at the hearing, Mr. Martinez and his witnesses alleged that the child would appear with unkept hair and dirty fingernails. These allegations were denied by Ms. Lagos and her witnesses.

Mr. Martinez testified that he has a three bedroom house that he shares with his wife and his mother, and the child has her own bedroom. The child has a good relationship with his current wife, who treats her like a daughter. His wife has a 19 year old daughter who recently married and does not live with them. However, she is available to assist with the child's homework. Mr. Martinez testified that he works from 6:30 A.M. to 3:00 P.M., so he would be able to pick up his daughter from school. Mrs. Martinez testified that she would be able to bring the child to school in the morning.

Several contentious encounters between Mr. Martinez and Ms. Lagos were related at the hearing. August 20, 2012 was the child's first day of kindergarten. Ms. Lagos testified that she had an appointment at 8:00 A.M., and then she had to work. She went to the school after her appointment to see if Mr. Martinez was there and whether he could stay with the child. She did not have the child with her when she appeared at the school. Mr. Martinez stated that he went to the school for the child's first day, and that Ms. Lagos showed up alone, telling him it was not necessary for the child to appear on the first day of school. He stated he had Ms. Lagos leave, pick up the child and bring her to school. At the close of the school day, there again was a dispute between the two of them as to who should take the child home. Shortly after this, they appeared before a hearing officer who set a provisional custody schedule.

A second encounter occurred when they were at worship at Good Shepard Church. Ms. Lagos was already seated when Mr. Martinez entered with the child. Ms. Lagos asked to see her for a minute, and Mr. Martinez responded no and requested that Ms. Lagos not come close when he had custody. Later, as the child was leaving her Sunday school classroom, she saw Ms. Lagos, and went over to show her a coloring book. The child was wearing a fake fingernail at the time. Ms. Lagos was holding the coloring book along with the child, and as Mr. Martinez grabbed the child, the child's fake nail came off. Mr. Martinez accused Ms. Lagos of hurting the child, to which Ms. Lagos responded that it was an accident.

A third event occurred on January 1, 2013. Mr. Martinez drove to Ms. Lagos' house and took the child away with him for several hours, even though it was Ms. Lagos' custody day.

The final event was related in which Ms. Lagos had some medicine to treat an infected mosquito bite. Mr. Martinez went to her house to retrieve the medicine, and she threw it on the ground in front of him. Ms. Lagos testified that she threw it because he requested that she do so.

Ms. Lagos also testified that she had to change her passwords on her banking and mortgage accounts because Mr. Martinez would access them to discover how much money she had and how much she owed on her condominium.

Also at the hearing, it was established that on three separate incidents, Ms. Lagos called the police to complain about Mr. Martinez's actions. She testified that on the first occasion, in August of 2011, she had a friend at her house, and she discovered that Mr. Martinez was at the window, listening to their conversation. After the friend left, Mr. Martinez came into the condo, and they argued. Mr. Martinez apparently stayed that night, and when he left the next morning, he took her cell phone and charger with him. This was not the first time he had taken items from her condo without her permission, so two days later, she called the police.

The second time Ms. Lagos called the police; she had received a call from Mr. Martinez informing her that he had taken the child to the doctor because she was ill. Ms. Lagos knew that Mr. Martinez was scheduled to work that evening, so she told him to bring the child to her if the child was ill. Ms. Lagos called for a police officer to go with her to Mr. Martinez's house, however when they knocked no one answered the door.

The third incident occurred in March of 2013. Ms. Lagos stated that Mr. Martinez had been following her as she drove to pick up a co-worker and to go to work, so she called the police. Mr. Martinez was stopped and he related to the officer that he was following Ms. Lagos in order to pick up the child, although it was not the appropriate time. According to Ms. Lagos, the police officer told Mr. Martinez to stop following her. At the hearing, Mr. Martinez denied following Ms. Lagos. He testified that he just happened to be in the area and he was surprised when he was stopped by the police.

Ms. Lagos, in response to cross-examination, stated that she did not file for any restraining orders, because Mr. Martinez would stop the offending behavior after she notified the police. She also stated that Mr. Martinez lowered his child support after she contacted the police.

The trial court, after considering the testimony, maintained the schedule of the hearing officer that provided for joint custody to the parties, with the mother as custodial parent during the school year and shared physical custody during the summer months. Mr. Martinez was awarded visitation during the school years on Tuesdays and Thursdays from the end of the school day until 7:00 P.M. and on every other weekend from Friday when school ends until Sunday at 7:00 P.M. Physical custody of the child during holidays was also set forth. The parties were also ordered to participate in co-parenting therapy.

In this appeal, Mr. Martinez argues that the trial court erred in failing to grant him physical custody, or in the alternative, to grant shared custody. He argues that the trial court made its determination based on the parties' relationship toward each other, and not on the best interest of the child. He further argues that the trial court erred in failing to address the child's current living situation.

In rendering judgment, the court orally noted that Mr. Martinez had control issues. The court also stated that the child's sleeping arrangement would have to be addressed in the future as she got older.

At the time of the hearing, the child was in school, and a shared weekly physical custody would cause disruption. In addition, Ms. Lagos had been the primary physical custodian for the entirety of the child's life. Thus, the trial court could have found that shared custody, with Ms. Lagos as the primary physical custodian during the school year was in the best interest of the child. Furthermore, the fact that the child's sleeping arrangement may need to be addressed in the future does not mandate that it be addressed in the present. All parties agreed that the child was happy and successful with the current custody arrangement. The trial court is not required to make a mechanical evaluation of every factor of La. C.C. art. 194. Every child custody case must be viewed based on its own particular facts and relationships involved, with the goal of determining what is in the best interest of the child.

Furthermore, the court of appeal cannot simply substitute its own findings for that of the trial court. The trier of fact is not disadvantaged by the review of a cold record and is in a superior position to observe the nuances of demeanor evidence not revealed in a record.

We find no manifest error in the trial court's factual determination that the best interest of the child is to have her mother as domiciliary custodian during the school year, and a sharing of custody with weekly exchanges during the summer months.

AFFIRMED.

Kirsch v. Kirsch

180 So. 3d 417 (La. App. 1 Cir. 2015)

THERIOT, J.

In this child custody case, the mother appeals a judgment in which the trial court granted sole custody of the parties' minor children to the father. For the following reasons, we affirm the judgment of the trial court.

FACTS & PROCEDURAL HISTORY

This matter involves a protracted and contentious custody dispute between Karl Kirsch and Kristin Kirsch [together, "the parties"]. The parties were married on January 12, 2001. Two children were born of the marriage: MK1, born August 16, 2001, and SK, born December 20, 2003. The parties separated and ceased living together in September 2011. . . .

[Kristin made several complaints to DCFS and to the police alleging Karl physically abused her and physically and sexually abused the children. There was apparently no merit in her complaints, and Karl alleged she coached the children into making false accusations against him.]

On September 9, 2013, the trial court signed a second judgment reiterating that Karl had been awarded sole custody, and, among other specific orders, provided that Kristin would have only supervised visitation on alternating weekends, and that neither party should publicly disclose any facts or details of the proceedings nor discuss them with the children.

STANDARD OF REVIEW

The court shall award custody of a child in accordance with the best interest of the child. La. C.C. art. 131. In determining the child's best interest, the court shall consider all the factors that are relevant to that specific case. La. C.C. art. 134. The trial court's decision in child custody matters is entitled to great weight and it will not be overturned absent a clear showing of an abuse of discretion.

DISCUSSION

Assignment of Error No. 1

In her first assignment of error, Kristin argues that the trial court erred in awarding sole custody to Karl and permitting only supervised visitation by Kristin because Karl failed to put forth evidence that such was in the best interests of the children, and because Karl failed to prove that Kristin coached the children to make false allegations against him.

Kristin also challenges the qualification of Investigator Brian Brown of the Louisiana Department of Justice, who testified regarding his belief that Kristin coached the children, as an expert witness in "criminal investigation of the sexual abuse of children." Brown was the SPD Detective who investigated the allegations of sexual abuse against Karl. However, as Kristin failed to object to the qualification of Brown as an expert at the trial on this matter, this issue may not be raised on appeal.

Generally, the court shall award custody to the parents jointly; however, if custody to one parent is shown by clear and convincing evidence to serve the best interest of the child, the court shall award custody to that parent. . . .

Considering the particular facts and the relationships involved in this case, we must determine if the trial court abused its discretion in finding by clear and convincing evidence that awarding sole custody of the children to Karl is in the childrens' best interest. Further, we must determine if the trial court's evaluations of credibility are reasonable.

The paramount consideration in any determination of child custody is the best interest of the child. In determining the best interest of the child, La. C.C. art. 134 enumerates twelve factors to be considered by the trial court. . . .

The list of factors set forth in Article 134 is non-exclusive, and the determination as to the weight to be given each factor is left to the discretion of the trial court. We here summarize both the evidence contained in the record before us and the trial court's analysis and conclusion based on the La. C.C. art. 134 factors for determining the best interest of the children, as follows:

Regarding the first La. C.C. art. 134 factor, the trial court concluded that the love, affection, and other emotional ties between each party and the children are equal between the parties. This is supported by the report of Dr. Klein, who conducted full mental health examinations of both parties pursuant to the Interim Consent Judgment and evaluated both children. In his report, Dr. Klein wrote that the children appeared to be equally bonded to both parents.

Regarding the second La. C.C. art. 134 factor, the trial court concluded without discussion that it was her belief that Karl has the greater capacity and disposition to give the child love, affection, and spiritual guidance and to continue the education and rearing of the child.

Regarding the third La. C.C. art. 134 factor, the trial court concluded that Karl has the greater capacity and disposition to provide the children with food, clothing, medical care, and other material needs. Karl has stable employment and demonstrated better judgment concerning financial matters; whereas Nurse Ann Troy, a nurse at Children's Hospital in New Orleans, who had examined MK after Kristin brought him to the ER alleging sexual abuse, reported that Kristin told her during a hospital visit that she had no money for food and gas and convinced Nurse Troy to give Kristen assistance. In addition, as found by the trial court, Kristin appears to be in denial about the children's medical needs and lacks the capacity to handle the children's medical needs, as demonstrated by her failure to provide the children with enough medication to last the duration of their visits with Karl and her refusal to accept doctor's recommendations of medications for the children. In light of the children's severe mental health issues, including previous threats and actions of physical violence against their parents and sexually acting out against other children, a thorough understanding of and ability to address the children's medical needs is vital, and Kristin's history demonstrates her lack of capacity to provide the children with such.

Regarding the fourth La. C.C. art. 134 factor — the length of time the child has lived in a stable, adequate environment, and the desirability of maintaining continuity of that environment — the trial court concluded that Karl can provide the children with the most stable and adequate home environment. This conclusion was based on evidence that the living conditions with Kristin have at times been poor, while Karl currently has a stable, adequate residence with his mother.

Regarding the fifth La. C.C. art. 134 factor — the permanence, as a family unit, of the existing or proposed custodial home or homes — the trial court found it significant that Kristin relies almost entirely on spousal support, which is likely to result in an inability to maintain her current residence at some point in time.

The sixth and seventh La. C.C. art. 134 factors, which consider the moral fitness of each party as it affects the welfare of the children, and the mental and physical health of the parties, respectively, involve closely interrelated issues of extreme significance.

With respect to Karl, Dr. Klein's report and testimony indicated that Karl tends to be suspicious and appears easily irritated, and regarding Kristin's allegations that Karl physically abused her, Dr. Klein stated that there was "reasonable concern that this may be a possibility." Dr. Klein described Karl as "always logical, coherent and orderly in his thinking" and reported that there was no indication that Karl has mood problems or instability in emotional functioning. Karl had no criminal history. The trial court ultimately found that Karl had no psychological problems of any significance.

In stark contrast, the trial court found that Kristin "presents a danger to these children at this point in time on many levels." The evidence and the trial testimony together demonstrate significant issues regarding both Kristin's moral fitness, her judgment, her credibility, and her mental health. Further, Dr. Klein testified that Kristin has a major depressive disorder and anxiety disorder; he also testified that she presented with a "malignant psychological picture" and the "data points toward severe psychological disturbance." Dr. Klein's report to the trial court indicated that Kristen is naïve, highly anxious, and has notable character issues, including being resentful, argumentative, suspicious, paranoid, and "has a long history of severe social maladjustment with a poor work history."

Kristin had on at least one occasion permitted individuals to stay in the home with the children, although she did not know the individuals well enough to tell Dr. Klein their last names. In addition, Kristin claimed to Dr. Klein that she had been diagnosed with cancer in 2009, but failed to follow up on the diagnosis or seek treatment. She also told Dr. Klein that she had been admitted to both Harvard and Yale after high school, though when questioned, she did not know where either school was located, and Dr. Klein testified that such an achievement would be very surprising given her psychological profile. Kristin has been arrested for breaking and entering and assault and battery, while one of the children was with her. No explanation or denial of this event was provided.

Investigator Brown's testimony, which overlapped with the contents of the DCFS records, fleshed out the history surrounding the sexual abuse allegations and provided further support for the conclusion that the children had been coached.

Brown testified that on October 19, 2011, the SPD received a call from Kelsey Bourgeois at DCFS relating to Kristin's allegation of sexual battery against Karl. One of Brown's colleagues met with Kristin the next day, and Kristin reported that MK had written "Dad hurt my butt" on the wall with his feces when the parties lived in California years earlier; that both children had commented that Karl had been engaged in "wee wee touching" with the boys; and that Kristin had personally seen MK put his mouth on SK's genitals and that Karl had made the children do this to him in the past.

On October 26, 2011, Brown arranged for a forensic interview of both children with representatives of DCFS at Hope House, which he observed on closed circuit television. SK stated that he couldn't remember what he was supposed to say, but what he told the other person was all true. Kristin calmly denied having coached the children when Brown confronted her. The DCFS employees both agreed with Brown that the children had been coached. On this issue, the trial court noted its belief that this matter was the only occasion it had ever seen DCFS "actually say that they believe the mother had coached the children."

Following the Hope House interviews, Karl passed a polygraph test. However, Kristin could not complete her polygraph test because she was "very upset, hysterical." After the attempted polygraph test, Kristin told Brown that she would consent to Karl having joint custody, which he testified was a "red flag," because "[s]omeone whose child is being molested by the parent would not agree to let them have any custody, at least in my experience."

On October 28, 2011, Brown spoke with Nurse Troy, a nurse at Children's Hospital in New Orleans, who had examined MK after Kristin brought him to the ER alleging sexual abuse. Troy found no evidence to corroborate Kristin's allegations and also felt that the story had been coached or rehearsed. Further, Troy felt tricked, as she had given Kristin money for food and gas. The investigation of these charges was closed on November 4, 2011, finding that Kristin lacked credibility and that there were numerous inconsistencies in her stories, as well as indications that the children had been coached and there was no physical evidence of abuse.

Brown testified that at one of the monthly meetings held to review investigations of alleged sexual abuse attended by individuals representing the St. Tammany Parish Sheriff's Office, the Covington Police Department, the DCFS and the District Attorney's Office, everyone present felt that MK and SK had been coached to assert false allegations of sexual abuse against Karl. In addition, DCFS received a phone call from Kristin's sister, who stated that she believed Kristin had fabricated the allegations.

Brown investigated other abuse allegations filed by Kristin. Shortly after closing the first investigation, Brown received a call from DCFS reporting that Kristin had accused Karl of placing marshmallows in the children's anuses and taught them to do it to each other. These charges were determined to be false.

In early 2012, the Jefferson Parish Sheriffs Office ["JPSO"] contacted Brown regarding an allegation submitted by Kristin that she had found blood in MK's underwear and that Karl had raped him. The substance was determined to be feces, and JPSO closed the investigation.

Brown testified that he considered arresting Kristin for filing false police reports, but after discussions with his supervisors, decided against it due to her fragile mental state.

Natalie Elyea, Kristin's maid of honor at her wedding to Karl, testified by deposition that Kristin has a propensity to falsely accuse people of abuse. Specifically, Elyea testified that Kristin accused her high school swim coach of sexually abusing her; accused her mother of physical abuse; and accused her sister of sexually abusing her.

Regarding an incident that occurred in the New Orleans French Quarter, one of several instances in which Kristin accused Karl of physical abuse, Elyea's testimony was consistent with Karl's and indicated that contrary to Kristin's allegations, Kristin was abusive to Karl and not the other way around. Ruby Kirsch, Karl's mother, also testified that she had seen Kristin be physically violent towards Karl.

The trial court concluded that Kristin is dishonest and a danger to the children and "has a long and extensive history of not telling the truth to the children, to the DCFS, to medical personnel, to authorities, to the Court." The trial court further stated:

> It was difficult, in listening to what she had to say and looking through all the testimony and the documentary evidence, it is difficult to understand is she delusional or is this malicious and intentional and directed at destroying this man's relationship with his children. And I am not so sure I even have to come to that conclusion. But I can tell you that if I do have to come to that conclusion, I do believe she coached her children.

> She has coached the most vulnerable of children willingly, maliciously, arbitrarily, in an effort to gain an advantage in this case, in an effort to destroy the relationship with their father, in an effort to alienate them from

their father. And the most vicious allegations that she could make, the most bizarre allegations that she could make were told to these children and they were coached to tell authorities, that's reprehensible.

This is consistent with Dr. Klein's report, in which he stated that "[i]t was not at all clear what had transpired other than there was either coaching and/or the children had been interviewed numerous times and have been contaminated and when they see a therapist they are expected to talk about the abuse," and his testimony, that "in reviewing all of the records and the experts who opined regarding the sexual molesta-tion, combined with some 20-something years as director of a sexual abuse treatment program—speaking about myself—I did not see any validity in the allegations."

Regarding the eighth La. C.C. art. 134 factor, the trial court concluded that the home, school, and community history of the children supported an award of cus-tody to Karl. In light of the fact that the children have moved previously, due to Karl's military service, it is unlikely that it would be significant for the children to move again. Further, Karl will have family support, whereas Kristin does not and has accused several of her own family members of physically and sexually abusing her.

Regarding the ninth La. C.C. art. 134 factor—the reasonable preference of the children—the trial court concluded that there was no credible evidence presented.

Regarding the tenth La. C.C. art. 134 factor, the trial court concluded that the will-ingness and ability of each party to facilitate and encourage a close and continuing relationship between the children and the other party was a huge factor in this case. In light of "the level of parental alienation that has been exhibited by the mother toward the father," the trial court found that Kristin has no ability to facilitate and encourage a relationship between the children and Karl. In contrast, the trial court found that Karl has a great ability to facilitate and encourage a relationship between Kristin and the children, as demonstrated by his continued willingness to allow her to be involved in the childrens' lives.

Regarding the eleventh La. C.C. art. 134 factor, the trial court concluded that the distance between the respective residences of the parties was negligible.

Regarding the twelfth La. C.C. art. 134 factor of responsibility for the care and rearing of the children previously exercised by each party, the trial court stated that despite the history of Kristin acting as the primary caregiver, such was not to be desired any longer for all of the above reasons. . . .

Having thoroughly reviewed the record and evidence in its entirety, and consid-ering the particular facts and the relationships involved in this case, we find no man-ifest error in the trial court's factual determination that Kristin coached the children into supporting false allegations of sexual abuse by their father. For this reason and the many others extensively detailed above, we find that the trial court did not abuse its discretion in finding that Karl has shown by clear and convincing evidence that awarding sole custody of the children to Karl is in the children's best interest. . . . This assignment of error is without merit. . . .

CONCLUSION

We find the trial court did not abuse its discretion in the awarding of custody. Furthermore, we find this court lacks jurisdiction over the remaining assignments of error.

DECREE

The August 8, 2013 judgment of the trial court is affirmed. Cost of this appeal is assessed to the appellant, Kristin Kay Kirsch.

D. Modification of Custody

Custody arrangements may be — and often are — modified. The Civil Code does not set forth specific rules governing modification. Jurisprudence, however, has made it clear that the same considerations — the best interest of the child — apply to custody modifications. Generally, the burdens of proof are also the same. The court should typically award joint custody to the parents. If, however, a party seeks a modification that results in sole custody, Civil Code article 132 still requires that party to show "by clear and convincing evidence [that sole custody would] serve the best interest of the child." Similarly, in accordance with Article 133, a court should only modify a custody arrangement to grant custody to a non-parent if there is sufficient evidence that "joint custody or sole custody to either parent would result in substantial harm to the child."

In addition to the general custody considerations, parties seeking modifications are required to make some additional evidentiary showings. In *Bergeron v. Bergeron*, the Louisiana Supreme Court made it clear that in order to seek a modification of custody, there must have been some material change in circumstances since the initial custody decree.[4] This had been the rule under earlier jurisprudence and is supported by policy considerations. As the court explained:

> Traditionally, to support an action for modification of a judgment of child custody, the plaintiff has been required to show that a change in circumstances materially affecting the welfare of the child has occurred since the prior order respecting custody. The reasons for the rule are that it is desirable that there be an end of litigation and undesirable to change the child's established mode of living except for imperative reasons. Moreover, to require a party to show a change in circumstances materially affecting the child's welfare before contesting an award of custody, that he previously has had a full and fair opportunity to litigate, protects his adversary and the child from the vexation and expense attending multiple unjustified lawsuits, conserves judicial resources, and fosters reliance on judicial actions by minimizing the possibility of inconsistent decisions.

---

4. Bergeron v. Bergeron, 492 So. 2d 1193 (La. 1986).

In *Bergeron*, the court additionally drew a distinction between "stipulated judgments" and "considered decrees." If the initial decree was the latter type, the *Bergeron* court explained that additional evidentiary showings were required for modification. An initial custody arrangement that is the result of a stipulated judgment is afforded less deference than an initial considered decree. A stipulated judgment—or consent judgment—is an agreement that the parties entered into on their own and submitted to the court for approval. The Civil Code encourages parents to reach these types of agreements, and courts will typically approve them without hearing testimony or other evidence. In contrast, a considered decree is the result of a more adversarial proceeding where the court hears testimony and considers other evidence in order to craft a custody arrangement on its own accord. The *Bergeron* court explained that if the initial decree was a stipulated judgment, then the party seeking modification need only show that there has been a material change in circumstances and that the best interest of the child warranted some other arrangement. If, however, the initial arrangement was the result of a considered decree, "then the party seeking a change bears a heavy burden of proving that the continuation of the present custody is so deleterious to the children as to justify removing them from the environment to which they are accustomed."[5] As the court explained, this approach was also supported by prior jurisprudence and by policy considerations:

> A heavy burden of proof in custody modification cases is justified for several reasons. In the usual civil case a mistaken judgment for the plaintiff is no worse than a mistaken judgment for the defendant. However, this is not the case in an action to change a permanent award of custody. The available empirical research data and psychiatric opinions indicate a need for strict standards that set clear boundaries for modification actions. There is evidence that more harm is done to children by custody litigation, custody changes, and interparental conflict, than by such factors as the custodial parent's post divorce amours, remarriage, and residential changes, which more often precipitate custody battles under liberal custody modification rules than conduct that is obviously harmful to the child, such as abuse or serious neglect, which justifies intervention to protect the child under the court's civil or juvenile jurisdiction. . . .

> The child has at stake an interest of transcending value in a custody modification suit—his best interest and welfare—which may be irreparably damaged not only by a mistaken change in custody but also by the effects of an attempted or threatened change of custody on grounds that are less than imperative. The consequences to the mental and emotional well being and future development of the child from an erroneous judgment, unjustified litigation, threat of litigation, or continued interparental conflict are usually more serious than similar consequences in an ordinary civil case. On the

---

5. *Id.*

other hand, we are convinced that in a narrow class of cases a modification of custody may be in the child's best interest even though the moving party is unable to show that the present custody is deleterious to the child. However, in order to protect children from the detrimental effects of too liberal standards in custody change cases, the burden of proof should be heavy and the showing of overall or net benefit to the child must be clear. To accommodate these interests, the burden of proof rule should be restated as follows: When a trial court has made a considered decree of permanent custody the party seeking a change bears a heavy burden of proving that the continuation of the present custody is so deleterious to the child as to justify a modification of the custody decree, or of proving by clear and convincing evidence that the harm likely to be caused by a change of environment is substantially outweighed by its advantages to the child.[6]

The following modification cases illustrate the various principles set forth in *Bergeron*. They also provide additional illustrations of how courts consider the various best interest of the child factors. *Mulkey v. Mulkey*, a Louisiana Supreme Court decision, reaffirms the *Bergeron* standard in the case of a considered decree. *Tinsley v. Tinsley* is case involving proposed modification of a consent judgment — to which the lower standard applies. *Tinsely* discusses what evidence is needed to show a material change in circumstances. *Tinsley* also illustrates some of the challenges of parenting (and being a child) in the age of social media.

Mulkey v. Mulkey
118 So. 3d. 357 (La. 2013)

JOHNSON, C.J.

In this custody dispute, the trial court ordered a change in custody, finding the father satisfied the requirements of *Bergeron v. Bergeron* by establishing that any harm caused by a modification of a 2004 custody decree would be substantially outweighed by its advantages to the child. The trial court's ruling was reversed by the court of appeal. We granted this writ application to review the correctness of the court of appeal's ruling. Because we find no abuse of discretion by the trial court in modifying custody, we reverse the ruling of the court of appeal and reinstate the ruling of the trial court.

FACTS AND PROCEDURAL HISTORY

Phillip Ray Mulkey ("Phillip") and Vicki Juanita Harris Mulkey Pyles ("Vicki") were married on June 26, 1993, and established their matrimonial domicile in Winnsboro, Louisiana. They had one child during their marriage, Matthew Harris Mulkey ("Matthew"), who was born on January 19, 1998. The couple was divorced by judgment rendered on March 5, 2001. The parties thereafter jointly entered into two

---

6. *Id.*

separate consent decrees regarding custody of Matthew. Essentially, the consent decrees provided the parents with seven-day alternating custodial periods with Matthew.

Ultimately, the consent decrees were not able to be maintained. In 2003, both parties petitioned the court to modify the custody plan then in effect. . . . After a trial, the court rendered judgment on June 29, 2003, awarding the parties joint custody of Matthew, with Vicki named the domiciliary parent. Vicki was also granted primary custody during the school year. The trial court signed a judgment to this effect on December 9, 2004. No modification was sought by the parties until 2011.

On July 28, 2011, Vicki filed a "Rule for Payment of Medical Expenses and Rule to Show Cause for Judgment of Past Due Medical Support, Contempt, and Attorneys Fees" alleging Phillip failed to pay his share of Matthew's uncovered medical expenses and extracurricular activities. In addition, Vicki requested an increase in child support.

In response, Phillip filed an "Answer and Reconventional Demand" seeking to be named the domiciliary parent. Phillip also requested that his child support obligation be terminated, and that Vicki be ordered to pay him child support. As grounds for the modification of custody, Phillip asserted several particular changes in circumstances since the previous custody order. Notably, Phillip asserted that Vicki voluntarily changed employment requiring night shift work, thus she is not home at night with Matthew; Matthew has a history of excessive absences and poor academic performance at school; Matthew has expressed a preference to live with Phillip; and Phillip has remarried and he now lives in a spacious home with Matthew's half-siblings, with whom Matthew has a close bond. . . .

In lengthy reasons for judgment, the trial court found that after the 2004 custody decree was rendered, there was a material change in circumstance in the lives of Vicki, Phillip, and Matthew. The court noted Matthew was five when the 2004 decree was rendered, and he is now fourteen, has matured, and his needs, activities and interests have changed. Matthew confirmed that he wanted to live with his father, testifying: "I've lived most of my life at my mama's [in Ruston] so I want to live down here [at my father's house in Winnsboro] for the rest of the time I have until I move and get my own house." After questioning Matthew at trial, the court determined he was mature enough to express his parental preference.

The court further noted that Vicki voluntarily changed her employment since custody was originally set, requiring her to frequently work nights. Thus, she was at work when Matthew went to bed and woke up and Matthew had to prepare his own breakfast each morning as well as several of his evening meals, which he generally eats by himself in his room. The court noted that at his father's house Matthew enjoys outdoor activities such as fishing, hunting and riding dirt bikes with Phillip and his cousins. Matthew is also involved in church and youth group activities offered at Life Church where Phillip and his family attend. Testimony revealed the family ate meals together, played games and watched television together.

The court also recognized that Matthew developed several medical conditions since the 2004 decree. He now has Type I diabetes, requiring Matthew to wear an insulin pump which is monitored throughout the day. Vicki also testified he has hypothyroidism and takes medication to control that condition. Vicki complained that Phillip did not participate in Matthew's medical care, and failed to monitor his insulin needs and dietary restrictions. Phillip stated he offered Matthew a balanced diet, but admitted that Matthew is primarily in charge of monitoring his insulin pump and adjusting his own medication. Phillip criticized Vicki for over-medicating Matthew, and claimed she failed to regularly inform him about Matthew's medical treatment.

Another change noted by the trial court was that Vicki's husband had developed medical problems since the 2004 trial, including depression, CREST Syndrome and Sarcoidosis. The court noted that as a result of these conditions and other extraneous reasons, he has been unable to maintain steady employment.

The court observed that in the past, Matthew excelled in school and won many academic awards until he reached seventh grade. His performance in the eighth grade revealed a significant decline, and he appears to prefer playing video games to doing school work. In addition, whereas he formerly participated in various extracurricular activities, the court noted Matthew reduced his activities in the eighth grade year. [The trial court found a material change in circumstances and that the *Bergeron* requirements were met. The court of appeal reversed.] . . .

Accordingly, the court of appeal reinstated the 2004 custody decree.

Phillip filed a writ application in this court, which we granted.

DISCUSSION

The primary consideration in a determination of child custody is the best interest of the child. This applies not only in actions setting custody initially, but also in actions to change custody. A considered decree is an award of permanent custody in which the trial court receives evidence of parental fitness to exercise care, custody, and control of children. In an action to change custody rendered in a considered decree, additional jurisprudential requirements set forth by this court in *Bergeron v. Bergeron*, *supra*, are also applied. There is no question in this case that the 2004 custody award is a considered decree. Thus, the burden of proof on the party seeking to modify custody is dictated by *Bergeron*.

In *Bergeron*, this court considered whether the heavy burden of proof rule in modification cases should be continued. That rule provided that "when a trial court has made a considered decree of permanent custody the party seeking a change bears a heavy burden of proving that the continuation of the present custody is so deleterious to the children as to justify removing them from the environment to which they are accustomed." While recognizing that the heavy burden of proof in custody modification cases was justified for several reasons, we were convinced that in a narrow class of cases a modification of custody may be in the child's best interest even though the moving party is unable to show that the present custody is deleterious to the child.

Recognizing that the heavy burden of proof rule could inflexibly prevent a modification of custody that is in the child's best interest, and also cognizant of the need to protect children from the detrimental effects of too liberal standards in custody change cases, we restated the burden of proof rule as follows:

> When a trial court has made a considered decree of permanent custody the party seeking a change bears a heavy burden of proving that the continuation of the present custody is so deleterious to the child as to justify a modification of the custody decree, or of proving by clear and convincing evidence that the harm likely to be caused by a change of environment is substantially outweighed by its advantages to the child.

Thus, when a party seeks to change custody rendered in a considered decree, the proponent of change must not only show that a change of circumstances materially affecting the welfare of the child has occurred since the prior order respecting custody, but he or she must also meet the burden of proof set forth in *Bergeron*.

Phillip asserts the court of appeal erred in finding he did not meet the burden of proof outlined in *Bergeron*. Phillip argues the court of appeal erroneously expanded the *Bergeron* test to require him to prove that the advantages of Matthew moving in with him were "clear and convincing." *Bergeron* only requires the advantages substantially outweigh the perceived harm of relocation. He notes the trial court and the court of appeal essentially agreed that, under the circumstances presented in this case, there was no harm in relocating Matthew from Ruston to Winnsboro. Further, the court of appeal did not deny the advantages for Matthew in Phillip's home, namely the significant connections Matthew had with friends, family and activities, combined with a more structured and traditional environment and schedule.

Phillip also suggests that if the instant case does not warrant a change in custody under the alternate ground in *Bergeron*, then no such case exists. He submits that in a case where both parents love the child, but the best interest of the child would be served by a modification of custody, without any harm to the child, application of *Bergeron*'s alternative ground is necessary. Phillip asserts the court of appeal's ruling effectively limits *Bergeron*'s intended application.

Vicki first argues the trial court's finding that a material change in circumstance had occurred since the rendition of the 2004 custody decree was an abuse of discretion. Although she was working night shifts at the time the request for modification was filed, her testimony at trial established she was returning to a regular forty-hour work week. Thus, her employment schedule should not be an issue.

Further, while Matthew's age and preference should be given consideration, it should not be a reason for a change of circumstances under the facts of this case. Vicki suggests that Phillip influenced Matthew prior to trial. Vicki further asserts that Matthew's weekends at his father's house were his "lazy time," as it consisted of weekends, holidays and summers without the pressure, stress and strains required by the routine of everyday life.

Vicki also asserts that Matthew's school performance is not a material change in circumstance. She argues that Matthew's poor school performance has to be considered in light of the facts and circumstances of this case. Matthew testified that eighth grade was harder for him, and the trial court also did not consider the impact Matthew's health may have had on his school performance. She also notes Phillip had very little involvement in Matthew's school activities in the past, never attending a parent/teacher conference, and only attending one football game to see Matthew perform in the band. Further, the trial court did not consider the impact of the trial itself on Matthew's school performance. Vicki asserts the stress of the custody trial placed great strain on Matthew's mental, physical, and emotional health, and this stress coincided with his poor performance in the eighth grade.

Vicki contends Phillip failed to meet the *Bergeron* standard of proving by clear and convincing evidence that a change in custody would provide substantial advantages to Matthew. The advantages alleged by the trial court were not demonstrated by clear and convincing evidence, as the trial court had to "read between the lines" of Matthew's testimony to make its decision. She argues this case does not fit the "narrow class" discussed in *Bergeron*. Here, the only advantages the trial court could offer was that Matthew would go to a new school, and already had family and friends in Winnsboro. She notes that Matthew has the same advantages with her in Ruston. The trial court also did not address the harm associated with Matthew's health because of his father's lack of interest therein. The possibility that Matthew might improve his grades at a new school in Winnsboro does not outweigh the potential harm of his medical issues being ignored by his father.

At the outset, we agree with the trial court's finding that a material change in circumstances has occurred since 2004. It is clear from the record that the dynamics of both households have changed since the previous custody order. Matthew's age, Vicki's change of employment and work schedule, Phillip's change in home environment and Matthew's academic performance are all changes that materially affect Matthew's welfare. Thus, we move on to consider whether the burden of proof of *Bergeron* was met. In the instant case, the lower courts found, and the parties agree, that the present custody decree is not deleterious to Matthew. Therefore, the narrow issue presented in this case is whether Phillip proved by clear and convincing evidence that the harm likely to be caused by a change of custody naming him as domiciliary parent is substantially outweighed by its advantages to Matthew.

After reviewing the record and considering the briefs and arguments of the parties, we find the court of appeal erred in reversing the trial court's ruling. We find no sufficient basis in the record to conclude the trial court's findings were manifestly erroneous. . . .

Vicki argues Matthew could be harmed by a change in custody because Phillip will ignore his medical problems. However, nothing in the trial court's reasons for judgment indicate the court had any concerns that Phillip would neglect Matthew's medical issues. Rather, the trial court apparently rejected Vicki's assertion that

Phillip did not participate in Matthew's medical care, and failed to monitor his insulin needs and dietary restrictions. The court noted Phillip's testimony that he offered Matthew a balanced diet, but Matthew is primarily in charge of monitoring his insulin pump and adjusting his own medication. Considering Matthew's age, it is not unreasonable for Phillip to allow him to assume some role in his own medical care. Additionally, Matthew has been in Phillip's care every other weekend, one-half of the major holidays, and most of the summers for the past nine years. There is no evidence his medical condition has deteriorated while he was in Phillip's custody.

Vicki also argues Phillip has not participated in Matthew's schooling or extra-curricular activities in the past. However, the trial court made a finding that granting custody to Phillip provided Matthew with the best chance to thrive and succeed in all areas of his adolescent life. The trial court further made a finding that "Phillip has proven to be a very capable father and husband who provides his family with a stable, loving home environment." Thus, despite his past actions, Phillip is now ready to assume a greater role in his son's life.

Additionally, Vicki suggests Phillip did not meet his burden by clear and convincing evidence because the trial court indicated it had to "read between the lines" to reach its decision. While the trial court stated it was "reading between the lines" to reach its conclusion, this is precisely why deference is given to the trial court's judgment. The trial court clearly observed certain nuances in Matthew's testimony which cannot be communicated by the record, but which convinced the court of Matthew's strong preference to live with his father and convinced the court a modification in custody would be in Matthew's best interest.

Every child custody case must be viewed based on its own particular facts and relationships involved, with the goal of determining what is in the best interest of the child. Our decision in *Bergeron* was not meant to tie the hands of a court when the facts and circumstances of a case and the needs of a child necessitate a change in custody. The record reveals that both parents love Matthew and have raised him well. The record further demonstrates that Matthew is a well-adjusted, appropriately mature teenager who has expressed a desire to live with his father and finish his high school years in Winnsboro. In determining the best interest of the child, a court is permitted to consider the child's custodial preference, if the court deems the child to be of sufficient age to express a preference. Matthew was fourteen years old at the time of trial, and the trial court found him to be a mature and grounded teenager, and was "impressed with Matthew's ability to communicate his sincere desire to live with his father the next four years before he reaches the age of majority." After reviewing the record, we find no error in the weight the trial court placed on Matthew's preference to live with his father. The record clearly shows that although Matthew loves his mother, and has a good relationship with her and his stepfather, he yearns for the family structure and interaction provided in his father's household. The record reveals that Matthew spends a lot of time alone at Vicki's house, where the family does not participate in many activities together. Matthew's preference to live with Phillip is based in large part on the routine, structure, family connection and interaction in his father's household. We find in this case, where the parents are relatively equally balanced in terms of caring for the child, the preference of a mature and grounded teenager such as Matthew is entitled to great weight. In this case, we find Matthew is entitled to live in an environment which supports his desire for a family life while he is still a minor. We see no error in the trial court's finding that Phillip is the parent "whose home environment can provide him with the greatest opportunity to thrive and succeed scholastically, spiritually, socially, emotionally and physically during this very important stage of his adolescent life, as he prepares for manhood."

Further, the court of appeal cannot simply substitute its own findings for that of the trial court. The determination of the trial court in child custody matters is entitled to great weight, and its discretion will not be disturbed on review in the absence of a clear showing of abuse. The trial court thoughtfully considered all of the trial testimony and evidence and set forth in great detail the reasons why a change in custody was justified and in Matthew's best interest. Given Matthew's age and demonstrated level of maturity, and considering the particular facts and circumstances of this case, we find the record supports the trial court's finding that Phillip has met the burden of *Bergeron* by proving that any harm caused by a modification of the 2004 custody decree would be substantially outweighed by its advantages to Matthew.

CONCLUSION

For the above reasons, we find the court of appeal erred in reversing the trial court's modification of custody. Phillip met the burden of *Bergeron* by proving that any harm caused by a modification of the 2004 custody decree would be substantially outweighed by its advantages to Matthew. Thus, we find no error in the trial court's ruling modifying the 2004 custody decree.

DECREE

REVERSED. RULING OF THE TRIAL COURT REINSTATED.

Tinsley v. Tinsley

211 So. 3d 405 (La. App. 1 Cir. 2017)

WELCH, J.

In this child custody dispute, the mother, Nicole Renee Nugent Tinsley, appeals a trial court judgment that, among other things, modified the parties' joint custodial arrangement to award the father, Jason Lee Tinsley, equal physical custody of the minor child, as well as certain decision making authority. For the reasons that follow, we reverse the judgment insofar as it modified the physical custodial arrangement and the authority of the domiciliary parent and we affirm the trial court's decision to deny Nicole Tinsley's request for injunctive relief.

I. FACTUAL AND PROCEDURAL HISTORY

The parties in this matter, Nicole Tinsley and Jason Tinsley, were married on March 10, 2001, and they had one child during their marriage: K.N.T., born

February 27, 2002. On July 28, 2011, Jason Tinsley filed a petition for divorce, seeking among other things, that the parties be awarded joint custody of their minor child, with each party having physical custody of the child on an equal basis, and that child support be calculated and fixed according to the child support guidelines. On July 29, 2011, Nicole Tinsley filed a petition for divorce also requesting that the parties be awarded joint custody of their minor child, that she be designated as the child's domiciliary parent, subject to specific custodial periods by Jason Tinsley, and that she be awarded child support. The two suits were subsequently consolidated in the trial court.

The parties subsequently entered into a stipulated (or consent) judgment providing that the parties would be awarded joint custody of the minor child, that Nicole Tinsley would be designated as the domiciliary parent, and that Jason Tinsley would have physical custody of the child in accordance with a specific schedule. . . .

On September 28, 2012, Jason Tinsley filed a rule for modification of custody, visitation, child support, and other ancillary matters. Therein, he claimed that there had been a material change in circumstances since the February 6, 2012 consent judgment and the filing of the rule and that it was in the best interest of the minor child to modify the physical custodial schedule so that the parties would share equal physical custody of the child. In response to this rule, the parties again entered into a stipulated judgment maintaining the award of joint custody with Nicole Tinsley designated as the domiciliary parent, but modifying Jason Tinsley's physical custodial schedule. The trial court signed this stipulated judgment regarding child custody and support on February 21, 2013.

On September 16, 2014, Jason Tinsley filed another rule for change in custody. In that rule, he alleged that since the February 21, 2013 stipulated judgment, there had been a material change in circumstances affecting the welfare of the minor child and that it was in the best interest of the minor child to modify the parties joint custody arrangement such that he should be designated as the minor child's domiciliary parent subject to specific physical custodial periods in favor of Nicole Tinsley, or alternatively, that the parties share equal physical custody of the minor child. In response, on January 20, 2015, Nicole Tinsley filed an answer generally denying the allegations of Jason Tinsley's rule and a reconventional demand requesting relief on various ancillary matters, including contempt for Jason Tinsley's failure to pay his pro-rata share of tutoring, counseling fees, and school registration for the child. Thereafter, on November 17, 2015, Nicole Tinsley also sought an injunction seeking to prohibit Jason Tinsley and his wife from posting embarrassing pictures of the minor child on their social media accounts.

After a full trial on the merits, which took place on January 21 and February 12, 2016, the trial court took the matter under advisement. On February 29, 2016, the trial court rendered judgment (with written reasons assigned) finding that Jason Tinsley had proven that there had been a material change in circumstances since the rendition of the previous custody judgment and that a modification of the parties' custodial arrangement was in the best interest of the child. Based on that factual finding, the trial court modified the parties' custodial arrangement to provide that the parties would share physical custody of the child on a week to week schedule, i.e., on a 50/50 basis. Although the trial court maintained Nicole Tinsley as the domiciliary parent, it modified her authority as the domiciliary parent by requiring the parties to mutually agree on the child's high school selection and her Attention Deficit Disorder ("ADD") treatment and medication and by granting Jason Tinsley the right to select the tutor for the minor child, with each party being responsible for their pro rata percentage of the cost of tutoring. The trial court also declined to enjoin Jason Tinsley and his new wife from posting embarrassing pictures of the minor child on social media. A judgment in conformity with the trial court's written reasons was signed by the trial court on March 15, 2016, and it is from this judgment that Nicole Tinsley has appealed. . . .

III. LAW AND DISCUSSION

A. Modification of Physical Custody and Authority of the Domiciliary Parent

1. General Legal Precepts: Child Custody and Domiciliary Parent

The paramount consideration in any determination of child custody is the best interest of the child. If the parents agree who is to have custody, the court shall award custody in accordance with their agreement unless the best interest of the child requires a different award. In the absence of agreement, or if the agreement is not in the best interest of the child, the court shall award custody to the parents jointly; however, if custody in one parent is shown by clear and convincing evidence to serve the best interest of the child, the court shall award custody to that parent.

In determining the best interest of the child, La. C.C. art. 134 enumerates twelve non-exclusive factors to be considered by the trial court. . . .

3. Burden of Proof: Modification of a Custody Plan

There is a distinction between the burden of proof needed to change a custody plan ordered pursuant to a considered decree and of that needed to change a custody plan ordered pursuant to a non-considered decree. A "considered decree" is an award of permanent custody in which the trial court receives evidence of parental fitness to exercise care, custody, and control of children. By contrast, a non-considered decree or uncontested decree is one in which no evidence is presented as to the fitness of the parents, such as one that is entered by default, by stipulation or consent of the parties, or is otherwise not contested.

Once a considered decree of permanent custody has been rendered by a court, the proponent of the change bears the heavy burden of proving that a change of circumstances has occurred, such that the continuation of the present custody arrangement is so deleterious to the child as to justify a modification of the custody decree, or of proving by clear and convincing evidence that the harm likely caused by a change of environment is substantially outweighed by its advantages to the child.

However, in cases where the underlying custody decree is a stipulated judgment, and the parties have consented to a custodial arrangement with no evidence as to parental fitness, the heavy burden of proof rule enunciated in *Bergeron* is inapplicable. Rather, a party seeking a modification of a consent decree must prove: (1) that there has been a change in circumstances materially affecting the welfare of the child since the original (or previous) custody decree was entered; and (2) that the proposed modification is in the best interest of the child.

First and foremost, on appeal, Jason Tinsley . . . claims that his burden of proof was to show (1) that there has been a material change in circumstances since the previous custody decree and (2) that the proposed modification was in the best interest of the child. In other words, he argues that "[t]here is no requirement [that he] prove the material change [in circumstances] affects the child's welfare." However, we find no merit to his argument. . . .

In addition, the well-established and often-cited jurisprudence from this court with regard to modifications of custody following a consent decree unequivocally provide that the change in circumstance must affect the welfare of the child. . . .

In this case, there is no dispute that the underlying custody decree (the February 21, 2013 custody decree) was a non-considered decree—it was a stipulated judgment wherein the parties agreed that they would have joint custody of the child, with Nicole Tinsley designated as the child's domiciliary parent, subject to Jason Tinsley having specific periods of physical custody. Therefore, in order to modify that custody plan, Jason Tinsley had to prove, and the trial court had to find: (1) that there had been a change in circumstances materially affecting the welfare of the child since the February 21, 2013 custody decree/stipulated judgment; and (2) that modification proposed by Jason Tinsley—i.e., that he be designated as the domiciliary parent subject to specific physical custodial periods in favor of Nicole Tinsley, or alternatively, that the parties share equal physical custody of the minor child with a modification in the authority of the domiciliary parent—was in the best interest of the child.

In the trial court's reasons for judgment, it found that Jason Tinsley met his burden of proving a material change in circumstances because: (1) Jason Tinsley had remarried since the February 21, 2013 judgment, (2) he had recently moved his residence closer to both the minor child's school and Nicole Tinsley's house, (3) the child's school performance had "suffered tremendously in recent years," and (4) the minor child had not been properly treated for ADD. In addition, after considering all of the evidence and the factors set forth in La. C.C. art. 134, the trial court found that a modification of custody was in the child's best interest and awarded the parties shared physical custody of the child on a week-to-week basis. Although the trial court maintained Nicole Tinsley as the domiciliary parent, it modified her authority as the domiciliary parent by requiring the parties to mutually agree on the child's high school selection and ADD treatment and medication and by granting Jason Tinsley the right to select the tutor for the minor child.

4. Material Change in Circumstances Affecting the Welfare of the Child

On appeal, Nicole Tinsley contends that the trial court's factual finding that there had been a material change in circumstances affecting the welfare of the minor child was manifestly erroneous because there was no evidence in the record establishing that either Jason Tinsley's remarriage or his move closer to the minor child's residence had any effect on the welfare of the child, the record established that the minor child's grades had improved (rather than suffered) since the rendition of the February 21, 2013 judgment, and the record failed to establish that the minor child was not being treated properly for ADD. We agree.

First, with respect to ADD, although Jason Tinsley claimed that the minor child had been diagnosed with ADD but was not being given her medication as prescribed, the record herein does not clearly establish whether the minor child was ever formally evaluated or diagnosed with ADD or whether it was being treated improperly.

According to Nicole Tinsley's testimony, the minor child was not formally evaluated for ADD. Nicole Tinsley stated that she initiated an appointment with the child's pediatrician to discuss whether the child had ADD and that Jason Tinsley was present for this appointment. She stated that the child's pediatrician did not perform any formal testing or evaluation to determine whether the child had ADD; instead, the pediatrician asked a few questions and then issued the child a prescription. Nicole Tinsley testified that she began giving the child her medication as prescribed on school days; however, she said that she did not give the child the medication on weekends or when the child was not in school because she was told by the pediatrician's office that it was not necessary at those times. According to Nicole Tinsley, shortly after the minor child commenced taking the medication, the child began complaining about headaches and stomachaches. When Nicole Tinsley reported this to the child's pediatrician, the pediatrician increased the dosage. However, when the child's headaches and stomachaches continued and did not subside, Nicole Tinsley called the pediatrician's nurse and the decision was made to wean the child off the medication. Jason Tinsley admitted that he was aware that Nicole Tinsley had discussed weaning the child off the medication with the child's pediatrician. The child's medical records from the pediatrician were not offered into evidence by either party.

According to Nicole Tinsley, none of the minor child's teachers have suggested to either her or Jason Tinsley that the minor child needed to be evaluated or treated for ADD. Nicole Tinsley stated that she would like to have the child formally evaluated for ADD; however, Jason Tinsley stated that he did not think that the ADD medication helped the child and he did not think that the child needed any additional testing or to be evaluated for ADD or any other learning disability.

Based on our review of the record, we find that it fails to establish any factual support for the trial court's conclusion that the minor child was being treated improperly for ADD. As such, the trial court's factual determination that this constituted a change in circumstances materially affecting the child was manifestly erroneous.

With respect to the minor child's school performance, we note that the evidence at trial established that the child has performed poorly at school for a number of years and this was not a "change" that has occurred since the rendition of the February 21, 2013 judgment. When the February 21, 2013 judgment was rendered, the minor child's poor grades were a major issue because Jason Tinsley specifically alleged in his October 5, 2012 rule to modify custody (the rule that led to the February 21, 2013 stipulated judgment) that the minor child was not adequately prepared for homework and/or tests while in the physical custody of Nicole Tinsley, that he was better suited to assist the child with her studies, and that he could ensure that the child kept up with her school work and remained in good standing. Despite these allegations and the child's poor school performance, Jason Tinsley entered into the February 21, 2013 stipulated judgment.

Furthermore, the record does not support the trial court's conclusion that the minor child's grades have "suffered" since the February 21, 2013 judgment. To the contrary, the minor child's report cards, which were offered into evidence, reflects that the child's grades have improved, albeit slightly, since the rendition of that judgment. At the time of the February 21, 2013 judgment, the minor child was in 5th grade and her grades for the third nine weeks in her core subjects were as follows: Religion—C; English—C; Math—C; Reading—D; Science—B; Social Studies—C. When Jason filed the rule to modify custody in September 2014, her most recent report card, from the end of 6th Grade (May 2014), reflected the following grades in her core subjects: Religion—C; English—F; Math—D; Reading—C; Science—C; Social Studies—C, and she was conditionally promoted to 7th grade. Just after Jason filed the rule (October 2014), the minor child received a report card for the first nine weeks of 7th grade, which reflected the following grades in her core subjects: Religion—B; English—B; Math—C; Reading—C; Science—D; Social Studies—C. Thus, the evidence established that the child did not have particularly stellar grades when the parties entered into the February 21, 2013 judgment, but since that time, the child's grades have slightly improved in some of her core subjects. Accordingly, we find the trial court's conclusion that there was a change in circumstances affecting the welfare of the child because the minor child's grades had suffered since the February 21, 2013 judgment was likewise not supported by the evidence and is clearly wrong.

Insofar as Jason Tinsley's move is concerned, the record reflects that at the time of the February 21, 2013 judgment, Jason Tinsley was residing in Zachary with Michelle Tinsley (his current wife, but then girlfriend). At trial, Jason Tinsley testified that he and Michelle were moving and about to "close" on a house in Central, which was closer to the child's current residence with her mother and Central High School—the high school that the child would likely attend. Notably, Zachary and Central are located adjacent to each other in the northern part of East Baton Rouge Parish. While this change in residence is certainly a change in the life of Jason and his wife, the record contains no evidence as to how this intra-parish move from Zachary to Central affects the welfare of the minor child.

Jason Tinsley contends that a move has been judicially recognized as a material change in [*Distefano*].

We find *Distefano* is distinguishable because *Distefano* involved an inter-parish move from East Baton Rouge Parish to Livingston Parish rather than an intra-parish move as in this case. In addition, the determination that the inter-parish move in

Distefano constituted a change in circumstances was based on the fact that the distance between the parties' residences was a major factor in the underlying judgment sought to be modified, whereas in this case, there is no evidence that the distance between Jason Tinsley's house in Zachary and Nicole Tinsley's house in Central was a factor under consideration in the underlying judgment or that this distance affected the custodial arrangement in any way. Accordingly, Jason Tinsley's intra-parish move was not per se a material change of circumstance materially affecting the child's welfare.

Jason Tinsley lived in East Baton Rouge Parish at the time the February 21, 2013 judgment was rendered, at the time he filed the rule requesting a modification of custody, and at the time of the trial of this matter. Absent some evidence as to how Jason Tinsley's move within East Baton Rouge Parish affects the welfare of the minor child, it cannot constitute a material change in circumstances affecting the welfare of the child. Accordingly, the trial court manifestly erred in concluding that Jason Tinsley's move was a material change in circumstances since the rendition of the February 21, 2013 judgment which warranted a modification of custody.

With respect to Jason Tinsley's remarriage, the record does indeed reflect that Jason Tinsley married Michelle Tinsley since the rendition of the February 21, 2013 judgment; again however, the record contains no evidence as to how this change affects the minor child. According to the testimony, Jason Tinsley and Nicole Tinsley separated in July of 2011, and in November or December of 2011, Jason Tinsley moved in with Michelle Tinsley. Therefore, at the time of the initial stipulated judgment of custody (the February 6, 2012) and the subsequent stipulated judgment (the February 21, 2013 judgment), Jason Tinsley and Michelle Tinsley were living together in the same house. Jason Tinsely married Michelle Tinsely on March 22, 2014, and approximately six months later, on September 16, 2014, Jason Tinsley filed the instant request for a modification of custody. Although Jason Tinsley was specifically asked how his marriage to Michelle Tinsley changed things (or affected) the minor child, he was unable to provide a response other than to say that his bond with Michelle had gotten "closer" since they were married and that he believed there was a "big difference," as far as commitment, between a marriage and dating somebody.

Jason Tinsley maintains that remarriage has been judicially recognized as a material change in circumstances warranting a modification of custody. . . . Therefore, he claims that his remarriage alone was a change in circumstance sufficient to warrant a modification of custody. We disagree. It is well-settled that a party's remarriage, by itself, does not constitute a change in circumstances materially affecting a child's welfare so as to warrant a change in custody. . . . Thus, while Jason Tinsley's remarriage was certainly a change in circumstances in his life, absent some evidence that this change affects the welfare of the minor child, his remarriage, by itself, does not constitute a change in circumstances warranting a modification of custody. And, although Jason Tinsley's remarriage could be considered a factor in a combination of factors constituting a change in circumstance, the record before us contained no other evidence establishing any changes in circumstance affecting the welfare of the minor child since the rendition of the February 21, 2013 stipulated judgment so as to warrant a modification of custody. Accordingly, we find the trial court's factual determination that Jason Tinsley's remarriage was a change in circumstances warranting a modification of custody is manifestly erroneous.

Since we have determined that the trial court erred in its finding, and that Jason Tinsley failed to prove, that there has been a material change in circumstances affecting the welfare of the minor child since the rendition of the February 21, 2013 stipulated custody judgment, a modification of the February 21, 2013 judgment was not warranted. As such, we must conclude that the trial court abused its discretion in modifying the physical custodial arrangement set forth in the February 21, 2013 judgment and in modifying the general authority of the domiciliary parent to make all decisions affecting the child. Accordingly, the March 15, 2016 judgment of the trial court is reversed insofar as it modified the parties' physical custodial schedule and modified the domiciliary parent's authority under La. R.S. 9:335 by requiring the parties to mutually agree on high school selection and ADD treatment and medication and by giving Jason Tinsley the right to select the tutor for the child.

B. Social Media Injunctive Relief

Lastly, on appeal, Nicole Tinsley contends that the trial court erred in failing to enjoin Jason Tinsley, and his wife, Michelle Tinsley, from posting embarrassing photos or comments about the minor child on social media. Nicole Tinsley sought this injunction based on an incident wherein Jason Tinsley, as a means of punishment, forced the minor child to post a picture of herself on her Instagram account holding a sign that said "I WILL BE A LEADER, NOT A LIAR!!" In addition, Jason Tinsley and his wife posted the same photo on their Instagram and Facebook pages, with Jason Tinsley making this photo his profile picture on his Facebook page. Nicole Tinsley contended that this form of discipline was inappropriate, humiliating, and demeaning, and therefore, she claimed that Jason Tinsley and his wife should be prohibited from posting such pictures on social media accounts.

The trial court denied Nicole Tinsley's request for the injunction because it interpreted the request as an attempt to dictate how Jason Tinsley would parent the minor child and did not find the social media activity improper such that Nicole Tinsley should be permitted to control the rearing of the minor while the child was in Jason Tinsley's physical custody.

Louisiana Code of Civil Procedure article 3601 provides that "[a]n injunction shall be issued in cases where irreparable injury, loss, or damage may otherwise result to the applicant. . . ." The issuance of a permanent injunction takes place only after a trial on the merits in which the burden of proof must be founded on a preponderance of the evidence; hence, the manifest error standard is the appropriate standard of review for the issuance of a permanent injunction.

At trial, Jason Tinsley did not dispute that he used Instagram to publicly punish the child for telling him a lie. According to Jason Tinsley, the child had a friend over to the house and the child and her friend asked if they could ride their bikes to a park, which was approximately one-third of a mile from his house. Jason Tinsley allowed them to go to the park, but told the child and her friend that while they were there, they were not to meet up with anyone else. Jason Tinsley testified that the child and her friend then went to the park and that they spent most of the day there. When the child and her friend got back to the house, he asked them if they saw or met up with anyone while at the park and they responded "no." The next day, he saw a picture on Instagram that either the minor child or her friend had posted. The picture was of the child and her friend at the park; however, there was also a boy in the picture. Jason Tinsley claims that when he showed them the picture, they started "backtracking." He took the friend home and had a conversation with the child about the incident. He then made the child write lines, he took the picture of the child with the sign, and made the child post it on her Instagram account and he posted it on his Facebook and Instagram accounts as well. He stated that he did this so that "the family" and "her friends" could see the picture and know what she had done. Jason Tinsley admitted that the child did not want to post the picture on her Instagram account and that he did not allow her to remove the picture from her account until the next day after school and that he removed it from his account several days later. Jason Tinsley stated that he made the child post the picture because when she went to school, she had to "own" what she did—that she made a choice to lie. Jason Tinsley admitted that he thought the child was probably embarrassed by the photo, but he did not think the child was humiliated. He testified that he believed the punishment was appropriate, and that he would do it again if need be. The minor child told the trial court that she was embarrassed and humiliated by the incident.

Based on our review of the record, we cannot say that the trial court's refusal to issue an injunction against Jason Tinsley and his wife with respect to social media was manifestly erroneous. The record reasonably supports the trial court's apparent determination that there was no irreparable injury, loss, or damage that could result to Nicole Tinsley or the minor child. However, we disagree with the trial court's characterization of Nicole Tinsley's request for an injunction as an attempt to control Jason Tinsley's parenting and with its conclusion that Jason Tinsley's use of social media was not improper.

Under the circumstances of this case, we find Jason Tinsley's use of social media—particularly his forced takeover of and publishing of content on a minor child's social media account—was clearly improper and inappropriate. Jason Tinsley staged an intentionally embarrassing picture of the minor child, he then posted the embarrassing picture of the minor child on his social media accounts, and he forced the minor child to post (or publish) the embarrassing picture of herself on her own social media account, all of which was for the sole purpose of punishing the child by notifying the child's family and friends (and Jason Tinsley's family and friends) of the child's transgression—an apparent lie about a boy being at a public park while the child was at the same park with a friend. It is hard to imagine a more improper or inappropriate use of social media by a parent than to use it punitively to publicly humiliate a minor child by requiring a child to publish a photograph of herself wearing the modem day equivalent of a scarlet letter to thereby notify the public of her wrong. Accordingly, we cannot say that Nicole Tinsley's request for an injunction was an attempt to control Jason Tinsley's parenting, but rather, was an attempt to protect the minor child from further improper or inappropriate punishment and public humiliation.

However, this court, like the trial court, is reluctant to interfere with a fit parent's constitutional right to parent and make decisions for their child as they see fit. Therefore, we cannot say that the trial court's ultimate conclusion that there was no irreparable injury, loss, or damage to occur to the child or Nicole Tinsley was clearly wrong. Therefore, the trial court's decision to deny Nicole Tinsley's request for an injunction is affirmed.

CONCLUSION

For all of the above and foregoing reasons, the March 15, 2016 judgment of the trial court is reversed insofar as it modified the parties' physical custodial schedule and modified the domiciliary parent's authority by requiring the parties to mutually agree on a high school selection and ADD treatment and medication and by giving Jason Tinsley the right to select the tutor for the minor child. In addition, the trial court's decision to deny Nicole Tinsley's request for injunctive relief is affirmed. All costs of this appeal are assessed to the plaintiff/appellee, Jason Lee Tinsley

REVERSED IN PART; AFFIRMED IN PART.

E. Custody in Non-Parent

See La. Civ. Code art. 133.

Occasionally, courts will award custody to a non-parent. Because of the constitutional interest parents have in the care and custody of their children, the burden of proof required to justify awarding custody to a non-parent is higher than in parental custody cases. Louisiana Civil Code article 133 requires a showing that custody with a parent "would result in substantial harm to the child." *Remirez v. Ramirez* illustrates the application or Article 133. That case also shows how Article 134 continues to be relevant in cases involving custody in a non-parent. *In re J.E.T.* involves a stipulated custody arrangement between a parent and a non-parent. That case, in reviewing recent jurisprudence, explains that such arrangements are permitted and discusses the relevant burden of proof required to modify such an agreement. *In re J.E.T.* also illustrates some of the difficulties same-sex parents have faced in having their parental rights recognized.

Ramirez v. Ramirez
124 So. 3d 8(La. App. 5 Cir. 2013)

Fredericka Homberg Wicker, Judge.

Elba Esperanza Ramirez ("Elba"), appeals the trial court's November 26, 2012 judgment granting her sister, Reyna Ramirez ("Reyna"), the sole custody, care, and control of Elba's minor child, Carlos Enrique Ramirez ("Carlos"). Elba argues the trial court erred in this judgment because: it did not consider whether the custody award to Reyna would result in substantial harm to the minor child; it did not evaluate all of La. C.C. art. 134's factors to determine the best interest of the child; and it did not determine whether appellee would provide the minor child a wholesome and stable environment. For the following reasons we find appellant's assignments to be without merit and affirm the trial court's judgment. . . .

DISCUSSION

In this appeal, Elba argues that the trial court erred in its November 26, 2012 judgment, both in its application of the law and in the conclusion it reached. In each assignment of error, Elba argues the trial court erred when it granted sole custody of Carlos to Reyna, with only "liberal visitation" to Elba. In her assignments, Elba argues the trial court erred: first, because it did not consider whether the award of custody to Elba would result in substantial harm to the minor child; second, because it did not evaluate all of the factors set in La. C.C. art. 134 for determining the best interest of the child; and third, because it failed to determine whether Reyna would provide a wholesome and stable environment for Carlos.

In this case, Reyna, a non-parent, petitioned for sole legal custody of Carlos, a minor child, and made Elba, the child's biological parent, a defendant. The determination of Reyna's petition is governed by Louisiana Civil Code article 133. . . .

This article provides for a dual test for divesting a biological parent of the custody of his or her child. As explained by the Third Circuit:

> [B]efore a trial court deprives a parent of the custody of his or her child, the trial court must first determine that an award of custody would cause substantial harm to the child. If so, then the courts look at the best interest of the child factors in Article 134 to determine if an award of custody to a non-parent is required to serve the best interest of the child.

The burden of proof on the non-parent requires a showing that the granting of custody to the parent would result in substantial harm by clear and convincing evidence.

La. C.C. art. 133 Comment (b) states that while "substantial harm" is a change in terminology from the previous law, it is not entirely new to Louisiana jurisprudence. . . .

"The concept of substantial harm under art. 133 includes parental unfitness, neglect, abuse, abandonment of rights, and is broad enough to include 'any other circumstances, such as prolonged separation of the child from its natural parents, that would cause the child to suffer substantial harm.'"

After the non-parent meets his or her burden of proving substantial harm, the court must consider the best interest of the child. . . .

"The primary consideration and prevailing inquiry is whether the custody arrangement is in the best interest of the child."

Here, we have no indication that the trial court, in making its determination, failed to follow the law as set forth in La. C.C. arts. 133 and 134. While neither party requested separate reasons for judgment from the trial court, the transcript reveals that the trial court did consider the substantial harm Elba's status as an undocumented immigrant could cause Carlos:

> You know, and the fact that if something happens and Elba has to be deported back to Honduras, she has custody of a child. The child goes back to Honduras. He has never lived in Honduras other than visit Honduras, and so now he's taken from here. I know the same thing could happen with Reyna, too, though. If the T.P.S. [Temporary Protective Status] somehow for some reason— . . . it's not extended, then she has to go back, too. But the chances are better with Reyna it appears than with Elba.

Thereafter, the trial court acknowledged that under the applicable La. C.C. art. 133, the burden of proof was on Reyna.

While there is a dearth of jurisprudence in Louisiana on how a parent's possible deportation affects a finding of substantial harm, other states have faced this issue. . . . [T]he Supreme Court of Texas ruled that the mere threat of deportation was insufficient to establish a child's endangerment. The Supreme Court of Nebraska . . . also found that mere deportation of a parent was not sufficient for the state to terminate her parental rights. In that case, the Supreme Court of Nebraska ruled for the parent, who was currently residing in Guatemala, despite the fact that her children had lived in the United States for their entire lives.

We agree that the fact that Elba is subject to deportation is not alone sufficient to support a finding that an award of custody to Elba would result in substantial harm to Carlos. Here, however, there is more than that possibility. Here, Elba's possible deportation, combined with the uncertainty created by Elba's history of delegating the responsibility for raising her other children to others, as well as her failure to support and keep in contact with Carlos, are sufficient for the trial court to have reasonably found that Carlos would have faced substantial harm if Elba was granted custody in this case.

Additionally, the transcript from the hearing on the petition indicates that the trial judge correctly applied La. C.C. art. 133 in making its decision. The transcript of the hearing clearly shows that the trial court correctly considered Carlos' best interest to be paramount, stating:

> Let me just tell Ms. Elba Ramirez and Ms. Reyna Ramirez, it's not about the two of you. It's about Carlos, and whatever decision I make will be in the best interest of the child. And if both of you really love Carlos and you want to do what's best for him, then you will put everything that happened behind you and try to move on and allow this child to enjoy all of his family, not just part of his family.

Here, the record reflects that the trial court heard testimony on: Carlos' emotional ties to the parties; the capacity of the parties to love and provide for Carlos; the condition of the parties' residences; the moral fitness of the parties and the people that they lived with; Carlos' school history; each party's willingness and ability to facilitate and encourage a close and continuing relationship between the child and the other party; the parties' ability to drive and the distance between them; and each party's history with regard to caring for and supporting Carlos. On the record before us, we cannot find that the trial court erred in applying the law. . . .

[W]e find that the trial court did not err in its failure to explicitly make findings on all of La. C.C. art. 134's factors for determining the best interest of the child. We find that the trial court's judgment here was legally sufficient when it stated that its judgment was made, "pursuant to La. C.C. art. 133." Accordingly, to the extent that Elba argues the trial court erred in failing to make certain findings explicitly, we find Elba's assignments to be without merit.

Furthermore, we cannot say that the trial court manifestly erred in its grant of custody to Reyna and liberal visitation to Elba. Here, the evidence established that Carlos has a close connection with Reyna and calls her his "mama." The evidence also establishes that Reyna has been Carlos' primary caretaker for almost his entire life, providing him almost all of his food, shelter, clothing, medical treatment, education, and family activities. The evidence showed that Elba currently resides in the United States illegally as an undocumented immigrant and has been deported from the United States three previous times. In contrast, Reyna has Temporary Protective Status in the United States and is legally therefore allowed to live and work in this Country. Under these circumstances, we cannot say that the trial court manifestly erred when it awarded Reyna legal custody of Carlos but also gave "liberal visitation" to Elba.

Accordingly, we find Elba's assignments to be without merit, and therefore affirm the trial court's judgment.

AFFIRMED

In re J.E.T.

211 So. 3d 575 (La. App. 1 Cir. 2016)

WHIPPLE, C.J.

In this appeal, the adoptive mother of the minor child challenges the trial court's judgment denying her request for modification of a stipulated judgment of custody rendered in 2005, through which she and her female partner were granted joint custody of her adoptive son, and further denying her request to relocate with the child to the state of Texas. For the following reasons, we affirm the judgment of the trial court. Additionally, the adoptive mother's "Motion for Leave to Attach Additional Documents" is denied as moot.

FACTS AND PROCEDURAL HISTORY

Jennifer Thomas (now Nolan) and Jacqueline Calandro were involved in an intimate relationship for seventeen years, during which time they lived together in

Walker, Louisiana. During their relationship, Nolan underwent several unsuccessful in vitro fertilization procedures. Thereafter, by a judgment of adoption dated May 2, 2005, Nolan adopted the minor child whose custody is at issue, who was sixteen months old at the time of the adoption. However, the child had been residing with Nolan and Calandro since the day after he was born. At the time that Nolan adopted the child, she and Calandro had been involved in a relationship for six years.

On May 12, 2005, ten days after the adoption, Nolan and Calandro jointly filed a "Motion to Implement and Establish Joint Custody" in the district court below, through which Nolan sought a court order allowing her to jointly share the "legal care, custody and control" of her adoptive son with Calandro. By judgment dated May 12, 2005, Nolan and Calandro were granted joint legal care, custody, and control of the minor child. . . .

Thereafter, Nolan and Calandro resided together with the minor child in Calandro's home in Walker, Louisiana until March of 2015, when Nolan moved out of the home. On June 23, 2015, approximately three months after ending her relationship with Calandro, Nolan married Scott Nolan, a colonel in the United States Army stationed in Austin, Texas.

On February 24, 2015, shortly before Nolan moved out of Calandro's home, Calandro filed a Rule to Show Cause, wherein, based on concerns that Nolan planned to relocate outside of the state of Louisiana with the minor child, she sought an order prohibiting either party from removing the child from the state and allocating physical custody of the minor child to her and Nolan on a week-to-week basis. An order was entered on March 2, 2015, prohibiting the parties from removing the minor child from the state of Louisiana until a hearing on the issue of physical allocation of custody could be held.

Nolan then filed a "Rule for Sole Custody and to Relocate the Minor Child" on September 28, 2015.2 In the rule, Nolan asserted that a material change in circumstances had occurred since the rendition of the 2005 stipulated judgment in that she and Calandro were no longer intimate partners, that she intended to relocate to Texas and that she was the only legal parent of the child. Thus, Nolan sought to have the 2005 stipulated judgment modified to reflect that she is the child's only legal parent, to grant her sole custody of the child, and further that she be allowed to relocate with the child to the state of Texas.

A hearing on the rules was conducted on November 4, 2015. By judgment dated November 17, 2015, the trial court denied Nolan's request to modify the award of joint custody to sole custody and further denied her request to relocate with the child to the state of Texas. The court further designated specific periods of physical custody for the parties in a Joint Custody Plan attached to the judgment.

From this judgment, Nolan appeals. . . .

VALIDITY OF THE MAY 12, 2005 STIPULATED JUDGMENT

On appeal, Nolan first contends that the May 12, 2005 stipulated judgment is an absolute nullity pursuant to this court's prior decision in *In re Melancon*. . . .

At the outset, we note that the May 12, 2005 judgment is a stipulated judgment between the parties. A consent or a stipulated judgment is a bilateral contract by which the parties adjust their differences by mutual consent, with each party balancing his hope of gain against his fear of loss. Its binding force arises from the voluntary acquiescence of the parties rather than the adjudication by the court.

Thus, generally, there is no right to appeal a stipulated or consent judgment . . . because "[a]n appeal cannot be taken by a party who confessed judgment in the proceedings in the trial court or who voluntarily and unconditionally acquiesced in a judgment rendered against him."

Moreover, the only remedy available to a party seeking to set aside a final judgment is a claim in nullity. The nullity of a final judgment may be demanded for vices of either form or substance. A vice of form renders the judgment an absolute nullity. Additionally, with regard to a consent judgment, which is a bilateral contract between the parties, a consent judgment may be absolutely null or void ab initio if it contains a condition that is contra bonos mores.

While relatively null judgments must be attacked directly and within the time limitation set forth in LSA-C.C.P. art. 2004, absolutely null judgments may be attacked collaterally, at any time, by rule or by any other method. Such a collateral attack may include the assertion of the absolute nullity of a judgment as an affirmative defense, such as in an answer, by exception, or by contradictory rule or motion.

In support of her argument that the May 12, 2005 stipulated judgment is an absolute nullity, Nolan contends that the judgment "should never have been signed by the district court" because there had been no determination pursuant to LSA-C.C. art. 133 that her sole custody of the minor child "would cause substantial harm to the child."

Custody matters are governed by Chapter 2, Section 3 of the Louisiana Civil Code. Pursuant to LSA-C.C. art. 132 therein, parents may consent to a custody arrangement as follows:

> If the parents agree who is to have custody, the court shall award custody in accordance with their agreement unless the best interest of the child requires a different award.

On the other hand, with regard to a court's award of custody to a non-parent, LSA-C.C. art. 133 provides as follows:

> If an award of joint custody or of sole custody to either parent would result in substantial harm to the child, the court shall award custody to another person with whom the child has been living in a wholesome and stable environment, or otherwise to any other person able to provide an adequate and stable environment.

In support of her contention that custody of the minor child herein should have been governed by LSA-C.C. art. 133 at the time the 2005 stipulated judgment was rendered and that it is accordingly absolutely null for lack of compliance with that article, Nolan relies upon this court's opinion in *Melancon* wherein this court found that a situation involving a parent's consent to shared custody between the parent and a non-parent was governed by LSA-C.C. art. 133, rather than article 132. Citing *Melancon*, Nolan asserts in her appellate brief that the 2005 stipulated judgment awarding her and Calandro joint custody should have never been signed because at the time of its rendition, no right of action was presented to the court, and the requested relief was not supported by the law of this state. Thus, she contends that the May 12, 2005 stipulated judgment is "illicit and contra bonos mores" and that the trial court erred in failing to recognize that it was absolutely null and void ab initio. However, in light of more recent Louisiana Supreme Court jurisprudence, we are constrained to conclude that the above statements in *Melancon* cannot be relied upon to support Nolan's position.

In *Melancon*, a minor child was conceived by artificial insemination and had only one known biological parent, her mother. Since the child's birth, the child and her biological mother resided with the petitioner, who was also a woman. The petitioner filed an unopposed petition to share custody of the child with the child's biological mother and attached to the petition the affidavit of the biological mother, in which she consented to joint custody of the minor child between herself and the petitioner. Thus, a consent judgment of joint custody was submitted to the trial court.

However, the trial court, on its own motion, raised and maintained an exception of no cause of action on the basis that the pleadings contained no allegation that an award of sole custody to the child's biological mother would cause substantial harm to the child, as required pursuant to LSA-C.C. art. 133 for an award of custody to a non-parent.

On appeal, the petitioner therein argued that since there was no dispute between her and the biological mother regarding the best interest of the child being served by the award of joint custody, the trial court should have awarded her joint custody pursuant to LSA-C.C. art. 132, which allows a parent to consent to a custodial arrangement. As to any claim under LSA-C.C. art. 132, this court sua sponte raised and maintained an exception of no right of action. Specifically, this court held that LSA-C.C. art. 132 discloses causes of action for shared or joint custody only to legal parents. Noting that the petitioner was not a legal parent, the court held that she was "not a member of the class of persons that has a legal interest in the subject matter of the litigation." Furthermore, with regard to any claim pursuant to LSA-C.C. art. 133, this court affirmed the trial court's judgment maintaining the exception of no cause of action, noting that the petitioner had failed to allege that sole custody by the parent would result in substantial harm to the child. In so ruling, as asserted by Nolan, the court in *Melancon* expressly concluded (in 2011) that "the law today simply does not permit a parent to share custody with a non-parent without a showing of substantial harm to the child."

However, the recent Louisiana Supreme Court decision in *Tracie F. v. Francisco D.*, casts serious doubt on the viability or validity of that statement in *Melancon*. In *Tracie F.*, the mother and father of a minor child and the maternal grandmother had all consented to a judgment whereby joint custody was awarded to the father and the grandmother, with the grandmother designated as the domiciliary parent. Thereafter, the father filed a rule to change custody, seeking sole custody or, alternatively, to be named the domiciliary parent. While the trial court modified the prior stipulated judgment of joint custody to award sole custody to the father, the appellate court reversed and reinstated the stipulated award of joint custody.

On review, the Louisiana Supreme Court first addressed the appropriate burden of proof that a parent must meet when the parent consents to an award of joint custody between the parent and the non-parent and later petitions to change the stipulated award. Rather than questioning a parent's right to consent to a stipulated judgment of joint custody with a non-parent, the Louisiana Supreme Court clearly recognized a parent's right to consent to such a judgment wherein the parent shares legal custody of the child with a non-parent. Noting that a stipulated judgment of custody is a judgment rendered when the parties consent to a custodial arrangement and no evidence of parental fitness is taken, the Louisiana Supreme Court acknowledged that "[i]ndeed, it is foreseeable that because of youth, impecunity, or other life situations, a parent might consent to a non-parent serving the role of a domiciliary parent." The Louisiana Supreme Court then articulated the appropriate burden of proof where "the parent has been fortunate enough to find such a person with whom to share joint custody," but later petitions to change the stipulated award of joint custody between the parent and non-parent. The Louisiana Supreme Court made no indication that such a stipulated judgment of joint custody between a parent and non-parent would be void ab initio as being contra bonos mores.

Based on the reasoning set forth by the Louisiana Supreme Court in *Tracie F.* and the Court's articulation of the appropriate burden of proof a parent must establish when seeking modification of a stipulated judgment (i.e., a stipulated judgment consented to by the parties with no prior determination of parental fitness) through which the parent had consented to joint custody between the parent and a non-parent, we must conclude that this court's 2011 statement in *In re Melancon*, that "the law today simply does not permit a parent to share custody with a non-parent without a showing [that sole custody by the parent would result in] . . . substantial harm to the child" is not an accurate statement of law. Rather, *Tracie F.* warrants the conclusion that stipulated judgments of joint custody between a parent and a non-parent are allowable and supported under the law of this state. . . . For these reasons, we find no merit to Nolan's contention that the trial court erred in failing to recognize the absolute nullity of the May 12, 2005 stipulated judgment awarding custody of the minor child to her and Calandro jointly.

APPROPRIATE BURDEN OF PROOF FOR MODIFICATION OF STIPULATED JUDGMENT OF JOINT CUSTODY

Nolan next argues that the trial court erred by applying the incorrect burden of proof when evaluating her request for a modification of custody. In declining to modify the May 12, 2005 stipulated joint custody judgment, the trial court herein charged Nolan, as the moving party, with the burden of proving that a material change in circumstances affecting the child had occurred and that the proposed modification to sole custody was in the child's best interest. Nolan contends, however, that the burden of proof herein should have been placed on Calandro, given her status as a non-parent, and that she should have had the burden of establishing, as in an initial contest of custody between a parent and non-parent pursuant to LSA-C.C. art. 133, that the grant of sole custody to Nolan, as the legal parent, would result in substantial harm to the child.

Nolan acknowledges that in *Tracie F.,* the Louisiana Supreme Court held that a parent, as the party seeking to modify a stipulated judgment that granted joint custody to the parent and a non-parent, had the burden, as in all other modification cases involving stipulated judgments, of proving that: (1) there has been a material change in circumstances since the original custody decree was entered, and (2) the proposed modification is in the best interest of the child. . . .

Nonetheless, Nolan maintains that all cases involving custody of a child between a parent and a non-parent require a LSA-C.C. art. 133 determination of parental fitness and tries to distinguish *Tracie F.* and *Varner* from the present case on the asserted basis that in both of those cases, "something negative was going on in the biological parents' lives at the time they entered into the respective stipulated judgments that demonstrated the action was in the best interest of the children involved." Hence, she contends that those cases involved "a determination of parental fitness by consent." In essence, she contends that because the parents in those cases were going through "something negative" in their lives, their actions in consenting to the granting of custody to a non-parent should be deemed also as consent to an implicit determination as to their unfitness. Thus, Nolan contends that the burden of proof imposed on the parents seeking modification of the consent judgments in those cases is inapplicable to this matter, where Nolan's fitness has never been addressed or even questioned.

To the contrary, however, the Louisiana Supreme Court in *Tracie F.* specifically recognized, in addressing a situation where there was a prior stipulated judgment of joint custody by a parent and non-parent, that a stipulated judgment is a judgment rendered by the court where the parties consent to the custodial arrangement and where no evidence of parental fitness is taken. Moreover, in articulating the appropriate burden of proof, the Louisiana Supreme Court specifically discussed and rejected the approach . . . that an initial consent judgment awarding custody to a parent and non-parent with the non-parent as domiciliary parent operates as an acknowledgement or determination both of the parent's unfitness and the fitness of the non-parent. Thus, any suggestion that the Court in *Tracie F.* established the appropriate burden of proof for modification of a stipulated judgment of custody between a parent and non-parent on the basis that the prior agreement by the parent therein to share custody with a non-parent implies some sort of determination of parental unfitness by consent of the parent is simply unfounded.

Accordingly, we find no merit to Nolan's assertion that the trial court, in applying the same burden later articulated by the Supreme Court in *Tracie F.,* imposed the incorrect burden of proof upon her when considering whether to modify the May 12, 2005 stipulated judgment of joint custody to an award of sole custody in her favor. . . .

JUDGMENT AFFIRMED.

F. Parental Visitation Rights

See LA. CIV. CODE art. 136–37.

Generally, if a parent is not afforded custody of a child, the parent will still be awarded visitation rights. Civil Code article 136 explains that a parent is entitled to "reasonable visitation rights unless the court finds, after a hearing, that visitation would not be in the best interest of the child." Article 137 specifically denies visitation rights in certain circumstances involving criminal activity. As *Leeper v. Leeper* demonstrates, denying a parent visitation rights usually involves severe factual scenarios.

Leeper v. Leeper
21 So. 3d 1006 (La. App. 2 Cir. 2009)

GASKINS, J.

This appeal arises from a judgment in which the trial court awarded sole custody of a seven-year-old boy to his father and refused to order that the child visit his mother in prison. . . .

We affirm the trial court judgment.

FACTS

The parents, Gerald and Karen Leeper, were married in January 2002 in Jefferson Parish following the September 2001 birth of their son. The mother was incarcerated from February 2002 to May 2004. After her release, the family lived together in Jefferson Parish.

In April 2006, the mother was sentenced to six years at hard labor for possession of cocaine; pursuant to a plea bargain, a charge of possession of hydrocodone was dismissed. In May 2006, a Jefferson Parish district court order designated the father as the domiciliary parent in a joint custody plan. Because the mother was in prison, no visitation was ordered; the court stated that the mother had reasonable contact with the child by phone or mail. The father and the child moved to Ouachita Parish that same month.

In March 2008, the father filed the instant petition for divorce and custody in Ouachita Parish. He requested sole custody of the child or, in the alternative, joint custody with domiciliary custody to him and reasonable contact by phone or mail with the mother. The father asserted that visiting with the mother in prison and/or contact with her had caused the child distress. He alleged that he and the child moved to Monroe due to threats by persons associated with the mother.

On April 14, 2008, the mother answered in proper person, requesting joint custody and visitation with the child. As to visitation, she cited a "caring parents" program at the prison. The trial court did not sign an order for the mother to be brought from prison to a hearing. . . . [The mother was not granted permission to attend the various hearings.]

On April 15, 2009, the HOC was held. The father and his attorney were present but the mother, who was served, did not appear. Various findings of undisputed fact were made, including the following. The father had not taken the child to the prison to visit the mother for more than a year. Previously, he had taken the child on some occasions; however, the child became upset during the visits and he had indicated a desire to not return to the prison to visit. During 2007 and early 2008, the mother attempted to maintain contact through cards and letters. Each parent contended that threats have been made by the other parent or persons associated with the other parent. The mother's release date from prison is in 2012. There were also statements that the mother had sought sexual encounters through ads in publications.

The hearing officer concluded that 10 of the 12 factors set forth in La. C.C. art. 134 favored the father and that the two remaining factors—preference of the child and willingness to encourage a relationship with the other parent—did not favor either party. As a result, sole custody to the father was found to be in the child's best interest. Additionally, the hearing officer found that visitation with the mother at the prison at St. Gabriel would place a substantial burden of travel on the father and the child and would likely be upsetting to the child. Instead, the hearing officer held that it would be in the child's best interest for the mother to communicate by mail. The hearing officer also stated that after her release, the mother can file pleadings seeking visitation. The HOC report was filed April 16, 2009.

On April 16, 2009, the trial court signed a judgment adopting and implementing the hearing officer's recommendations. . . .

The mother appeals from the trial court judgment. She requests that joint custody of the child be granted and that the child be compelled to visit her in prison.

LAW

The paramount consideration in any determination of child custody is the best interest of the child. La. C.C. art. 131. In order to obtain an award of sole custody, the parent seeking custody must prove by clear and convincing evidence that sole custody, as opposed to joint custody, is in the best interest of the child. La. C.C. art. 132. A parent not granted custody or joint custody of a child is entitled to reasonable visitation rights unless the court finds, after a hearing, that visitation would not be in the best interest of the child. La. C.C. art. 136.

The jurisprudence emphasizes that the best interest of the child is the sole criterion for determining a noncustodial parent's right to visitation. Because each case depends on its own facts, the determination regarding visitation is made on a case-by-case basis. Great weight is given to the trial court's determination, and the court's judgment will not be overturned unless a clear abuse of discretion is shown. . . .

A prisoner has a right of access to state and federal civil courts. However, this right does not necessarily include the right to be physically present at the trial of a civil suit. Generally, prisoners who bring civil actions have no right to be personally present in court at any stage of the action. Lawful incarceration brings about the necessary withdrawal or limitation of many privileges and rights, among which is the right of a prisoner to plead and manage his action in court personally.

It is not unusual for individuals who are incarcerated to be parties to civil litigation, either as plaintiff or defendant, and a writ of habeas corpus ad testificandum is the means for such individuals to be present in court. Prisoners who are parties to litigation utilize this mechanism to obtain their presence in court.

The determination of whether a prisoner-party in a civil action should appear personally in court for the trial of the action rests in the discretion of the trial court.

DISCUSSION

The record shows that the mother was served with the notice for the HOC. While the mother filed requests to be present at other proceedings, she did not file one specifically for the HOC. Accordingly, since she failed to take the necessary steps to secure her presence at the hearing, she cannot complain now that she was not there. Nor can she be heard to complain about the fact that her absence from the HOC waived her right to object to the recommendations in the HOC report, which the trial court then adopted and implemented in its judgment.

Furthermore, even assuming arguendo that the mother's "motion to appeal" filed on March 6, 2009, could be construed as a request to be present at the HOC, nothing in the record indicates an abuse of the trial court's discretion in denying the same. As an incarcerated inmate, the mother had no absolute right to be physically present at such a hearing.

The record demonstrates that the mother has been absent for most of the child's life due to her incarcerations for criminal activities. The father has been the child's primary caregiver since infancy. Under the circumstances of the instant case, we find no error in the trial court's determination that the father proved by clear and convincing evidence that granting him sole custody was in the child's best interest. On the issue of visitation, the hearing officer and the trial court found that visitation at the prison was not in the best interest of the child. The father indicated that the prior visits to the mother in prison were distressing to this young child. We find that the trial court's refusal to force the child to visit the mother in the confines of a state prison — an activity which upset the child in the past — is not an abuse of discretion.

We note that following her release from prison, the mother will have the opportunity to seek a modification of custody and/or visitation. In the meantime, the mother is allowed to reasonably maintain her relationship with the child through communication by mail.

CONCLUSION

The judgment of the trial court is affirmed. Costs of this appeal are assessed against the mother, Karen Leeper.

G. Visitation Rights of Non-Parents

See LA. CIV. CODE art. 136; LA. REV. STAT. § 9:344.

A number of states, including Louisiana, have enacted laws allowing non-parents (such as grandparents) to seek visitation with a child. These statutes can, in some cases, infringe on the constitutional rights of parents to determine the care, custody, and control of their minor children. The issue reached the Supreme Court in *Troxel v. Granville*, below.

Troxel v. Granville

530 U.S. 57 (2000)

Justice O'CONNOR announced the judgment of the Court and delivered an opinion, in which THE CHIEF JUSTICE, Justice GINSBURG, and Justice BREYER join.

Section 26.10.160(3) of the Revised Code of Washington permits "[a]ny person" to petition a superior court for visitation rights "at any time," and authorizes that court to grant such visitation rights whenever "visitation may serve the best interest of the child." Petitioners Jenifer and Gary Troxel petitioned a Washington Superior Court for the right to visit their grandchildren, Isabelle and Natalie Troxel. Respondent Tommie Granville, the mother of Isabelle and Natalie, opposed the petition. The case ultimately reached the Washington Supreme Court, which held that § 26.10.160(3) unconstitutionally interferes with the fundamental right of parents to rear their children.

I

Tommie Granville and Brad Troxel shared a relationship that ended in June 1991. The two never married, but they had two daughters, Isabelle and Natalie. Jenifer and Gary Troxel are Brad's parents, and thus the paternal grandparents of Isabelle and Natalie. After Tommie and Brad separated in 1991, Brad lived with his parents and regularly brought his daughters to his parents' home for weekend visitation. Brad committed suicide in May 1993. Although the Troxels at first continued to see Isabelle and Natalie on a regular basis after their son's death, Tommie Granville informed the Troxels in October 1993 that she wished to limit their visitation with her daughters to one short visit per month.

In December 1993, the Troxels commenced the present action by filing, in the Washington Superior Court for Skagit County, a petition to obtain visitation rights with Isabelle and Natalie. The Troxels filed their petition under two Washington statutes, Wash. Rev.Code §§ 26.09.240 and 26.10.160(3) (1994). Only the latter statute is at issue in this case. Section 26.10.160(3) provides: "Any person may petition the court for visitation rights at any time including, but not limited to, custody proceedings. The court may order visitation rights for any person when visitation may serve the best interest of the child whether or not there has been any change of circumstances." At trial, the Troxels requested two weekends of overnight visitation per month and two weeks of visitation each summer. Granville did not oppose visitation altogether, but instead asked the court to order one day of visitation per month with no overnight stay. In 1995, the Superior Court issued an oral ruling and entered a visitation decree ordering visitation one weekend per month, one week during the summer, and four hours on both of the petitioning grandparents' birthdays.

Granville appealed, during which time she married Kelly Wynn. Before addressing the merits of Granville's appeal, the Washington Court of Appeals remanded the case to the Superior Court for entry of written findings of fact and conclusions of law. On remand, the Superior Court found that visitation was in Isabelle's and Natalie's best interests. . . .

Approximately nine months after the Superior Court entered its order on remand, Granville's husband formally adopted Isabelle and Natalie.

The Washington Court of Appeals reversed the lower court's visitation order and dismissed the Troxels' petition for visitation, holding that nonparents lack standing to seek visitation under § 26.10.160(3) unless a custody action is pending. In the Court of Appeals' view, that limitation on nonparental visitation actions was "consistent with the constitutional restrictions on state interference with parents' fundamental liberty interest in the care, custody, and management of their children." Having resolved the case on the statutory ground, however, the Court of Appeals did not expressly pass on Granville's constitutional challenge to the visitation statute.

The Washington Supreme Court granted the Troxels' petition for review and, after consolidating their case with two other visitation cases, affirmed. The court disagreed with the Court of Appeals' decision on the statutory issue and found that the plain language of § 26.10.160(3) gave the Troxels standing to seek visitation, irrespective of whether a custody action was pending. The Washington Supreme Court nevertheless agreed with the Court of Appeals' ultimate conclusion that the Troxels could not obtain visitation of Isabelle and Natalie pursuant to § 26.10.160(3). The court rested its decision on the Federal Constitution, holding that § 26.10.160(3) unconstitutionally infringes on the fundamental right of parents to rear their children. In the court's view, there were at least two problems with the nonparental visitation statute. First, according to the Washington Supreme Court, the Constitution permits a State to interfere with the right of parents to rear their children only to prevent harm or potential harm to a child. Section 26.10.160(3) fails that standard because it requires no threshold showing of harm. Second, by allowing " 'any person' to petition for forced visitation of a child at 'any time' with the only requirement being that the visitation serve the best interest of the child," the Washington visitation statute sweeps too broadly. "It is not within the province of the state to make significant decisions concerning the custody of children merely because it could make a 'better' decision." The Washington Supreme Court held that "[p]arents have a right to limit visitation of their children with third persons," and that between parents and judges, "the parents should be the ones to choose whether to expose their children to certain people or ideas." Four justices dissented from the Washington Supreme Court's holding on the constitutionality of the statute.

We granted certiorari, and now affirm the judgment.

II

. . . The nationwide enactment of nonparental visitation statutes is assuredly due, in some part, to the States' recognition of these changing realities of the American family. Because grandparents and other relatives undertake duties of a parental nature in many households, States have sought to ensure the welfare of the children therein by protecting the relationships those children form with such third parties. The States' nonparental visitation statutes are further supported by a recognition, which varies from State to State, that children should have the opportunity to benefit from relationships with statutorily specified persons—for example, their grandparents. The extension of statutory rights in this area to persons other than a child's parents, however, comes with an obvious cost. For example, the State's recognition of an independent third-party interest in a child can place a substantial burden on the traditional parent-child relationship. . . .

The Fourteenth Amendment provides that no State shall "deprive any person of life, liberty, or property, without due process of law." We have long recognized that the Amendment's Due Process Clause, like its Fifth Amendment counterpart, "guarantees more than fair process." The Clause also includes a substantive component that "provides heightened protection against government interference with certain fundamental rights and liberty interests."

The liberty interest at issue in this case—the interest of parents in the care, custody, and control of their children—is perhaps the oldest of the fundamental liberty interests recognized by this Court. . . .

In light of this extensive precedent, it cannot now be doubted that the Due Process Clause of the Fourteenth Amendment protects the fundamental right of parents to make decisions concerning the care, custody, and control of their children.

Section 26.10.160(3), as applied to Granville and her family in this case, unconstitutionally infringes on that fundamental parental right. The Washington nonparental visitation statute is breathtakingly broad. According to the statute's text, "[a]ny person may petition the court for visitation rights at any time," and the court may grant such visitation rights whenever "visitation may serve the best interest of the child." § 26.10.160(3) (emphases added). That language effectively permits any third party seeking visitation to subject any decision by a parent concerning visitation of the parent's children to state-court review. Once the visitation petition has been filed in court and the matter is placed before a judge, a parent's decision that visitation would not be in the child's best interest is accorded no deference. Section 26.10.160(3) contains no requirement that a court accord the parent's decision any presumption of validity or any weight whatsoever. Instead, the Washington statute places the best-interest determination solely in the hands of the judge. Should the judge disagree with the parent's estimation of the child's best interests, the judge's view necessarily prevails. Thus, in practical effect, in the State of Washington a court can disregard and overturn any decision by a fit custodial parent concerning visitation whenever a third party affected by the decision files a visitation petition, based solely on the judge's determination of the child's best interests. The Washington Supreme Court had the opportunity to give § 26.10.160(3) a narrower reading, but it declined to do so.

Turning to the facts of this case, the record reveals that the Superior Court's order was based on precisely the type of mere disagreement we have just described and nothing more. The Superior Court's order was not founded on any special factors that might justify the State's interference with Granville's fundamental right to make decisions concerning the rearing of her two daughters. To be sure, this case involves a visitation petition filed by grandparents soon after the death of their son—the father of Isabelle and Natalie—but the combination of several factors here compels our conclusion that § 26.10.160(3), as applied, exceeded the bounds of the Due Process Clause.

First, the Troxels did not allege, and no court has found, that Granville was an unfit parent. That aspect of the case is important, for there is a presumption that fit parents act in the best interests of their children. . . .

Accordingly, so long as a parent adequately cares for his or her children (i.e., is fit), there will normally be no reason for the State to inject itself into the private realm of the family to further question the ability of that parent to make the best decisions concerning the rearing of that parent's children.

The problem here is not that the Washington Superior Court intervened, but that when it did so, it gave no special weight at all to Granville's determination of her daughters' best interests. More importantly, it appears that the Superior Court applied exactly the opposite presumption. In reciting its oral ruling after the conclusion of closing arguments, the Superior Court judge explained:

> "The burden is to show that it is in the best interest of the children to have some visitation and some quality time with their grandparents. I think in most situations a commonsensical approach [is that] it is normally in the best interest of the children to spend quality time with the grandparent, unless the grandparent, [sic] there are some issues or problems involved wherein the grandparents, their lifestyles are going to impact adversely upon the children. That certainly isn't the case here from what I can tell."

The judge's comments suggest that he presumed the grandparents' request should be granted unless the children would be "impact[ed] adversely." In effect, the judge placed on Granville, the fit custodial parent, the burden of disproving that visitation would be in the best interest of her daughters. The judge reiterated moments later: "I think [visitation with the Troxels] would be in the best interest of the children and I haven't been shown it is not in [the] best interest of the children."

The decisional framework employed by the Superior Court directly contravened the traditional presumption that a fit parent will act in the best interest of his or her child. In that respect, the court's presumption failed to provide any protection for Granville's fundamental constitutional right to make decisions concerning the rearing of her own daughters. . . . In an ideal world, parents might always seek to cultivate the bonds between grandparents and their grandchildren. Needless to say, however, our world is far from perfect, and in it the decision whether such an intergenerational relationship would be beneficial in any specific case is for the parent to make in the first instance. And, if a fit parent's decision of the kind at issue here becomes subject to judicial review, the court must accord at least some special weight to the parent's own determination.

Finally, we note that there is no allegation that Granville ever sought to cut off visitation entirely. Rather, the present dispute originated when Granville informed the Troxels that she would prefer to restrict their visitation with Isabelle and Natalie to one short visit per month and special holidays. In the Superior Court proceedings Granville did not oppose visitation but instead asked that the duration of any visitation order be shorter than that requested by the Troxels. While the Troxels requested two weekends per month and two full weeks in the summer, Granville asked the Superior Court to order only one day of visitation per month (with no overnight stay) and participation in the Granville family's holiday celebrations. . . . The Superior Court gave no weight to Granville's having assented to visitation even before the filing of any visitation petition or subsequent court intervention. The court instead rejected Granville's proposal and settled on a middle ground, ordering one weekend of visitation per month, one week in the summer, and time on both of the petitioning grandparents' birthdays. Significantly, many other States expressly provide by statute that courts may not award visitation unless a parent has denied (or unreasonably denied) visitation to the concerned third party.

Considered together with the Superior Court's reasons for awarding visitation to the Troxels, the combination of these factors demonstrates that the visitation order in this case was an unconstitutional infringement on Granville's fundamental right to make decisions concerning the care, custody, and control of her two daughters. The Washington Superior Court failed to accord the determination of Granville, a fit custodial parent, any material weight. In fact, the Superior Court made only two formal findings in support of its visitation order. First, the Troxels "are part of a large, central, loving family, all located in this area, and the [Troxels] can provide opportunities for the children in the areas of cousins and music." Second, "[t]he children would be benefitted from spending quality time with the [Troxels], provided that that time is balanced with time with the childrens' [sic] nuclear family." These slender findings, in combination with the court's announced presumption in favor of grandparent visitation and its failure to accord significant weight to Granville's already having offered meaningful visitation to the Troxels, show that this case involves nothing more than a simple disagreement between the Washington Superior Court and Granville concerning her children's best interests. The Superior Court's announced reason for ordering one week of visitation in the summer demonstrates our conclusion well: "I look back on some personal experiences. . . . We always spen[t] as kids a week with one set of grandparents and another set of grandparents, [and] it happened to work out in our family that [it] turned out to be an enjoyable experience. Maybe that can, in this family, if that is how it works out." As we have explained, the Due Process Clause does not permit a State to infringe on the fundamental right of parents to make child rearing decisions simply because a state judge believes a "better" decision could be made. Neither the Washington nonparental visitation statute generally—which places no limits on either the persons who may petition for visitation or the circumstances in which such a petition may be granted—nor the Superior Court in this specific case required anything more. Accordingly, we hold that §26.10.160(3), as applied in this case, is unconstitutional.

Because we rest our decision on the sweeping breadth of §26.10.160(3) and the application of that broad, unlimited power in this case, we do not consider the primary constitutional question passed on by the Washington Supreme Court—whether the Due Process Clause requires all nonparental visitation statutes to include a showing of harm or potential harm to the child as a condition precedent to granting visitation. We do not, and need not, define today the precise scope of the parental due process right in the visitation context. . . .

There is thus no reason to remand the case for further proceedings in the Washington Supreme Court. As Justice KENNEDY recognizes, the burden of litigating a domestic relations proceeding can itself be "so disruptive of the parent-child relationship that the constitutional right of a custodial parent to make certain basic determinations for the child's welfare becomes implicated." In this case, the litigation costs incurred by Granville on her trip through the Washington court system and to this Court are without a doubt already substantial. As we have explained, it is apparent that the entry of the visitation order in this case violated the Constitution. We should say so now, without forcing the parties into additional litigation that would further burden Granville's parental right. We therefore hold that the application of §26.10.160(3) to Granville and her family violated her due process right to make decisions concerning the care, custody, and control of her daughters.

Accordingly, the judgment of the Washington Supreme Court is affirmed.

It is so ordered.

Chapter 15

Child Support

A. History & Evolution of Child Support

Both common law and civil law have long recognized that parents have a natural obligation to support and educate their children. In *Greenspan v. Slate*, the New Jersey Supreme Court explained that this natural law concept is express in the civil codes of many countries:

> The course of the Roman law and the modern civil law of Western Europe, which is based on it, suggests that the common law rule, which we are now discarding in favor of the equitable doctrine, may be merely an instance of early undeveloped law. In the Roman law the duty of a father to support his child was enforced only by criminal proceedings, but in the modern civil law the obligation of the parents is direct:
>
> 'The duty of taking care of the children's support until such time as they are capable of supporting themselves is primarily incumbent on the father. Their physical care is primarily incumbent on the mother. In the event that the father is indigent the duty to take care of the children's support and in the event of the father's death (the duty to take care of) the children's education in general, is primarily incumbent on the mother. In the event that the mother shall not survive (the father) or is indigent, such duty is incumbent upon the paternal grandparents or, subordinately, on the maternal grandparents.' Austrian Civil Law, sec. 143.
>
> 'Spouses are jointly obligated, by reason of the sole fact of contracting marriage, to feed, support and educate their children.' French Civil Code, Art. 203.
>
> 'Relatives in the line of direct descendants are under the obligation of supporting each other.' German Civil Code, sec. 1601.
>
> 'Only the one who is incapable of supporting himself is entitled to support. An infant unmarried child may require his parents to support him although he own property, to the extent to which the income from his property and from his own work are not sufficient for his support.' *Ibid.*, sec. 1602.
>
> 'Duties towards the Children.— Marriage imposes upon both spouses the duty to support and to give an education and instruction to the issue.

393

Education and instruction must conform to moral principles.' Italian Civil Code, Art. 147.

'Contribution to the Burdens. — The duty of supporting and of giving an education and instruction to the issue is borne by the father and by the mother in proportion to their property, including in the mother's contribution income from her dowry. If the parents do not have sufficient means, such duty falls on the other ascendants according to their order of proximity to the infants.' *Ibid.*, Art. 148.

'The father and the mother and the child owe each other the care and assistance which are required in the interest of the family.' Swiss Civil Code, Art. 271.

'The father and the mother shall bear the expenses for the support and education of the child (and they shall share in them) according to their matrimonial regime. If they are in need or if the child causes extraordinary expenses or under other exceptional circumstances, the supervising (judicial) authority may allow the father and the mother to subject the property of the infant child to contribution for his support and education to the extent fixed by it.' *Ibid.*, Art. 272.[1]

Common law likewise recognized a natural obligation of parents to support their children. This obligation, however, was difficult if not impossible to enforce from a legal perspective. Drawing inspiration, in part, from modern civil codes, American courts and legislatures began to devise rules that required a father to provide support for his minor children in accordance with his means. By the early 1900s, most American states had laws requiring support and contemplating a legal process for obtaining it.

The federal government became involved in child support and related issues — eventually resulting in some measure of similarity among the states. Title IV of the Social Security Act of 1935 — the Aid to Dependent Children Act — established a partnership between state and federal governments under which states received federal funding to help provide support to children of poor parents. After several failed efforts to improve child support programs over the years, Congress enacted the Family Support Act of 1974 — also known as Title IV-D of the Social Security Act. This amendment began an era of increased federal oversight and involvement in child support and related matters. This trend continued through subsequent amendments. The 1984 Child Support Enforcement Amendments, for example, required states to implement various enforcement mechanisms to facilitate collection of child support — such as wage garnishments, real estate liens, and deductions from state and federal income tax refunds. The 1984 Amendments also established a national advisory panel on child support guidelines to develop some advisory guidelines for

---

1. Greenspan v. Slate, 97 A.2d 390 (N.J. 1953).

determining child support awards. A few years later, the Family Support Act of 1988 mandated that states enact mandatory (rather than advisory) child support guidelines by 1994.

States were required to enact, and then periodically update, child support guidelines which considered a number of factors prescribed by federal law. States were, however, given some latitude in deciding how to implement these requirements. Nationally, several models of implementing the child support guidelines emerged: (1) the income shares model; (2) the percentage of income model; and (3) the Melson formula.

Income Shares. The income shares model is by far the most widely adopted child-support model—it has been adopted by at least 39 states, including Louisiana. This model is based on the underlying theory that the child should not suffer the economic consequences of divorce or non-marital parentage. This idea is clearly expressed in La. Rev. Stat. § 9:315:

> The premise of these guidelines as well as the provisions of the Civil Code is that child support is a continuous obligation of both parents, children are entitled to share in the current income of both parents, and children should not be the economic victims of divorce or out-of-wedlock birth. The economic data underlying these guidelines, which adopt the Income Shares Model, and the guideline calculations attempt to simulate the percentage of parental net income that is spent on children in intact families incorporating a consideration of the expenses of the parties, such as federal and state taxes and FICA taxes. While the legislature acknowledges that the expenditures of two-household divorced, separated, or non-formed families are different from intact family households, it is very important that the children of this state not be forced to live in poverty because of family disruption and that they be afforded the same opportunities available to children in intact families, consisting of parents with similar financial means to those of their own parents. . . .
>
> In intact families, the income of both parents is pooled and spent for the benefit of all household members, including the children. Each parent's contribution to the combined income of the family represents his relative sharing of household expenses. This same income sharing principle is used to determine how the parents will share a child support award.

Generally, income shares models are based on the idea that support should be determined by considering the income levels of each parent and their relative custodial time.

Melson Formula. The Melson Formula is a variation of the income shares approach developed by (and named after) a Delaware judge. The main difference between the Melson Formula and a typical income shares model is that the Melson formula also considers the economic needs of the parents. The Melson approach is used in

Delaware, Hawaii, and Montana. The Delaware Supreme Court described the origin and purpose of the formula as follows:

> The Melson Formula is named after its judicial craftsman, Judge Elwood F. Melson, Jr. of the Family Court of the State of Delaware. The formula was developed by Judge Melson in response to the directive of 13 Del.C. § 514. . . .

> Almost immediately, several other judges in the Family Court began to apply Judge Melson's formula in child support cases. Each Family Court judge that used the formula found it to be an effective analytical model, by which to discharge the statutory directive of 13 Del.C. § 514. Approximately one year after its articulation by Judge Melson, his formula was being used by a majority of the Family Court judges.

> The gradual, but steady, expansion of the use of Judge Melson's formula within the judiciary of the Family Court raised a practical concern. The Family Court is, and has been, required by statute, to "[m]ake and publish [Family] Court rules governing policies, processes, practices, and procedures, which shall be uniform throughout the state." 10 Del. C. § 907(5). In order to provide a uniform method of determining support obligations, the judges of the Family Court unanimously adopted the Melson Formula, as a rebuttable presumption, to be used in support cases, effective January 26, 1979.

> The basic principles of the Melson Formula have been summarized as follows:

>> Parents are entitled to keep sufficient income to meet their most basic needs in order to encourage continued employment.

>> Until the basic needs of children are met, parents should not be permitted to retain any more income than that required to provide the bare necessities for their own self-support.

>> Where income is sufficient to cover the basic needs of parents and all dependents, children are entitled to share in any additional income so that they can benefit from the absent parent's higher standard of living.[2]

Percentage of Income. Unlike the income shares model and the Melson formula, the percentage of income approach sets support by reference simply to the obligor's income. The income of the primary custodial parent is not typically considered in calculating the support owed by the other parent. Nine states use the percentage of income model.

---

2. Dalton v. Clayton, 559 A.2d 1197 (Del. 1989).

B. Child Support Guidelines in General

See La. Civ. Code art. 141–42; La. Rev. Stat. § 9:315–315.47.

Federal law makes the role of state child-support guidelines clear:

> There shall be a rebuttable presumption, in any judicial or administrative proceeding for the award of child support, that the amount of the award which would result from the application of such guidelines is the correct amount of child support to be awarded. A written finding or specific finding on the record that the application of the guidelines would be unjust or inappropriate in a particular case, as determined under criteria established by the State, shall be sufficient to rebut the presumption in that case.[3]

In accordance with the federal mandate, La. Rev. Stat. § 9:315.1 provides that the Louisiana guidelines create a rebuttable presumption of correctness. The statute also delineates the situations in which deviation is permitted. In *Stogner v. Stogner*, below, the Louisiana Supreme Court addressed the enforceability of and the role of the courts in reviewing stipulated agreements.

Stogner v. Stogner
739 So. 2d 762 (La. 1999)

Knoll, Justice.

This modification for child support matter concerns a stipulated (consent) judgment and the applicable standard required for a change of circumstances in requesting a modification. The adequacy of the stipulated child support judgment raises the issues to what extent, if any, are the guidelines applicable and the function of the trial judge as gatekeeper to assure adequacy and consistency in child support awards.

FACTS AND PROCEDURAL HISTORY

Benita and Robert Stogner were married in Washington Parish on June 26, 1981. They had two children, Jeremy born on September 20, 1987, and Timothy born on July 14, 1990. Benita and Robert separated on January 15, 1994. On April 6, 1994, the trial court, by stipulation of the parties, awarded joint custody of the two minor children to the Stogners, with Benita being the domiciliary parent and Robert paying $400 per month for the support of the children. Subsequently, on June 29, 1994, the trial court granted a judgment of divorce, finding Benita at fault in the termination of the marriage, and incorporated the provisions of the April 6, 1994, judgment which pertained to custody, visitation, and support.

Thereafter, on October 28, 1996, approximately two years later, Benita filed a rule nisi for increase of child support. In her petition, Benita alleged that a change of circumstances had occurred and that the child support set initially in 1994 was

---

3. 42 U.S.C. § 667 (2017).

established without regard for the child support guidelines. The testimony at this hearing showed that at the time of the consent judgment Benita earned $6.81 per hour and Robert had a yearly salary of $63,234.97. In contrast, at the time of Benita's motion, her hourly wage had increased to $10.50 per hour and Robert's annual salary had decreased to $61,183.22. In its ruling, the trial court held that although the original child support was set in complete disregard of the guidelines, it was done pursuant to the agreement between the parties, and that Benita agreed to this amount with the benefit of legal representation. It further held that this amount would remain unless it could be shown that a change of circumstances had occurred. Accordingly, finding no proof of a change of circumstances, the trial court denied Benita's motion for an increase.

Later, on a motion for new trial, Benita urged that according to La. R.S. 9:315.1(D) the trial court should have considered the guidelines even though the parties had proposed an amount of child support to which both agreed. In its denial of the motion for new trial, the trial court held that a review of the proposed stipulation pursuant to La. R.S. 9:315.1(D) was discretionary with the trial court, and was intended to occur at the time of the agreement, not when judicial examination was urged years later.

In an unpublished opinion the Court of Appeal, First Circuit, found that no proof of a substantial change of circumstances had been established. It further concluded that the trial court had not erred when it did not exercise its option to review the proposed stipulation in light of the statutory guidelines as provided in La. R.S. 9:315.1(D). . . .

We granted Benita's writ application to consider the lower courts' rulings regarding the discretion of the trial court under La. R.S. 9:315.1(D) and the change that must be shown in a modification action. For the following reasons, we reverse and remand this matter to the trial court, finding that the trial court based its ruling on the stipulated judgment of June 29, 1994, which it then approved without the trial court first considering the guidelines in reviewing the adequacy of the stipulated amount, La. R.S. 9:315.1(A) and (D), and without giving specific oral or written reasons warranting a deviation from the guidelines, La. R.S. 9:315.1(B), all of which rendered this judgment an abridgment of the legislative intent in the enactment of the statutory guidelines, and an error of law. . . .

LEGAL ANALYSIS

STIPULATED JUDGMENTS AND THE APPLICABILITY OF THE GUIDELINES

The lower courts relied upon the stipulated judgment of June 29, 1994, in denying Benita a modification of child support. Therefore, we must determine if the adequacy of that stipulated judgment was properly decided and warranted the downward deviation, in assessing the correctness of the denial of the modification.

In assessing the modification of child support, the lower courts, focusing only on Paragraph (D) of La.R.S. 9:315.1, found that there was no duty on the part of the trial court to review the adequacy of the stipulated amount in the initial judgment. After considering Paragraph (D) in light of the entirety of La.R.S. 9:315.1 and reflecting on the legislative intent in that enactment, we find that the trial court's role in instances where child support has been stipulated is greater than that assigned in the lower courts heretofore.

When a law is clear and unambiguous and its application does not lead to absurd consequences, the law shall be applied as written and no further interpretation may be made in search of the intent of the legislature. However, when a law is susceptible of different meanings, "it must be interpreted as having the meaning that best conforms to the purpose of the law."

Legislative intent is the fundamental question in all cases of statutory interpretation, and rules of statutory construction are designed to ascertain and enforce the intent of the statute. It is likewise presumed that it is the intention of the legislative branch to achieve a consistent body of law. The meaning and intent of a law is determined by consideration of the law in its entirety and all other laws on the same subject matter, and a construction should be placed on the provision in question which is consistent with the express terms of the law and with the obvious intent of the lawmaker in enacting it.

La. Civ. Code art. 227 provides that parents, by the very act of marrying, contract together the obligation of supporting, maintaining, and educating their children. The obligation to support their children is conjoint upon the parents and each must contribute in proportion to his or her resources. As a complement to that obligation, La.R.S. 9:315–315.15 provides a detailed set of guidelines that the courts are mandated to follow in setting the amount of child support in "any proceeding to establish or modify child support filed on or after October 1, 1989." These child support guidelines were enacted in 1989 for a twofold purpose: to address the inconsistency in the amounts of child support awards and as an appropriate solution to the inadequacy of the amounts of these awards. Under this system of guidelines, the Legislature adopted an income shares approach which combines the adjusted monthly gross income of both parties in arriving at the amount of support owed. As stated in La.R.S. 9:315.1(A) the amount determined by the guideline formula is presumed to be in the child's best interest. Moreover, the parental obligation to pay child support must be implemented within the body of law contained in the Louisiana Child Support Guidelines. As such, the guidelines are intended to fairly apportion between the parents the mutual financial obligation they owe their children, in an efficient, consistent, and adequate manner.

It is likewise provided in the legislation that there may be deviation from the guidelines if the application of the guidelines would not be in the best interest of the child or would be inequitable to the parties. In this instance, it is incumbent upon the trial court to "give specific oral or written reasons for the deviation, including a finding as to the amount of support that would have been required under a mechanical application of the guidelines and the particular facts and circumstances that warranted a deviation from the guidelines." As such, the function of the guidelines to provide adequacy and consistency in child support awards is served through the establishment of a method of deviation which requires the introduction of an evidentiary basis for such departure into the record.

Prior to the enactment of the child support guidelines, the jurisprudence had further recognized that parents may enter into a consent judgment to establish child support. In accordance with that jurisprudence, it is likewise envisioned in the guidelines that there will be instances where the parents will stipulate (consent) to an amount of child support. In that regard, La.R.S. 9:315.1(D) provides:

> The court may review and approve a stipulation between the parties entered into after the effective date of this Part as to the amount of child support to be paid. If the court does review the stipulation, the court shall consider the guidelines set forth in this Part to review the adequacy of the stipulated amount, and may require the parties to provide the court with the income statements and documentation required by R.S. 9:315.2.

It is this provision on which we now focus our attention.

In the present case, the lower courts read Paragraph (D) in isolation, concluding that review of the stipulated amount in light of the guidelines was discretionary. We find this a flawed reading of this statutory provision which defeats the purpose of the legislature's intent to ensure adequate and consistent child support awards.

A reading of the lower courts' rulings makes it evident that the one thing not considered was the overriding provision of La.R.S. 9:315.1(A) wherein the legislature provided that the guidelines must be used "in any proceeding to establish or modify child support." In light of that mandate, we find that the opening sentence's use of the words "court may review and approve the stipulation" in La.R.S. 9:315.1(D) means that although the parents may present a stipulation for consideration, the trial court is not bound to follow it and may choose to use the guidelines instead. In this context, we find that the opening phrase of the second sentence of Paragraph (D), "If the court does review the stipulation," simply means that if the trial court does not categorically reject the proposed stipulation, i.e., it chooses to entertain the stipulation, the trial court "shall consider the guidelines . . . to review the adequacy of the stipulated amount." To assume, as the lower courts did herein, that the reviewing role of the trial court was discretionary creates an anomaly that cannot be reconciled with the mandated application of the guidelines to the establishment or modification of child support provided in Paragraph (A) of La.R.S. 9:315.1. Moreover, such a reading would impermissibly find the guidelines inapplicable.

As directed by the codal articles and jurisprudence in the interpretation of statutes, we find that consideration of the legislative impetus to enact the guidelines convinces us that the language of Paragraph (D) must yield to the mandated review requirements established in Paragraph (A). With that in mind, it is clear that the focal point of Paragraph (D) is its insistence in the second sentence that when the trial court reviews the agreement proposed by the parents, it "shall consider the guidelines . . . to review the adequacy of the stipulated amount." This the trial court did not do in the present case. Nor did it give any reasons warranting a deviation from the guidelines.

We hasten to add that although we find that the adequacy of the stipulated amount must be evaluated in light of the guideline's considerations, the trial court is not foreclosed from approving the amount to which the parents have stipulated (consented).

As authorized in La.R.S. 9:315.1(B), the trial court, after reviewing the proposed stipulation in light of the considerations enunciated in La.R.S. 9:315.1(C), may nevertheless approve a deviation from the guidelines provided it specifies for the record, either orally or in writing, the reasons for the deviation. Such an approach underscores the integral role of the trial court as gatekeeper in this area of paramount importance. If properly performed in accordance with the guidelines, this judicial review will further assure the adequacy and consistency of child support awards, foster evenhanded settlements, and preserve a record for the evaluation of later proceedings to modify initially stipulated child support awards.

This analysis is not to be viewed as an abrogation of that body of law which has recognized that a consent (stipulated) judgment is by its nature a bilateral agreement between the parties wherein the parties adjust their differences by mutual consent and thereby put an end to a lawsuit with each party balancing the hope of gain against the fear of loss. Notwithstanding the freedom of the parties to so agree, parties must remember that their agreements may not "derogate from laws enacted for the protection of the public interest." In the present instance, it is clear that the stipulated child support recognized in the judgment must conform with the public policy codified in the child support guidelines with its concomitant best interest presumption and mandated adequacy review provisions. Accordingly, we find that pursuant to La.R.S. 9:315.1(A) and (D), the trial court should have "consider[ed] the guidelines set forth [and] . . . review[ed] the adequacy of the stipulated amount, ..." before the stipulated judgment was presented to it for signature, and further, the trial court should have given oral or written reasons warranting the deviation from the guidelines, La.R.S. 9:315.1(B).

Since the stipulated judgment of June 29, 1994, was not given proper consideration by the trial court, it was error for the lower courts to rely upon this flawed judgment in denying Benita a modification of child support.

C. Effect of Custodial Arrangement

See La. Rev. Stat. § 9:315.8–.10.

Custody arrangements are sometimes driven by the effect they will have on child support obligations. In an income shares state, like Louisiana, the custodial arrangement can have a significant effect on the calculation of child support. Louisiana — like some other income shares states — is a so-called "deviation factor" state. Certain custodial arrangements will allow — or even require — the court to deviate from the guidelines. Louisiana's child support statutes contemplate two different types of joint custody arrangements: regular joint custody and shared custody. Shared custody, per

La. Rev. Stat. § 9:315.9, is a joint custody arrangement where "each parent has physical custody of the child for an approximately equal amount of time." Joint custody arrangements that fall short of that time allocation are simply called "joint custody."

If the arrangement qualifies as shared custody, then the statutes provide for an automatic and fixed deviation from the child support guidelines. This deviation recognizes that when the parents have approximately equal physical custody of the child, then many costs are duplicated and/or provided in-kind while the child is in each parent's care. In practice, courts do not require a strict 50/50 time-split. Jurisprudence tends to be more lenient. *Mendoza v. Mendoza*, below, discusses the somewhat nebulous dividing line between joint custody and shared custody and illustrates how much power is sometimes afforded to the trial court in making that determination.

If the joint custody arrangement does not qualify as shared custody, a deviation from the guidelines may still be allowed. La. Rev. Stat. § 9:315.8 gives the court the discretion to allow a deviation from the guidelines if "the person ordered to pay child support has physical custody of the child for more than seventy-three days." This arrangement is sometimes referred to as "extraordinary visitation."

Louisiana recognizes one additional type of custody arrangement that may affect child support—so-called "split custody." La. Rev. Stat. § 9:315.10 explains that split custody exists when "each party is the sole custodial or domiciliary parent of at least one child to whom support is due." In a split custody arrangement, the statute provides that the court should compute the amount of support each parent would owe the other and then calculate the net difference.

Mendoza v. Mendoza
170 So. 3d 1119 (La. App. 5 Cir. 2015)

Robert A. Chaisson, Judge.

In this appeal, Glenroy Mendoza seeks review of a portion of the trial court's August 14, 2014 judgment denying his request for shared custody and the trial court's corresponding use of Obligation Worksheet A contained in LSA-R.S. 9:315.20. In addition, Mr. Mendoza contends that the trial court erred in not extending his custody on alternating weekends to include overnight visitation on Sundays. For the reasons that follow, we find no error in the trial court's rulings. Furthermore, we deny Candace Meads Mendoza's request for attorney's fees.

FACTS AND PROCEDURAL HISTORY

On June 2, 2007, defendant/appellant, Glenroy Mendoza, and plaintiff/appellee, Candace Meads Mendoza, were married and established their matrimonial domicile in Jefferson Parish. One child was born of this union on November 29, 2010. Ms. Mendoza filed a petition for divorce on August 12, 2013, based on the parties living separate and apart for the requisite amount of time. Thereafter, the parties appeared for conferences before a domestic hearing officer address various ancillary issues relating to child custody and support. In accordance with the recommendations of the hearing officer, the parties were awarded joint custody of the child with Ms. Mendoza being designated as the domiciliary parent. Mr. Mendoza was awarded custody every Monday and Wednesday overnight from after work until the child was returned to day care the next day and alternating weekend visitation from Friday after work until Sunday night. In accordance with the awarding of joint custody, child support was calculated based on Worksheet A.

The parties filed objections to various recommendations made by the hearing officer, and the district court thereafter conducted a hearing on the objections. At the hearing, Mr. Mendoza argued that the custody agreement should be considered shared custody, pointing out that Ms. Mendoza's Sunday night visitation is the only additional period preventing custody from being shared equally between the parties. On August 14, 2014, the trial court issued a judgment denying Mr. Mendoza's objections to these particular recommendations of the hearing officer. The pertinent part of that judgment reads as follows:

> IT IS FURTHER ORDERED, ADJUDGED AND DECREED that Defendant's objection to the recommendation of the Hearing Officer regarding the calculation of child support is DENIED, as this Court determines that the custody in this matter is joint, rather than shared, and that child support, thus, must be calculated according to Worksheet A.

Mr. Mendoza now appeals this judgment.

DISCUSSION

Mr. Mendoza first complains that the trial court erred in its decision to deny his request for shared custody and in thereafter denying his request for calculation of child support on Worksheet B. Mr. Mendoza contends that their custodial arrangement constitutes shared custody, pointing out that the only custodial period that Ms. Mendoza enjoys that he does not is the overnight Sunday time frame.

LSA-R.S. 9:315.8 provides for the setting of child support in joint custody cases and provides that Worksheet A is to be utilized in calculating child support. According to LSA-R.S. 9:315.8(E), joint custody means "a joint custody order that is not shared custody as defined in R.S. 9:315.9." A shared custody agreement is specifically excluded from the provisions of LSA-R.S. 9:315.8.

LSA-R.S. 9:315.9 sets forth the formula for calculating child support when the parents have shared custody. LSA-R.S. 9:315.9(A)(1) defines shared custody as "a joint custody order in which each parent has physical custody of the child for an approximately equal amount of time." In determining whether a particular arrangement is shared, LSA-R.S. 9:315.9 does not bind the trial court to a threshold percentage determined solely on the number of days; rather, the statute mandates an "approximately equal amount of time." . . . "It is obvious from a reading of LSA-R.S. 9:315.8(E)(2) that when the legislature intends to fix a threshold parameter, it does so." Therefore, the trial court has discretion in determining whether a particular arrangement constitutes shared custody justifying the application of LSA-R.S. 9:315.9.

In the present case, the trial court determined that the custodial arrangement between the parties constituted joint custody. Based on our calculations, Mr. Mendoza has custody of the child approximately 46.44 percent of the time, and Ms. Mendoza has custody approximately 53.56 percent of the time. Our review of the jurisprudence clearly illustrates that there is no bright line rule as to what constitutes shared custody so as to trigger the application of LSA-R.S. 9:315.9.

In *Martello v. Martello* . . . the custody arrangement gave the father custody of the children approximately 42.85 percent of the time. The trial court awarded joint custody, without an express determination of whether the split of physical custody constituted shared custody, and utilized Worksheet A, rather than Worksheet B, in calculating the basic child support obligation. The appellate court found "no error or abuse of discretion in the trial court's apparent conclusion that the joint custody order in this case did not provide each parent with physical custody of the child for an 'approximately equal' amount of time." Therefore, the trial court did not err in computing child support on Worksheet A.

In *DeSoto v. DeSoto* . . . the father had custody of the child 45 percent of the time, and the mother had custody of the child 55 percent of the time. The trial court determined that this custodial arrangement constituted joint custody and utilized Worksheet A for calculating child support. The appellate court noted that the custody arrangement met the statutory definition of shared custody, but nonetheless determined that the trial court did not abuse its discretion in finding otherwise.

In *Janney v. Janney* . . . the trial court found a shared custody arrangement where the father had custody of the child 45.3 percent of the time. The appellate court found no error or abuse of discretion in the trial court's conclusion that the joint custody order provided each parent with physical custody of the child for an "approximately equal" amount of time, and therefore, the court did not err in computing child support in accord with the formula in LSA-R.S. 9:315.9 and Worksheet B.

In *Broussard v. Rogers* . . . the parties had a custodial arrangement identical to the one at issue. In that case, the father had custody of the child every other weekend from Friday afternoon until Sunday night and two overnights per week. The trial court determined that this agreement constituted shared custody, in that the mother had the other weekends from Friday afternoon and the two other nights during the week. This Court found that the trial court did not abuse its discretion in finding a custodial arrangement identical to the one at issue constituted shared custody or in its utilization of Worksheet B in calculating child support.

In light of *Broussard* . . . we acknowledge that the custodial arrangement in this case could meet the definition of shared custody. However, given the fact that there is no bright line rule as to what custody split constitutes shared custody, and taking into consideration the trial court's discretion in determining whether a particular arrangement constitutes shared custody, we cannot say that the trial court abused its discretion in determining that the custodial arrangement amounted to joint custody, or in its utilization of Worksheet A for calculating the child support obligation.

On appeal, Mr. Mendoza also contends that the trial court erred by not extending his custody on alternating weekends to include overnight visitation on Sundays.

In every child custody determination, the primary consideration is the best interest of the child. LSA-C.C. art. 132 provides that in the absence of an agreement between the parties, the trial court shall award joint custody to the parents. Where there is joint custody, "to the extent it is feasible and in the best interest of the child, physical custody of the children should be shared equally." Nonetheless, a trial court's finding that joint custody is in the best interest of the child does not necessarily require an equal sharing of physical custody. Substantial time rather than strict equality of time is mandated by the legislative scheme providing for joint custody of children.

Each child custody case must be viewed in light of its own particular set of facts and circumstances, with the paramount goal of reaching a decision that is in the best interest of the child. On appellate review, the determination of the trial court in establishing custody is entitled to great weight and will not be disturbed absent a clear showing of an abuse of discretion.

There is no requirement that the trial court give the parties an exactly equal amount of time of physical custody. Accordingly, we cannot say that the trial court abused its discretion in its custody award.

For the foregoing reasons, we affirm the trial court judgment which determined that the custodial arrangement amounted to joint custody and which utilized Worksheet A to calculate the child support obligation. In addition, we affirm the award of child custody. Furthermore, we deny Ms. Mendoza's request for attorney's fees and assess the costs of appeal against Mr. Mendoza.

AFFIRMED

D. Enforcement Mechanisms

See La. Rev. Stat. § 9:315.26–.47; § 13:4611; § 14:75.

As required by federal law, Louisiana has enacted a number of measures aimed at ensuring enforcement of child support orders. These measures include income assignment orders, wage garnishments, tax liens, license suspensions, contempt of court, criminal penalties, and jail time. In recent years, some extreme cases of indigent parents being imprisoned for non-payment of child support obligations have raised serious constitutional and policy questions. Some of those questions are addressed in

Turner v. Rogers, below, which considers a parent's right to counsel in child support proceedings.

Turner v. Rogers

131 S. Ct. 2501 (2011)

Justice BREYER delivered the opinion of the Court.

South Carolina's Family Court enforces its child support orders by threatening with incarceration for civil contempt those who are (1) subject to a child support order, (2) able to comply with that order, but (3) fail to do so. We must decide whether the Fourteenth Amendment's Due Process Clause requires the State to provide counsel (at a civil contempt hearing) to an indigent person potentially faced with such incarceration.

We conclude that where as here the custodial parent (entitled to receive the support) is unrepresented by counsel, the State need not provide counsel to the noncustodial parent (required to provide the support). But we attach an important caveat, namely, that the State must nonetheless have in place alternative procedures that assure a fundamentally fair determination of the critical incarceration-related question, whether the supporting parent is able to comply with the support order.

I

A

South Carolina family courts enforce their child support orders in part through civil contempt proceedings. Each month the family court clerk reviews outstanding child support orders, identifies those in which the supporting parent has fallen more than five days behind, and sends that parent an order to "show cause" why he should not be held in contempt. The "show cause" order and attached affidavit refer to the relevant child support order, identify the amount of the arrearage, and set a date for a court hearing. At the hearing that parent may demonstrate that he is not in contempt, say, by showing that he is not able to make the required payments. If he fails to make the required showing, the court may hold him in civil contempt. And it may require that he be imprisoned unless and until he purges himself of contempt by making the required child support payments (but not for more than one year regardless).

B

In June 2003 a South Carolina family court entered an order, which (as amended) required petitioner, Michael Turner, to pay $51.73 per week to respondent, Rebecca Rogers, to help support their child. (Rogers' father, Larry Price, currently has custody of the child and is also a respondent before this Court.) Over the next three years, Turner repeatedly failed to pay the amount due and was held in contempt on five occasions. The first four times he was sentenced to 90 days' imprisonment, but he ultimately paid the amount due (twice without being jailed, twice after spending two or three days in custody). The fifth time he did not pay but completed a 6–month sentence.

After his release in 2006 Turner remained in arrears. On March 27, 2006, the clerk issued a new "show cause" order. And after an initial postponement due to Turner's failure to appear, Turner's civil contempt hearing took place on January 3, 2008. Turner and Rogers were present, each without representation by counsel.

The hearing was brief. The court clerk said that Turner was $5,728.76 behind in his payments. The judge asked Turner if there was "anything you want to say." Turner replied,

> "Well, when I first got out, I got back on dope. I done meth, smoked pot and everything else, and I paid a little bit here and there. And, when I finally did get to working, I broke my back, back in September. I filed for disability and SSI. And, I didn't get straightened out off the dope until I broke my back and laid up for two months. And, now I'm off the dope and everything. I just hope that you give me a chance. I don't know what else to say. I mean, I know I done wrong, and I should have been paying and helping her, and I'm sorry. I mean, dope had a hold to me."

The judge then said, "[o]kay," and asked Rogers if she had anything to say. . . . After a brief discussion of federal benefits, the judge stated,

> "If there's nothing else, this will be the Order of the Court. I find the Defendant in willful contempt. I'm [going to] sentence him to twelve months in the Oconee County Detention Center. He may purge himself of the contempt and avoid the sentence by having a zero balance on or before his release. I've also placed a lien on any SSI or other benefits."

The judge added that Turner would not receive good-time or work credits, but "[i]f you've got a job, I'll make you eligible for work release." When Turner asked why he could not receive good-time or work credits, the judge said, "[b]ecause that's my ruling."

The court made no express finding concerning Turner's ability to pay his arrearage (though Turner's wife had voluntarily submitted a copy of Turner's application for disability benefits). Nor did the judge ask any followup questions or otherwise address the ability-to-pay issue. After the hearing, the judge filled out a prewritten form titled

> "Order for Contempt of Court," which included the statement:

> "Defendant (was) (was not) gainfully employed and/or (had) (did not have) the ability to make these support payments when due."

But the judge left this statement as is without indicating whether Turner was able to make support payments.

C

While serving his 12–month sentence, Turner, with the help of pro bono counsel, appealed. He claimed that the Federal Constitution entitled him to counsel at his contempt hearing. The South Carolina Supreme Court decided Turner's appeal after he had completed his sentence. And it rejected his "right to counsel" claim. The court pointed out that civil contempt differs significantly from criminal contempt. The former does not require all the "constitutional safeguards" applicable in criminal proceedings. . . . And the right to government-paid counsel, the Supreme Court held, was one of the "safeguards" not required.

Turner sought certiorari. In light of differences among state courts (and some federal courts) on the applicability of a "right to counsel" in civil contempt proceedings enforcing child support orders, we granted the writ. . . .

III

A

We must decide whether the Due Process Clause grants an indigent defendant, such as Turner, a right to state-appointed counsel at a civil contempt proceeding, which may lead to his incarceration. This Court's precedents provide no definitive answer to that question. This Court has long held that the Sixth Amendment grants an indigent defendant the right to state-appointed counsel in a criminal case. And we have held that this same rule applies to criminal contempt proceedings (other than summary proceedings).

But the Sixth Amendment does not govern civil cases. Civil contempt differs from criminal contempt in that it seeks only to "coerc[e] the defendant to do" what a court had previously ordered him to do. A court may not impose punishment "in a civil contempt proceeding when it is clearly established that the alleged contemnor is unable to comply with the terms of the order." And once a civil contemnor complies with the underlying order, he is purged of the contempt and is free. . . .

Consequently, the Court has made clear (in a case not involving the right to counsel) that, where civil contempt is at issue, the Fourteenth Amendment's Due Process Clause allows a State to provide fewer procedural protections than in a criminal case.

This Court has decided only a handful of cases that more directly concern a right to counsel in civil matters. And the application of those decisions to the present case is not clear. On the one hand, the Court has held that the Fourteenth Amendment requires the State to pay for representation by counsel in a civil "juvenile delinquency" proceeding (which could lead to incarceration). Moreover, in *Vitek v. Jones,* 445 U.S. 480, 496–497 (1980), a plurality of four Members of this Court would have held that the Fourteenth Amendment requires representation by counsel in a proceeding to transfer a prison inmate to a state hospital for the mentally ill. Further, in *Lassiter v. Department of Social Servs. of Durham Cty.,* 452 U.S. 18 (1981), a case that focused upon civil proceedings leading to loss of parental rights, the Court wrote that the "pre-eminent generalization that emerges from this Court's precedents on an indigent's right to appointed counsel is that such a right has been recognized to exist only where the litigant may lose his physical liberty if he loses the litigation."

And the Court then drew from these precedents "the presumption that an indigent litigant has a right to appointed counsel only when, if he loses, he may be deprived of his physical liberty."

On the other hand, the Court has held that a criminal offender facing revocation of probation and imprisonment does not ordinarily have a right to counsel at a probation revocation hearing. And, at the same time, *Gault*, *Vitek*, and *Lassiter* are readily distinguishable. The civil juvenile delinquency proceeding at issue in *Gault* was "little different" from, and "comparable in seriousness" to, a criminal prosecution. In *Vitek*, the controlling opinion found no right to counsel. And the Court's statements in *Lassiter* constitute part of its rationale for denying a right to counsel in that case. We believe those statements are best read as pointing out that the Court previously had found a right to counsel "only" in cases involving incarceration, not that a right to counsel exists in all such cases. . . .

B

Civil contempt proceedings in child support cases constitute one part of a highly complex system designed to assure a noncustodial parent's regular payment of funds typically necessary for the support of his children. Often the family receives welfare support from a state-administered federal program, and the State then seeks reimbursement from the noncustodial parent. Other times the custodial parent (often the mother, but sometimes the father, a grandparent, or another person with custody) does not receive government benefits and is entitled to receive the support payments herself.

The Federal Government has created an elaborate procedural mechanism designed to help both the government and custodial parents to secure the payments to which they are entitled. These systems often rely upon wage withholding, expedited procedures for modifying and enforcing child support orders, and automated data processing. But sometimes States will use contempt orders to ensure that the custodial parent receives support payments or the government receives reimbursement. Although some experts have criticized this last-mentioned procedure, and the Federal Government believes that "the routine use of contempt for non-payment of child support is likely to be an ineffective strategy," the Government also tells us that "coercive enforcement remedies, such as contempt, have a role to play." South Carolina, which relies heavily on contempt proceedings, agrees that they are an important tool.

We here consider an indigent's right to paid counsel at such a contempt proceeding. It is a civil proceeding. And we consequently determine the "specific dictates of due process" by examining the "distinct factors" that this Court has previously found useful in deciding what specific safeguards the Constitution's Due Process Clause requires in order to make a civil proceeding fundamentally fair. As relevant here those factors include (1) the nature of "the private interest that will be affected," (2) the comparative "risk" of an "erroneous deprivation" of that interest with and without "additional or substitute procedural safeguards," and (3) the nature and magnitude of any countervailing interest in not providing "additional or substitute procedural requirement[s]."

The "private interest that will be affected" argues strongly for the right to counsel that Turner advocates. That interest consists of an indigent defendant's loss of personal liberty through imprisonment. The interest in securing that freedom, the freedom "from bodily restraint," lies "at the core of the liberty protected by the Due Process Clause." And we have made clear that its threatened loss through legal proceedings demands "due process protection."

Given the importance of the interest at stake, it is obviously important to assure accurate decisionmaking in respect to the key "ability to pay" question. Moreover, the fact that ability to comply marks a dividing line between civil and criminal contempt. . . . That is because an incorrect decision (wrongly classifying the contempt proceeding as civil) can increase the risk of wrongful incarceration by depriving the defendant of the procedural protections (including counsel) that the Constitution would demand in a criminal proceeding. And since 70% of child support arrears nationwide are owed by parents with either no reported income or income of $10,000 per year or less, the issue of ability to pay may arise fairly often.

On the other hand, the Due Process Clause does not always require the provision of counsel in civil proceedings where incarceration is threatened. And in determining whether the Clause requires a right to counsel here, we must take account of opposing interests, as well as consider the probable value of "additional or substitute procedural safeguards."

Doing so, we find three related considerations that, when taken together, argue strongly against the Due Process Clause requiring the State to provide indigents with counsel in every proceeding of the kind before us.

First, the critical question likely at issue in these cases concerns, as we have said, the defendant's ability to pay. That question is often closely related to the question of the defendant's indigence. But when the right procedures are in place, indigence can be a question that in many—but not all—cases is sufficiently straightforward to warrant determination prior to providing a defendant with counsel, even in a criminal case. Federal law, for example, requires a criminal defendant to provide information showing that he is indigent, and therefore entitled to state-funded counsel, before he can receive that assistance.

Second, sometimes, as here, the person opposing the defendant at the hearing is not the government represented by counsel but the custodial parent unrepresented by counsel. The custodial parent, perhaps a woman with custody of one or more children, may be relatively poor, unemployed, and unable to afford counsel. Yet she may have encouraged the court to enforce its order through contempt. She may be able to provide the court with significant information. And the proceeding is ultimately for her benefit.

A requirement that the State provide counsel to the noncustodial parent in these cases could create an asymmetry of representation that would "alter significantly the nature of the proceeding." Doing so could mean a degree of formality or delay that would unduly slow payment to those immediately in need. And, perhaps more important for present purposes, doing so could make the proceedings less fair overall, increasing the risk of a decision that would erroneously deprive a family of the support it is entitled to receive. The needs of such families play an important role in our analysis.

Third, as the Solicitor General points out, there is available a set of "substitute procedural safeguards," which, if employed together, can significantly reduce the risk of an erroneous deprivation of liberty. They can do so, moreover, without incurring some of the drawbacks inherent in recognizing an automatic right to counsel. Those safeguards include (1) notice to the defendant that his "ability to pay" is a critical issue in the contempt proceeding; (2) the use of a form (or the equivalent) to elicit relevant financial information; (3) an opportunity at the hearing for the defendant to respond to statements and questions about his financial status, (e.g., those triggered by his responses on the form); and (4) an express finding by the court that the defendant has the ability to pay. In presenting these alternatives, the Government draws upon considerable experience in helping to manage statutorily mandated federal-state efforts to enforce child support orders. It does not claim that they are the only possible alternatives, and this Court's cases suggest, for example, that sometimes assistance other than purely legal assistance (here, say, that of a neutral social worker) can prove constitutionally sufficient. But the Government does claim that these alternatives can assure the "fundamental fairness" of the proceeding even where the State does not pay for counsel for an indigent defendant.

While recognizing the strength of Turner's arguments, we ultimately believe that the three considerations we have just discussed must carry the day. In our view, a categorical right to counsel in proceedings of the kind before us would carry with it disadvantages (in the form of unfairness and delay) that, in terms of ultimate fairness, would deprive it of significant superiority over the alternatives that we have mentioned. We consequently hold that the Due Process Clause does not automatically require the provision of counsel at civil contempt proceedings to an indigent individual who is subject to a child support order, even if that individual faces incarceration (for up to a year). In particular, that Clause does not require the provision of counsel where the opposing parent or other custodian (to whom support funds are owed) is not represented by counsel and the State provides alternative procedural safeguards equivalent to those we have mentioned (adequate notice of the importance of ability to pay, fair opportunity to present, and to dispute, relevant information, and court findings).

We do not address civil contempt proceedings where the underlying child support payment is owed to the State, for example, for reimbursement of welfare funds paid to the parent with custody. Those proceedings more closely resemble debt-collection proceedings. The government is likely to have counsel or some other competent representative. And this kind of proceeding is not before us. Neither do we address what due process requires in an unusually complex case where a defendant "can fairly be represented only by a trained advocate."

IV

The record indicates that Turner received neither counsel nor the benefit of alternative procedures like those we have described. He did not receive clear notice that his ability to pay would constitute the critical question in his civil contempt proceeding. No one provided him with a form (or the equivalent) designed to elicit information about his financial circumstances. The court did not find that Turner was able to pay his arrearage, but instead left the relevant "finding" section of the contempt order blank. The court nonetheless found Turner in contempt and ordered him incarcerated. Under these circumstances Turner's incarceration violated the Due Process Clause.

We vacate the judgment of the South Carolina Supreme Court and remand the case for further proceedings not inconsistent with this opinion.

It is so ordered.

Chapter 16

Jurisdiction and the U.S. Constitution

A. Divorce Actions

In the era of fault-based divorce, a handful of jurisdictions established themselves as "divorce mills." In essence, some jurisdictions would allow non-residents to obtain a fairly quick divorce after residing in the jurisdiction for a short period of time. Often, only one spouse would appear in the proceeding, and he or she would obtain a default judgment against the other spouse. Typically, once the divorce was complete, the spouse would return back to his or her home state and sometimes remarry. These divorce mills raised a number of constitutional and policy questions for courts and for the spouses involved.

In a pair of decisions involving the same litigants, the Supreme Court weighed in on the jurisdiction required to issue a divorce judgment and the ability of another state to attack that judgment. In *Williams I*, below, the Supreme Court held that divorce was more akin to an *in rem* action than to an *in personam* action. Accordingly, it was not necessary for the court to have personal jurisdiction over the defendant spouse in order to issue a divorce judgment entitled to full faith and credit in other states. In reaching this conclusion, the Court overruled its earlier decision in *Haddock v. Haddock*. In *Williams II*, also below, the court discussed the circumstances under which a court in one state could bring a collateral attack on the divorce judgment issued in the other state. In particular, the *Williams II* court allowed North Carolina to challenge the underlying decision regarding domicile made by the Nevada court. The cases that follow *Williams I* and *Williams II* further illustrate and refine these points.

Williams vs. North Carolina (Williams I)
317 U.S. 287 (1942)

Mr. Justice Douglas delivered the opinion of the Court.

Petitioners were tried and convicted of bigamous cohabitation under § 4342 of the North Carolina Code, 1939, and each was sentenced for a term of years to a state prison. The judgment of conviction was affirmed by the Supreme Court of North Carolina. The case is here on certiorari.

Petitioner Williams was married to Carrie Wyke in 1916 in North Carolina and lived with her there until May, 1940. Petitioner Hendrix was married to Thomas

413

Hendrix in 1920 in North Carolina and lived with him there until May, 1940. At that time petitioners went to Las Vegas, Nevada and on June 26, 1940, each filed a divorce action in the Nevada court. The defendants in those divorce actions entered no appearance nor were they served with process in Nevada. In the case of defendant Thomas Hendrix service by publication was had by publication of the summons in a Las Vegas newspaper and by mailing a copy of the summons and complaint to his last post office address. In the case of defendant Carrie Williams a North Carolina sheriff delivered to her in North Carolina a copy of the summons and complaint. A decree of divorce was granted petitioner Williams by the Nevada court on August 26, 1940, on the grounds of extreme cruelty, the court finding that 'the plaintiff has been and now is a bona fide and continuous resident of the County of Clark, State of Nevada, and had been such resident for more than six weeks immediately preceding the commencement of this action in the manner prescribed by law'. The Nevada court granted petitioner Hendrix a divorce on October 4, 1940, on the grounds of willful neglect and extreme cruelty and made the same finding as to this petitioner's bona fide residence in Nevada as it made in the case of Williams. Petitioners were married to each other in Nevada on October 4, 1940. Thereafter they returned to North Carolina where they lived together until the indictment was returned. Petitioners pleaded not guilty and offered in evidence exemplified copies of the Nevada proceedings, contending that the divorce decrees and the Nevada marriage were valid in North Carolina as well as in Nevada. The State contended that since neither of the defendants in the Nevada actions was served in Nevada nor entered an appearance there, the Nevada decrees would not be recognized as valid in North Carolina. . . . Petitioners excepted to these charges. The Supreme Court of North Carolina in affirming the judgment held that North Carolina was not required to recognize the Nevada decrees under the full faith and credit clause of the Constitution (Art. IV, § 1) by reason of *Haddock v. Haddock*, 201 U.S. 562. . . . Accordingly, we cannot avoid meeting the *Haddock v. Haddock* issue in this case by saying that the petitioners acquired no bona fide domicil in Nevada. . . . Rather we must treat the present case for the purpose of the limited issue before us precisely the same as if petitioners had resided in Nevada for a term of years and had long ago acquired a permanent abode there. In other words, we would reach the question whether North Carolina could refuse to recognize the Nevada decrees because in its view and contrary to the findings of the Nevada court petitioners had no actual, bona fide domicil in Nevada, if and only if we concluded that *Haddock v. Haddock* was correctly decided. But we do not think it was.

The *Haddock* case involved a suit for separation and alimony brought in New York by the wife on personal service of the husband. The husband pleaded in defense a divorce decree obtained by him in Connecticut where he had established a separate domicil. This Court held that New York, the matrimonial domicil where the wife still resided, need not give full faith and credit to the Connecticut decree, since it was obtained by the husband who wrongfully left his wife in the matrimonial domicil, service on her having been obtained by publication and she not having entered an appearance in the action. But we do not agree with the theory of the *Haddock* case that, so far as the marital status of the parties is concerned, a decree of divorce granted under such circumstances by one state need not be given full faith and credit in another.

Article IV, § 1 of the Constitution not only directs that 'Full Faith and Credit shall be given in each State to the public Acts, Records, and Judicial Proceedings of every other State' but also provides that 'Congress may be general Laws prescribe the Manner in which such Acts, Records and Proceedings shall be proved, and the Effect thereof.' Congress has exercised that power. . . . Congress has provided that judgments 'shall have such faith and credit given to them in every court within the United States as they have by law or usage in the courts of the State from which they are taken.' Chief Justice Marshall stated . . . that 'the judgment of a state court should have the same credit, validity, and effect, in every other court in the United States, which it had in the state where it was pronounced, and that whatever pleas would be good to a suit thereon in such state, and none others, could be pleaded in any other court in the United States.' That view has survived substantially intact. This Court only recently stated that Art. IV, § 1 and the Act of May 26, 1790 require that 'not some but full' faith and credit be given judgments of a state court. Thus even though the cause of action could not be entertained in the state of the forum either because it had been barred by the local statute of limitations or contravened local policy, the judgment thereon obtained in a sister state is entitled to full faith and credit. Some exceptions have been engrafted on the rule laid down by Chief Justice Marshall. . . .

The historical view that a proceeding for a divorce was a proceeding in rem was rejected by the *Haddock* case. We likewise agree that it does not aid in the solution of the problem presented by this case to label these proceedings as proceedings in rem. Such a suit, however, is not a mere in personam action. Domicil of the plaintiff, immaterial to jurisdiction in a personal action, is recognized in the *Haddock* case and elsewhere as essential in order to give the court jurisdiction which will entitle the divorce decree to extraterritorial effect, at least when the defendant has neither been personally served nor entered an appearance. The findings made in the divorce decrees in the instant case must be treated on the issue before us as meeting those requirements. For it seems clear that the provision of the Nevada statute that a plaintiff in this type of case must 'reside' in the State for the required period requires him to have a domicil as distinguished from a mere residence in the state. Hence the decrees in this case like other divorce decrees are more than in personam judgments. They involve the marital status of the parties. Domicil creates a relationship to the state which is adequate for numerous exercises of state power. Each state as a sovereign has a rightful and legitimate concern in the marital status of persons domiciled within its borders. The marriage relation creates problems of large social importance. Protection of offspring, property interests, and the enforcement of marital responsibilities are but a few of commanding problems in the field of domestic relations with which the state must deal. Thus it is plain that each state by virtue of its command over its domiciliaries and its large interest in the institution of marriage can alter within its own borders the marriage status of the spouse domiciled there, even though the other spouse is absent. There is no constitutional barrier if the form and nature of the substituted service meet the requirements of due process. Accordingly it was admitted in the *Haddock* case that the divorce decree though not recognized in New York was binding on both spouses in Connecticut where granted. And this Court in *Maynard v. Hill*, 125 U.S. 190, upheld the validity within the Territory of Oregon of a divorce decree granted by the legislature to a husband domiciled there, even though the wife resided in Ohio where the husband had deserted her. It therefore follows that, if the Nevada decrees are taken at their full face value (as they must be on the phase of the case with which we are presently concerned), they were wholly effective to change in that state the marital status of the petitioners and each of the other spouses by the North Carolina marriages. Apart from the requirements of procedural due process not challenged here by North Carolina, no reason based on the Federal Constitution has been advanced for the contrary conclusion. But the concession that the decrees were effective in Nevada makes more compelling the reasons for rejection of the theory and result of the *Haddock* case.

This Court stated in *Atherton v. Atherton*, that 'A husband without a wife, or a wife without a husband, is unknown to the law.' But if one is lawfully divorced and remarried in Nevada and still married to the first spouse in North Carolina, an even more complicated and serious condition would be realized. . . . Under the circumstances of this case, a man would have two wives, a wife two husbands. The reality of a sentence to prison proves that that is no mere play on words. Each would be a bigamist for living in one state with the only one with whom the other state would permit him lawfully to live. Children of the second marriage would be bastards in one state but legitimate in the other. And all that would flow from the legalistic notion that where one spouse is wrongfully deserted he retains power over the matrimonial domicil so that the domicil of the other spouse follows him wherever he may go, while if he is to blame, he retains no such power. But such considerations are inapposite. As stated by Mr. Justice Holmes in his dissent in the *Haddock* case, they constitute a 'pure fiction, and fiction always is a poor ground for changing substantial rights.' Furthermore, the fault or wrong of one spouse in leaving the other becomes under that view a jurisdictional fact on which this Court would ultimately have to pass. Whatever may be said as to the practical effect which such a rule would have in clouding divorce decrees, the question as to where the fault lies has no relevancy to the existence of state power in such circumstances. The existence of the power of a state to alter the marital status of its domiciliaries, as distinguished from the wisdom of its exercise, is not dependent on the underlying causes of the domestic rift. As we have said, it is dependent on the relationship which domicil creates and the pervasive control which a state has over marriage and divorce within its own borders. . . . It is one thing to say as a matter of state law that jurisdiction to grant a divorce from an absent spouse should depend on whether by consent or by conduct the latter has subjected his interest in the marriage status to the law of the separate domicil acquired by the other spouse. But where a state adopts, as it has the power to do, a less strict rule, it is quite another thing to say that its decrees affecting the marital status of its domiciliaries are not entitled to full faith and credit in sister states. Certainly if decrees of a state altering the marital status of its domiciliaries are not valid throughout the Union even though the requirements of procedural due process are wholly met, a rule would be fostered which could not help but bring 'considerable disaster to innocent persons' and 'bastardize children hitherto supposed to be the offspring of lawful marriage,' or else encourage collusive divorces. These intensely practical considerations emphasize for us the essential function of the full faith and credit clause in substituting a command for the former principles of comity . . . and in altering the 'status of the several states as independent foreign sovereignties' by making them 'integral parts of a single nation.'

It is objected, however, that if such divorce decrees must be given full faith and credit, a substantial dilution of the sovereignty of other states will be effected. For it is pointed out that under such a rule one state's policy of strict control over the institution of marriage could be thwarted by the decree of a more lax state. But such an objection goes to the application of the full faith and credit clause to many situations. It is an objection in varying degrees of intensity to the enforcement of a judgment of a sister state based on a cause of action which could not be enforced in the state of the forum. . . . Such is part of the price of our federal system.

This Court, of course, is the final arbiter when the question is raised as to what is a permissible limitation on the full faith and credit clause. But the question for us is a limited one. In the first place, we repeat that in this case we must assume that petitioners had a bona fide domicil in Nevada, not that the Nevada domicil was a sham. We thus have no question on the present record whether a divorce decree granted by the courts of one state to a resident as distinguished from a domiciliary is entitled to full faith and credit in another state. Nor do we reach here the question as to the power of North Carolina to refuse full faith and credit to Nevada divorce decrees because, contrary to the findings of the Nevada court, North Carolina finds that no bona fide domicil was acquired in Nevada. In the second place, the question as to what is a permissible limitation on the full faith and credit clause does not involve a decision on our part as to which state policy on divorce is the more desirable one. It does not involve selection of a rule which will encourage on the one hand or discourage on the other the practice of divorce. That choice in the realm of morals and religion rests with the legislatures of the states. Our own views as to the marriage institution and the avenues of escape which some states have created are immaterial. It is a Constitution which we are expounding—a Constitution which in no small measure brings separate sovereign states into an integrated whole through the medium of the full faith and credit clause. Within the limits of her political power North Carolina may, of course, enforce her own policy regarding the marriage relation—an institution more basic in our civilization than any other. But society also has an interest in the avoidance of polygamous marriages . . . and in the protection of innocent offspring of marriages deemed legitimate in other jurisdictions. And other states have an equally legitimate concern in the status of persons domiciled there as respects the institution of marriage. So when a court of one state acting in accord with the requirements of procedural due process alters the marital status of one domiciled in that state by granting him a divorce from his absent spouse, we cannot say its decree should be excepted from the full faith and credit clause merely because its enforcement or recognition in another state would conflict with the policy of the latter. Whether Congress has the power to create exceptions . . . is a question on which we express no view. It is sufficient here to note that Congress in its sweeping requirement that judgments of the courts of one state be given full faith and credit in the courts of another has not done so. And the considerable interests involved and the substantial and far-reaching effects which the allowance of an exception would have on innocent persons indicate that the purpose of the full faith and credit clause and of the supporting legislation would be thwarted to a substantial degree if the rule of *Haddock v. Haddock* were perpetuated.

Haddock v. Haddock is overruled. The judgment is reversed and the cause is remanded to the Supreme Court of North Carolina for proceedings not inconsistent with this opinion.

It is so ordered.

Reversed and remanded with directions.

Williams vs. North Carolina (Williams II)
325 U.S. 226 (1945)

Mr. Justice FRANKFURTER delivered the opinion of the Court.

This case is here to review judgments of the Supreme Court of North Carolina, affirming convictions for bigamous cohabitation, assailed on the ground that full faith and credit, as required by the Constitution of the United States, was not accorded divorces decreed by one of the courts of Nevada. [*Williams I*] decided an earlier aspect of the controversy. It was there held that a divorce granted by Nevada, on a finding that one spouse was domiciled in Nevada, must be respected in North Carolina, where Nevada's finding of domicil was not questioned though the other spouse had neither appeared nor been served with process in Nevada and though recognition of such a divorce offended the policy of North Carolina. The record then before us did not present the question whether North Carolina had the power 'to refuse full faith and credit to Nevada divorce decrees because, contrary to the findings of the Nevada court, North Carolina finds that no bona fide domicil was acquired in Nevada.' This is the precise issue which has emerged after retrial of the cause following our reversal. Its obvious importance brought the case here. . . .

Under our system of law, judicial power to grant a divorce—jurisdiction, strictly speaking—is founded on domicil. The framers of the Constitution were familiar with this jurisdictional prerequisite, and since 1789 neither this Court nor any other court in the English-speaking world has questioned it. Domicil implies a nexus between person and place of such permanence as to control the creation of legal relations and responsibilities of the utmost significance. The domicil of one spouse within a State gives power to that State, we have held, to dissolve a marriage whereso-ever contracted. In view of [*Williams I*], the jurisdictional requirement of domicil is freed from confusing refinements about 'matrimonial domicil'. . . . Divorce, like marriage, is of concern not merely to the immediate parties. It affects personal rights of the deepest significance. It also touches basic interests of society. Since divorce, like marriage, creates a new status, every consideration of policy makes it desirable that the effect should be the same wherever the question arises.

It is one thing to reopen an issue that has been settled after appropriate opportu-nity to present their contentions has been afforded to all who had an interest in its adjudication. This applies also to jurisdictional questions. After a contest these can-not be relitigated as between the parties. But those not parties to a litigation ought not to be foreclosed by the interested actions of others; especially not a State which is concerned with the vindication of its own social policy and has no means, cer-tainly no effective means, to protect that interest against the selfish action of those outside its borders. The State of domiciliary origin should not be bound by an unfounded, even if not collusive, recital in the record of a court of another State. As to the truth or existence of a fact, like that of domicil, upon which depends the power to exert judicial authority, a State not a party to the exertion of such judicial author-ity in another State but seriously affected by it has a right, when asserting its own unquestioned authority, to ascertain the truth or existence of that crucial fact.

These considerations of policy are equally applicable whether power was assumed by the court of the first State or claimed after inquiry. This may lead, no doubt, to conflicting determinations of what judicial power is founded upon. Such conflict is inherent in the practical application of the concept of domicil in the context of our federal system. . . . 'Neither the Fourteenth Amendment nor the full faith and credit clause . . . requires uniformity in the decisions of the courts of different states as to the place of domicil, where the exertion of state power is dependent upon domicil within its boundaries. . . .' If a finding by the court of one State that domicil in another State has been abandoned were conclusive upon the old domiciliary State, the policy of each State in matters of most intimate concern could be subverted by the policy of every other State. This Court has long ago denied the existence of such destructive power. The issue has a far reach. For domicil is the foundation of pro-bate jurisdiction precisely as it is that of divorce. The ruling in *Tilt v. Kelsey*, 207 U.S. 43, regarding the probate of a will, is equally applicable to a sister-State divorce decree: 'The full faith and credit due to the proceedings of the New Jersey court do not require that the courts of New York shall be bound by its adjudication on the question of domicil. On the contrary, it is open to the courts of any state, in the trial of a col-lateral issue, to determine, upon the evidence produced, the true domicil of the deceased.'

Although it is now settled that a suit for divorce is not an ordinary adversary pro-ceeding, it does not promote analysis, as was recently pointed out, to label divorce proceedings as actions in rem. But insofar as a divorce decree partakes of some of the characteristics of a decree in rem, it is misleading to say that all the world is party to a proceeding in rem. All the world is not party to a divorce proceeding. What is true is that all the world need not be present before a court granting the decree and yet it must be respected by the other forty-seven States provided—and it is a big proviso—the conditions for the exercise of power by the divorce-decreeing court are validly established whenever that judgment is elsewhere called into question. In short, the decree of divorce is a conclusive adjudication of everything except the jurisdictional facts upon which it is founded, and domicil is a jurisdictional fact. To permit the necessary finding of domicil by one State to foreclose all States in the protection of their social institutions would be intolerable.

But to endow each State with controlling authority to nullify the power of a sister State to grant a divorce based upon a finding that one spouse had acquired a new domicil within the divorcing State would, in the proper functioning of our federal system, be equally indefensible. No State court can assume comprehensive attention to the various and potentially conflicting interests that several States may have in the institutional aspects of marriage. The necessary accommodation between the right of one State to safeguard its interest in the family relation of its own people and the power of another State to grant divorces can be left to neither State. . . .

What is immediately before us is the judgment of the Supreme Court of North Carolina. We have authority to upset it only if there is want of foundation for the conclusion that that Court reached. The conclusion it reached turns on its finding that the spouses who obtained the Nevada decrees were not domiciled there. The fact that the Nevada court found that they were domiciled there is entitled to respect, and more. The burden of undermining the verity which the Nevada decrees import rests heavily upon the assailant. But simply because the Nevada court found that it had power to award a divorce decree cannot, we have seen, foreclose reexamination by another State. Otherwise, as was pointed out long ago, a court's record would establish its power and the power would be proved by the record. Such circular reasoning would give one State a control over all the other States which the Full Faith and Credit Clause certainly did not confer. If this Court finds that proper weight was accorded to the claims of power by the court of one State in rendering a judgment the validity of which is pleaded in defense in another State, that the burden of overcoming such respect by disproof of the substratum of fact—here domicil—on which such power alone can rest was properly charged against the party challenging the legitimacy of the judgment, that such issue of fact was left for fair determination by appropriate procedure, and that a finding adverse to the necessary foundation for any valid sister-State judgment was amply supported in evidence, we can not upset the judgment before us. And we cannot do so even if we also found in the record of the court of original judgment warrant for its finding that it had jurisdiction. If it is a matter turning on local law, great deference is owed by the courts of one State to what a court of another State has done. But when we are dealing as here with an historic notion common to all English-speaking courts, that of domicil, we should not find a want of deference to a sister State on the part of a court of another State which finds an absence of domicil where such a conclusion is warranted by the record.

When this case was first here, North Carolina did not challenge the finding of the Nevada court that petitioners had acquired domicils in Nevada. For her challenge of the Nevada decrees, North Carolina rested on *Haddock v. Haddock*, 201 U.S. 562. Upon retrial, however, the existence of domicil in Nevada became the decisive issue. The judgments of conviction how under review bring before us a record which may be fairly summarized by saying that the petitioners left North Carolina for the purpose of getting divorces from their respective spouses in Nevada and as soon as each had done so and married one another they left Nevada and returned to North Carolina to live there together as man and wife. Against the charge of bigamous cohabitation under § 14-183 of the North Carolina General Statutes, petitioners stood on their Nevada divorces and offered exemplified copies of the Nevada proceedings. The trial judge charged that the State had the burden of proving beyond a reasonable doubt that (1) each petitioner was lawfully married to one person; (2) thereafter each petitioner contracted a second marriage with another person outside North Carolina; (3) the spouses of petitioners were living at the time of this second marriage; (4) petitioners cohabited with one another in North Carolina after the second marriage. The burden, it was charged, then devolved upon petitioners 'to satisfy the trial jury, not beyond a reasonable doubt nor by the greater weight of the evidence, but simply to satisfy' the jury from all the evidence, that petitioners were domiciled in Nevada at the time they obtained their divorces. The court further charged that 'the recitation' of bona fide domicil in the Nevada decree was 'prima facie evidence' sufficient to warrant a finding of domicil in Nevada but not compelling 'such an inference'. If the jury found, as they were told, that petitioners had domicils in North Carolina and went to Nevada 'simply and solely for the purpose of obtaining' divorces, intending to return to North Carolina on obtaining them, they never lost their North Carolina domicils nor acquired new domicils in Nevada. Domicil, the jury was instructed, was that place where a person 'has voluntarily fixed his abode . . . not for a mere special or temporary purpose, but with a present intention of making it his home, either permanently or for an indefinite or unlimited length of time.'

The scales of justice must not be unfairly weighted by a State when full faith and credit is claimed for a sister-State judgment. But North Carolina has not so dealt with the Nevada decrees. She has not raised unfair barriers to their recognition. North Carolina did not fail in appreciation or application of federal standards of full faith and credit. Appropriate weight was given to the finding of domicil in the Nevada decrees, and that finding was allowed to be overturned only by relevant standards of proof. There is nothing to suggest that the issue was not fairly submitted to the jury and that it was not fairly assessed on cogent evidence.

State courts cannot avoid review by this Court of their disposition of a constitutional claim by casting it in the form of an unreviewable finding of fact. This record is barren of such attempted evasion. What it shows is that petitioners, long-time residents of North Carolina, came to Nevada, where they stayed in an auto-court for transients, filed suits for divorce as soon as the Nevada law permitted, married one another as soon as the divorces were obtained, and promptly returned to North Carolina to live. It cannot reasonably be claimed that one set of inferences rather than another regarding the acquisition by petitioners of new domicils in Nevada could not be drawn from the circumstances attending their Nevada divorces. It would be highly unreasonable to assert that a jury could not reasonably find that the evidence demonstrated that petitioners went to Nevada solely for the purpose of obtaining a divorce and intended all along to return to North Carolina. Such an intention, the trial court properly charged, would preclude acquisition of domicils in Nevada. And so we can not say that North Carolina was not entitled to draw the inference that petitioners never abandoned their domicils in North Carolina, particularly since we could not conscientiously prefer, were it our business to do so, the contrary finding of the Nevada court.

If a State cannot foreclose, on review here, all the other States by its finding that one spouse is domiciled within its bounds, persons may, no doubt, place themselves in situations that create unhappy consequences for them. This is merely one of those untoward results inevitable in a federal system in which regulation of domestic relations has been left with the States and not given to the national authority. But the occasional disregard by any one State of the reciprocal obligations of the forty-eight States to respect the constitutional power of each to deal with domestic relations of those domiciled within its borders is hardly an argument for allowing one State to deprive the other forty-seven States of their constitutional rights. Relevant statistics happily do not justify lurid forebodings that parents without number will disregard the fate of their offspring by being unmindful of the status of dignity to which they are entitled. But, in any event, to the extent that some one State may, for considerations of its own, improperly intrude into domestic relations subject to the authority of the other States, it suffices to suggest that any such indifference by a State to the bond of the Union should be discouraged not encouraged.

In seeking a decree of divorce outside the State in which he has theretofore maintained his marriage, a person is necessarily involved in the legal situation created by our federal system whereby one State can grant a divorce of validity in other States only if the applicant has a bona fide domicil in the State of the court purporting to dissolve a prior legal marriage. The petitioners therefore assumed the risk that this Court would find that North Carolina justifiably concluded that they had not been domiciled in Nevada. Since the divorces which they sought and received in Nevada had no legal validity in North Carolina and their North Carolina spouses were still alive, they subjected themselves to prosecution for bigamous cohabitation under North Carolina law. The legitimate finding of the North Carolina Supreme Court that the petitioners were not in truth domiciled in Nevada was not a contingency against which the petitioners were protected by anything in the Constitution of the United States. . . .

We conclude that North Carolina was not required to yield her State policy because a Nevada court found that petitioners were domiciled in Nevada when it granted them decrees of divorce. North Carolina was entitled to find, as she did, that they did not acquire domicils in Nevada and that the Nevada court was therefore without power to liberate the petitioners from amenability to the laws of North Carolina governing domestic relations. And, as was said in connection with another aspect of the Full Faith and Credit Clause, our conclusion 'is not a matter to arouse the susceptibilities of the states, all of which are equally concerned in the question and equally on both sides. . . .'

Affirmed.

Sherrer v. Sherrer
334 U.S. 343 (1948)

Mr. Chief Justice VINSON delivered the opinion of the Court.

We granted certiorari in this case . . . to consider the contention of petitioners that Massachusetts has failed to accord full faith and credit to decrees of divorce rendered by courts of sister States.

Petitioner Margaret E. Sherrer and the respondent, Edward C. Sherrer, were married in New Jersey in 1930, and from 1932 until April 3, 1944, lived together in Monterey, Massachusetts. Following a long period of marital discord, petitioner, accompanied by the two children of the marriage, left Massachusetts on the latter date, ostensibly for the purpose of spending a vacation in the State of Florida. Shortly after her arrival in Florida, however, petitioner informed her husband that she did not intend to return to him. Petitioner obtained housing accommodations in Florida, placed her older child in school, and secured employment for herself.

On July 6, 1944, a bill of complaint for divorce was filed at petitioner's direction in the Circuit Court of the Sixth Judicial Circuit of the State of Florida. The bill alleged extreme cruelty as grounds for divorce and also alleged that petitioner was a 'bona fide resident of the State of Florida.' The respondent received notice by mail of the pendency of the divorce proceedings. He retained Florida counsel who entered a general appearance and filed an answer denying the allegations of petitioner's complaint, including the allegation as to petitioner's Florida residence.

On November 14, 1944, hearings were held in the divorce proceedings. Respondent appeared personally to testify with respect to a stipulation entered into by the parties relating to the custody of the children. Throughout the entire proceedings respondent was represented by counsel. Petitioner introduced evidence to establish her Florida residence and testified generally to the allegations of her complaint. Counsel for respondent failed to cross-examine or to introduce evidence in rebuttal.

The Florida court on November 29, 1944, entered a decree of divorce after specifically finding 'that petitioner is a bona fide resident of the State of Florida, and that this court has jurisdiction of the parties and the subject matter in said cause . . .' Respondent failed to challenge the decree by appeal to the Florida Supreme Court.

On December 1, 1944, petitioner was married in Florida to one Henry A. Phelps, whom petitioner had known while both were residing in Massachusetts and who had come to Florida shortly after petitioner's arrival in that State. Phelps and petitioner lived together as husband and wife in Florida, where they were both employed, until February 5, 1945, when they returned to Massachusetts.

In June, 1945, respondent instituted an action in the Probate Court of Berkshire County, Massachusetts, which has given rise to the issues of this case. Respondent alleged that he is the lawful husband of petitioner, that the Florida decree of divorce is invalid, and that petitioner's subsequent marriage is void. Respondent prayed that he might be permitted to convey his real estate as if he were sole and that the court declare that he was living apart from his wife for justifiable cause. Petitioner joined issue on respondent's allegations.

In the proceedings which followed, petitioner gave testimony in defense of the validity of the Florida divorce decree. The Probate Court, however, resolved the issues of fact adversely to petitioner's contentions, found that she was never domiciled in Florida, and granted respondent the relief he had requested. The Supreme Judicial Court of Massachusetts affirmed the decree on the grounds that it was supported by the evidence and that the requirements of full faith and credit did not preclude the Massachusetts courts from reexamining the finding of domicile made by the Florida court.

At the outset, it should be observed that the proceedings in the Florida court prior to the entry of the decree of divorce were in no way inconsistent with the requirements of procedural due process. We do not understand respondent to urge the contrary. The respondent personally appeared in the Florida proceedings. Though his attorney he filed pleadings denying the substantial allegations of petitioner's complaint. It is not suggested that his rights to introduce evidence and otherwise to conduct his defense were in any degree impaired; nor is it suggested that there was not available to him the right to seek review of the decree by appeal to the Florida Supreme Court. It is clear that respondent was afforded his day in court with respect to every issue involved in the litigation, including the jurisdictional issue of petitioner's domicile. Under such circumstances, there is nothing in the concept of due process which demands that a defendant be afforded a second opportunity to litigate the existence of jurisdictional facts.

It should also be observed that there has been no suggestion that under the law of Florida, the decree of divorce in question is in any respect invalid or could successfully be subjected to the type of attack permitted by the Massachusetts court. The implicit assumption underlying the position taken by respondent and the Massachusetts court is that this case involves a decree of divorce valid and final in the State which rendered it; and we so assume.

That the jurisdiction of the Florida court to enter a valid decree of divorce was dependent upon petitioner's domicile in that State is not disputed. This requirement was recognized by the Florida court which rendered the divorce decree, and the principle has been given frequent application in decisions of the State Supreme Court. But whether or not petitioner was domiciled in Florida at the time the divorce was granted was a matter to be resolved by judicial determination. Here, unlike the situation presented in [*Williams II*] the finding of the requisite jurisdictional facts was made in proceedings in which the defendant appeared and participated. The question with which we are confronted, therefore, is whether such a finding made under the circumstances presented by this case may, consistent with the requirements of full faith and credit, be subjected to collateral attack in the courts of a sister State in a suit brought by the defendant in the original proceedings.

The question of what effect is to be given to an adjudication by a court that it possesses requisite jurisdiction in a case, where the judgment of that court is subsequently subjected to collateral attack on jurisdictional grounds, has been given frequent consideration by this Court over a period of many years. Insofar as cases originating in the federal courts are concerned, the rule has evolved that the doctrine of res judicata applies to adjudications relating either to jurisdiction of the person or of the subject matter where such adjudications have been made in proceedings in which those questions were in issue and in which the parties were given full opportunity to litigate. The reasons for this doctrine have frequently been stated. '. . . It is just as important that there should be a place to end as that there should be a place to begin litigation. After a party has his day in court, with opportunity to present his evidence and his view of the law, a collateral attack upon the decision as to jurisdiction there rendered merely retries the issue previously determined. There is no reason to expect that the second decision will be more satisfactory than the first.'

This Court has also held that the doctrine of res judicata must be applied to questions of jurisdiction in cases arising in state courts involving the application of the full faith and credit clause where, under the law of the state in which the original judgment was rendered, such adjudications are not susceptible to collateral attack. . . .

We believe that the decision of this Court in the *Davis* case and those in related situations are clearly indicative of the result to be reached here. Those cases stand for the proposition that the requirements of full faith and credit bar a defendant from collaterally attacking a divorce decree on jurisdictional grounds in the courts of a sister State where there has been participation by the defendant in the divorce proceedings, where the defendant has been accorded full opportunity to contest the jurisdictional issues, and where the decree is not susceptible to such collateral attack in the courts of the State which rendered the decree.

Applying these principles to this case, we hold that the Massachusetts courts erred in permitting the Florida divorce decree to be subjected to attack on the ground that petitioner was not domiciled in Florida at the time the decree was entered. Respondent participated in the Florida proceedings by entering a general appearance, filing pleadings placing in issue the very matters he sought subsequently to contest in the Massachusetts courts, personally appearing before the Florida court and giving testimony in the case, and by retaining attorneys who represented him throughout the entire proceedings. It has not been contended that respondent was given less than a full opportunity to contest the issue of petitioner's domicile or any other issue relevant to the litigation. There is nothing to indicate that the Florida court would not have evaluated fairly and in good faith all relevant evidence submitted to it. Respondent does not even contend that on the basis of the evidence introduced in the Florida proceedings, that court reached an erroneous result on the issue of petitioner's domicile. If respondent failed to take advantage of the opportunities afforded him, the responsibility is his own. We do not believe that the dereliction of a defendant under such circumstances should be permitted to provide a basis for subsequent attack in the courts of a sister State on a decree valid in the State in which it was rendered. . . .

It is urged further, however, that because we are dealing with litigation involving the dissolution of the marital relation, a different result is demanded from that which might properly be reached if this case were concerned with other types of litigation. It is pointed out that under the Constitution, the regulation and control of marital and family relationships are reserved to the States. It is urged, and properly so, that the regulation of the incidents of the marital relation involves the exercise by the States of powers of the most vital importance. Finally, it is contended that a recognition of the importance to the States of such powers demands that the requirements of full faith and credit be viewed in such a light as to permit an attack upon a divorce decree granted by a court of a sister State under the circumstances of this case even where the attack is initiated in a suit brought by the defendant in the original proceedings.

But the recognition of the importance of a State's power to determine the incidents of basic social relationships into which its domiciliaries enter does not resolve the issues of this case. This is not a situation in which a State has merely sought to exert such power over a domiciliary. This is, rather, a case involving inconsistent assertions of power by courts of two States of the Federal Union and thus presents considerations which go beyond the interests of local policy, however vital. In resolving the issues here presented, we do not conceive it to be a part of our function to weigh the relative merits of the policies of Florida and Massachusetts with respect to divorce and related matters. Nor do we understand the decisions of this Court to support the proposition that the obligation imposed by Article IV, § 1 of the Constitution and the Act of Congress passed thereunder, amounts to something less than the duty to accord full faith and credit to decrees of divorce entered by courts of sister States. The full faith and credit clause is one of the provisions incorporated into the Constitution by its framers for the purpose of transforming an aggregation of independent, sovereign States into a nation. If in its application local policy must at times be required to give way, such 'is part of the price of our federal system.'

This is not to say that in no case may an area be recognized in which reasonable accommodations of interest may properly be made. But as this Court has heretofore made clear, that area is of limited extent. We believe that in permitting an attack on the Florida divorce decree which again put in issue petitioner's Florida domicile and in refusing to recognize the validity of that decree, the Massachusetts courts have asserted a power which cannot be reconciled with the requirements of due faith and credit. We believe that assurances that such a power will be exercised sparingly and wisely render it no less repugnant to the constitutional commands.

It is one thing to recognize as permissible the judicial reexamination of findings of jurisdictional fact where such findings have been made by a court of a sister State which has entered a divorce decree in ex parte proceedings. It is quite another thing to hold that the vital rights and interests involved in divorce litigation may be held in suspense pending the scrutiny by courts of sister States of findings of jurisdictional fact made by a competent court in proceedings conducted in a manner consistent with the highest requirements of due process and in which the defendant has participated. We do not conceive it to be in accord with the purposes of the full faith and credit requirement to hold that a judgment rendered under the circumstances of this case may be required to run the gantlet of such collateral attack in the courts of sister States before its validity outside of the State which rendered it is established or rejected. That vital interests are involved in divorce litigation indicates to us that it is a matter of greater rather than lesser importance that there should be a place to end such litigation. And where a decree of divorce is rendered by a competent court under the circumstances of this case, the obligation of full faith and credit requires that such litigation should end in the courts of the State in which the judgment was rendered.

Reversed.

Johnson v. Muelberger

340 U.S. 581 (1951)

Mr. Justice REED delivered the opinion of the Court.

The right of a daughter to attack in New York the validity of her deceased father's Florida divorce is before us. She was his legatee. The divorce was granted in Florida after the father appeared there and contested the merits. The issue turns on the effect in New York under these circumstances of the Full Faith and Credit Clause of the Federal Constitution, Art. 4, § 1.

Eleanor Johnson Muelberger, respondent, is the child of decedent E. Bruce Johnson's first marriage. After the death of Johnson's first wife in 1939, he married one Madoline Ham, and they established their residence in New York. In August 1942, Madoline obtained a divorce from him in a Florida proceeding, although the undisputed facts as developed in the New York Surrogate's hearing show that she did not comply with the jurisdictional ninety-day residence requirement. The New York Surrogate found that 'In the Florida court, the decedent appeared by attorney and interposed an answer denying the wrongful acts but not questioning the allegations as to residence in Florida. The record discloses that testimony was taken by the Florida court and the divorce granted Madoline Johnson. Both parties had full opportunity to contest the jurisdictional issues in the court and the decree is not subject to attack on the ground that petitioner was not domiciled in Florida.'

In 1944 Mr. Johnson entered into a marriage, his third, with petitioner, Genevieve Johnson, and in 1945 he died, leaving a will in which he gave his entire estate to his daughter, Eleanor. After probate of the will, the third wife filed notice of her election to take the statutory one-third share of the estate, under § 18 of the New York Decedent Estate Law, McK.Consol.Laws, c. 13. This election was contested by respondent daughter, and a trial was had before the Surrogate, who determined that she could not attack the third wife's status as surviving spouse, on the basis of the alleged invalidity of Madoline's divorce, because the divorce proceeding had been a contested one, and '[s]ince the decree is valid and final in the State of Florida, it is not subject to collateral attack in the courts of this state.'

The Appellate Division affirmed the Surrogate's decree per curiam, the New York Court of Appeals reversed. The remittitur remanded the case to the Surrogate 'for further proceedings not inconsistent with' the opinion of the Court of Appeals. But in light of the record before us we assume that the requirement of Florida for a residence of 90 days as a jurisdictional basis for a Florida divorce is no longer open as an issue upon return of these proceedings to the Surrogate's Court. Accordingly the judgment under review is a final decree.

The Court of Appeals held that the Florida judgment finding jurisdiction to decree the divorce bound only the parties themselves. This followed from their previous opportunity to contest the jurisdictional issue. As the court read the Florida cases to allow Eleanor to attack the decree collaterally in Florida, it decided she should be equally free to do so in New York. The Court of Appeals reached this decision after consideration of the Full Faith and Credit Clause. Because the case involves important issues in the adjustment of the domestic-relations laws of the several states, we granted certiorari.

The clause and the statute prescribing the effect in other states of judgments of sister states are set out below. This statutory provision has remained substantially the same since 1790. There is substantially no legislative history to explain the purpose and meaning of the clause and of the statute. From judicial experience with and interpretation of the clause, there has emerged the succinct conclusion that the Framers intended it to help weld the independent states into a nation by giving judgments within the jurisdiction of the rendering state the same faith and credit in sister states as they have in the state of the original forum. The faith and credit given is not to be niggardly but generous, full. '[L]ocal policy must at times be required to give way, such 'is part of the price of our federal system.'

This constitutional purpose promotes unification, not centralization. It leaves each state with power over its own courts but binds litigants, wherever they may be in the Nation, by prior orders of other courts with jurisdiction. 'One trial of an issue is enough.' 'The principles of res judicata apply to questions of jurisdiction as well as to other issues,' as well to jurisdiction of the subject matter as of the parties.' The federal purpose of the clause makes this Court, for both state and federal courts, the 'final arbiter when the question is raised as to what is a permissible limitation on the full faith and credit clause. . . .'

It is clear from the foregoing that, under our decisions, a state by virtue of the clause must give full faith and credit to an out-of-state divorce by barring either party to that divorce who has been personally served or who has entered a personal appearance from collaterally attacking the decree. Such an attack is barred where the party attacking would not be permitted to make a collateral attack in the courts of the granting state. This rule the Court of Appeals recognized. It determined, however, that a 'stranger to the divorce action,' as the daughter was held to be in New York, may collaterally attack her father's Florida divorce in New York if she could have attacked it in Florida.

No Florida case has come to our attention holding that a child may contest in Florida its parent's divorce where the parent was barred from contesting, as here, by res judicata. . . .

We conclude that Florida would not permit Mrs. Muelberger to attack the Florida decree of divorce between her father and his second wife as beyond the jurisdiction of the rendering court. In that case New York cannot permit such an attack by reason of the Full Faith and Credit Clause. When a divorce cannot be attacked for lack of jurisdiction by parties actually before the court or strangers in the rendering state, it cannot be attacked by them anywhere in the Union. The Full Faith and Credit Clause forbids.

Reversed.

B. Personal Jurisdiction and Minimum Contacts

Unlike divorce, many cases involving family law issues do require personal jurisdiction over the defendant. Actions involving spousal support and child support, for example, are actions that typically result in money judgments—rather than status determinations. As such, courts typically need personal jurisdiction over the defendant in order to render a judgment. In *Kulko v. California*, below, the Supreme Court weighed in on the minimum contacts necessary to support personal jurisdiction in a case involving child support.

Kulko v. California
436 U.S. 84 (1978)

Mr. Justice MARSHALL delivered the opinion of the Court.

The issue before us is whether, in this action for child support, the California state courts may exercise in personam jurisdiction over a nonresident, nondomiciliary parent of minor children domiciled within the State. For reasons set forth below, we hold that the exercise of such jurisdiction would violate the Due Process Clause of the Fourteenth Amendment.

I

Appellant Ezra Kulko married appellee Sharon Kulko Horn in 1959, during appellant's three-day stopover in California en route from a military base in Texas to a tour of duty in Korea. At the time of this marriage, both parties were domiciled in and residents of New York State. Immediately following the marriage, Sharon Kulko returned to New York, as did appellant after his tour of duty. Their first child, Darwin, was born to the Kulkos in New York in 1961, and a year later their second child, Ilsa, was born, also in New York. The Kulkos and their two children resided together as a family in New York City continuously until March 1972, when the Kulkos separated.

Following the separation, Sharon Kulko moved to San Francisco, Cal. A written separation agreement was drawn up in New York; in September 1972, Sharon Kulko flew to New York City in order to sign this agreement. The agreement provided, inter alia, that the children would remain with their father during the school year but would spend their Christmas, Easter, and summer vacations with their mother. While Sharon Kulko waived any claim for her own support or maintenance, Ezra Kulko agreed to pay his wife $3,000 per year in child support for the periods when the children were in her care, custody, and control. Immediately after execution of the separation agreement, Sharon Kulko flew to Haiti and procured a divorce there; the divorce decree incorporated the terms of the agreement. She then returned to California, where she remarried and took the name Horn.

The children resided with appellant during the school year and with their mother on vacations, as provided by the separation agreement, until December 1973. At this time, just before Ilsa was to leave New York to spend Christmas vacation with her mother, she told her father that she wanted to remain in California after her vacation. Appellant bought his daughter a one-way plane ticket, and Ilsa left, taking her clothing with her. Ilsa then commenced living in California with her mother during the school year and spending vacations with her father. In January 1976, appellant's other child, Darwin, called his mother from New York and advised her that he wanted to live with her in California. Unbeknownst to appellant, appellee Horn sent a plane ticket to her son, which he used to fly to California where he took up residence with his mother and sister.

Less than one month after Darwin's arrival in California, appellee Horn commenced this action against appellant in the California Superior Court. She sought to establish the Haitian divorce decree as a California judgment; to modify the judgment so as to award her full custody of the children; and to increase appellant's child-support obligations. Appellant appeared specially and moved to quash service of the summons on the ground that he was not a resident of California and lacked sufficient "minimum contacts" with the State under *International Shoe Co. v. Washington*, 326 U.S. 310, 316, (1945), to warrant the State's assertion of personal jurisdiction over him. . . .

II

The Due Process Clause of the Fourteenth Amendment operates as a limitation on the jurisdiction of state courts to enter judgments affecting rights or interests of nonresident defendants. It has long been the rule that a valid judgment imposing a personal obligation or duty in favor of the plaintiff may be entered only by a court having jurisdiction over the person of the defendant. The existence of personal jurisdiction, in turn, depends upon the presence of reasonable notice to the defendant that an action has been brought and a sufficient connection between the defendant and the forum State to make it fair to require defense of the action in the forum. In this case, appellant does not dispute the adequacy of the notice that he received, but contends that his connection with the State of California is too attenuated, under the standards implicit in the Due Process Clause of the Constitution, to justify imposing upon him the burden and inconvenience of defense in California.

The parties are in agreement that the constitutional standard for determining whether the State may enter a binding judgment against appellant here is that set forth in this Court's opinion in *International Shoe Co. v. Washington, supra*: that a defendant "have certain minimum contacts with [the forum State] such that the maintenance of the suit does not offend 'traditional notions of fair play and substantial justice.'" While the interests of the forum State and of the plaintiff in proceeding with the cause in the plaintiff's forum of choice are, of course, to be considered . . . an essential criterion in all cases is whether the "quality and nature" of the defendant's activity is such that it is "reasonable" and "fair" to require him to conduct his defense in that State.

Like any standard that requires a determination of "reasonableness," the "minimum contacts" test of *International Shoe* is not susceptible of mechanical application; rather, the facts of each case must be weighed to determine whether the requisite "affiliating circumstances" are present. We recognize that this determination is one in which few answers will be written "in black and white. The greys are dominant and even among them the shades are innumerable." But we believe that the California Supreme Court's application of the minimum-contacts test in this case represents an unwarranted extension of *International Shoe* and would, if sustained, sanction a result that is neither fair, just, nor reasonable.

A

In reaching its result, the California Supreme Court did not rely on appellant's glancing presence in the State some 13 years before the events that led to this controversy, nor could it have. Appellant has been in California on only two occasions, once in 1959 for a three-day military stopover on his way to Korea, and again in 1960 for a 24-hour stopover on his return from Korean service. To hold such temporary visits to a State a basis for the assertion of in personam jurisdiction over unrelated actions arising in the future would make a mockery of the limitations on state jurisdiction imposed by the Fourteenth Amendment. Nor did the California court rely on the fact that appellant was actually married in California on one of his two brief visits. We agree that where two New York domiciliaries, for reasons of convenience, marry in the State of California and thereafter spend their entire married life in New York, the fact of their California marriage by itself cannot support a California court's exercise of jurisdiction over a spouse who remains a New York resident in an action relating to child support.

Finally, in holding that personal jurisdiction existed, the court below carefully disclaimed reliance on the fact that appellant had agreed at the time of separation to allow his children to live with their mother three months a year and that he had sent them to California each year pursuant to this agreement. . . . [T]o find personal jurisdiction in a State on this basis, merely because the mother was residing there, would discourage parents from entering into reasonable visitation agreements. Moreover, it could arbitrarily subject one parent to suit in any State of the Union where the other parent chose to spend time while having custody of their offspring pursuant to a separation agreement. As we have emphasized:

> "The unilateral activity of those who claim some relationship with a nonresident defendant cannot satisfy the requirement of contact with the forum State. . . . [I]t is essential in each case that there be some act by which the defendant purposefully avails [him]self of the privilege of conducting activities within the forum State. . . ."

The "purposeful act" that the California Supreme Court believed did warrant the exercise of personal jurisdiction over appellant in California was his "actively and fully consent[ing] to Ilsa living in California for the SCHOOL YEAR . . . AND . . . SEN[DING] her to California for that purpose." We cannot accept the proposition that appellant's acquiescence in Ilsa's desire to live with her mother conferred jurisdiction over appellant in the California courts in this action. A father who agrees, in the interests of family harmony and his children's preferences, to allow them to spend more time in California than was required under a separation agreement can hardly be said to have "purposefully availed himself" of the "benefits and protections" of California's laws.

Nor can we agree with the assertion of the court below that the exercise of in personam jurisdiction here was warranted by the financial benefit appellant derived from his daughter's presence in California for nine months of the year. This argument rests on the premise that, while appellant's liability for support payments remained unchanged, his yearly expenses for supporting the child in New York decreased. But this circumstance, even if true, does not support California's assertion of jurisdiction here. Any diminution in appellant's household costs resulted, not from the child's presence in California, but rather from her absence from appellant's home. Moreover, an action by appellee Horn to increase support payments could now be brought, and could have been brought when Ilsa first moved to California, in the State of New York; a New York court would clearly have personal jurisdiction over appellant and, if a judgment were entered by a New York court increasing appellant's child-support obligations, it could properly be enforced against him in both New York and California. Any ultimate financial advantage to appellant thus results not from the child's presence in California, but from appellee's failure earlier to seek an increase in payments under the separation agreement. The argument below to the contrary, in our view, confuses the question of appellant's liability with that of the proper forum in which to determine that liability.

B

In light of our conclusion that appellant did not purposefully derive benefit from any activities relating to the State of California, it is apparent that the California Supreme Court's reliance on appellant's having caused an "effect" in California was misplaced. This "effects" test is derived from the American Law Institute's Restatement (Second) of Conflict of Laws § 37 (1971), which provides:

> "A state has power to exercise judicial jurisdiction over an individual who causes effects in the state by an act done elsewhere with respect to any cause of action arising from these effects unless the nature of the effects and of the individual's relationship to the state make the exercise of such jurisdiction unreasonable."

While this provision is not binding on this Court, it does not in any event support the decision below. As is apparent from the examples accompanying § 37 in the Restatement, this section was intended to reach wrongful activity outside of the State causing injury within the State . . . or commercial activity affecting state residents. Even in such situations, moreover, the Restatement recognizes that there might be circumstances that would render "unreasonable" the assertion of jurisdiction over the nonresident defendant.

The circumstances in this case clearly render "unreasonable" California's assertion of personal jurisdiction. There is no claim that appellant has visited physical injury on either property or persons within the State of California. The cause of action herein asserted arises, not from the defendant's commercial transactions in interstate commerce, but rather from his personal, domestic relations. It thus cannot be said that appellant has sought a commercial benefit from solicitation of business from a resident of California that could reasonably render him liable to suit in state court; appellant's activities cannot fairly be analogized to an insurer's sending an insurance contract and premium notices into the State to an insured resident of the State. Furthermore, the controversy between the parties arises from a separation that occurred in the State of New York; appellee Horn seeks modification of a contract that was negotiated in New York and that she flew to New York to sign. . . .

Finally, basic considerations of fairness point decisively in favor of appellant's State of domicile as the proper forum for adjudication of this case, whatever the merits of appellee's underlying claim. It is appellant who has remained in the State of the marital domicile, whereas it is appellee who has moved across the continent. Appellant has at all times resided in New York State, and, until the separation and appellee's move to California, his entire family resided there as well. As noted above, appellant did no more than acquiesce in the stated preference of one of his children to live with her mother in California. This single act is surely not one that a reasonable parent would expect to result in the substantial financial burden and personal strain of litigating a child-support suit in a forum 3,000 miles away, and we therefore see no basis on which it can be said that appellant could reasonably have anticipated being "haled before a [California] court". . . . To make jurisdiction in a case such as this turn on whether appellant bought his daughter her ticket or instead unsuccessfully sought to prevent her departure would impose an unreasonable burden on family relations, and one wholly unjustified by the "quality and nature" of appellant's activities in or relating to the State of California.

III

In seeking to justify the burden that would be imposed on appellant were the exercise of in personam jurisdiction in California sustained, appellee argues that California has substantial interests in protecting the welfare of its minor residents and in promoting to the fullest extent possible a healthy and supportive family environment in which the children of the State are to be raised. These interests are unquestionably important. But while the presence of the children and one parent in California arguably might favor application of California law in a lawsuit in New York, the fact that California may be the "'center of gravity'" for choice-of-law purposes does not mean that California has personal jurisdiction over the defendant. And California has not attempted to assert any particularized interest in trying such cases in its courts by, e.g., enacting a special jurisdictional statute.

California's legitimate interest in ensuring the support of children resident in California without unduly disrupting the children's lives, moreover, is already being served by the State's participation in the Revised Uniform Reciprocal Enforcement of Support Act of 1968. This statute provides a mechanism for communication between court systems in different States, in order to facilitate the procurement and enforcement of child-support decrees where the dependent children reside in a State that cannot obtain personal jurisdiction over the defendant. California's version of the Act essentially permits a California resident claiming support from a nonresident to file a petition in California and have its merits adjudicated in the State of the alleged obligor's residence, without either party's having to leave his or her own State. New York State is a signatory to a similar Act. Thus, not only may plaintiff-appellee here vindicate her claimed right to additional child support from her former husband in a New York court . . . but also the Uniform Acts will facilitate both her prosecution of a claim for additional support and collection of any support payments found to be owed by appellant.

It cannot be disputed that California has substantial interests in protecting resident children and in facilitating child-support actions on behalf of those children. But these interests simply do not make California a "fair forum," in which to require appellant, who derives no personal or commercial benefit from his child's presence in California and who lacks any other relevant contact with the State, either to defend a child-support suit or to suffer liability by default.

IV

We therefore believe that the state courts in the instant case failed to heed our admonition that "the flexible standard of *International Shoe*" does not "heral[d] the eventual demise of all restrictions on the personal jurisdiction of state courts." In

McGee v. International Life Ins. Co., we commented on the extension of in personam jurisdiction under evolving standards of due process, explaining that this trend was in large part "attributable to the . . . increasing nationalization of commerce . . . [accompanied by] modern transportation and communication [that] have made it much less burdensome for a party sued to defend himself in a State where he engages in economic activity." But the mere act of sending a child to California to live with her mother is not a commercial act and connotes no intent to obtain or expectancy of receiving a corresponding benefit in the State that would make fair the assertion of that State's judicial jurisdiction.

Accordingly, we conclude that the appellant's motion to quash service, on the ground of lack of personal jurisdiction, was erroneously denied by the California courts. The judgment of the California Supreme Court is, therefore,

Reversed.

Chapter 17

Jurisdiction and Venue in Family Law Matters

A. Federal vs. State Jurisdiction

Unlike state courts, federal courts are vested with limited subject matter jurisdiction. Article III of the U.S. Constitution sets forth the outer limits of federal court jurisdiction—which includes "cases . . . arising under the Constitution, the laws of the United States, and treaties made, or which shall be made, under their authority." Federal legislation further defines the limits of federal court jurisdiction. For example, 28 U.S.C. § 1331 vests federal district courts with original jurisdiction in "all civil actions arising under the Constitution, laws, or treaties of the United States."

Family law issues sometimes find themselves in federal court pursuant to § 1331 "federal question jurisdiction" when the issue at hand touches on a federal law, a constitutional right, or both. In *Zablocki v. Redhail*, 434 U.S. 374 (1978), Redhail brought a class action in federal district court pursuant to 42 U.S.C. § 1983 arguing that a Wisconsin statute that precluded him from obtaining a marriage license violated his (and others') Fourteenth Amendment equal protection and due process rights. Section 1983 allows a civil action whenever a state law results in "the deprivation of any rights, privileges or immunities secured by the Constitution." Section 1331, in turn, vests federal courts with original jurisdiction over § 1983 claims. Similarly, some of the petitioners in *Obergefell v. Hodges*, 135 S. Ct. 2585 (2015), brought § 1983 claims in federal district court arguing that state prohibitions on same-sex marriage violated various constitutionally protected rights.

Federal court jurisdiction is more limited in cases that do not involve federal law or constitutional challenges. Civil actions involving matters of only state law are generally reserved for the state courts. However, 28 U.S.C. § 1332 confers federal district courts with original jurisdiction in "all civil actions where the matter in controversy exceeds the sum or value of $75,000" and is between litigants with diversity of citizenship such as "citizens of different states." Many family law matters could, conceivably, be properly brought in federal court pursuant to § 1332 "diversity jurisdiction." For example, a divorce action where a spouse sought spousal support or property in excess of $75,000 from a spouse who was domiciled in a different state would seem to meet the criteria for § 1332 jurisdiction. However, the so-called "domestic relations exception" to diversity jurisdiction precludes many family law matters from being heard by federal courts. *Ackenbrandt v. Richards*, below, explores the history and limits of the domestic relations exception.

Ankenbrandt v. Richards

504 U.S. 689 (1992)

Justice WHITE delivered the opinion of the Court.

This case presents the issue whether the federal courts have jurisdiction or should abstain in a case involving alleged torts committed by the former husband of petitioner and his female companion against petitioner's children, when the sole basis for federal jurisdiction is the diversity-of-citizenship provision of 28 U.S.C. § 1332.

I

Petitioner Carol Ankenbrandt, a citizen of Missouri, brought this lawsuit on September 26, 1989, on behalf of her daughters L.R. and S.R. against respondents Jon A. Richards and Debra Kesler, citizens of Louisiana, in the United States District Court for the Eastern District of Louisiana. Alleging federal jurisdiction based on the diversity-of-citizenship provision of § 1332, Ankenbrandt's complaint sought monetary damages for alleged sexual and physical abuse of the children committed by Richards and Kesler. Richards is the divorced father of the children and Kesler his female companion. On December 10, 1990, the District Court granted respondents' motion to dismiss this lawsuit. . . . [T]he court concluded that this case fell within what has become known as the "domestic relations" exception to diversity jurisdiction, and that it lacked jurisdiction over the case. The court also invoked the abstention principles announced in *Younger v. Harris*, 401 U.S. 37 (1971), to justify its decision to dismiss the complaint without prejudice. The Court of Appeals affirmed in an unpublished opinion.

We granted certiorari limited to the following questions: "(1) Is there a domestic relations exception to federal jurisdiction? (2) If so, does it permit a district court to abstain from exercising diversity jurisdiction over a tort action for damages?" and "(3) Did the District Court in this case err in abstaining from exercising jurisdiction under the doctrine of *Younger v. Harris*?"

We address each of these issues in turn.

II

The domestic relations exception upon which the courts below relied to decline jurisdiction has been invoked often by the lower federal courts. The seeming authority for doing so originally stemmed from the announcement in *Barber v. Barber*, 21 How. 582 (1859), that the federal courts have no jurisdiction over suits for divorce or the allowance of alimony. In that case, the Court heard a suit in equity brought by a wife (by her next friend) in Federal District Court pursuant to diversity jurisdiction against her former husband. She sought to enforce a decree from a New York state court, which had granted a divorce and awarded her alimony. The former husband thereupon moved to Wisconsin to place himself beyond the New York courts' jurisdiction so that the divorce decree there could not be enforced against him; he then sued for divorce in a Wisconsin court, representing to that court that his wife had abandoned him and failing to disclose the existence of the New York decree. In a suit brought by the former wife in Wisconsin Federal District Court, the former husband alleged that the court lacked jurisdiction. The court accepted jurisdiction and gave judgment for the divorced wife.

On appeal, it was argued that the District Court lacked jurisdiction on two grounds: first, that there was no diversity of citizenship because although divorced, the wife's citizenship necessarily remained that of her former husband; and second, that the whole subject of divorce and alimony, including a suit to enforce an alimony decree, was exclusively ecclesiastical at the time of the adoption of the Constitution and that the Constitution therefore placed the whole subject of divorce and alimony beyond the jurisdiction of the United States courts. Over the dissent of three Justices, the Court rejected both arguments. After an exhaustive survey of the authorities, the Court concluded that a divorced wife could acquire a citizenship separate from that of her former husband and that a suit to enforce an alimony decree rested within the federal courts' equity jurisdiction. The Court reached these conclusions after summarily dismissing the former husband's contention that the case involved a subject matter outside the federal courts' jurisdiction. In so stating, however, the Court also announced the following limitation on federal jurisdiction:

> "Our first remark is—and we wish it to be remembered—that this is not a suit asking the court for the allowance of alimony. That has been done by a court of competent jurisdiction. The court in Wisconsin was asked to interfere to prevent that decree from being defeated by fraud.
>
> "We disclaim altogether any jurisdiction in the courts of the United States upon the subject of divorce, or for the allowance of alimony, either as an original proceeding in chancery or as an incident to divorce a vinculo, or to one from bed and board."

As a general matter, the dissenters agreed with these statements, but took issue with the Court's holding that the instant action to enforce an alimony decree was within the equity jurisdiction of the federal courts.

The statements disclaiming jurisdiction over divorce and alimony decree suits, though technically dicta, formed the basis for excluding "domestic relations" cases from the jurisdiction of the lower federal courts, a jurisdictional limitation those courts have recognized ever since. The *Barber* Court, however, cited no authority and did not discuss the foundation for its announcement. Since that time, the Court has dealt only occasionally with the domestic relations limitation on federal-court jurisdiction, and it has never addressed the basis for such a limitation. Because we are unwilling to cast aside an understood rule that has been recognized for nearly a century and a half, we feel compelled to explain why we will continue to recognize this limitation on federal jurisdiction. . . .

B

That Article III, § 2, does not mandate the exclusion of domestic relations cases from federal-court jurisdiction, however, does not mean that such courts necessarily must retain and exercise jurisdiction over such cases. Other constitutional provisions explain why this is so. Article I, § 8, cl. 9, for example, authorizes Congress "[t]o constitute Tribunals inferior to the supreme Court" and Article III, § 1, states that "[t]he judicial Power of the United States, shall be vested in one supreme Court, and in such inferior Courts as the Congress may from time to time ordain and establish." The Court's cases state the rule that "if inferior federal courts were created, [Congress was not] required to invest them with all the jurisdiction it was authorized to bestow under Art. III."

This position has held constant since at least 1845, when the Court stated that "the judicial power of the United States . . . is (except in enumerated instances, applicable exclusively to this Court) dependent for its distribution and organization, and for the modes of its exercise, entirely upon the action of Congress, who possess the sole power of creating the tribunals (inferior to the Supreme Court) . . . and of investing them with jurisdiction either limited, concurrent, or exclusive, and of withholding jurisdiction from them in the exact degrees and character which to Congress may seem proper for the public good." We thus turn our attention to the relevant jurisdictional statutes.

The Judiciary Act of 1789 provided that "the circuit courts shall have original cognizance, concurrent with the courts of the several States, of all suits of a civil nature at common law or in equity, where the matter in dispute exceeds, exclusive of costs, the sum or value of five hundred dollars, and . . . an alien is a party, or the suit is between a citizen of the State where the suit is brought, and a citizen of another State." The defining phrase, "all suits of a civil nature at common law or in equity," remained a key element of statutory provisions demarcating the terms of diversity jurisdiction until 1948, when Congress amended the diversity jurisdiction provision to eliminate this phrase and replace in its stead the term "all civil actions."

The *Barber* majority itself did not expressly refer to the diversity statute's use of the limitation on "suits of a civil nature at common law or in equity." The dissenters in *Barber*, however, implicitly made such a reference, for they suggested that the federal courts had no power over certain domestic relations actions because the court of chancery lacked authority to issue divorce and alimony decrees. Stating that "[t]he origin and the extent of [the federal courts'] jurisdiction must be sought in the laws of the United States, and in the settled rules and principles by which those laws have bound them," the dissenters contended that "as the jurisdiction of the chancery in England does not extend to or embrace the subjects of divorce and alimony, and as the jurisdiction of the courts of the United States in chancery is bounded by that of the chancery in England, all power or cognizance with respect to those subjects by the courts of the United States in chancery is equally excluded." Hence, in the dissenters' view, a suit seeking such relief would not fall within the statutory language "all suits of a civil nature at common law or in equity." Because the *Barber* Court did not disagree with this reason for accepting the jurisdictional limitation over the issuance of divorce and alimony decrees, it may be inferred fairly that the jurisdictional limitation recognized by the Court rested on this statutory basis and that the disagreement between the Court and the dissenters thus centered only on the extent of the limitation.

We have no occasion here to join the historical debate over whether the English court of chancery had jurisdiction to handle certain domestic relations matters, though we note that commentators have found some support for the *Barber* majority's interpretation. Certainly it was not unprecedented at the time for the Court to infer, from what it understood to be English chancery practice, some guide to the meaning of the 1789 Act's jurisdictional grant. We thus are content to rest our conclusion that a domestic relations exception exists as a matter of statutory construction not on the accuracy of the historical justifications on which it was seemingly based, but rather on Congress' apparent acceptance of this construction of the diversity jurisdiction provisions in the years prior to 1948, when the statute limited jurisdiction to "suits of a civil nature at common law or in equity. . . ."

When Congress amended the diversity statute in 1948 to replace the law/equity distinction with the phrase "all civil actions," we presume Congress did so with full cognizance of the Court's nearly century-long interpretation of the prior statutes, which had construed the statutory diversity jurisdiction to contain an exception for certain domestic relations matters. With respect to the 1948 amendment, the Court has previously stated that "no changes of law or policy are to be presumed from changes of language in the revision unless an intent to make such changes is clearly expressed." With respect to such a longstanding and well-known construction of the diversity statute, and where Congress made substantive changes to the statute in other respects, we presume, absent any indication that Congress intended to alter this exception, that Congress "adopt[ed] that interpretation" when it reenacted the diversity statute.

III

In the more than 100 years since this Court laid the seeds for the development of the domestic relations exception, the lower federal courts have applied it in a variety of circumstances. Many of these applications go well beyond the circumscribed situations posed by *Barber* and its progeny. *Barber* itself disclaimed federal jurisdiction over a narrow range of domestic relations issues involving the granting of a divorce and a decree of alimony . . . and stated the limits on federal-court power to intervene prior to the rendering of such orders:

> "It is, that when a court of competent jurisdiction over the subject-matter and the parties decrees a divorce, and alimony to the wife as its incident, and is unable of itself to enforce the decree summarily upon the husband, that courts of equity will interfere to prevent the decree from being defeated by fraud. The interference, however, is limited to cases in which alimony has been decreed; then only to the extent of what is due, and always to cases in which no appeal is pending from the decree for the divorce or for alimony."

The *Barber* Court thus did not intend to strip the federal courts of authority to hear cases arising from the domestic relations of persons unless they seek the granting or modification of a divorce or alimony decree. The holding of the case itself sanctioned the exercise of federal jurisdiction over the enforcement of an alimony decree that had been properly obtained in a state court of competent jurisdiction. Contrary to the *Barber* dissenters' position, the enforcement of such validly obtained orders does not "regulate the domestic relations of society" and produce an "inquisitorial authority" in which federal tribunals "enter the habitations and even into the chambers and nurseries of private families, and inquire into and pronounce upon the morals and habits and affections or antipathies of the members of every household." And from the conclusion that the federal courts lacked jurisdiction to issue divorce and alimony decrees, there was no dissent. . . .

Subsequently, this Court expanded the domestic relations exception to include decrees in child custody cases. In a child custody case brought pursuant to a writ of habeas corpus, for instance, the Court held void a writ issued by a Federal District Court to restore a child to the custody of the father. "As to the right to the control and possession of this child, as it is contested by its father and its grandfather, it is one in regard to which neither the Congress of the United States nor any authority of the United States has any special jurisdiction. . . ."

We conclude, therefore, that the domestic relations exception, as articulated by this Court since *Barber*, divests the federal courts of power to issue divorce, alimony, and child custody decrees. Given the long passage of time without any expression of congressional dissatisfaction, we have no trouble today reaffirming the validity of the exception as it pertains to divorce and alimony decrees and child custody orders.

Not only is our conclusion rooted in respect for this long-held understanding, it is also supported by sound policy considerations. Issuance of decrees of this type not infrequently involves retention of jurisdiction by the court and deployment of social workers to monitor compliance. As a matter of judicial economy, state courts are more eminently suited to work of this type than are federal courts, which lack the close association with state and local government organizations dedicated to handling issues that arise out of conflicts over divorce, alimony, and child custody decrees. Moreover, as a matter of judicial expertise, it makes far more sense to retain the rule that federal courts lack power to issue these types of decrees because of the special proficiency developed by state tribunals over the past century and a half in handling issues that arise in the granting of such decrees.

By concluding, as we do, that the domestic relations exception encompasses only cases involving the issuance of a divorce, alimony, or child custody decree, we necessarily find that the Court of Appeals erred by affirming the District Court's invocation of this exception. This lawsuit in no way seeks such a decree; rather, it alleges that respondents Richards and Kesler committed torts against L.R. and S.R., Ankenbrandt's children by Richards. Federal subject-matter jurisdiction pursuant to § 1332 thus is proper in this case. We now address whether, even though subject-matter jurisdiction might be proper, sufficient grounds exist to warrant abstention from the exercise of that jurisdiction.

IV

The Court of Appeals, as did the District Court, stated abstention as an alternative ground for its holding. . . . It is axiomatic, however, that "[a]bstention from the exercise of federal jurisdiction is the exception, not the rule." *Colorado River Water Conservation Dist. v. United States*, 424 U.S. 800, 813 (1976). Abstention rarely should be invoked, because the federal courts have a "virtually unflagging obligation . . . to exercise the jurisdiction given them."

The courts below cited *Younger v. Harris*, 401 U.S. 37 (1971), to support their holdings to abstain in this case. In so doing, the courts clearly erred. *Younger* itself held that, absent unusual circumstances, a federal court could not interfere with a pending state criminal prosecution. Though we have extended *Younger* abstention to the civil context . . . we have never applied the notions of comity so critical to *Younger*'s "Our Federalism" when no state proceeding was pending nor any assertion of important state interests made. In this case, there is no allegation by respondents of any pending state proceedings, and Ankenbrandt contends that such proceedings ended prior to her filing this lawsuit. Absent any pending proceeding in state tribunals, therefore, application by the lower courts of *Younger* abstention was clearly erroneous.

It is not inconceivable, however, that in certain circumstances, the abstention principles developed in *Burford v. Sun Oil Co.*, 319 U.S. 315 (1943), might be relevant in a case involving elements of the domestic relationship even when the parties do not seek divorce, alimony, or child custody. This would be so when a case presents "difficult questions of state law bearing on policy problems of substantial public import whose importance transcends the result in the case then at bar." Such might well be the case if a federal suit were filed prior to effectuation of a divorce, alimony, or child custody decree, and the suit depended on a determination of the status of the parties. Where, as here, the status of the domestic relationship has been determined as a matter of state law, and in any event has no bearing on the underlying torts alleged, we have no difficulty concluding that *Burford* abstention is inappropriate in this case.

V

We thus conclude that the Court of Appeals erred by affirming the District Court's rulings to decline jurisdiction based on the domestic relations exception to diversity jurisdiction and to abstain under the doctrine of *Younger v. Harris*, *supra*. The exception has no place in a suit such as this one, in which a former spouse sues another on behalf of children alleged to have been abused. Because the allegations in this complaint do not request the District Court to issue a divorce, alimony, or child custody decree, we hold that the suit is appropriate for the exercise of § 1332 jurisdiction given the existence of diverse citizenship between petitioner and respondents and the pleading of the relevant amount in controversy. Accordingly, we reverse the decision of the Court of Appeals and remand the case for further proceedings consistent with this opinion.

It is so ordered.

B. Interstate Jurisdiction; In General

See 26 U.S.C. § 1738A (PKPA); La. Rev. Stat. § 13:1801 *et seq.* (La. UCCJEA); La. Child. Code art. 1301.1 *et seq.* (La. UIFSA).

The *Williams* and *Kulko* decisions and their progeny demonstrate that it is possible for multiple states to have jurisdiction over a particular family law matter. While those cases remain good law, over the years, states have enacted a number of "uniform" statutes aimed at addressing jurisdictional issues in cases involving child custody and support. Presently, every state has adopted the Uniform Interstate Family Support Act (UIFSA) and the Uniform Child Custody Jurisdiction and Enforcement Act (UCCJEA), or comparable predecessor uniform acts.

The UCCJEA sets forth rules for determining which state has jurisdiction to make an initial child custody determination. Once a court has exercised jurisdiction, the UCCJEA generally vests that court with continuing exclusive jurisdiction over the matter in order to prevent duplicative and conflicting proceedings. The UCCJEA bases initial jurisdiction on four potential grounds: home state, significant connections, last resort, and emergency. The Act establishes a strong preference for home state jurisdiction. Home state is defined in La. Rev. Stat. § 13:1802 as follows:

> (7)(a) "Home state" means the state in which a child lived with a parent or a person acting as a parent for at least six consecutive months immediately before the commencement of a child custody proceeding. In the case of a child less than six months of age, the term means the state in which the child lived from birth with any of the persons mentioned. A period of temporary absence of any of the mentioned persons is part of the period.

La. Rev. Stat. § 13:1813 explains that, generally, initial jurisdiction rests with the court in the home state. If, however, there is no home state or the home state has declined jurisdiction, then a state with significant connections may exercise jurisdiction. If there is no such state, or the state with significant connections has declined jurisdiction, then any court can exercise jurisdiction as a sort of "last resort" jurisdiction. La. Rev. Stat. § 13:1816 vests courts with temporary emergency jurisdiction under appropriate circumstances.

The UIFSA sets forth rules for determining which state has initial jurisdiction to make a determination of child support. In many respects, the UIFSA and the UCCJEA are similar. Like the UCCJEA, the UIFSA vests courts with continuing exclusive jurisdiction in an effort to prevent duplicative and conflicting proceedings. The UIFSA also establishes a preference for home state jurisdiction.

Albitar v. Albitar, below, demonstrates the interaction of the various constitutional principles set forth in *Williams* and *Kulko*, as well as the relevance of the UCCJEA.

One goal of the UCCJEA was to eliminate duplicative and conflicting proceedings in different states. As demonstrated by the two *Marsalis* cases, below, this goal has not always been achieved.

Albitar v. Albitar

197 So. 3d 332 (La. App. 5 Cir. 2016)

WICKER, J.

In this proceeding for divorce, custody, and ancillary matters, defendant, Zouhair K. Albitar, assigns error to the trial court's judgment denying his exceptions of lack of personal and subject matter jurisdiction and the trial court's judgment awarding plaintiff, Michelle Lee Lannes Albitar, sole custody of the parties' minor child, as well as child and spousal support, and injunctive relief related to the pending divorce proceeding. For the reasons fully discussed herein, we affirm the trial court's judgments.

PROCEDURAL AND FACTUAL HISTORY

On June 25, 2015, plaintiff filed a "Petition for Divorce in Accordance with Louisiana Civil Code Article 102 (with Children) and Ancillary Relief Related Thereto," in the Twenty-Ninth Judicial District Court for the Parish of St. Charles. In her petition, plaintiff alleged that she and defendant were married in New Orleans, Louisiana, in 2002, and that one child was born of the marriage in 2009. Plaintiff's petition asserted that she was domiciled in St. Charles Parish, Louisiana, and therefore jurisdiction and venue were proper in St. Charles Parish. In her petition, plaintiff also sought interim spousal support and child support in her favor, and an order granting her exclusive use and possession of a 2005 Infiniti QX56. Plaintiff further requested that the trial court issue a temporary restraining order restraining defendant from alienating any community property, harassing plaintiff, or removing the minor child from St. Charles Parish without the express consent of plaintiff or by order of the trial court issued subsequent to a contradictory hearing. Lastly, plaintiff sought an order granting her permanent sole custody of the minor child and designation as the primary domiciliary parent.

Simultaneous to filing her petition, plaintiff filed a motion and order to appoint a curator, alleging that defendant resided outside of the United States of America and that defendant's whereabouts were unknown to plaintiff. On July 8, 2015, the trial court appointed a curator ad hoc to represent defendant, and service of plaintiff's petition was made on the curator ad hoc. [Defendant raised various exceptions based on jurisdiction. The court found in favor of plaintiff.]

LAW AND ANALYSIS

. . . .

The Merits

In his first assignment of error, defendant argues that the trial court erred in denying his exceptions to plaintiff's petition, because the trial court lacked personal and subject matter jurisdiction over the various claims related to plaintiff's petition for divorce.

Jurisdiction, a term with multiple meanings, primarily indicates the power to adjudicate. Subject matter jurisdiction, defined by La. C.C.P. art. 2 as "the legal power and authority of a court to hear and determine a particular class of actions or proceedings, based upon the object of the demand, the amount in dispute, or the value of the right asserted," is an essential element for every civil action. In every civil case in Louisiana, the court must have not only subject matter jurisdiction, but also either (1) personal jurisdiction under La. C.C.P. art. 6, (2) property jurisdiction under La. C.C.P. art. 8 or 9, or (3) status jurisdiction under La. C.C.P. art. 10.

Jurisdiction over the Divorce and Ancillary Matters

In her petition, plaintiff sought, inter alia, a judgment of divorce after the delays required by La. C.C. art. 102, along with orders awarding plaintiff interim spousal support, exclusive use of a vehicle, and injunctive relief related to the pending divorce proceedings. Defendant argues that the trial court erred in granting plaintiff's requested relief because it lacked subject matter jurisdiction to render those orders and lacked jurisdiction over defendant's person.

La. C.C.P. art. 10 provides that a Louisiana trial court has jurisdiction over a divorce action, if at the time of filing, one or both of the spouses are domiciled in Louisiana. Moreover, under La. C.C.P. art. 3941, the venue of a divorce action is jurisdictional and cannot be waived. The proper venue for a divorce action is the parish where either party is domiciled or in the parish of the last matrimonial domicile. There is no dispute that defendant was not domiciled in Louisiana at the time plaintiff filed her petition, nor do the parties dispute that the last matrimonial domicile was outside of Louisiana. Therefore, the only issue we address is whether plaintiff was domiciled in St. Charles Parish at the time she filed her petition.

The domicile of a natural person is the place of his habitual residence. La. C.C.P. art. 38. Domicile is maintained until acquisition of a new domicile. La. C.C.P. art. 44. A natural person changes domicile when he moves his residence to another location with the intent to make that location his habitual residence. Proof of one's intent to establish or change domicile depends on the circumstances. A sworn declaration of intent recorded in the parishes from which and to which he intends to move may be considered as evidence of intent. La. C.C.P. art. 45.

In establishing domicile, intent is based upon the actual state of facts and not what one declares them to be. The circumstances indicating establishment of a domicile include where a person sleeps, takes his or her meals, has established his or her household, and surrounds himself or herself with family and the comforts of domestic life.

The determination of plaintiff's intent to establish domicile in St. Charles Parish is a question of fact; the trial court's findings of fact are not disturbed on appeal unless they are clearly wrong or manifestly erroneous. Reversal is warranted only if the appellate court finds that a reasonable factual basis for the trial court's finding does not exist in the record, and that the finding is clearly wrong on the record. . . .

It is undisputed that plaintiff was physically residing in St. Charles Parish at the time she filed her petition. Therefore our inquiry turns to whether the evidence shows that plaintiff possessed the requisite intent to make St. Charles Parish her habitual residence at the time she filed her petition.

Louisiana jurisprudence offers guidance as to relevant circumstances to consider in determining whether a spouse has shown the requisite intent to change domicile. Factors relevant to this appeal include a spouse changing his or her driver's license or voter registration to reflect an address within the new domiciliary parish, and arranging for child care within the new domiciliary parish.

At the hearing on defendant's exceptions, plaintiff introduced the declarations of intent to change domicile from Texas to St. Charles Parish, which plaintiff executed before a notary and two witnesses on June 24, 2015. Additionally, plaintiff introduced her personal driver's license, issued on January 14, 2014, reflecting a St. Charles Parish address, and her voter registration card, reflecting that she registered to vote in St. Charles Parish on August 6, 2014. Plaintiff also introduced a "Temporary Residency Verification" form required for the minor child to attend St. Charles Parish schools, notarized on June 24, 2015, wherein plaintiff attested to residing in St. Charles Parish with her father at the same address listed on her previously issued driver's license.

Defendant asserts that plaintiff's declarations of intent and temporary residency verification, which plaintiff executed one day prior to filing her petition, demonstrate that plaintiff did not possess a bona fide intent to establish St. Charles as her domicile; rather, defendant argues, plaintiff is attempting to manufacture jurisdiction in St. Charles Parish. Defendant alleges that plaintiff and the minor child were domiciliaries of Saudi Arabia for at least four years prior to the date plaintiff filed her petition and that they returned to the United States for a vacation rather than to remain there. In support of his argument, plaintiff filed numerous documents purporting to reflect translated Saudi Arabian government documents showing that plaintiff and the minor child were issued travel visas within Saudi Arabia during the marriage and that the minor child attended school in Saudi Arabia during the year prior to plaintiff filing her petition.

Plaintiff concedes that she visited Saudi Arabia during 2015 for several months to attempt to reconcile with defendant, but that she returned to St. Charles Parish, where she had previously established domicile, in May of 2015 after the reconciliation attempts failed.

Upon review of the competent evidence introduced at the hearing, we find that plaintiff became a domiciliary of St. Charles Parish as early as 2014. On June 24, 2015, plaintiff executed declarations of intent to change domicile, wherein she attested by authentic act that she moved to St. Charles Parish in mid-2014 with the intent to abandon her former domicile and establish St. Charles Parish as her new domicile. Though the declarations of intent and temporary residency verification were not executed until one day prior to commencing these proceedings, plaintiff's attestations therein were corroborated by her driver's license, reflecting a St. Charles Parish address and an issuance date in 2014, and her voter's registration card, reflecting plaintiff's registration to vote in St. Charles Parish in 2014. Furthermore, the residential real estate listing agreement for the former family home supports the conclusion that plaintiff had no intent to return to Texas.

While plaintiff admitted to travelling to Saudi Arabia for an extended visit in 2015, the record is devoid of any evidence showing plaintiff's intent to relinquish her St. Charles Parish domicile and establish Saudi Arabia as her new domicile. None of the Saudi Arabian documents introduced by defendant bear the certifications required by La. C.E. art. 902(3) to authenticate foreign public documents, nor was there any extrinsic evidence introduced to authenticate either the documents themselves or the accompanying translations. Moreover, even if admissible, the travel visas and residence permits introduced by defendant fail to positively establish plaintiff's and the minor child's physical presence in Saudi Arabia; rather, this evidence would merely show that plaintiff and the minor child had governmental permission to travel therein. Considering the foregoing evidence, we find no manifest error in the trial court's finding that plaintiff was domiciled in St. Charles Parish prior to filing her petition. Accordingly, we find that the trial court has jurisdiction over the divorce proceedings pursuant to La. C.C.P. art. 10.

However, only the marital status is subject to adjudication under the status jurisdiction conferred by La. C.C.P. art. 10. Ancillary claims for alimony or support require personal jurisdiction over the nonresident defendant who owes the personal obligation. Thus, we must determine whether the trial court had personal jurisdiction over defendant, as required to issue the ancillary support orders.

When reviewing a trial court's legal ruling on a declinatory exception of lack of personal jurisdiction, an appellate court applies a de novo standard. However, the trial court's factual findings underlying the decision are reviewed under the manifest error standard of review.

The Louisiana long-arm statute, La. R.S. 13:3201, provides for the exercise of personal jurisdiction over a nonresident defendant. Subsection B of the statute provides that jurisdiction under the long-arm statute extends to the limits allowed by due process. Thus, "if the assertion of jurisdiction meets the constitutional requirements of due process the assertion of jurisdiction is authorized under the long arm statute."

This due process requirement has evolved into a two-part test. In order to subject a nonresident defendant to personal jurisdiction, the defendant must have certain minimum contacts with the forum state such that the maintenance of the suit does not offend traditional notions of fair play and substantial justice.

The "minimum contacts" prong is satisfied by a single act or actions by which the defendant "purposefully avails itself of the privilege of conducting activities within the forum state, thus invoking the benefits and protections of its laws." This "purposeful availment" must be such that the defendant "should reasonably anticipate being haled into court" in the forum state. This part of the test ensures that the defendant will not be haled into a jurisdiction solely as a result of a random, fortuitous, or attenuated contact, or by the unilateral activity of another party or a third person. If the defendant deliberately engages in significant activities within a state, or creates continuing obligations between himself and residents of the forum, he manifestly has availed himself of the privilege of conducting business there. Because his activities are shielded by the benefits and protections of the forum's laws, it is presumptively not unreasonable to require the defendant to submit to the burdens of litigation in that forum.

The second part of the due process test centers around the fairness of the assertion of jurisdiction. Once minimum contacts are established, these contacts may be considered in light of other factors to determine whether the assertion of personal jurisdiction would comport with "fair play and substantial justice." Thus, once the plaintiff meets his burden of proving minimum contacts, "a presumption of reasonableness of jurisdiction arises" and "the burden then shifts to the opposing party to prove the assertion of jurisdiction would be so unreasonable in light of traditional notions of fair play and substantial justice as to overcome the presumption of reasonableness created by the defendant's minimum contacts with the forum." In determining this fundamental fairness issue, the relevant considerations are: (1) the defendant's burden; (2) the forum state's interest; (3) the plaintiff's interest in convenient and effective relief; (4) the judicial system's interest in efficient resolution of controversies; and (5) the state's shared interest in furthering fundamental social policies.

Applying the law to the facts of this case, we find that defendant had sufficient minimum contacts with the state of Louisiana to reasonably anticipate being haled into court in Louisiana. The record reflects that plaintiff and defendant were married in New Orleans in 2002 and that both of plaintiff's parents reside in Louisiana. At the hearing on plaintiff's petition, plaintiff's mother testified that during the course of the parties' marriage, defendant directed some of his mail, including bank statements, to be delivered to her address in Kenner, Louisiana. Additionally, in 2013 and 2014, the parties employed an accountant located in Metairie, Louisiana to prepare their tax returns. Because defendant deliberately engaged in activities shielded by the benefits and protections of Louisiana law, we find it presumptively reasonable to require that he submit to the burdens of litigation in Louisiana.

Turning to the issue of fundamental fairness, we find that assertion of jurisdiction is not so unreasonable as to offend the traditional notions of fair play and substantial justice. Having already concluded that the trial court had jurisdiction over the divorce proceeding, we find that Louisiana has a significant interest in adjudicating those ancillary claims for support and injunctive relief which are intricately intertwined with the divorce proceeding. For that same reason, we find that the assertion of jurisdiction over those ancillary matters would further the judiciary's interest in efficiently resolving all of the related claims asserted within plaintiff's petition and would further plaintiff's interest in obtaining convenient and effective relief. Finally, we find that Texas, where the parties co-owned real estate and filed joint tax returns, may be an alternative forum state possessing jurisdiction over defendant's person. Given defendant's current residence in the distant country of Saudi Arabia, we find that any burden imposed on defendant by requiring litigation in Louisiana, as opposed to the alternative forum of our nearby neighboring state of Texas, is insignificant.

Accordingly, we find no error in the trial court's denial of defendant's exception of lack of personal jurisdiction.

Jurisdiction over Custody Matters

In his second assignment of error, defendant argues that even if the trial court had jurisdiction over plaintiff's petition for divorce and ancillary matters related thereto, the trial court did not have jurisdiction over any matters related to the custody proceedings under the UCCJEA.

Under La. Const. art. V, § 16(A), the trial court in St. Charles Parish had subject matter jurisdiction to adjudicate the particular class of action, i.e., child custody and support matters. However, the UCCJEA grafts a second tier of inquiry onto the question of subject matter jurisdiction for Louisiana courts considering child custody issues. A Louisiana court may have subject matter jurisdiction, but must decline that jurisdiction based on jurisdictional limitations imposed by the UCCJEA. These limitations further the UCCJEA's purposes, including avoiding jurisdictional competition, assuring that custody litigation takes place in the state with which the child and his family have the "closest connection" and where relevant evidence is located, promoting a stable home environment, deterring abductions, and encouraging cooperation among the courts of different states. Although likened to subject matter jurisdiction, the choice of the optimum jurisdiction to resolve custody battles under the UCCJEA actually focuses on the strength of connections between the minor child and the state, more akin to a personal jurisdiction analysis. However, our lower courts have generally approached the limitations imposed by the UCCJEA as equivalent to declarations of subject matter jurisdiction which mandate that the jurisdictional requirements of the UCCJEA be met when the custody request is filed.

The UCCJEA provides four alternatives as a basis for a state to assert jurisdiction: (1) "home state" jurisdiction; (2) "significant connection" jurisdiction; (3) "emergency" jurisdiction; and (4) "residual" jurisdiction. The UCCJEA defines "home state" as:

> [T]he state in which a child lived with a parent or a person acting as a parent for at least six consecutive months immediately before the commencement of a child custody proceeding. In the case of a child less than six months of age, the term means the state in which the child lived from birth with any of the persons mentioned. A period of temporary absence of any of the mentioned persons is part of the period.

La. R.S. 13:1802(7)(a).

At the hearing on defendant's exceptions, plaintiff introduced certified copies of her two declarations of intent to change domicile, which were recorded in both Harris County, Texas, and St. Charles Parish. Within these filings, which are in authentic form, plaintiff averred that in May of 2014 she moved from Harris County, Texas to St. Charles Parish, where she remained at the time she filed her petition. At the hearing, plaintiff testified that, since the minor child's birth, he has lived solely with plaintiff in either Texas or St. Charles Parish.

As he argued in support of his first assignment of error, defendant again asserts that plaintiff and the minor child lived with defendant in Saudi Arabia for the majority of the child's life. Defendant further asserts that shortly before filing her petition, plaintiff and the child were living in Saudi Arabia with defendant and returned to the United States for a temporary visit. In support of his exception, defendant points to the Saudi Arabia documents introduced at the exception hearing. For the reasons discussed above, we will not consider these documents in our de novo review.

Upon review of the competent evidence in the record, we find that plaintiff's authentic declarations of intent to change domicile, corroborated by her testimony, updated driver's license, and updated voter registration, established that the minor child began living in Louisiana more than twelve months prior to commencing the custody proceedings and for a period exceeding six consecutive months. The totality of competent evidence in the record reflects that any absence from Louisiana during the period leading up to the commencement of these custody proceedings was a "temporary absence" within the definition of home state as provided by La. R.S. 13:1802.

We also find that litigation of the custody proceeding in Louisiana comports with the purposes of the UCCJEA. Plaintiff testified that she has been the minor child's sole care giver since his birth and that the child has only ever resided in Louisiana and Texas. Furthermore, the record reflects that the child's maternal grandparents live in Louisiana. By contrast, plaintiff testified that though she and defendant co-owned their family home in Texas, defendant spent the majority of his time abroad and only returned to Texas for a few days each year, and defendant has put forth no other evidence demonstrating a potential connection between the child and Texas or any other state. This evidence demonstrates that Louisiana is the state with the "closest connection" to the child and that relevant evidence, in the form of family members' testimony, is located in Louisiana. Moreover, there is no evidence in the record of any proceedings pending in a Texas court, assuring us that assertion of jurisdiction by a Louisiana court will not promote jurisdictional competition. Finally, the evidence demonstrates that the child resided in Louisiana with his mother and grandfather for more than a year preceding the commencement of these proceedings, persuading this Court that litigation in Louisiana will further promote a stable home environment for the minor child.

Accordingly, we find no error in the trial court's denial of defendant's exception of subject matter jurisdiction over the custody proceedings.

CONCLUSION

For the foregoing reasons, we find no error in the trial court's denial of defendant's exceptions and grant of plaintiff's petition, and we affirm the trial court's November 3, 2015, and November 17, 2015 judgments.

AFFIRMED

Marsalis v. Marsalis

52 So. 3d 295 (La. App. 3 Cir. 2010)

MARC T. AMY, Judge.

The trial court entered judgment, granting, among other things, the parties joint custody of their children. The defendant appeals and asserts that the trial court erred in rendering judgment under the Uniform Child Custody Jurisdiction and Enforcement Act (UCCJEA), La.R.S. 13:1801, et seq., due to similar proceedings pending in Texas. For the following reasons, we affirm.

Factual and Procedural Background

Candace Marsalis instituted this matter in St. Landry Parish by filing a "Petition for 102 Divorce and Child Custody Pursuant to R.S. 13:1801 et seq. (U.C.C.J.E.A.)" on September 10, 2009. She alleged that she and her husband, James Frank Marsalis, were married in November 1992 in Ouachita Parish and had been living separate and apart since July 2009. The petition explained that the couple had six minor children who resided with Ms. Marsalis in Arnaudville, Louisiana.

The petition alleged that Mr. Marsalis was domiciled in Texas, although, earlier in the year, his domicile was in Louisiana, "where he owns a home." Ms. Marsalis pointed out that Mr. Marsalis had filed for divorce and custody of the minor children in Texas. However, Ms. Marsalis alleged that the Texas court lacked jurisdiction under the UCCJEA and sought a determination that Louisiana is the home state of the children pursuant to La.R.S. 13:1813(A)(1) due to the children having been domiciled in Louisiana "for more than six months before the commencement of the State of Texas proceeding." She asserted that she "and the minor children were temporarily in the State of Texas from late April of 2009 to August of 2009[.]" Ms. Marsalis further alleged that, pursuant to La.R.S. 13:1813, not only is Louisiana the children's home state, but that the children have significant connections with Louisiana and that substantial evidence regarding the past and future care, protections, training, and personal relationships exists in this state.

In addition to a custody determination, Ms. Marsalis sought child support, spousal support, and use and occupancy of the matrimonial domicile in Arnaudville pending partition of the community property.

As exhibits to the petition, Ms. Marsalis attached a copy of the petition in the Texas proceeding and letters regarding the children's contacts in Louisiana from a health care provider and a minister.

On September 15, 2009, and on consideration of the "petition and annexed attachments," the trial court signed an order recognizing Louisiana "as having proper jurisdiction of this proceeding as it is the 'home state' of the minor children."

The record indicates that, subsequently, and upon Ms. Marsalis's motion, a hearing officer conference scheduled for October 1, 2009 was rescheduled for November 10, 2009. However, Ms. Marsalis's counsel later sought the appointment of a private process server due to an inability to serve the petition on Mr. Marsalis in Texas. She attached an "Affidavit of Service Attempts" from the Panola County, Texas Sheriff's Department, which listed four attempts with no contact. The trial court signed the order appointing a private process server on November 6, 2009.

The hearing on the merits of the underlying matter was held on December 7, 2009. The trial court explained that it had received correspondence from Mr. Marsalis, who did not appear at the hearing, seeking a continuance of the hearing date. After addressing the contents of the letter on the record, the trial court entered the letter into evidence and proceeded with the hearing.

Ms. Marsalis testified regarding her marriage to Mr. Marsalis, their long-term residence in Louisiana, their decision to move to Texas in April 2009, and her return to Louisiana in August 2009 with the children. The trial court determined that Louisiana had jurisdiction to consider the custody question and that no other state had such jurisdiction. It also determined that it had jurisdiction to consider the divorce.

Ultimately, the trial court rendered judgment, awarding the parties joint custody of the minor children and designating Ms. Marsalis as the domiciliary parent. The trial court ordered that Mr. Marsalis would have reasonable visitation as agreed upon by the parties. The trial court further ordered Mr. Marsalis to provide child support at a designated rate, and spousal support. It awarded Ms. Marsalis use and occupancy of the marital domicile. The trial court later denied Mr. Marsalis's motion for new trial.

Mr. Marsalis appeals, assigning the following as error:

> The trial court clearly erred in rendering judgment before staying its proceedings and communicating with the Texas court as required by La.R.S. 13:1801, et seq. (Uniform Child Custody Jurisdiction and Enforcement Act).

Discussion

Mr. Marsalis contends that the trial court's judgment must be reversed as it failed to stay the custody proceeding and contact the court in Panola County, Texas in order to determine if it had jurisdiction to proceed. He contends that this procedure is required by La.R.S. 13:1818.

However, Mr. Marsalis's argument assumes that the Texas court had jurisdiction. The record does not contain evidence supporting this contention. At the hearing, the trial court determined both that Louisiana had jurisdiction of the custody matter and that no other state had jurisdiction. In reaching this conclusion, the court stated:

The Court will find that, as to the children, that the Court has jurisdiction of these children, due to the fact that there is no other State Court that has jurisdiction, that the children have lived all of their lives in Louisiana, and the last six of which have been in St. Landry Parish, except for the months of April 12, 2009 through August 9, 2009, where they lived in Texas for a period of approximately four (4) months, during an attempted reconciliation between the parents.

Thus, the Louisiana court made a finding of initial jurisdiction in keeping with La.R.S. 13:1813(A)(2), which states:

A. Except as otherwise provided in R.S. 13:18161, a court of this state has jurisdiction to make an initial child custody determination only if:

. . . .

(2) A court of another state does not have jurisdiction or a court of the home state of the child has declined to exercise jurisdiction on the ground that this state is the more appropriate forum under R.S. 13:1819 or 1820; and

(a) The child and the child's parents, or the child and at least one parent or a person acting as a parent, have a significant connection with this state other than mere physical presence.

(b) Substantial evidence is available in this state concerning the child's care, protection, training, and personal relationships.

The record supports a determination that Louisiana had jurisdiction pursuant to La.R.S. 13:1813(A)(2).

First, the evidence does not indicate that another state has jurisdiction. Recall that Mr. Marsalis, who seemingly asserts that the Texas court has jurisdiction over the custody matter, did not appear at trial to advance or support his position. Instead, Ms. Marsalis presented evidence regarding contacts in Louisiana. She explained that the couple and their children had lived in Louisiana during their marriage, that each of the six children were born in Louisiana, and that the couple's marital home was in Arnaudville. She testified that the children had been schooled in Louisiana and not in any other state. The parties and their children left Louisiana and moved to Texas in April 2009. However, Ms. Marsalis and the children returned to Louisiana four months later, in August 2009. Ms. Marsalis explained that she and the children intend to stay in Louisiana permanently, as this is their "home."

With regard to the potential of the Texas court having jurisdiction, the only evidence arguably in support of this view is the petition instituting the Texas proceedings and a letter that the trial court indicated was faxed to it prior to the hearing. Although the trial court entered the letter into evidence, its contents, at most, indicate that a proceeding was pending in Texas and, although Mr. Marsalis was residing in Texas, he was working in North Dakota. The letter revealed nothing regarding the children's presence or contacts in Texas. Instead, the letter addressed Mr. Marsalis's request for a continuance.

For these reasons, the only evidence presented supports a determination that no other state, including Texas, had jurisdiction pursuant to La.R.S. 13:1813(A)(2). Also, the evidence indicates that the children and Ms. Marsalis had significant connections to this state other than mere physical presence. See La.R.S. 13:1813(A)(2)(a). Indeed, the children lived their entire lives, other than approximately four months, in Louisiana. Finally, and again due to the children's long term presence and schooling in Louisiana, "[s]ubstantial evidence is available in this state concerning the child's care, protection, training, and personal relationships." La.R.S. 13:1813(A)(2)(b).

With this overlay as to the trial court's determinations regarding jurisdiction, we turn to Mr. Marsalis's precise argument that La.R.S. 13:1818 required the trial court to stay its proceedings and contact the Panola County court. Indeed, in light of the trial court's awareness of the Texas proceedings, consideration of La.R.S. 13:1818 would be arguably appropriate, insofar as it relates to simultaneous proceedings and provides, in pertinent part, that:

> A. Except as otherwise provided in R.S. 13:1816, a court of this state may not exercise its jurisdiction under this Subpart if, at the time of the commencement of the proceedings, a proceeding concerning the custody of the child has been commenced in a court of another state having jurisdiction substantially in conformity with this Act, unless the proceeding has been terminated or is stayed by the court of the other state because a court of this state is a more convenient forum under R.S. 13:1819.

> B. Except as otherwise provided in R.S. 13:1816, a court of this state, before hearing a child custody proceeding, shall examine the court documents and other information supplied by the parties pursuant to R.S. 13:1821. If the court determines that a child custody proceeding has been commenced in a court in another state having jurisdiction substantially in accordance with this Act, the court of this state shall stay its proceeding and communicate with the court of the other state. If the court of the state having jurisdiction substantially in accordance with this Act does not determine that the court of this state is a more appropriate forum, the court of this state shall dismiss the proceeding.

However, Mr. Marsalis's argument overlooks the fact that the trial court made a finding that no other state had jurisdiction. Paragraph A of La.R.S. 13:1818 provides that a Louisiana court may not exercise its jurisdiction if a custody matter is proceeding "in a court of another state having jurisdiction substantially in conformity" with the UCCJEA. Again, the trial court expressly stated that no other state had jurisdiction over the matter and, as explained above, Mr. Marsalis's failure to appear at the hearing and produce his own evidence left little on which the trial court could have determined that Texas had jurisdiction.

Next, Mr. Marsalis contends that La.R.S. 13:1818(B) required the trial court to confer with the Texas court prior to proceeding with its own custody hearing.

However, we find no indication in the record that the trial court violated the requirements of Paragraph B. Instead, Paragraph B provides that a Louisiana court shall stay its proceeding and communication with the court of another state, only "[i]f the court determines that a child custody proceeding has been commenced in a court in another state having jurisdiction" substantially in accordance with the UCCJEA. While Ms. Marsalis apprized the court of the Texas proceeding, Mr. Marsalis failed to submit evidence indicating that Texas was a forum "having jurisdiction" under the UCCJEA. See La.R.S. 13:1818(B).

We recognize that Mr. Marsalis asserts that jurisprudence required the trial court to stay the custody hearing, pending its communication with the Texas court. However, the cases cited by Mr. Marsalis are distinguishable from the present matter insofar as they are cases in which another state has been found to have jurisdiction or the other state's jurisdiction is presumed. In the present case, however, the trial court determined that no other state had jurisdiction over this matter. In fact, the party seemingly contesting Louisiana's jurisdiction failed to produce evidence showing otherwise.

Finally, we note that Mr. Marsalis contends that Ms. Marsalis is essentially lodging a collateral attack on any rulings issued by the Texas court. This assertion lacks merit. In fact, and again, the record contains no evidence regarding the Texas proceedings other than Ms. Marsalis's attachment of the Texas petition to the petition instituting this matter. Any products of the Texas proceeding were not before the trial court and are not properly before this court.

This assignment lacks merit.

DECREE

For the foregoing reasons, the judgment of the trial court is affirmed. All costs of this proceeding are assigned to the appellant, James Frank Marsalis.

AFFIRMED.

CHATELAIN, J., dissents in part and assigns written reasons.

CHATELAIN, Judge, dissenting in part.

Although I agree with that portion of the majority opinion that finds the statutory requirements for initial Louisiana jurisdiction are met, for the reasons below, I respectfully dissent from that portion of the majority opinion which finds that the trial court was not required to determine whether Texas had jurisdiction substantially in accordance with the UCCJEA. I find the trial court erroneously concluded that Louisiana was the Marsalis children's home state and, therefore, that its ruling that no other state had jurisdiction was also improper. I would reverse the portion of the judgment awarding child custody and child support and remand for the trial court to consider whether Texas would have "significant connection" jurisdiction substantially under La.R.S. 13:1813(A)(2). . . .

In re Marsalis

338 S.W.3d 131 (Ct. App. Tex. Texarkana 2011)

Before Morriss, C.J., Carter and Moseley, JJ.

OPINION

Opinion by Justice Moseley.

This case is a tale of competing and parallel actions for divorce in two sister states: Texas and Louisiana. Since the date of different occurrences have a distinct impact on a complete understanding of this case, a chronology of events is helpful at the outset.

1. James Frank Marsalis, his wife Candice Rae, and their six children had lived in Louisiana for several years, where they owned a home. James commenced working in Texas and was commuting back and forth between his workplace and his home, spending nights in both places. James' parents resided in Panola County, Texas. After some temporary moves back and forth and visits with James' parents, in order to maintain a more stable marriage, all of the Marsalis family moved from Louisiana to Panola County, Texas, in 2009 and placed their home and property in Louisiana on the market for sale. According to James, this move took place March 21; Candice testified at the Panola County hearing that it occurred April 14.

2. Apparently, the effort to achieve the marital stability they sought by moving to Texas failed. James filed a suit July 29, 2009, in Panola County, Texas; this action sought a dissolution of the marriage, a disposition of their community property, and a child custody adjudication of the couple's six children.

3. After James filed for divorce (August 9), Candice took the children and returned to reside in the still-unsold house in Louisiana where the family had previously resided.

4. In September, Candice filed an action for divorce in St. Landry Parish, Louisiana, attaching a copy James' Texas petition for divorce to her pleading. Candice then filed a special appearance and plea in abatement before the Panola County court, arguing that under the Uniform Child Custody Jurisdiction and Enforcement Act (UCCJEA), the Panola County court lacked subject-matter jurisdiction over the children because the children had not lived in Texas for six consecutive months prior to the filing of the divorce.

5. On December 7, a hearing was held in the Louisiana divorce action. James was not present.

6. James filed an amended petition in the Panola County action on December 16.

7. On January 5, 2010, James' Louisiana attorney presented objections to the form and content of the proposed Louisiana divorce decree. A hearing was held on the following day and the Louisiana court, rejecting James' objections, entered a divorce decree. At some point thereafter, James appealed the grant of the Louisiana divorce decree.

8. On January 11, Candice caused a copy of the Louisiana divorce decree to be filed with the District Clerk in Panola County.

9. On January 19, the judge in Panola County entered an order overruling Candice's special appearance and plea in abatement, finding that it had "subject matter jurisdiction over the parties and all matters in controversy. . . ."

10. A hearing on the merits of the Panola County action was held on February 4 and a final decree of divorce was entered March 12, which dissolved the marriage, divided the community property, and adjudicated custody of the children. Candice filed an appeal of that judgment of divorce.

11. The Louisiana Court of Appeals for the Third Circuit issued an opinion on December 8, 2010, affirming the judgment of divorce entered by the St. Landry Parish, Louisiana, District Court.

In her sole point of error, Candice contends that the trial court erred by denying her special appearance and objections to the court's jurisdiction to adjudicate custody, maintaining that Louisiana, not Texas, was the children's home state and, therefore, the Texas trial court lacked subject-matter jurisdiction to adjudicate custody.

We affirm the Texas trial court's judgment of divorce because no other court of any other state would have jurisdiction under Section 152.201 of the Texas Family Code.

At the time the Texas suit was filed, no other state had jurisdiction under the
UCCJEA

Both Texas and Louisiana have adopted the UCCJEA.

Subject-matter jurisdiction exists when the nature of the case falls within a general category of cases that the court is empowered, under applicable statutory and constitutional provisions, to adjudicate. Subject-matter jurisdiction is essential to the authority of a court to decide a case. Subject-matter jurisdiction over custody issues is governed by the UCCJEA. That Act provides mandatory jurisdictional rules for an original child custody proceeding. A Texas court must have subject-matter jurisdiction under the UCCJEA in order to make a child custody determination.

Whether a court has subject-matter jurisdiction is a question of law that we review de novo. Subject-matter jurisdiction is never presumed and cannot be waived.

Section 152.201 of the Texas Family Code governs the initial child custody jurisdiction of courts in the State of Texas and allows Texas courts to make an initial child custody determination only if the statutory requirements are fulfilled. In making a determination regarding jurisdiction, the location of the parties and the children is a vital factor. Because the parties and the children were not within either Texas or Louisiana during the entire period of time set out in the above chronology of events, we must first determine the critical date upon which inquiry of the surrounding circumstances of the parties should be applied. Jurisdiction is determined based upon circumstances existing at the time suit is filed in Texas. Here, suit was filed in

Panola County, Texas, on July 29, 2009. Accordingly, we look to the status of the parties and the children on that date: July 29, 2009.

We will summarize the four possible bases of jurisdiction in Texas and then examine whether any of the four authorizes a Texas court to conduct this custody determination.

(1) Home State Jurisdiction — Under the UCCJEA, a state has jurisdiction if that state was one in which a child lived with a parent for at least six consecutive months immediately before the commencement of a child custody proceeding or was the home state of the child within six months before the commencement of the proceeding and the child is absent from the state, but a parent continues to live in that state. The word "lived" connotes physical presence. . . . The UCCJEA suggests that the child's physical location is the central factor to be considered when determining the child's home state.

Both James and Candice concentrate their arguments on the issue of home state jurisdiction. Although James adamantly argues that Texas was the children's home state, Candice disputes that. Candice maintains that the children's four-month stay in Texas was merely a temporary stay, making Louisiana the children's home state. The first cogent issue in determining whether Texas was the home state is a determination of whether the children were physically present in Texas for six consecutive months preceding James' filing on July 29, 2009. James testified that he, Candice, and the children visited his parents in Texas in late January 2009, "preempting [sic] to talking about moving into a house down the street from them," and that the family "started to move [to Texas] in February." However, James clarified that the children moved to Texas on March 21, 2009, "[w]ith visitations [in Texas] before then." We observe that neither a "start to move" nor visitations within the State suffice for this determination. Therefore, we determine that the evidence presented by James is that the children moved to Texas on March 21. Candice testified that the children did not move to Texas until April 14, 2009 (in her words, to begin a "new start" in their lives). James and Candice concur that Candice and the children moved from Texas back to Louisiana on August 9, 2009. Irrespective of whether the children's move to Texas occurred in March or in April, six months had not elapsed before July 29, when James filed his petition for divorce in Panola County. . . .

As stated above, we determine jurisdiction based upon the circumstances as they existed on July 29, 2009, the date that the Texas action was filed. On that date, no one impacted by the dissolution of the marriage (not Candice, not James, and none of the children) lived in Louisiana. The subsequent decision by Candice to return to Louisiana did not abrogate that fact. Therefore, Louisiana could not have been the children's home state. On the other hand, the record establishes that the children were not physically present in Texas for six consecutive months before July 29, 2009. Rather, the record reflects that the children lived in Texas for (at most) five months before that date, although James and Candice had discussed in January a move to Texas, and that the children visited Texas frequently between February and March 21, 2009, before moving to Texas. Such sporadic presence in Texas does not satisfy the requirement that the children be physically present in Texas for six consecutive months.

The facts clearly show that although Louisiana was not the home state of the children at the date of commencement, neither was Texas.

(2) Significant Connection Jurisdiction—A Texas court may also have jurisdiction if no court from another jurisdiction qualifies as the home state of the child under (1) above or the home state court of the child has declined to exercise jurisdiction on the ground that such court is an inconvenient forum or due to unjustifiable conduct (such as kidnapping) by a person seeking to invoke that court's jurisdiction, and: (1) the child and at least one parent have a significant connection with Texas other than mere physical presence; and (2) "substantial evidence is available [in Texas] concerning the child's care, protection, training, and personal relationships. . . ."

Here, the record indicates that the children lived in Texas for about four months, that they frequently visited Texas before moving here, and that James and several coworkers stayed at a house in Texas during their "week on, week off" work week. In addition, it was shown that James' parents also lived in Texas, but no evidence was presented that this family relationship had a great impact on the children. These circumstances do not satisfy to provide substantial evidence of the children's care, protection, training, and personal relationships while in Texas. Therefore, Texas cannot exercise original jurisdiction under the significant connection provision.

(3) More Appropriate Forum Jurisdiction—A Texas court has jurisdiction if all courts having jurisdiction under (1) or (2) above have declined to exercise jurisdiction, finding Texas the more appropriate forum.

Texas courts do not acquire jurisdiction under this provision because there is no evidence that all courts having jurisdiction have declined to exercise jurisdiction or found that Texas courts are the more appropriate forum.

(4) Default Jurisdiction—A Texas court has jurisdiction if no court of any other state would have jurisdiction under (1), (2), or (3) above.

Because there are no courts of any other states having jurisdiction in this case, the trial court properly exercised subject-matter jurisdiction to adjudicate custody of the children under the default provisions of Section 152.201(a)(4) of the Texas Family Code. Accordingly, we overrule Candice's point of error and affirm the trial the court's judgment of divorce.

A. Louisiana judgment, competing jurisdiction, and comity

Several weeks after James commenced the Texas divorce and custody action, Candice, on September 10, 2009, filed a divorce and custody action of her own in St. Landry Parish, Louisiana (attaching a copy of James' Texas original petition to her pleading). That case was docketed as number 09-C-4858-B in the Louisiana court. A hearing on Candice's petition in the Louisiana case was scheduled December 7, 2009. Although James sent a handwritten pro se letter to the Louisiana court requesting a continuance, the motion was denied, statedly because of James' failure to provide a return address or other means of contacting him regarding an alternate hearing date. A hearing on the petition was held, but neither James nor anyone purporting to represent him was present for the hearing.

Judging from the recitations in the reported case mentioned below, the evidence produced at the hearing was that Candice and the children considered Louisiana their home, that the children had spent their entire lives (except for the months spent in Texas) living in Louisiana, and that she provided evidence regarding the past and future care, protection, training, and personal relationships with emphasis on the connections these things had with Louisiana. Based on the evidence before it, the trial court ruled that Louisiana was the children's home state. The court's judgment adjudicated custody and awarded spousal support, child support, and the use and occupancy of the marital residence in Louisiana. The judgment was affirmed on appeal to the Court of Appeals of Louisiana, Third Circuit. Other than taking note of James' letter, the trial court made no inquiry into the circumstances or jurisdictional basis of the previously filed Texas action.

In an effort to not ignore the benefits of comity, we have researched and examined the Louisiana appellate opinion in Marsalis. Apparently, James' sole point on appeal in that case complained of the entry of a judgment before staying its proceedings and communicating with the Texas court, a mandate of the UCCJEA. Rather than finding that Louisiana possessed home state jurisdiction (as found by the Louisiana trial court), the court of appeals held that Louisiana had jurisdiction based upon significant connections. The Louisiana appellate court noted that James' letter failed to make any allegations regarding the children's presence or connections in Texas, found that "the only evidence presented supports a determination that no other state, including Texas, had jurisdiction [over the children]," and stated that "the evidence indicates that the children and [Candice] had significant connections to [Louisiana] other than mere physical presence." Despite the trial court making no inquiry beyond the pleadings into the previously filed Texas action, the court held that the Louisiana trial court was not required to stay its proceedings or contact the Texas trial court under the UCCJEA's simultaneous proceeding provision because there was no evidence that Texas had jurisdiction substantially in accordance with the UCCJEA. Interestingly, however, there was likewise no evidence given that the Texas court did not have jurisdiction.

Here, the Texas trial court had the advantage of hearing testimony and evidence regarding the children from both James and Candice, whereas the Louisiana courts only had evidence presented by Candice. As per our ruling above, on the date James filed his petition in Texas, neither parent nor any of the children lived in Louisiana and no state other than Texas would have had jurisdiction under the UCCJEA. Therefore, at the time Candice filed her petition in Louisiana, Texas already had jurisdiction in accord with the UCCJEA under Section 152.201(a)(4), although it appears that the Louisiana court did not take that into account. Because Texas already had jurisdiction at the time the Louisiana suit was filed, the Louisiana trial court could not exercise jurisdiction over the case. Accordingly, the Louisiana trial court's judgment and child support and custody orders were entered without jurisdiction.

The Marsalises find themselves in a situation of competing custody orders, parallel appeals, relitigation of custody issues, and interstate jurisdictional competition—the very problems the UCCJEA was enacted to prevent. Since the support orders entered in the two respective actions for divorce do not comport with each other, it is extremely likely that confusion as to the enforceability of each will become an issue in the future. Each of the trial courts became aware of the pendency of custody actions in the other state. Perhaps this judicial conflict would not have arisen if either trial court had seen fit to make contact with the other (even if they were not absolutely required under the UCCJEA to do so and even if such a communication between the courts of the respective states did not result in a resolution of the conflict).

We affirm the judgment of the trial court.

Concurring Opinion by Justice CARTER.

JACK CARTER, Justice, concurring.

This result should be avoided. Some issues can best be resolved by a negotiated resolution, and this statute gives the trial judges the opportunity to do just that. Trial courts in different jurisdictions are encouraged to communicate when it is known that custody matters are filed in more than one state. After that conference, a trial court may decline to exercise jurisdiction if it finds that another state is the more appropriate forum. We have searched to determine if, as an appellate court, we have the authority to decline jurisdiction and resolve this matter relying on the doctrine of comity so that these parties would have only one court to answer to. But our function is to review the trial court record for error, not to attempt to make a policy determination that even though the trial court order is legally correct, we should reverse that order based on our judgment of what would serve the best interest of all parties.

Having found jurisdiction in the trial court in Texas, where the first action was filed, we may not simply "throw it back to Louisiana." I concur in the judgment.

Index